P9-DGU-543

DISCARD

UNIVERSITY OF CONNECTICUT — GROTON, CONN. — SOUTHEASTERN BRANCH LIBRARY

DEC 2 1970

WILLIAM
THE CONQUEROR

THE NORMAN IMPACT UPON ENGLAND

William the Conqueror, from the Bayeux Tapestry

WILLIAM
THE CONQUEROR

THE NORMAN IMPACT UPON ENGLAND

DAVID C. DOUGLAS

Fellow of the British Academy,
Emeritus Professor of History in the
University of Bristol

1964

UNIVERSITY OF CALIFORNIA PRESS

BERKELEY AND LOS ANGELES

© *David C. Douglas 1964*
University of California Press
Berkeley and Los Angeles
California

Printed in Great Britain

CONTENTS

Abbreviations   *page* vii
Preface   xi
Prologue   3

PART I · THE YOUNG DUKE

1. Birth and Inheritance   15
2. Accession and Minority (1035–1047)   31
3. The War for Survival (1047–1060)   53

PART II · THE DUKE IN HIS DUCHY

4. The Duke and the New Aristocracy   83
5. The Ecclesiastical Revival   105
6. The Rule of Duke William   133

PART III · THE ESTABLISHMENT OF
THE ANGLO-NORMAN KINGDOM

7. Normandy and England (1035–1065)   159
8. The Conquest of England (January 1066–March 1067)   181
9. The Defence of the Anglo-Norman Kingdom (March 1067–
   November 1085)   211

PART IV · THE KING IN HIS KINGDOM

10. *Willelmus Rex*   247
11. The Feudal Polity   265
12. The Royal Administration   289
13. The King in the Church   317
14. The End of the Reign (Christmas 1085 – 9 September 1087) 346
    Epilogue   367

APPENDICES

A. The birth of William the Conqueror and the connexions of
   Herleve   *page* 379
B. The chronology of Duke William's campaigns between 1047
   and 1054   383
C. The marriage of William and Matilda   391
D. The sequence of events in 1066   396
E. The chronology of King William's campaigns between 1073
   and 1081   401
F. On poisoning as a method of political action in eleventh-
   century Normandy   408

   Select chart pedigrees   417
   Select Bibliography   427
   Schedule of selected dates   449
   Index   457

MAPS

I. Normandy in the time of William the Conqueror   454
II. England and Normandy in the time of William the Conqueror 456

ABBREVIATIONS

The following abbreviations are used in the footnotes. For some other books short titles are used, and these are fully extended in the bibliography.

AS. Chron.	Anglo-Saxon Chronicle. [Cited by version and year.]
Bayeux Tapestry.	This is cited by reference to the plates in the edition by F. M. Stenton (1957), and by reference to the plates in *E.H.D.*, vol. II.
Cal. Doc. France.	J. H. Round, *Calendar of Documents preserved in France*, vol. I (1899). [Cited by number.]
Carmen.	*Carmen de Hastingae Proelio* (often attributed to 'Guy of Amiens').
Cart. Bayeux.	*Antiquus Cartularius ecclesiae Baiocensis* (*Livre Noir*), ed. V. Bourrienne, 2 vols. (1902, 1903).
Cart. Îles Norm.	*Cartulaire des Îles normandes* (Soc. Jersiaise, 1918–1924).
Cart. S. Père Chartres.	*Cartulaire de Saint-Père de Chartres*, ed. Guerard (1840).
Cart. S. Trin. Roth.	*Chartularium Monasterii Sanctae Trinitatis de Monte Rothomagi*, ed. A. Deville (1840).
Chartes de Jumièges.	*Chartes de l'Abbaye de Jumièges*, ed. J. J. Vernier, 2 vols. (1916).
D.B.	Domesday Book, 2 vols. (Record Commission, 1783).
E.H.D.	*English Historical Documents*, vol. II, ed. D. C. Douglas and G. W. Greenaway (1953).
Eng. Hist. Rev.	*English Historical Review.*
Flor. Worc.	Florence of Worcester. [Cited from the edition by B. Thorpe, 2 vols., 1848, 1849.]
Gall. Christ.	*Gallia Christiana* (16 vols. of varying date).
Lanfranc. Epp.	*Lanfranci Epistolae.* [Cited by number from the series given in *Pat. Lat.*, vol. CL.
Le Prévost, *Eure.*	*Mémoires et Notes de M. Auguste Le Prévost pour servir à l'histoire du Département de l'Eure*, 3 vols. (1862–1869).

Lot, *Saint-Wandrille.*	F. Lot, *Études critiques sur l'abbaye de Saint-Wandrille* (1912).
Mon. Ang.	W. Dugdale, *Monasticon Anglicanum*, 6 vols. in 8 (1817–1830).
Ord. Vit.	Ordericus Vitalis, *Historia Ecclesiastica*, ed. A. Le Prévost and L. Delisle, 5 vols. (1838–1855).
Pat. Lat.	*Patrologiae Latinae Cursus Completus*, ed. J. P. Migne.
R.A.D.N.	*Recueil des Actes des Ducs de Normandie (911–1066)*, ed. M. Fauroux (1961). [The deeds are cited by number.]
Rec. Hist. Franc.	*Recueil des Historiens des Gaules et de la France* ('Dom Bouquet'), 24 vols. of varying dates.
Regesta.	*Regesta Regum Anglo Normannorum*, vol. 1, ed. H. W. C. Davis (1913); vol. II (1956), ed. C. Johnson and H. A. Cronne.
R. Hist. Soc.	Royal Historical Society. [The *Transactions* are cited by series and volume.]
Will. Jum.	William of Jumièges, *Gesta Normannorum Ducum*, ed. J. Marx (1914).
Will. Malms.	William of Malmesbury. [His *Gesta Regum* is cited from the edition by W. Stubbs, 2 vols. (1887, 1889); his *Gesta Pontificum* from the edition by N. E. S. A. Hamilton (1870).]
Will. Poit.	William of Poitiers, *Gesta Guillelmi Ducis Normannorum et Regis Anglorum*, ed. R. Foreville (1952).

TO
Evelyn Douglas

PREFACE

In 1963 I was appointed Ford's Lecturer in English History to the University of Oxford, and my first obligation in connexion with this book is to the Electors to that Lectureship whose invitation not only did me honour, but impelled me to bring to a conclusion certain studies in Anglo-Norman history which had occupied much of my leisure for more than twenty years. The present volume differs in its arrangement, and in its more extended content, from the lectures I delivered on the same theme. But my gratitude for the stimulus thus given me is not thereby in any way diminished.

The importance of the subject here considered has been reflected in the continuous interest it has excited over the centuries, and in the continuous propaganda it has inspired. None the less, it is hoped that a new study of William the Conqueror and his times can be justified, and the particular purpose of this book will be apparent to readers of its introductory chapter. Briefly, my aims have been to eschew the controversies of the past; to bring French and English scholarship here into closer relation; and, throughout, to base my study upon the original testimony, some of which has, I believe, been given a new cogency as a result of recent criticism. For this reason, a somewhat full citation of the authorities has been supplied since this seems emphatically to be a case where readers should be given the opportunity of testing for themselves the adequacy of the evidence as well as the contrasted interpretations which have been placed upon it. It is believed, however, that those who wish to do so will be able to read the text independently of the citations which support it, and more detailed discussion of certain difficult questions has been relegated to appendices.

A glance at the bibliography will indicate how heavily I am indebted to the work of others, but it will not suffice to record the many personal kindnesses I have received in connexion with this work. These are, in fact, too numerous to be individually acknowledged, but I here offer my grateful thanks to all those who have helped me in so many ways.

I must, however, allude specially to all my friends in the University of Bristol. My pupils have taught me more than they perhaps realize, and among them I would particularly mention Dr David Walker and Mr Peter Hull. As for my colleague Mr James Sherborne, he has increased my existing debt to him by his valuable criticism of much that I have written. I am obliged to Mr Freke for help in the preparation of the maps, and I cannot be sufficiently grateful for the inexhaustible patience and interest of my secretary, Miss Kathleen Hek.

In a very special sense, too, I have been indebted to the encouragement given me over the years by my friends, Sir Frank Stenton, Professor V. H. Galbraith, and Mr Douglas Jerrold. Dom David Knowles and Professor Richard Southern have, moreover, been so kind as to read and comment upon much of the book in the later stages of its preparation. I must be careful not to implicate any of these distinguished writers in such errors of statement or interpretation as may remain in my book, but the bare recital of their names will indicate the magnitude of the obligations I have incurred.

Even so, the greatest debts remain to be recorded. It was that fine feudal scholar, Mr Lewis Loyd, who first directed my attention constructively to Anglo-Norman history, and who, with characteristic generosity, allowed me to profit without stint from his instruction, and from his own researches. Again, it was Mrs Germaine Mason, my colleague in the University of Bristol, who, at a later date, with equal generosity, led me to a fresh appreciation of many of the problems of French literature and history. My debt to these two scholars, now, alas, both dead, is not to be expressed in a sentence. I only wish that this book was more worthy of their memory, and of their friendship.

Certainly, no author has ever been more fortunate in the kindness of others, and throughout the whole protracted undertaking my wife has played her own essential part. Without her, it would never have been sustained. She would not wish me to speak in detail of her indispensable share in our common work, or of all that this book owes to her. The dedication is gratefully hers by right.

D.C.D.

Bristol, 1964

PROLOGUE

PROLOGUE

The subject of this book is William the Conqueror. Its object is to consider the Norman impact upon England. It seeks to show how, within the lifetime of one man, and largely through his acts, a single province of Gaul was enabled to effect the conquest of an ancient kingdom, and it attempts to analyse the character and the results of that conquest. These topics (it will be further suggested) may challenge attention not only for their intrinsic importance, but also by reason of their enduring relevance to the subsequent development of England and of western Christendom. And they are made the more interesting by being inseparably connected with one of the most spectacular biographies of history.

In one sense the theme is familiar. No medieval king of England is more famous than William the Conqueror, and no event in the whole of English history has been more discussed than the Norman conquest. To call attention to the massive tradition of scholarship[1] which has been inherited by the student of Anglo-Norman history in this period, it would, indeed, be unnecessary to do more than recollect, for example, how the seventeenth-century labours of André Duchesne and Jean Pommeraye in France were matched by those of their great English contemporaries – Selden, Spelman, and Dugdale; how the eighteenth-century editions of Wilkins and Bessin still together offer material for comment; or how this topic was later enriched by Stapleton and Freeman in England; by Haskins in America; by Steenstrup in Denmark; and by Auguste Le Prévost, Henri Prentout, and Léopold Delisle in France.

Nor does this activity show any signs of abating. In England new editions are providing students of this subject with fresh opportunities, and the fine collection of early Norman charters which has just appeared at the hands of Madame Fauroux has made more accessible than ever before a wide range of indispensable material.[2] Such textual studies are,

---

[1] Most of the older works are cited in C. Gross, *Sources and Literature of English History* (ed. 1915), and in E. Frère, *Manuel de bibliographe normand* (1858, 1860) – a wholly admirable work. Cf. also Douglas, *Norman Conquest and British Historians* (1937), and the select bibliography given below on pp. 427–447.

[2] *Recueil des Actes des Ducs de Normandie* (*Mémoires de la Société des Antiquaires de Normandie*, vol. xxxvi, 1961). Cited hereafter as *R.A.D.N.*

moreover, being matched by new efforts at interpretation. Thus in England the origins of Anglo-Norman feudalism are being subjected to re-examination, and the ecclesiastical history of the age is being displayed with ever-increasing elaboration. At the same time, in France, a new approach to Anglo-Norman history is being successfully made by Professors M. de Bouard, Jean Yver, Lucien Musset, and their colleagues in the university of Caen. The list could, of course, be easily extended and it would include the fundamental work associated with Dom David Knowles and Sir Frank Stenton. But even the bare mention of a few selected names may indicate the continuing interest which the subject excites. It might also serve to raise a doubt whether anything new can be added to this accumulated erudition.

Nevertheless, a reconsideration of this theme may perhaps be justified if only because wide differences of opinion still appear in the work of its most distinguished exponents; and these disagreements extend even to the largest issues involved. Thus French scholars remain sharply divided on the relative importance of the Scandinavian factor in the growth of Normandy; and in respect of the development of Anglo-Norman feudalism, new theories are now being propounded in opposition to those of John Horace Round, who himself reacted so vigorously against his predecessors. Again (to quote no more instances) the appraisal of the ecclesiastical consequences to England of the Norman conquest as supplied in the work of Heinrich Böhmer or Z. N. Brooke may be contrasted with that offered by Professors Stenton and Darlington. Examples could be multiplied, but these may suffice to point the paradox. There is, of course, no finality in historical research, and the ebb and flow of criticism and correction is essential to its vitality. None the less the situation here revealed is surely remarkable. Despite the fact that the history of William the Conqueror and of the Norman conquest of England has been assiduously studied for three centuries, few periods of our history remain more the subject of controversy.

There is, moreover, another reason why a fresh examination of this theme may not be without profit. The modern student of Anglo-Norman history finds himself today in a quite extraordinary position. He is not only the heir to a great tradition of scholarship: he is also subject to the influence of an even longer tradition of propaganda. The treatment accorded to William the Conqueror and to the Norman conquest of England is, indeed, one of the curiosities of English literature, and it is surely strange how consistently over the centuries the history of this distant age should have prompted statesmen and lawyers, pamphleteers and ecclesiastics into a war of words inspired by current controversies or immediate political stress.[1] Arguments concerning the Norman conquest cover almost the entire span of English prose. Thus even before the death of Queen Elizabeth I, Archbishop Matthew Parker and his associates were seeking in the Old English Church uncorrupted by the Normans a prototype of the reformed establishment they were called upon to administer; and few indeed of the contentions – political and religious – which vexed England during the seventeenth century were debated without some reference either to the Conqueror or to the Norman conquest. Here, for example, the common lawyers came into conflict not only with the supporters of the king but with the new historiography, and it may be recalled how important to the Levellers was their conception of the 'Norman yoke'.[2] In the eighteenth century the debate was vigorously continued in the constitutional sphere; and in the nineteenth it became even more highly coloured under the influence of liberal and national sentiments.

The result has been truly astonishing. The posthumous career of William the Conqueror in controversial literature is almost as remarkable as his actual career in eleventh-century history. For generations he has remained, so to speak, a figure in contemporary politics. He has been presented in terms of Whig theory, of sectarian fervour, and of modern nationalism. He has been hailed as one of the founders of English greatness, and as the cause of one of the most lamentable of English defeats. He has been pictured as the special enemy of protestantism, and as one of the most strenuous opponents of the papacy. He has been envisaged as both the author, and also as the subverter, of the English Constitution. In France, too, the tradition, though distinct, has not been dissimilar. William of Normandy has there been saluted as a French national hero. He has also been denounced as a champion of superstition and as an enemy of the people, so that Calvinists and Revolutionaries were led savagely to desecrate his tomb, and to scatter his remains. Was he not representative of that 'feudalism' which has still formally to be renounced by all new members of the Legion of Honour? Few personalities in history have been more praised and blamed for acts in which they had no share.

[1] Douglas, *op. cit.*; also *English Scholars*, chaps. III and VI.
[2] J. A. Pococke, *Ancient Constitution and the Feudal Law* (1957); C. Hill, *Democracy and the Labour Movement* (1959).

It is, indeed, important to realize how persistent has been this polemical tradition, and to recall the lengths to which, even in comparatively recent times, it has been exploited. As an example, there might be cited the utterances of two men who on all grounds may be revered as eminent Victorians – that is to say, distinguished men in a most distinguished age. Here, for instance, is Thomas Carlyle in 1858 echoing in some sense the sentiments of John Milton, but writing in a manner wholly his own:

Without the Normans [he exclaims] what had it ever been? A gluttonous race of Jutes and Angles capable of no great combinations; lumbering about in pot-bellied equanimity; not dreaming of heroic toil and silence and endurance, such as lead to the high places of the Universe, and the golden mountain tops where dwell the spirits of the Dawn.[1]

The exclamation may well provoke surprise. But it could be matched (in the opposite sense) by remarks made a few years earlier by Edward Freeman in connexion with the establishment of the present School of Modern History in the university of Oxford:

We must recognize [wrote Freeman, when debating the new Examination Statute of 1850] the spirit which dictated the Petition of Right as the same which gathered all England round the banners of Godwin, and remember that the 'good old cause' was truly that for which Harold died on the field and Waltheof on the scaffold.[2]

These, it will be recalled, were notable men who were justly revered by their contemporaries as exponents of history. And the fact that they could write in such a way about an episode of eleventh-century history testifies to the strength of the controversial tradition which they inherited and which they sought to pass on to us their successors. Nor were they wholly unsuccessful in so doing. Even today it is very evident that the influence of this long polemical tradition has not wholly evaporated, and it is something against which every student of eleventh-century English history should be set on guard.

And if a special obligation is thus imposed upon a biographer of William the Conqueror to avoid such controversies as extraneous to his subject; to attempt objectivity; and to eschew anachronistic sentiments; so also should he strive to place the general problems with which he is concerned in their widest contemporary setting. Beyond doubt, the

---

[1] *Frederick the Great*, vol. I, p. 415; quoted by W. Stubbs, *Constitutional History* (ed. 1891), vol. I, p. 236. Cf. J. Milton, *History of Britain* (ed. 1695), pp. 356, 357.
[2] *Life and Letters* (ed. W. R. W. Stephens), vol. I, p. 125.

latter half of the eleventh century witnessed a turning-point in the history of western Christendom, and beyond doubt Normandy and the Normans played a dominant part in the transformations which then occurred. By the conquest of a great kingdom they effected a political regrouping of north-western Europe with lasting consequences both to France and England. They assisted the papacy to rise to a new political of political dominance, and they became closely associated with the reforming movement in the Church which the papacy came to direct. They contributed also to a radical modification of the relations between eastern and western Europe with results that still survive. The Norman conquest of England may thus in one sense be regarded as but part of a far-flung endeavour, the implications of which were to stretch even into the sphere of culture. The Normans by linking England more straitly to Latin Europe helped what may be called the Romance-speaking peoples to achieve that dominance in western culture which they exercised during the twelfth-century renaissance, so that, for example, the great monastic movements of that age, crusading senti-ment and troubador song, the new universities and the learning that was fostered therein, all came from a world that was centred upon France, and which included not only the England which the Normans conquered but the Italy which the Normans helped to transform.[1]

This transference of power and influence was a prime factor in the making of Europe, and the Norman contribution to it, though inspired by many diverse motives, was undoubtedly considerable. But it was not inevitable, and it came from a province which some forty years before the Norman conquest of England showed but few signs of its future achievement. On the day when William the Conqueror was born it could hardly have been foreseen. When he died after a career which was in every way astonishing, its results were already assured.

Here, then, is a problem which invites solution. How had the Norman power which was to be so notably exhibited under William the Con-queror been attained? How had the special characteristics of Normandy at that time been acquired? And what were the factors of Norman policy which was then brought to its culmination? These questions, it would seem, lie across the threshold of our subject. But even to pose them indicates an important conclusion. It is that the long debate on the consequences to England of the Norman conquest can no longer be profitably sustained unless a fresh attempt be made to appraise, for its

[1] Cf. R. W. Southern, *Making of the Middle Ages*, especially pp. 15–57.

own sake, the social and political character of the Normandy which confronted England in 1066. This conviction is at all events implicit in the chapters which here follow, and it has determined their sequence. If the Norman achievement at its zenith cannot be dissociated from the career of the greatest of the Norman dukes, it is certainly not to be explained solely by reference to a single personality. To discriminate, in this sense, among the causes – general and personal – of the Norman impact upon England, and of the highly individual results it entailed is, in fact, a primary object of the present study, and one which is largely responsible for the pattern of this book.

William was the outstanding member of an exceptional dynasty, and he ruled over an exceptional province of Gaul. What he accomplished was thus in large measure due to his inheritance.[1] But the circumstances of his birth and of his accession were also exceptional,[2] and before he could be assured of his heritage he was forced into a hazardous struggle which tested his courage, and annealed his character.[3] On the outcome of that struggle, which involved not only Normandy but a large part of northern France, the subsequent strength of ducal Normandy was largely to depend, and only after its successful conclusion could William complete the consolidation of the duchy on which his power was henceforth to be based. In that work, too, he was dependent upon social and political movements which had begun before his accession. The Norman military successes in the eleventh century were directly dependent on the rise in the province of a new secular aristocracy,[4] and the quality of the influence which Normandy was to exercise during the life of William the Conqueror was conditioned by the ecclesiastical revival which at the same time transformed the Church in the province of Rouen.[5] It was William's achievement not only to foster and co-ordinate these movements but also to dominate them. Only thus is to be explained the success of his rule over Normandy, and the subsequent expansion of Norman influence overseas.[6]

The same considerations apply also to William's later career. He was placed in a position of crucial importance at a critical moment in the political development of western Europe, but he was capable of turning that situation to his own advantage, and to the profit of the Norman duchy. The Scandinavian impact on Europe in the tenth and eleventh centuries had already bound together the fates of Normandy and

[1] Chap. 1. [2] Chap. 2. [3] Chap. 3.
[4] Chap. 4. [5] Chap. 5. [6] Chap. 6.

England, and posed for the future the fundamental question whether, for the remainder of the Middle Ages, England should be linked to Latin Europe rather than to the Scandinavian lands. That problem, complicated by so many personal and political factors, dominated Anglo-Norman relations until the climax of 1066, and to its solution William undoubtedly made his own individual contribution.[1] Prepared and made possible by previous history, the conquest of England owed its accomplishment, and many of its major consequences, to his initiative, and the Anglo-Norman kingdom was established through him.[2] Its continued existence was, however, long in doubt and its defence, conducted through years of hazard, displayed to the full the energy and capacity of its ruler. That defence (as will here be suggested) was a unified endeavour involving a continuous series of interconnected operations on both sides of the Channel, and it was the essential prerequisite for the fulfilment of William's constructive work.[3]

William's claim to be considered as a man of original genius must rest ultimately upon his rule of the conjoint realm which he created and defended. In 1066 he achieved royalty with all the sanctified authority which this implied.[4] By thus acquiring a special status in the secular and ecclesiastical world of the eleventh century, he found himself possessed of new opportunities and resources. He used them to the full, and in a manner that was characteristically his own. He established in England the new aristocracy he brought from overseas, and through its agency he modified the structure of England's society by the application of new principles of social organization which were in turn to react upon the province from which he came.[5] Yet, both in Normandy and in England he was faithful to tradition, and in England, especially, it became a cardinal feature of his administration to respect, and to utilize, the customs of the kingdom he had conquered.[6] Similarly, William brought to England the influence of the ecclesiastical revival which had taken place in Normandy under his rule, and the Church in England whose organization was thereby remodelled was brought into a new relationship with the movement of reform which in the time of Hildebrand was beginning to pervade the politics of Europe. Nevertheless, William's ecclesiastical policy as a consecrated king of England remained highly individual, and the position he came to occupy in the European Church was scarcely less notable than that which he filled in the European

---

[1] Chap. 7. [2] Chap. 8. [3] Chap. 9.
[4] Chap. 10. [5] Chap. 11. [6] Chap. 12.

secular order.[1] Nor was there any abatement of his activities as age advanced. The last twenty months of his reign were to involve a final crisis in the defence of his realm, and also the production of the greatest written memorial to his administration. His work did not cease until his tragic death and still more terrible funeral.[2]

His life possessed an heroic quality and men soon found little difficulty in applying to him phrases comparable with those used in lauding the fabled Charlemagne in the 'Song of Roland'.[3] In view of this, and still more because of the later controversies of which he was the object, it is not easy to make a sober estimate of what he accomplished. Certainly this could only be achieved, if at all, by a direct study of the contemporary evidence such as here has been attempted. It deserves note, therefore, that, considering the remote period from which it derives, such evidence is surprisingly plentiful. A bare recital of a few selected items may of itself suffice to display its abundance. It is not merely that the great king left in Domesday Book his own magnificent record of the kingdom he had conquered, or that the Bayeux Tapestry supplied shortly after the event a unique pictorial representation of the central episode of his career. The whole period is illustrated in the Anglo-Saxon Chronicle, and is completely covered in one of its recensions, whilst writers in England of the next generation, such as William of Malmesbury, Simeon of Durham, Eadmer, and the so-called 'Florence of Worcester', give full prominence to the events of these years. Again, a fascinating early life of Edward the Confessor, together with the lives and letters of Archbishop Lanfranc, may by themselves suffice to indicate how fully the historical narrative of this age can be supplemented by the biographies and the correspondence it produced. Equally copious are the charters. Nearly three hundred instruments issued by William the Conqueror as king between 1066 and 1087 have been calendared, and to these can be added a considerable number of private deeds, most of which have been reproduced in print from original or cartulary texts.

The extended scope of the evidence deriving from England is fairly well known, but the fact that the Norman sources of Anglo-Norman history in this period are likewise abundant is less generally appreciated on this side of the Channel. The Norman annals[4] are, it is true, less full

---

[1] Chap. 13.　　　　　　　　　　　　　　　　[2] Chap. 14.
[3] Cf. the phrases in AS. Chron., s.a. 1087, with those used in the *Chanson de Roland* (vv. 371–374 and vv. 2331, 2332). Cf. Douglas, *French Studies*, vol. XIV (1960), pp. 99–114.
[4] *Mon. Germ. Hist. Scriptores*, vol. XXVI, pp. 489–495.

than their Anglo-Saxon counterparts, but as has recently been demonstrated, they present features of unusual interest,[1] whilst the *Acta* of the archbishops of Rouen[2] are not only interesting in themselves, but are representative of a fairly large class of material. In William of Jumièges, whose account continues until 1070–1071, we have a contemporary Norman chronicler of good standing,[3] and his work is given colour by the treatise on the Conqueror composed about the same time by William of Poitiers. It is, moreover, particularly fortunate that the production of both these writers, whose work stands in close but at present undefined relation to each other, should in the next generation have fallen under the notice of an author of some genius. The interpolations made by Ordericus Vitalis to the seventh book of the chronicle of William of Jumièges are of particular value,[4] and most, if not all, of the lost portion of the work of William of Poitiers is embodied in Orderic's own great *Historia Ecclesiastica*, which must be judged the most valuable single narrative source of Anglo-Norman history in this period.

Nor is there any lack of documentary material deriving from the duchy at this time. The records of the Norman church councils are both copious and informative. Norman private charters of the eleventh century are also fairly numerous, and in addition to those still awaiting investigation in the *Archives* of Eure and Seine-Maritime many of them are in print, though, being scattered through many volumes of varying date and accuracy, they are difficult of access. Again, many of the charters issued by William himself after 1066 are likewise of Norman origin. But it is the pre-Conquest ducal texts that are here particularly noteworthy. There is a widespread impression in England that such instruments are rare. On the contrary, they are very numerous. It deserves considerable emphasis that not less than one hundred and thirty charters, issued or subscribed by William as duke of Normandy between 1035 and 1066, are extant and in print[5] – a number which approximates fairly closely to that of all the genuine surviving charters and writs issued by Edward the Confessor during the whole of his reign for the whole of England. If less is known of pre-Conquest Normandy than of pre-Conquest England it is assuredly not because of lack of testimony. Perhaps the evidence has

---

[1] J. Laporte, *Annales de Jumièges* (1954), pp. 7–23.

[2] *Rec. Hist. Franc.*, vol. XI, pp. 70 *et sqq.* Cf. E. Vacandard, *Rev. catholique de Normandie*, vol. III, p. 123.

[3] Separated from its later additions in the edition of J. Marx (1914). Cited hereafter as 'Will. Jum.'.

[4] L. Delisle, *Bibliothèque de l'École de Chartes*, vol. LXXI (1910).

[5] *R.A.D.N.*, pp. 242–449.

been somewhat neglected by English scholars. At all events this essential material remains the least worked source of Anglo-Norman history in this age.

The biographer of William the Conqueror has in short no reason to complain of lack of evidence. The difficulty lies in its assessment. It is by no means easy, for example, to elucidate the interrelation between the various narrative sources; the interpretation of Domesday Book is notoriously difficult; and there are few harder tasks than to criticize eleventh-century charters in respect of their form, their dating, and their authenticity. A further problem is posed by the special character of the subject, and the uneven spread of the testimony. Legend gathered very quickly about William the Conqueror, and much that is frequently related of him is fabulous. Much more, though probably true, derives from evidence that is very scanty. There is here, therefore, a special necessity to recall the salutary caution of Mabillon that the duty of the historian is not only to proclaim certainties as certain and falsehoods as false, but also uncertainties as dubious. For this reason a modern study of the Conqueror must include much criticism of evidence relating to points of detail.[1] But the investigation can none the less be justified by the wider issues that were involved. For these in truth were fundamental, and the consequences of what then occurred are still alive among us today. Seldom can a decisive and constructive epoch in history be examined more directly through the contemplation of a particular series of events – and in one man's life.

[1] For this reason a somewhat full citation of the original testimony has been given in the footnotes to the pages which follow.

Part I

THE
YOUNG DUKE

Chapter 1

BIRTH AND INHERITANCE

William the Conqueror – Duke William II of Normandy, King William I
of England – was born at Falaise in 1027 or 1028, and probably during
the autumn of the latter year.[1] He was the bastard son of Robert I, sixth
duke of Normandy, by Herleve, a girl of that town. His parentage was thus
remarkable. Little is known about his mother, for contemporary writers
are discreetly silent about her origins. Later testimony, however, indicates
that her father's name was probably Fulbert, and there is substantial evidence to suggest that this 'Fulbert' was a tanner.[2] Herleve's connexion
with the duke was none the less to advance not only her own fortunes but
those of her kinsfolk. Fulbert was apparently given a subordinate office at
the ducal court, and Herleve's brothers, Osbert and Walter, appear as
witnesses to important charters.[3] Herleve, herself, shortly after the Conqueror's birth, was married off to Herluin, *vicomte* of Conteville, and to
him she was to bear two very distinguished sons, namely Odo, the famous
bishop of Bayeux and subsequently earl of Kent, and Robert, count of
Mortain, later one of the largest landowners in eleventh-century England.
The whole subsequent history of north-western Europe was thus to be influenced by the offspring of this obscure but remarkable girl, who died it
would seem in or about 1050.[4] Students of genetics, and of 'hereditary
genius', may, moreover, be tempted to comment on the youth of William's
parents. Robert cannot have been more than twenty-one at the time of
his connexion with Herleve, and in all likelihood he was younger, possibly
in his seventeenth year.[5] The girl herself was probably no older.

[1] Below, Appendix A.

[2] Other occupations have been suggested; *e.g.* that he was a man who prepared corpses
for burial. The tradition that he was a tanner is, however, strong, and the tanneries at
Falaise were famous.

[3] Ord. Vit., interp. Will. Jum., p. 157; *R.A.D.N.*, no. 102, and perhaps Lot, *Saint-Wandrille*,
no. 20.   [4] Below, Appendix A.

[5] This may be inferred from the date of the marriage of Robert's parents. The traditional
date for the marriage of Richard II and Judith, namely 1008, can hardly be accepted, but
even if the marriage be placed five years earlier, the implications are remarkable. In that case,
allowing for the normal periods of pregnancy, Robert, who was junior to his brother Richard III,
could not, at the earliest, have been born before 1005. But to place his birth as early as this it is
necessary to stretch all the evidence to the limit of possibility, by assuming that among the six
children of Richard II by Judith the two elder sons were before any of the three girls – a fact
for which there is no evidence. See Douglas, in *Eng. Hist. Rev.*, vol. LXV (1950), pp. 289–303.

If, however, William's mother was of humble stock, his father belonged to one of the most interesting families of Europe. For he was the direct descendant of Rolf the Viking, who, after a career of depredation, had, in or about 911, been recognized as a legitimate ruler in Neustria by the emperor, Charles III ('the Simple'), and had thereafter passed on his power in an unbroken succession to his son William, nicknamed 'Longsword' (died 942), to his grandson Duke Richard I (942–966), and to his great-grandson Duke Richard II, the Conqueror's grandfather, who was to survive until within three years of William's birth. Little more than a century thus separated the establishment in Gaul of the Viking Rolf from the birth of his most illustrious descendant, and William's inheritance, which he was so signally to enlarge, derived in large measure from the position acquired in the Viking dynasty in Gaul, and from the manner in which their power had been developed.[1]

Rolf,[2] known to his Frankish posterity as Rollo, was probably of Norwegian stock, being the son of Rögnvald, earl of Möre, and before his formal establishment in Gaul he had a long career as a Viking, raiding not only in France but also, as it seems, in Scotland and Ireland. In 911, having entered Gaul afresh, perhaps by way of the Loire valley, he was defeated in a pitched battle outside the walls of Chartres, and it was after this that he and his followers were given lands by the emperor in the valley of the lower Seine. Whether this famous grant of lands and recognition was made (as tradition later asserted) after a formal interview between Charles and Rolf at Sainte-Clair-sur-Epte is questionable, and the application of the term 'treaty' to these arrangements is undoubtedly too precise. What, however, is certain is that before 918 Rolf and his followers already held considerable lands in this region, and that they had been formally confirmed in possession of them by the emperor.[3] Equally certain is that in token of the new position he was henceforth to occupy in Gaul, Rolf accepted baptism at the hands of the archbishop of Rouen.[4]

His power was steadily to grow. The muniments of Jumièges, Saint-Ouen and Le Mont-Saint-Michel, taken in conjunction with the narrative of Flodoard of Rheims, indicate that the earliest demesne of the

[1] Douglas, *Rise of Normandy* (1949); published separately, and also in the *Proceedings* of the British Academy for that year.

[2] The controversial literature concerning him is considered by Douglas, in *Eng. Hist. Rev.*, vol. LVII (1942), pp. 417–436. The name may represent O. Norse *Hraithulfr*; or O. Swed. *Hrithulf*.

[3] *Rec. Actes – Charles III* (ed. Lauer), no. XCII.

[4] Prentout *Étude sur Dudon*, pp. 250–259.

dynasty was confined to an area bounded by the Epte, the Orne, and the sea: it was concentrated in the district lying on both sides of the Seine between Les Andelys and Vernon, and stretched to the west nearly as far as Évreux, and to the east along the Epte towards Gisors. Between 911 and 918 Rolf was also in possession of Rouen itself and of certain districts on the sea-coast dependent on that city, and by 925 he was apparently established as far to the east as Eu. Westward, however, the progress was to be much more gradual. Not until 924 was the rule of the new family extended from the Orne to the Vire, and only in 933 (after the death of Rolf) was it carried by his son William Longsword as far west as the Couesnon.[1]

These frontiers (which were to endure) are of the highest interest. For they were not imposed by Nature. Indeed, the Normandy over which William was eventually to rule may be regarded as an expression of history rather than as a product of geographical conditions. Its physical structure was diversified, and it possessed on the landward side no clearly defined natural boundaries.[2] The Bresle and the Epte on the east, the Sélune and the Couesnon on the west, are small streams, and in the south the Avre, marked as it was to be by the strongholds of Nonancourt, Tillières and Verneuil, was a strategic line rather than a natural frontier. By contrast, the great valley of the Seine running through the midst of the province, and dividing it, led past the debatable land of the Vexin into the very heart of France. Up and down that waterway there was always constant passage which linked Normandy to Burgundy, and Rouen to Paris. Even between Rouen and Orléans is no great distance, and the rivers which lie in between are neither large nor formidable. Thus, though eleventh-century Normandy was a highly individual land, it was always linked to France. Two of the ancient road systems of Gaul passed across it.[3] The route from Marseilles and Lyons to the English Channel, by way of Paris and Mantes, followed the Seine valley to meet the sea at Lillebonne and Harfleur. Similarly, the road which united the Channel with the valley of the Loire proceeded from Tours to Le Mans, and then on to Sées and Bayeux. To and fro along these roads, as up and down the valley of the Seine, there passed a commerce of merchandise and ideas which flowed across the frontiers which were the product of historical circumstance.

[1] Douglas, *Rise of Normandy*, pp. 7–9.
[2] Vidal de la Blache, *Tableau de la géographie de la France* (Lavisse, *Histoire de France*, vol. I, part I, pp. 171–183).
[3] Powicke, *Loss of Normandy* (1913), pp. 14 and 15.

Not only were the land frontiers of Normandy insubstantial, but the region they enclosed was geographically divided. The distinction between Upper and Lower Normandy is, in this respect, well marked. The east of the province is grouped naturally round the reaches of the lower Seine, for the wide district bounded by the Bresle and Epte, the Avre, the uplands of Perche, and those of the upper Vire is all dominated by the great river which flows through its midst. Within these areas there are defined regions marked by their own peculiarities, but all are united in a common territorial structure which has produced an open countryside of cornfields, orchards, and of farm life. This land makes a contrast with the country which lies to the west, which forms, geologically, the eastern bastion of the Breton *massif*. Here the fertile plain gives place to moorlands, and to the south of the Bessin, the *Bocage normand* resembles the Breton Vendé more closely than it does the country of the Seine valley. Lower Normandy looks westward and feels the western sea. Its maritime connexions link it with Brittany rather than to the Seine basin. The western seaboard of the Cotentin, rocky and forbidding, here meets the north shore of Brittany, and, with it, encloses a bay which might serve as the frontier of a single province, while the point at which the coasts intersect might appear the natural site for a provincial capital. Attempts were, indeed, actually made in the eighth century to give political expression to this geographical demand.[1] They were not to endure. None the less, if today the estuary of the Couesnon marks the western boundary of the Norman land, this is due, not to Nature, but to the historical process which created medieval Normandy. And, even so, the distinction between Upper and Lower Normandy was long to persist. It substantially modified the heritage of William the Conqueror, and at one point in his career was nearly to bring destruction upon him.

The duchy to which William succeeded in 1035 thus owed its political definition not to Nature but to an historical development which in the eleventh century was already of long duration. It was the Roman administrators who perhaps first realized that the great coastal curve which stretches from Eu to Barfleur (and which, unlike the coast of Picardy, faces north) might impart a special identity to the lands it bounds. At all events, they established here the administrative province of Lugdunensis Secunda, which about the year 400, according to the

---

[1] Solomon of Brittany thus included the Cotentin in his dominion, and an attempt was made to erect Dol into a metropolitan see (*Chronique de Nantes* (ed. Merlet), pp. 26–28).

Notitia Provinciarum et Civitatum, comprised the territory appurtenant to the seven cities of Rouen (the provincial capital), Bayeux, Avranches, Évreux, Sées, Lisieux, and Coutances.[1] This, as might be said, was the first political definition of medieval Normandy, and here as elsewhere in Gaul the permanence of the Roman arrangements was to be assured by the Church. The provincial organization, as described in the time of Honorius, was coeval with the introduction of Christianity into this region. Rouen had become a Christian metropolis by the close of the fourth century, and there are reasons for believing that the bishopric of Bayeux, where Christianity was preached at a very early date, was established shortly after 400. Bishops from Avranches, Évreux, and Coutances took part in the council of Orléans in 511, whilst in 533 there is specific reference to a bishop of Sées, and in 538 to a bishop of Lisieux.[2] Before the end of the sixth century, therefore, the Norman bishoprics had been firmly established in the ancient Roman *civitates*, and thus it was that the traditions of the Second Lyonnaise were to be carried into Merovingian Neustria and beyond. The results were to influence the whole subsequent history of Normandy. The identity of the province was to survive even the Viking devastations of the ninth century. And in the eleventh century, Normandy could still be defined as roughly coincident not only with Lugdunensis Secunda but also, and more particularly, with the ecclesiastical province of Rouen and its six dependent bishoprics.

By 933, therefore, the conquests of the new Viking dynasty had been made to stretch over an ancient administrative province, but they had not overpassed its bounds. Their limitations were thus as remarkable as their extent. Less than a hundred years before the birth of William the Conqueror, the rule of the Scandinavian family to which he belonged had been halted at frontiers which were indicated not by physical conditions but by a long process of earlier history. The crucial question thus arises as to how far his political inheritance – how far the character of the Normandy which he came to rule – had been modified during the ninth and tenth centuries by the Scandinavian settlements in Neustria.[3]

It is generally agreed that Normandy in 1066 was an exceptional

---

[1] Stapleton, *Rot. Scacc. Norm.*, vol. I, pp. xxxvii–xxxviii.

[2] *Gall. Christ.*, vol. XI, p. 136; Prentout, *La Normandie* (1910), p. 33.

[3] On this much debated question, see M. de Bouard, 'De la Neustrie carolingien à la Normandie féodale' (*Bull. Inst. Historical Research*, vol. XXVIII (1955), pp. 1–14); J. Yver, 'Le développement du pouvoir ducale en Normandie' (*Atti del Congresso di Studi Ruggierani*, Palermo, 1955); and L. Musset, 'Les domaines de l'époque franque et les destinées du régime domainiale du IXe au XIe siècle' (*Bull. Soc. Antiq. Norm.*, vol. XLIX (1942), pp. 9–98).

province, and it is both plausible and very usual to account for its individuality by reference to the intrusion of a Scandinavian population into this area of Gaul. Nor is evidence wanting to support this suggestion. The number of Rolf's followers who were given land in Neustria is not known, but the region in which they were settled had then been subject to continuous visitations from Scandinavia for nearly a hundred years. The exceptional violence of the Viking attack in the valley of the lower Seine is well attested, and Norman chroniclers of a later date are unanimous in asserting that considerable depopulation then took place. Due allowance must here be made for exaggeration, but the testimony albeit late is not to be wholly set aside easily. The process, moreover, did not end with the coming of Rolf. It is known that considerable migration into this region took place during the central decades of the tenth century, and the agrarian revolt in Normandy which marked its close was so remarkable both for its date and for its organization that it might be tempting to explain it by the survival among a newly settled warrior peasantry of traditions of personal freedom comparable to those which the peasantry of the North Mercian Danelaw retained until the time of Domesday Book.[1]

A similar conclusion might be suggested by reference to the Church in Neustria. Later writers were naturally prone to magnify the devastation caused by the pagan adversaries of Christendom, but there is no doubt that during the earlier half of the tenth century the ecclesiastical life which had formerly distinguished the province of Rouen had been disrupted. The surviving lists of Norman bishops show gaps at this time which are eloquent testimony to what had occurred. In the tenth century the see of Coutances-Saint-Lô seems to have lost all connexion with a district that had lapsed into paganism, and no less than five successive bishops of Coutances resided at Rouen.[2] In the Avranchin conditions were equally bad, and late in the tenth century a bishop of Sées is to be found using stones from the city wall to rebuild his cathedral.[3] The monastic collapse was even more pronounced, and it is probable that in the third decade of the tenth century not a single monastery remained in the Norman land.

It would appear, also, that despite the baptism of Rolf, the Viking dynasty itself only slowly renounced the traditions of its pagan past. It

---

[1] Dudo (ed. Lair), pp. 129–131; Will. Jum., pp. 7–13; F. Lot, 'La grande invasion normande 856–861' (*Bibliothèque de l'École de Chartes*, vol. LXIX, pp. 5–62).

[2] L. B. de Glanville, *Prieuré de Saint-Lô*, vol. I (1890), pp. 21–24.

[3] Ord. Vit., interp. Will. Jum., pp. 165–168.

is not impossible that Rolf reverted to paganism before his death, and it is certain that a pagan reaction swept through the province after the murder of his son William Longsword in 942. In the ensuing years the whole province was given over to warfare between rival Viking bands, and during the early reign of Rolf's grandson, Richard I, the chief supporter of settled order appears to have been not the duke but the French king, Louis d'Outre-Mer, who in 942 overthrew the pagan Sihtric, and who in 945 suffered defeat at the hands of the Viking Harald.[1] Sixteen years later a veritable crisis developed, and the terrible war which ravaged the province between 961 and 965 reproduced many of the worst features of the ninth century.[2] The settlement which marked its close was, however, to prove decisive. In 965 Duke Richard I made a pact with Lothair at Gisors, and in the following year he was to restore the monastery of Le Mont-Saint-Michel with the king's approval.[3] It was an arrangement comparable with that of 911, and, as marking a stage in the development of Normandy, it was to prove scarcely less important.

From this time forward the position of the Viking dynasty was rapidly to change. It entered into closer relations with the political and ecclesiastical authorities of Gaul, and at the same time Normandy itself became ever more susceptible to Latin and Christian influences. But, even so, the Scandinavian affinities of the province endured, and Normandy continued to be in one sense a peripheral part of the Scandinavian world, sharing in its commerce and its interests, and to some extent participating also in its Viking adventures. In the closing decades of the tenth century, Ethelred II of England was moved to protest that Viking raiders of England were receiving hospitality and assistance in the Norman ports, and it was not for nothing that as late as 996 Richer, the chronicler of Rheims, could refer to a Norman duke as the Viking leader, *pyratarum dux*.[4] Even more striking perhaps is the fact that in 1014, within fifteen years of the birth of William the Conqueror – his grandfather, Duke Richard II, could welcome in his Christian capital of Rouen a pagan host from Scandinavia which under the leadership of Olaf and Lacman had recently spread devastation over a considerable area of north-western Gaul.[5]

[1] Flodoard, *Annales* (ed. Lauer), p. 63; Lauer, *Louis d'Outre Mer*, pp. 100, 287.
[2] F. Lot, *Les derniers Carolingiens* (1891), pp. 346–357.
[3] *Rec. Actes Lothaire et Louis V* (ed. Halphen), no. XXIV; Prentout, *Étude sur Dodon*, pp. 447–451.   [4] Ed. Waitz (1877), p. 180.
[5] Will. Jum., pp. 85–87; *Translatio S. Maglorii (Bibliothèque de l'École de Chartes*, vol. LVI, pp. 247, 248).

In face of such evidence it would be rash to minimize the Scandinavian factor in the making of Normandy. None the less, it might be easy to overestimate its importance. It is becoming increasingly open to question whether Scandinavia in the ninth and tenth centuries could have produced such a large surplus population as to account for such extensive migrations as are currently postulated.[1] And apart from this general question, the particular conditions in Neustria might merit closer consideration. The exhaustive examination which has recently been undertaken of Norman place-names as they are revealed in texts of the tenth and eleventh centuries, has displayed a surprising number of Latin-Scandinavian hybrids, and this has been held to indicate that the settlement of large groups of peasant warriors from Scandinavia in Neustria was, to say the least, exceptional.[2] Still more significant is it that on many large estates in the province, the events of the early tenth century do not seem to have interrupted a tenurial continuity which here proceeded with scarcely less modification than elsewhere in northern Gaul.[3] Doubtless Scandinavian influence varied from district to district in Neustria, and certainly it was stronger in the west than in the east. But already by the second quarter of the tenth century, Scandinavian speech had become generally obsolete in Rouen, though it persisted in Bayeux,[4] and the later assimilation of Normandy into the culture of France was eventually to be so rapid, and finally to be so complete, that of itself it might suggest an administrative and political continuity between Carolingian Neustria and ducal Normandy.

There is, moreover, positive evidence to show that such continuity did in fact take place. It is inevitable in this matter to turn first to the Church, which was the natural repository of the traditions of Christian Neustria. The baptism of Rolf had been the cardinal feature of the arrangements of 911–912, and it imposed upon the new ruler ecclesiastical obligations which he may not wholly have evaded. His reputed attempt to resuscitate the earlier religious life of Neustria must be regarded as an exaggeration of later writers, but some concessions may have been exacted from the newly converted Viking, and some of his alleged benefactions, particularly those to Saint-Ouen in Rouen,

[1] Cf. P. H. Sawyer, in *Birmingham Univ. Hist. Journal*, vol. VI (1958), pp. 1–17.

[2] See the notable series of articles by J. Adigard des Gautries in *Annales de Normandie* (1947), *et sqq.* Cf. Stenton, in R. Hist. Soc., *Transactions*, series 4, vol. XXVII, p. 6.

[3] Musset, *op. cit.*

[4] Dudo (ed. Lair), p. 221. Cf. Adémar de Chabannes (ed. Chavanon (1897)), p. 148: 'Many of them received the Christian faith, and forsaking the language of their fathers accustomed themselves to Latin speech.'

may in fact have been made. The reputation of his son William Longsword as a friend of the Church, though likewise unduly magnified by his posterity, rests, however, on surer foundations. The evidence of the charters of three religious houses gives at least some support to later legends that he was interested in the re-foundation of the Neustrian monasteries, and that he was particularly associated with the re-establishment of Jumièges.[1]

Not, however, until after 965 did the process gather momentum. The pact between Richard I and Lothair marked the beginning of a period wherein Norman monasticism became, under ducal initiative, subjected to the influence of great monastic reformers from outside the province. Thus late in the tenth century, Mainard was to introduce into Normandy the ideas of Saint Gérard de Broigne from Ghent, and early in the eleventh, a more fundamental inspiration came with the advent, by ducal invitation, of William of Volpiano who brought to the duchy the full force of Cluniac teaching from Dijon. As a result, through the agency of the Viking dynasty, four of the greatest monasteries of Carolingian Neustria had been re-established before the accession of Duke William,[2] and other new foundations had been made.[3] At the same time the organization of the province of Rouen was being reconstituted. A famous charter of Duke Richard I in 990 displayed the Norman bishoprics once more in full action.[4] The manner in which this ecclesiastical revival was begun, and how it was extended and developed in the time of William the Conqueror, will be considered in some detail later in this book, for it conditioned his personal achievement, and it substantially affected the character of the Norman impact upon England. Here it must suffice to note that the duchy to which Duke William succeeded in 1035 might already be regarded as an ecclesiastical unit fortified by ancient traditions that had been revived by the ducal house.

The same continuity between Carolingian Neustria and ducal Normandy is suggested by many features of the political structure of the duchy at the time of the Conqueror, and by reference to the manner in which it had been developed. There can be little doubt, for instance, that the grant by Charles the Simple to Rolf vested the Viking leader with some at least of the rights and responsibilities of a Carolingian

---

[1] Douglas, *Rise of Normandy*, p. 13; J. G. Philpot, *Maistre Wace, a Pioneer in Two Literatures* (1925), pp. 85–127.
[2] Jumièges; Saint Wandrille; Le Mont-Saint-Michel; Saint-Ouen.
[3] *e.g.* Fécamp; Bernay; Holy Trinity, Rouen; Cerisy-la-Forêt.
[4] *R.A.D.N.*, no. 4.

count,[1] and it is certain that 'count' was a title much favoured by early members of his family. What was the formal practice of Rolf and William Longsword in this matter is not known, since apparently they did not normally issue written instruments to confirm their gifts.[2] But the Icelandic writer, Ari the Learned, could in the eleventh century refer to Rolf as *Ruðu jarl*, and a charter for Jumièges which passed in 1012 could describe his son as count of Rouen.[3] In like manner the Latin *Lament* for William Longsword, which was composed about the end of the tenth century, saluted Richard I as count of Rouen,[4] and the usage was thereafter very frequently followed in official documents. In a charter given to Fécamp in 990 Richard I styled himself 'count and consul', and between 1006 and 1026 not less than nine charters of the time of Richard II spoke of him as count.[5] Other titles were used alongside this, and with the advance of the eleventh century that of 'duke' came to predominate. But in many of his charters William's father, Robert I, is styled count, and the practice was kept up by the Conqueror himself.[6]

Much more was here involved than merely formal usage. By acquiring the traditional title of count, the Viking dynasty not only vested itself with the sanctions of legitimacy, but it could in consequence lay claims to important privileges and powers. The Carolingian count by virtue of his office had wide rights to the profits of public justice, and fiscal rights also over the imperial estates which lay within his jurisdiction.[7] All these advantages seem to have accrued to the new rulers of Neustria, and they did so, moreover, at a time, and in conditions, when they might be especially valuable. With the decline of the central authority, the counts everywhere gained more independence, and they could in addition now exploit to their own benefit the imperial estates which had been entrusted to their administration. This process, as is well known, took place throughout northern Gaul. But in tenth-century Neustria the situation was particularly favourable to the ruling family. For owing to the prolonged Viking wars, and owing to the rapid expansion of the power of the new dynasty between 919 and 933, there had survived in the whole wide region between the Bresle and the

---

[1] J. Yver, *op. cit.*, p. 186.　　　　　　　　　　[2] *R.A.D.N.*, nos. 36, 53.

[3] *Ibid.*, no. 14, *bis*; *Origines Islandicae* (ed. Vigfusson and York Powell), vol. i, p. 187.

[4] Lair, *Guillaume Longue-Epée* (1893), pp. 66–68. Cf. Adémar de Chabannes (1897), p. 189: 'Ricardus Rothomagensis comes.'

[5] *R.A.D.N.*, no. 4 and nos. 9, 17, 18, 22, 23, 29, 32, 44, and 46.

[6] *Ibid.*, nos. 64, 65, 73, 80, and pp. 239–454.

[7] Cf. Fustel de Coulanges, *Transformations de la royauté* (1922), pp. 421–434.

Couesnon, between the Avre and the sea, no rival count who could dispute power with the newly established counts of Rouen.[1] The significance of this fact to the growth of ducal authority in Normandy was certainly very considerable, and its consequences were to be seen in the political structure of the duchy in the time of the Conqueror. Duke William II after his accession was to find himself surrounded by counts. But the comital houses to which they belonged were all then of a very recent establishment, and all of them without exception were closely connected with the ducal dynasty itself.

The process by which this had taken place was to entail results of such importance to the future that it deserves some illustration.[2] The first private individual to be styled count in Normandy was Rodulf of Ivry, half-brother of Duke Richard I, who assumed the title between 1006 and 1011, and thereafter several of the sons of that duke were similarly designated, perhaps by reason of their birth. Archbishop Robert of Rouen, for instance, claimed to be also count of Évreux, and in 1037 he was to pass on the dignity to his eldest son Richard. Again, about 1015 two illegitimate sons of Duke Richard I, Godfrey and William, became counts, the latter being certainly count of Eu; and after their deaths, Gilbert of Brionne, the son of Godfrey, was a count, whilst William's son, Robert, was before 1047 recognized as count of Eu. In Lower Normandy a similar development occurred. About 1027, there was established in the extreme west of the province a certain Count Robert, who was very probably one of Duke Richard I's bastards: he may well have been count of Mortain as was certainly William Werlenc, who was possibly his son and who survived until after 1050. Apart from the Conqueror's father, who may have been count of the Hiémois before he became duke, no other count can be discovered in Normandy before 1050 with the exception of William, son of Duke Richard II, who very early in the Conqueror's reign was made count of Arques.[3]

Here may be found a further indication of the manner in which the Viking dynasty had been enabled to extend and make effective over the whole of Neustria the comital powers which it had itself inherited from the Carolingian past. Indeed, the appearance as count of cadet members of the reigning family may well have been connected with some scheme of defence for the Viking province as a whole. The earliest Norman

[1] Yver, *op. cit.*, p. 186.
[2] For what here follows, see the evidence given in Douglas, 'The Earliest Norman Counts' (*Eng. Hist. Rev.*, vol. LXI (1946), pp. 129–156).
[3] Will. Jum., p. 119.

counts appear to have been established at Ivry, Eu, and Mortain. The first faced the count of Chartres, the second guarded the eastern border of Normandy, whilst Mortain lay across the line of Breton advance by way of Pontorson. These were frontier districts even as were the principal earldoms over which at a later date the Conqueror was to set his *comites* in England.[1] There is thus no reason to suppose that the advancement to comital status of members of the ducal family during the earlier half of the eleventh century indicated any diminution of the ducal authority. Rather, it may be considered as part of a settled policy by which the Viking dynasty, relying on earlier traditions, had extended its own administrative power.

The same conclusion could be reinforced by reference to the *vicomtes* who were likewise a characteristic feature of eleventh-century Normandy. Even as the duke had for long been the sole count in Normandy so also had *vicomtes* been established in the province before the local counts. A *vicomte* of Arques can, for instance, be found in that district before a count was set over it,[2] and those regions of Normandy such as the Cotentin, the Avranchin, and the Bessin which were to produce the greatest families of *vicomtes* never in this period possessed a count of their own. The early development of the office is also noteworthy. Not less than twenty *vicomtes* can be personally identified in Normandy between 1015 and 1035, and the number was soon to be increased.[3] Equally significant is it that the *vicomtes* seem from their first appearance in ducal Normandy to have been agents of the ducal administration, and regular suitors to the ducal court where they performed many of the functions later discharged by the household officials. It is in fact impossible to escape the conclusion that the *vicomte* in eleventh-century Normandy was not simply (as his title implies) the deputy of a count: he was more specifically the deputy of the count of Rouen who had become duke of Normandy.

Both the Norman *comtés* and the Norman *vicomtés* which had come into existence by the time of Duke William II thus derived much of their special character from an earlier process of history. They were

[1] Below, pp. 294–296.

[2] Rainald was *vicomte* of Arques before 1026 (Chevreux et Vernier, *Archives de Normandie*, plate IX). William was not made count of Arques until after 1035.

[3] I have noted the following among those named as *vicomtes* in charters between 1015 and 1035: Nigel; Tescelin (and Richard his son); Thurstan (Goz); Alfred the Giant; Richard; Wimund; Odo; Siric; Geoffrey; Rainald; Goscelin (son of Hedo); Ersio; Aymon; Hugh; Rodulf; Anschetil; Gilbert; Erchembald; Gerard. The careers of many of them, or of their descendants in the reign of Duke William II, will be illustrated below.

based, moreover, not upon new territorial units but upon the administrative divisions of Carolingian Neustria which had themselves survived the Viking wars.[1] If the Conqueror's father was count of the Hiémois he presided over a district whose earlier identity is illustrated in a long series of Merovingian and Carolingian texts; and the count of Évreux exercised jurisdiction over the ancient Evreçin which had enjoyed an individual life in the eighth and ninth centuries. The *comté* of Eu likewise represented a territory which was distinct in the time of Rolf. And it was the same with the *vicomtés*. The Cotentin is mentioned, for instance, in a sixth-century *Life* of Saint Marculf; the Avranchin was similarly defined at an early date; and the Bessin was of very ancient origin. A similar development might be detected in the church. In the reconstruction of the Norman church which was characteristic of the eleventh century, many of the dioceses which were then reconstituted, and many of the archdeaconries which were then established, were based, albeit with considerable modification, on the ancient territorial units.

The continuity here revealed deserves comment. The characteristic subdivision of Carolingian Neustria had been the *pagus*. But at the time when Rolf was established in Gaul, the *pagi* within the western empire were everywhere beginning to disintegrate, though their disruption was not to become general before the end of the tenth century.[2] Rolf and his immediate successors, therefore, possessed of special powers through their unique comital status in Neustria, were here given the special opportunity to arrest, or to postpone, a disintegration which was taking place with great rapidity elsewhere. It would seem that they seized it, and continued for some time to preserve the *pagi* as units of their own administration. At the beginning of the second quarter of the eleventh century, for example, the *pagi* of Saire, Hague, and Bauptois in the extreme north of the Cotentin were given in their entirety by the Conqueror's uncle Duke Richard III to his wife Adela, and about 1040 a charter could correctly describe the newly constituted *comté* of Arques as the Pays de Talou.[3] The growth of a new feudal order based upon tenure and service was soon to mask the earlier growth. Nevertheless, the conformity of eleventh-century Normandy, as a whole, and in its parts, to ancient areas and institutions of government merits full

[1] Le Prévost, 'Les anciennes divisions territoriales de la Normandie' (Soc. Antiq. Norm., *Mémoires*, vol. XI (1840), pp. 1–19). What follows in this paragraph is derived from that remarkable article.
[2] J.-F. Lemariginer, in *Mélanges – Halphen* (1951), pp. 401–410.
[3] *R.A.D.N.*, no. 58; *Chartes de Jumièges*, vol. I, no. XX; Musset, *op. cit.*, p. 96.

emphasis. The Viking dynasty had thus acquired through special circumstances a special authority. Its very survival during the tumultuous years of William's minority was, as will be seen, to depend in no small measure on this fact.

The debt of ducal Normandy to older political and ecclesiastical institutions lends a special interest to the relationship which at the time of William's birth had been established between the Norman dynasty and the ruling house of France. For this too is only to be explained by reference to an earlier development. Whatever may have been the precise terms on which the grant of land was made to Rolf by Charles III – and these are open to dispute[1] – there is no doubt that vassalage was claimed, and if its practical implications were often ignored by Rolf and his immediate successors, it seems also that they were sometimes acknowledged. The solemn reception of Louis d'Outre Mer at Rouen by William Longsword in 942 was probably a recognition of this relationship, and the subsequent murder of the duke later in that year may not have been unconnected with it. Again, if the famous story of the abduction of the young Duke Richard I by the French king undoubtedly contains legendary elements, it may well represent the assertion of an overlord of his right to bring up the infant son of a defunct vassal at his own court.[2]

What, however, is more relevant to the Conqueror's inheritance is that this vassalage, always claimed and sometimes recognized, was in due course to be transferred to the rising house of Capet, and in this development, too (though there were earlier connexions between the two families), the period following the settlement of 965 was to prove decisive. In 968 Richard I formally recognized Hugh the Great as his overlord, and after the royal coronation of Hugh Capet in 987, the French kings of the new family consistently regarded the Norman dukes as their vassals.[3] Moreover, throughout his long reign, the Conqueror's grandfather, Duke Richard II, repeatedly discharged the duties which such vassalage implied.[4] The consequences to the future were to be

---

[1] Flodoard (Annales (ed. Lauer), pp. 39. 55, 75), three times seems to speak of formal commendation, and Charles's diploma of 918 (Rec. Actes Charles III (ed. Lauer), no. XCII) states that the grant was made for the defence of the kingdom (pro tutela regii). On the other hand, the same charter speaks of the grants as being made to 'the Normans of the Seine' – Nortmannis sequanensibus – a plural form of words inappropriate to a feudal grant as later understood.

[2] Flodoard, Annales, p. 84; Richer (ed. Waitz), p. 53; Dudo (ed. Lair), p. 209.

[3] R.A.D.N., no. 3; Lot, Fidèles ou Vassaux? pp. 177–192.

[4] Douglas, Rise of Normandy, p. 12.

profound. Indeed, the relationship was in due course to prove an important factor in the survival of both the dynasties concerned. In 1031 – some three years after the birth of William – the young King Henry I of France, flying from the wrath of his mother, Constance, took refuge in Rouen, and calling on the Norman duke for support was thereby enabled to regain his kingdom.[1] Correspondingly, in 1047, it was the intervention of Henry I on behalf of his Norman vassal which then rescued the young Duke William from destruction.[2]

Of less intrinsic interest, but equally indicative of the increasing participation of the Norman dynasty in the affairs of Gaul, were the relations which had developed about the same time between the ducal house and Brittany. The future pattern of these relations was in fact set during the first decade of the eleventh century by two notable marriages.[3] The former of these was a union between Hawisa, daughter of Duke Richard I of Normandy, and Geoffrey of Rennes, who was subsequently count of Brittany. The latter was a marriage between Duke Richard II of Normandy and Judith of Brittany who was Geoffrey's sister. These two marriages followed closely upon each other, and there is reason to suppose that they were also connected as part of a common design to safeguard the welfare of the two families. Such, at all events, was the result. On Geoffrey's departure in 1008 on the pilgrimage during which he died, his two sons Alan III and Eudo, then of tender age, were left under the tutelage of their Norman mother, and in consequence Richard II, who was both brother and brother-in-law to Hawisa, immediately began to play a dominant part in the government of Brittany.[4] Similarly, after Richard II's death, and particularly after William's succession as duke in 1035, Alan III of Brittany, the son of Geoffrey, was to find himself deeply involved, and highly influential, in Norman affairs.[5]

The Norman inheritance of William the Conqueror was thus made up of many diverse elements, and in particular it derived from two contrasted traditions. The extent of Scandinavian influence upon the growth of Normandy has perhaps sometimes been overestimated, but its consequences were none the less considerable, and it helped to

---

[1] Will. Jum., p. 105; Lot, *Saint-Wandrille*, no. 13.

[2] Below, pp. 48–50.

[3] Will. Jum., p. 88; *Ann. S. Michel* (Delisle, *Robert de Torigni*, vol. ii, p. 231); Douglas, *Eng. Hist. Rev.*, vol. lxv (1950), pp. 289–291.

[4] La Borderie, *Historie de Bretagne*, vol. iii, pp. 8–10.

[5] Below, pp. 36–38.

distinguish the province over which William came to rule from its neighbours in Gaul. On the other hand, the family to which William's father belonged, and which was itself a characteristic product of Scandinavian expansion, had from the start rested its power on other and more ancient foundations which it sought to strengthen rather than to destroy. It had been established by imperial grant; it had utilized and vitalized the administrative institutions of the Carolingian age; it had associated itself with the Capetian rulers of France; and it had linked its fortunes with those of the Church in the province of Rouen. The process by which this had been achieved was gradual. Before the pact of Gisors in 965 the Scandinavian affinities of Normandy, though weakening, remained strong. Between 965 and 1028 they became subordinate, as the duchy became increasingly absorbed in the surrounding Latin and Christian civilization of France. As a result, the Normandy, which under the leadership of William the Conqueror was in the third quarter of the eleventh century to reorientate the history of England, was French in its speech, in its culture, and in its political ideas.

Such was the heritage to which William the Conqueror was eventually to succeed. But would the bastard boy at Falaise ever be permitted to grasp it? And, if seized, could he retain it? And how might it be so exploited as to deflect the future development of western Christendom?

Chapter 2

ACCESSION AND MINORITY

1035–1047

Little is known of William's childhood, and it must be presumed that it was passed in the obscurity of his mother's home at Falaise. Later, legends inevitably developed that his greatness was immediately recognized, and his future achievements anticipated.[1] But there is no evidence to warrant this supposition. Posterity might dwell on the romantic circumstances of his birth, but sentiment could not alter the facts of the situation nor mask William's essential illegitimacy. William, although to be in due course styled 'the Conqueror'[2] or 'the Great',[3] was for his contemporaries emphatically 'William the Bastard'. Nor is there any reason to suppose that during his infancy he was ever considered as a possible successor to the Norman duchy. It is noteworthy that his father never sought to legitimize him by making Herleve his wife.

Nevertheless, during these years there was emerging that pattern of Norman politics which was to make possible his eventual accession, and to provide the background to his minority as duke. His grandfather, Richard II, had died on 23 August 1026,[4] after a reign of nearly twenty years, leaving six children by his Breton wife, namely three daughters[5] and three sons,[6] of whom the eldest was Richard, and the second Robert, the Conqueror's father. It was the former of these, then perhaps about eighteen years of age, who succeeded as Duke Richard III in

---

[1] William of Malmesbury (*Gesta Regum*, vol. II, p. 285) was, before 1125, telling that Robert first saw Herleve when she was dancing in the road (washing her clothes in a stream is another version – cf. Benoit (ed. Michel), vol. II, pp. 555–557), and forthwith brought her into the castle. And that night, after William's conception, Herleve dreamt that a tree grew out of her body whose branches overshadowed all Normandy and England. It is a good story.

[2] For an early example of this, see Douglas, *E.H.D.*, vol. II, no. 69.

[3] Freeman, *Norman Conquest*, vol. II, note T.

[4] Cf. Douglas, in *Eng. Hist. Rev.*, vol. LXV (1950), pp. 289–303.

[5] Will. Jum., p. 88. The girls were (i) Adeliza who married Rainald of Burgundy – their son Guy was to play a large part in Norman history; (ii) Eleanor who married Baldwin IV of Flanders; and (iii) an unnamed daughter who died young and unmarried.

[6] Besides Richard and Robert there was a son named William who became a monk at Fécamp and died young.

1026, whilst Robert apparently became count of the Hiémois.[1] The arrangement, however, proved unstable. Robert disputed his brother's position, and established himself at Falaise. As a result, during the autumn of 1026 and the early months of 1027, hostilities persisted between them. Then on 5 or 6 August 1027, Richard III suddenly died.[2] Posterity was not slow to accuse Robert of fratricide, and though this cannot be proved, he was certainly the chief gainer by his brother's death. For though Richard III had left a young legitimate son named Nicholas, the child was immediately relegated first to the monastery of Fécamp and then to that of Saint-Ouen in Rouen,[3] and it was Robert, who was himself scarcely more than a boy, who became the sixth duke of Normandy.

He was to rule Normandy for nine years,[4] but in view of the circumstances in which he had acquired power it is not surprising that his reign should have opened with violence. The civil war between him and his brother had divided the duchy, and invited further disorder. There is evidence, for instance, that the new secular aristocracy, whose rise to power in the province was to be so notable a feature of this period,[5] took advantage of the situation to advance their fortunes by private war against their neighbours, whilst many of the less fortunate in these struggles were, about this time, to depart from the duchy in order to rehabilitate themselves elsewhere and particularly in southern Italy.[6] There is testimony, too, that many of them, such as the family of Montgomery, took the opportunity to enrich themselves at the expense of the church, and that they often did so with the connivance of the duke.[7] It is small wonder, therefore, that the monastic records and annals became filled with complaints, or that the duke himself should have fallen under ecclesiastical censure.[8] By 1028, indeed, matters were approaching a crisis. In that year Robert, archbishop of Rouen, who had apparently endeavoured to restrain the young duke, was besieged by him at Évreux, and was forced into exile, whereupon he promptly

---

[1] Will. Jum., p. 97. But the matter is not wholly certain (Douglas, *Eng. Hist. Rev.*, vol. LXI (1946), pp. 145, 146). It is significant that Robert was at Falaise in the Hiémois when he encountered Herleve.

[2] Douglas, *Eng. Hist. Rev.*, vol. LXV (1950), pp. 289–303.

[3] *Gall. Christ*, vol. XI, cols. 141–144. His public career was none the less to be interesting.

[4] His reign is surveyed in Will. Jum., pp. 97–114.

[5] Below, chap. 4.

[6] F. Chalandon, *Domination normande*, vol. I, pp. 88–111.

[7] Below, pp. 90–92.

[8] Will. Jum., p. 100; *Miracula S. Wulframni* (Soc. Hist. Norm., *Mélanges*, vol. XIV (1938), p. 47); *R.A.D.N.*, no. 66.

laid Normandy under an interdict.[1] Nor were Robert's early troubles circumscribed by the bounds of his duchy, for during the opening years of his reign he found himself at war with his cousin Alan III of Brittany, who may perhaps (by reason of his parentage) have hoped himself to succeed to the Norman duchy.[2] In these circumstances, there was some danger that in the vivid phrase of Hugh of Flavigny, Normandy might become 'debauched' with anarchy.[3]

By 1031, however, the situation had been largely retrieved, and the chief agent in effecting the recovery was the metropolitan archbishop of Rouen. Robert, archbishop of Rouen, was in many ways a most remarkable man. Brother to Duke Richard II, he had been appointed to the metropolitan see as early as 989, and ever since he had been closely associated in the government of the duchy. He appears, for instance, as a witness to not less than fourteen charters of Richard II.[4] He was reputedly responsible for the conversion of the future Saint Olaf in 1014, and he was certainly a munificent benefactor of the abbey of Saint-Père of Chartres.[5] But his interests were by no means exclusively ecclesiastical. He took to wife a woman named Herleve, and by her he had three sons: Richard, Ralph of Gacé, and William.[6] Further, according to later testimony, he was count of Évreux at the same time as he was archbishop of Rouen.[7] Certainly, he held the lands which later pertained to the *comté* of Évreux, and equally certainly his son, Richard, became count of Évreux immediately after his father's death.[8] Robert, thus, might be said to have combined in himself, by his inheritance, and through his career, many of the ducal, aristocratic, and even ecclesiastical traditions which were later to provide the basis of Norman might. Possessed of such power, so diversely derived, and himself ruthless, mundane, and capable, his support was by 1030 essential to his young nephew, the duke of Normandy.

The archbishop's recall from exile thus became imperative, and with it a general stabilization of the duchy began. The interdict was lifted, and the reconciliation between Duke Robert I and his uncle was marked by the issue of one of the most interesting charters of the period[9] whereby the duke and archbishop, apparently by way of treaty, confirmed the possessions of the cathedral church of Rouen. Equally

---

[1] Letter of Fulcher of Chartres (*Pat. Lat.*, vol. CXLI, cols. 224, 225).
[2] Will. Jum., p. 106. [3] *Mon. Germ. Hist. Scriptores*, vol. VIII, p. 401.
[4] Douglas, *Eng. Hist. Rev.*, vol. LXI (1946), pp. 132, 133.
[5] *Cart. S. Père Chartres*, vol. I, p. 115. [6] Ord. Vit., vol. II, p. 365. [7] *Ibid.*
[8] *Chartres de Jumièges*, vol. I, no. XIX; *R.A.D.N.*, no. 92. [9] *R.A.D.N.*, no. 67.

significant was the ending of the Breton war. The archbishop brought his two nephews together at Le Mont-Saint-Michel, and persuaded them to a truce whose terms are uncertain, but which possibly included the performance of homage by Alan to Duke Robert.[1] What was more important, however, was that by these means the archbishop had once more renewed the advantageous connexion between the two dynasties which had been characteristic of the latter years of Duke Richard II. Alan was left free to consolidate his position in Brittany against his numerous rivals. Robert was liberated from menace on the western border of his duchy, and might hope for support from Alan III in any policy he might adopt at home.

From this time forward until his death in 1037 Archbishop Robert of Rouen was to be the dominant force in Normandy, and responsible, in part at any rate, not only for the increased prosperity of the duchy during the remainder of the reign of Duke Robert I, but also in large measure for the conditions which were to make possible the succession of William in 1035. During these years, for instance, there can be seen forming a powerful group of Norman magnates who were specially pledged to Robert's support. Prominent among them was Gilbert of Brionne, the count, a grandson of Duke Richard I, and the ancestor of a family which was to be very notable both in Normandy and England.[2] A man of large possessions, particularly in central Normandy, and of unbounded ambition, he became closely associated with Duke Robert about this time, and is to be found frequently witnessing his charters.[3] Nor was he alone in this respect, for during these same years a yet more interesting person is to be found with the young duke. This was Osbern whose sister Gunnor had married Duke Richard I, and who was himself to found the fortunes of one of the greatest of those feudal families whose rise in Normandy will hereafter have to be considered.[4] Already by 1034 he had become one of the foremost of the new territorial lords in the province, and it was symptomatic of the improved position of Duke Robert that such a man should have been now content to serve as *dapifer*, or steward, in the ducal household.[5]

Such, then, was the position of the ducal power in Normandy during the last year of the reign of Robert I. The elements of disorder inherent

[1] Lobineau, *Histoire de Bretagne* (1707), vol. I, p. 91; La Borderie, *Histoire de Bretagne*, vol. III, p. 9.   [2] Below, pp. 86, 87.
[3] *Vita Herluini* (ed. Robinson, *Gilbert Crispin*, p. 88); *R.A.D.N.*, nos. 64, 65, 67, 70, 80, 85.
[4] Below, pp. 89, 90.   [5] *R.A.D.N.*, nos. 69, 82. Cf. Ord. Vit., vol. III, p. 229.

in a society which was in a state of flux had, of course, by no means been suppressed, and it is significant that even after his reconciliation with Archbishop Robert, the duke was compelled to resort to arms when Hugh, bishop of Bayeux, refused the ducal orders and fortified himself in his castle of Ivry.[1] Nevertheless the duke's authority had been preserved and strengthened, and his prestige outside his duchy was considerable. Rulers of other lands were eager to obtain his support, or at least respected his enmity. His relations with Cnut the Great will hereafter call to be examined, and Ethelred II of England together with his wife and two sons had already sought protection in Normandy.[2] Baldwin IV of Flanders was for a short time at his court, and he had made an ally of Alan III of Brittany.[3] Most important of all, he had by the prompt discharge of his feudal duty in 1031 placed the king of France in his debt.[4] At home he had gained the adherence of a strong group among the rising aristocracy, and he had secured the support of the powerful archbishop of Rouen, who, more than anyone else, could make his rule respected and effective.

It was in these circumstances that late in 1034 Duke Robert made the sudden and astounding resolve to depart forthwith on pilgrimage to Jerusalem.[5] The secular irresponsibility of the decision naturally provoked an outraged opposition on the part of those Norman magnates who had assisted him to build up his power. Yet Robert was not to be dissuaded, and in seeking to account for an act which seems to baffle modern explanation, it must be remembered that he was here moved by one of the strongest impulses of the age.[6] Thus Fulk Nerra, the terrible count of Anjou, had in 1002 gone to Jerusalem to expiate his crimes, and, despite great hardships, he was twice to return there.[7] Similarly, in 1008, Geoffrey of Brittany had likewise set forth on pilgrimage to the Holy Land.[8] And soon Sweyn Godwineson, brother of King Harold II of England, a man whose violence and brutality had caused him to be condemned as 'nithing', or worthless, by his associates,[9] was to set out for Jerusalem, and to perish from cold in the Anatolian mountains on the journey.[10] Such, moreover, were but

---

[1] Will. Jum., p. 102.   [2] Below, pp. 162, 163.   [3] Will. Jum., p. 104.
[4] Above, pp. 28, 29.   [5] Will. Jum., p. 111.
[6] Cf. Musset, in *Annales de Normandie*, October 1962.
[7] K. Norgate, *England under Angevin Kings*, vol. I, pp. 153, 192–196.
[8] *Ann. Mont S. Michel*, s.a. 1008; *Hist. S. Flor. Saumur* (Marchegay and Mabille, *Églises d'Anjou*, p. 261); Morice, *Hist. de Bretagne, Preuves*, vol. I, col. 354.
[9] AS. Chron., 'C', s.a. 1049.
[10] Freeman, *Norman Conquest*, vol. II, note BB; Runciman, *Crusades*, vol. I, p. 47.

outstanding examples of this particular exhibition of penitence operating in the most unlikely quarters. The strange atmosphere of the eleventh century was charged with violent emotions resulting in lurid crimes and fantastic penances. And the idea of pilgrimage was pervasive. Already the shrine of Saint Michael at Monte Gargano was attracting a steady stream of pilgrims, particularly from Normandy, and about 1026 a Norman duke had sponsored the great pilgrimage associated with Richard, abbot of Saint-Vanne.[1] Certainly, the impulse to pilgrimage was strong, and perhaps Robert felt some special need to attempt to gain by such means a private absolution. It was later alleged that he wished to purge himself from guilt in the death of his brother.[2] At all events, in the contemporary circumstances, it is not wholly inexplicable that the call to Jerusalem should have been answered by a young man who seems always to have combined within himself a violent lack of scruple with a strain of romantic rashness.

Resolute in his determination, he therefore convoked a notable meeting of Norman magnates, who, led by the archbishop, sought in vain to turn him from his purpose. They urged with truth that it was folly for him now to leave a duchy which he had acquired only after warfare, and which he had only with difficulty retained. They added, with equal truth, that he could point to no man who might be able, or who could be trusted, to safeguard his interests during his absence; nor in the event of his failing to return was there any heir who could expect to succeed him without dispute. Robert's resolve was however formed, and at length he even secured some support. He brought forward his infant son, his bastard by Herleve, and persuaded the magnates to recognize William as his heir. They did so, and swore the customary oaths of fealty and obedience. Shortly afterwards, Duke Robert departed from Normandy.[3]

He was never to return. The story of his pilgrimage passed speedily into legend: men told of the splendour of his retinue, and how his wealth and magnificence had impressed even the emperor of the East. They added praise for his devotion, and extolled the lavish generosity with which he endowed the Holy Sepulchre.[4] Though there is evidently here much exaggeration the whole story should not be dismissed as false. Other Norman dukes had been noted for their benefactions to the Holy Land, and Wace who tells the story of Robert's pilgrimage in greatest

---

[1] Runciman, *loc. cit.*; Southern, *Making of the Middle Ages*, pp. 51–54.
[2] Below, Appendix F.   [3] Will. Jum., p. 111.   [4] *Miracula S. Wulframni, loc. cit.*

detail was here relying, in part at any rate, upon traditions which had long been current.[1] Robert's pilgrimage undoubtedly inspired the admiration of contemporaries whose sentiments respecting it were perhaps further influenced by its unfortunate conclusion. On his homeward journey the young duke was stricken with mortal sickness while passing through Asia Minor. The usual stories of poisoning were current as early as 1053, and were soon to be elaborated.[2] What is certain is that Robert, sixth duke of Normandy, styled by posterity the 'Magnificent', died at the Bythinian Nicaea on one of the first three days of July 1035.[3] The Norman reign of William the Conqueror had begun.

It could hardly have opened in less auspicious conditions. Even apart from the fact that the new duke was a child of some seven years of age, his illegitimacy would itself have made it inevitable that his accession would be challenged, and his survival in 1035 was due in the first instance to the support of the group which had gathered round Duke Robert I during the closing years of his reign. The first guardians of Duke William were thus the chief supporters of his father: the archbishop of Rouen, Count Alan of Brittany, and Osbern the powerful steward at the court. To them must also be added a certain Turchetil or, as he is also styled, Turold, who is asserted to have been the *pedagogus* or even the *nutricius* of the infant duke.[4] Little is known of the functions of the office thus strangely described, but Turchetil, who possessed lands at Neufmarché, was the ancestor of a family which was to play a significant part in the history both of Normandy and Wales, and to give Duke William notable support at a later crisis in his reign.[5] In 1035, however, Turchetil must have been of lower standing than the other *tutores* of the duke, though he was a significant figure in the small group which assisted William to secure his inheritance.

The most important person in Rouen during the critical autumn of 1035 was undoubtedly the elderly archbishop. He might, indeed, by reason of his descent have claimed the succession for himself, but doubtless in view of his advancing years, and his ecclesiastical office, he

---

[1] *Roman de Rou* (ed. Andresen), vol. II, pp. 148, 149; Haskins, *Norman Institutions*, pp. 268–272.

[2] Below, Appendix F.

[3] The date is fixed by the necrologies of Jumièges, Saint-Évroul, and Le Mont-Saint-Michel (*Rec. Hist. Franc.*, vol. XXIII, pp. 420, 487, 579). The place is given in Will. Jum., p. 114; in Ord. Vit., vol. I, p. 179; vol. II, p. 11; vol. III, p. 224; and also by Rodulf Glaber (ed. Prou, p. 108).

[4] Ord. Vit., vol. I, p. 180; vol. II, p. 369; vol. III, p. 229; interp. Will. Jum. (ed. Marx), p. 156.

[5] Ord. Vit., vol. III, p. 42. His grandson was Bernard of Neufmarché, lord of Brecknock.

preferred not to contemplate any further extension of his power. He was, however, uniquely placed to dominate the crisis. The metropolitan see of Rouen had always since the days of Rollo been placed in a special relationship with the ducal dynasty, and Robert had not only his office to buttress his authority but also the extensive lands of the *comté* of Évreux which he had acquired. Moreover, it was he who had been first among the counsellors of Duke Robert at the close of his reign, and it was he also who had brought together his Norman and Breton nephews, doubtless thereby securing for William the support of Alan III. It may again have been the archbishop who by virtue of his connexions in France brought about what was not the least significant event of Norman history in 1035. Shortly before, or shortly after, Robert's departure from Normandy the 'consent' to William's succession had been obtained from King Henry,[1] and it is probable that at this time the boy was actually sent to the king in order to perform homage to his royal overlord as successor to the Norman duchy.[2]

None the less, even with the support of the archbishop of Rouen, and with the recognition of King Henry, the position of the young duke was extremely precarious, and it was fortunate for him that overt opposition from those members of the dynasty whom he had supplanted could for various reasons be postponed for a time. Thus Nicholas, who as son of Duke Richard III was perhaps nearest in succession in the legitimate line and who had been placed in the monastery of Saint-Ouen by Robert I when still a boy, now showed no disposition to dispute William's accession. Indeed he was always to be a loyal supporter of his cousin under whom he was in about 1042 to become abbot of the monastery over which he was to preside for fifty years.[3] More formidable opposition might, however, have been expected from Mauger and William, the sons of Duke Richard II by Papia, or even from 'Guy of Burgundy', who through his mother Adeliza was grandson of that duke. In the event all of these were in due course to lead formidable revolts, but they evidently did not as yet feel strong enough to rebel. In 1035 neither Mauger nor William had attained the positions of authority which they were soon to attain, and Guy was not as yet possessed of those lands in central Normandy from which he was later to draw his strength.[4] Archbishop Robert backed by his prestige and position could thus control the situation with the aid of the ducal officials.

[1] Rodulf Glaber (ed. Prou), p. 108.
[2] Wace, *Roman de Rou* (ed. Andresen), vol. II, p. 150.
[3] *Gall. Christ.*, vol. XI, cols. 141–143.   [4] Below, pp. 48, 49.

Detailed evidence of the conditions prevailing in Normandy during the first critical months of the reign of Duke William II is naturally hard to obtain, but a charter of this time is illuminating in this respect. This was issued by Hugh, bishop of Bayeux, between August 1035 and March 1037.[1] In it the bishop notes the depredations which had taken place on the lands of his bishopric 'after the death of Duke Richard [II] and after the death of Duke Robert [I]', and states that he had determined to have his rights restored and safeguarded. He therefore brought a suit before a court which consisted of 'Robert the archbishop, Eudo the count,[2] Nigel the *vicomte*', and other magnates who had rights of justice in the kingdom;[3] and it was this court which after hearing the plea gave judgment in his favour. The procedure is in every way notable. It will be observed that the archbishop is clearly the dominant figure in the proceedings whilst the young duke is not mentioned. On the other hand, the presence of the *vicomte* and the other lords possessed of judicial rights indicates that the ducal administration was being continued.

Even this measure of stability depended, however, directly upon the personal power of Archbishop Robert, and when that prelate died on 16 March 1037,[4] the situation degenerated with disastrous rapidity. So violent was the confusion which ensued that it has proved tempting to assume that the men who were involved in it were moved by a simple liking of disorder for its own sake. Yet this underrates their capacity, for they were later to prove their ability, and few of them had not much to lose if sheer chaos had been allowed to prevail. It is useful, therefore, to attempt to analyse the motives which impelled the chief participants in these sanguinary struggles. The chief feudal families of a highly competitive nobility which was only now rising to its full power were compelled by the decline in the ducal authority to take their own measures to safeguard their newly won possessions, and tempted to enlarge these by

[1] *Cart. Bayeux*, vol. I, p. 27, no. XXI. The date is determined by the fact that the death of Duke Robert is recorded, whilst Archbishop Robert is still alive.

[2] There was no Norman count of this name, I believe, at this time. It might be tempting to consider Odo II, count of Blois, who died 11 November 1037, but the reference may rather be to Eudo of Penthièvre, a count of Brittany.

[3] 'Robertus, scilicet archiepiscopus, Odo comes, et Niellus vicecomes, alii-que seniores justiciam regni obtinentes.'

[4] The death of Archbishop Robert I in 1037 is well established but the modern authorities such as *Gallia Christiana*, Vacandard, and Bourrienne do not seem to have given it further precision. Perhaps this is because, very strangely, it does not appear in the obituary of Rouen Cathedral (*Rec. Hist. Franc.*, vol. XXIII, p. 358). None the less, in the necrology of Le Mont-Saint-Michel, there appears the obituary of *Robertus archiepiscopus Rotomagensis* (*ibid.*, p. 577). This could refer either to Robert I or Robert II who died in 1221. But Robert II is known to have died in May (*Gall. Christ.*, vol. XI, col. 60), so it must be Robert I who is here designated.

the sword at the expense of their neighbours. The ducal dynasty in its turn (which could in one sense be regarded as the most important feudal family in the province) was similarly placed, and whilst many of its members were ready to dispute with William the title of duke, none of them could wish that the authority of the count of Rouen should be completely destroyed. Indeed at one crisis in the minority they were notably to act together in the interests of order. Finally, there was the French king who might well feel that during the minority of his vassal he had a direct responsibility to maintain his own rights in the duchy.

What was of immediate moment was the question of who should obtain control of the young duke, and in consequence the ducal household was for some years given over to such shocking disorder that almost all those who had closely supported William at his accession were to perish by violence. Count Alan III died suddenly, either in 1039, or more probably in October 1040.[1] His place as chief tutor was taken by Gilbert, the count, who had been another of the intimates of Duke Robert I, but within a few months Gilbert himself was murdered, when out riding, by assassins acting under the orders of Ralph of Gacé, one of the sons of Archbishop Robert.[2] About the same time Turchetil was likewise assassinated.[3] And Osbern the steward was killed at Vaudreuil after a scuffle in the very bedchamber of the boy duke.[4] William's household was in fact becoming a shambles, and some idea of the conditions which had come to prevail therein may be gathered from the story that Walter, the brother of Herleve, was wont at this time to sleep in the company of Duke William his nephew, and frequently at night was forced to fly for safety with his charge to take refuge in the cottages of the poor.[5] It is not surprising that these years left a lasting impression on the character of the boy who was chiefly involved.

The crimes which disgraced the ducal household at this time were of such dramatic horror that they might easily mask the more fundamental issues of the crisis. In truth, they formed the background to a concerted movement by members of the ducal dynasty to obtain a more active control of its affairs. In particular, this period saw the rise to dominance of Mauger and William, the sons of Duke Richard II by Papia. In, or shortly after, 1037[6] Mauger was appointed archbishop of Rouen in

[1] Ord. Vit., vol. II, p. 369; vol. III, p. 225; La Borderie, *Histoire de Bretagne*, vol. III, p. 13.
[2] Ord. Vit., interp. Will. Jum. (ed. Marx), pp. 153, 154.
[3] Will. Jum., p. 116.   [4] *Ibid.* Cf. *R.A.D.N.*, no. 96.   [5] Ord. Vit., vol. III, p. 229.
[6] E. Vacandard, in *Rev. catholique de Normandie*, vol. III, p. 103.

succession to Robert, whilst William his full brother became count of Arques.[1] The appointments may in some sense be held to have been made in the interests of the dynasty. It is noteworthy, for instance, that William received his *comté* of Arques as a benefice to be held specifically in return for his discharging the loyal service of a vassal to the duke,[2] whilst Mauger as archbishop took immediately a prominent position in the government of the duchy. He appears among the witnesses to many ducal charters of these early years, and he can sometimes be watched as presiding over the court of the young duke, whose attestation occasionally follows after that of the archbishop. The situation resulting from the advancement of these two brothers can in fact be seen very clearly in a charter which was issued about 1039.[3] By it Count William, styling himself 'son of Duke Richard', gave land to the abbey of Jumièges, and among the leading attestations to the act these are given in the following order: 'Mauger the archbishop; William, count of the Normans; William, the count's "master";[4] and William, count of Arques'. The two brothers were clearly advancing towards a dominating position in the duchy. After 1040 it was Mauger, archbishop of Rouen, who was in chief control, backed by William, count of Arques, and possibly by Nicholas, abbot of Saint-Ouen. But other members of the family were also moving towards a position of greater importance. Chief of these was Ralph of Gacé,[5] the murderer of Count Gilbert, and the son of Archbishop Robert, whilst at about this time Guy of Burgundy, grandson of Duke Richard II, received both Vernon and also Count Gilbert's castle of Brionne.[6] Clearly the ducal family was not going to relinquish its power without a struggle.

But the province of Normandy was lapsing into a fell disorder. The confusion of these years cannot, it is true, be illustrated in full detail, but enough is known to mark the minority of William after 1037 as one of the darkest periods of Norman history. Long-standing feuds among the secular aristocracy were reopened, and each crime was made the occasion for further bloodshed. Most of the great families whose rise will have to be considered as part of the growth of a new nobility in the

[1] Will. Jum., p. 119.

[2] Hic enim Willelmus a duce jam in adolescentia pollente comitatum Talogi percipiens, obtentu beneficii, ut inde existeret fidelis.

[3] *R.A.D.N.*, no. 100.

[4] Was he a personal guardian or tutor to the boy? He appears also in a charter for Sigy (*R.A.D.N.*, no. 103).

[5] Ord. Vit., interp. Will. Jum. (ed. Marx), pp. 159, 161.

[6] Will. Jum., p. 122; Will. Poit., p. 16; Ord. Vit., vol. III, p. 230.

province were involved at this time in violence or disaster. Thus Bjarni of Glos-la-Ferrières, a vassal of Osbern the steward, avenged the murder of his lord by killing William of Montgomery.[1] Roger of Tosny, having ravaged the lands of his neighbour Humphrey 'of Vieilles', was in due course assassinated by Humphrey's son Roger 'of Beaumont',[2] and the feud was continued by the house of Clères who were dependants of the family of Tosny.[3] Again, Hugh of Montfort-sur-Risle and Walkelin of Ferrières both perished in the private war they waged against each other,[4] and the family of Bellême conducted against the sons of Geré of Échauffour an onslaught which was marked by unspeakable crimes.[5]

A feature of the private wars which ravaged Normandy at this time was the use made therein of castles. Some of the ducal fortresses which had sometimes been built of stone were seized by the magnates to whom they had been entrusted. Thus William Talvas of Bellême established himself at Alençon, Hugh, bishop of Bayeux, at Ivry, and Thurstan Goz at Tillières. At the same time a large number of smaller fortifications of a different type were hastily erected.[6] These were wooden structures built on artificial mottes, surrounded by palisades and encircled by moats which might be filled with water.[7] Undoubtedly a family needed to be of some standing to erect such a stronghold for its own use, and to man it, but they became sufficiently numerous during these years to give a special character to the civil warfare which was convulsing the province. It was from them that the families who were most directly involved in these disorders could conduct hostilities against each other, and defend themselves from the onslaught of their enemies.

It is true that the record of these disorders has survived for the most part in the writings of monastic chroniclers who may perhaps have been disposed to paint them in too lurid colours, and in consequence the disturbances of the time have perhaps been exaggerated.[8] Certainly the ducal administration never seems during these years wholly to have collapsed, and this must have been directly due to the tradition of public authority which the Viking dynasty had inherited and developed from Carolingian Neustria.[9] It could be illustrated in several directions. The Bayeux charter to which reference has been made indicates that

[1] Ord. Vit., interp. Will. Jum. (ed. Marx), p. 157.
[2] *Ibid.*, vol. I, p. 180; vol. II, pp. 40, 41; vol. III, p. 229.
[3] *Ibid.*, vol. III, pp. 426, 427.   [4] Will. Jum., p. 116.
[5] Ord. Vit., interp. Will. Jum. (ed. Marx), pp. 159, 161, 162.
[6] J. Yver, 'Châteaux forts' (*Bull. Soc. Antiq. Norm.*, vol. LIII (1957), pp. 53–57).
[7] De Bouard, *Guillaume le Conquérant* (1958), p. 33.
[8] De Bouard, in *Annales de Normandie*, October 1959, p. 174.   [9] Above, pp. 22–29.

between 1035 and 1037 recognized legal sanctions were still appealed to and applied,[1] and even after the death of Archbishop Robert there is evidence that some attempt was made – and not wholly without success – to maintain this situation. Though Thurstan Goz was to lead a rebellion from Tillières, nearly all the *vicomtes* between 1035 and 1046 regularly discharged their duties, and the vice-comital attestations to ducal charters in this period are not infrequent.[2] Again, the bishops of Normandy seem in general to have given their corporate support to the child ruler, and most if not all the ducal revenues as from the *comté* of Rouen will be found to have been regularly collected at this time.[3] The duke, or those who acted for him, seem also to have had a specifically ducal force at their disposal since if the testimony of a later writer can be believed, at the worst period of the disorders, Ralph of Gacé, who was then dominant at the ducal court, could be described as 'head of the armed forces of the Normans' (*princeps militie Normannorum*), and as such he seems to have commanded a considerable body of troops which he used to good purpose.[4] In short, the ancient traditions of ducal authority, and some of the administrative machinery which might give it effect, survived during these years and contributed much to preserving the integrity of the Norman duchy through this critical decade. How important this was will be seen in the lethal situation which at once arose in 1047 when the western *vicomtes* at last revolted.

Nevertheless, the conditions of William's minority were sufficiently terrible. The feudal families were becoming ever more desperately involved in an internecine struggle with each other, and the plight of humbler folk in the duchy can be imagined. Not the least significant feature of these years is the action by groups of peasantry who organized themselves (sometimes under their parish priests) for corporate defence. When the sons of Soreng sought to dominate the district round Sées, a savage struggle ensued, in the course of which the cathedral itself was partially burnt. But they were at last captured and killed by the men of the countryside.[5] The power of the ducal government to dispense local justice was evidently becoming severely restricted, and perhaps for this reason men in the duchy were being led to look elsewhere for means to mitigate disorder.

It was during these years that there occurred in Normandy a most

---

[1] Note that the reference is to those exercising justice as of right in the kingdom (*regni*), not the duchy (above, pp. 38, 39).

[2] *e.g. R.A.D.N.*, nos. 92, 102, 103.

[3] Below, pp. 133, 135.

[4] Ord. Vit., interp. Will. Jum. (ed. Marx), p. 159.

[5] Will. Jum., pp. 165, 167.

interesting juridical development which was to entail wide consequences in the future. During the tenth and early eleventh centuries
there had been made, first in southern and central France, and later
in Burgundy, the famous attempt of the Church to rescue public order
by means of the institution known as the Truce of God,[1] whereby, under
episcopal sanction, an undertaking was made to prohibit private warfare
during certain days of the week, or during certain seasons of the
Christian year. Among the ecclesiastics who were foremost in propagat-
ing the Truce of God none were more influential than Odilon, abbot of
Cluny, and Richard, abbot of Saint-Vanne of Verdun.[2] Consequently
it is remarkable that although Richard of Saint-Vanne had close
connexions with the Norman ducal court in the latter years of Duke
Richard II, and during the reign of Duke Robert I,[3] no attempt was
made by him or anyone else to introduce the Truce into Normandy at
that time. The reason must be that the ducal authority was then
considered to be itself capable of preserving public order by means of
judicial processes which were generally respected.[4] Now, however, the
situation had radically changed, and in 1041–1042 Richard of Saint-
Vanne, acting, it would seem, with the approval of those in charge of
ducal policy, made a strong move to bring the Truce of God to the
duchy.[5] The methods he employed are somewhat obscure since no
ecclesiastical council seems to have been called at this time, and it is
more probable that an individual approach was made to the bishops of
the province.[6] The attempt, however, failed. The private interests of the
rising feudal families to which the bishops belonged proved too strong.
And though some five years later, in changed circumstances, the earlier
effort of Richard of Saint-Vanne was at last to be fruitful, in the meantime the Truce was rejected by Normandy, and the disintegration of
public order proceeded apace.[7]

It is indeed a matter of some wonder that the young duke survived
the troubles of his minority, and the explanation must in part be sought
outside Normandy. One of the decisive factors of Norman history at this
time is to be found in the policy of the king of France. The position of

[1] On all that concerns the introduction of the Truce of God in Normandy, see M. de
Bouard, 'Trève de Dieu' (*Annales de Normandie*, (October 1959), pp. 168–189). This fundamental article in my opinion supersedes all that had been written before on the subject, and
in particular it corrects my own ill-advised remarks on this topic in *Cambridge Historial
Journal*, vol. XIII (1957), pp. 114, 115.
[2] H. Dauphin, *Le Bienheureux Richard* (1946), pp. 254–264.   [3] De Bouard, *loc. cit.*
[4] *Ibid.*   [5] Hugh of Flavigny (*Mon. Germ. Hist. Scriptores*, vol. XIII, p. 403).
[6] De Bouard, *op. cit.*, p. 117.   [7] Hugh of Flavigny, *loc. cit.*

King Henry I in respect of Normandy during these years was mis-represented by Norman chroniclers who wrote at a time when the relations between the ducal house and the French monarchy were being transformed, and who for patriotic reasons were prone to depict such relations as those existing between independent sovereign princes. Nor has this misconception been wholly avoided by some modern scholars.[1] In truth, however, as has been seen, the vassalage of the duke of Normandy had for long been admitted, and sometimes enforced; and it had now become of high importance. Even as Duke Robert I had in 1031 acknowledged and assisted King Henry I as his natural lord,[2] so now, on the accession of a minor in Normandy, the French king claimed and exercised his feudal rights over the duchy. King Henry's recognition and support for the child duke had been an essential feature of the arrangements of 1035, and it was largely owing to the French king that those arrangements were to endure.

The 'consent' which had been given by King Henry to the accession of Duke William was of cardinal importance. The king could claim right of wardship over the infant heir of a defunct vassal, and by so doing he made himself to some extent responsible for that vassal's safety. It is significant therefore that not only had William been sent to do homage in person to the king at the time of his father's pilgrimage, but that, at some subsequent date, Henry invested the duke with the insignia of knighthood.[3] Throughout the minority the king claimed, and exercised, direct rights over Normandy, and regarded William as being in some special sense under his protection. When after 1040, for example, Gilbert of Brionne, the count, became tutor to the duke, he was considered as acting in that capacity as the deputy of the French king,[4] and a later writer was probably correct in saying that during these years King Henry treated Normandy as if it were *fiscus regalis* – part of the royal demesne.[5]

Only in the light of such considerations can be explained the confused political history of Normandy during this period, or the French king's intervention therein. Thus, some time after 1040, Henry is to be found investing Tillières-sur-Avre,[6] a fortress which had originally been built

[1] Freeman, *Norman Conquest*, vol. II (1860), pp. 199, 203.
[2] Will. Jum., p. 105: 'per fidei debitum sibi'.
[3] Will. Malms., *Gesta Regum*, vol. II, p. 286.
[4] Gislebertus comes tutor pupilli constituitur; tutela tutoris regi Francorum Henrico assignatur – Will. Malms., *ibid.*, p. 285.
[5] Henry of Huntingdon, *Historia Anglorum* (ed. Arnold), pp. 189, 190.
[6] Will. Jum., p. 117.

by Duke Richard II as a bastion against the counts of Chartres,[1] but which, after the cession of the territory of Dreux by Odo of Blois to King Robert, had faced the ancestral possessions of the house of Capet. The fortress was at this time in charge of Gilbert Crispin,[2] an under-tenant of Count Gilbert, and the uncle of a distinguished abbot of Westminster.[3] Crispin refused to surrender it, but many Norman notables supported the king, who was thus enabled to capture the stronghold and in due course to dismantle it.[4] Again, when shortly afterwards the French king decided once more to intervene in the Norman anarchy a strictly similar situation immediately developed. Now, Henry entered the Hiémois, and passed on into the valley of the Orne, where he stormed the town of Argentan.[5] On this occasion, also, he had Norman support. For Thurstan Goz, who was to be the ancestor of the earls of Chester, and who was then *vicomte* of Exmes, at once co-operated with the French troops and himself occupied Falaise. There he was invested by Ralph of Gacé, who had control of the boy duke, and after considerable fighting Falaise was recaptured. Thurstan was sent into exile (from which he was soon to be recalled), and King Henry returned towards Paris, but not before he had regained the fortress of Tillières, and placed his own garrison within its walls.[6]

The conduct of the French king in these events was bitterly con-demned by later Norman chroniclers as exhibiting base ingratitude towards the dynasty to which in part he owed his throne.[7] There is, however, little reason to suppose that Henry was at this time ever anxious to supplant the young vassal whose succession in Normandy he had recognized. The French king had cause, moreover, to view the anarchy within the Viking province with some dismay, the more espe-cially as it affected a large area of northern France. The concern of Brittany with the Norman succession had been displayed in the career of Alan III, and there was always a possibility that the Norman crisis might have repercussions also in Flanders. Baldwin V, who succeeded to the rule of Flanders in 1035, was already trying to play off the emperor against the French king whose sister he had married, and he watched the Norman situation with deep interest. He is indeed reported to have given positive assistance to Duke William during the minority,[8] and tradition later asserted that it was during these years that there was

[1] Will. Jum., pp. 84, 87.   [2] *Ibid.*, p. 117.   [3] J. A. Robinson, *Gilbert Crispin*, p. 14.
[4] Will. Jum., p. 117.   [5] *Ibid.*, p. 118.   [6] *Ibid.*
[7] *Ibid.*, p. 117.   [8] Chronicle of Tours (*Rec. Hist. Franc.*, vol. XI, p. 107).

first formed the project of a marriage between William and Baldwin's daughter Matilda.[1] The implications of the Norman crisis were thus widespread, and certainly no king reigning in Paris could afford to neglect its possible repercussions on the political balance of northern France.

King Henry's intervention in Norman politics at this time is thus to be explained, not as the incursion of a foreign prince, but as the attempt of an overlord to safeguard his rights, and to improve his position, during the minority of one of his chief vassals. For this reason he always had support from within Normandy, not only from among the warring groups of magnates but also, as it would seem, from those who might well have considered that in the royal power might be found a hope for the eventual restoration of order out of chaos. Indeed, during the minority of Duke William the policy of the French king appears on the whole to have been directed towards safeguarding the position of the young duke against those who sought either to supplant him or to make him a passive agent of their will. Certainly, William stood in need of any such intervention as might be available, for during this period he could hardly make any personal contribution to the government of his duchy. Towards its close, however, there were already signs that he was beginning to discriminate among his counsellors, and to act on his own initiative.[2] But his personal authority was still weak, and he was strictly dependent upon such Norman factions as would support him, and still more on the backing of his royal overlord. And it was thus that on the threshold of manhood he was suddenly called upon to assume independently his own responsibilities, and to face a new crisis in his affairs.

In the late autumn of 1046 the disorder in Normandy which had ravaged the duchy since March 1037 began to crystallize into a co-ordinated assault upon the young duke. Hitherto, the continued existence of his nominal authority had depended in large measure upon the mutual rivalry between the contending factions in the duchy, and more particularly upon the continued operation of the ducal administration which in its turn was directly dependent upon the loyal support of his *vicomtes*. Now, a wider-spread and more closely organized movement of revolt took place. Based upon Lower Normandy, it involved many of the foremost feudal families of the duchy, and its most dangerous feature was the implication of the two principal *vicomtes* of the west. Its

---

[1] Below, pp. 391–393.   [2] Will. Jum., p. 122.

avowed object, moreover, was the overthrow of William and the substitution of a new ruler for the duchy.

The prime mover in this revolt was Guy of Burgundy, one of the possible successors to the dukedom in 1035, and now possessed of the important strongholds of Vernon on the Seine, and of Brionne on the Risle, which he had received on the death of Count Gilbert.[1] This man now sought to make himself duke, and he rallied to his support a very powerful group of Norman magnates.[2] These came, moreover, not only from the neighbourhood of Guy's own possessions in middle Normandy but more particularly from the west, and the army which was to come very near to destroying Duke William was to be led by Nigel I, *vicomte* of the Cotentin, and Rannulf I, *vicomte* of the Bessin.[3] These were joined by many lords from Lower Normandy, and especially by a group of magnates established in the district of the Cinglais situated between Caen and Falaise.[4] Among them were Ralph Tesson, lord of Thury (now Thury-Harcourt), Grimoald of Plessis,[5] and Haimo *dentatus*, lord of Creully, the ancestor of a family later to be famous in England.[6] It was a formidable rebellion and it threatened the very identity of Normandy.

According to later tradition, the revolt began with an attempt, sponsored, it was said, by Grimoald of Plessis, to capture and murder the duke as he tarried at Valognes in the heart of his enemies' territory.[7] Being warned of his danger, however, William managed to make a hurried escape by night, and riding hard through the darkness he forded the estuary of the Vire at low tide. Morning saw him at Ryes, where he received succour, and at length he reached Falaise.[8] The story of that famous ride may well contain legendary elements, but at least it may serve to emphasize the extreme plight of the young duke at this crisis. One resource alone remained to him: he could appeal to his overlord. William, therefore, hastened to the king of France whom he found at Poissy, and throwing himself at his feet he claimed as a faithful vassal

---

[1] Will. Poit., p. 14; Will. Malms., *Gesta Regum*, vol. II, p. 286; Ord. Vit., vol. III, p. 230.

[2] Will. Poit., p. 16.

[3] Will. Jum., p. 122.

[4] On this district and its lords, see F. Vaultier, Soc. Antiq. Norm., *Mémoires*, vol. x (1837), pp. 1–256.

[5] Wace, *Roman de Rou* (ed. Andresen), vol. II, vv. 3773 *et sqq.*; 3863 *et sqq.*

[6] Will. Malms., *Gesta Regum*, vol. II, p. 287; Pezet, *Barons de Creully*, pp. 16, 17.

[7] *Roman de Rou*, vv. 3657–3750.

[8] The legend says that he was welcomed by Hubert of Ryes, father of Eudo the steward, later famous as sheriff of Essex. Many of Eudo's tenants in England came from the neighbourhood of Ryes.

the succour of his suzerain.[1] The French king, moreover, felt himself directly involved in this threat to one of the greatest of the French fiefs, and it is thus that his subsequent action should be explained. Later Norman writers were to represent the transaction as a pact between equals, and it is possible that Henry may have recalled the support given to his dynasty seventeen years before by Duke Robert I. But the circumstances were now very different, and such an interpretation cannot be sustained. The young duke was in desperate straits, and it was as the king's liegeman that he pleaded his cause. Correspondingly it was as overlord of Normandy that Henry could regard the rebellion against his vassal as directed in some measure against himself. Thus was the French king moved to take perhaps the most momentous decision of his reign. Early in 1047 he entered Normandy at the head of an army resolved to rescue Duke William from his enemies.

The French army advanced towards Caen by way of Mézidon. There it was met by some sparse levies which Duke William had managed to raise from Upper Normandy. These had made their way with difficulty over the marshy plain of the Val d'Auge, passing Argentan and encamping at the side of the Laison in the neighbourhood of the royal host. The next day, very early, the king moved through Valmeraye where he heard Mass, and then proceeded to the plain of Val-ès-Dunes,[2] a featureless stretch of country bounded by the hamlets of Serqueville, and Begrenville, Bill, and Airan – villages whose place in the annals of war was to be re-emphasized in the twentieth century. It was there that the royal army encountered the force of the rebels who, advancing from the west, had previously effected a crossing of the river Orne.

The battle of Val-ès-Dunes which ensued was a decisive event in the development of Normandy, but few details of the engagement have been preserved. It seems, however, that no great generalship was displayed by either side, and the battle consisted of isolated conflicts between detached forces of cavalry. No use was made of supporting arms, and nothing is heard of the employment of the archers whose action was to be so successfully co-ordinated with that of mounted troops nineteen years later at Hastings. Long-range weapons do not appear to have been used, and if infantry were present their part of the battle was negligible. Those accounts of the battle which are most nearly contemporary are short. William of Jumièges merely says:

[1] Will. Jum., p. 123; Ord. Vit., vol. I, p. 182.
[2] *Roman de Rou*, vol. II, vv. 3807–3815.

The king and the duke, unafraid of the strength and enmity of their enemies, offered them battle, and after many engagements between groups of cavalry inflicted a great slaughter on their foes, who at last were seized with panic, and took refuge in flight, throwing themselves into the waters of the Orne.[1]

The account given by William of Poitiers though more rhetorical is hardly less brief:

The greater part of the Normans fought [he says] under the banner of iniquity, but William, chief of the avenging host, was undismayed by the sight of their swords. Hurling himself upon his enemies he terrified them with slaughter.... Most of them perished in the difficult country: some met their death on the field of battle, crushed or trampled upon by those who fled; and many of the horsemen with their mounts were drowned in the river Orne.[2]

It is probably legitimate, however, to supplement these short accounts by means of the magnificent battle picture painted in the twelfth century by Wace,[3] for the *Roman de Rou*, which is so often untrustworthy, is here of unusual value, since its author was for many years a cleric at Caen, where he had every opportunity for becoming acquainted with local traditions, and his minute descriptions leave little doubt that he himself actually visited the field of battle. According to the information supplied by Wace it would seem that before the engagement began the rebel forces were somewhat disorganized by the defection of Ralph Tesson to the side of the duke, but even so the struggle was extremely bitter. During its earlier stages King Henry was unhorsed by Haimo *dentatus*, who was, however, himself killed before he could inflict a mortal wound upon his royal master.[4] Elsewhere in the field Duke William was giving proof of that personal prowess in battle for which he was later to be famous, by striking down with his own hand a certain Hardez from Bayeux, noted as a great warrior and a faithful vassal of Rannulf of Avranches. Later Rannulf himself lost heart, and with his flagging energies the tide of battle began to turn against the insurgents. Nigel of the Cotentin long put up a strenuous and desperate resistance, but it was unavailing. The defeat became a rout as panic seized the rebel host which began to break up into small bands and to fly in great disorder. And the river Orne completed the destruction of the army.

Great was the mass of fugitives [concludes Wace], and fierce the pursuit. Horses were to be seen running loose over the plain, and the field of battle was covered with knights riding haphazard for their lives. They sought to

---

[1] Will. Jum., p. 123.
[2] Will. Poit., pp. 12–18.
[3] *Roman de Rou*, vol. II, vv. 3865 *et sqq.*
[4] Will. Malms., *Gesta Regum*, vol. II, p. 287.

escape to the Bessin, but feared to cross the Orne. All fled in confusion, and strove to cross between Allemagne and Fontenay by fives and sixes and threes. But the pursuers were at their heels bent on their destruction. Many of them were driven into the Orne, and there killed or drowned, and the mills of Borbillon were stopped with dead bodies.[1]

The defeat of the western *vicomtes* at Val-ès-Dunes was to prove a decisive event in the career of Duke William, and in the development of Normandy, and though its full consequences were only slowly to be disclosed some indication of its significance was immediately to be supplied. In October 1047 outside Caen, and in near proximity to the battlefield, there met an ecclesiastical council[2] at which were present not only the duke but most of the chief prelates of Normandy, notably Archbishop Mauger and Nicholas, abbot of Saint-Ouen, who were both of the ducal house.[3] It was a solemn assemblage, and in it the Truce of God, which had been rejected in Normandy five years previously in the time of Richard of Saint-Vanne, was formally proclaimed, whilst those present swore to observe it taking their oaths on holy relics and particularly on those of Saint-Ouen which had been brought from Rouen for the purpose.[4] The exact nature of the Truce which was thus proclaimed can only be considered by reference to texts which were compiled at a later date,[5] but its terms are reasonably certain. Private war was prohibited from Wednesday evening until Monday morning, and during the seasons of Advent, Lent, Easter, and Pentecost.[6] In this the arrangements followed a pattern with which other regions of France had already been made familiar.

The value of any such legislation depended, however, always on the efficacy of the means by which it could be enforced, and here the Norman arrangements were of a type not paralleled elsewhere at this date except in Flanders, and in the province of Rheims.[7] Here as elsewhere the chief sanctions were ecclesiastical, for the Truce itself was an institution of the Church, and it was the prelates of the Church who were primarily held responsible for its enforcement. At the council of Caen therefore the chief penalties invoked against those who might violate the Truce were excommunication and the denial to the offender of all

---

[1] *Roman de Rou*, vol. II, vv. 4155–4170.
[2] De Bouard, *op. cit.*, pp. 172–174. The Acts of the Council are indicated in the texts printed in Bessin, *Concilia*, p. 39.
[3] De Bouard, *op. cit.*, p. 175.
[4] *Miracula S. Audoeni* (*Acta Sanctorum*, August, vol. IV, pp. 834, 835).
[5] De Bouard, *op. cit.*, pp. 176–179.   [6] Bessin, *Concilia*, *loc. cit.*
[7] De Bouard, *op. cit.*, pp. 186, 187.

spiritual benefits which the Church alone could bestow.[1] But in the ordinances enacted at Caen the secular power was also invoked, and not the least important feature of what was decreed was the express exclusion from the Truce of the king and the duke, who were permitted to wage war during the prohibited periods and allowed to maintain forces to enable them to do so in the public interest.[2] Here again there is a clear indication of the authority still recognized as being vested in the ducal office,[3] and it was this combination of secular and ecclesiastical sanctions that at a later date was to enable the duke to transform the Truce of God in Normandy into the more effective *pax ducis*[4] which in due course he was to make to prevail over all his dominion.

The proclamation of the Truce of God at Caen in October 1047 was a matter of rejoicing, particularly among the peasantry,[5] but at the time it must have seemed doubtful whether it would prove operative even over the restricted region where it was first to be applied. For in the light of what is known of later history it would be easy to exaggerate what were the immediate consequences of the battle of Val-ès-Dunes. Norman chroniclers writing after the conquest of England when the Conqueror was at the height of his power could rightly discern in the battle the beginnings of the Conqueror's dominance in his duchy.[6] 'The Normans,' exclaimed William of Poitiers, 'feeling themselves mastered, all bowed their necks before their lord.'[7] Such rhetoric should not, however, be taken at its face value, and in any case it had to wait on subsequent events for its justification. In 1047 many hazards had still to be overcome before even order and security could be restored to the duchy. The victory of Val-ès-Dunes had in truth been decisive, but it had been won by the king rather than by the duke, and William's own power was still both precarious and circumscribed. He had escaped from the imminent threat of destruction, and he had emerged from tutelage. But his future was still perilous and uncertain. The minority was over: the duke's war for survival was about to begin.

---

[1] Bessin, *Concilia, loc. cit.*   [2] *Ibid.*
[3] De Bouard, *op. cit.*, pp. 187, 188.
[4] Especially at the council of Lillebonne in 1080.
[5] *Miracula S. Audoeni*: 'Gaudent omnes et maxime agricolae.'
[6] Yver, 'Châteaux forts' (*Bull. Soc. Antiq. Norm.*, vol. LIII (1957), p. 48).
[7] Will. Poit., p. 18.

Chapter 3

THE WAR FOR SURVIVAL

1047–1060

The period 1047–1060 is of cardinal importance in the history of Normandy. Often dismissed as comprising merely a welter of disconnected political disturbances, it none the less possessed its own cohesion, and without doubt it entailed momentous consequences for the future. It began with the revolt which in 1047 came near to annihilating the ducal power, and it reached its second crisis when in 1052–1054 the duke was forced to withstand not only a hostile confederation formed by his own magnates, but also a coalition of French fiefs led by the king of France. During these fourteen years the duke of Normandy was almost continually at war. Until after 1054 his survival was always in some doubt, and not until after 1060 could it at last be regarded as fully assured.

The unity of this period in the development of Normandy needs therefore to be stressed. The opening battle in these campaigns – Val-ès-Dunes – is properly to be considered as marking the end of the anarchic minority of the duke, and setting the seal on his authority. Yet the critical engagement on the banks of the Orne was but one episode in the duke's struggle for survival, and it was the beginning of a long period of uninterrupted warfare. The disturbances of these years are in short to be regarded not as a series of isolated revolts, but rather as embodying a prolonged crisis which lasted in the most acute form from 1046 to 1054; and the threat to the Norman future was no less formidable at Mortemer than it had been at Val-ès-Dunes. Only after 1054 can there be discerned a relaxation of the tension, and no subsequent menace to the integrity of Normandy was ever so severe during the Conqueror's reign as that which had been continuous between 1046 and 1054. Varaville in 1057 was an engagement of only minor importance, and the deaths of the count of Anjou and the king of France in 1060 did but give final assurance that the perils which had been faced during the previous fourteen years had at last been surmounted.

The condition of Normandy, and its place in the European order, was in fact so different in 1066 from what it had been in 1046 that it would be easy to underestimate the hazards which attended this transformation. It was not merely the survival of Duke William that was at stake. The events of this period assuredly offer the strongest testimony of the indomitable purpose of the young man who was the principal actor in this embattled drama, but these related campaigns decided much more than his own personal fate. The antagonism between Upper and Lower Normandy which was partially reflected in the conflict of 1047 had for political purposes been resolved by 1060; and the same period witnessed the beginning of the long struggle between Anjou and Normandy for the dominance of north-western Gaul. Finally, a yet more fundamental change was made at this time in the relations between the duke of Normandy and the king of France – a change which has been justly described as marking nothing less than a 'turning-point of history'.[1] The ultimate consequences of these developments were, indeed, to stretch into the far future, and were not in fact to be fulfilled until the establishment of Henry, count of Anjou, as King Henry II of England. The confused, but always interconnected, events of these years, when such large issues were still in question, thus deserve careful examination, for the outcome of the crisis which they reflected, and determined, was sensibly to affect the fortunes of Normandy and Anjou, of France and England, for more than a century and a half.

On the morrow of the battle of Val-ès-Dunes, Duke William was still not secure in his duchy. Nor did that battle mark the end of the warfare of which it formed a part. King Henry himself left Normandy shortly after his victory,[2] but hostilities continued without interruption. It is in fact perhaps indicative of the duke's continuing insecurity at this time that most of the surviving leaders of the revolt were to escape somewhat lightly. Nothing is known of the immediate fate of Rannulf of the Avranchin, but he was not deprived of his *vicomté* and he was to transmit it to his son.[3] Nigel of the Cotentin was in more desperate plight, but he too was treated with considerable leniency. He was forced to go into exile in Brittany, but before long he returned; by 1054 he was re-established in his vice-comital lands, and nearly all his forfeited possessions were restored to him.[4] As for Guy of Burgundy, although wounded, he managed to escape from the battlefield with a

[1] F. Lot, *Fidèles ou Vassaux?*, p. 198: 'un tournant d'histoire'.
[2] Will. Jum., p. 123.
[3] Below, pp. 92, 93.
[4] Delisle, *Saint Sauveur*, pp. 20, 21.

considerable force, and he promptly fortified himself in his stronghold of Brionne.[1]

The reduction of Brionne with the minimum of delay was thus imposed upon the duke as an imperative necessity if his authority was to be restored, and it was a considerable check to his fortunes when he failed to take it by storm. He was thus compelled to invest it, and to undertake an operation which might prove to be disastrously protracted. He certainly did not minimize either the importance or the difficulty of his task. He erected large siege-works on both banks of the Risle and, in particular, wooden towers which might make the siege closer and at the same time protect his own investing troops against sorties by the garrison.[2] Even these measures, however, for long proved ineffective, and it would seem that nearly three years elapsed before the castle surrendered.[3] The length of this operation, indeed, deserves some emphasis. For the delay was fraught with peril for the duke, and it postponed any reimposition of his authority over a united duchy. So long as Brionne remained untaken, Duke William could never proceed with any confidence much beyond the neighbourhood where his principal enemy, the potential leader of a new rising, was established. There is in fact no record of Duke William's presence in Upper Normandy at any time during the years 1047–1049, and it is possible that during these years Rouen itself passed out of his control. Excluded from the richest part of his duchy, and with a strong castle in central Normandy holding out against him, William remained throughout the period 1047–1049 in an equivocal position. It was probably not until the beginning of 1050, after Guy had surrendered and been banished from Normandy, that William was at last able once more to re-enter his own capital.[4]

During these years William's authority was in fact largely circumscribed by the extent of the power he had recently regained in Lower Normandy, and the fact was to entail considerable consequences. He found himself established in precisely that part of the duchy which had come most tardily under the control of the counts of Rouen, and it is possible that he realized that here might be provided an opportunity of mitigating that dichotomy between Upper and Lower Normandy

[1] Will. Poit., p. 18; Ord. Vit., vol. III, p. 232.
[2] Will. Poit., p. 21.
[3] Ord. Vit., vol. III, p. 342; vol. IV, p. 335.
[4] Will. Poit., p. 18. He says that after William re-entered Rouen, he punished those who had recently revolted against him in the city.

which had always tended to impair the political unity of the duchy. At all events, it is significant that the growth of Caen to a position of greater importance begins about this time.[1] By the end of the first quarter of the eleventh century a cluster of villages had been formed at the juncture of the Orne and the Odon, and the importance of this site was evidently recognized in 1047 when it was chosen as the meeting-place of the council which proclaimed the Truce of God. Thenceforward William, who doubtless appreciated the strategic and commercial advantages of this position, took positive action during the ensuing years to foster the growth of an urban agglomeration at this place, providing it with walls of stone and perhaps with a castle, and making it also one of his principal residences. The regard he had for it is displayed today in the two magnificent abbey-churches which remain the glory of the town, and it is significant that at the last William was to be buried, not like his ancestors in Rouen or Falaise, but at Caen. Although not an episcopal city, Caen rose during his lifetime to be the second town in Normandy, and its early growth owes more to William the Conqueror than to any other single man. The rise of Caen during the Conqueror's reign is thus symptomatic of his eventual success in integrating Upper and Lower Normandy finally into a single political unit.

It was, likewise, during the period immediately following the battle of Val-ès-Dunes that the rise of Anjou began to introduce a new factor into Norman politics. The relations between Normandy and Anjou, which were to colour so much of the history of the twelfth century and eventually to result in the formation of a great continental empire, entered on their first critical phase between 1047 and 1052, and it was then that there began to take shape a new political grouping in north-western France which was vitally to affect the future. So wide-reaching were to be the results of this development, and so fraught was it with immediate peril to the duke, that its obscure origins in Angevin policy need here to be watched in so far as these hazardously affected the subsequent course of William's career, and modified the fortunes of the duchy over which he ruled.

Hitherto, the expansion of Anjou had been directed southward. It had been achieved mainly at the expense of the counts of Blois,[2] and so successfully that in 1044, a bare three years before Val-ès-Dunes, King

---

[1] De Bouard, *Guillaume le Conquérant*, pp. 58–61.
[2] Norgate, *England under Angevin Kings*, vol. I, pp. 143–185.

Henry I had been constrained to give formal recognition to Angevin dominance over Touraine.[1] Henceforth Anjou, holding in Tours the key to the Loire valley, could block the Roman road of Capetian governance which ran from Paris to Orléans and onward into Poitou.[2] In this way was justified the political insight of earlier counts of Anjou who had realized that their power could best be based upon a control of the Loire, and it was Geoffrey Martel, who, succeeding as count in 1040, reaped the reward of their endeavour. Brutal, unprincipled, crude, and strong, Geoffrey lacked finesse in his ambitions and statesmanship in his policies. But he had in his character much of the hammer after which he was named, and his achievements are not to be minimized. From 1044 until his death in 1060 he was always a formidable menace to the duke of Normandy, and for most of that period he was a stronger force than Duke William in the affairs of northern France.

It is not surprising that such a man finding himself now secure in the south should at once strive to push northward in his conquests. And the *comté* of Maine presented itself as the obvious field for his operations. For Maine at this time was in a state of great disorder. It was precisely during the earlier half of the eleventh century that a new feudal aristocracy arose in Maine. Such families as those of Mayenne, Château-Gonthier, Craon, Laval, and Vitré were being established in their possessions and in many cases there is charter evidence to show that the early eleventh-century lord was the original grantee.[3] In face of this development the comital house of Maine found itself unable to exercise any effective control, and after the death of Herbert 'Wake-Dog' about 1035,[4] his successor Count Hugh IV was engaged in constant warfare with his vassals, many of whom had now fortified themselves in newly built castles.[5] Among these, moreover, there was one feudal family which was to play a crucial part in the wider conflict which ensued. For at the exact point whereat Capetian, Norman and Angevin interests were to meet, there was established the house of Bellême.

Neither the French king, nor the count of Anjou, nor the young duke of Normandy, could ignore the family of Bellême, for it controlled a region that was vital to all of them – a wild stretch of hilly country on the border between Maine and Normandy which held the key to

---

[1] Halphen, *Comté d'Anjou* (1906), p. 48.
[2] Powicke, *Loss of Normandy* (1913), vol. II, p. 14.
[3] B. de Broussillon, *Maison de Craon* (1893), vol. I, pp. 18 *et sqq.*; *Maison de Laval* (1895), chap. I; R. Latouche, *Comté du Maine* (1910), pp. 60–62, 116–127.
[4] Latouche, *op. cit.*, pp. 22–31.   [5] *Ibid.*, pp. 60–62.

important lines of communications. At Bellême itself, six roads converged linking Maine with the Chartrain and with Normandy. Through Alençon passed the old Roman way from Le Mans to Falaise. And in the single gap in the ridge between Alençon and Domfront there ran yet another Roman road leading towards Vieux.[1] It had for long been the ambition of the first house of Bellême[2] to obtain control of this vital district and by 1040, that ambition had been virtually fulfilled. The family held Bellême itself nominally from the king of France, Domfront from the count of Maine, and Alençon from the duke of Normandy. But in reality it was possible for the lords of Bellême to act as virtually independent of their various overlords, and to play these off one against the other.[3] Moreover, the power of the family had been yet further increased by the dominating position it had acquired in the church. Between 992 and 1055 three successive bishops of Le Mans – Siffroi, Avejot, and Gervais – were connexions of the family of Bellême,[4] and in 1035 Yves, then head of the family, became bishop of Sées.[5]

Such was the situation in Maine when shortly after the battle of Val-ès-Dunes, the count of Anjou began to extend his activities northwards. In the extreme south of Maine, and near the Angevin border, was the fortress of Château-du-Loir whereat was established Gervais, bishop of Le Mans,[6] and it was this stronghold that Geoffrey Martel now attacked.[7] He failed to take the castle, which was partially burnt during the operation,[8] but he had the good fortune to capture the bishop, whom he promptly threw into prison.[9] A situation was clearly arising which the French king could not ignore, the more especially, when in 1050, Pope Leo IX, who had made unavailing protests against the imprisonment of Gervais,[10] formally excommunicated the count of Anjou.[11] Finally, on 26 March 1051, Count Hugh IV of Maine

---

[1] J. Boussard, in *Mélanges – Halphen* (1951), pp. 43, 44.

[2] On this family, see G. H. White, R. Hist. Soc., *Transactions*, series 4, vol. XXXI (1940), pp. 67–68.

[3] Lemarignier, *Hommage en Marche* (1945), pp. 65, 66.

[4] Latouche, *op. cit.*, pp. 132–136. Siffroi (d. *c.* 1000) was brother-in-law to Yves of Bellême (d. after 1005), and Avejot (d. *c.* 1032) was the son of that Yves. Gervais, bishop of Le Mans (1038–1055), was nephew of William of Bellême who died in 1027.

[5] *Gall. Christ.*, vol. XI, cols. 680–682.

[6] The original grantee was Haimo, the father of Gervais: he was already established there by 1007 (Latouche, *op. cit.*, p. 62).   [7] *Ibid.*, pp. 27–28.

[8] *Cart. Château-du-Loir* (ed. E. Vallé (1906)), no. 27.

[9] *Actus pontificum Cenomannis* (*Rec. Hist. Franc.*, vol. XI, p. 136).

[10] Already at the opening of the council of Rheims (3–6 October 1049) Leo IX was concerned with the imprisonment of Gervais.

[11] *Act. pont. Cenomm.* (*Rec. Hist. Franc.*, vol. XI, p. 138).

died,[1] and the citizens of Le Mans immediately offered their town to Count Geoffrey. The count of Anjou at once seized his opportunity and occupied the capital of Maine.[2]

The crisis which ensued inexorably involved not only the French king but the Norman duke. Hugh's widow Bertha with her son Herbert and her daughter Margaret were expelled from Maine.[3] At the same time, Gervais, who at last obtained his release by ceding Château-du-Loir to Count Geoffrey, repaired to the Norman court, and together with other exiles ceaselessly urged the duke to take action in Maine.[4] Duke William must have realized that his own interests were now involved, and in any case he could hardly have refused assistance to his royal overlord on whose support he relied. Hostilities had in fact become inevitable and it is possible that about this time the duke joined the king in blockading the Angevin stronghold of Mouliherne near Baugé.[5] Whether this engagement (which is only reported in William of Poitiers) ever took place, or whether in that case it should be referred (as is probable) to the spring of 1051 is doubtful. Soon, however, the war was to be extended up to the very border of Normandy. Once secure in Le Mans after the cession of the town in March 1051, Geoffrey moved north-eastward and occupied the fortresses of Domfront and Alençon. The Norman duchy was now directly threatened by the Angevin expansion and its duke was forced into action.[6]

In the late summer or early autumn of 1051,[7] therefore, Duke William, with the approval of King Henry, entered the territory of Bellême to dispute with the count of Anjou the possession of the key fortresses of this region. His first advance was towards Domfront, and so immediate did the threat appear that Count Geoffrey at once hurried

---

[1] *Necrologie de la Cathédrale du Mans* (ed. Busson and Ledru), p. 72; Latouche, *op. cit.*, p. 29; Halphen, *Comté d'Anjou*, p. 73.

[2] *Act. pont. Cenomm. (Rec. Hist. Franc.*, vol. XI, p. 138).

[3] Latouche, *op. cit.*, p. 29.   [4] *Act. pont. Cenomm., loc. cit.*

[5] Everything connected with the episode at Mouliherne, including its date, is obscure. It may have taken place in 1048 (Halphen, *op. cit.*, p. 72), though in that case it must have been before October when the king was at Carignan, near Sedan. The action could, however, be better referred to the spring of 1051 (Prentout, *Duc de Normandie*, p. 146). There is, however, nothing in Will. Poit. (the sole authority) to connect it with the operations round Domfront.

[6] Will. Poit., pp. 23, 34–36; Will. Jum., pp. 124–126.

[7] The traditional date of 1048 for this campaign is only to be rejected with hesitation. Accepted by Halphen (*op. cit.*) when that notable scholar was a very young man, his conclusion has been very generally followed. Henri Prentout (*Duc de Normandie*, pp. 140–143) has, however, shown good reason why it is unacceptable, and in this he has been followed by de Bouard, though without further comment (*op. cit.*, p. 41). Some of the evidence is set out below (Appendix B), and I have few doubts in assigning the operation round Domfront and Alençon to the autumn of 1051 and the early spring of 1052.

to the rescue.[1] After considerable fighting the count was compelled to retire, and perhaps owing to a threat to Anjou by King Henry from Touraine, he subsequently left Maine.[2] Even so, William could not take Domfront by storm, and after constructing siege-works similar to those he had used at Brionne, he settled down to besiege it. But in the absence of his chief opponent he was not content merely with the prolonged blockade which certainly lasted for a considerable time during the months of winter.[3] One night, therefore, leaving a section of his force in front of Domfront, he suddenly moved under cover of darkness to Alençon. He achieved surprise, stormed the town, and having inflicted horrible barbarities upon the defenders, he placed his own garrison within its walls. Then he moved back to Domfront, and so great was the fear excited by the atrocities he had sanctioned at Alençon that the inhabitants of Domfront determined to surrender in return for a promise of mercy and protection. Duke William thus found himself in possession of the two strongholds.[4]

The importance of this campaign was considerable. Alençon and Domfront were both in the future to stand in need of defence, but the duke had retained his overlordship over the one, and added the other to his dominion. The customs of Normandy thus soon came to prevail also in Domfront, whilst the surrounding district of the Passais was gradually to be absorbed in the duchy.[5] A certain stabilization of this frontier had thus been achieved in the interests of Normandy, and the results were reflected in the changing position of the house of Bellême within the feudal structure of north-western France. The lords of Bellême were always to prove difficult subjects, but though the Capetian kings were ever ready to assert direct overlordship over them, the Norman dukes from this time forward were able to treat them more and more as vassals, and the new situation was forcibly expressed in one of the most important feudal alliances of this period. About this time Roger II of Montgomery, whose family had risen to power with the support of Duke Robert I, acquired for wife Mabel, daughter of William Talvas of Bellême.[6] She was heiress of a large part of the

---

[1] Will. Poit., p. 40.　　[2] *Ibid.*, p. 42.　　[3] *Ibid.*, p. 38.　　[4] Will. Jum., p. 126.
[5] Lemarignier, *Hommage en Marche*, pp. 19, 20, 35.
[6] The *Complete Peerage* (vol. xi, p. 686) places the marriage 'probably between 1050 and 1054'. The inference taken from the date of the birth of Roger's son, Robert of Bellême (*ibid.*, p. 689, note j), is valueless, since the date of Robert's birth is in fact unknown, and since it is uncertain whether any or all of the daughters of Roger II of Montgomery by Mabel of Bellême were born before Robert, who was himself the second son of that marriage. The date suggested by Jean Marx (Will. Jum., p. 125) of '1048–1049' is evidently based on the assumption that the Domfront campaign took place in those years.

Bellême lands, and her marriage was yet further to advance the fortunes of Montgomery. Henceforth the fortunes of Bellême were to be linked to those of Normandy, and with a family already closely associated with the Norman ducal house.

The control obtained by the duke over the debatable territory of Bellême was in the future to provide William with a base from which he might extend his authority westward. But this development was still remote in 1051, for Geoffrey was for long to remain the dominant force in Maine. Nor is it perhaps always realized how great a threat to the duke was latent in this war. Throughout, it would appear, he was surrounded by treachery,[1] and any failure would undoubtedly have provoked a widespread revolt. In the event, however, his position was to be substantially strengthened by his success, and it is noteworthy that in this campaign William had been particularly assisted not only by Roger of Montgomery (who had a special interest in the Bellême inheritance) but also by William fitz Osbern, the son of Duke Robert's murdered steward.[2] These young men were to be among the architects of the Norman conquest of England, and their presence along with others with William in front of Domfront indicates that the duke was already attracting to his support rising members of the new Norman nobility, who were now willing to stake their personal fortunes on his survival.

He was in truth almost immediately to stand in need of all the support he could inspire, for his fate was now to be perilously inter-twined with a political movement which was to influence much of the future of France and England, and which after all but destroying the Norman power was to determine much of the subsequent character of Norman policy. Hitherto, the survival of the duke had depended in large measure upon the French king. During the minority Normandy had been treated almost as if it were part of the royal demesne of France. The prime feature of Val-ès-Dunes had been the action of King Henry; and in the subsequent wars the duke had discharged his feudal duty to the king. In 1052, however, the ancient connexion between the Norman dynasty and the house of Capet was disrupted. Val-ès-Dunes had been won by the king for the duke; Alençon had been stormed by William when fighting against the enemies of Henry; but when, shortly after the fall of Domfront, Duke William had to face a rebellion comparable in magnitude with that of 1047, he did so, not with Capetian assistance,

[1] Will. Poit., p. 36. [2] *Ibid.*, p. 38.

but in opposition to the armed strength of the French king. There thus took place a transformation in the long-established relations between the Norman duchy and the French monarchy, and as a result a new epoch opened wherein Normandy was no longer to appear as the vassal and supporter of the Capetian monarchy, but henceforth, for a hundred and fifty years, as its most formidable opponent in Gaul.

This transformation in political filiations was, if judged by its future consequences, one of the most important events in the Norman reign of Duke William, but the manner in which it was accomplished is difficult to ascertain. It would seem, however, that the change must have been initiated by the king rather than the duke. The warfare between Henry and Geoffrey had dragged on inconclusively, and it may have become clear to the French king that he had little to gain from its continuance. At all events, a *rapprochement* between the count and the king took place during the first half of 1052, and a definite reconciliation between them was completed before 15 August of that year when the king and the count were together in amity at the royal court at Orléans.[1] William on his part was bound to be concerned at this development. It would seem that he hurried to the king for he is himself to be found on 20 September 1052 in the royal presence at Vitry-aux-Loges,[2] where he doubtless strove to hinder the reconciliation between Henry and Count Geoffrey. He failed; and in fact this was the last time he was ever to be present as a friend at the court of the French king. The new alliance between Henry and Geoffrey at once began to take shape, and its critical consequences for Normandy were immediately to be disclosed. Anjou and Normandy had already been brought into direct collision, and now the former protector of the duke of Normandy had passed over to the duke's most dangerous opponent in northern Gaul. It only needed a formidable rebellion to break out within the duchy, and in connexion with the new alliance, to produce one of the most acute crises of Norman history. And such a rebellion was immediately foreshadowed when in the midst of the siege of Domfront, William, count of Arques, suddenly and without excuse, deserted from the ducal army, renounced his vassalage, and departed to his own lands in eastern Normandy.[3]

The establishment of this man as count of Arques had been one of the

---

[1] Charter printed in *Rec. Hist. Franc.*, vol. xi, p. 590; cf. Soehnée, *Actes d'Henri I*, no. 91.
[2] Charter printed in *Rec. Hist. Franc.*, vol. xi, p. 588. For date, see Soehnée, *op. cit.*, no. 92.
[3] Will. Poit., p. 52.

features of the minority, and in 1052 he and his full brother Mauger, now archbishop of Rouen, could between them exercise an overwhelming authority over the whole of Upper Normandy. In view, therefore, of the critical situation now developing in north-western France their support might almost have seemed essential to the survival of the young duke. From the first, however, William, count of Arques, seems always to have shown himself ill-disposed towards his nephew whom with some complacency he despised as illegitimate.[1] He was in fact overwhelmingly ambitious, and having failed to become duke himself, he perhaps hoped to establish himself as an independent ruler east of the Seine.[2] Not without reason did William of Poitiers assert that his efforts to increase his own power and to diminish that of the duke were constant and of long duration.[3] His importance as an opponent may, further, be gauged not only by the extent of his possessions, which were vast,[4] but also by the frequency with which his attestation was sought in order to fortify private charters. He appears about this time as witness to deeds relating to Jumièges and Saint-Ouen, to Saint-Wandrille, and Holy Trinity, Rouen.[5] Nor was it only from his brother, the archbishop, that he might expect to receive support in his designs. He had already married a sister of Enguerrand II, count of Ponthieu, and his son Walter might expect to succeed him.[6] Here in truth was a most formidable connexion based on Upper Normandy which by itself might have seemed capable of menacing the existence of the ducal power.

The formation within Normandy of this powerful coalition in opposition to the duke was, moreover, effected at the same time as the king of France and the count of Anjou were making their own alliance, and by 1052 the two developments, which were not wholly dissociated, had combined to threaten the ducal authority with extinction. It is in fact in the light of these events that the change in the traditional relationship between the duke of Normandy and the French monarchy is best to be appraised. Duke William had at this time nothing to gain by an assertion of independence from the French monarchy such as was the delight of later Norman chroniclers to acclaim, and for a long time he seems to have been very reluctant even to recognize the breach that had been made.[7] Both Norman and later English writers thus insist that he

[1] Ord. Vit., vol. III, p. 232. [2] Will. Poit., p. 52. [3] *Ibid.*
[4] He had lands as far west as the forest of Brotonne (*R.A.D.N.*, no. 100).
[5] *R.A.D.N.*, nos. 113 (Jumièges), 103 (Sigy); Lot, *Saint-Wandrille*, nos. 22, 29 (*R.A.D.N.*, nos. 108, 125); Chevreux et Vernier, *Archives de Normandie*, plate IV; *Cart. S. Trin. Roth.*, p. 447, no. 50.
[6] Lot, *Saint-Wandrille*, no. 15. [7] Will. Poit., p. 26; Will. Malms., p. 289.

showed himself averse from engaging in any personal conflict with his overlord. King Henry, on the other hand, having made peace with the count of Anjou, appears to have hoped that his dominance over Normandy could be sustained by means of a powerful faction within the duchy which would support the French king against the duke. Only in part therefore was the significance of the ensuing war to be explained by Ordericus Vitalis when he accurately reported that Count William of Talou rebelled with the counsel of Archbishop Mauger his brother, and that together these succeeded in bringing the king of France to their aid.[1] King Henry after his negotiations with Anjou had a still more positive part to play in the drama. He assumed it: and the significance of his action was perhaps felt by a monk of Holy Trinity, Rouen, who saw fit to date one of his charters by reference to the event.[2] The king and the duke were now at war, and a new era had opened in the relations between France and Normandy.

Certainly, the threat to the ducal dynasty was lethal; for if the full strength of this coalition from Talou and Rouen, from Paris, Anjou, and Ponthieu, could ever have been brought at one time in unison to attack the duke, it is very doubtful whether he could have survived. As it was, the hostilities opened on Norman soil where the insurgents had acquired a great accession of strength from the great fortress which the count of Talou had recently built on the heights overlooking Arques.[3] This famous castle, whose erection marked an epoch in the development of Norman military architecture, was designed to be impregnable to direct assault. It was perhaps built of stone, and further strengthened by a deep surrounding fosse which can still be seen. The erection of such a castle by a count who was notoriously ill-disposed towards his nephew must have been a source of great disquiet to the duke, and according to William of Poitiers he early placed a garrison of his own within it. Whether he was in fact able to take this step against the magnate who had certainly built the castle for his own use is a little doubtful, as must also be the assertion that the ducal garrison afterwards betrayed the fortress to the count. In any case, at the opening of hostilities the castle of Arques was in full possession of the count of Talou, and his revolt was based upon it.

Strong in his great fortress, the count of Arques could begin to make

[1] Ord. Vit., vol. I, p. 184.
[2] *Cart. S. Trin. Roth.*, no. VII (*R.A.D.N.*, no. 130).
[3] Will. Jum., p. 119; Will. Poit., p. 54; A. Deville, *Château d'Arques*.

himself supreme in the surrounding countryside, and at first he seems
to have encountered little opposition except in one quarter where an
interesting family group decided to withstand him. In what is now the
small village of Hugleville,[1] some twelve miles south of Arques, there
was established a certain Richard who was related to the ducal house
since his mother, Papia, who had married Gulbert, *advocatus* of Saint-
Valéry, was herself a daughter of Duke Richard III.[2] This man who
was in due course to build the little town of Auffay,[3] had erected for
himself a stronghold near Saint-Aubin between Hugleville and Arques.
Here he stood against the count and brought to his assistance Geoffrey
of Neufmarché[4] and Hugh of Morimont,[5] the two sons[6] of that Turchetil
who had about 1040 been killed while acting as guardian of the ducal
court. Geoffrey of Neufmarché had, moreover, previously married one
of Richard's III's daughters,[7] and so it was a close connexion of related
magnates, all of whom had in different ways become associated with the
ducal dynasty, that now determined to resist the count of Arques. At
first their opposition was ineffective, and Hugh of Morimont with
certain of his followers was slain after an encounter with the men from
Arques at Esclavelles.[8] The family connexion of Saint-Valéry and
Auffay was soon to play a great part in Norman history, but for the
moment their opposition to the count of Arques was checked. The
count could, in fact, now boast that he had on his side 'almost all the
inhabitants of the county of Talou'.[9]

The news of the count's overt rebellion came to Duke William when
he was in the Cotentin.[10] He may already have unsuccessfully summoned
the count to appear before him, or it may have been a report of the
betrayal of the castle which first reached him.[11] At all events he acted
with speed. He set out at once with a very few followers, and riding
rapidly eastward, was joined on his way by a small body of men from
Rouen who had already without success striven to prevent the provision-
ing of Arques. On his arrival at the castle he engaged in a skirmish with
some of the count's men outside the walls and drove them back within

[1] Seine-Maritime; cant. Longueville.
[2] Ord. Vit., vol. III, pp. 41–42 and 483–484. *Robert de Torigni* (ed. Delisle), vol. I, pp. 33–34.
[3] Ord. Vit., vol. III, p. 42.   [4] Seine-Maritime; cant. Gournai.
[5] Morimont is a hamlet of Esclavelles near Neufchâtel.
[6] Ord. Vit., vol. III, pp. 42, 43; *R.A.D.N.*, no. 104.
[7] The full brother of this girl was Gulbert of Auffay, who was present at the battle of
Hastings, founded the abbey of Auffay in 1079, and died 14 or 15 August 1087.
[8] Ord. Vit. (vol. III, p. 45) places this fighting later – at the time of the action at Saint-
Aubin in October 1053.
[9] Ord. Vit., vol. III, p. 42.   [10] Will. Poit., p. 54.   [11] Will. Jum., p. 119.

the fortress. Then realizing that the castle was not to be taken by storm, he determined to besiege it, and following his earlier practice, he erected a large wooden tower by means of which he might threaten the defenders from outside. Having done this, he left Walter Giffard to conduct the siege and himself retired in order to prepare to meet any relieving force that might come from outside to the assistance of the beleaguered garrison.[1]

The duke's prime purpose was to invest the castle of Arques before the count of Talou could be joined by his allies from outside Normandy. In this he was so far successful that when in the autumn of 1053[2] King Henry in company of Count Enguerrand of Ponthieu entered Normandy by way of the Scie valley, he found Arques already cut off, and an opposing force lying between him and the stronghold.[3] It therefore became the king's major objective to bring reinforcements and provisions to the garrison. Duke William, whose chief hope was to prevent such assistance reaching Arques, still seems to have been reluctant to oppose his overlord in person, but on 25 October[4] some of his followers succeeded in ambushing a part of the French force near Saint-Aubin and in cutting it to pieces. The casualties were heavy, and Enguerrand himself was among the slain.[5]

This engagement which brought consternation to the defenders of Arques was a decided reverse for the enemies of the duke, and it is therefore little wonder that his panegyrists were concerned to emphasize its importance.[6] King Henry was able to give some help both in men and material to the garrison, but he was compelled soon to withdraw. Thereafter the castle could be starved into surrender, and late in 1053 it yielded on the sole condition that the lives of the garrison should be spared. The fortress of Arques, so essential to the governance of Upper Normandy, thus passed into the hands of the Norman duke. Count William of Arques was granted terms of surprising leniency, but he was constrained to leave the duchy, and he fled to the court of Eustace, count of Boulogne. He troubled Normandy no more.[7]

---

[1] The sequence of events here followed is that given by Will. Poit., which is not wholly consistent with that supplied by Will. Jum. or by Wace (*Roman de Rou*, vol. ii, pp. 167 *et sqq.*).
[2] Below, Appendix B.   [3] Will. Poit., pp. 58–60.
[4] The date is fixed by the obituary of Enguerrand (C. Brunel, *Actes des Comtes de Ponthieu*, p. iv).   [5] Will. Poit., p. 58; Will. Jum., p. 120.
[6] Will. Poit., p. 50. According to a later chronicler (*Rec. Hist. Franc.*, vol. xi, p. 330) the dying cries of Enguerrand were heard by his sister on the walls of Arques. It is a good story which might even be true, for less than a mile separates the castle from Saint-Aubin-sur-Scie, and the exact site of the engagement is unknown.
[7] Will. Poit., p. 60; Will. Jum., p. 120.

Whilst the fall of Arques was of the first importance, the capture of the fortress did not itself decide the campaign. Already Count Geoffrey of Anjou was making his preparations, and on the western borders of Normandy there were men who were ready to support him. Thus even while Arques was being besieged, many magnates elsewhere in Normandy rebelled, and the men of Moulins which lay near the territory of Bellême actually gave up their town to Guy-William of Aquitaine, the brother-in-law and ally of the count of Anjou. The king of France in his turn was only delayed for a very short while by the defeat of his men on the Scie. It is not certain how long the reduction of Arques took after the action at Saint-Aubin on 25 October 1053, but several weeks were probably occupied in this task, and Duke William can hardly have been master of the fortress much, if at all, before December. Yet before the beginning of February 1054 the coalition arrayed against the duke was ready for joint action, and a large double invasion of Normandy then took place.[1]

The offensive planned by the French king was organized on a wide scale. The main body of the invaders assembled under the king at Mantes, and entered the *comté* of Évreux which was given over to pillage. In this body were troops drawn from all over north-western France, from Berri, for example, from Sens, Blois, and Tourraine and it would seem that there were also men from Anjou perhaps with Count Geoffrey at their head. The other body of invaders was recruited chiefly from the north-eastern fiefs of the French king and placed under the leadership of Odo, his brother, together with Rainald, count of Cleremont, and Guy, count of Ponthieu, who was doubtless eager to avenge the death of his own brother who had fallen the previous year outside the walls of Arques. This force entered eastern Normandy and immediately began a widespread devastation. It was in all a formidable attack. Full allowance must be made for the exaggerations of later Norman chroniclers who were naturally prone to magnify the threat to the duchy. But their remarks receive some independent confirmation, and it would seem that a very considerable part of the feudal strength of the Capetian monarchy had been mobilized against Normandy.[2]

It was at this moment of peril that Duke William's previous capture of Arques saved him from destruction for he was able to collect a

[1] Will. Poit., pp. 62, 65; Will. Malms., *Gesta Regum*, vol. II, p. 290; Ord. Vit., vol. III, pp. 234-238.
[2] Will. Poit., pp. 68-72. Freeman (*Norman Conquest*, vol. III, pp. 144, 164) denies that Geoffrey was present, but Will. Jum. (p. 129) mentions him.

defending force from all over his duchy without the menace of a hostile fortress within his own borders. Wace gives a long list of the magnates who rallied to his support,[1] and more reliable writers indicate that there was a wide response to his summons.[2] This was in itself a notable achievement. For whilst it is very significant that many of the men particularly noted by William of Poitiers as having taken part in the campaign seems to have been as much concerned to preserve their own estates as to defend the duchy,[3] none the less their interests had clearly become identified with those of their ruler. William's force was at any rate large enough for it to be divided into two contingents operating respectively to the west and east of the Seine. The duke himself with men from middle Normandy faced the invaders who were advancing under the French king through the Évreçin.[4] On the other side of the river, Robert, count of Eu, with Hugh of Gournay, Walter Giffard, Roger of Mortemer, and the young William of Warenne, came out from their own lands to withstand the eastern incursion under Count Odo and Count Rainald.[5]

The French force under Odo and the counts seems to have been unprepared for this levy from eastern Normandy. Having entered the duchy by way of Neufchâtel-en-Bray, it advanced to the neighbourhood of Mortemer, and there gave itself up to unrestrained rape and pillage. Widely scattered and demoralized, it thus offered itself as an easy target for attack, and when the troops of the count of Eu rapidly advanced they achieved surprise, and fought with an initial advantage which was ultimately to prove decisive. The engagement lasted many hours and was fiercely contested, but no discipline could apparently be imposed on the French force, and the slaughter was considerable. It is unfortunate that no detailed account which merits credence has survived of this battle which was to be of decisive importance, but of the issue there could be no doubt. Odo and Rainald escaped with difficulty; Guy, count of Ponthieu, was captured; and their force was dispersed. So complete was the Norman victory that when the news of the battle reached the two opposing forces on the other side of the Seine, the king

---

[1] *Roman de Rou* (ed. Andresen), vol. II, pp. 224, 225.

[2] Will. Poit., p. 72.

[3] Many of the magnates such as the count of Eu, Hugh of Gournai, William of Warenne, and Walter Giffard mentioned as having taken part in the battle of Mortemer came from that neighbourhood.

[4] For example, Ralph of Tosny, who was with the duke west of the Seine (Ord. Vit., vol. III, p. 238), was a great landowner in Central Normandy.

[5] Will. Poit., p. 70.

of France decided to withdraw. The duke of Normandy had been saved.[1]

The battle of Mortemer reflected a major crisis in Norman history, and never again was Duke William to be faced by so formidable a threat to the continued existence of his power. Within Normandy the results were immediately apparent as the strong coalition which had been arrayed against him began rapidly to break up. The king of France and the count of Anjou had departed, and William, count of Arques, who had already gone into exile, lost all hope of return. His *comté* was forfeit; his son, Walter, disinherited; and for the remainder of Norman history Talou was never to possess a count of its own, but was directly subject to the duke at Rouen. Even more noteworthy were the consequences to the archbishop of Rouen. Very soon after Mortemer, perhaps in 1055,[2] but more probably in 1054,[3] an ecclesiastical council, meeting at Lisieux in the presence of Hugh, bishop of that see, together with other bishops of the province and under the presidency of Ermenfrid, bishop of Sitten, the papal legate, solemnly deposed Mauger and appointed a reforming archbishop of a new type to succeed him.[4] Duke William's power had been firmly re-established in Upper Normandy, and his victory might even seem to have had the blessing of the church.

It is therefore reasonable to conclude that at Mortemer a turning-point in the Norman reign of Duke William had been reached and passed, and it is interesting to consider how far he had himself been personally responsible for the achievement. Before 1046 he can hardly have had much influence on the conduct of affairs, and he clearly played a subordinate part in the campaign which culminated at Val-ès-Dunes.

---

[1] *Ibid.*, p. 72; Will. Jum., p. 130; Ord. Vit., vol. III, pp. 237, 238.

[2] The Norman annals give this date which has been generally accepted, but it is based on doubtful evidence. The charter which might support it has been printed in *R.A.D.N.* (no. 133), and in *Cart. Îles normandes* (p. 185, no. 116). It has also been calendared in *Cal. Doc. France* (no. 710). All three editors assign this instrument to 25 December 1054, and since it is subscribed by Mauger as archbishop this would imply that he had not been deposed at that time. The charter could, however, in my opinion, be dated with equal plausibility (according to modern reckoning) at 25 December 1053, for Christmas was frequently taken to mark the beginning of the new year.

[3] The *Acta* of the archbishops of Rouen (*Rec. Hist. Franc.*, vol. XI, p. 70) speak of Mauger as having been deposed by the authority of Leo IX, who died 19 April 1054. This by itself is not wholly conclusive. But a charter for Le Mont-Saint-Michel (*R.A.D.N.*, no. 132), which all the elements of a complicated date seem to place in 1054, is witnessed by Mauger's successor Maurilius as archbishop. The matter is not removed from doubt, but I have only slight hesitation in assigning Mauger's deposition to 1054.

[4] Bessin, *Concilia*, pp. 46, 47.

But his energy at that time was remarkable and his influence was not negligible, whilst in the succeeding years he moved rapidly into a position of greater prominence. His personal prowess during the warfare in Maine was noted with admiration,[1] and he now began to show for the first time those qualities of efficient leadership which were later so signally to impress his generation. It is not known whether the planned methods of siege-work which he employed successively at Brionne, Domfront, and Arques were of Norman origin, but certainly the young duke used them with great effect, and his night march to Alençon, by which he achieved surprise, was a remarkable tactical feat. During the war in Maine he also exhibited for the first time that calculated combination of ferocity and leniency which was later to mark so much of his career. The horrible savagery with which he treated those who resisted him at Alençon was used as an example to the defenders of Domfront, who were offered pardon and protection in return for surrender. It was a device which he continually repeated and with notable results, both in Normandy and England. His successes in this warfare certainly caused him to be surrounded at this time with an ever-increasing regard, and the widespread support he received during the crisis of 1052–1054 was undoubtedly due to the prestige he had acquired by his character and through his acts.

He now reaped the reward of his endeavours. But if his position in Normandy after 1054 was stronger than it had ever been before, there was still to be much fighting before there could be formal peace between him and the French king. Yet the duke was able to take the offensive, and it was probably at this time that William fitz Osbern was charged with the fortification of Breteuil over against Tillières.[2] Meanwhile negotiations between the duke and the king proceeded. The details of these have been lost, and even the date and terms of the ensuing agreement are uncertain. It would seem, however, that by the end of 1055 Duke William had become formally reconciled to his overlord, and on terms which were not disadvantageous to himself. The French king, it would appear, obtained the release of some of his vassals who had been captured at Mortemer, and in return he is said to have confirmed William in possession of all the lands which the duke had taken from Count Geoffrey.[3]

The count of Anjou, however, could hardly be expected to acquiesce

[1] Will. Jum., p. 127; Will. Poit., p. 44.
[2] Ord. Vit. (Will. Jum., p. 180); Benoit (ed. Michel), vol. III, p. 132.
[3] Will. Poit., p. 74.

in these arrangements, and it is probably to the years 1054 and 1055[1] that should be referred a renewal of hostilities between Normandy and Anjou. These were concentrated once again in the border country around Domfront, where Duke William had garrisoned the strongholds of Mont Barbet and Ambrières.[2] Once again, also, a great border family became involved in these disputes. In 1054 Mayenne, which is some seven miles from Ambrières, was held by a certain Geoffrey, the son, as it seems, of Haimo 'de Medano', who was established as early as 1014.[3] This Geoffrey of Mayenne held land not only in Maine but also in the diocese of Chartres, and he was later found witnessing charters in favour both of Marmoutier and Le Mont-Saint-Michel.[4] His position was in fact (on a smaller scale) analogous to that occupied by the lords of Bellême, and it was in his interests likewise to prevent too close a definition as to who were his immediate overlords: the counts of Maine or Anjou, the king of France, or the duke of Normandy. Faced by the Norman advance, he now appealed to Geoffrey of Anjou, and the count immediately responded. He called to his assistance Guy-William of Aquitaine and Count Eudo of Brittany, and together with Geoffrey of Mayenne they moved against Ambrières. Duke William thereupon came to rescue the stronghold, and he compelled the besiegers to withdraw. Geoffrey of Mayenne was himself captured, and carried off to Normandy, where he was compelled to do homage. Thus the vassalage of another of the great border families was passing to Normandy.[5]

It would be easy, none the less, to overemphasize the duke's success on this occasion. Whatever he may have achieved at Ambrières, his exploits at this time do not seem sensibly to have affected the Angevin dominance over Maine. In August 1055, when Bishop Gervais was translated to Rheims, the count of Anjou was able without difficulty to secure the appointment to the vacant see of Le Mans of his own nominee Vougrin, who had formerly been abbot of Saint Sergius at Angers,[6] and throughout these years there can be little doubt that

---

[1] Will. Poit. (p. 74) states that there was much fighting between the battle of Mortemer (February 1054) and the truce between William and King Henry (? 1055). In particular, he assigns to this period operations round Ambrières. Will. Jum. (p. 127) places an attack on Ambrières at the time of the Domfront campaign, and this may well have taken place. But the same writer alludes to the seizure of 'two townships' in Maine after Mortemer, and Ordericus, interpolating this passage (p. 184), says this action was in the neighbourhood of Ambrières.

[2] Ord. Vit., interp. Will. Jum., p. 184.   [3] *Cart. S. Vincent du Mans*, no. IV.
[4] *Cart. S. Père Chartres*, pp. 149, 184, 193, 211, 403; Round, *Cal. Doc. France*, no. 1168; *Cart. S. Michel de l'Abbayette*, no. 5.
[5] Will. Poit., pp. 66–78.   [6] Latouche, *op. cit.*, pp. 32, 79.

Geoffrey Martel continued to be master of Maine. As such, he remained a perpetual menace to the Norman duke, and the natural centre of any coalition against Normandy which might be formed. Thus it was that King Henry, anxious to avenge the defeat of Mortemer, again turned to the count of Anjou, and charters indicate that he was associated very closely with him during the early months of 1057.[1] The same alliance which had dominated the crisis of 1054 thus once more came into being, and immediately precipitated a new attack on Normandy. It was in August 1057 that there thus occurred a combined invasion of the duchy by the king of France and the count of Anjou.[2]

On this occasion the king and the count entered Normandy by way of the Hiémois with the object of laying waste the whole of that district, and pushing their destruction northward towards Bayeux and Caen. Duke William, however, still seems to have been reluctant to oppose his French overlord in person, and he contented himself with massing a considerable force in the neighbourhood of Falaise, where by means of spies he kept himself informed of the movements of the enemy. In due course his opportunity came. Glutted with pillage, the invaders reached the Dives at the ford near Varaville, and proceeded to cross the river. When part of the force was across, the incoming tide made it impossible for the remainder to follow. William thereupon launched a savage attack on those who had not effected the crossing, and according to his panegyrists inflicted something like a massacre upon them. So heavy were the losses sustained by the French that, as we understand from the Norman writers, the king of France felt he had no option but to beat a hasty retreat. Never again was he to invade Normandy at the head of a hostile army.[3]

The so-called battle of Varaville does not possess the same critical significance in the history of Normandy as does that of Mortemer, and its importance has been overestimated. Unlike Mortemer, it is scarcely noticed by the annalists who record the earlier battle. William of Poitiers and William of Jumièges are almost the only early writers to describe it; William of Malmesbury very briefly repeats their story;

---

[1] The king and the count were together at Tours on 19 January 1057, and at Angers on 1 March 1057 (*Rec. Hist. Franc.*, vol. XI, pp. 592, 593; Soehnée, *op. cit.*, nos. 106, 107).

[2] Not 1058, as has been very generally supposed. The correct date has been established by J. Dhondt (*Normannia*, vol. XII (1939), pp. 465–486; also *Revue Belge de Philologie et d'histoire*, vol. XXV (1946), pp. 87–109). That the expedition took place in August (of 1057) is indicated by the remark of Wace (*Roman de Rou*, vol. II, pp. 238) that the crops were still on the ground and ready for harvest.

[3] Will. Jum., p. 131; Will. Poit., pp. 80–82.

but most of the chroniclers, including Ordericus himself, pass by this campaign with little or no notice;[1] and it is not until the time of Wace that the full Norman tradition of a great victory is developed.[2] It might therefore be wise to suspect some exaggeration here in a Norman tradition which is so little corroborated. Nevertheless, in the years 1057–1060 there seems to have been a significant extension of the Norman influence in Maine. It will be recalled that after the death of Count Hugh of Maine in 1051, Herbert his son had been driven into exile by Geoffrey Martel. He now turned with some confidence towards the Norman duke for support against his Angevin supplanter. William, on his side, was quick to see the advantage that might be gained by promoting Herbert's claims under his own direction. As a result, and some time after 1055, a notable pact was made between them. By it, Herbert promised to marry a daughter of the Norman duke, and engaged his sister Margaret to marry William's son, Robert. Moreover, it was agreed that in the event of Herbert's dying without children the *comté* of Maine should pass to the duke of Normandy.[3] From this time forward Herbert could be regarded as William's protégé, if not his vassal, and it was in this capacity that during these years he began to recover some authority in Maine.[4] Duke William, on his part, might see opening up before him the distant prospect of adding Maine eventually to his own dominion.

In the meantime, however, it was with King Henry that the Norman duke was most closely engaged. After Varaville he could take the initiative, and soon he is to be found on the south-western frontier of his duchy. Here there was a district which was to provide the occasion for long disputes between the dukes of Normandy and the kings of France. In Carolingian times the whole region between the Andelle and the Oise had formed a single *pagus* – the Vexin – but after the establishment of the Viking dynasty, the northern part of this had been made an effective part of Normandy, whilst the section south of the Epte containing the towns of Mantes and Pontoise passed under the control of local counts.[5] In the time of William's father, one of these, named Dreux,

---

[1] *Gesta Regum*, vol. II, p. 291. The Norman annals are all silent on this campaign, and the name Varaville is not mentioned by either Will. Poit. or Will. Jum.

[2] *Roman de Rou*, vol. II, pp. 236 *et sqq.*; Benoit (ed. Michel), vol. II, pp. 14 *et sqq.*

[3] Will. Poit., p. 88; Ord. Vit., vol. II, pp. 102, 252; C. W. David, *Robert Curthose*, pp. 7, 8.

[4] A charter given by Herbert of La Milesse between August 1055 and 14 November 1060 is assented to by his lords, Geoffrey, count of Anjou, and Herbert of Maine (*Cart. S. Vincent du Mans*, no. 303).

[5] Le Prévost, Soc. Antiq. Norm., *Mémoires*, vol. XI (1840), pp. 20–25. Cf. Stenton, *Anglo-Saxon England*, p. 611.

came under the overlordship of Duke Robert, and after Dreux's death his eldest son, Walter, continued in this vassalage.[1] The French Vexin was, however, always liable to cause disturbance, and its counts were in fact to play an important part in the relations between Normandy, France, and England during the central decades of the eleventh century. For Dreux had married a sister of Edward the Confessor, and his son, Ralph, was to have a notable career in England,[2] whilst Walter, on his part, by subsequently claiming the *comté* of Maine, was to precipitate one of the most important of William's continental wars.[3]

In 1058, however, the Norman overlordship in the French Vexin was not immediately threatened, and it was slightly to the west of this district – that is to say on the northern borders of the Chartrain – that William now began hostilities against King Henry. According to one account it was about this time that he regained Tillières which he had lost during the minority,[4] and certainly he now succeeded in capturing the French king's stronghold of Thimert, some twelve miles from Dreux.[5] Between 29 June and 15 August 1058[6] King Henry therefore came to lay siege to this fortress, and there opened the last episode in the war between him and Duke William. The siege of Thimert was in fact to last almost as long as the siege of Brionne. Several royal charters are dated by reference to it in 1058 and 1059, and it was still continuing when Philip I was consecrated on 23 May of the latter year.[7] The contest was, however, losing its significance, and there were already tentative negotiations for a truce. According to a Norman chronicler, the bishops of Paris and Amiens were sent to Normandy by Henry on an embassy designed to bring about a peace,[8] and the fact that about this time William and many of his magnates are to be found near Dreux[9] suggests that a personal interview may have taken place between the king and the duke. None the less the war dragged on. It is unlikely that the siege of Thimert was over in August 1060, and it is probable that King Henry died before peace was concluded with Duke William.[10]

The negotiations of Duke William with Herbert of Maine and with

[1] Ord. Vit., vol. III, p. 224.
[2] Round, *Studies in Peerage and Family History*, pp. 147, 149.
[3] Below, pp. 173, 174.
[4] Ord. Vit., interp. Will. Jum. (ed. Marx), p. 184.
[5] On what follows, see R. Merlet, in *Moyen Age*, vol. XVI, 1903.
[6] Dhondt, *Normannia*, vol. XII, p. 484.
[7] *Rec. Hist. Franc.*, vol. XI, pp. 431, 598; Soehnée, *op. cit.*, no. 116.
[8] Chronicle of Fécamp (*Rec. Hist. Franc.*, vol. XI, p. 364).
[9] *Cart. S. Père Chartres*, vol. I, p. 153 (*R.A.D.N.*, no. 147).
[10] Merlet, *op. cit.*, vol. XVI (1903), p. 208.

the French king, together with the desultory fighting which accompanied them, form a fitting epilogue to the long period of almost uninterrupted warfare which occupied the Norman duke from 1047 to 1060. During these years the duke of Normandy was engaged in a continuous struggle for survival, and it falsifies the character of this prolonged crisis in the Norman fortunes to treat its various episodes in isolation. The siege of Brionne began within a few weeks of Val-ès-Dunes, and Brionne was scarcely taken before the opening of the war in Maine. The campaign round Domfront and Alençon was in turn directly linked to the revolt of Count William of Arques, and this merged into the invasion of Normandy by King Henry which was repelled at Mortemer. Thus while it is true that the battle of Val-ès-Dunes marks the beginning of the effective reign of Duke William, it is equally true that his authority was never undisputed or secure during the seven years which followed the victory on the banks of the Orne, and during the last two years of that period, the revolutionary change which turned the king of France from a friend into an enemy provided a new and most formidable element of danger. In retrospect it may even appear a matter of wonder that the ducal power was enabled in this period to survive the onslaught which was directed against it from so many quarters, and its preservation reflects authentically not only the strong tradition of ducal authority which was never allowed to disappear but also the indomitable character of the future conqueror of England.

Between 1054 and 1060 the tension was relaxed, but it remained acute. The joint invasion of the duchy by King Henry and Count Geoffrey in 1057 gave some indication of the danger which was still latent. Even after Varaville, Maine continued to be an Angevin rather than a Norman dependency, and until his death Geoffrey Martel was a stronger force in north-western Gaul than was the young Duke William. On his other frontier, it is true, the duke was now able, albeit with some reluctance, to take the offensive against his overlord, though the Capetian monarchy had large reserves of strength which might again be turned against Normandy. But the tide had evidently turned in favour of the duke before two events completed the deliverance which had been so hardly earned. On 4 August 1060 King Henry I died, leaving the French realm in the hands of his son Philip, who passed under the guardianship of William's father-in-law, Baldwin V, count of Flanders.[1] And on 14 November 1060 there occurred the death of

---

[1] *Rec. Actes – Philippe I* (ed. Prou), p. xxviii.

Geoffrey Martel, which removed William's greatest rival in the west, and plunged both Anjou and Maine into a civil war in which the Norman duke might take his profit.[1] Thus the stage was cleared for a new act in the personal drama of Duke William, and there opened for the architect of Norman greatness a new era of Norman opportunity.

Certainly his success in surmounting the difficulties which faced him between 1046 and 1060 had been due in large measure to his own personality. Consequently it is noteworthy that the politics of these years, and their hazards, were throughout this period further complicated by a series of events which were in a special sense personal to himself. Before 1049, that is to say shortly after the battle of Val-ès-Dunes, plans had been made for a marriage between the duke and Matilda, daughter of Baldwin V, count of Flanders, by Adela, daughter of Robert II, king of France.[2] The projected marriage was, however, forbidden by Leo IX at the council of Rheims in October 1049, and though, in the report of the council, no specific reason for the prohibition is given, it is generally assumed that the ground for the objection was that William and Matilda were within the prohibited degrees of relationship.[3] The marriage none the less took place. Perhaps in 1050, probably in 1051, and at all events not later than 1052,[4] Baldwin V brought his daughter to Eu, where the marriage was celebrated, and the duke forthwith conducted his bride with fitting pomp to Rouen. Not until 1059, however, was the papal sanction to the union obtained from Pope Nicholas II at the second Lateran Council.[5]

The marriage of Duke William, and the circumstances in which it took place, were sensibly to affect the position of the duke in his duchy, and indeed the place he was to occupy in the political structure of western Europe. And no event in his career has given rise to more controversial discussion.[6] Much speculation has, for instance, taken place as to the ecclesiastical objections to the match, and the nature of the consanguinity (if such existed) between William and Matilda. At one time it was held that when William sought her hand, Matilda was already the wife of a certain Gerbod, by whom she had a daughter, Gundrada, who later became the wife of William of Warenne, the first earl of Surrey. This, however, has now been finally disproved, and it is in the highest degree improbable that Matilda was married to anyone

---

[1] Halphen, *op. cit.*, p. 12.
[3] Hefele-Leclerc, *Histoire des Conciles*, vol. IV, p. 1018.
[5] Will. Jum., pp. 127, 128.

[2] Below, Appendix B.
[4] Below, Appendix B.
[6] Below, Appendix B.

before the Conqueror. Some other explanation has therefore to be sought for the ecclesiastical ban on the marriage. It has thus been suggested that both William and Matilda were cousins in the fifth degree, being both directly descended from Rolf the Viking. It has also been suggested that the ground for the probition was a marriage, which is alleged to have been contracted (though it was certainly not consummated) between Duke Richard III of Normandy and Adela (Matilda's mother) before the latter was married to Baldwin V. Finally it has been suggested (perhaps with greater probability) that the prohibition was based on the fact that after the death of Baldwin V's mother, Ogiva, his father, Baldwin IV, had married a daughter of Duke Richard II of Normandy. All these theories have difficulties to overcome, and the matter may well therefore be left in some suspense.

It is thus much more profitable to consider William's marriage, the opposition it excited, and the political consequences it entailed, in relation to the politics of the age. Viewed against the background of the duke's war for survival, it is not difficult to conjecture the motives which impelled him to seek the match. After Val-ès-Dunes he was still strictly dependent upon the loyalty of a few trusted magnates, and on the support of his overlord the king of France. Consequently, it is noteworthy that the duke was, as it seems, urged to the marriage by his followers, and it is equally significant that Matilda was the niece of the French king.[1] The marriage must furthermore have in itself seemed highly advantageous to a young man labouring under the stigma of bastardy, and as yet only partially in possession of his inheritance. Moreover, the rising power of Flanders under Baldwin V was involved,[2] and might well have appeared to offer to the Norman duke the prospect of a useful alliance. In any circumstances, therefore, such a marriage might be expected to increase the influence of Normandy in Gaul, and its results were to be more profitable than even the astute duke could have foreseen in 1049. Much was to happen in the ensuing decade, and William was, in particular, to lose the support of his royal overlord. But after the deaths of Count Geoffrey and King Henry I in 1060 when Baldwin V had become guardian to Philip I, the earlier marriage between William and Matilda of Flanders thus began in some measure to condition the pattern of power in north-western Europe that formed the essential background to the Norman conquest of England.

[1] Will. Jum., p. 127.
[2] Grierson, in R. Hist. Soc., *Transactions*, series 4, vol. XXIII (1941), pp. 95 *et sqq.*

It is, perhaps, harder to understand why the count of Flanders should have welcomed the project, but such was apparently the case,[1] and here too the explanation may be sought in the political situation then prevailing in Europe. Baldwin V was already engaged in turning Flemish policy in the direction of France and away from the empire.[2] His own marriage to Adela the daughter of the French king had been of great moment to him,[3] and it was to be the corner-stone of Franco-Flemish relations for the ensuing forty years.[4] Moreover, in 1049, his affairs were approaching a crisis, for in that year both he and his ally, Duke Godfrey of Upper Lorraine, were being hard pressed by Emperor Henry III,[5] and the repercussions of this struggle were felt even in England, where Edward the Confessor collected a fleet to serve if necessary against the count of Flanders.[6] Finally, the pope – Leo IX – was also involved, being still himself committed to the imperial cause.[7] The two opposing interests at the council of Rheims were thus neatly defined. Baldwin V might feel constrained to receive favourably the project of marriage between his daughter and a loyal vassal of the French king who had recently been rescued by his overlord at Val-ès-Dunes. The pope, by contrast, must have viewed with some alarm the prospect of the confederation against the emperor being so substantially strengthened.

The prohibition thus conformed broadly to the grouping of political forces in western Europe in 1049, and in the event the marriage was postponed. When, about 1052–1053 it did take place, the situation had changed in so far as Duke William and the French king were no longer allies but enemies. But the war in Germany still dragged on, and Baldwin V cannot have wished to renounce the alliance, the more especially as he had become more directly involved at this time in the turbulent politics of England. He had evidently not forgotten the action of the Confessor in 1049. In or before 1051, he had given his half-sister Judith in marriage to Tosti, son of Earl Godwine, when the latter was still one of Edward's opponents, and in 1052 he sponsored the armed return of Godwine to England in the king's despite.[8] In 1053, therefore, the count of Flanders was still himself in need of allies, so that he had little reason to do other than welcome the marriage of William and Matilda. And the marriage itself was notably to affect the course not only of Flemish but also of French and Anglo-Norman history.

[1] Will. Poit., pp. 52–54.   [2] Lot, *Fidèles ou Vassaux?*, p. 13.
[3] Will. Jum., pp. 103–104.   [4] Flach, *Origines de l'ancienne France*, vol. IV, p. 71.
[5] Grierson, *op. cit.*, p. 98.   [6] AS. Chron., 'C', *s.a.* 1049.
[7] Grierson, *loc. cit.*   [8] Below, pp. 169, 170.

The general political implications of this important marriage were, however, only slowly to be disclosed, and at the beginning of the project, the ecclesiastical opposition to the match must have sensibly increased the difficulties of Duke William within his own duchy. It is significant that Norman writers of the period seem to have been very reluctant to discuss the ban, or the reasons for its imposition, and their silence was later to be broken only by legends which, however picturesque, are historically valueless.[1] The matter was evidently one of great delicacy. A strong tradition supports the view that the marriage was, for whatever reason, a matter of deep concern to the Norman church, and it has even been suggested that the very strong contingent of Norman bishops at the council of Rheims in 1049 had been sent there by the duke in the hope that they might prevent the ban being promulgated. After the prohibition had been pronounced it would seem that an influential party in the province of Rouen was actively hostile to the marriage,[2] and it was later asserted that Archbishop Mauger's denunciation of the match was one of the causes of his eventual banishment.[3] Disloyalty could certainly, in this matter, cloak itself in the garments of righteousness, and jealous enemies of the duke might find themselves in company with ecclesiastical reformers. According to writers from Le Bec, Normandy was actually placed under an interdict at some time during this period.[4]

The situation was certainly dangerous for a young ruler whose own position was precarious, and whose own title was weakened by illegitimacy. It is not surprising therefore that after the improvement in his fortunes in the years following Mortemer, the duke took active steps to try to effect a reconciliation with the papacy, and it is further significant that the long controversy about the marriage which then took place should have played its part in developing the personal relationship between Duke William and Lanfranc, then prior of Le Bec, whose later co-operation was to be the basis of the ecclesiastical policy of the

---

[1] The most picturesque of these derives from the Chronicle of Tours (*Rec. Hist. Franc.*, vol. XI, p. 348). It tells that the duke, who had been sustained by Baldwin V, asked for the count's daughter in marriage. The girl declared that she would never marry a bastard. Whereupon, Duke William went secretly to Bruges where she was living and forced his way into her bedroom, where he beat and kicked her. The girl then took to her bed, but was so impressed with the treatment she had received that she declared that she would never marry anyone else. The tale may be regarded as of more interest to the student of psychology than to the student of history.

[2] Milo Crispin, *Vita Lanfranci* (*Opera* (ed. Giles), vol. I, p. 286); Ord. Vit., interp. Will. Jum. (ed. Marx), pp. 181–182.

[3] Will. Malms., *Gesta Regum*, vol. II, p. 327.

[4] Milo Crispin, *loc. cit.*; *Chronique du Bec* (ed. Porée), p. 190.

Anglo-Norman kingdom. Since, however, the duke was never at any time prepared to recognize any bar to his marriage, negotiations inevitably moved slowly. Not until 1059 did the reconciliation eventually take place, and then apparently only on conditions. Pope Nicholas II removed the ban but (as is alleged) only in return for a promise that the duke and his wife should each build and endow a monastic house at Caen.[1] Certainly, these two magnificent churches can be regarded as symbolizing an important feature of the growth of eleventh-century Normandy. A close interconnexion between temporal and ecclesiastical authority within the duchy was to prove one of the chief sources of Duke William's Norman power, and the long controversy over his marriage was mainly important in so far as it impeded or retarded the realization of that harmony, which today at Caen is still so strikingly represented in stone.

William's marriage, and his eventual reconciliation with the papacy which had taken place by 1060, form a fitting counterpart to the duke's war for survival and its successful conclusion. After 1054, and more particularly between 1060 and 1066, the duke strengthened his duchy so that he could undertake a successful foreign invasion. It must, however, be emphasized that only twelve years and seven months separated Mortemer from Hastings, and less than seven years elapsed between the death of King Henry and William's own coronation at Westminster. The interval was too short for even the ablest ruler to attain such power had he not been able to rely upon earlier institutions of government which had escaped destruction during the period of confusion, and had he not been able, also, to link to his purpose the social and ecclesiastical movements which in his time were sweeping with exceptional force through an exceptional province. In particular, his political power was to derive from the rise of a remarkable secular aristocracy, from a notable revival in the Norman church, and from the duke's control and co-ordination of both these movements. These developments have now therefore to be considered, for much of the future history both of Normandy and England was to depend upon them. The culminating achievement of William the Conqueror was to be securely based upon the developing strength of Normandy during the decades immediately preceding the Norman conquest of England, and to the position then attained by the duke in his duchy.

[1] Milo Crispin, *loc. cit.*; *Chronique du Bec* (ed. Porée), p. 190.

Part II

THE DUKE
IN HIS DUCHY

Chapter 4

THE DUKE AND
THE NEW ARISTOCRACY

By 1060 the political position of Duke William had been stabilized as a result of fourteen years of continuous war. He had moved out of his perilous minority, and freed himself from dependency upon the king of France. He had withstood a combined assault from Paris and from Anjou; and the deaths of Count Geoffrey and King Henry had removed from his path his two most formidable opponents in Gaul. Never before, during his reign, had Normandy been so secure from attack, and its ruler was now offered the opportunity yet further to strengthen his position during the six years which were to elapse before he undertook the invasion of England. He was in his early thirties, and it is small wonder that what he had accomplished had won for him an ever-increasing prestige. This appears in all the comments of contemporaries. Of itself, therefore, it merits some attention since it was to make a real contribution to what he was later to achieve.

A warrior age salutes a warrior, and in the young William it found a warrior to salute. Tall in stature and of great physical strength, his personal exploits in battle (particularly in the campaigns of 1051 and 1052) had attracted notice, and more sober contemporaries might already have detected in him a commander of considerable capacity. Yet these attributes (which were shared by many of his contemporaries) do not suffice by themselves to account for the special admiration with which in 1060 he was beginning to be surrounded. An explanation has therefore to be sought in his more individual qualities. Brutal himself, it was not merely through successful brutality that he had been able to elicit support from so many of the ruthless men who might have been expected to withstand him. Doubtless, fortune had sometimes favoured him, and certainly Norman chroniclers, writing after 1066, were liable to offer him fulsome adulation. But when all deductions have been made, his courage in adversity had in fact been outstanding, and it commands admiration. There must, moreover, have been a wonderful tenacity of purpose in this young man, who threatened by murder in infancy and menaced by treachery in adolescence, had none the less saved himself by long years of war conducted against great odds. His success in his struggle between 1046 and 1060 must in the last resort be adjudged as in some measure a triumph of character.

The value of the prestige he had acquired was to be abundantly displayed in the future. But by itself it will not explain the power of the Norman duchy which confronted England in the third quarter of the eleventh century. If in 1066 the Norman duke in the Norman duchy could aspire to become, by force of arms, one of the dominant rulers of Europe, this was due in the first instance to the political structure of pre-Conquest Normandy. In particular it depended upon the results of two movements which had already by 1066 been brought to fruition in the province, namely the rise of a very remarkable aristocracy, and a most notable revival in the Norman church. The one supplied the sinews of Norman strength, the other gave a special direction to Norman policy. Both these movements had started before Duke William II began his effective rule, but both gathered new impetus under his direction; and he was to be signally successful in co-ordinating them to his own advantage. To these developments – aristocratic, ecclesiastical, and ducal – attention must now be turned, for they were to mould the future, and to provide not only the force but also much of the character of the Norman impact upon England. The greatest period of Norman achievement did not begin until they had taken place, or before they had been fused together by a great constructive statesman to provide the overmastering energy of a province which in 1066 was unique in Christendom.

Of these developments the rise of the Norman feudal aristocracy must, both for its causes and its consequences, challenge immediate attention. For it is by no means easy to ascertain with any precision why it took place. General theories of lordship and vassalage will clearly not of themselves suffice to account for the rise of an exceptional aristocracy in an exceptional province, and if actuality is to be given to the inquiry, reference must be made to the particular families which then arose. An endeavour must be made to determine how they acquired such power, and how their doing so affected their relations with the duke. Such an investigation must inevitably on occasion be concerned with points of detail, but it can be justified by the magnitude of the issues which were involved. Even so (as must be confessed) the evidence is somewhat intractable. The statements of later chroniclers respecting the ancestors of their patrons are notoriously suspect, and in the case of Normandy a special problem is posed in connexion with the pedigrees which, late in the twelfth century, Robert of Torigny added to the chronicle of William of Jumièges.[1] These famous genealogies have been widely used by modern scholars, but it is usually hazardous to rely on them unless they can be corroborated by independent testimony. In short, any account of the rise of that Norman secular aristocracy which was under the duke to effect the Norman conquest, and to give a new nobility to England, must not only be related to individual families: it must also be firmly based upon the testimony of the Norman charters.

Four such families may here therefore be selected as illustrating this development which was to be of such importance to Europe. The first of these is the house of Tosny.[2] Its earliest undoubted member is a certain Ralph de Tosny, and this man (who may be styled Ralph II) or perhaps another Ralph who was possibly his father (and may thus be styled Ralph I) was the original grantee of Tosny,[3] which had belonged to the see of Rouen in the time of Hugh, archbishop of Rouen, from 942 to 990. Ralph II, about whom there is definite information, was in 1013 or 1014 entrusted by Duke Richard II with the defence of Tillières,[4] but just before this, or shortly after, he is to be found in Italy, and when and where he died is not known. He was succeeded as lord of Tosny by his son Roger I who, likewise, had a varied career, both within and outside Normandy. At some time he went adventuring to Spain,[5] and he is known to have married a woman named Godehildis, who later (after Roger's death) became the wife of Richard, count of Évreux. Roger himself perished in one of the feuds of the minority, for in, or shortly after, 1040 he was slain in private war by Roger of Beaumont. This disaster, however, did not prevent Roger's son by Godehildis – Ralph III – from succeeding to Tosny, and he too played a prominent part in Norman politics. Ralph III was active against the king of France in the campaign of 1054, and later he fought at Hastings.[6] Nevertheless, it was always in Normandy that his chief interests lay, and before his death, which occurred before 24 March

[1] Ed. Marx, pp. 320–329.

[2] *Complete Peerage* (G. H. White), vol. XII, part I, pp. 753 *et sqq.*

[3] Eure, cant. Gaillon.

[4] Will. Poit., p. 64; Pfister, *Robert le Pieux*, p. 213.

[5] On a possible literary inference deriving from Roger's Spanish exploits, see Douglas, 'Song of Roland and the Norman Conquest of England' (*French Studies*, vol. XIV (1960), pp. 110, 111).

[6] Will. Poit., p. 197.

1102, he had become, within the duchy, a benefactor of many religious houses, including Saint-Évroul, La Croix-Saint-Leuffroi, Le Bec-Hellouin, and Jumièges.[1]

Tosny is the earliest family to be discovered in Normandy wherein a territorial appellation is found to be descendable in the manner of a surname, and the succession which has here been displayed is thus of exceptional interest. Similarly, the marriage alliances formed by members of this family are symptomatic of its growing power. Not only did the widow of Roger I marry a count of Évreux, but his sister linked Normandy to Maine, by allying herself with Guy de Laval, and one of his daughters married William fitz Osbern, steward of Normandy, and later earl of Hereford.[2] Nor was the Old English aristocracy itself to be unaffected by the Tosny fortunes, for Ralph IV of Tosny (the son of the man who fought at Hastings) married a daughter of Waltheof, son of Earl Siward of Northumbria.[3] A better illustration of the expanding influence of a rising Norman family in the eleventh century could hardly be obtained.

The rise of Tosny was, however, not to be unchallenged even in central Normandy, for some twenty miles to the west of it lay Beaumont on the Risle which was to give its name to an equally illustrious and bitterly hostile house.[4] The first member of this family who possessed Beaumont was Humphrey 'of Vieilles' who was probably the son of one 'Thorold of Pont-Audemer', and more doubtfully grandson of a certain 'Torf'.[5] This Humphrey was a supporter of Duke Robert I in whose company he is frequently to be found, and before 1035 he founded at Préaux near Pont-Audemer two monasteries: Saint-Pierre for men, and Saint-Léger for women.[6] He died before 1047 and was succeeded by his son Roger, soon to be styled 'of Beaumont', who first brought the family to greatness. For a long time, however, its fortunes were precarious, since during the minority of Duke William a fierce struggle took place between Beaumont and Tosny in which not only Roger II of Tosny but also Robert the brother of Roger of Beaumont perished.[7] Nevertheless, Roger of Beaumont himself prospered. Leaving Vieilles, he established himself on the neighbouring hill of Beaumont,

[1] Ord. Vit., vol. II, p. 404; vol. IV, p. 183.
[2] *Cal. Doc. France*, no. 1171; Le Prévost, *Eure*, vol. I, p. 415.
[3] Ord. Vit., vol. IV, p. 198; *Vita et Passio Waldevi* (ed. Michel), p. 126.
[4] *Complete Peerage*, vol. VII, pp. 521–523.
[5] Ord. Vit., vol. II, p. 14; vol. III, p. 339; Robert of Torigny, interp. Will. Jum., p. 324.
[6] *Complete Peerage*, vol. VII, p. 521, note 'c'.
[7] Ord. Vit., vol. II, p. 370; vol. III, p. 426.

where he built a famous castle, and there he remained in power throughout the Conqueror's lifetime.[1] He did not take part in the campaign at Hastings, but was represented at that battle by his eldest son, Robert.[2] His own interests, in fact, remained in Normandy, though in 1086 he is recorded as possessing some estates in Dorset and Gloucestershire.[3] But his two sons, Robert and Henry, became great landowners in England and in due course respectively earls of Leicestershire and Warwick. Thus it was that a man who had been active in Norman politics in the time of Duke Robert I survived until after the time of Domesday Book, and having established the fortunes of a great Norman family, left behind him two sons who were to acquire English earldoms. The rise of Beaumont can in truth be described as both rapid and spectacular.

Few Norman families of the eleventh century were more powerful than those of Tosny and Beaumont, but the same period also witnessed the rise of many lesser houses, and of these the first family of Vernon may be taken as an example. When, some time between 1032 and 1035, Duke Robert I gave land to Saint-Wandrille at Sierville, some ten miles north of Rouen, he did so with the consent of a certain 'Hugh of Vernon',[4] and other documents show that the family of Hugh had already become possessed of other estates in this district,[5] for in 1053 William 'of Vernon', together with his father Hugh, who had by now become a monk, gave to Holy Trinity, Rouen, land at Martainville within five miles of the city.[6] It is probable, moreover, that the full lordship of Vernon passed to this family at some time between these two dates. Early in his reign Duke William had given Vernon to his cousin Guy of Burgundy, and Guy's disgrace and forfeiture after 1047[7] may well have provided the opportunity for the rise of the new family. A charter for Saint-Père of Chartres,[8] which was passed before 1061, and probably before 1053, shows that at that time the family had then obtained full lordship of Vernon, together with its castle;[9] and William of Vernon retained this lordship until after the Norman conquest, his last recorded act being in 1077 when he made a grant to the monastery of Le Bec.[10] It is rare indeed that the origin of a Norman territorial

---

[1] He was a constant witness to ducal charters before 1066. See *R.A.D.N.*, *passim*.
[2] Will. Poit., p. 197.　　　　　　　[3] D.B., vol. I, fols. 80, 168.
[4] Lot, *Saint-Wandrille*, p. 54, no. 14.
[5] *Cart. S. Trin. Roth.*, no. LXX; p. 460, no. LXXVIII.
[6] *Ibid.*, p. 441, no. XXXVII.　　　[7] Ord. Vit., vol. III, p. 230; vol. IV p. 335
[8] *Cart. S. Père Chartres*, p. 178.　　[9] *Cart. S. Trin. Roth.*, no. LXX.
[10] *Neustria Pia*, p. 442; Porée, *L'abbaye du Bec*, vol. I, p. 373.

family of the second class can be illustrated with this particularity from the independent charters of four religious houses.

Finally, there may be taken the instance of the family of Montfort-sur-Risle.[1] The first known ancestor of this house is Thurstan of Bastembourg who appears in a ducal charter of 1027 as possessed of land at Pont-Authou, and who, perhaps, also subscribed two charters for Saint-Wandrille which passed at the ducal court at about the same time.[2] This Thurstan had a daughter, with whom the notorious Geré of Échauffour fell in love at first sight while dining with her father,[3] and also two sons – William Bertram, who can perhaps be seen in charters for Le Mont-Saint-Michel, and Hugh I of Montfort (some five miles from Pont-Authou) who perished in private war with Walchelin of Ferrières during the anarchy.[4] It was, however, the son of Hugh I, namely Hugh II of Montfort, who finally established the fortunes of the house. He was one of the leaders of the Norman forces at Mortemer, and between 1060 and 1066 attested ducal charters for Bayeux and Caen.[5] He fought at Hastings, and so influential had he become by that time that in 1067 he was left in England to assist in the government of the kingdom during William's absence and placed in charge of the important castle of Dover.[6] In due course he was to become a great landowner in England, and in Normandy to add to his *hereditas* of Montfort the distinct honour of Coquainvillers.[7]

The four families, whose origins have here been briefly illustrated, may safely be regarded as typical of the Norman aristocracy which came to supply the greater part of Norman strength in the time of William the Conqueror. It will be noted, moreover, that in all these cases the family only acquired the lands from which it took its feudal name during the earlier half of the eleventh century. At a later date the family of Tosny might claim descent from an uncle of Rolf,[8] but its association with Tosny only started with Ralph II or Ralph I, and its feudal greatness only began with Ralph III. In like fashion the lords of Beaumont might subsequently cite remote ancestors, but the authentic history of their house really starts with Humphrey of Vieilles, and their full power was only

[1] Douglas, *Domesday Monachorum*, pp. 65–70.
[2] *Chartres de Jumièges*, vol. I, p. 41, no. XII; Lot, *Saint-Wandrille*, nos. 9, 14.
[3] Ord. Vit., interp. Will. Jum., p. 163.
[4] *Cal. Doc. France*, nos. 703, 704; Will. Jum., p. 116.
[5] Will. Poit., p. 73; *R.A.D.N.*, no. 219; *Regesta*, vol. I, no. 4.
[6] Will. Poit., p. 267. See also below, pp. 207, 208.
[7] *Cart. S. Ymer-en-Auge* (ed. Breard), no. I; *Cal. Doc. France*, no. 357.
[8] Ord. Vit., interp. Will. Jum., p. 157.

attained under a man who was to survive the Conqueror. Again, the first family of Vernon has been shown to have acquired its domainal lands between 1035 and 1053, whilst the house of Montfort-sur-Risle began about the same time with Thurstan of Bastembourg, and only achieved greatness with a man who is recorded in Domesday Book. The history of these families therefore points inexorably to an important conclusion. The Norman aristocracy which surrounded Duke William, and which he led to the conquest of England, was in his time of comparatively recent growth.

The manner in which this new aristocracy acquired its lands can only be sparsely demonstrated in the available documents, for the surviving texts are not sufficiently numerous to reveal in any comprehensive fashion what was the distribution of land in Normandy before the establishment of the great feudal honours. The pedigrees of Robert of Torigny suggest, however, that the advancement of the kindred of the Duchess Gunnor, widow of Richard I, may have been a factor in the rise of many Norman houses during the latter years of the reign of his son,[1] and there is charter evidence which indicates that some at least of these families acquired lands which had formerly belonged to the ducal dynasty. Thus among the possessions of the Duchess Judith, first wife of Duke Richard II, was a large block of territory in the Lieuvin.[2] After her death most of this went to the abbey of Bernay,[3] but some of the manors do not seem to have been thus disposed, and of these Ferrières-Saint-Hilaire and Chambrais which had both belonged to the Duchess Judith became the special endowment of one of the new Norman houses. Walchelin of Ferrières was clearly established at that place before his death about 1040, and Chambrais (which is the modern Broglie) probably came into the possession of this family at about the same time, since Chambrais, situated but three miles from Ferrières, was at a later date held by the lords of Ferrières in demesne, and afterwards became the head of their Norman barony.[4]

A clearer example of the acquisition by a feudal family of lands, which had earlier been part of the ducal demesne, can be seen in the descent of the possessions of Count Rodulf, half-brother to Duke Richard I.[5] Among the lands held by this man were estates situated on the Risle near Saint Philibert; estates on the Eure, including Cocherel,

---

[1] Will. Jum., pp. 320–329; cf. G. H. White, in *Genealogist*, New Series, vol. xxxvii, p. 57.
[2] *R.A.D.N.*, no. 11.　　[3] *Ibid.*, no. 35.
[4] Will. Jum., p. 116; Ord. Vit., vol. i, p. 180.
[5] Douglas, *Eng. Hist. Rev.*, vol. lix (1944), pp. 62–64; vol. lxi (1946), p. 131.

Jouy, and, it would seem, Pacy; lands dependent on Breteuil; and lands centred on Ivry. Many of these lands, particularly those on the Eure, were inextricably intermingled with the earliest demesne of the Norman dukes and must have come to Rodulf through his stepfather or his half-brother. Their subsequent devolution is thus of particular interest. Part of the Ivry lands went to the count's eldest son Hugh, bishop of Bayeux, whilst the barony of Saint Philibert passed through the count's second son, John, bishop of Avranches, to that cathedral church. But the larger part of Rodulf's possessions, including the honour of Pacy and the distinct honour of Breteuil, descended through the count's daughter, Emma, to her husband Osbern, the steward of Duke Robert I, and one of the guardians of the infant William. And Osbern was typical of the new aristocracy which at this time was rising to power. Few of his wide estates had been held by his father Herfast, whose meagre *hereditas* passed eventually to the monastery of Saint Père of Chartres.[1] Osbern's own extensive lands were acquired by him between 1020 and 1040. Carved out of the original demesne of the ducal dynasty, they passed after 1040 to Osbern's great son, William fitz Osbern, the future earl of Hereford, and became the endowment of one of the greatest feudal honours of Normandy.

If the new magnates thus enriched themselves with lands which had previously been in lay possession, they also effected a considerable spoliation of the Church. It was not for nothing that an ecclesiastical synod before 1046 denounced prelates in the province who gave lands to laymen.[2] When Ralph II of Tosny went to Apulia he was already known by the name of his chief Norman possession which had from an early date belonged to the cathedral church of Rouen, and if this particular alienation may perhaps be explained by the kinship between Ralph and Archbishop Hugh, none the less about the same time other archiepiscopal estates centred on Douvrend passed likewise into lay hands.[3] Similarly, Robert, bishop of Coutances, was accused of having bestowed cathedral prebends on his relatives to be held by them as lay fiefs.[4] It is probable, however, that the older monasteries of Normandy were the chief victims. As late as 1025, for instance, the abbey of Bernay was in possession of Vieilles, Beaumont, and Beaumontel which had been given to the monks by the Duchess Judith,[5] but shortly afterwards

[1] *Cart. S. Père Chartres*, vol. I, p. 108.   [2] Bessin, *Concilia*, p. 42, cl. X.
[3] Valin, *Duc de Normandie, Preuves*, no. 1; Stapleton, in *Archaeological Journal*, vol. III, pp. 6–7.
[4] *Gall. Christ.*, vol. XI; *Instrumenta*, col. 218.   [5] *R.A.D.N.*, nos. 11, 35.

Humphrey 'de Vetulis' obtained Vieilles, and Beaumont was ceded to him before 1035.[1] The best example of this process might, however, be taken from the history of the family of Montgomery which seems to have acquired many of its earliest possessions from monastic lands. Roger I, the first ascertainable member of that house, is reported to have abstracted lands in the possession of Bernay,[2] and between 1028 and 1032 he seems to have acquired Vimoutiers,[3] which in 1025 had been held by the monks of Jumièges.[4] Again, a charter of Duke Richard II displays Troarn with its dependencies as belonging to the abbey of Fécamp, and in 1025 this abbey also held Airan and Almenèches. Yet Troarn and Airan appear to have been possessed by Roger I of Montgomery, while Almenèches is known to have belonged at some time to his son Roger II.[5] Three of the oldest monastic houses of Normandy clearly had reason to regret the rise of Montgomery in the second quarter of the eleventh century.

Such transactions may safely be regarded as representative, for our knowledge of them depends upon the chance survival of texts from a remote age, and on the possibility of making certain identifications of the places mentioned in them. The spoliation of the Norman church by the new Norman aristocracy must have been considerable, and the numerous new religious houses, which in the latter part of the eleventh century were founded by these magnates, were often endowed by them with lands which had fairly recently been taken from the older ducal foundations. It should, however, be noted that these ecclesiastical alienations would tend to figure with undue prominence in the documents, and the transference of lay lands must also have been extensive, even though for the most part it was unrecorded. Only because the monastery of Saint-Taurin of Évreux was interested in the property is anything known of the manner in which Meules, which was part of the ducal demesne in the time of Duke Richard I, passed into the hands of the family of Gilbert of Brionne, the count, to supply at last a territorial name for the first Norman sheriff of Devon.[6]

The large-scale transference of landed property which created the new Norman aristocracy involved a tenurial revolution which coloured

---

[1] *Gall. Christ.*, vol. XI; *Instrumenta*, col. 199; Robert of Torigny, *De Immuatatione Ordinis Monachorum* (*Mon. Ang.*, vol. VI, p. 1063).

[2] Robert of Torigny, *loc. cit.*   [3] *Chartes de Jumièges*, vol. I, no. XII.

[4] *Ibid.*, no. XIII, but the editor's comments need correction.

[5] *R.A.D.N.*, no. 34; Sauvage, *L'abbaye de Troarn, Preuves*, no. I; *Chartes de Jumièges*, no. XII.

[6] Douglas, *Rise of Normandy*, p. 19.

the whole history of the duchy during the Norman reign of Duke William II. For while the beginnings of this social movement may be referred to the first half of the eleventh century (though not earlier) its end had not been fully accomplished even on the eve of the Norman conquest. The disorders in the duchy between 1035 and 1060 provided plentiful opportunity for men of the new aristocracy to win estates and power by means of the sword, and each crisis within that period involved the fate of families which were later to rise to dominance in Normandy and England. The disturbances of the minority directly concerned the fortunes of Tosny, Beaumont, Montgomery, Ferrières, and Montfort, whilst the campaigns of 1047 and 1051 not only brought misfortune to many magnates in Lower Normandy but also influenced the rise of men as far to the east as William of Vernon. But probably the greatest changes in this period occurred after the forfeiture of William, count of Arques, in 1053. The count's possessions had stretched west-ward across the Seine,[1] and in that region Beaumont and Montfort were ready to take advantage of his disgrace, whilst within the Pays de Talou itself the upheaval must have been even wider spread. Thus, while Bolbec, some twenty miles from Le Havre, seems to have been the original home of the Giffards,[2] they were enabled about this time to establish themselves at Longueville in the heart of the Pays de Talou, and this was to remain the head of their Norman honour.[3] Similarly, the establishment of Warenne at Bellencombre certainly took place during these years, and as a result of these events.

The rise of this aristocracy inevitably presented a problem of special urgency to Duke William, the more especially as several of these families not only obtained extensive possessions but also acquired official positions within the duchy. Emphasis has already been laid on the importance of the *vicomte* in bridging the transition between Carolingian Neustria and ducal Normandy, and in providing an instrument of administration for the descendants of Rolf. It was therefore a matter of great moment when during the earlier half of the eleventh century many of the chief Norman *vicomtés* themselves passed into the hereditary possession of some of the most important of the feudal families. Nigel of Saint Sauveur, *vicomte* of the Cotentin, who rebelled in 1047, was either the son or possibly the grandson of the first man known to have held

---

[1] *Chartes de Jumièges*, no. XX.

[2] G. H. White, in *Genealogist*, New Series, vol. xxxvii, p. 59. 'Osbern of Bolbec' seems none the less a somewhat nebulous figure.

[3] Stapleton, *Rot. Scacc. Norm.*, vol. I, p. civ.

this office, and he was himself a lord of great power. He was to regain his *vicomté* after Val-ès-Dunes, and to survive until long after the Norman conquest.[1] Equally notable were the hereditary *vicomtes* of the Avranchin. Richard, later *vicomte* of Avranches, who was established by 1046,[2] and who was perhaps also lord of Creully,[3] was the son of Thurstan Goz, likewise a *vicomte*,[4] and he was to continue in that office at least as late as November 1074.[5] The Bessin, too, produced an outstanding dynasty of *vicomtes*. At the beginning of Duke William's reign the *vicomte* of the Bessin was Rannulf, who was the son of a *vicomte* named Anschitil.[6] He married a daughter of Duke Richard III[7] and was among the defeated rebels at Val-ès-Dunes. None the less, the office continued in the family, for he was succeeded by another Rannulf (II) who was established at Avranches before the Norman conquest, and who survived until after April 1089.[8] Moreover, this second Rannulf married Maud, daughter of Richard, *vicomte* of the Avranchin, thus linking together two powerful vice-comital dynasties which were later in turn to determine the succession of the earldom of Chester.[9]

These descents have far more than merely a genealogical interest. They reflect the rise of great feudal families whose possession of the vice-comital office was to influence the growth of Normandy and the fate of England. Moreover, whilst the greatest vice-comital dynasties were to be found in Lower Normandy – in the Cotentin, the Avranchin, and the Bessin – the same process could be watched elsewhere in the duchy. In 1054, for example, one Rainald was *vicomte* of Arques.[10] His possessions passed in due course to Goscelin, son of Hedo, *vicomte* of

---

[1] On all that concerns the family of St Sauveur, and the *vicomté* of the Cotentin in this period, see L. Delisle, *Saint-Sauveur* (1867).

[2] *R.A.D.N.*, no. 110.

[3] L. Musset, *Actes Inédits de XIᵉ Siècle*, pp. 8, 9. (This is *Bull. Soc. Antiq. Norm.*, vol. LII, 1954.)

[4] His reputed father was 'Ansfrid the Dane', and his career is illustrated in many charters between 1015 and 1040 (*R.A.D.N.*, *passim*).

[5] *Cart. Bayeux*, vol. I, nos. 2, 3; *Cal. Doc. France*, no. 1211.

[6] *R.A.D.N.*, no. 111. The career of Anschitil is illustrated in many other charters of an early date, particularly in those of Saint-Wandrille (*e.g.* Lot, *op. cit.*, nos. 13, 14).

[7] *Gall. Christ.*, vol. XI; *Instrumenta*, col. 70; Robert of Torigny (ed. Delisle), vol. I, p. 34.

[8] *Cart. Bayeux*, no. IV.

[9] It seems to have been generally assumed that there were only two Rannulfs, *vicomtes* of the Bessin, at this time, namely Rannulf 'Meschin' who became earl of Chester in 1120, and Rannulf his father who married Maud, daughter of Richard, *vicomte* of the Avranchin. Chronology, however, makes it imperative to distribute them into three: namely (i) Rannulf, son of Anschitil, who fought in 1047 at Val-ès-Dunes; (ii) Rannulf, presumably his son, who occurs in or before 1066; and (iii) Rannulf 'Meschin'.

[10] Chevreux et Vernier, *Archives de Normandie*, plate IX. For date, see Haskins, *op. cit.*, p. 258.

Rouen,[1] and Goscelin's daughter married a certain Godfrey who in turn became *vicomte* of Arques.[2] The feudal connexion thus exhibited between the *vicomtés* of Arques and Rouen in these years is not un-remarkable since it affected the social structure of Upper Normandy at a critical period. But farther to the west, in the centre of the duchy, a more striking manifestation of the same process was taking place. Between July 1031 and July 1032 there was included in a charter for Saint-Wandrille the sign of 'Roger, *vicomte* of the Hiémois', and this was none other than Roger I of Montgomery.[3] His father is unknown, and his career is obscure, but he was to be succeeded by his famous son, Roger II, who was to bring the family to its full power. Already in 1051, as has been seen, Roger II of Montgomery was distinguishing himself round Domfront, and at about the same time he made his brilliant marriage with Mabel, heiress to many of the lands of Bellême.[4] From that time forward his career was bound up with that of William the Conqueror, but he was still proud to be *vicomte* of the Hiémois even after (about 1075) he had become the first earl of Shrewsbury.[5]

The establishment of the great vice-comital families was fraught with danger to the ducal power. But it also provided Duke William with a great opportunity which in the event he was not slow to seize. The *vicomte* had been, and was to remain, the chief agent of ducal adminis-tration, so that while the acquisition of *vicomtés* in hereditary possession might in a special way challenge the ducal authority, it might also be made to provide the means whereby prominent members of the new nobility could be made to act, like their predecessors in this office, as deputies of the count of Rouen. As will be seen,[6] Duke William was enabled, even in the changed conditions, continuously to employ his *vicomtes* as agents of his administration, but his success in so doing none the less depended directly upon his solution of the more general problem which confronted him in respect of the aristocracy. For the vice-comital families were but a section of that aristocracy, and their rise was but part of the same process which at the same time led to the advancement of other families of equal or greater power. The progress of Tosny and

---

[1] Martène and Durand, *Thesaurus Anecdotorum*, vol. i, col. 167; *R.A.D.N.*, no. 72; Valin, *op. cit.*, *Preuves*, no. I. He is usually described as having been *vicomte* of Arques, but this can hardly have been the case since he appears in charters alongside of Rainald, *vicomte* of Arques (Chevreux et Vernier, *op. cit.*, plate IX), and also alongside of Godfrey, Rainald's successor as *vicomte* of Arques (*Cart. S. Trin. Roth.*, no. I). That Goscelin was *vicomte* not of Arques but of Rouen is indicated by no. IX of the same cartulary.

[2] *Ibid.*   [3] Lot, *Saint-Wandrille*, no. 13.

[4] Above, pp. 90, 91.   [5] Below, pp. 294, 295.   [6] Below, pp. 141–144.

Beaumont, for example, was not essentially different from that of the hereditary *vicomtes* of the Cotentin and the Bessin, and the possession of the *vicomté* of the Hiémois was as much a result as a cause of the enrichment of Montgomery. The crucial task for Duke William was thus in this matter the same throughout. It was to maintain his own position within a social structure which throughout his reign was being progressively modified by the rapid acquisition of landed wealth by members of a new nobility.

For the establishment in Normandy between 1030 and 1060 of so many of the families which were later to dominate the feudal province entailed also the advancement of their dependants, and contributed to the formation of a new political organization of the duchy based upon lordship and vassalage. The chief tenants of the greater Norman lords in England after the Conquest often bore territorial names which reveal their families as near neighbours of their lords in Normandy;[1] and it is impossible to avoid the conclusion that they owed their rise to power to an earlier connexion with the great feudal houses from whom they were later to hold their widely scattered English estates. Sometimes indeed positive evidence of this can be found in pre-Conquest Norman documents. The connexion between Pantulf and Montgomery, for instance, which was to be so strikingly exhibited in Shropshire at the time of Domesday Book may thus, for instance, be confidently referred back to the time of Roger I of Montgomery, who between 1027 and 1035 issued for the abbey of Jumièges a charter which is subscribed with the sign of 'William Pantulf'.[2]

The best example of the early growth of Norman vassalage may, however, be found in the dependency of Clères upon Tosny which likewise was to continue in England after the Conquest. At the end of the eleventh century, Gilbert of Clères, the son of Roger I of Clères, gave land at La Puthenaye to the abbey of Conches with the assent of Ralph (III) of Tosny 'to whose fief it belongs'.[3] Similarly, the same Ralph of Tosny, between 1071 and 1083, confirmed to the abbey of Croix-Saint-Leuffroi all the possessions of Gilbert's son Ralph who had become a monk.[4] Moreover, shortly before the Conquest, Gilbert's father – Roger I of Clères – made a grant to Saint-Ouen of Rouen with the assent of his lord Ralph (III) of Tosny,[5] and at about the same time

[1] Below, pp. 270, 271. [2] D.B., vol. I, fols. 257, 257b; *Chartes de Jumièges*, no. XIII.
[3] *Gall. Christ.*, vol. XI; *Instrumenta*, col. 132; Delisle-Berger, *Rec. Actes – Henry II*, vol. I, p. 553.
[4] Lebeurier, *Notice – sur Croix-Saint-Leuffroi*, p. 46, no. III.
[5] Le Prévost, *Eure*, vol. III, p. 467.

he gave land to the abbey of Conches for the soul of his former overlord Roger (I) of Tosny, and with the assent of Ralph (III) of Tosny who was then the chief lord of the fief.[1] It is seldom, indeed, that early Norman vassalage can be illustrated with this particularity, and in this case the connexion between the two families can be noticed at an even more remote date. Among the numerous acts of violence characteristic of Duke William's minority two are in this respect especially heinous. Roger I of Tosny was killed by Roger of Beaumont, and shortly afterwards Robert of Beaumont (Roger's brother) was assassinated by Roger I of Clères.[2] In the light of subsequent evidence it is impossible not to regard this latter act as the revenge of a vassal for the murder of his overlord. The dependence of Clères upon Tosny (which in fact was to continue until the thirteenth century) can thus be traced back to the beginning of the reign of Duke William.

Such early connexions between Norman families are challenging, but it would be wrong to deduce from them a conclusion that before the Norman conquest the structure of Norman society had as yet been made to conform to an ordered feudal plan. Norman charters of the period 1035–1066 reveal unmistakably in the duchy a society which was based upon vassalage, but with equal certainty they display a social structure in which feudal arrangements had not as yet been reduced to a uniform pattern capable of precise definition in the interests of the duke as feudal overlord. Dependent tenure is, however, to be met with on every side, and gifts of land seem normally to have required the consent of a superior. When a certain Urso, about 1055, gave land to Holy Trinity, Rouen, he asserted the previous consent of his lord (who was dead), and also the approval of his lord's wife and sons;[3] and when, about the same time, Ansfred, son of Osbern the *vicomte*, granted his hereditary possessions to the same monastery, he did so with the consent of 'my lords Emma, the wife of Osbern the steward, and her sons William and Osbern'.[4] Such vassalage could in fact be very widely illustrated, but it would seem impossible to define it in terms characteristic of later feudal society; and the drafters of Norman charters at this time made little attempt to do so. Right down to the Norman conquest the most common word for a dependent estate in Normandy was the older term *beneficium*. About 1050 Rodulf I of Warenne, for instance, assigned to Holy Trinity, Rouen, land which had previously pertained to the 'old benefice' of a

[1] *Gall. Christ.*, vol. XI; *Instrumenta*, col. 132. Round, *Cal. Doc. France*, no. 625. Ord. Vit., vol. II, p. 403; vol. v, p. 180.   [2] Ord. Vit., vol. I, p. 180; vol. II, pp. 40, 41.
[3] *Cart. S. Trin. Roth.*, no. X.   [4] *Ibid.*, no. XLIX.

certain Roger,[1] and when Guidmund gave land in Normandy to Saint-Père of Chartres he did so with deference 'to my lord William the count from whom I hold it as a benefice'.[2] In like manner when Guazo in 1060 founded the priory of Croth in the Évreçin, his endowments were made with the consent of his lord Hugh Bardo, 'part of whose benefice they were'.[3]

The terminology of the Norman charters of this time is characteristic of an age in which feudal obligations have not yet been fully defined and few of these deeds use any of the terms of feudal status in anything like the precise sense they subsequently acquired. The word *baro*, for instance, is rare in Norman documents of this period, and much more frequent is the vaguer term *fidelis* (liegeman). Thus Gilbert, son of Erchembald the *vicomte*, is the *fidelis* of Osbern the steward;[4] Oylard is the *fidelis* of the Countess Lesceline of Eu;[5] and Roger, son of Humphrey, is the *fidelis* of Duke William.[6] Most significant of all is the vague connotation in these texts of the word *miles*, which later acquired the meaning of 'knight'. The father of William of Warenne can, for instance, be described as a *miles*;[7] so also can the founder of the priory of Croth; and so also can a multitude of lesser men. It would indeed be very rash even to suppose that at this time the word *miles* inevitably designated a mounted warrior. Many of these men undoubtedly fought on horseback at Val-ès-Dunes and Mortemer, but it would be difficult to assert what was the precise status of those seven *equites* given to the abbey of Saint-Ouen by Osbern of Écquetot before 1066,[8] or that of Atselin *equitis mei* whose land Duke William himself, about 1050, confirmed to the monastery of Saint-Wandrille.[9]

There thus seems little warranty for believing that anything resembling tenure by knight-service, in the later sense of the term, was uniformly established, or carefully defined, in pre-Conquest Normandy. Such definition as was attained in the duchy during the Conqueror's reign is recorded for the most part in Norman charters issued after the conquest of England. Nor is there anything in the testimony to suggest that before the Conquest, Normandy had been made generally familiar with the 'feudal incidents' which half a century later were so carefully to be discussed after the coronation of King Henry I of England. In all the texts that have been examined there would

---

[1] *Ibid.*, no. XXX.
[2] *Cart. S. Père Chartres*, vol. I, p. 145.
[3] Le Prévost, *Eure*, vol. I, p. 570.
[4] *Cart. S. Trin. Roth.*, no. VI (*R.A.D.N.*, no. 96).
[5] *Ibid.*, no. LXIX.
[6] *R.A.D.N.*, no. 128.
[7] Le Prévost, *Eure*, vol. III, p. 324.
[8] *Ibid.*, vol. II, p. 38.
[9] *R.A.D.N.*, no. 109.

appear to be only one mention before 1066 of the payment of a 'relief', and this occurs in a charter which was issued only a very few years before the Norman conquest.[1]

The evidence reveals within the duchy between 1035 and 1066 a society in a state of flux, and it must in this sense qualify any such generalization as that 'Norman society in 1066 is a feudal society, and one of the most fully developed feudal societies in Europe'.[2] Dependent tenure, of various kinds and in different degrees, was widespread through Normandy, but there seems little reason to believe that feudal law and feudal obligations were generally accepted and enforced in the duchy at this time in the manner characteristic of a later age. The feudal order which the Conqueror was able to impose upon England before his death was much more developed, and much more centralized, than anything that can be discovered in Normandy before 1066, and it was his success in his kingdom which enabled him to attain in his duchy a part of those feudal objectives which might otherwise have eluded him. If Normandy gave feudal principles to England, England under the Conqueror profoundly influenced Normandy in the matter of feudal practice. Before 1066 older notions of vassalage were still widespread in Normandy, and still imperfectly co-ordinated in a regular feudal scheme. It was therefore a vital problem for Duke William whether he could so link his own interests with those of the aristocracy which surrounded him between 1047 and 1066 as ultimately to dominate the developing social order to which they belonged. And upon the outcome of this endeavour was to depend much of the future history of two countries, for if it had failed, the Norman conquest of England would have been impossible.

The character of Duke William's success in this matter can only be appraised in relation to the difficulties he faced and the manner in which he overcame them. During the earlier years of his reign the duke's position in the new social order might seem to have depended less on the enunciation of legal theory than upon the creation of such personal, and particular, loyalties as the young ruler could elicit from the magnates who surrounded him. In the midst of a social transformation controlled by great families eager to extend their newly won power, it was essential for the duke judiciously to favour the fortunes of those upon whom he could rely. This he seems to have done from an early

---

[1] *Gall. Christ.*, vol. IX; *Instrumenta*, col. 132; Le Prévost, *Eure*, vol. III, p. 467.
[2] Haskins, *Norman Institutions*, p. 5.

date as a matter of definite policy. William fitz Osbern and Roger II of Montgomery, themselves still 'young warriors', had already in 1051 been selected by the duke for his special confidence,[1] and both these men consistently enjoyed their master's support in their advance to power, and co-operated with him closely, both in Normandy and England. To reward such men could, however, before 1066, only be done by impoverishing the ducal demesne, or at the expense either of their fellow magnates in Normandy or of the Norman church, so that the policy was always fraught with the danger of open conflict.

It may, therefore, be regarded as a sign of the growing strength of the duke that in 1055 or 1056[2] he was able very summarily to disinherit William Warlenc, count of Mortain, and to establish in that *comté* his own half-brother Robert, who later guarded Norman England from the Sussex rape of Pevensey, and became one of the richest English landowners. Often, however, the advancement of the duke's supporters came about with greater hazard. One of his first acts appears to have been to grant the *comté* of Arques to his uncle, William, on the understanding that the new count, 'having obtained this benefice would in return remain faithful in all things to the duke'. The confidence was woefully misplaced as the great revolt of 1052–1054 was to prove, but the count's defeat, as has been seen, enriched several other families, and the duke was able to use this situation in its turn to his advantage. It was, for instance, by William's direct intervention that the count's forfeiture was made to entail the decline of Mortemer and the rise of Warenne.

The early history of Warenne[3] may indeed serve as an excellent demonstration of the duke's feudal policy during these critical years, and at the same time illustrate how, as a result of that policy, a particular family might be made to rise from small beginnings to great power. At the opening of the reign, Warenne was of little account. A certain Rodulf of Warenne can be discerned holding some estates near Rouen,[4] and he apparently survived until 1074.[5] He had, moreover, two sons, Rodulf the elder and William.[6] As a younger son this William can have

---

[1] Will. Poit., p. 38.
[2] William 'Werlenc' was still witnessing charters as count about this time (*R.A.D.N.*, nos. 161, 162).
[3] L. C. Loyd, 'The Origin of the Family of Warenne' (*Yorks. Arch. Soc. Journal*, vol. XXXI (1933), pp. 97–113).
[4] *Cart. S. Trin. Roth.*, nos. XXVII, XXIX, XL, XLI; *Mon. Ang.*, vol. VI, p. 1101.
[5] *Cart. S. Trin. Roth.*, no. XXXV.
[6] *Ibid.*, no. XXXI.

inherited little of the meagre *hereditas* of his father.[1] Yet it was none the less this man who established the greatness of the house. In the campaign of 1052–1054 he distinguished himself by his special loyalty to the duke, and though still a young man (*tiro legitimus*), he was, after the fall of the count of Arques, singled out by the duke for special favour. It is specially recorded that when, after the critical campaign, Roger of Mortemer forfeited a large part of his Norman lands, the castle of Mortemer itself was bestowed upon William of Warenne.[2] Nor was this all; for the extensive lands later held by Warenne in the neighbourhood of Mortemer must have been acquired at the same time and as a result of the same forfeiture. Such at least must have been the origin of the Warenne possessions round Bellencombre (some fifteen miles from Mortemer), and those situated in the region of Dieppe some eighteen miles to the north of Bellencombre. It was a notable advance, but even the acquisition of these lands was not of itself sufficient to raise Warenne to the front rank of the Norman aristocracy. Only after 1066 was this to be achieved, and then too as a consequence of continuing service as a specially trusted adherent of the Conqueror.

To establish relationships such as these, which might assure him faithful service from important men in his duchy was a cardinal feature of the policy of Duke William during his Norman reign, and upon his success in this matter depended to a large extent the position he was eventually to occupy in the feudal order that was soon to be established. The suppression of successive revolts in these years did not merely enable the duke to survive; it enabled him in each case to reward his friends out of the lands of his defeated enemies, and very gradually to mould the developing feudalism of Normandy according to a pattern that might subserve his own interests. The process, which must be sharply contrasted with the more sudden introduction of military feudalism into England, was in Normandy a slow one, and only after a considerable time did it make possible the practical application in the duchy of those feudal principles which the Normans were so soon to introduce into England. In his kingdom, the Conqueror, by interpreting Norman feudal custom in a sense advantageous to himself, was enabled to assume, as if by legal right, a position in the feudal order to which he had long aspired, but which he never wholly attained in Normandy before the Norman conquest.

[1] Loyd, *op. cit.*, pp. 106–110.   [2] Ord. Vit., vol. III, p. 237.

It would therefore be misleading to describe the aristocratic structure of pre-Conquest Normandy in the light of the conditions prevailing in England, or indeed in Normandy, at the close of the Conqueror's reign. In particular, there would seem no reason to suppose that before 1066 the greater Norman magnates had been made generally to regard their position as depending upon ducal grant, or as conditional on their performing military service for the duke with a specified number of trained and equipped knights. The principle of the 'service owed', the *servitium debitum*, precisely defined and rigidly enforced, was one of the cardinal features of feudal organization in the Anglo-Norman kingdom between 1070 and 1087.[1] But it is very doubtful how generally it had been applied in the duchy before the Norman conquest of England. The magnates who were most directly concerned had, as has been seen, established many military tenures on their own lands, but, as must be supposed, they had done this in their own interest, being compelled in a fiercely competitive society to take all possible measures to safeguard the possessions they had so recently won. The feuds during the minority in which so many members of these families perished made it necessary for them to attract to their support as many dependents as possible, and the persistence of private war as a recognized institution in Normandy certainly encouraged sub-infeudation far in excess of any demands that the duke might have felt himself able to make.

Perhaps, indeed, there may here be discerned a factor of feudal development which has received less attention than it deserves and which is particularly applicable to the situation here being discussed. It is generally assumed that the imposition of a fixed *servitium debitum* was in the interests, and for the benefit, of the ruler, and such was undoubtedly the case in England after the Norman conquest. But in pre-Conquest Normandy the situation may have been different. The fixed payment of the 'relief' was welcomed at a later date by the feudal tenants of the king as protecting them against arbitrary and excessive demands. A fixed *servitium debitum* may on occasion have been likewise welcomed as conferring a similar benefit in a changing society wherein the increasing authority of the duke might have appeared to menace an aristocracy already entrenched in power. In other words, the imposition in such cases may sometimes have occurred by mutual consent, and have approached very closely to a free bargain. At all events, it was not until after the conquest of England that William was

---

[1] Below, pp. 281–283.

able to attempt a uniform regulation of Norman vassalage in his own interests.

None the less, it deserves full emphasis that the imposition of *servitia debita* in Normandy began to be widely made during the reign of Duke William II. Indeed there is testimony to show the manner in which the burden was imposed in his time, and sometimes on estates which had not been so burdened when they were originally acquired. Thus in 1072 the abbey of Saint-Évroul owed the service of two knights,[1] and since this was not a ducal foundation it is difficult to see how a conditional service to the duke would have been attached to the original grant of these lands, and in any case the *servitium debitum* of this abbey could not have come into existence before its re-establishment about 1050. There is, again, reason to suppose that no defined service attached either to the Breteuil or the Ivry baronies when these were in the possession of Count Rodulf early in the eleventh century, and the later service of five knights owed to the duke by the count of Meulan cannot have been established before the acquisition of Beaumont-le-Roger, with its dependencies, by the family between 1026 and 1035, and may very possibly be of still later origin.[2] Finally, the service of five knights owed in the twelfth century to the duke by Hugh of Mortemer must derive from the partial restoration of the Mortemer lands after their forfeiture in 1054.[3] It is rarely possible to supply such specific illustrations from the surviving testimony. But it may be added as very probable that before his rebellion in 1047 Grimoald had been made to perform knight-service for his lands at Plessis,[4] and that between 1060 and 1066 John, bishop of Avranches, rendered a service of five knights in respect of the honour of Saint-Philibert.[5]

The results of such arrangements were so substantially to increase the military strength of Normandy that it is important to realize how gradually, and with what difficulty, they were achieved in the time of Duke William. At the time of his accession the process can scarcely have begun. The Norman exodus to Italy in the time of his father may be diversely explained, but it is inconceivable that a ruler able to exact a *servitium debitum* regularly from his magnates would, like Duke

---

[1] *Red Book of Exchequer* (ed. Hall), p. 626.
[2] *Ibid.* Cf. Ord. Vit., vol. III, pp. 263, 336.
[3] *Ibid.*
[4] Haskins, *op. cit.*, pp. 16, 17, and the authorities there cited. The inference may, however have been pushed somewhat too far.
[5] *Ibid.* Cf. Le Prévost, *Eure*, vol. III, p. 183.

Robert I, have allowed so many of them to depart with their followers to distant lands.[1] Moreover, the disorder which afflicted Normandy between 1037 and 1047, followed by the continuous war which lasted until 1054, must have prohibited any more general application of ducal rights in this matter. The point, indeed, deserves some emphasis. The period which elapsed between the accession of Duke Robert (1028) and the battle of Mortemer (1054) was precisely that in which the new aristocracy established itself in Normandy. But during these years there can have been little opportunity for formal assertion of the military demands of the duke over his magnates. If the special position of the duke in the military organization of Normandy, and his legal claims on the service of his magnates, were more generally recognized in 1066 than they had been three decades earlier, this must be attributed to particular arrangements which Duke William had from time to time been able to make with individuals, and more especially to his rule over his duchy during the twelve years which preceded the Norman conquest of England.

By the beginning of 1066 the process was well advanced. It seems certain that before the Norman conquest of England, contractual military service had been imposed on all the older Norman monasteries, and on most, if not all, of the Norman bishops. It had been imposed also upon many, if not on most, of the lay magnates. This for the duke was a practical success of a high order. On the other hand, it is by no means certain that even in 1066 the Norman secular aristocracy had been brought uniformly to accept the principle that they held their lands conditionally upon service, or that at that time they had generally, or in a formal manner, recognized the duke as head of a unified feudal order dependent upon the regular discharge of specified military obligations. Only after William had successfully imposed such legal doctrine on his followers in a newly conquered kingdom was he able at last to apply it generally, and as a matter of principle, to his Norman duchy.

Feudal organization developed gradually in Normandy in connexion with the tumultuous rise of a new aristocracy: it was not imposed rapidly, as in England, by the administrative policy of a prince. All the more noteworthy, therefore, was William's success in bringing this movement so much under his control during his own hazardous reign as duke; for the men who at this time first arise to greatness in Normandy were themselves remarkable. Their vigour was astonishing, and if the

---

[1] Stenton, *Anglo-Saxon England*, p. 551.

superabundant virility which was apparent in their private lives was in part responsible for bringing them to dominance in their own province, none the less many of them early learnt that political sagacity which won for them the panegyric of William of Poitiers.[1] Yet, stained as they were with many of the worst vices of a violent age, and as yet unorganized in any rigid feudal scheme, they were in very truth unamenable to control. Consequently, it is wholly noteworthy that they found in William a leader able to dominate them by his personality, and capable also of directing their immense energy into the paths of constructive statesmanship. Only thus were these men enabled to claim the future for their inheritance, so that much of the history of Normandy and of England was to be a record of their acts. Not the least of the achievements of William the Conqueror was that before 1066 he made to subserve his purpose the ambitions and the divergent interests of the most remarkable secular aristocracy produced in eleventh-century Europe.

[1] Will. Poit., p. 149.

Chapter 5

THE ECCLESIASTICAL REVIVAL

The developing strength of Normandy during the reign of Duke William was due in the first instance to the rise of a new aristocracy, and to the identification of its interests with those of the duke. But the growth of Norman power during this period was never wholly secular, either in its causes or consequences, and the achievement of William the Conqueror was to depend also in large measure on an ecclesiastical revival in the province, which had already begun at the time of his accession, but which gathered increasing momentum in his time. The interconnexion between the secular and ecclesiastical strength of Normandy was, in fact, to become so close by the third quarter of the eleventh century that there is even some danger of forgetting that it was then of comparatively recent growth. The collapse of ecclesiastical life in the province of Rouen at the time of the Viking wars was in truth only slowly repaired. The first definite evidence that the bishoprics of Normandy had been fully reconstituted comes from a text of 990.[1] And of the ten principal religious houses existing in Normandy at the time of William's accession, only four had been reconstituted before 1000,[2] and four more had been founded or re-established since his birth.[3] These facts deserve some emphasis. The ecclesiastical development of Normandy during the earlier half of the eleventh century was almost as remarkable as the growth at the same time of its secular strength, and unless it be explained no assessment of what was accomplished by the greatest Norman duke can hope to be adequate.

Two major factors can be watched in this process. In the first place, there was a monastic revival which began under ducal sponsorship and continued on highly original lines. And secondly there took place a reorganization of the Norman church by a strong group of bishops acting in close co-operation with the duke. Of these, it was the monastic movement which was to entail the more notable consequences. Indeed the growth of Norman monasticism during the decades immediately

[1] *R.A.D.N.*, no. 4.   [2] Jumièges, Le Mont-Saint-Michel, Saint-Wandrille, Saint-Ouen.
[3] Cerisy, Montivilliers, Holy Trinity, Rouen, and Saint-Amand. Fécamp had been reconstituted in 1001, and Bernay established about 1026.

preceding the Norman conquest was so remarkable that it has properly attracted the attention of a long succession of historians, and even now its dramatic character may still excite wonder. Less than a hundred years before the accession of William the Conqueror it is probable that not a single monastery survived in the province of Rouen. The houses were desolate, the congregations dispersed. A few of these had, it is true, maintained a precarious existence by migration. Thus certain of the monks of Jumièges had departed to Haspres in the diocese of Cambrai, whilst others from Fontanelle had gone to Picardy and subsequently to Flanders.[1] But in general the destruction had been complete. Yet little more than a century later – on the eve of the Norman conquest of England – Normandy, plentifully filled with religious houses, was renowned for its monastic life.

Scarcely less notable than the rapidity of this spectacular transformation was the part played by the Viking dynasty in bringing it about. It is possible that, by virtue of the comital status he had acquired, Rolf had been given custody of the abbeys within the *comté* of Rouen, but later assertions of his monastic benefactions must be received with some caution.[2] On the other hand, a very strong tradition asserts that his son William Longsword had been actively interested in projects to resuscitate monastic life in his dominion.[3] In particular, he is said to have welcomed back to Jumièges monks from that congregation who were at Haspres, and to have begun the rebuilding of that monastery to which he brought other monks from the abbey of Saint-Cyprien at Poitiers.[4] Legend undoubtedly magnified the part played by William Longsword as a champion of Christianity, but it would be rash to assert that later Norman monasticism owed nothing to his acts.

The pagan reaction which followed his murder arrested any progress in this direction which may have been made, and it was not until after the pact between Duke Richard I and Lothair in 965 that any appreciable advance can be discerned. Here again, moreover, the primary impulse seems to have come from the ducal dynasty, and now it was to be reinforced by an influence radiating from the abbey of Saint Peter's, Ghent, under the direction of Saint Gérard of Brogne. The impact of this Flemish movement upon Normandy could, for instance, be

---

[1] Prentout, *Étude sur Dudon*, p. 300; *Inventio S. Wulframni* (Soc. Hist. Norm., *Mélanges*, vol. xiv (1938), pp. 1–83).

[2] Douglas, in *Eng. Hist. Rev.*, vol. lvii (1942), p. 433.

[3] Lair, *Guillaume Longue-Epée* (1893) ; *Hist. de Jumièges* (ed. Loth), vol. i, pp. 122–126.

[4] Will. Jum., p. 38; Ord. Vit., vol. ii, p. 8; Robert of Torigny (ed. Delisle), vol. ii, p. 192.

illustrated with particular clarity in the fortunes of the dispersed congregation of Fontanelle which, as has been seen, had after some wanderings reached Flanders. A desire to re-establish the ancient monastery of Fontanelle had long inspired the followers of Saint Gérard. And in 960 to 961 there departed from Ghent to Normandy a small party of monks under the leadership of one of Gérard's disciples named Mainard. These obtained from Duke Richard I the devastated site of Fontanelle, and there they began to reconstruct a new religious house in honour of Saint-Wandrille. Other monks came in due course to join them, and Mainard acquired books and ornaments from Ghent. The re-establishment of Fontanelle under its new style of Saint-Wandrille was thus achieved.[1]

The work of Mainard in Normandy entailed considerable consequences. He only remained a few years at Fontanelle which after his departure seems to have suffered a decline. But in due course Duke Richard transferred him to Le Mont-Saint-Michel. The reconstitution of the famous sanctuary on the Mount was indeed one of the most important acts of Richard the Fearless. Carried out by the ducal energy, with the authority of the pope, and with the collaboration of Archbishop Hugh of Rouen, it was confirmed by a charter of Lothair.[2] Monks were installed in place of canons, and the community received possessions and privileges.[3] Mainard himself was to rule this community for twenty-five years, and his influence, supported by the duke, was widespread.[4] Jumièges, for instance, received new ducal grants at this time, and Saint-Ouen experienced a revival. In short, the significance of the latter part of the reign of Richard I in the growth of Norman monasticism has perhaps been unduly minimized, and Mainard's own career and achievements would probably repay a closer study. The effects of the Flemish monastic revival on the English church in the age of Dunstan and Ethelwold have been well established. Its influence on the development and monastic life in Normandy has been less generally appreciated.

The dominant external influence on the Norman monasticism which was to be developed under William the Conqueror as duke, was, however, derived not from Flanders but from Cluny, or at least from the

---

[1] *Inventio S. Wulframni (op. cit.,* p. 32) ; Lot, *Saint-Wandrille,* pp. xl–xlv.
[2] *Rec. Actes de Lothair et de Louis V* (ed. Halphen), no. XXIV.
[3] *Gall. Christ.,* vol. XI, col. 513; J. Huynes, *Hist. – du Mont-St-Michel* (ed. Beaurepaire), vol. I, pp. 149–151.
[4] He died 16 April, 991 (*Rec. Hist. Franc.,* vol. XXIII, p. 579).

movement which, starting at Cluny, achieved new life at centres such as Dijon.[1] The transition can best be watched in connexion with yet another Norman monastery. Among the ecclesiastical benefactions of Duke Richard I none were more notable than those to Fécamp to which he was particularly attached. There he established a community of secular canons to serve the fine new church which he had built. But the canons, as it would seem, proved unworthy of their task, and some time late in his reign Duke Richard I took the important step of appealing to Maieul, abbot of Cluny, to send monks to replace them. The appeal was at first unsuccessful but after the duke's death it entailed a decisive result. In 1001 at the invitation of Duke Richard II, there came to Fécamp, William of Dijon, whose arrival was to inaugurate a new era in the monastic growth of Normandy.[2] He was to remain abbot of Fécamp for more than a quarter of a century, and in due course to pass on his policy to his great successor Abbot John, who survived until 1079.[3] His influence was, in fact, to determine the character that Norman monasticism assumed during the reign of William the Conqueror.

William of Volpiano, or of Dijon,[4] was of noble Piedmontese stock. He had been at Cluny under Maieul and had been sent in 989 by that abbot to reform the ancient monastery of Saint-Benigne of Dijon. From there his activities rapidly spread so that it was to a man of high reputation in the European church that Duke Richard II made his appeal. At first the famous abbot was reluctant to undertake the mission, alleging the barbarous conditions still surviving in the Viking province. But at length the duke's insistence prevailed, and though William of Dijon never confined his attention to Normandy, it was there that his greatest work was done. As a result, Norman monasticism was henceforth dominated not only by Cluniac ideas, but on the individual adaptation of those ideas supplied by his highly original mind. The earliest centre of this development was of course Fécamp itself, where a new monastic community was forthwith established, but the great abbot's influence speedily radiated throughout the province. Thus he is alleged to have introduced reforms at Saint-Ouen and Jumièges, and according to a later writer he also had Le Mont-Saint-

---

[1] Knowles, *Monastic Order*, pp. 83, 89.

[2] *Liber de Revelatione* (*Pat. Lat.*, vol. CLI, col. 699); Leroux de Lincy, *Essai – sur Fécamp* (1840), pp. 5–9.

[3] Knowles, *op. cit.*, p. 85.

[4] For what follows, see Watkin Williams in *Downside Review*, vol. LII, pp. 520–534.

Michel 'under his rule'.[1] Moreover, such was his ascendancy that when in the ten years before the Conqueror's accession new ducal foundations were made in Normandy, these in their turn were modelled according to his ideas. Bernay in this manner was founded in about 1026 by the Duchess Judith,[2] and of the same character were the two monasteries set up during the reign of Duke Robert I, the one at Cerisy-la-Forêt, and the other dedicated to the Holy Trinity on Saint Catherine's Mount at Rouen.[3] Of similar pattern were two nunneries: the one established at Montivilliers, and the other dedicated to Saint-Amand in Rouen.[4]

The reviving Norman monasticism which Duke William inherited in 1035 and which was so signally to be developed during his reign had thus become Cluniac in spirit, even as it had been ducal in direction. Traces of the earlier influence from Flanders remained, it is true, at Le Mont-Saint-Michel and at Saint-Wandrille, whence it might in part be transmitted to the daughter houses of Fontanelles at Préaux and Grestain. But the main stimulus was now from Cluny, whose influence, modified by William of Dijon and Richard of Saint-Vannes, was predominant.[5] Nor could the ducal connexion with the movement be ignored or its essential character masked. It is noteworthy that among the foundations made by Norman dukes before 1035 all save two were made on the sites of ancient religious houses, so that this endeavour can legitimately be held to reflect a conscious attempt made by the Viking dynasty to revive the flourishing ecclesiastical life of Neustria, which had been all but annihilated in the Viking wars.

Further justification for this opinion could be found if reference was made to the endowments which the new ducal monasteries had received. For these were, as it would seem, frequently made from lands which had previously been held by the abbeys that had been destroyed, or from estates over which the dukes, by virtue of an earlier tradition of secular authority, had come to claim custody. Thus Cerisy-la-Forêt in the time of Duke William's father received estates which had earlier belonged to the destroyed abbeys of Deux-Jumeaux, Saint-Fromond, and Saint-Marculf, whilst Holy Trinity, about the same time, acquired some of the lands of the earlier monastery of Saint-Philibert.[6] Other

---

[1] Robert of Torigny (ed. Delisle), vol. I, p. 193.
[2] Le Prévost, *Eure*, vol. I, p. 285; A. Goujou, *Histoire de Bernay*, chap. II.
[3] *Mon. Ang.*, vol. VI, p. 1073; *R.A.D.N.*, no. 61.
[4] Le Cacheux, *Saint Amand*, chap. I; the 'foundation charter' (p. 242) is, however, a forgery.
[5] H. Dauphin, *Le Bienheureux Richard* (1946), pp. 260–264.
[6] Le Musset, 'Les destins de la propriété monastique' (*Jumièges – XIIIᵉ Centenaire*, pp. 49–55).

restitutions of a similar nature were undoubtedly made in this period, and even apart from these the direct benefactions of the ducal house were most notable. Of the ten religious houses which William found in existence in Normandy at the time of his accession – Jumièges, Saint-Wandrille, Le Mont-Saint-Michel, Saint-Ouen, Fécamp, Bernay, Cerisy, Montivilliers and Holy Trinity, Rouen, and Saint-Amand – all owed their foundation or re-establishment, directly or indirectly, to ducal action. The young Duke William thus succeeded to a tradition of monastic patronage which had become a characteristic feature of Norman ducal authority.

Moreover, while the ducal dynasty had established itself as the guardian of monastic life within Normandy, so also were the re-established Norman monasteries linking their own temporal fortunes to those of the duchy. Before the Viking wars, the monasteries of this region had held estates widely scattered throughout Gaul. Thus Fontanelles in addition to its possessions in the valley of the Lower Seine had held lands in Picardy, in Provence, in Saintonge, and in Burgundy, whilst Jumièges had possessed estates in Anjou, Maine, Poitou, and the Vexin.[1] Even after the restorations which were gradually and imperfectly made during the tenth century, the Norman monasteries still sought to retain their rights over possessions outside as well as within Normandy. During the three decades before William's accession, however, this policy was reversed, and the Norman monasteries now began to show themselves anxious to concentrate their landed wealth within the dominions of the Norman duke. Thus Jumièges in 1012 ceded one of its Poitevin estates to the abbey of Bourgeuil in exchange for lands near Vernon, and in 1024 dispensed with Haspres by a similar arrangement with the monks of Saint-Vedast of Arras.[2] The abbey of Saint-Wandrille adopted the same procedure,[3] and from this time forward, with the partial exception of the abbey of Le Mont-Saint-Michel, the Norman monasteries appear to have renounced until after 1066 any policy of enriching themselves outside the duchy. By 1035 they had come in short to identify their territorial fortunes with the secular development and expansion of Normandy itself.

The development of Norman monasticism during the reign of Duke William was thus conditioned by a complex tradition which had

---

[1] Lot, *Saint-Wandrille*, pp. xiii–xxviii; Musset, *op. cit.*, p. 50.
[2] *R.A.D.N.*, nos. 14 *bis*, 26.　　　　[3] Musset, *op. cit.*, p. 50.

already linked the dynasty with monastic restoration, and was merging the interests of the reformed monasteries with those of the Norman duchy. Nevertheless, the new reign was to witness a phase of monastic growth in Normandy which was in every way notable, and which was marked by its own especial features. Not only was the earlier tradition sustained, but its operation was enlarged, and this was brought about by a new wave of enthusiasm and of patronage. In 1035, as has been seen, all the religious houses of the province had owed their eleventh-century existence to the ducal dynasty. Now a new influence was brought to bear on this growth. Already in 1030 it was at the instigation of Goscelin, *vicomte* of Rouen, and Emmeline his wife, that Duke Robert I had granted the foundation charter to Holy Trinity, Rouen,[1] to which the venerated relics of Saint Catherine had come some time between 1033 and 1054.[2] And Goscelin and Emmeline had also been influential, a few years later, in establishing the nunnery of Saint-Amand.[3] It was typical of a new type of patronage that was soon to be dominant in the duchy. After Robert I's death no new ducal monastery was to be founded in Normandy until in 1063 William and Matilda set up their twin houses at Caen. None the less, between 1035 and 1066 at least twenty new religious houses were established in the duchy. They owed their origin to members of the new aristocracy, and this fervent activity is not the least surprising feature of the acts of that astonishing group of interrelated families. It commands attention, even though it may baffle full explanation.

For this movement was sudden. Not only had the new nobility taken little direct share in the earlier monastic foundations, but in their rise to power they had frequently enriched themselves at the expense of the Church. Jumièges, Saint-Wandrille, and Le Mont-Saint-Michel had all, for example, suffered particular losses in this respect.[4] Yet between 1035 and 1050, when the ducal power was in partial eclipse, this same competitive aristocracy addressed itself to the development of Norman monastic life and, until 1066, took over much of the patronage which had earlier been exercised by the dukes. This endeavour was in fact so general that it commanded the admiring eulogy of a later monk. At this

---

[1] *R.A.D.N.*, no. 61.

[2] R. Fawtier, 'Les Reliques rouennaises de Sainte Catherine d'Alexandrie' (*Analecta Bollandiana*, vol. xli (1923), pp. 357–368). M. Fawtier shows that Hugh of Flavigny's story of the relics, and of the foundation, is not to be relied upon.

[3] M. J. Le Cacheux, *op. cit.*, chap. I.

[4] Above, pp. 80–91.

time, remarked Ordericus Vitalis, in a famous passage,[1] the nobles of Normandy, imitating the actions of their dukes, vied with one another in monastic benefactions to such an extent that any one of these magnates held himself cheap if he had not established, and endowed, clerks, or monks, on his estates. In such language there may of course be detected overtones of enthusiasm. But the factual record of the origins of Norman monasteries supplied by Robert of Torigny shows that there was here no undue exaggeration.[2]

It is indeed hard to avoid monotony in recalling the particular foundations made by the new aristocracy in Normandy between 1035 and 1066, for few of the great feudal families whose rise then took place failed to contribute something to this endeavour. Thus about 1035 Roger I of Tosny established a monastery at Châtillon, and about the same time Humphrey of Vieilles founded two houses at Préaux – the one, Saint-Pierre, for men, and the other, Saint-Léger, for women.[3] The Countess Lesceline and her son Robert, count of Eu, were responsible for the abbey of Saint-Pierre-sur-Dives, and later the same Count Robert set up the abbey of Saint-Michel-du-Tréport.[4] Herluin, *vicomte* of Conteville, his wife Herleve, and his son Robert, count of Mortain, founded the abbey of Grestain; and before 1055 Ralph Tesson, a member of a notable family in middle Normandy, established the monastery of Fontenay.[5] William fitz Osbern, son of Duke Robert's steward, in like manner established the abbey of Lire, and subsequently followed this up with a similar foundation at Cormeilles.[6] In Upper Normandy, the house of Saint Victor-en-Caux was set up by Roger of Mortemer as a priory of Saint-Ouen, whilst farther to the west Odo 'au Capel' and Robert Bertram, both of whom held for a time the title of *vicomte* of the Cotentin, respectively established the monasteries of Lessay and Beaumont-en-Auge.[7] Finally (to cite no more examples), the family of Montgomery was responsible during these years for no less

[1] Ord. Vit., vol. II, p. 12.

[2] The *De Immuatatione Ordinis Monachorum* is printed in the edition of the works of Robert of Torigny by L. Delisle (vol. II, pp. 184–207). The tract is, on the whole, more accurate than the individual notices supplied by the author in his other writings.

[3] Robert of Torigny (*op. cit.*, vol. II, pp. 197, 199); *Gall. Christ.*, vol. XI; *Instrumenta*, cols. 199–203; Douglas, in *French Studies*, vol. XIV (1960), pp. 110, 111.

[4] Robert of Torigny (*op. cit.*, vol. II, pp. 200, 201); *Gall. Christ.*, vol. XI; *Instrumenta*, cols. 153–157.

[5] Robert of Torigny (*op. cit.*, vol. II, pp. 202, 203); *Cart. – Fontenay le Marmion*, ed. L. Saige (Monaco, 1895), p. xviii.

[6] Robert of Torigny, *op. cit.*, vol. II, p. 198; Guéry, *Hist. – de Lire* (1917), chap. I. The foundation charter (pp. 563–567) is grievously inflated.

[7] Robert of Torigny (*op. cit.*, vol. II, pp. 201, 202); *Gall. Christ.*; *Instrumenta*, cols. 13, 224–228.

than three foundations: Saint-Martin at Sées, Saint-Martin at Troarn, and the nunnery at Almenèches.[1] It was by any standard a most vigorous movement of patronage, and it must further be noted that these men did not confine their benefactions to those houses which they themselves had founded. Roger I of Tosny made lavish gifts not only to his own foundation at Châtillon but also to Lire, whilst his son Ralph III was a benefactor of Saint-Évroul, La Croix-Saint-Leuffroi, and Jumièges.[2] Richard, count of Évreux, likewise, made gifts to Jumièges; and Saint-Wandrille could count among its benefactors William, count of Arques, and Roger of Beaumont.[3] Among those who endowed the nunnery of Saint-Amand in Rouen was Baldwin, son of Gilbert of Brionne, and William fitz Osbern, in addition to founding Lire and Cormeilles, made substantial gifts to Holy Trinity, Rouen.[4]

As a result of this widespread activity, Normandy before 1066 had become famous throughout north-western Europe for the number of its monasteries. But their distribution within the duchy needs also to be remarked. Of the ten ducal houses no less than eight lay within a restricted area round Rouen. In the metropolitan city itself there were three: Saint-Ouen, Holy Trinity, and Saint-Amand. A little farther down the Seine were Jumièges and Saint-Wandrille, whilst near its mouth was Montivilliers, and some fifteen miles north-east of this was Fécamp. On the other side of the capital but not far distant from it was Bernay. Only Le Mont-Saint-Michel – a shrine of immemorable antiquity – lay isolated on its island facing the Atlantic, and it was not until about 1030 that Cerisy-la-Forêt was established in the diocese of Bayeux. In short, the ducal monasteries were concentrated very notably in the region dominated by the Christian capital of the dukes.

The aristocratic endowments were to enlarge this area since the new foundations were made on the estates of the nobles who established them. None the less, it was still central Normandy that continued to receive the bulk of the new religious houses. The majority of these were in fact in the area watered by the Seine, the Risle, the Touques, and the Dives. Le Bec was but some twenty miles from Jumièges, less from Bernay, and only about fifteen miles from the two religious houses at Préaux. A circle of some fifteen miles radius could be made to include Préaux, Cormeilles, and Grestain, all situated between the Risle and

---

[1] Robert of Torigny (*op. cit.*, vol. II, pp. 199, 200); R. N. Sauvage, *Saint-Martin-de-Troarn* (1911), pp. 3–31.
[2] *Complete Peerage*, vol. XII, pp. 756, 759.
[3] *R.A.D.N.*, nos. 92, 129; Lot, *Saint-Wandrille*, no. 41.　　　　[4] *R.A.D.N.*, nos. 118, 182.

the Touques, whilst a circle of twelve miles radius could be made to surround the monasteries of Châtillon, Saint-Taurin, and Lire which lay between the Risle and the Seine. Lire, moreover, was but about twenty miles from Saint-Évroul, and Saint-Évroul less than that distance from the neighbouring houses of Almenèches and Saint-Martin of Sées. On the Dives, also were Troarn and, some twelve miles distant from it, the abbey of Saint-Pierre. The multiplication of monastic foundations at this period in central Normandy is indeed most notable.

Outside this area, however, the foundations were less numerous. Between 1059 and 1066 there was, it is true, a definite movement of colonization from Fécamp which included not only a migration to Bonneville-sur-Touques, where in due course the priory of Saint Martin-du-Bosc was founded, but also a mission of monks farther to the west which resulted eventually in the establishment of the priory of Saint-Gabriel by the lords of Creully.[1] In the diocese of Bayeux there was also Fontenay, not far from Cerisy-la-Forêt, whilst Saint-Vigor arose outside the walls of the cathedral city. Again, at Le Tréport the counts of Eu erected their own monastic bastion of Normandy towards the east, and when Lessay arose to look upon the Atlantic from the west of the Cotentin, it was a symbol of an extension of the movement, this time into the most distant part of a backward diocese. Despite all these foundations, it none the less remains true that before 1066 the monasteries of Normandy were still concentrated in the central area of the duchy.

Even so, the scope of the aristocratic endowment of Norman monasticism between 1035 and 1066 remains so astonishing that it is necessary to consider the motives which inspired it. It would of course be rash to consider these transactions simply as benefactions, or the endowments themselves as simply gifts. In the eleventh century was beginning the movement which was in due course to make the monasteries of western Europe depots of credit for secular lords, and certainly the greater Norman monasteries, such as Fécamp under Abbot John, played their full part, during the latter half of that century, in the development of a money economy in the duchy.[2] Even before 1066 many of the new Norman nobility were beginning to use the monasteries of the duchy as agents whereby they could make available some of their recently

---

[1] Chevreux et Vernier, *Archives de Normandie*, plate V; L. Musset, 'Actes Inédites' (*Bull. Soc. Antiq. Norm.* (1954), pp. 8–10).

[2] Cf. R. Génestal, 'Du Rôle des monastères comme établissements de crédit' (1901).

acquired landed wealth as expendable cash, and the endowment of a monastery with estates in return for an annual payment to be made to the 'donor' was one of the means by which this could be effected. Nor should it be forgotten that the establishment of a monastery might provide a means for increasing the wealth of a great estate, and it is not without significance that many of the Norman foundations were situated in proximity to land ready for new colonization or exploitation.[1]

Yet whilst the part played by the Norman aristocracy in promoting the monastic life of the duchy is certainly in some measure thus to be explained, it can hardly be attributed solely to economic causes. More complex motives are also to be discerned. In an age when prestige counted for much, something may have been due to rivalry in this matter between the greater families as was apparently the case at Saint-Évroul between the houses of Montgomery and Grandmesnil.[2] Reputations thus questionably coveted could also be disreputably enhanced. It is certain, for instance, that in many cases the new foundations were enriched by lands which had been illegitimately taken from the older monasteries of Normandy. Thus both Troarn and Almenèches received from the house of Montgomery estates which had formerly belonged to Fécamp,[3] and Ralph Tesson endowed his own abbey of Fontenay with some lands which had previously been given by the Duchess Judith to Bernay.[4] All this is true. But the eleventh-century mind is not to be interpreted by indiscriminate cynicism any more than it is to be judged in terms of credulous sentimentality; and it is perhaps permissible in this connexion to recall how many of these ruthless men retired to end their lives in the abbeys which they had enriched.[5]

There was at any rate one monastery founded at this time in Normandy whose establishment might reasonably be cited as illustrating the influence of private spirituality on secular history.[6] About 1035

[1] J. Sion, *Paysans de Normandie* (1909), p. 131.
[2] Ord. Vit., vol. II, pp. 20–60.   [3] *R.A.D.N.*, no. 34.
[4] Gifts by Ralph I and Ralph II of Tesson to Fontenay include estates in the Cinglais at Thury, Essay, and Fresnay-le-Vieux which figure in the *dotalicium* of Judith (*R.A.D.N.*, no. 11), but there is no proof that these went with Judith's other lands to Bernay. On these estates, see also Vaultier in Soc. Antiq. Norm., *Mémoires*, vol. x (1837).
[5] Thus Goscelin, *vicomte* of Rouen, became a monk of Holy Trinity, and his wife entered Saint-Amand. The Countess Lesceline of Eu entered religion, while both Humphrey of Vieilles and his son Roger of Beaumont passed their last days at Saint-Peter, Préaux (*Gall. Christ.*, vol. XI, cols. 728, 729; Ord. Vit., vol. II, p. 163; vol. III, pp. 33, 426). Many other examples could be given but these will suffice to point the conclusion.
[6] Of the voluminous literature on the origins of Le Bec, there may be cited: A. Porée, *L'abbaye du Bec* (1901); J. A. Robinson, *Gilbert Crispin* (1911); M. D. Knowles, *Monastic Order* (1940), pp. 88–91.

a certain knight of Count Gilbert of Brionne, named Herluin, being moved by an impulse towards the religious life, sought to satisfy his desire first as a lay-brother, and then as a monk, in one of the existing monasteries of the province. This was without success, and so, with two followers, he retired to one of his estates at Bonneville near the Risle, where he was joined by a few more men of like mind, and in 1039 the little company moved to Le Bec-Hellouin, where they began a community life of great simplicity and where their church was consecrated by Archbishop Mauger on 23 February 1041.[1] There was, as will be seen, no desire to inaugurate a monastic movement, or to acquire wealth, prestige, or external influence. Yet such was the origin of what was soon to be for a period the most famous monastery of western Europe, sending its members to preside over bishoprics and abbeys, and imparting its culture of mind and spirit to a large area of western Christendom.

The rapid rise of Le Bec to fame may be dated from the entry into this little community of one whose career was to be part of Anglo-Norman history. When Lanfranc entered Le Bec, about 1042, he was already some thirty-five years of age and had won fame as a teacher in North Italy and at Avranches. For three years he obtained on the banks of the Risle the obscurity for which he craved, but his genius was not to be suppressed, and in due course he became prior under Herluin and resumed his teaching. Pupils thus began to come to Le Bec from all parts, and the fame of Le Bec grew. It was in fact already celebrated as a house of studies when about 1060 another man, even more remarkable, entered its walls. This was Anselm, the future archbishop of Canterbury. The consummation was thus rapidly achieved. The prayers of Herluin, the genius of Lanfranc, the sanctity of Anselm, together with the outstanding religious life of their companions, produced at length an influence that was worthy of their endeavour. Le Bec, 'in a little over a quarter of a century from being an wholly obscure venture which was in a sense a reaction from the monasticism around it, came to rival and surpass its neighbours in their most typical activities, and to be the model and the mistress of Norman monasticism'.[2]

A monastery which between 1058 and 1063 had within its walls 'two of the most powerful intelligences and more than two of the most saintly men of a great formative epoch'[3] inevitably stands apart in respect of its individual pre-eminence. It would, however, be wrong to dissociate its achievement too sharply from the general monastic growth of the

---

[1] Porée, *op. cit.*, vol. I, p. 43.   [2] Knowles, *op. cit.*, p. 92.   [3] *Ibid.*, p. 89.

Norman province at this time. During these years not only did the Norman monasteries multiply, but they were established in close relation to the great reforming movement which was beginning to sweep over north-western Europe, and they were linked together by their progressive acceptance of the Cluniac discipline. William of Dijon had introduced the reforms at Fécamp and Bernay, whilst his disciples performed the same task at Jumièges, Le Mont-Saint-Michel, and Saint-Ouen; and from these houses the new discipline was rapidly to spread by stages throughout the new foundations.[1] Thus Fécamp gave the first abbots to the Tosny foundation at Conches, and the Montgomery house at Troarn. Le Mont-Saint-Michel supplied an abbot and monks to the monastery of Saint-Vigor at Bayeux. In like manner, Jumièges gave the first abbot to the Grandmesnil foundations at Saint-Évroul, and this latter monastery supplied several of the early abbots of William fitz Osbern's foundation at Lire. But the houses established by the Norman nobility at this time probably owed most in this respect to Saint-Ouen. The first five abbots of Holy Trinity, Rouen, came from this abbey, and Holy Trinity passed on the succession by supplying the first abbots not only of the count of Eu's foundations at Le Tréport and Saint-Pierre-sur-Dives, but also of William fitz Osbern's monastery at Cormeilles. Cerisy-la-Forêt, likewise, took its first superior from Saint-Ouen. And from Saint-Ouen too came the first abbots of the reformed house of La Croix-Saint-Leuffroi, of Roger of Mortemer's abbey of Saint-Victor-en-Caux, and of Robert Bertram's foundation at Beaumont-en-Auge.

Most of the monasteries established in Normandy before 1066 have been mentioned in this summary list, and among the omissions are some which are themselves very significant. Le Bec, as has been seen, was the result of an indigenous movement, which, whilst representing a highly distinguished form of monastic life, was in many ways unique. Nevertheless, despite its individuality, it came to conform in many respects to the prevailing pattern and handed on its own discipline directly to the abbey of Lessay, and later to the ducal foundation of Saint-Stephen's, Caen.[2] Again, at Saint-Wandrille there probably survived traditions from the earlier movement in Flanders, and these may have been in some sense handed on to the Beaumont foundation at Préaux, to Herluin's house at Grestain, and perhaps also to Ralph Tesson's house

---

[1] Robert of Torigny, *op. cit.*, vol. II, pp. 184–206.
[2] *Ibid.*, vol. II, p. 202. The first four abbots of Lessay came from Le Bec, and the fifth from Saint-Stephen's, Caen, where Lanfranc was abbot.

at Fontenay.[1] But even here the exception is in part illusory, for there seems no doubt that Saint-Wandrille was itself reformed from Fécamp about 1063.[2] In general, therefore (with the exception of Le Bec), the Norman monasteries before the Norman conquest can be regarded as a closely confederated group with observance in the main deriving from Cluny. Founded either by the ducal dynasty, or by the rival members of a highly competitive aristocracy, they yet, through their connexions with one another, came to serve as a cohesive force within Normandy. They thus contributed not only to the ecclesiastical character but also to the political unity of the duchy ruled by Duke William.

So outstanding was the monastic development of Normandy during the reign of Duke William that it is easy to forget that this, though the chief, was not the sole factor in promoting the ecclesiastical revival which was to condition the impact of Normandy on Europe in his time. It is proper to contrast the fine spirituality exhibited, for example, by Richard of Saint-Vannes, or in the monastery of Le Bec, with the mundane interests of the contemporary secular church, and it is very true that the reform of the Norman church was primarily monastic rather than episcopal in its essence. Yet the Norman bishops between 1035 and 1066 formed a group of prelates which was in many ways remarkable.[3] They were, it is true, out of touch with the reforming ideals which were radiating from Cluny and its offshoots, and their conception of the episcopal office had little in common with that envisaged by later reformers. They therefore attracted censure which in many cases their private lives did much to justify. None the less they were never negligible, and much of what they wrought endured.

If, however, the ecclesiastical development of Normandy between 1035 and 1066 owed something to the bishops who then held office within the province of Rouen, the contrast between these men and those responsible for the monastic reforms none the less remains striking. Though precision as to dating is hard to obtain, the episcopal succession in Normandy between 1035 and 1066 is well established, and the bare recital of the names which it involves reveals the cardinal fact that the Norman episcopacy during the reign of Duke William is overwhelmingly representative of the new secular aristocracy which was then being

---

[1] Robert of Torigny, *op. cit.*, pp. 199, 202. [2] Will. Poit., p. 134.
[3] Douglas, 'The Norman Episcopate before the Norman Conquest' (*Cambridge Historical Journal*, vol. XIII (1957), pp. 101–116).

established in the duchy, and which was itself closely connected with the ducal dynasty. The see of Rouen before 1055 was held by two sons of Norman dukes, namely Robert and Mauger. The bishopric of Bayeux was occupied first by Hugh, son of Count Rodulf, half-brother to Duke Richard I, and then after 1049–1050 by Odo, half-brother of Duke William himself. John, who became bishop of Avranches in 1060, and subsequently archbishop of Rouen, was another of Count Rodulf's sons, and Hugh who was made bishop of Lisieux in 1049–1050 was the son of William, count of Eu, and grandson of Duke Richard I. Geoffrey, who became bishop of Coutances in 1049, was a Mowbray, and Yves, bishop of Sées throughout this period, was head of the great family of Bellême. Again, William, son of Gérard Flaitel, who was made bishop of Évreux some time after 1040, was the relative and probably the first cousin of Radbod, a former bishop of Sées; and one of Radbod's sons was William who became archbishop of Rouen in 1079. Such facts deserve close consideration. They indicate unmistakably that the Norman episcopate, during the reign of Duke William, was dominated by a small close-knit aristocratic group whose principal filiations could be displayed within the scope of two very restricted and connected pedigree sketches.

Such men were often hardly to be distinguished as to character and policy from their lay kinsfolk, and many of them had children by unions which were recognized, if not regular.[1] Owing their appointment to their dynastic connexions they were naturally concerned to further the fortunes of the families to which they belonged, and as members of the new aristocracy in Normandy they were deeply committed to the maintenance of that nobility in power. As a result the establishment of great lords in ecclesiastical office led naturally to such a situation as was created when Archbishop Robert of Rouen became also count of Évreux, or when Yves added the bishopric of Sées to his secular inheritance of Bellême. It was by a logical extension of these ideas that Odo, bishop of Bayeux, was later to become earl of Kent, and both he and Geoffrey, bishop of Coutances, acquired, as individuals rather than as bishops, lands in England which in their extent and wealth could be compared with the very greatest of the temporal baronies constituted by the Norman conquest. Such conditions, unedifying in themselves, were particularly shocking to commentators writing in the time of

---

[1] Richard, son of Archbishop Robert, was count of Évreux, and a son of Odo of Bayeux was a familiar figure at the court of King Henry I of England.

St Anselm who were convinced that the root of evil in the church was the mingling of sacred and secular things, and it is little wonder that, especially by comparison with the monastic reformers, the Norman bishops before the Norman conquest should have been branded with an evil reputation by posterity.

Nevertheless, it would perhaps be rash to indulge here in too sweeping a condemnation. There is doubtless little to be said in favour of Archbishop Robert as a prelate, but he was certainly a stabilizing force in the duchy, and Mauger, who was universally criticized, at least convoked, early in his pontificate, a synod at Rouen which vigorously denounced simony before the papacy had launched with Leo IX its great reforming campaign. Geoffrey of Coutances in his turn might be dismissed too readily as an able secular administrator who enriched himself out of the spoils of the Conquest, for his administration of his diocese was notable; he left a great cathedral for his memorial, and he is said to have combined his zeal for his bishopric with considerable personal austerity.[1] Even of Odo of Bayeux an adverse judgment might well admit modification. His overwhelming ambitions were a source of strife, his ruthless oppressions made him hated, and his private life was a source of scandal. Nevertheless, the see of Bayeux enjoyed great benefits from his rule, and his patronage was both lavish and well directed. Certainly a prelate whose political career affected the fortunes of both Normandy and England so signally cannot be dismissed as negligible, and perhaps the twelfth-century monk was just as well as charitable when he concluded that in this extraordinary man virtues and vices were strangely mingled.[2] Finally, with Hugh of Lisieux and John of Avranches we come upon prelates who were personally distinguished and of high repute. There is little doubt that the former deserved the attractive eulogy pronounced upon him by William of Poitiers, who knew him well.[3] And as for John of Avranches, his abilities were later to be fully displayed as archbishop of Rouen, and when he was still bishop of Avranches he won for himself by his writings an assured place in the history of the liturgy of the western church.

These prelates all belonged, however, to an older ecclesiastical tradition which was attacked and condemned by the reformers of the succeeding generation, and only one occupant of a Norman see before

---

[1] Le Patourel, *Eng. Hist. Rev.*, vol. LIX (1944), pp. 129 *et sqq.*
[2] Ord. Vit., vol. II, p. 222; vol. III, pp. 263, 264.
[3] Will. Poit., pp. 136–142.

the Conquest can be said to have conformed to later notions of episcopacy. This was Maurilius who in exceptional circumstances became
archbishop of Rouen in May 1055 after the deposition of Mauger.
Maurilius[1] was not a Norman, nor was he connected with the Norman
aristocracy. Born about 1000 in the neighbourhood of Rheims, he had
received his training at Liége, and later been *scholasticus* in the chapter
of Halberstadt. He then became a monk at Fécamp, whence he migrated
to live a hermit's life at Vallombrosa. From there he was called to
become abbot of the Benedictine house of Saint Mary of Florence, but
the rigour of his rule inspired a revolt among the monks, and he
returned once more to Fécamp. And it was from Fécamp that he was
brought in 1054–1055 to undertake the duties of the metropolitan archbishop of Normandy. His remarkable career had thus been passed in
the most vital centres of European intellectual and spiritual life; he had
experienced the learning of Liége, the spiritual fervour of Vallombrosa,
the Cluniac monasticism of William of Dijon. Even so, his advancement
to the archbishopric was surprising. A new and extraneous element was
thus introduced into the secular hierarchy of the province of Rouen, and
the personal influence of such a man with such experience must have
been very great.

Nevertheless, the individual contribution made by Maurilius to the
ecclesiastical development of Normandy might be exaggerated. It was
the duke who was chiefly responsible for his appointment, and throughout his pontificate the duke was to exercise an ever-increasing power
over the Norman church. In 1055 William had just surmounted the
great crisis of his Norman reign, and it was perhaps owing to him as
much as to the ageing archbishop that during the decade preceding the
Norman conquest there was a further quickening in the ecclesiastical
life of the province. The duke may even have appreciated the contrast
between the influence on the Norman episcopate and that of the
Norman monasteries, and conscious that each had much to contribute
to the welfare of his duchy, he may have sought to harmonize them by
the advancement of a distinguished monk to the archiepiscopal see.
Certainly, he was fortunate in having as archbishop during these years
a man whose saintly character inspired widespread respect. None the
less it would be unwise to distinguish what occurred in the ecclesiastical

[1] The chief authority for Maurilius is the *Acta Archiepiscoporum Rothomagensium*. Vacandard
showed that the section relating to Maurilius is a nearly contemporary text, whereas
subsequent sections were added somewhat later by a monk of Saint-Ouen (*Rev. catholique
de Normandie*, vol. III (1893), p. 117).

life of Normandy after 1055 from what had been accomplished before.[1] The monastic revival took on increased momentum, but the original impetus was still the same, and among the bishops of Normandy Maurilius was always an exceptional figure. The achievements of these bishops between 1035 and 1066 must thus be considered as a whole (with no break at 1054), and as the work under the duke of an episcopal group which, with the single exception of Maurilius, was made up of selected members of the newly established aristocracy of Normandy.

Called upon to administer a recently disorganized church in a province which long remained subject to disorder, these prelates displayed in full measure the vigour of their class, and though many of them were lamentably lacking in spirituality they affected a notable reconstruction. Many of them, notably Hugh of Lisieux, John of Avranches, Geoffrey of Coutances, and Odo of Bayeux, were praised for the benefits they conferred on their sees, and if such eulogy might of itself be considered suspect, it could be supported by more precise testimony. In 1035 the bishoprics of the province of Rouen still felt the effects of earlier disintegration, and even in 1050 they remained in need of further rehabilitation. The well-organized bishoprics characteristic of medieval Normandy may thus be contrasted sharply with those in existence in 1035, and much of the transformation was the work of the bishops who presided over the Norman church during the reign of Duke William.

Their work in this respect can be suitably assessed in the first instance by reference to the archidiaconate in Normandy,[2] for the archdeacon was an essential agent in the ordered administration of any medieval bishopric. The Norman archdeaconries of the thirteenth century, together with the rural deaneries into which they were then divided, are well known, and a long series of twelfth-century instruments testifies to the earlier prevalence of archdeaconries and to the activities of their holders. Further, this chain of testimony can be stretched into the eleventh century itself. The archidiaconate as an office was fully recognized in the provincial council summoned by Mauger about 1040, and evidence exists relative to its institution at Rouen, at Coutances, and at Lisieux. More precisely the four archdeacons who witnessed a notable charter of Odo, bishop of Bayeux,[3] can reasonably be held to represent

---

[1] As will be seen later, there was a continuity of conciliar practice between Mauger and Maurilius.

[2] For what follows, see Douglas, *op. cit.*, pp. 108–110. [3] *Cart. Bayeux*, no. XXII.

the four archdeaconries which were later attached to that church, whilst the five territorial archdeaconries later established in the diocese of Sées must likewise have been represented in the five named archdeacons who between 1040 and 1065 ratified a gift by Bishop Yves to the abbey of Saint-Vincent du Mans. [1] By contrast, apart from the two archdeacons, presumably of Rouen, who attested a charter of Archbishop Robert for Chartres in 1024,[2] it might be hard to find a reference to a particular archdeacon in Normandy before the time of Duke William. The office would seem to have been re-established in the duchy by the bishops who presided over the Norman sees in his time.

The archdeacon was, however, only one of the dignitaries normally attached to a cathedral church, for a secular cathedral in the Middle Ages was distinguished by the character and composition of its chapter. The Norman cathedral chapters were fully established in the thirteenth century, and in many respects they can be traced back through the twelfth and even into the latter part of the eleventh century.[3] For Sées and Avranches early evidence is lacking, but there is definite testimony that the very peculiar chapter of Coutances took its origin with Bishop Geoffrey. The first reference to the decanal office at Évreux comes from the last quarter of the eleventh century, and there seems little doubt that the bulk of the chapter of Lisieux was set up in the time of Bishop Hugh. At Bayeux the chapter is cited in a charter of Bishop Odo,[4] and most of the dignitaries who later composed it are mentioned by name in the instrument. Finally, though the titles of the officials concerned were in due course to be somewhat varied, there is no doubt that the chapter of the metropolitan cathedral of Rouen was in all essentials fully reconstituted during the Norman reign of Duke William.[5] Doubtless, here as elsewhere in Normandy, the conquest of England stimulated the process, for a chapter needed money for its upkeep, and some of these prelates, notably Geoffrey of Coutances and Odo of Bayeux, devoted to this purpose revenues that they had derived from England. But the essential work had been done during the preceding decades, and there seems no doubt that the highly individual chapters of the Norman cathedrals began to take shape under the bishops who were appointed to the Norman sees between 1035 and 1066.

Such an achievement was of importance to the growth of the Norman

[1] *Cart. S. Vincent du Mans*, no. 545.   [2] *Cart. S. Père Chartres*, p. 116.
[3] For details, see Douglas, *op. cit.*, pp. 110–114.
[4] *Cart. Bayeux*, no. XXII.   [5] Douglas, *op. cit.*, p. 109.

church, and whilst the work of these bishops needed the correction which the monastic reformers could supply, the two activities should not be considered as if they were in opposition the one to the other. It is true that shortly before the advent of Duke William certain of the Norman monasteries had succeeded in asserting, 'according to the privileges of Cluny', an exemption from episcopal jurisdiction: the right, in theory, to elect their own abbots, and sometimes the distinct privilege of collecting the episcopal dues from a specified number of 'exempt' churches.[1] But it is doubtful how far such privileges were extended or enforced between 1035 and 1066, and when in 1061 an agreement was made after controversy between John, bishop of Avranches and the abbey of Le Mont-Saint-Michel, the compromise achieved was indicative of the superior judicial authority of the bishop.[2] From the opposite point of view the bishops on their part can be seen as giving substantial support to the monastic movement. Maurilius, himself a monk, took the lead in this matter by standing as the friend of Saint-Ouen, Jumièges, Le Tréport, and Saint-Ymer;[3] but he did not stand alone, and many of his episcopal colleagues added their own benefactions to those of their kinsfolk. William, bishop of Évreux, was a benefactor of the house of Saint-Taurin, whilst Hugh, bishop of Lisieux, joined his mother, the Countess Lesceline of Eu, in her grants to Holy Trinity, Rouen.[4] In like manner Geoffrey, bishop of Coutances, seems to have been concerned to sponsor a revival of monastic life in a distracted diocese, and the gifts of Odo, bishop of Bayeux, were not confined to his cathedral.[5]

The resuscitation of ecclesiastical life in the province of Rouen was in fact due to many agencies and was manifested in many ways. It was, for instance, reflected in an architectural revival which has attracted the admiring attention of critics.[6] The earliest surviving eleventh-century church in Normandy is probably that of Bernay, and it was marked by many novel features. Moreover, the other great monastic churches which arose during these years conformed generally to the same plan which is found not only at Bernay but also at Le Mont-Saint-Michel, Holy Trinity, Rouen, and Saint-Taurin at Évreux; and again at Saint-

---

[1] J.-F. Lemarignier, *Privilèges d'Exemption*, esp. pp. 44–84.
[2] *Ibid.*, p. 152; E. A. Pigéon, *Diocèse d'Avranches*, pp. 658–660.
[3] *R.A.D.N.*, no. 213; Le Prévost, *Eure*, vol. I, p. 152; vol. II, p. 32; *Cart. S. Michel du Tréport* (ed. Laffleur de Kermingant), pp. i–xxxii; *Cart. S. Ymer en Auge* (ed. Bréard), no. I.
[4] *Gall. Christ.*, vol. XI; *Instrumenta*, col. 126; *Cart. S. Trin. Roth.*, no. LXIX.
[5] *Gall. Christ.*, vol. XI, cols. 354, 870.
[6] See A. W. Clapham, *English Romanesque Architecture after the Conquest* (1934), chap. I – on which what here follows is based.

Ouen, Montivilliers, Lire, Lessay, and Jumièges. Here, then, was a concerted movement which promoted a distinct architectural style, and which though not peculiar to Normandy has been held to have produced in the duchy what was structurally 'the most logical of the various schools of Romanesque'.[1] Yet while 'it was the monastic revival which gave the necessary impetus to the architectural revival in Normandy'[2] at this time, the bishops of the province also made their own contribution to it. Recent excavations in the crypt of Rouen cathedral have thrown fresh light on the great church built by Maurilius,[3] and traces can still be seen at Bayeux of the cathedral begun by Bishop Hugh, and completed with characteristic magnificence by Bishop Odo.[4] A new cathedral is known to have been begun at Lisieux before 1049, and it was finished by Bishop Hugh and dedicated by him on 8 July 1060.[5] Finally, at Coutances, Geoffrey left his own memorial in a great church whose structure still survives in parts of the present cathedral.[6]

Nor was it only in architecture that the ecclesiastical renaissance in Normandy at this time found expression. It was the same with learning and literature. The Cluniac discipline with its stress on formal worship, and with its multiplication of the hours of liturgical observance, was, as is well known, somewhat indifferent to the development of monastic scholarship and teaching. Its application to Normandy, however, was to entail different results. William of Dijon was himself a man of wide cultural interests who held that part of the monastic function was to study and to teach. As a consequence, intellectual and educational interests were to become strong at Fécamp from an early date. The schools at Fécamp established at this time have in particular attracted much attention.[7] It has been held, for instance, that they were open not only to ecclesiastics but to lay-folk, and it would seem that free lodging was provided for some of the students. Perhaps there has here been some exaggeration, and certainly the Fécamp schools were not unique in Normandy for they had their counterparts, as it would seem,

---

[1] *Ibid.*, p. 8.　　　　　　　　　　[2] *Ibid.*, p. 12.

[3] G. Lanfry, *La Cathédrale dans la Cité romane et en Normandie ducale* (1957), pp. 20–46. Among earlier works on Rouen cathedral may be mentioned those of E. H. Langlois, who was not only a competent antiquarian but an exquisite draftsman (see P. Chirol, *Étude sur E-H Langlois* (1922)). A good account of the earlier erudition is given in A. Alinne and A. Loisel, *La Cathédrale de Rouen avant l'incendie de 1100* (1904).

[4] *Gall. Christ.*, vol. XI, col. 353; *Will. Poit.*, p. 240.

[5] *Will. Poit.*, p. 138; *Ord. Vit.*, vol. II, p. 308.

[6] *Gall. Christ.*, vol. XI, col. 219; E. A. Freeman, *Sketches of Travel*, pp. 80–83.

[7] Watkin Williams, *op. cit.*, p. 529; Knowles, *op. cit.*, p. 490.

at Saint-Ouen and Holy Trinity, at Le Mont-Saint-Michel, and perhaps at Jumièges and Saint-Évroul.[1] Their main function seems to have been to train monks for the cloister, but the educational activity prosecuted in Normandy before the Norman conquest was undoubtedly notable.

The scholarly interests of Fécamp, as established in the time of William of Dijon, and the influence it exercised on those other Norman houses to which it sent superiors reached its climax in the work of a writer of the first importance. John (or Johanellinus), abbot of Fécamp from 1031 to 1079, was one of the makers of Norman monasticism.[2] A Lombard, like Lanfranc he came to Normandy early in the eleventh century, and throughout his long life he was prominent in the affairs of the duchy. But it was in the sphere of learning, and more particularly of devotional literature, that his finest work was done.[3] His surviving letters are of interest, and he was apparently versed in the medical knowledge of the day. It was, however, through other productions that he was to establish himself as a 'spiritual guide and writer unique among his contemporaries'. So notable and so influential were his devotional treatises that paradoxically their very excellence was for long to contribute to their author's anonymity. One of his treatises was, for instance, attributed to St Augustine, and when another was published in 1539 it was assigned to John Cassian. None the less his work has endured. The moving and beautiful prayers in preparation for Mass which have found their place in the *Missale Romanum*[4] (where they are attributed to St Ambrose) were, in fact, written by this eleventh-century abbot of Fécamp whose pervasive inspiration thus continues today.

In surveying the intellectual revival associated with the ecclesiastical development of Normandy before the Norman conquest, it is inevitable that attention should be turned chiefly towards Le Bec. The schools of Le Bec were not in their origin essentially different from those established at Fécamp and elsewhere, but they advanced to a unique distinction under the direction of Lanfranc, who began to teach there in 1045 or 1046, and who raised the new abbey on the banks of the Risle to the status of a centre of European education. The political achievements of Lanfranc relate chiefly to the period after 1066, but his

[1] See Delisle in his great introduction to the edition of Ord. Vit.
[2] *Gall. Christ.*, vol. XI, cols. 206, 207.
[3] A. Wilmart, *Auteurs spirituels et textes devots du Moyen Age latin* (1932), pp. 101–125.
[4] In the Latin-English Missal published by Burns and Oates in 1949 these will be found on pp. 664–672. See also: J. Leclerc and J. P. Bonnes, *Un maître de la vie spirituelle* (1946).

greatest work in scholarship and teaching was done when he was a monk at Le Bec, for it was then that he made his widely read Biblical and patristic commentaries, and compiled his treatise against Berengar, the importance of which in the development of medieval theology has recently been emphasized.[1] His prestige as a teacher was moreover immense, and he numbered among his pupils an astonishingly large number of men who were subsequently to attain to high positions. Among them, for instance, might be mentioned William 'Bonne-Ame', later archbishop of Rouen, three abbots of Rochester, Gilbert Crispin, abbot of Westminster, and a large group of abbots in England and France.[2] Such a list (which is by no means exhaustive) may occasion surprise. It is certainly sufficient to testify to the intellectual influence of Le Bec before the Norman conquest, even if it be not added that among Lanfranc's pupils was Anselm himself, who became a monk at Le Bec in 1060, and who was soon to win for himself a permanent place as a doctor of the Church.

Le Bec at its zenith stands distinct. But its brilliance must, none the less, be taken into account in any assessment of the ecclesiastical revival in the Norman land wherein it grew. Nor should its brilliance be allowed to obscure the work which at the same time was being done in other Norman monasteries. The picture of Saint-Évroul before the Norman conquest painted in the twelfth century by Ordericus Vitalis is doubtless at times distorted by enthusiasm; but it is none the less substantially authentic, and the obvious sympathy between this writer and his abbey makes it legitimate to consider his own great book, perhaps the most brilliant historical work produced in Normandy or England in his time, as at once a description and a reflection of the intellectual interests prevailing in the more favoured monasteries of Normandy in the middle of the eleventh century. Nor did Saint-Évroul stand alone. Its library, for example, if respectable, was not outstanding, and it had its counterparts in other monasteries such as Fécamp, Lire, and doubtless other places.[3] The list of scholar monks who achieved at least a temporary fame in Normandy before the Conquest is not negligible, and there seems to have been a definite policy to place these in positions of responsibility. Thus (to select but a few names) Thierry was known as a scholar at Jumièges before he became the first

[1] R. W. Southern, in *Essays – F. M. Powicke* (1948), pp. 28–48.
[2] Porée, *L'abbaye du Bec*, vol. I, pp. 103, 104.
[3] Ord. Vit., introduction by Léopold Delisle. Cf. J. P. Martin, *La bibliothèque d'Avranches; les manuscrits du Mont St Michel* (1924).

abbot of Saint-Évroul, and Isembard, the first abbot of Holy Trinity, Rouen, had been praised for his earlier eminence in liberal studies when at Saint-Ouen.[1] Again, Durand, first abbot of Troarn, who at Saint-Ouen had been Isembard's pupil, was justly described as 'learned'; and Ainard, the first abbot of Saint-Pierre-sur-Dives, was known as a teacher of music who also composed widely read verses in honour of Saint Catherine.[2] Gerbert, abbot of Saint-Wandrille, could actually be compared to Lanfranc as a scholar,[3] and though this was a fantastic overestimate, modern students of history have had abundant reason to be grateful for the sober and interesting chronicle written by William of Jumièges while a monk at that house.

It was not to be expected that the Norman bishops of this time, immersed as they were in practical affairs, should personally participate in this literary activity. But they cannot be dissociated from it, and two of them made an individual contribution thereto. Maurilius of Rouen was with justice reputed for his erudition, and as for John of Avranches, his *De Officiis Ecclesiasticis* has been widely recognized by modern commentators for its importance in the development of the liturgy of the western church.[4] Maurilius and John, of course, stood apart, in this matter, from their episcopal colleagues, but their fellow bishops in Normandy were by no means indifferent to the development of letters, and many of them discharged with high distinction the duties of patronage.[5] Most notable in this respect were, for instance, Geoffrey, bishop of Coutances, and Odo, bishop of Bayeux. Geoffrey's princely munificence became indeed something of a legend in medieval Normandy, and though many of his benefactions were made after 1066 out of the spoils of conquest, it is specifically stated that most of them took place at an earlier date.[6] Nor can there be any doubt that many of these were directed towards fostering scholarship and the arts, for he is stated to have provided his church with numerous service books, many of which

---

[1] Ord. Vit., vol. II, pp. 42, 95; *Hist. Litt. de la France*, vol. VII (1746), p. 70.

[2] Ord. Vit., vol. II, pp. 29, 247, 292, 411.   [3] *Ibid.*, vol. III, p. 240.

[4] R. Delamare, Le '*De Officiis ecclesiasticis*' de *Jean d'Avranches* (1923); Southern, *St. Anselm*, pp. 41, 42.

[5] They brought books from overseas. Archbishop Robert, for example, elicited from his sister Emma in England the gift of a magnificent liturgical work which passed eventually to the archbishop's son William and thence to William's wife, Hawise (Ord. Vit., vol. II, p. 41). This is distinct from the so-called 'Missal of Robert of Jumièges' (Bradshaw Soc., vol. XI, 1896), which is recorded in a contemporary charter (*Chartes de Jumièges*, no. XXIII), and was perhaps given to Jumièges by Robert when bishop of London. See further on this: J. B. L. Tolhurst, in *Archaeologia*, vol. LXXXIII (1933), pp. 29–41.

[6] *Gall. Christ.*, vol. XI; *Instrumenta*, col. 220; Le Patourel, *op. cit.*

were decorated by the best manuscript workers of the time; and among the earlier gifts to Coutances were beautiful altar vessels of gold and silver, and richly wrought vestments. Due allowance must, of course, be made for exaggeration, but there can be little question that during the fifteen years which elapsed between 1049 and 1066 Geoffrey of Coutances laboured constructively to transform an enfeebled Church in a demoralized diocese into a cathedral worthy of an imperial duchy.[1]

The patronage of Odo, bishop of Bayeux, was even more notable, and it is attested with greater particularity. His munificent encouragement of craftsmanship may be illustrated in his enrichment of the fabric and ornaments of his cathedral, and there is little doubt that he was largely responsible for the development of the cathedral school at Bayeux.[2] Moreover, at a later date, the Bayeux Tapestry itself most probably took its origin from his initiative,[3] and it has even been suggested, though with less probability, that his patronage may have contributed to the production of the *Chanson de Roland* in the earliest complete form now known to us.[4] Be that as it may, Odo of Bayeux was clearly in touch with neighbouring prelates of intellectual eminence such as Marbod of Rennes, and perhaps Hildebert of Tours, and it was in connexion with his patronage of young scholars that his activities were most notable. It was, for instance, his practice to send promising young clerics from his diocese at his own expense to study in the centres of European scholarship, and more particularly at Liége;[5] and many of the men he selected as fitting recipients of his support were afterwards to win for themselves high rank in the Anglo-Norman church. Thus, among the scholars who were sustained by Odo at Liége was Thurstan, later to be an unfortunate abbot of Glastonbury, and William of Rots, subsequently dean at Bayeux and abbot of Fécamp.[6] The most remarkable results of this enlightened patronage could, however, be discerned in connexion with two young clerics named Thomas and Samson, sons of a certain Osbert and Muriel of whom little further is known.[7] Both of these youths were sent to Liége by their bishop, and their subsequent

[1] Cf. Toustain de Billy, *Hist. de Coutances* (ed. 1874), vol. I, p. 123.
[2] *Gall. Christ.*, vol. XI, cols. 353, 354.
[3] E. Maclagan, *The Bayeux Tapestry* (1943), p. 27.
[4] P. Andrieu-Guitrancourt, *L'Empire normand et sa civilization* (1952), pp. 386–391: 'Le Turpin de la légende et Odon de Bayeux sont un même personnage.' But see Douglas, in *French Studies*, vol. XIV (1960), p. 103.
[5] Ord. Vit., vol. III, p. 265.
[6] Ord. Vit., vol. II, pp. 129, 244; vol. IV, pp. 269, 272.
[7] C. T. Clay, *Yorks. Arch. Journal*, vol. XXXI (1945), pp. 1, 2.

careers were spectacular. Thomas became in due course treasurer of Bayeux, and then, from 1070 to 1100, archbishop of York, whilst Samson, who was likewise for a time treasurer at Bayeux, was bishop of Worcester from 1096 to 1115.[1] Whatever judgment may be passed on the political activities of Odo, bishop of Bayeux, he must certainly be reckoned as one of the great patrons of the age.

There is no mistaking the vigour of the intellectual life which was beginning to develop in the Norman church, and particularly in the Norman monasteries during the period immediately preceding the Norman conquest of England. Even if the outstanding achievement of Le Bec were to be regarded as exceptional, the range of these activities would remain impressive. It extended from the writing of history to theological controversy, from medicine to devotional literature, from verse-making to the cultivation of music in which the Norman monasteries of the eleventh century seem to have excelled.[2] It is true, of course, that many of the most distinguished exponents of the monastic life in Normandy at this time were drawn from elsewhere – particularly from North Italy and the Rhineland.[3] But the mere fact that such men chose the Viking province for their home and were welcomed therein is itself a matter of large significance. It must be taken into account alongside the native endeavour. It was the counterpart of the patronage of scholarship by Norman bishops and the lavish endowment of Norman monasteries by the Norman aristocracy. Strong in the aspirations of a brightening renaissance not peculiar to itself, the Norman church of this age was already beginning to impart by its very vigour something of its own to the intellectual revival which was to be characteristic of twelfth-century Europe.

The vitality of the Norman church at this time, and its unity, could not be better illustrated than in the councils which were held in the province of Rouen during these decades. Thus while no texts have survived to record any meeting of an ecclesiastical council in Normandy during the tenth century, there can be no question that there was considerable conciliar activity in the duchy during the Norman reign of Duke William. The bishops of that period were wont to summon diocesan synods with some regularity, and numerous councils of the

---

[1] Two of Samson's sons, Thomas and Richard, became respectively archbishop of York (1109–1119) and bishop of Bayeux (1108–1113).

[2] Ord. Vit., vol. II, pp. 94–96, 247.

[3] e.g. John of Fécamp and Lanfranc. From the Rhineland came, for instance, Isembard of Saint-Ouen, Ainard of Saint-Pierre-sur-Dives, and Archbishop Maurilius.

whole province were also held.[1] It is true that a record of their acts has only been preserved in a few cases, and that it is often difficult to assign precise dates for their meetings. But the evidence here is none the less remarkable. Thus, early in his pontificate, and certainly before 1048, Mauger convoked a provincial council in Rouen whose acts are extant, and it was at an ecclesiastical assemblage held outside Caen in October 1047 that the Truce of God was proclaimed. In 1054 or 1055 a provincial council at Lisieux ratified the deposition of Mauger, and it is probable that either in 1055 or at some date between 1055 and 1063 Maurilius held a council at Rouen.[2] More certainly on 1 October 1063, Maurilius held a provincial council at Rouen,[3] and in 1064 there met another provincial council at Lisieux whose acts have survived,[4] whilst a synod was held at Caen in July 1066 on the occasion of the dedication of the abbey of Holy Trinity.[5]

Our knowledge of these assemblies depends upon the chance survival of particular texts, but the testimony is at all events sufficient to indicate the scope of this activity and its character. The proceedings at these councils conforms to the general pattern of the reforming legislation in the western church at this time, and offers a fresh indication of the manner in which these reforms were starting to pervade the Viking duchy. The first council of Mauger, for instance, denounced simony, and in the councils that were held in the time of Maurilius, legislation was consistently passed respecting clerical celibacy, the conduct of parish clergy, and the controversial aspects of the teaching of Berengar.[6] None the less, the Norman councils of this period had their own special features. It is, for example, surely remarkable that some years before, in 1049, Leo IX introduced his reforms at the council of Rheims, a Norman council summoned by Mauger, an archbishop of no high repute, should have legislated against the traffic in ecclesiastical offices, and should have taken measures designed to provide the province of

---

[1] The *Ordo provincialis concilii celebrandi*, which was inserted into the 'Benedictional of Archbishop Robert' (Bradshaw Soc., vol. xxiv (1903), p. 154) apparently in the latter half of the eleventh century, assumes that two provincial councils are held each year, and though this practice was probably not followed before the Norman conquest, the statement is significant. Bishop John of Avranches in 1061 claimed the right to hold two diocesan synods each year (E. A. Pigéon, *Diocèse d'Avranches*, pp. 658–660).

[2] Bessin, *Concilia*, p. 47. It is possible, however, that this is the council which met in 1063.

[3] *Ibid.*, p. 49.

[4] Edited by L. Delisle from a MS. in Trinity College, Cambridge, and printed in *Journal des Savants* (1901), pp. 516–521.

[5] *R.A.D.N.*, no. 231.

[6] Bessin, *Concilia*, pp. 47, 49; *Journal des Savants* (1901), p. 517, cl. I, II, and III.

Rouen with an instructed clergy.[1] There seems here to have been a continuity of policy between Mauger and Maurilius, and the acts of those councils held in the time of the latter archbishop were related both to earlier and to later legislation.[2] The ecclesiastical policy of William the Conqueror between 1066 and 1087, which entailed such important results for England and for western Europe, was in fact to flow easily out of the ecclesiastical legislation which took place in the Norman Church during his reign as duke.

For there can be no doubt that before 1066 the duke himself took a prominent part in the conciliar activity which took place in his duchy. He was perhaps too young to be at the first council of Mauger, but he was at the council at Caen in 1047, and it would seem that he was present, along with the papal legate, at the council of Lisieux in 1054–1055, and again at the council at Rouen in 1063. The important council of Lisieux of 1064 was in its turn held 'under William the most noble duke of the Normans'.[3] In the light of this testimony, there would thus seem no reason to question the emphatic assertion of William of Poitiers that the Norman ecclesiastical councils of this period met 'at the command and with the encouragement of the duke'. William, it was said, was careful to attend their meetings and to be the 'arbiter' of their proceedings. He was, it is added, always unwilling to learn at second-hand about matters which he held to be of such importance to the welfare of his duchy.[4]

Before 1066 his concern had indeed been amply rewarded. The Norman church during his reign had so waxed in strength as to win widespread admiration of contemporaries for its vigour, its aspirations, and its intellectual life. The men, so diverse in character and yet so personally outstanding, who had risen to eminence within it were themselves sufficient to give it distinction. An ecclesiastical province of no abnormal size which at the beginning of 1066 could be represented by men of such contrasted distinction as Odo of Bayeux and Geoffrey of Coutances, Maurilius of Rouen, John of Avranches, and Hugh of Lisieux, Lanfranc of Saint-Stephen's, John of Fécamp, Herluin of Le Bec, and the young Anselm was assuredly not to be ignored. It is not surprising, therefore, that its subsequent influence was to be pervasive. The Norman ecclesiastical revival had in short been made in its turn to subserve the developing strength of Normandy under the rule of Duke William.

[1] Bessin, *Concilia*, p. 41, canons VI and VIII. [2] Below, pp. 331–335.
[3] *Journal des Savants* (1901), p. 517. [4] Will. Poit., p. 124.

Chapter 6

THE RULE OF DUKE WILLIAM

William's rule over Normandy during the decades preceding the Norman conquest must be considered in direct relation to the aristocratic and ecclesiastical developments which we have examined. To harmonize these movements, and to control them, was here the major object of his policy; and the measure of his success in so doing is reflected in the contrast between his weakness in 1046 and his strength in 1066. In 1035 it might have seemed doubtful whether the ducal authority could survive: in 1066 it was secure, and the duke could regard himself as the firmly established ruler of one of the strongest and most united provinces of Gaul. The transformation is itself so remarkable, and its consequences were in the event to prove so far-reaching, that it is important to consider how far and in what manner the ducal administration of Normandy during these years had contributed to this result.

The greatest asset which accrued to the boy who succeeded in 1035 lay in those rights which were held by tradition to pertain to the ducal office. He might claim to be able to declare law throughout the duchy, and within limits to be competent to dispense justice; he might mint money and levy certain taxes; and as 'lord of Normandy'[1] he had at least in theory a military force at his disposal. Whether such claims could ever be made effective on behalf of the infant ruler was of course doubtful, but it was surely in recognition of them that he was brought as a child with his tutor into the ducal court to pronounce judgment, or that as a very young man he was called in 1047 to take a prominent part in the ecclesiastical council which proclaimed the Truce of God. Such ideas could on occasion be turned to practical effect, and, as has been seen, the duke's survival during the minority may have been due in large measure to them. Later they were to be exploited with ever-increasing vigour as the duke's personal authority grew, and they helped him to maintain and to enhance his special position within a social order which was itself in a state of flux.

Nowhere were they to prove more important than in connexion with

[1] *Consuetudines et Justicie* (Haskins, *Norman Institutions*, p. 281).

the rights which might thus be exercised by the duke in exploiting the economic resources of his duchy. For these were very considerable. Pre-Conquest Normandy has recently been termed by an English scholar an 'impoverished duchy',[1] but there is little warranty for such a description. There is evidence to suggest that Normandy at that time was (comparatively speaking) thickly populated and that the cultivation of its soil was extensive. The Scandinavian connexions of the province had promoted a considerable external trade, and men from Normandy, looking out over their own especial sea, had kept commercial contact with the northern world from which their rulers came. Rouen was a prosperous port, and its prosperity was reflected elsewhere in the duchy. The rise of Caen during these years has already been noted, and Bayeux was evidently also growing in importance. Indeed there is even testimony to indicate the formation in Normandy about this time of what has been termed an 'aristocracy of money'.[2] Ernald of Bayeux, chaplain successively to Richard II, Robert I, and Duke William, could be described in a contemporary text as 'powerful in possessions and houses both within and outside the city which he had purchased with his own gold and silver'.[3]

Again, the lavish ecclesiastical endowments characteristic of the period are significant in this respect, since they could not have been undertaken without considerable financial support. Cathedral chapters need money for their establishment, and the numerous monastic foundations of the time of themselves presuppose the existence of surplus wealth. Some idea of the degree to which it was in fact expendable can be gathered from the fact that within a circle of twenty-five miles in the neighbourhood of Rouen there existed in 1066 no less than five great monasteries: Saint-Ouen, Holy Trinity, Saint-Georges de Boscherville, Jumièges, and Saint-Wandrille. All of these had been founded, or had been re-established, before the Norman conquest, and all of them together with the cathedral church of Maurilius were, in the time of Duke William II, adorned with new buildings. Pre-Conquest Normandy could with greater propriety be described as a rich province rather than as a poor one.

There is good reason to believe that the ducal dynasty derived full benefit from these conditions. The largess of the Norman duke was

---

[1] Galbraith, *Making of Domesday Book*, p. 45.
[2] L. Musset, *Annales de Normandie*, vol. IX (1959), pp. 285–299.
[3] Stapleton, *Archaeologia*, vol. XXXVII (1839), pp. 26–37.

known early in the eleventh century as far as Mount Sinai, and the liberality of the Conqueror's father when on his last pilgrimage passed into legend.[1] These stories were evidently based on some reality, and there is little doubt that William inherited considerable hoarded wealth. He had, moreover, his own means of augmenting it. He possessed, of course, his own very large estates, but it appears that he was less exclusively dependent upon his demesnes and forests than were most of his fellow rulers in Gaul.[2] He had also what might be called his public revenues as duke, some of which had descended to him from Carolingian times. And these were numerous. Many of the items of ducal revenue specified in the earliest surviving fiscal record of the province – the 'Rolls of the Norman Exchequer' of 1180 – can be traced back to the Conqueror's reign and beyond.[3] And in particular there might be noted the *graverie* – the chief direct tax of the age which is well attested, together with the officials who were charged with its collection.[4] Scarcely less important were the rights which the duke possessed in customs and tolls, and his toll-collectors – *telonarii* – were evidently men of considerable social standing.[5]

How far before the Norman conquest such payments were taken in money must depend upon the extent to which a money economy had come to prevail in Normandy at this time. The extreme rarity of surviving coins from pre-Conquest Normandy might suggest that they were never very plentiful, but reference to the precious metals and to their circulation are not infrequent in the texts.[6] The case of Ernald of Bayeux which has already been cited is significant in this respect, and after 1066 the circulation of money in the duchy was certainly considerable. This was, of course, due in large measure to profits taken from the English adventure, but earlier wars of conquest had enriched William's predecessors, and it is unlikely that the treasure then amassed had been dissipated before his accession. Nor is evidence lacking of the minting of money in Normandy at this time. A text drawn up shortly after the Conqueror's death refers to the ducal mints at Rouen and Bayeux,[7] and there seems no reason to doubt that these had been set up before

---

[1] Southern, *Making of the Middle Ages*, pp. 53, 54.

[2] Cf. Musset, 'Aristocratie d'argent' (*Annales de Normandie*, vol. IX, 1959).

[3] Haskins, *op. cit.*, p. 39.

[4] Musset, *op. cit.*, p. 289; *Cart. S. Trin. Roth.*, nos. LXXIII, LXXX, LXXXVII.

[5] Haskins, *op. cit.*, p. 47; Musset, *op. cit.*, p. 290. One of these *telonarii* can be ranked among the *optimates* (*Cart. S. Père Chartres*, p. 146).

[6] Musset, *op. cit.*, pp. 285, 286.

[7] *Consuetudines et Justicie*, cl. XIII (Haskins, *op. cit.*, p. 283).

1066. At least four ducal moneyers established about this time are known by name,[1] and two of these belonged to a family which was to exercise considerable influence. Thus Rannulf the moneyer held that office very early in Duke William's reign, and one of his sons, Osbern, succeeded his father as moneyer before 1066,[2] whilst another son, who was likewise implicated in Duke William's financial transactions, was in due course to pass over into England.[3] Some suggestion of the extent of William's revenues as duke before the Conquest is in fact given by the standing of the men who were responsible for their administration, and while it would be difficult to attempt any precise reckoning of his income from all sources at this time, there is at least one impressive indication that it must have been large. In the spring and early summer of 1066 he was able to maintain a very large force of mercenaries in his service, and we are expressly told that he did so without impoverishing the countryside on which they were quartered.[4]

The administrative problem which faced Duke William during his Norman reign was thus not what rights he might claim as duke, but how far, in circumstances of peculiar difficulty, he could translate those rights into practice. It was here that his relation with the new Norman aristocracy became of such paramount importance. For by 1050 that aristocracy was dominant in both secular and ecclesiastical affairs, and the ducal administration had been conducted and developed in a duchy wherein power had become concentrated to a remarkable degree in the hands of a few great families of which that of the duke was the chief.[5] The nexus of authority that resulted could in fact be plentifully illustrated. At the centre was the duke himself. His two half-brothers were respectively bishop of Bayeux and count of Mortain, and the counts of Évreux and Eu were his cousins. William fitz Osbern, perhaps the most powerful magnate of central Normandy, who was the duke's steward, was descended on both sides from the ducal house. An uncle of William fitz Osbern was bishop of Avranches, and the brother of the count of Eu was bishop of Lisieux. Again, Rannulf I, *vicomte* of the Bessin, married the duke's first cousin, and her brother, or half-brother, was abbot of Saint-Ouen. The brother of the count of Eu was bishop of Lisieux, the bishop of Coutances was a Mowbray, and the bishop of Sées uncle to the wife of Roger II of Montgomery. Elsewhere the same connexions

---

[1] Musset, *op. cit.*, pp. 290 *et sqq.*; *Cal. Doc. France*, nos. 711, 712.
[2] Musset, *op. cit.*, p. 292. [3] Below, pp. 303, 304.
[4] Will. Poit., p. 152, and see below, pp. 191, 192. [5] Above, pp. 83–104.

had been reinforced by the characteristic marriage alliances of the period, such as that of Montgomery with Bellême, Beaumont with Grandmesnil, or fitz Osbern with Tosny. Such facts have more than a genealogical interest. They illustrate how completely, before 1066, a few powerful families, dominated by that of the duke, had spun over the whole of Normandy a web of authority from which none of its inhabitants could escape.

It is misleading, therefore, to dissociate the resuscitation of ducal power in Normandy under Duke William from the rise of the feudal aristocracy at that time. There was, of course, truth in the bitter complaint attributed to the Conqueror on his death-bed that his worst foes had always been those from his own duchy, and of his own family.[1] But the rapid increase of Norman strength in the twenty years preceding the Norman conquest is not to be explained by reference to a continued opposition between the Norman duke and the Norman magnates. In the early part of his reign William, by himself, would never have been strong enough to withstand a concerted attack from the great men of the duchy, and, from the start, there was always a party of magnates which was ready to support him. And, as time went on, the interests of the greater Norman families were seen to be becoming ever more notably linked with those of the duke, until at last a situation was reached in which the duke could demand, and increasingly receive, their support, whilst they in turn could usually rely on the duke to sustain them.

Duke William's contribution in bringing about this result has already in part been indicated. It was exemplified, for instance, in the manner in which he extended the feudal obligations of his magnates. It was also displayed in the individual and constructive share he took in the government of the Norman church during his Norman reign. Such a policy could not, however, have been implemented apart from the personal prestige he gained during his wars between 1047 and 1060. The men with whom he had to deal in his duchy were crude and violent, but many of them were also shrewd and politic, and they would never have accepted the control of any man whose own character and exploits had not won their respect. No better illustration of William's dominance, and the manner in which it was built up, could, in fact, be found than in his relations with Lanfranc, who, when prior of Le Bec, had been estranged from the duke in the matter of William's marriage. Their

[1] Ord. Vit., vol. III, p. 229.

later co-operation was to be a factor in the subsequent history of the Anglo-Norman kingdom, and it is highly significant that their reconciliation was brought about largely through the influence of William fitz Osbern, who was himself one of the architects of the Norman conquest of England.[1] Upon such personal relationships was much of William's later policy to depend.

The task which here confronted William as he approached maturity was to implement the inherent rights of his dynasty in the midst of a changing society, and, as far as might be, to implicate the newly established feudal aristocracy with the administrative authority that traditionally pertained to a Norman duke. It was an endeavour that was to affect the whole social structure of Normandy, but its operation was most noteworthy – and most critical – in connexion with those institutions where the interests of the duke and his magnates most strongly converged, where opposition between them might have proved disastrous, and where, if harmony could be achieved, the results would be most far-reaching. Chief of these were the *comtés* and the *vicomtés* which by the middle of the eleventh century had become inseparably connected with the feudal nobility, but which remained also as units essential to the ducal administration. It was in fact an indispensable prerequisite for the development of Norman strength during these years that William should be able to utilize the Norman *comtés* and the Norman *vicomtés* in the government of his duchy.

In the case of the *comtés* his policy might be said to have been fairly clearly indicated by previous history. As has been seen, the Norman counts did not make their appearance until the first quarter of the eleventh century, and their establishment at that time could be considered in some sense as an extension of the comital power of the duke. These men were all drawn from the ducal family; their *comtés* were situated at strategic points suitable for the defence of the duchy; and the one danger that might ensue from these arrangements was personal disloyalty on the part of a member of the ruling family against its head. After William's accession this in fact took shape with the rebellion of William, count of Arques, but with his forfeiture in 1054 the solidarity of the group was re-established, and it was further strengthened when in, or shortly after, 1055, Duke William found himself strong enough to dispossess William Werlenc, count of Mortain, apparently upon a very flimsy excuse, and to set up in his place his own half-brother Robert, the

[1] *Vita Herluini* (Robinson, *Gilbert Crispin*, p. 27); Will. Malms., *Gesta Pontificum*, p. 150.

son of Herluin and Herleve.[1] By 1060, therefore, the Norman counts had come to form a small aristocratic group whose cohesion could hardly be matched elsewhere in contemporary Europe. They owed their allegiance not to a king to whom they were unconnected by blood, but to a duke to whom they were nearly related. Prominent members of the feudal aristocracy, they had at the same time become inextricably involved in the ducal administration of Normandy.

Much more crucial was William's problem in connexion with the *vicomtés* which, as has been seen, had now passed into hereditary possession of the new feudal families. On his ability to make these perform, as deputies to the count of Rouen, the duties formerly inherent in the vice-comital office in Normandy, much of the success of Duke William's administration was in fact to depend. The manner in which this was brought about thus deserves some illustration. It would seem, for example, that in his time, and before 1066, the collection of ducal revenue and the discharge of ducal payments had become recognized as part of the obligations of any Norman *vicomte*, however personally distinguished. Shortly after the Conquest, the *vicomte* of Avranches was held responsible for paying annually to the church of Saint Stephen, Caen, the sum of eighty pounds from the ducal manor of Vains;[2] and shortly before the Conquest the *vicomté* of the Hiémois was similarly charged with paying on behalf of the duke an annual sum to the monks of Saint-Martin of Sées.[3] These men belonged to the most powerful section of the Anglo-Norman aristocracy, for the one was father of Hugh, earl of Chester, and the other was Roger of Montgomery, himself soon to become earl of Shrewsbury. That they should at this period have thus been content to serve as the fiscal agents of the duke is in every way notable. Nor is there any doubt that the practice of farming the Norman *vicomtés*[4] was in operation before the Conquest, and at an early date certain Norman monasteries were enriched by grants assessed not on individual estates but upon *vicomtés* as a whole.[5] It is clear therefore that, before 1066, the Norman *vicomté* could be regarded as, in some sense, a fiscal unit dependent upon the court of Rouen, and that at the same period some of the greatest among the Norman magnates were, as *vicomtes*, actively administering the fiscal policy of the duke.

[1] Ord. Vit., vol. II, p. 259; vol. III, p. 246.
[2] Haskins, *op. cit.*, appendix E, no. 1; Delisle-Berger, *Rec. Actes – Henri II*, vol. I, p. 345.
[3] Haskins, *op. cit.*, Appendix E, no. 11.
[4] *Ibid.*, pp. 42, 43.   [5] *R.A.D.N.*, no. 99.

Equally clear is the evidence which shows that at this time the *vicomtes* in Normandy were being regularly employed as agents and executants of the ducal justice. Between 1070 and 1079 Richard, *vicomte* of the Avranchin, was ordered by Duke William to summon the men of Caen so that judgment might be pronounced between Ralph Tesson and the abbey of Fontenay,[1] and in 1080 at the council of Lillebonne the *vicomtes* of Normandy were specifically entrusted with enforcing the Truce of God on behalf of the duke.[2] About the same time Rannulf, *vicomte* of the Bessin, heard a plea in which he gave judgment in favour of the abbey of Le Mont-Saint-Michel, whilst Richard, *vicomte* of the Avranchin, was one of the judges who, about 1076, pronounced sentence against Robert Bertram.[3] These examples have been taken from the period immediately subsequent to the Norman conquest, but it seems clear that they reflected earlier conditions. Some time before 1028 the duke of Normandy, having given judgment in favour of the see of Rouen, in respect of a disputed estate, forthwith sent Goscelin, son of Hedo (who was *vicomte* of Rouen), and Richard, the *vicomte*, son of Tescelin, to give effect to the decision of his court.[4] And when between 1035 and 1037 the bishop of Bayeux sought justice, his case was heard in the presence among others of Nigel, *vicomte* of the Cotentin.[5] Evidently at the beginning of the reign the *vicomtes* of Normandy were numbered among these 'lords who conducted the justice of the kingdom', and it was to be one of the achievements of Duke William to make this judicial position to depend ever more strictly on the ducal court.

Probably the most important responsibilities of the Norman *vicomtes* were military. Just as the Norman *comtés* of the eleventh century can be seen in relation to a scheme for the defence of the duchy, so also can the *vicomtés*, and their holders, be likewise regarded. The great *vicomtes* of the Cotentin, the Avranchin, and the Bessin faced both Brittany and the sea, and the *vicomté* of the Hiémois with its centre at Exmes looked south across the debatable frontier into Maine. More specifically was the Norman *vicomte* from his first appearance the normal custodian of a ducal castle. Nigel, who had previously repelled an English invasion of the Cotentin, was entrusted by Duke Richard II with the defence of Tillières, and he was, likewise, at a later date to hold the castle of Le

---

[1] *Gall. Christ.*, vol. XI; *Instrumenta*, cols. 61–65; *Regesta*, vol. I, no. 117.
[2] Ord. Vit., vol. II, p. 316.   [3] Delisle, *Saint Sauveur, Preuves*, nos. 35, 36.
[4] Valin, *Duc de Normandie, Preuves*, no. 1.   [5] *Cart. Bayeux*, vol. I, no. 21.

Homme which had formerly belonged to Richard III and subsequently to Guy of Burgundy.[1] Alfred 'the Giant', another *vicomte* of the time of Duke Richard II, was similarly one of the custodians of the castle of Cherrieux, which likewise was in due course to pass into the keeping of the *vicomtes* of the Cotentin. Thurstan Goz, yet another of the early *vicomtes*, was associated with the custody of the ducal castle of Falaise; and the castle of Saint-James de Beuvron, which was built by Duke William in connexion with the Breton war of 1064, was confided to Richard, *vicomte* of the Avranchin.[2]

Some of the Norman castles of this period such as Arques and Brionne, and possibly Tillières and Falaise, were constructed of stone, but most of them were doubtless of the 'motte and bailey' type with which England after the Conquest was to be made familiar. All alike, however, had become pivotal points in the defence of Normandy and in the maintenance of order within the duchy. Castles were already in fact becoming essential to the efficient conduct of warfare, and it is small wonder that within Normandy the dukes should have wished to retain full control over them. Indeed, before 1035 it would seem to have been exceptional in Normandy for a castle to be held by a magnate other than a *comte* or *vicomte*; and the men who did succeed in acquiring castles of their own were usually themselves of the highest status and power.[3] Nor is it without significance that many of the most important of the early 'private' castles in Normandy were situated, like Échauffour, Laigle, and Montreuil-l'Argille, in districts where the ducal authority was perhaps less effective.[4] The Norman dukes were well aware of the peril of castles passing out of their control, and the fact that ducal castles had been so constantly placed in the charge of *vicomtes* illustrates from a new angle the connexion between the early *vicomtes* and the counts of Rouen.

No aspect of the disturbances following William's accession was, therefore, more menacing than the attempt of certain *vicomtes* to gain for themselves full possession of the castles with which they had been entrusted. Thurstan Goz defied the duke from the castle of Falaise, and Nigel of the Cotentin obtained from Guy of Burgundy the castle of Le Homme which in due course he was to hold against his young master.[5] Such developments were symptomatic of the general threat to

---

[1] Will. Jum., pp. 76, 84; Yver, *Châteaux forts*, pp. 39–48.
[2] Will. Jum., pp. 105, 106, 272.   [3] Yver, *op. cit.*, p. 57.
[4] Ord. Vit., vol. II, pp. 23, 27, 295; Yver, *op. cit.*, pp. 40, 41.
[5] Will. Jum., p. 118; Yver, *op. cit.*, p. 46.

ducal authority during these years; and the *vicomtes* were by no means the only magnates in the duchy who at this time sought to buttress power by building strongholds from which they could advance their fortunes by force of arms. But in the case of the *vicomtes* the menace was particularly grave. The revolt of the western *vicomtes* in 1047 was rightly regarded as a special treason, and it is noteworthy that after Val-ès-Dunes there was a widespread destruction of many of the illicit castles that had been built. 'Happy battle', exclaimed William of Jumièges with some exaggeration, 'that in a single day caused all the castles to fall.'[1] In this, as in so many other ways, the suppression of the rebellion of 1047 was of cardinal importance in preventing the vice-comital power in Normandy from passing out of ducal control, and thereafter William was able with ever-increasing success to reimpose upon Normandy the doctrine that the Norman *vicomte* was the agent of the duke, holding office at his pleasure, charged with specific duties on his behalf, and in the last resort removable at his will.

The degree to which this was accomplished before 1066 was due in the first instance to William's own successful wars, and to the dominant position he eventually attained within the feudal structure of Normandy. But he seems at the same time to have attempted to alter in some measure the character of the *vicomtés* themselves, seeking to create, albeit under the old name, new and smaller units of administration. The full results of this development were not to be attained until the twelfth century. But its beginnings can be legitimately assigned to the reign of the Conqueror, and to the period before 1066. Thus a charter of Duke William which passed before the Conquest alludes to the *vicomté* of Gavray, and subsequent texts reveal this to have been a comparatively small jurisdiction established within the Cotentin.[2] Again, Ordericus Vitalis speaks of a *vicomté* of Orbec as already established before 1091.[3] And when, before 1066, Herluin, the husband of the Duke William's mother, became a *vicomte* he was given the small *vicomté* of Conteville, about which nothing is previously known.[4] The evidence is admittedly scanty, but the establishment of little *vicomtés*, such as these, must have affected the character of the office which was held by the great Norman *vicomtes* before the Conquest. It betokened the beginnings of a change

[1] Will. Jum., p. 123; Yver, *op. cit.*, p. 48.
[2] *Mon. Ang.*, vol. VI, p. 1073; *R.A.D.N.*, no. 99; Powicke, *Loss of Normandy*, p. 114.
[3] Ord. Vit., vol. III, p. 371.
[4] Douglas, *Domesday Monachorum*, pp. 27, 28; Powicke, *op. cit.*, p. 108.

whereby the number of the Norman *vicomtes* was increased at the same time as their personal importance tended to diminish.

In the sphere of local government, therefore, the development of ducal power in Normandy during these years can be seen in the extent to which William made important men in the duchy serve as ducal officials who were not merely his domainal agents, but officers in charge of large administrative districts. Correspondingly, the growing co-operation between William and his magnates in the administration of Normandy as a whole can be illustrated in the activities of the ducal court during this period, and here the resuscitation of the traditional powers pertaining to the duke was also to be displayed. The composition of that court attracted, indeed, the attention of contemporary chroniclers. William of Poitiers spoke in glowing terms of the ecclesiastical and lay counsellors by whom William was surrounded, mentioning in particular the bishops of Normandy, and (among the laity) the counts of Eu and Mortain, Roger of Beaumont, William fitz Osbern, and Roger of Montgomery.[1] The statement is, of course, tainted with rhetoric, and it refers to the latest period in the duke's Norman reign. But it may be confirmed with some particularity by the attestations to ducal charters between 1035 and 1066.

Attendance at the ducal court naturally varied with the events of these tumultuous years, since it depended not only on the business to be transacted but also on the ability of the duke at any given time to enforce the presence of particular notables in the duchy. None the less a general pattern can be discerned which differs little from the description given by the chronicler. Thus in 1038–1039, at the very beginning of the reign, an instrument ratified by the ducal court was attested by the duke himself, by Hugh, bishop of Évreux, and by Adso, the *vicomte*.[2] Again, some time between 1049 and 1058, a formal charter of the duke was subscribed in his presence by Hugh, bishop of Lisieux, Roger of Montgomery, William fitz Osbern, Robert, the duke's half-brother, and Richard, *vicomte* of the Avranchin.[3] With the growth of the duke's power, his court naturally became more imposing, and within a few months of the invasion of England it can be watched in full session. On 18 June 1066 a charter,[4] which can be dated by reference to the famous comet, was subscribed by the duke, his wife Matilda, his son Robert, his half-brother Robert, count of Mortain, Archbishop Maurilius, the

---

[1] Will. Poit., pp. 135, 149; Ord. Vit., vol. II, p. 121.
[3] *Ibid.*, no. 140.
[2] *R.A.D.N.*, no. 92.
[4] *Regesta*, vol. I, no. 4.

bishops of Évreux, Bayeux, and Avranches, William fitz Osbern, and
Roger Montgomery in his capacity of *vicomte* of the Hiémois.

Such examples (selected from among many) go far to suggest that
the chronicler's description of the duke's entourage on formal occasions
was accurate in its essentials. A full session of the ducal court might be
expected to include members of the duke's family such as his wife, his
eldest son, and his half-brothers.[1] Among the lay magnates, moreover,
the most frequent witnesses are precisely those whom William of Poitiers
described as his most constant counsellors: that is to say, the counts of
Eu, Mortain, and Évreux, William fitz Osbern, Roger of Beaumont,
and Roger of Montgomery – to whom should perhaps be added Ralph
Tesson and the elder Walter Giffard.[2] Again, the presence of high
ecclesiastics is also normal. Abbots, with the exception of Nicholas of
Saint-Ouen, son of Duke Richard III, appear perhaps less frequently
than might be expected, but all the occupants of the Norman sees
were constantly in attendance at the ducal court, in particular the
two archbishops in their turn (Mauger and Maurilius), Odo of Bayeux,
Hugh of Lisieux, William of Évreux, and John of Avranches.[3] Further,
an executive act of the duke was usually witnessed by one or more of his
vicomtes, among whom the *vicomtes* of the Cotentin and the Avranchin
were prominent. Such were in fact the main elements of the ducal court
during William's Norman reign, but this *curia* could always be enforced,
and the presence of visiting magnates, both lay and ecclesiastical, is a
feature of the period. A remarkable charter of Duke Robert I[4] had been
subscribed not only by the French king but by the exiled English
athelings, Edward and Alfred. Charters of Duke William between 1035
and 1066 were in like manner attested by Walter, count of the Vexin,
Gervais, bishop of Le Mans, Hugh, count of Maine, Waleran, count of
Meulan, and perhaps by Robert of Jumièges when archbishop of
Canterbury.[5]

The ducal court appears to have met at irregular intervals, and at
various places as occasion required, though there is some evidence to
suggest a practice of holding an Easter meeting at Fécamp.[6] The *curia*
also varied greatly in size, but at its centre there can already be detected

---

[1] *e.g. R.A.D.N.*, nos. 138, 141, 158, 202.   [2] *R.A.D.N., passim.*

[3] *e.g. R.A.D.N.*, nos. 100, 129, 229, 230; cf. *Cal. Doc. France*, nos. 709, 710, 1165, 1167, 1172.

[4] *R.A.D.N.*, no. 69.

[5] *Ibid.*, nos. 104, 107, 113, 137. The assignation of the date of 1055 to the last-named deed
is not certain and the list of witnesses presents difficulty. Lot (*Saint-Wandrille*, no. 17) suggests
the visit of Robert, archbishop of Canterbury, but the ascription is not certain.

[6] Haskins, *op. cit.*, p. 55.

the beginnings of a household administration charged particularly with the ducal administration. It will be recalled that during the reign of King Henry I of France, the Capetian household began to take on its later form. Instruments of that king were very frequently expedited by Baldwin the chancellor, and during the reign of Philip I the royal *diplomata* start to be regularly attested by the four great officers – the steward, the constable, the chamberlain, and the butler.[1] Such a development might reasonably be expected to have found some reflection in Normandy, and in fact several of the counterparts of the great officers of the court of Paris make their appearance in the duchy between 1035 and 1066. Chief among these was the steward. There can be no doubt that during the reign of Duke Robert I the office of steward in Normandy was held by no less a personage than Osbern, son of Herfast, and nephew of the Duchess Gunnor, who himself married Emma the daughter of Count Rodulf, half-brother to Duke Richard I. He is described as steward by the chroniclers,[2] and as steward he witnessed charters for Saint-Wandrille and for Holy Trinity, Rouen.[3] Doubtless because of his office, he became after 1035 one of the guardians of the young duke, and about 1040 he was murdered while in attendance on his young master.[4]

The association of the Norman stewardship with one of the most powerful families of the new nobility was itself a fact of considerable importance. Osbern, however, was not the only steward at the ducal court during these years,[5] and though, after his death, his office was inherited by his famous son William fitz Osbern, early charters of Duke William are also attested by other stewards. Such, for instance, was Gerard *senescallus*, who appears in several of these instruments;[6] and of even greater interest is Stigand, *dapifer*. For this Stigand was not only himself steward, but, even during his lifetime, the title of *dapifer* was apparently held also by his son, Odo, until his death in 1063 at the age of twenty-six.[7] Moreover, Stigand, in 1054, witnessed as *dapifer* a charter which is attested by William fitz Osbern without further designation.[8] It cannot therefore be asserted with complete confidence that no interval elapsed between the death of Osbern and the time when William fitz Osbern assumed the office which his father had held. But it is certain

[1] Prou, *Rec. Actes – Philippe I*, pp. l–liii. [2] Ord. Vit., vol. III, p. 229.
[3] *R.A.D.N.*, nos. 69, 82. [4] Will. Jum., p. 116.
[5] Harcourt, *His Grace the Steward*, p. 7. [6] *R.A.D.N.*, *passim*.
[7] P. Eudeline, *Hist. de Hauteville* (1948), plate II; *R.A.D.N.*, no. 158.
[8] *R.A.D.N.*, no. 188.

that before the end of the Norman reign of Duke William, William fitz Osbern, closest among the duke's advisers, was also steward at the ducal court, and his great personal distinction inevitably gave an additional prestige to the office.[1]

The importance of the steward in the pre-Conquest court in Normandy was due less to the office than to the personal standing of the men who held it. But some parallel to this development can be seen in respect of the chamberlainship. Many pre-Conquest Norman charters are attested by Radulfus *camerarius* or *cubicularius*, and this was none other than Ralph, son of Gerald, lord of Tancarville.[2] He appears as chamberlain as early as 1035,[3] and during the Norman reign of Duke William he was constantly in attendance at court. He died, as it seems, before 1066, when his son Ralph inherited an office which, like that of the Norman steward, had grown in dignity owing to the personal importance of its holder.[4] Similarly, the existence of the office of butler at the Norman court during this period is well attested. Charters for Jumièges, Holy Trinity, Rouen, and Coulombes are attested by Hugh *pincerna* or *buticularius*, and one text shows that this was Hugh of Ivry, a man of some standing in Normandy, who later crossed over with his duke to England, but none the less continued as butler in Normandy, surviving apparently until after 1086.[5] As to the fourth of the great Capetian officials – the constable – there is less evidence in pre-Conquest Normandy. But when at a later date Robert of Ver became one of the constables in England, he did so by inheritance from the family of Montfort-sur-Risle. And this family, which held the 'honour of the constable' (*honor constabulariæ*) in England, was well established in Normandy before the Norman conquest, and then already closely associated with the Norman duke.[6]

There remains the chancellorship; and here the Capetian parallel needs particularly to be considered. Before 1060, as has been seen, many of the French royal *diplomata* had been formally subscribed by a certain Baldwin who acted regularly as chancellor. Moreover, the evolution elsewhere of chanceries from organized groups of court chaplains is well known, and the clerical element in the pre-Conquest court

---

[1] Will. Jum., p. 117; cf. *Cart. S. Trin. Roth.*, no. LXVII.

[2] *R.A.D.N.*, nos. 138, 204; *Cart. Îles Norm.*, nos. 298, 299, 300; Le Prévost, *Eure*, vol. III, p. 467 (*R.A.D.N.*, no. 191).

[3] *R.A.D.N.*, no. 89.

[4] *Complete Peerage*, vol. x, Appendix F.

[5] *R.A.D.N.*, nos. 138, 188, 233; Round, *King's Serjeants*, pp. 140, 141.

[6] Douglas, *Domesday Monachorum*, pp. 65–67; Round, *Geoffrey de Mandeville*, p. 326.

of Duke William was evidently considerable. Thus Theobald and Baldwin witnessed as chaplains one of the duke's charters for Marmoutier about 1060, and Rannulf the chaplain attested another charter for that house at a slightly later date.[1] Indeed, the biography of one of the duke's chaplains has in this connexion a particular interest. This was Herfast who subscribed the earlier of the two Marmoutier charters mentioned above, and who, three years after the Norman conquest, was to appear in an English charter with the title of *cancellarius*,[2] being perhaps, though not certainly, the first man in England to be so styled.[3] His career has therefore attracted attention, and there have even been some who have not hesitated to conclude therefrom the presence of a chancery in pre-Conquest Normandy, and the importation of this institution from the duchy into the kingdom.

It is, however, extremely unlikely that any organized chancery existed, either in fact or name, in Normandy during the Norman reign of Duke William. Herfast is not known to have been given the title of chancellor before he came to England,[4] and the clerks of William's chapel do not appear with any regularity as witnesses to the ducal charters of the period.[5] Moreover, the character of the ducal charters which were issued between 1035 and 1066 itself forbids any assumption that there existed at this time in Normandy a ducal *scriptorium* whose work followed a regular pattern, or whose activities were inspired by an established tradition.[6] There is, for instance, nothing to be found in Normandy to correspond with the formalized writs which, during these years, were being regularly produced by the *scriptorium* of Edward the Confessor.[7] By contrast, the ducal charters of this period exhibit such diversities of structure that it is tempting to suppose that they must often have been compiled in the religious houses for whose benefit they were granted, and there is positive evidence to show that this practice was followed.[8] It would seem, in short, that the development of

---

[1] *R.A.D.N.*, no. 141; cf. *Cart. Îles Norm.*, nos. 297, 300.

[2] *Regesta*, vol. I, no. 28.

[3] Harmer, *Anglo-Saxon Writs*, pp. 59–61.

[4] In three Norman charters of the early eleventh century (*R.A.D.N.*, nos. 18, 34; Pommeraye, *Saint-Ouen*, p. 422) persons appear under the style of chancellor, but it would be very rash to argue from the phraseology of the texts in their present form. Reference may be made in this connexion to *Nouveau Traité de Diplomatique*, vol. IV, p. 255, and to plate III in Haskins's, *Norman Institutions*. Whatever conclusions should be drawn on this matter, it remains true that there does not seem to be any reference to the title of chancellor in any text emanating from Normandy during the reign of Duke William II.

[5] Haskins, *op. cit.*, p. 52.

[6] Fauroux, *R.A.D.N.*, pp. 40–47.

[7] Below, pp. 292–294.

[8] *R.A.D.N.*, no. 134.

the duke's chapel into an organized chancery had before the Norman conquest made little or no progress.

The official household of the duke of Normandy was in 1066 still in a transitional stage of development, as was that of the French king, and there may well have been some mutual influence between them. Many of the great officials characteristic of the French royal household – notably the steward, the butler, and the chamberlain – were already at that time well established in Normandy, and they were surrounded by lesser functionaries, such as the marshal,[1] and the numerous ushers (*hostiarii*), who appear fairly frequently as witnesses to the charters.[2] It would thus be erroneous to suppose that this household had as yet achieved the organization that it was later to assume. Whilst the titles of master butler and master chamberlain may have been used in Normandy before the Conquest,[3] it would seem that the principal officers of the Norman household at this time were not as yet clearly distinguished from lesser officials with the same titles, and no regular order of precedence among them was as yet established. There can be no doubt that in the time of William fitz Osbern the steward was the most important official of the Norman household, and here the development antedated that of the French household, where the pre-eminence of the steward was not established until after 1071.[4] But even in Normandy claims to priority for the chamberlainship seem to have been made by the family of Tancarville at an early date.[5] The organization of the household of the Norman duke was still, it would seem, dependent upon personalities rather than upon institutional growth, or administrative tradition. It was, nevertheless, important that some of the greatest feudatories of Normandy should at this time have been serving as household officers of the duke, for their doing so inevitably gave additional strength to his court.

The charters show that this court met fairly regularly even in the early years of the minority. Two instruments for two religious houses, which were passed about 1040, indicate, for instance, the extreme youth of the duke, who was apparently present with a guardian at courts which, it would seem, were presided over by Mauger, archbishop of Rouen.[6]

---

[1] Ilbert and Milo appear as marshals in Normandy before 1066 (*Complete Peerage*, vol. XI, Appendix E).
[2] Haskins, *op. cit.*, p. 51. [3] *Complete Peerage*, vol. X, Appendix F.
[4] Prou, *Rec. Actes – Philippe I*, vol. I, p. cxxxvi.
[5] A. Deville, *S. Georges de Boscherville*, pp. 57–62.
[6] *R.A.D.N.*, no. 100; *Gall. Christ.*, vol. XI; *Instrumenta*, col. 12.

A court of this nature was also, doubtless, held when, at about the same time, the *comté* of Arques was bestowed on Mauger's brother William.[1] Again, between 1045 and 1047 the duke's confirmation of gifts to Jumièges was made in a court attended by three counts, and by William fitz Osbern.[2] And after Val-ès-Dunes the ducal court seems to have been enlarged. It was a *curia* of distinction that about 1050 met to ratify grants that had been made to the abbey of Le Mont-Saint-Michel,[3] and in 1051 it was in the presence of a full court that the monastery of Saint-Wandrille sought to vindicate its rights.[4]

Such records are impressive, and they indicate the continuity of the ducal administration during the troubles of the minority. None the less, it is significant that most of William's pre-Conquest charters come from the period subsequent to Mortemer, and that their subscriptions display a *curia* that was ever growing in size and importance. It would be hard to find in the earlier charters evidence of a court comparable to that which late in the duke's Norman reign attested the duke's confirmation of the gifts made to his half-brother Odo to the church of Bayeux,[5] or the court which some time in 1066 confirmed at Fécamp the restitutions then made to the monastery of Coulombes.[6] The growing prestige of the duke was in fact being displayed in the assembly which surrounded him. And on the eve of the Norman conquest William was able to collect in his support a most notable court which attracted the attention of contemporary writers. That neither William of Malmesbury nor William of Poitiers[7] were exaggerating in their admiring descriptions of this assemblage is confirmed by the subscriptions to the charter which was issued on 17 June 1066 for Holy Trinity, Caen.[8] The list, replete with illustrious names, both secular and ecclesiastical, reflects the existence of a ducal court in Normandy of which any prince in contemporary Europe might have been proud.

This was essentially a feudal court whose function it was to give general support and counsel to the lord, though, as the presence of the *vicomtes* might suggest, there was perhaps always scope within this assembly for the expression of those traditional ducal powers which Duke William inherited, and which he was to revive. The business of the court before 1066 seems, however, to have been largely undifferentiated. There is, for instance, little to suggest that any fully developed

---

[1] Will. Jum., p. 119.   [2] *R.A.D.N.*, no. 113.   [3] *Ibid.*, no. 110.
[4] Chevreux et Vernier, *Archives de Normandie*, plate IV (*R.A.D.N.*, no. 124).
[5] *R.A.D.N.*, no. 219.   [6] *Ibid.*, no. 230.
[7] *Gesta Regum*, p. 299; Will. Poit., p. 149.   [8] *Regesta*, vol. I, no. 4.

financial organization had been formed in ducal Normandy before the Norman conquest. It is true that there are references to a *camera* (or treasury) in the time of Duke Richard II,[1] and the process of collecting the miscellaneous revenue to which Duke William was entitled, and of occasionally granting tithes out of it, implies of itself not only some system of accounting, however crude, but also perhaps the existence of officials specially devoted to this work.[2] The importance of the chamberlainship in the hands of the family of Tancarville is significant in this respect, but the progress towards the formation of anything that might be legitimately termed a finance bureau seems to have been very limited before 1066. It was a full *curia*, and not a part thereof, which about 1042 confirmed to Cerisy-la-Forêt the tithes of certain *vicomtés*,[3] and later a similar assembly ratified to Montivilliers the grant of a hundred shillings in the *prévôté* of Caen.[4] Before the Conquest it was still the court as a whole which under the duke was concerned with the ducal revenue as with all other aspects of the duke's affairs.

The acts of the ducal court during the Norman reign of Duke William for which most evidence has survived are naturally those which concerned the confirmation by the duke of land or privileges to religious houses. It was at a full court that about 1050 the duke confirmed the foundation of the monastery of Saint-Désir at Lisieux by Bishop Hugh and his mother, the Countess Lesceline of Eu; and a similar court some ten years later ratified the gift by Nigel of Saint-Sauveur to Marmoutier of six churches in the island of Guernsey.[5] About 1054 the benefactions of Gilbert Crispin to Jumièges were attested in the presence of Duke William by William, bishop of Évreux, Stigand the steward, Hugh the butler, William fitz Osbern, and others;[6] whilst at a little later date a larger assembly of a similar character ratified the gifts made by Roger of Clères to the Tosny foundation of Conches.[7] Such transactions which normally involved the granting of a charter are for that reason of course exceptionally well recorded. But there is little doubt that they occupied much of the attention of the ducal court during this period.

Formal ratification of ownership was at times hardly to be distinguished from the settlement of claims that had long been in dispute, and it is in this connexion that the judicial work of the ducal court can best in the first instance be considered. Records of several pleas of the time have survived, and they merit attention. Between 1063 and 1066 there

---

[1] Haskins, *op. cit.*, pp. 40, 41.   [2] *Ibid.*   [3] *R.A.D.N.*, no. 99.
[4] *Ibid.*, no. 171.   [5] *Ibid.*, nos. 140, 141.   [6] *Ibid.*, no. 188.   [7] *Ibid.*, no. 191.

was a long dispute between the abbey of Marmoutier and that of Saint-Pierre-de-la-Couture at Le Mans respecting the land which Guy of Laval had given to Marmoutier near his castle of Laval for making a 'borough'.[1] At length when Duke William was holding his court at Domfront 'he held a plea on this matter', and ordered that the monks of Marmoutier should offer the ordeal, but that Reinald, abbot of Saint-Pierre, need only swear that he had never given the property in dispute. Abbot Reinald refused the oath, and the property was therefore restored to the monks of Marmoutier. 'Thus the plea which had so long remained in doubt was finally determined by means of a public and lawful judgment.' Again, in 1066, there occurred a long dispute between the church of Avranches and Roger of Beaufou, nephew of Bishop John, respecting the lordship of Saint-Philibert which Roger claimed by inheritance from his uncle. In this instance, also, the matter was brought into the ducal court, and a complicated settlement was there made, judgment at length being given on 18 June 1066 in general favour of the church at Avranches.[2] Finally, it may be noted how after a long dispute respecting a mill at Vains, Abbot Rannulf of Le Mont-Saint-Michel in like manner asked for the judgment of the duke's *curia*, and the resulting charter records that only after a careful examination of all the points at issue was the mill declared to belong to the monks of the Mount.[3]

Narratives such as these, together with the charters with which they are connected, tempt speculation on the nature of ducal justice in this period. But here it would be rash to attempt too great precision. In one sense the ducal court at this time could be regarded as but the greatest of the feudal courts in Normandy, and as administering on behalf of the duke a judicial authority which was not readily distinguishable in respect of secular affairs from that enjoyed by his greater vassals over their own tenants.[4] The older view that, alone among the great feuda-tories of France, the duke of Normandy had a monopoly of *haute justice* within his dominion cannot be justified by evidence from before the Norman conquest.[5] Many of the greater magnates of Normandy at that time, such as Roger of Beaumont or the count of Évreux, certainly

---

[1] *Ibid.*, no. 159.   [2] *Ibid.*, no. 229.

[3] *R.A.D.N.*, no. 148; Lechaudé d'Anisy, *Grands Rôles*, p. 196; *Cal. Doc. France*, nos. 711, 712. Cf. *Regesta*, vol. I, no. 92.

[4] J. Goebel, *Felony and Misdemeanour*, p. 283.

[5] Cf. Luchaire, *Manuel des Institutions*, pp. 245, 246, criticized by F. M. Powicke (*Loss of Normandy*, p. 52).

exercised very wide judicial rights, and it is very doubtful whether until after 1066 William was able to make generally recognized in Normandy the doctrine that they held these rights only by virtue of a specific grant from the duke.[1] Whatever may have been strict legal theory, it would seem that the growing importance of the ducal court between 1047 and 1066 could better be explained by reference to more practical considerations. It was during these years that William was able to assert more clearly his feudal rights over his vassals, and his increasing power made it ever more desirable that any important transaction should have the sanction of his former confirmation. Not without reason did Robert, abbot of Saint-Wandrille from 1048 to 1063, declare on one occasion: 'I took care to bring this charter to William lord of the Normans, and he confirmed it with the sign of his authority with the agreement of many of his own lords.'[2]

Nevertheless, there remained in Normandy those pre-feudal traditions which distinguished the judicial authority of the duke from that of his Norman vassals, and the political events of Duke William's reign were to strengthen their influence. The comital authority acquired in the tenth century by the Viking counts of Rouen remained as a source of potential strength to the descendants of Rolf, and now the changing relations between Duke William and the French king imparted to such prerogatives an enhanced significance. So long as the duke of Normandy remained the vassal of the king of France, he could be regarded in a sense as merely the holder of an exceptionally privileged 'immunity'. But after the events of 1052–1054 the authority of the French king was vitally impaired in Normandy, and other notions favouring the judicial independence of the duke were inevitably put forward. In this respect the position occupied by the duke in the church of the province of Rouen was to prove especially important. William's ancestors, having acquired special responsibilities towards the Church, had exercised these to their own advantage, and William himself was from the start directly to be implicated in ecclesiastical affairs. In the judicial sphere, for example, the introduction of the Truce of God in 1047 was here of particular significance, for not only had the duke been involved in its inception, but he was in due course to assume increasing responsibility for its execution, so that before his death the *Treuga Dei* in Normandy was to become scarcely distinguishable from the *pax Ducis*.[3] The

[1] Haskins, *op. cit.*, p. 29, note 112; cf. Le Prévost, *Eure*, vol. III, pp. 96, 97.
[2] *R.A.D.N.*, no. 153.   [3] Goebel, *op. cit.*, chap. V.

THE RULE OF DUKE WILLIAM

influence of this development might easily be exaggerated for the period 1047 to 1066, but it would probably be true to say that 'by slowly assuming responsibility for the sworn peace, the Norman dukes succeeded in establishing a prerogative over certain causes criminal which gave them an authority more far reaching than they had theretofore exercised as lords paramount'.[1]

Whatever may have been the precise influence of the enforcement of the Truce of God in developing the judicial prerogatives of the duke, there can be no question that these were enhanced in a more general way by the position assumed by Duke William between 1047 and 1066 within the Norman church. As has been seen, he took a personal share in most of the ecclesiastical councils of the province of Rouen during these years, and at the same time the greater prelates of Normandy were, like their lay kinsfolk, regular suitors to the ducal court.[2] In this compact duchy coincident with an ecclesiastical province, and dominated both secularly and ecclesiastically by a small group of interrelated families, any clear-cut demarcation between the two spheres of administration was almost impossible. And the duke's authority was thereby increased, since he was himself the apex of this closely integrated social structure. As his traditional powers as duke were progressively made to reinforce his feudal rights, so also did it become ever more difficult to define with any precision any ecclesiastical matters with which, in the duchy, he and his court might not feel themselves concerned.

There are indeed indications that, even before 1066, the intimate relation between the Norman duke and the Norman church was imparting to William's position as a ruler an ecclesiastical sanction different from that claimed by his fellow feudatories in Gaul. It is unlikely that before 1066 a Norman duke was at his installation ever blessed by any special consecration peculiar to his office, and according to a later tradition the essential act in the recognition of a duke of Normandy lay in his being girt with a sword.[3] On the other hand, the significance of the original baptism of Rolf was not forgotten, or the propaganda which had sought to display William Longsword as the dedicated champion of the Church; and if the presence of the archbishop of Rouen was always held to be essential to the installation of a duke of Normandy, this can hardly have been solely because of that prelate's position in the

---

[1] *Ibid.*, p. xxvi.   [2] Above, pp. 130–132.
[3] This happened in the case of Richard, son of King Henry II, when he became duke of Normandy (*Histoire de Guillaume le Maréchal* (ed. Meyer), vol. 1, v. 9556).

feudal structure of the province.[1] It has, moreover, been suggested that *Laudes* of the *Christus vincit* type such as had been chanted at the coronation of Charlemagne were sung when a Norman duke was accepted,[2] but this though possible cannot be proved, and there is no evidence that any Norman duke before 1066 was either anointed or crowned.[3] It is, however, noteworthy that at an early date, and probably before 1066,[4] a litany sung at important church festivals in the cathedral of Rouen contained a special acclamation on behalf of Duke William.[5] And this is the more remarkable in that no such particular salutation is known to have been used in any similar litany for any other lay magnate who was not of royal or imperial rank.[6] It would be as easy to underestimate as to exaggerate the implications of such a usage. Duke William of Normandy, exceptional in this matter among the magnates of Gaul, was before 1066 being accorded, in virtue of his ducal office, special powers and special responsibilities within the Norman Church. And he was thereby enabled to claim a certain religious sanction for his administrative acts.

During the decades preceding the Norman conquest of England, the aristocratic and ecclesiastical development of Normandy had been merged under the rule of Duke William II into a single political achievement. It might perhaps be summarized by saying that in 1065 a man might go from end to end of the duchy without ever passing outside the jurisdiction, secular or ecclesiastical, of a small group of interrelated great families with the duke at their head. The new aristocracy, now firmly established, had sponsored the monastic revival in the Norman church: correspondingly, the Norman bishops, drawn from that same aristocracy, were giving order to the province of Rouen which had itself become almost coincident with the Norman duchy. And at the centre of this interconnected progress was the duke. He had identified the ambitions of the aristocracy with his own political aims, and he had gone some way towards enforcing their feudal obligations towards himself. He had imposed his control likewise upon the reformed Norman church so that with some justice he might pose as the champion of the church in one of the most progressive provinces of western

---

[1] L. Valin, *Duc de Normandie*, p. 44.
[2] E. H. Kantorowicz, *Laudes Regiae* (1946), pp. 19, 166–171.
[3] *Ibid.*, pp. 170, 178.
[4] Julien Loth, *La Cathédrale de Rouen* (1879), pp. 553–562.
[5] 'Guillelmo Normannorum duci salus et pax continua.'
[6] E. H. Kantorowicz, *op. cit.*, p. 170.

Christendom. Thus had been attained that intense concentration of power in this province of Gaul which was among the most remarkable political phenomena of eleventh-century Europe. Here also was to be the basis of the greatest Norman achievement which was now about to be fulfilled under the leadership of Duke William – the establishment of the Anglo-Norman kingdom.

Part III

THE ESTABLISHMENT
OF THE
ANGLO-NORMAN
KINGDOM

Part III

THE ESTABLISHMENT
OF THE
ANGLO-NORMAN
KINGDOM

Chapter 7

NORMANDY AND ENGLAND

1035 - 1065

The Norman conquest of England was prepared and made possible by
the growth of Norman power during the earlier half of the eleventh
century, and by the consolidation of the duchy under the rule of Duke
William II. To explain why that Conquest was undertaken, and to
account for its success and its peculiar consequences it is necessary,
however, to consider not only the character of the Norman duchy in
his time but also the development of Norman policy during the same
period. Not otherwise is it to be understood why, and how, the medieval
destinies of England were during the third quarter of the eleventh
century to be deflected from Scandinavia towards Latin Europe by a
descendant of the Viking Rolf.

An intimate political relationship between Normandy and England
was part of the inheritance of Duke William.[1] The great Viking leaders
of the ninth century had transferred their operations indiscriminately
on both sides of the Channel, and the resulting settlements were associated both in the origin and in their character. In one sense the
Danelaw can be regarded as the English Normandy, and Normandy
the French Danelaw, inasmuch as in both cases similar problems arose
as to their assimilation into the older political order in which they were
planted. More direct political connexions inevitably ensued. Both
Athelstan and William Longsword were concerned with the fate of
Louis d'Outre-Mer,[2] and after the intensification of the Viking on-
slaughts towards the end of the tenth century, the interrelations between
the two dynasties became more pronounced. Ethelred II of England
(who had to bear the brunt of these attacks) was naturally interested in
what might be the policy of the Viking province of Gaul, and the
Norman dukes were not always unwilling to turn the situation to their
own advantage. The matter was clearly one of general importance to
western Europe, and it is not altogether surprising that Pope John XV
himself felt constrained to intervene. As a result a remarkable assembly

[1] Above, chap. I.   [2] Freeman, *Norman Conquest*, vol. 1, pp. 197–205.

met at Rouen in March 991 under the presidency of the papal envoy.[1] It consisted (as it would seem) of Roger, bishop of Lisieux, and other Norman notables, together with Æthelsige, bishop of Sherborne, and two English thegns.[2] There it was agreed that neither the duke nor the king should henceforth aid the enemies of the other, and the pact aptly symbolized both the special position which Normandy was attaining in western Christendom, and also the developing relationship between the ruling families of Normandy and England.

As the eleventh century advanced, the connexion became ever closer. The treaty of 991 was evidently only partially effective, for a Norman tradition which has some claims to credence refers to an unsuccessful English attack on the Cotentin in 1000, and if this in fact took place it was probably in the nature of a cutting-out operation designed to inflict punishment on a Viking fleet which after raiding England was refitting in the Norman harbours.[3] Something more was, therefore, necessary to cement between the English king and the Norman duke an alliance which was becoming increasingly necessary to both. And this took place with the famous marriage in 1002 between Emma, sister of Duke Richard II, and Ethelred II of England.[4] The full consequences of this momentous match were only to be revealed during the reign of the Conqueror himself, but even before his birth some of its implications became apparent. For when in 1013 Sweyn Forkbeard was successful in his last, and greatest, invasion of England, and the West Saxon royal family took refuge in flight, it was, as if inevitably, to Normandy that they turned. In the autumn of 1013 Emma arrived in the duchy with her two sons Edward and Alfred, and there they were joined in January 1014 by Ethelred himself.[5] It was from Normandy, and with Norman backing, that in the next month Ethelred II returned to England to wage his last unavailing war against Sweyn's son, Cnut the Great.[6]

---

[1] See the papal letter given in Will. Malms., *Gesta Regum*, vol. I, pp. 191–193. The letter is not wholly satisfactory in its present state, but in substance it is probably genuine (Stenton, *Anglo-Saxon England*, p. 371).

[2] Will. Malms. refers to Bishop Roger. The bishop of Lisieux was the only Norman bishop at this date with that name, and he appears in a charter of 990 (*R.A.D.N.*, no. 4). It is not inconceivable, however, that Will. Malms. made a mistake over the name and that Robert, archbishop of Rouen, is intended.

[3] The story is only found in Will. Jum. (p. 76), and must be treated with caution. It may be noted, however, that a Viking fleet in 1000 on leaving England went to Normandy, and that in the next year the coast of England opposite Normandy was ravaged, so perhaps there is some confirmation (AS. Chron., 'C', *s.a.* 1000, 1001).

[4] AS. Chron., 'C', *s.a.* 1002.

[5] *Ibid.*, *s.a.* 1013, 1014.

[6] Campbell, *Encomium Emmae*, vol. XLIV.

The fates of Normandy and England were in fact becoming inter-twined. Thus in 1013, during the same months when Sweyn was con-ducting his attack upon England, Olaf and Lacman were ravaging Brittany, and after their depredations they were received as guests in Rouen by Duke Richard II.[1] It is small wonder that the king of France was alarmed, and the assembly of Gaulish notables that he convoked at Coudres was a measure of his concern.[2] The danger was averted when Richard, perhaps by bribery, divested himself of his pagan allies, and the changing character of Norman policy at this period was further illustrated when Olaf – later to be the patron saint of the Scandinavian world – received baptism from the archbishop of Rouen.[3] Much of the future was here foreshadowed, and the situation was given further precision, when, after the death of Ethelred II, Emma joined her fortunes to those of his Scandinavian supplanter, and in July 1017 became the wife of Cnut the Great,[4] who was now king of England and soon to be the lord of a wide Scandinavian empire. All these events concerned Normandy no less than England. Nor was it merely the ruling families in the two countries that were affected. The political filiations of England with Scandinavia, the changing position of Normandy within Gaul, were equally and reciprocally involved. And the consequences were to be far-reaching.

Duke William's relations with England were thus conditioned by an interconnexion between the duchy and the kingdom, which had been formed before his birth. But if he was here the heir to a tradition, he none the less transformed it. His achievements in this matter, the manner in which they were accomplished, and the personalities who were involved have, therefore, always to be regarded in relation to those larger political problems which were posed before his time, but which were to be given a special and permanent solution as a result of his acts. At the time of his birth the political pattern which was to result from the relation between England, France, and the Scandinavian world had not been determined; and it was Normandy, uniquely placed within that pattern, which was, through Duke William, to give it final shape. Duke William's policy towards England may thus be seen to possess, even in its complex details, a logical coherence. It progressively involved the chief powers of western Europe. And it culminated in one of the most dramatic episodes of history.

[1] Above, p. 21. [2] Pfister, *Robert le Pieux*, pp. 214, 215.
[3] *Acta Sanctorum* (Palmé), July, vol. VIII, p. 125. [4] AS. Chron., 'C', *s.a.* 1017.

Even during his boyhood some of the many issues involved in this critical situation were being given more precise definition. It would seem that shortly after Cnut's establishment as king of England, the English athelings, Edward and Alfred, Emma's children by her first marriage, returned to Normandy as exiles. Their influence upon the formation of Norman policy at this time is not easy to determine, but it was not negligible. The remarriage of their mother and the friendship which prevailed between Cnut and Duke Richard II towards the end of the latter's reign must have kept them for some years in the background. After 1028, however, there is testimony to suggest that they may have been in fairly close attendance on Duke Robert I, so that William must often have seen them at his father's court. A charter given by Duke Robert for Fécamp about 1030 is, for instance, subscribed with their signs,[1] as is also a gift to Saint-Wandrille made by Robert in 1033.[2] Certain other texts also deserve consideration in this respect. Thus a charter of Duke William for Le Mont-Saint-Michel, which if genuine would fall in, or shortly before, 1042, contains in an early copy the attestation *Haduardus rex*.[3] The authenticity of this deed has, however, been legitimately questioned, and partly on the assumption that Edward would not have used the title of king at that time.[4] On the other hand, a charter given by Duke Robert to Fécamp between 1032 and 1035 commands greater confidence, and in both the early copies in which this deed survives there occurs the sign of *Edwardi regis*.[5] It is, of course, very probable that in this text (as in the suspect charter of Duke William for Le Mont-Saint-Michel) the royal title was given to Edward by a scribe writing after his accession to the English throne in 1042. The matter cannot, however, be regarded as finally settled, and whether Edward did, or did not, use the royal style at this early date, the Norman charters in which his name occurs give strong support to the statements of the Norman chroniclers that the English athelings in their exile kept alive at the Norman court their claims to the throne of England.

Nor is there any doubt that these claims were recognized and fostered by William's father. It was during this period, for example, that Goda, Edward's sister, who was with her brother in Normandy, was given in marriage to Dreux, count of the Vexin, who was Duke Robert's friend

[1] *R.A.D.N.*, no. 70.
[2] *Ibid.*, no. 69: accepted as genuine by Lot (*Saint-Wandrille*, no. 13) and by Round (*Cal. Doc. France*, no. 1422).　　　　[3] *R.A.D.N.*, no. 111; *Cart. Îles Norm.*, plate I.
[4] Haskins, *Norman Institutions*, p. 261.
[5] *R.A.D.N.*, no. 85; Haskins, *op. cit.*, plates IV and V.

and ally,[1] and beyond question the relations between Normandy and Cnut steadily deteriorated during Duke Robert's reign. It was later alleged, and it is widely believed, that the enmity between the two princes was caused by an intimate personal quarrel between them. Cnut, it is said, in order to propitiate the Norman duke gave Robert his sister Estrith, whom Robert married and subsequently repudiated. The evidence for this tale is, however, most unsatisfactory, and there is no need to have recourse to such a story to explain Robert's attitude towards England and its Danish ruler.[2] Robert may (as his apologists suggest) have been genuinely moved by the plight of the athelings, but at all events he had every reason to be apprehensive at the rapid extension of Cnut's power in the Viking world. As a result he was drawn into hostility with Cnut and became implicated in English affairs on the side of the dispossessed West Saxon dynasty. A statement by an early Norman chronicler even asserts that he planned an invasion of England on behalf of Edward and Alfred, and collected ships for that purpose. The story, which is unconfirmed, should be treated with caution, but it cannot be summarily dismissed. According to the narrative, the fleet actually set sail for England, but being harassed by a storm was diverted to Brittany to aid the Norman troops who were there engaged against Count Alan III.[3]

Cnut and Robert both died in 1035, and Anglo-Norman relations thereupon entered a new phase. In both countries the succession involved grave problems. In England, Cnut's designated heir seems to have been Harthacnut, Cnut's son by Emma, but in 1035 this man was in Denmark, and his half-brother, Harold 'Harefoot', succeeded in getting himself recognized as joint king despite the opposition of Emma and of Godwine, the powerful earl of Wessex.[4] In Normandy the troubles of William's minority were beginning. In these circumstances any Norman intervention in English affairs was clearly impossible, and the athelings who were still in the duchy were left to look after their own fortunes. And one year after the Conqueror's accession there occurred an event which was to have an enduring influence upon his subsequent policy. In 1036 Alfred the brother of Edward came to England from Normandy, ostensibly to visit his mother Emma. His advent was embarrassing to all parties in England and particularly to the supporters of Harold Harefoot with whom Earl Godwine was now

---

[1] Above, pp. 73, 74.   [2] Douglas, in *Eng. Hist. Rev.*, vol. LXV (1950), pp. 292–295.
[3] Will. Jum., p. 110.   [4] Stenton, *op. cit.*, p. 414.

joined. As a result, Godwine seized Alfred with his followers before they could reach Emma. He put many of the atheling's companions to death, and delivered Alfred himself to an escort of Harold Harefoot's men who took him on board ship, and there blinded him before bringing him to Ely, where he died from his mutilation.[1] It was a crime which shocked the conscience of even that callous age, and it was to leave a legacy of suspicion and hatred. There is good reason to believe that Edward, later king of England, always held Godwine guilty of his brother's murder, and that he never forgave the earl.[2] Moreover, it soon became clear that if in the future there was to be further Norman intervention in English affairs, the terrible fate of the Atheling Alfred might be cited as a justification.[3]

The conditions prevailing in Normandy and England at this time were such as to prevent the development of any settled policy between them. The death of Archbishop Robert of Rouen in 1037 precipitated increased disturbance in the duchy, and the English situation likewise became increasingly dominated by the rivalries of contending factions. Harold Harefoot was recognized as sole king from 1037 until his early death in June 1040, when Harthacnut became king in his turn.[4] Already, however, some of the English magnates were looking across the Channel for a successor, and in 1041 the Atheling Edward was invited to come from Normandy to England. It must have demanded considerable courage for him to accept such an invitation in view of what had so recently happened to his brother. None the less he crossed the Channel, became a member of the household of Harthacnut, and (as it seems) was recognized, at least by one faction, as the successor to the English throne.[5] On the other hand, there were Scandinavian princes whose claims could not be easily ignored. Sweyn Estrithson, of Denmark, though still a youth, might, as Cnut's nephew, be said to have an hereditary interest, whilst Magnus, king of Norway, had, apparently in 1038 or 1039, entered into a pact with Harthacnut that in the event of either of them dying without direct heirs the survivor should inherit his kingdom.[6] A critical situation was thus created when on 8 June 1042 Harthacnut, then no more than twenty-three years old, died suddenly 'as he stood at his drink'.[7]

It is not wholly certain whether the Atheling Edward was in

[1] AS. Chron., 'C', s.a. 1036; Campbell, op. cit., p. lxiii.
[2] Will. Malms., Gesta Regum, vol. 1, p. 240; and below, Appendix F.
[3] Will. Poit., pp. 11–13.   [4] AS. Chron., 'C', s.a. 1040.   [5] Ibid., s.a. 1041.
[6] Stenton, op. cit., p. 415.   [7] AS. Chron., 'C', s.a. 1042.

Normandy or England at the time of Harthacnut's death, but he was at once acclaimed king by a strong party in England 'as was his natural right'.[1] For some months it would seem that his position may have been doubtful, but he was at length fully recognized, and crowned on Easter Day 1043.[2] The event was clearly of major importance not only to England but also to Normandy. Edward, of course, owed his acceptance to the fact that he was the representative of the ancient and honoured West Saxon dynasty. But he was none the less in a special sense the protégé of Normandy, where he had spent so many years of his exile, and the Norman ducal house might well feel itself to some extent committed to his cause. Duke William himself was, it is true, only some fourteen years old at this time and his own position was precarious, but the connexion thus established was to prove of special consequence to the later development of his policy towards England.

Normandy was thus concerned from the start with the fortunes of the new king of England, who had been placed in a situation of some hazard. Edward had succeeded despite the claims of Scandinavian princes; there remained a very strong Scandinavian element in his court;[3] and the Danelaw districts in England had strong Scandinavian sympathies. It is not surprising therefore that the opening years of the reign of Edward the Confessor should have been coloured by an imminent threat from Scandinavia, and marked by the efforts which were made to withstand it. In 1043, for instance, Edward, supported by the earls of Wessex, Northumbria, and Mercia seized the person of Emma, who was apparently scheming on behalf of Magnus, and confiscated her property. In 1045 Magnus planned a large-scale invasion of England, and was only prevented from sailing because of his own war with Sweyn Estrithson of Denmark. Sweyn actually appealed to Edward for help, which was refused, and the menace to England became more acute when Magnus, having expelled him from Denmark, was once more ready to invade England. The sudden death of Magnus on 25 October 1047 may indeed have saved Edward from disaster, but the menace none the less remained. In 1048 the south-eastern shires were harried by a considerable Scandinavian force, and if the object on this occasion was plunder, it is clear that aspirations for the political reconquest of England were being fostered in the northern courts.[4]

---

[1] *Ibid.*, s.a. 1042. [2] *Ibid.*, s.a. 1043.
[3] Oleson, *Witenagemot in the Reign of Edward the Confessor*, Appendix B.
[4] AS. Chron., 'C', s.a. 1043; 'D', s.a. 1045, 1047 (equals 1046, 1048); 'E', s.a. 1043 (equals 1045).

Edward's hope of combating this threat depended upon the support he could elicit from his magnates, and here too he found himself in a position of difficulty. For the earldoms which had been created by Cnut as administrative provinces had now fallen into the hands of powerful families who between them exercised jurisdiction over the greater part of England. To implement any consistent policy therefore, Edward had in the first instance to reconcile the bitter rivalries of his great earls— Siward of Northumbria, Leofric of Mercia, and Godwine of Wessex— and if possible to use them to his own advantage. The struggles among them which ensued, and in particular the rise to dominance during these years of Godwine, earl of Wessex, was thus of major concern to the English king, and by implication a matter of moment to Normandy also. In 1045 Earl Godwine, presumably as the price of his allegiance, had forced the king to marry his daughter Edith,[1] and from that time forward the increase of the power of Godwine though not undisputed was constant. He had, it is true, to overcome the opposition of the other earls, and this, as in 1049, sometimes resulted in violent disorder. But by 1050 the family of Godwine had come to dominate the English scene. The earl of Wessex himself held all southern England from Cornwall to Kent; his eldest son Sweyn, whose career had been ruthless and disreputable, held five shires in the south-western Midlands; whilst Harold, his second son, was established as earl in Essex, East Anglia, Cambridgeshire, and Huntingdonshire. It was a concentration of power in the hands of a single family that was in itself a menace to the royal authority, and it was especially repugnant to the king since it had been achieved by the man who was charged with his brother's murder.[2]

In these circumstances it was inevitable that the king should endeavour to form his own party, and it was natural that he should turn to the connexions he had made during his exile, and in particular to the Norman duchy which had for so long given him hospitality and protection.[3] Thus Norman clerks began to appear in the royal household, and transferences of property in favour of Normans were made in the country. In Sussex, for instance, Steyning, then a port, was given to the abbey of Fécamp,[4] and Osbern the brother of William fitz Osbern, and

---

[1] AS. Chron., 'E', loc. cit. [2] Stenton, op. cit., p. 553.

[3] Round, Feudal England, pp. 317–341.

[4] Edward's declaration to this effect (Harmer, Anglo-Saxon Writs, p. 16) is not above suspicion. Harold had retaken Steyning in 1065, but Fécamp possessed it in 1086 (D.B., vol. I, fol. 17). That a grant was in fact made before 1066 is indicated by two confirmations by William (Regesta, vol. I, no. 1; Chevreux et Vernier, Archives, plates VIII). The matter is further discussed by D. Matthew, Norman Monasteries and their English Possessions, pp. 38–41.

himself a clerk, was established at Bosham which commanded the harbour of Chichester.[1] In the west, a more significant development took place in connexion with the advancement of Ralph, nicknamed 'the Timid', the son of Dreux, count of the Vexin, who had married Edward's sister. This man had come to England with the king in 1041, and received extensive lands in Herefordshire, Worcestershire, and Gloucestershire. In due course he became earl of Herefordshire, and under him a Norman colony was established. Richard, son of Scrob (a Norman), was settled in Herefordshire before 1052, and about the same time another Norman, nicknamed 'Pentecost', acquired the important manors of Burghill and Hope. Before 1050, or shortly afterwards, both these men constructed castles: 'Richard's castle' near Hereford, and the more famous stronghold of Ewias Harold which dominated the Golden Valley.[2] More important, however, was the king's success in introducing Norman prelates into the church. About 1044 Robert, abbot of Jumièges, was made bishop of London;[3] in 1049 Ulf, another Norman, became bishop of Dorchester, the see which stretched across England to include Lincoln;[4] and in 1051, after Robert of Jumièges had been promoted to Canterbury, William, a Norman clerk in the king's household, was appointed bishop of London.[5]

The infiltration of Normans into England during these years has attracted much comment, but it might be easy to exaggerate the originality of the king's policy in this respect. There is reason to believe that a group of men from Normandy had followed Edward's mother to England at the time of Emma's marriage to Ethelred II, and though these receded into the background after her marriage to Cnut, they can be regarded as the precursors of the men who responded to her son's invitation.[6] Edward's Norman policy was in short only partially dictated by his personal predilections: it flowed naturally out of the previous relations between Normandy and England. Nor, except in the Church, did it at first entail any very widespread consequences. It is to be remembered that during these years Edward could expect no personal support from Duke William who was himself engaged in a struggle for survival, and the greater men of Normandy were likewise too fully

---

[1] Will. Malms., *Gesta Pontificum*, pp. 201, 202; D.B., vol. I, fol. 17. He became bishop of Exeter in 1072.　　　　[2] Stenton, *op. cit.*, p. 554.

[3] Freeman, *op. cit.*, vol. II, p. 69.　　　　[4] AS. Chron., 'C', *s.a.* 1049.

[5] *Ibid.*, 'D', *s.a.* 1052 (equals 1051); 'E', *s.a.* 1048 (equals 1051).

[6] R. L. G. Ritchie, *Normans in England before Edward the Confessor* (Exeter, 1948).

occupied in establishing themselves in the duchy to pay much attention to England. Among the laymen who came to England from overseas during these years, few except Earl Ralph the Timid were of the first rank, and no Norman layman at this time seems to have been given possessions in England of very wide extent. None the less the tenacity with which the king pursued his Norman policy in opposition to Earl Godwine between 1042 and 1051 was bringing the affairs of the duchy and the kingdom into ever closer juxtaposition. And when in 1051 Edward found himself at last able to confront Earl Godwine on a major issue of policy, the relationship between Normandy and England was brought to a crisis.

The narratives which describe this crisis are mutually contradictory, and much controversy has taken place as to its immediate causes and consequences.[1] What is certain is that, very early in 1051, Robert of Jumièges, then bishop of London, was translated to the metropolitan see of Canterbury, and shortly afterwards, in the same year, the citizens of Dover were involved in an affray with the retinue of Eustace of Boulogne, the king's brother-in-law, who was returning to France after a visit to King Edward. Edward called in Earl Godwine to punish the citizens, but the earl, being perhaps already outraged by the appointment of Robert of Jumièges, refused to do so, and forthwith collected levies in all the earldoms under the control of his family in order to oppose the king. On his part, the king appealed to the loyalty of his subjects, called for the assistance of the Norman party he had created, and managed also to obtain the support of Earls Siward and Leofric against the rebellious earl of Wessex. The two northern earls thus came with troops to the king at Gloucester where they were joined by Earl Ralph, and they sent to their earldoms for further reinforcements. It was a trial of strength, and Edward was victorious. The opposing armies were disbanded by mutual consent, but Godwine and his sons were ordered to appear before the royal council in London to answer for their misconduct. When they refused to do so, they were condemned to banishment as rebels and forced to fly the country. It was a notable triumph for the king. Indeed, as a contemporary remarked: 'It would have seemed remarkable to everyone in England if anyone had told them that it could happen because he [Godwine] had been exalted so high even to the point of ruling the king and all England, and his sons were earls, and in the favour of the king, and his daughter married to

---

[1] B. Wilkinson, 'Freeman and the Crisis of 1051' (*Bull. John Rylands Library*, 1938).

the king.'[1] Edward had been forced to wait long for his deliverance, but by the end of 1051 it seemed complete.

The events of 1051 are, however, chiefly important in this context because they brought to a logical conclusion the earlier development of Anglo-Norman relations which we have been concerned to watch. Edward was childless; a feature of his triumph in 1051 had been his repudiation of his wife who was Godwine's daughter;[2] and there can be no reasonable doubt that before the end of 1051 he had nominated William of Normandy as his heir. It is, moreover, to 1051 itself that in all probability this grant should be assigned.[3] One authority even seems to suggest that in 1051 the duke came over to England to receive the grant in person.[4] But this, although very generally believed, is most unlikely[5] – if only for the fact that William was desperately concerned with affairs in Normandy throughout that year.[6] It is more probable that, as another narrative states,[7] Robert of Jumièges was sent to acquaint the duke of the bequest, and that he did so between mid-Lent and 21 June 1051, when on his way to Rome to seek his *pallium* as archbishop of Canterbury. The rebellion of the earl of Wessex may even have been caused by knowledge of this transaction, and the affair at Dover would in that case have to be regarded as only a secondary cause of the upheaval which followed. At all events, by the end of 1051, Godwine and his sons had been banished from England; the king who had for long received Norman support was master of his English kingdom; and Duke William of Normandy was his designated heir.

If the conditions prevailing in England at the close of 1051 had been allowed to continue, it is even possible that the political union of Normandy and England under the royal rule of a Norman duke might have been peacefully achieved. Events on both sides of the Channel were, however, at once to modify this situation. In England the year 1052 saw the re-establishment of Godwine and his sons by force of arms. The great earl had taken refuge in Flanders whilst his sons Harold and Leofwine fled to Ireland. From these countries a co-ordinated and brilliantly organized attack upon England was made by sea. It was overwhelmingly successful, and the king was forced to submit. He was compelled to readmit Godwine and his sons to their English dignities,

---

[1] AS. Chron., 'D', *s.a.* 1052 (equals 1051). [2] *Ibid.*
[3] Stenton, *op. cit.*, p. 553. [4] AS. Chron., 'D', *s.a.* 1052.
[5] The whole matter is discussed by me in *Eng. Hist. Rev.*, vol. LXVIII (1953), pp. 526–534; but see also Oleson, in *Eng. Hist. Rev.*, vol. LXII (1957), pp. 221–228.
[6] Above, pp. 55–69, and below, Appendix B. [7] Will. Jum., pp. 132, 133.

and to receive back to favour Godwine's daughter Edith as his wife. Whilst moreover some of the king's continental advisers, such as Ralph the Timid and William, bishop of London, were allowed to remain in England, most of the members of the Norman party were sent ignominiously into exile, including Robert the archbishop of Canterbury. A counter-revolution had in fact taken place, and its consequences were to be profound.[1]

The expulsion of Robert of Jumièges raised, for instance, the question of the metropolitan see he held, and a new element was introduced into Anglo-Norman politics when his place was promptly filled by Stigand, bishop of Winchester.[2] This man, whose reputation as a churchman was not untarnished,[3] had been a strong supporter of Godwine, and his promotion was clearly due to the triumphant earl. But the substitution of such a prelate, by such means, for an archbishop who had not been canonically deposed offered a challenge to the movement of ecclesiastical reform which was now being sponsored by the papacy. Stigand was in fact to be excommunicated and declared deposed by no less than five successive popes, and even in England his position was held to be so equivocal that prelates hesitated to be consecrated by him.[4] From 1052 onwards, therefore, the family of Godwine was to find itself out of favour with the reforming party in the Church, and for this reason it incurred the constant opposition of the papacy. William in Normandy could, by contrast, take considerable advantage from this situation, and he was to exploit it. The support which in 1066 he was to receive from the papacy was in fact partly inspired not only by the reformed state of the province of Rouen but also by the ecclesiastical situation which had been created in England twelve years earlier. And one of the inevitable consequences of the Norman conquest when it came was to be the final deposition of Stigand.

In 1052, however, the victory lay with the family of Godwine. The royal authority in England had been challenged and defeated, and the Norman policy of the king had been broken. Nor could the ultimate consequences of this to the future development of Anglo-Norman relations be other than catastrophic. The events of 1052 (as has been shrewdly observed) 'established the house of Godwine so firmly in power that neither the king nor any rival family could ever dislodge it.

---

[1] AS. Chron., s.a. 1052.   [2] AS. Chron., 'E', s.a. 1053.
[3] He continued to hold Winchester with Canterbury in plurality.
[4] Stenton, op. cit., p. 460.

It reduced the Normans in England to political insignificance, and thereby decided that if the duke of Normandy was ever to become king of England it could only be through war.'[1]

Whether the duke of Normandy would ever be strong enough forcibly to assert his claims on England was, however, in 1052 still very doubtful. Between 1052 and 1054 the duke was facing one of the great crises of his Norman reign, and this was not to be resolved until after the battle of Mortemer. Not before 1060 was he to be wholly free from peril. Every stage in the very confused history of England during these years was thus to be of vital concern to his future, and he must have watched with intense interest the manner in which death was changing the pattern of English politics at this time. In 1053 Earl Godwine died,[2] and since Sweyn, his eldest son had died on pilgrimage in 1052, the leadership of the family passed to his second son Harold. Two years later occurred the death of Earl Siward, and the Northumbrian earldom was given to Harold's brother Tosti, thus further increasing the power of the family.[3] Finally in 1057 two other deaths were to take place which were of great consequence to the future. In that year Earl Leofric of Mercia passed from the scene, leaving his earldom to his son Ælfgar, and on 21 December 1057 there died Earl Ralph the Timid[4] who, as a grandson of Ethelred II through his mother Goda, might have been considered as one of the possible claimants to the English throne. He passed on his claims to his brother Walter, count of the Vexin.

It was against this rapidly changing background that between 1053 and 1057 there was formed a plan to deflect the English succession away from Normandy and to substitute for Duke William a member of the West Saxon royal house. This was Edward, son of Edmund Ironsides, who since 1016 had been in exile in Hungary. He was quite unknown in England, but negotiations were opened for his return,[5] and eventually in 1057 he arrived in England accompanied, as it would seem, by his wife Agatha and his three children– Margaret, Edgar, and Christina.[6] It was an important occasion, for he came in state, with the support of the emperor, a great noble with much treasure. As was the case with Alfred in 1036, therefore, his advent was recognized as having deep political significance, and again, as in the case of Alfred, his

---

[1] *Ibid.*, pp. 558, 559.   [2] AS. Chron., 'D', *s.a.* 1053; below, Appendix F.
[3] *Ibid.*, *s.a.* 1055.   [4] *Ibid.*, *s.a.* 1057.
[5] Stenton, *op. cit.*, p. 563.   [6] Ritchie, *Normans in Scotland*, p. 8.

coming was the prelude to tragedy. He died in mysterious circumstances before he could reach the royal court. 'We do not know,' exclaimed a contemporary, 'for what reason it was brought about that he was not allowed to visit his kinsman King Edward. Alas, it was a miserable fate and grievous to all the people that he so speedily ended his life after he came to England.'[1] The words, it is true, do not in themselves warrant any specific accusation of foul play, but the phrases seem almost designed to invite suspicion, and there were many powerful men in England to whom Edward's arrival, like that of Alfred fifteen years earlier, must have been unwelcome. Nor was his removal without advantages to some of them. At all events, from this time forward Harold, earl of Wessex, seems to have begun to think of the succession for himself.

After 1057 the pre-eminence of Earl Harold in England rapidly became more marked. No royal atheling remained in the country to overshadow his prestige, and the deaths of Earls Leofric and Ralph enabled him once more to increase the territorial possessions of his house. He himself annexed Herefordshire; East Anglia passed into the hands of his brother Gyrth; whilst Leofwine, another brother, was given an earldom stretching from Buckinghamshire to Kent.[2] As a result of these arrangements Harold and his brothers, Tosti, Gyrth, and Leofwine, controlled the whole of England under the king with the exception of the Mercian earldom under Ælfgar which now had been diminished in size. It is little wonder that Ælfgar felt himself menaced. He was constantly in rebellion during these years, seeking support from Griffith, king of North Wales, and even from Scandinavian raiders. Sometimes in exile, and sometimes in precarious possession of Mercia, he survived until after 1062.[3] After his death his earldom passed to his young son Edwin, who could offer no effective opposition to the great earl of Wessex. By 1064, therefore, Harold had reached the apogee of his power, and it is little wonder that an annalist could refer to him as 'under-king' (sub-regulus).[4] Nor could it be any longer doubted that he was hoping eventually to acquire the royal dignity itself.

A new factor was thus intruded into the impending question of the English succession, and it was not only the duke of Normandy whose interests were challenged. Walter, count of the Vexin, for instance, might feel himself concerned as the grandson of Ethelred II, as might also Eustace, count of Boulogne, who as the second husband of Goda

---

[1] AS. Chron., 'D', s.a. 1057.
[2] Stenton, op. cit., p. 566.
[3] Oleson, Witenagemot, p. 117.
[4] Flor. Worc., vol. I, p. 224.

was the Confessor's brother-in-law.[1] More formidable reactions to Harold's rise might, however, be expected from Scandinavia, for after the death of Magnus the kingdom of Norway had fallen to Harold Hardraada, half-brother to St Olaf, a man whose adventures were already legendary, and whose ambitions were boundless. He certainly considered that the pact between Harthacnut and Magnus had given him a claim to the English throne, and he was ready to seize any opportunity to enforce it. The developing ambitions of the earl of Wessex thus presented to Harold Hardraada a challenge which he could hardly ignore. It is significant, therefore, that in 1058 his son attacked England on his father's behalf with a large fleet collected from the Hebrides and from Dublin,[2] and though the attempt was not successful, it clearly foreshadowed the larger invasion which Harold Hardraada was himself to make in 1066.

None the less, it was Duke William of Normandy who was most directly concerned with the developments which were taking place in England. Few political relationships in northern Europe were closer than that which had grown up between Normandy and England during the earlier half of the eleventh century, and this connexion had been fortified by the circumstances of Edward's accession, and more particularly by the promise of the English succession to the Norman duke. William was, moreover, just at this time himself attaining a position from which he could effectively assert the rights which he considered to have devolved upon him. The feudal and ecclesiastical consolidation of Normandy under its duke was now far advanced, and William's situation in France was much improved. The battle of Mortemer in 1054 was the last of the great crises of William's Norman reign, and the deaths of Geoffrey of Anjou and of Henry, king of France, in 1060 removed two most formidable rivals from his path. The same years that witnessed the rise of Earl Harold in England thus also saw the advancement of Duke William to a pre-eminent position in northern France, and in 1062 he was given the opportunity of turning that pre-eminence to practical advantage. The war of Maine which ensued was in fact to be of cardinal importance in producing the conditions that were necessary to the success of his English enterprise four years later.

It will be recalled that after the occupation of Le Mans by Geoffrey Martel in 1051, Duke William had sponsored the cause of the exiled Count Herbert II of Maine, and that a pact had been made between

---

[1] Round, *Studies in Peerage and Family History*, pp. 147–155.   [2] Stenton, *op. cit.*, p. 597.

them by which it was agreed that if Herbert died without children, Maine should pass to the Norman duke.[1] At the same time Herbert engaged himself to marry a daughter of the duke, whilst Robert, the duke's son, was betrothed to Margaret the infant sister of Herbert. So long as Geoffrey Martel lived, such arrangements were of little consequence, but after 1060 they began to be significant, and on Herbert's death on 9 March 1062[2] they precipitated a crisis. Duke William immediately claimed Maine on behalf of his son, whilst a strong party in Maine led by the border lord, Geoffrey of Mayenne, determined to resist him by putting forward as their candidate for the succession Walter, count of the Vexin, who had married Herbert's aunt Biota.[3] The situation was of particular interest since two of the most disputed fiefs of France were called in question by a single challenge: Maine which had for so long been a battle-ground between Normandy and Anjou, and the Vexin which had been similarly debatable between the duke of Normandy and the French king. William's reply to this challenge was thus understandably vigorous. Norman troops began to harry the Vexin while the duke himself invaded Maine. The war was prolonged, but before the end of 1063 William, who had captured Le Mans, had already begun to consolidate his conquest of the *comté*. The fortifications of Le Mans were strengthened; Mayenne was taken and sacked; and probably about this time the duke reconstructed his castles at Mont Barbet and Ambrières. By the beginning of 1064 he had made himself the effective master of Maine.[4]

The Norman acquisition of Maine altered the balance of power in Gaul in a manner that was substantially to affect the course of events during the next critical decade. It helped to ensure that the duke need fear no interference from northern France in any enterprise he might undertake overseas. Count Walter and his wife Biota, who after the fall of Le Mans had been taken into custody, died shortly afterwards in suspicious circumstances,[5] and the comital house of the Vexin, robbed of its chief members, passed under the leadership of a collateral branch. Walter was succeeded by his cousin Ralph of Crépi, or of Valois, whose policy towards Normandy had still to be disclosed. Similarly, the successful campaigns of 1062–1063 had freed William at last from the Angevin menace. After the death of Geoffrey Martel in 1060 a struggle

[1] Above, pp. 72, 73.　　　　　　　　　　[2] Latouche, *Comté du Maine*, p. 33, note 3.
[3] *Ibid.*, pp. 113–115.
[4] Will. Poit., pp. 91–93; Will. Jum., pp. 130, 184; Prentout, *Guillaume le Conquérant* (1936), pp. 149–153.　　　　　　　　　[5] Below, Appendix F.

for the Angevin succession developed, and for the next decade no Angevin count was to be able as heretofore to use Maine as an effective base for operations against Normandy. Finally, William's position in respect of the French royal house had also been strengthened. Since 1060 the young King Philip I, himself a minor, was the ward of the count of Flanders,[1] and able to exercise as yet no personal control over the conduct of affairs, and now just at the time when the Capetian monarchy was in eclipse the duke of Normandy had enhanced his prestige, and multiplied his resources by the conquest of Maine.

In 1064, therefore, Duke William might feel that his chance of eventually winning the long promised realm of England had been substantially improved, but he must also have realized that the rising fortunes of the earl of Wessex had erected a formidable obstacle across his path. The new security of the duke in Gaul had been won during the same years as the earl had so signally prospered in England, and now, as the life of Edward the Confessor ebbed to its close, the two men confronted each other across the Channel as possible rivals for the succession to the childless king. It was a situation which called for dramatic treatment, and it was soon to receive worthy commemoration in the famous stitchwork of the Bayeux Tapestry. The story there displayed was of course only one factor in the developing crisis which was overtaking northern Europe, but it was none the less an essential feature of that crisis. The connexion between England and Normandy which had been developing inexorably since 1035 was already in 1064 becoming crystallized into an individual opposition between two of the most remarkable personalities of eleventh-century Europe.

The relations of Duke William and Earl Harold, and their modification during the last two years of the Confessor's reign, thus possess a general importance as well as the personal interest which attaches to one of the most picturesque and controverted episodes of history. In 1064[2] (as it would seem) Earl Harold set sail from Bosham in Sussex on a mission to Europe. Almost every detail of his ensuing adventures, and their purpose, has been made the subject of controversy and no finality can be claimed for any single interpretation which may be put upon them.[3] Following the three earliest accounts[4] of these events which have survived, it may, however, seem reasonable to suggest that the earl of

---

[1] Fliche, *Philippe I*, chap. I.

[2] It is highly probable though not absolutely certain that the visit took place in that year.

[3] Douglas, *Eng. Hist. Rev.*, vol. LXVIII (1953), pp. 535–545; Oleson, *ibid.*, vol. LXXII (1957), pp. 221–228.   [4] Will. Jum., pp. 132, 133; Will. Poit., pp. 100–106; Bayeux Tapestry.

Wessex on this occasion had been commanded by the Confessor to proceed to Normandy in order formally to confirm in the presence of William the grant of the succession to the English throne which had previously been made by the king to the duke. Earl Harold, doubtless, had little liking for this task, but he may well have felt it unwise to disobey the king's order, and he may also have hoped to derive some personal advantages from its execution.[1] At all events he set out, but encountering a stiff wind he was blown out of his course and compelled to make a forced landing near the mouth of the Somme on the coast of the *comté* of Ponthieu.[2] There, 'according to the barbarous custom of the country,' he was seized by Guy, the reigning count, 'as if he were a shipwrecked mariner,' and thrown in prison within the castle of Beaurain situated some ten miles from Montreuil.[3]

The situation presented an immediate opportunity to Duke William which he was quick to seize. Perhaps the Norman duke was aware that Harold's journey was connected with the promise which had previously been given by Edward, and he appreciated at once the advantages he might obtain from personal contact with the earl of Wessex in circumstances highly favourable to himself. He therefore lost no time in demanding the person of Harold from Count Guy (who since 1054 could be regarded as in some sense a vassal of Normandy),[4] and he perhaps agreed to pay the count some ransom. Count Guy on his part felt it prudent or profitable to accede at once to the duke's request. He brought Harold to Eu, where the duke with a troop of armed horsemen came to receive him. The earl was thereupon conducted with honour to Rouen.[5] And either at Rouen,[6] or perhaps at Bayeux,[7] but more probably in the presence of an assembly of magnates held at Bonneville-sur-Touques,[8] Earl Harold was brought to swear his famous oath of fealty to the Norman duke, with particular reference to the impending question of the English succession. William of Jumièges states baldly that the earl 'swore fealty regarding the kingdom with many oaths',[9] whilst the Bayeux Tapestry indicates the solemn character

---

[1] He may have wished to safeguard his eventual position in the event of Duke William's success, and it is very probable that members of his family were at the Norman court as hostages to safeguard the duke's succession, and Harold may have wished to obtain their release.   [2] Bayeux Tapestry, plates VI, VII. There is no suggestion of a shipwreck.

[3] Will. Poit., pp. 100–102; Bayeux Tapestry, plates IX, X – 'Belrem' (*E.H.D.*, vol. II, p. 242).

[4] Ord. Vit., vol. II, pp. 237, 238.   [5] Will. Poit., p. 102.   [6] Ord. Vit., vol. II, p. 217.

[7] Bayeux Tapestry, plates XXVIII, XXIX – 'Bagias'.   [8] Will. Poit., p. 102.

[9] Will. Jum., p. 133: 'Facta fidelitate de regno plurimis sacramentis.'

of the transaction, and emphasizes the relics on which the oath was taken.[1] William of Poitiers, however, records the terms of the undertaking which was so solemnly given.[2] The earl swore to act as the duke's representative (*vicarius*) at the Confessor's court; he engaged himself to do everything in his power to secure the duke's succession in England after the Confessor's death; and in the meantime he promised to maintain garrisons in certain strongholds, and particularly at Dover. About the same time, and as part of these arrangements, Duke William vested the earl as his vassal with the arms of Norman knighthood, and (as it seems) also entered into an undertaking whereby the earl became pledged to marry one of the duke's daughters.

Such are the only facts given in the earliest accounts of this famous transaction, though legend was soon to add many embellishments to the story. Whether, as Eadmer suggested,[3] Harold acted under duress on this occasion, or was the subject of trickery,[4] must remain in doubt. Certainly, the position of the earl in Normandy was a difficult one. He may well have hesitated to defy the orders of his king, and the forceful desires of the duke who at this time was both his host and his protector. On the other hand, it is not impossible that he willingly consented to what took place, and perhaps even (as William of Malmesbury asserted) he acted here on his own initiative.[5] The perils which surrounded his own designs on the English throne were very obvious, for such an attempt could only succeed if he could obtain sufficient support at home to override the rights of surviving members of the English royal house and the claims of strong Scandinavian princes. The earl may thus perhaps have thought to safeguard his future position in the event of his own failure or the duke's success. And he may have felt that in any case he could later repudiate the oath, or plead that it had been taken under compulsion.

Whatever may have been Harold's motives on this occasion, there can be no doubt that William's policy had been clearly conceived, and the newly established relationship between the two men was demonstrated before Harold returned to England,[6] when the duke associated the earl with him as his vassal in a venture which was yet further to

[1] Plates XXVIII, XXIX (*E.H.D.*, vol. ii, p. 251).
[2] Will. Poit., pp. 104–106, 230.   [3] *Historia Novorum* (ed. Rule), p. 8.
[4] The story that the oath was taken on concealed relics is of later date. It appears in Wace, *Roman de Rou* (ed. Andresen), vol. ii, p. 258. Plate XXIX, Bayeux Tapestry, may be studied in this connexion.   [5] *Gesta Regum*, vol. i, p. 279.
[6] Will. Poit. and the Bayeux Tapestry differ as to the sequence of events, the latter placing the Breton campaign before the taking of the oath.

strengthen William's power on the eve of the English crisis. The acquisition of Maine which had been accomplished by 1064 had stabilized the western frontier of William's duchy. There remained, however, Brittany as a potential menace that needed to be removed. Since the death of Alan III in 1040 the nominal ruler of Brittany had been his young son, Conan II, whose interests were protected, albeit with great difficulty, by his mother Bertha, and opposed by his uncle Eudo of Penthièvre.[1] The result was prolonged disturbance, and it was not until 1057 that Conan was able to assert his own authority as sole ruler. Even so, he was dependent upon the precarious allegiance of the new feudal nobility which had arisen in Brittany.[2] Here was therefore another opportunity for Duke William. In 1064 Conan was engaged in operations against the Breton rebels near the stronghold of Saint-James-de-Beuvron which William had erected near the Norman border.[3] Some of the rebels, notably Riwallon of Dol, thereupon appealed to the duke, who forthwith invaded Brittany with the earl of Wessex in his force. He crossed the estuary of the Couesnon with some difficulty, and advanced to the relief of Riwallon, who was besieged in Dol. The town fell to the Norman assault, and Conan retreated towards Rennes. William thereupon moved to Dinant, which he captured. He then retired, leaving Conan to take his revenge in due course upon Riwallon, who was sent into exile.[4]

The details of William's Breton war of 1064 are highly obscure, but the results of this inconclusive fighting were considerable. A powerful Brittany, active and hostile on his western frontier, might have been a grave menace to Duke William during 1066, and in 1064 this danger was by no means to be ignored. The declaration alleged to have been made by Conan that he would resist any expedition made by William against England may safely be regarded as apocryphal,[5] but it represented what might very well have proved a disturbing factor in the development of Norman policy at this time. It had therefore been an astute move on William's part to foster opposition to Conan among the

---

[1] Lobineau, *Histoire de Bretagne*, vol. I, pp. 93–98; La Borderie, *Histoire de Bretagne*, vol. III, pp. 14–23; Durtelle de Saint Sauveur, *Histoire de Bretagne*, vol. I, p. 118. The chaotic condition of Brittany under Bertha is well illustrated in the remarkable charter printed by Morice, *Histoire de Bretagne: Preuves*, vol. I, col. 393.

[2] The character of that nobility in Brittany at this time is revealed in a charter of Conan (*Cart. de Redon*, p. 23); Morice, *op. cit., Preuves*, vol. I, col. 408; see also La Borderie, *Les Neufs Barons de Bretagne* (1905), pp. xiii, xiv.   [3] Will. Poit., p. 106.

[4] Will. Poit., pp. 106–112; Durtelle de Saint Sauveur, *op. cit.*, p. 119; Bayeux Tapestry, plates XXI–XXIV (*E.H.D.*, vol. II, pp. 248, 249).

[5] Ord. Vit., interp. Will. Jum., pp. 193, 194; and below, Appendix F.

Breton magnates, and his raids into Brittany in 1064 also served to turn Conan's attention elsewhere than Normandy during the critical years that followed. In 1065 Conan is to be found at Blois seeking an alliance against Anjou, and all through 1066 he was engaged in operations in Angevin territory until he died suddenly in December of that year while besieging Château-Gonthier.[1] His death was a further stroke of good fortune for William, but even more important was the fact that the duke had already created a powerful party of his own in Brittany. No less than four of the sons of Count Eudo of Penthièvre were to follow Duke William across the Channel, and together with many other Bretons to receive in due course large estates in England.

It is impossible not to admire the high competence of Duke William's policy in 1063–1064, or the manner in which it was steadfastly directed towards the eventual fulfilment of his English purpose. Full advantage had been taken of the weakness of the Capetian and Angevin dynasties; Maine had been added to his resources; and a strong faction in Brittany had become favourable to his cause. Finally, one of the most formidable of his potential opponents had publicly given an undertaking, recognized as sacrosanct by the feudal and ecclesiastical opinion of Europe, to support the duke's claim upon England, or at all events not to oppose it. During this same year, also, this same English magnate had been publicly displayed as the duke's vassal in a campaign which was indirectly to facilitate the later deployment of Norman arms in England. When before the end of 1064 Earl Harold returned to England, laden with gifts from Rouen,[2] his position as a possible rival to Duke William for the English throne had, in the public opinion of Europe, become irreparably compromised.

The advantage gained over the earl of Wessex by Duke William in 1064 was soon to be increased by events within England itself. In the autumn of 1065 a rebellion occurred in Northumbria against Earl Harold's brother, Tosti, who had been earl since 1055.[3] The revolt rapidly spread and the rebels, having massacred many of the earl's supporters in the north, took it upon themselves to proclaim Tosti an outlaw. They then offered his earldom to Morcar, the brother of Earl Edwin of Mercia, and in order to compel the king to confirm their acts, they marched southward in force to Northampton. Earl Harold tried to

---

[1] La Borderie, *Histoire de Bretagne*, vol. III, p. 20; Le Baud, *Histoire de Bretagne*, p. 157. He apparently captured Pouancé and Segré before his death.   [2] Will. Jum., p. 133.
[3] B. Wilkinson, 'Northumbrian Separatism in 1065 and 1066' (*Bull. John Rylands Library*, vol. XXXII (1939), pp. 504–526).

arrange some compromise in favour of his brother, but he failed to do so, and King Edward was forced to recognize Morcar as earl of Northumbria. Tosti and his wife Judith fled from England to take refuge with Judith's half-brother, Count Baldwin V of Flanders.[1] Earl Harold's position in England was thus seriously weakened by these events which removed his brother from an important earldom and substituted in his place, and against the wishes of the earl of Wessex, a member of the Mercian house of Leofric who had no reason to feel friendly to any representative of the family of Godwine.

The immediate advantage which thus accrued to Duke William is obvious. But there was a further implication of the Northumbrian revolt which was equally significant. It is wholly remarkable that despite the bitterness of the dispute of 1065 there seems to have been no desire on the part of the rebels to establish a separate kingdom north of the Humber.[2] King Edward had been compelled to accept an earl of whom he disapproved, but his status as the sole legitimate king over all England had been preserved for his successor. England, albeit comprising two ecclesiastical provinces and three great earldoms, was evidently conceived as a single kingdom whose political identity must override the differences inherent in the individual traditions of its several parts. At the same time as the resources of the earl of Wessex had been diminished, the unity of the inheritance which Edward the Confessor would leave to his successor had been sustained and indeed re-emphasized. The prize was soon to be disputed: its integrity remained unimpaired.

The long developing relationship between Normandy and England had thus at last produced a situation which involved the medieval destiny of a large part of northern Europe. The aged childless king, revered and qualifying for sainthood, was approaching his final problems. Earl Harold of Wessex, weakened by the events of 1064–1065, was still strong, and might yet acquire sufficient support in England to hold the crown he coveted. In the northern world, Harold Hardraada, representing a very strong tradition that England's true links were with the Baltic lands, was reaching the climax of his power as king of Norway, and must soon put to the test his long expressed claim to the English throne. These were no mean opponents for the duke of Normandy who, having welded a unique province into a political unity, was now, at the beginning of 1066, brought to the crisis of his fate.

[1] AS. Chron., 'C' 'D', *s.a.* 1065. [2] Wilkinson, *loc. cit.*

Chapter 8

THE CONQUEST OF ENGLAND

January 1066 – March 1067

On 5 January 1066 Edward the Confessor died childless, and the question of the English succession which had for so long loomed over northern Europe immediately entered on its final phase. Nor could there be any doubt that its settlement would involve war, or that in the conflict a crucial part must be played by Duke William whose policy towards England had been so consistently developed during the previous fifteen years. The chief actors in the ensuing drama had in fact already been brought to the forefront of the stage: Earl Harold of Wessex; Harold Hardraada, king of Norway; Tosti, the exiled earl of Northumbria; and Duke William himself. The personal rivalry between these men reflected, moreover, with considerable accuracy, the wider issues of politics which (as has been seen) had been created by the earlier relations between Normandy, Scandinavia, and England. The future of the English monarchy (and its character) was in truth but one of the issues which were at stake. The position of England for the remainder of the Middle Ages in relation to Scandinavia and Latin Europe was also to be determined, and the political and ecclesiastical structure of western Christendom was to be substantially modified. Contemporary observers were fully conscious that a crisis was at hand, and it is little wonder that many were ready to see a portentous significance in the comet which now began to illuminate the skies of western Europe.[1]

Duke William must have been aware for several weeks that the English king was dying, but even so the immediate challenge which he received must have contained an element of surprise. On the morrow of the Confessor's death – on the very day of his funeral[2] – Earl Harold

---

[1] 'When beggars die there are no comets seen.' The comet of 1066 (apparently 'Halley's comet') is mentioned with emphasis in Will. Jum. (p. 133) and is shown engagingly in the Bayeux Tapestry (plate XXXV; *E.H.D.*, vol. II, p. 255). The AS. Chron. ('C', *s.a.* 1066) says it first appeared on 24 April, and this is confirmed by *R.A.D.N.* (no. 299). To it Freeman devoted one of his most fascinating appendixes (*Norman Conquest*, vol. III, note M), and collected references to it from as far apart as Anjou and Poland. What is chiefly remarkable about the more distant references is the frequency with which they connect the comet with the English crisis.　　　　[2] Will. Poit., p. 146.

Godwineson, having obtained the support of a group of English magnates who were in London,[1] had himself crowned as king, as it would seem by Aldred, archbishop of York,[2] in the Confessor's new abbey of Saint Peter of Westminster. The indecent haste of these proceedings indicates that the earl's seizure of the throne was premeditated, and that he feared opposition. It is very probable, however, that the Confessor on his death-bed, either of his own free will or under persuasion, had nominated the earl as his successor,[3] and the solemn coronation by a metropolitan archbishop might supply a religious sanction to his new dignity. Finally, it might be argued that the perilous circumstances of the time demanded quick action. It was known that a new attack on England from Scandinavia was imminent, and Tosti, the earl's brother, following the precedent set by the family in 1052, might be expected very soon to attempt to return from Flanders by force. In these conditions, strong leadership was demanded, and such leadership could best be found in the earl of Wessex, who was already the most powerful man in England. For these reasons the chief surviving member of the old royal house, Edgar, son of Edward the atheling, who was then a lad, was set aside; and an earl, with no pretensions to royal descent, was allowed to acquire the English throne. It was, in itself, something of a revolution, and the act bore the appearance of a *coup d'état* executed with extreme speed and great resolution.

Harold Godwineson himself realized that he was staking his fortunes on force. None the less he could plead necessity, and he could command support. A chronicler of the next generation did not hesitate to regard him as, in every way, a legitimate king of England. He had been nominated by Edward the Confessor – wrote 'Florence of Worcester'[4] – he had been chosen by the chief magnates of all England, and he had been ceremoniously hallowed. Moreover, he was to prove a just king, and he was to labour for the defence of his realm. It was a notable

---

[1] Flor. Worc., vol. I, p. 226; Will. Malms., *Gesta Regum*, p. 280.

[2] Flor. Worc. (vol. I, p. 224) declares that Harold was crowned by Aldred, and this was probably the case. But Will. Poit. (p. 146) and Ord. Vit. (vol. II, p. 219; vol. IV, p. 432) state that Harold was crowned by Stigand. The Bayeux Tapestry (plate XXXIV; *E.H.D.*, vol. II, p. 255) shows Stigand performing an act evidently not unconnected with Harold's accession as king. Perhaps therefore the matter should not be regarded as finally settled.

[3] AS. Chron., 'C', 'D', *s.a.* 1065; 'E', *s.a.* 1066. But was undue pressure used by the group depicted in the Bayeux Tapestry as surrounding the dying king (plate XXXIII; *E.H.D.*, vol. II, p. 254)? Some support for this suspicion is given by the *Vita Edwardi* (ed. F. Barlow, pp. lxxiv, 77), which hints that Edward's intelligence was then impaired, and which indicates that at the last the king was 'broken with age and knew not what he said'.

[4] Flor. Worc., vol. I, p. 224.

tribute made after death to a defeated monarch who had shown himself an outstanding soldier and a brave man. Moreover, it receives some confirmation in the fact that the royal administrative system seems to have continued unimpaired under his direction.[1] Nevertheless, there was always something equivocal in Harold Godwineson's position as king. One of the most ancient royal dynasties of Europe had been set aside by a prominent member of a family which in the past had often been ruthless in the pursuit of power, and the act generated resentment in many quarters of England.[2] It was not only because of threats from overseas that (as a contemporary observer wrote) Harold 'met little quiet as long as he ruled the realm'.[3]

At the opening of his reign, it was even doubtful whether he would secure recognition outside his own earldom of Wessex. Little is known of the composition of the assembly which, in London, on the Confessor's death, acclaimed him as king. The fact that it was so rapidly summoned might suggest that it consisted merely of local personalities hastily collected to give assent to a decision already made by the powerful earl. On the other hand, the illness of the Confessor may have brought to London important men from outside Wessex. How far (as was later asserted)[4] any of those present dared to oppose the earl is likewise doubtful: the result could certainly be afterwards paraded as a unanimous acclamation.[5] But the acquiescence of many, and especially of Edwin and Morcar, earls respectively of Mercia and Northumbria, must at best have been half-hearted, and disaffection immediately broke out in the northern province.[6] In consequence, very early in his reign, Harold moved up to York, and with the aid of Wulfstan, bishop of Worcester, and doubtless also of Aldred the archbishop, he succeeded in stifling the opposition. This, however, could only be regarded as a temporary measure, and in order to retain the allegiance of Edwin and Morcar he consented, probably during the early months of his reign, to marry their sister Edith, the widow of Griffith of Wales.[7]

A king, so placed, was insecurely poised to withstand the assaults which might at any time be delivered against him by his banished brother, or by the powerful king of Norway. Indeed, if an apologia is to be made for Harold Godwineson, earl of Wessex, who became the last Anglo-Saxon king of England, it should surely be based not on later

---

[1] Stenton, *Anglo-Saxon England*, pp. 573, 574.   [2] Will. Malms., *Gesta Regum*, p. 280.
[3] AS. Chron., 'C', *s.a.* 1065.   [4] Will. Malms., *op. cit.*, p. 297.   [5] Flor. Worc., *loc. cit.*
[6] Will. Malms., *Vita Wulstani* (ed. Darlington), p. 22.   [7] Stenton, *op. cit.*, p. 523.

considerations of national patriotism (to which he was probably a stranger), nor on constitutional arguments (derived from later Whig doctrine) as to the doubtful legality of his royal title, but upon the manner in which a great warrior and a courageous man battled for nine months against adverse circumstances which, to the ultimate benefit of England, at last overwhelmed him.

To Duke William, Harold's seizure of power came as a personal affront as well as a political challenge. He had long recollections of Edward's original bequest of the English crown, and more recent remembrance of Harold's oath and vassalage. His reaction, therefore, to the news from England was swift. A protest was immediately sent to the English court,[1] but this was a formality, for the duke realized from the first that his whole political future now depended upon his ability to vindicate his claims by force. The chronology of the duke's acts during the earlier half of 1066 is somewhat confused, but their nature and purpose is clear, as is also the ultimate end to which they were all so steadfastly directed. During this critical interval, Duke William of Normandy secured the support of his vassals. He fostered divisions among his rivals. He successfully appealed to the public opinion of Europe. And he made the preparations essential for equipping the expedition which was, at last, to take him to victory overseas.

One of his first acts after he received the news of Harold's coronation was to take counsel with his magnates, and in particular with that inner circle of the new Norman nobility which had shared in his rise to power. Many of these men appear at first to have been doubtful about the risks of a projected attack on England, and a later tradition asserts that it was William fitz Osbern who persuaded them that the adventure was practicable.[2] At all events, a notable unity of purpose was early achieved, and this was deliberately fostered by the duke in a series of assemblies. William of Malmesbury asserts that a great council was held at Lillebonne, and Wace (though without naming a place) likewise speaks in detail of a large assembly which was brought enthusiastically to support Duke William's designs.[3] Again, it appears that when he was supervising the building of his ships on the Dives, the duke took council with some of his magnates at Bonneville-sur-Touques, and the project of the English invasion was certainly discussed in the great concourse of

---

[1] Will. Jum., p. 133.
[2] Will. Poit., p. 149; Ord. Vit., vol. II, p. 122; Wace, *Roman de Rou*, vol. II, pp. 270–275.
[3] Will. Poit., p. 149; Will. Malms., *Gesta Regum*, p. 299.

Norman notables, secular and ecclesiastical, who assembled at Caen in June 1066 for the dedication of the abbey of Holy Trinity.[1] How many of these assemblies were held, or what was their precise character, cannot be ascertained, but there can be no doubt that during these months the duke lost no opportunity of associating his magnates with his plans, and in view of his earlier struggles to establish his authority, the support which he was able to elicit was wholly remarkable.

Co-operation of this type was essential if the hazardous venture was to be given any chance of success. Even so, it might have seemed dangerous to leave the duchy denuded of its ruler, and of much of its armed strength. Special steps were taken therefore by the duke to provide for the administration of his duchy during his absence. Thus the Duchess Matilda assumed special responsibilities during these critical months,[2] in association with her son Robert, who was then some fourteen years of age. Robert had already appeared alongside his mother as witness to ducal charters, and in 1063, when he was less than twelve years old, he is specifically described in an instrument for Saint-Ouen as the heir designate to his parents. In 1066 his position as the future ruler of Normandy thus became crucial when his father was about to set out on an expedition from which he might never return, and it would seem that at home during the spring or summer of that year, Duke William, at one of the assemblies of his magnates, solemnly proclaimed Robert as heir to the duchy, and exacted from the chief men of Normandy an oath of fidelity to his son.[3] Robert's special position at this time seems to have been recognized even outside the boundaries of the duchy, for Bartholomew, abbot of Marmoutier, sent one of his monks to Rouen, asking for confirmation of Duke William's gifts to that house, and this was given by Robert, 'at the request of his father, who was then preparing to cross the sea and to make war against the English'.[4]

Nevertheless, the duke's own experiences in youth must have made him conscious how inadequate might prove such oaths of fidelity at a time of crisis, and a province notoriously susceptible to anarchy could not be left with confidence to the unaided tutelage of a woman and a boy. Prominent members of the new aristocracy were therefore directly associated with the administration of Normandy during the duke's absence. Chief among these was Roger of Beaumont, already an

---

[1] R.A.D.N., no. 231; Ord. Vit., vol. II, p. 125.   [2] Will. Poit., p. 260.
[3] R.A.D.N., nos. 158, 213; David, Robert Curthose, p. 12.   [4] R.A.D.N., no. 288.

elderly man, who was to be represented at Hastings by his son Robert, subsequently to become count of Meulan and earl of Leicester.[1] With him was Roger of Montgomery, who likewise remained behind in Normandy to assist the duchess.[2] Other trusted men were left in their company, among whom was Hugh, son of Richard, the powerful *vicomte* of the Avranchin, and himself eventually earl of Chester.[3] These arrangements, interesting in themselves, are mainly significant as illustrating once again the close association at this time between the Norman aristocracy and the Norman duke. It is in every way notable that no revolt occurred in Normandy during the critical period of the English venture. On the contrary, the bulk of the new Norman nobility were eager to support an extremely hazardous enterprise, and even to stake their personal fortunes on its success.

Nor was the Church in Normandy neglected at this crisis. Perhaps it was natural that Norman prelates should be anxious to obtain confirmations of grants before the duke left his duchy, and doubtless on their part Duke William and his followers wished to settle their relations with Norman religious houses before their departure. At all events, a very interesting group of surviving charters testifies in this respect to the urgency of the situation. Lanfranc was appointed to Saint Stephen's, Caen, in 1063, and on 18 June 1066, the dedication ceremony of Holy Trinity in the same town gave occasion for the ratification of the lavish endowment of Matilda's new foundation.[4] About the same time, the duke confirmed Fécamp in possession of land at Steyning in Sussex, the grant to take effect only if God should give him the victory in England.[5] In June, also, the rights of the see of Avranches over certain disputed properties were comprehensively ratified by the duke in a notable charter.[6] Similar action was also taken by many of the duke's followers, often in his presence, and with the sanction of his court. Thus it was recorded that Roger of Montgomery, with the assent of the duke, had in 1066 given land at Giverville to Holy Trinity, Rouen, at the time when 'the duke of the Normans set out across the

---

[1] Will. Poit., pp. 193, 260.

[2] Ord. Vit., vol. II, p. 178. In view of the author's connexions with the family, this is decisive against other evidence.

[3] A Whitby tradition (*Mon. Ang.*, vol. I, p. 149) asserts that Hugh of Avranches and William de Percy arrived in this country in 1067.

[4] Macdonald, *Lanfranc*, p. 56. Lanfranc was probably appointed to Saint Stephen's, Caen, in 1063. The gifts to Holy Trinity, Caen, were made in 1066 and are recorded in *R.A.D.N.* no. 231.

[5] *Regesta*, vol. I, no. 1.   [6] *R.A.D.N.*, no. 229.

sea with his fleet'.[1] Lesser men followed the same example. Roger, son of Turold, 'being about to set to sea with Duke William', gave a small estate in Sotteville-lès-Rouen to Holy Trinity, and similar grants were made in the same circumstances by Erchembald, the son of Erchembald the *vicomte*, and also by 'a certain knight', named Osmund de Bodes, who in the event was to perish on the expedition.[2] Such charters may reasonably be taken as representative of a larger number of similar instruments which have not survived, and they serve to illustrate from a new angle the temper prevailing in Normandy on the eve of the expedition to England.

Not only with his own duchy was Duke William concerned at this time. He was also at pains to justify his cause before the public conscience of Europe. At some undetermined date within the first eight months of 1066 he appealed to the papacy, and a mission was sent under the leadership of Gilbert, archdeacon of Lisieux, to ask for a judgment in the duke's favour from Alexander II.[3] No records of the case as it was heard in Rome have survived, nor is there any evidence that Harold Godwineson was ever summoned to appear in his own defence. On the other hand, the arguments used by the duke's representatives may be confidently surmised. Foremost among them must have been an insistence on Harold's oath, and its violation when the earl seized the throne. Something may also have been alleged against the house of Godwine by reference to the murder of the atheling Alfred in 1036, and to the counter-revolution of 1052. The duke could, moreover, point to the recent and notable revival in the province of Rouen, and claim that he had done much to foster it. For these reasons, the reforming papacy might legitimately look for some advantage in any victory which William might obtain over Harold. Thus was the duke of Normandy enabled to appear as the armed agent of ecclesiastical reform against a prince who through his association with Stigand had identified himself with conditions which were being denounced by the reforming party in the Church. Archdeacon Hildebrand, therefore, came vigorously to the support of Duke William, and Alexander II was led publicly to proclaim his approval of Duke William's enterprise.[4]

The success of the duke in thus obtaining a formal judgment in his favour from the highest ecclesiastical tribunal in Europe was to entail far-reaching consequences, and its significance is not to be appraised

[1] *Cart. S. Trin. Roth.*, no. XXXIX. [2] *Ibid.*, nos. XLVII, LVII, LXIII.
[3] Will. Poit., p. 152; Ord. Vit., vol. II, p. 122. [4] Jaffé, *Monumenta Gregoriana*, pp. 414–416.

without some reference to a complex of ideas which at this time was beginning to be formed in western Christendom. Duke William's propaganda was, in fact, admirably attuned not only to papal policy but also to sentiments which in the third quarter of the eleventh century were beginning to pervade the self-conscious Norman world. Ever since the battle of Civitate (1053) and the synod of Melfi (1059) the papacy had become increasingly dependent on an alliance with the Normans from which it could not escape, and the Normans on their side had been quick to appreciate the solid advantages they might obtain, say in Spain or Italy or Sicily, by posing as the champions in a holy war. The full implications of these ideas will hereafter be discussed in greater detail, for they helped to mould the character of William's royalty, and the influence which he and his fellow Normans were to exercise on England and on Europe.[1] Already in 1066, however, they must have contributed to the outcome of the important negotiations between the pope and the Norman duke. It was by no means out of keeping with the general character of papal and Norman endeavour in this age that, in the event, Duke William was to fight at Hastings under a papal banner, and with consecrated relics round his neck.[2] The venture had been made to appear – and in western Europe it was widely regarded – as something in the nature of a crusade.

It was a triumph of diplomacy. The attack upon Harold was never henceforth to be generally considered as a matter of pure aggression, and potential opposition from other European princes was thus to some degree forestalled. The duke, moreover, took other measures to exploit this advantage. The precise relations at this time between Duke William and the young King Philip I of France, who was then under the tutelage of Baldwin V, count of Flanders, are difficult to determine. Later tradition asserted that there was an interview between them, and more nearly contemporary writers suggest that the formal recognition of Robert as the duke's heir was made in the presence of King Philip and with his consent.[3] Be this as it may, it is certain that many men from France and Flanders were in due course to join in the English venture. Nor did William refrain from eliciting support, or at least neutrality, from other princes. Envoys were sent to the imperial court; and Henry IV, or the counsellors on whom the young emperor depended, were induced to make some public declaration in favour of the Norman duke.[4]

[1] Below, pp. 247–264.
[2] Will. Poit., pp. 155, 185.
[3] David, *Robert Curthose*, p. 12.
[4] Stenton, *op. cit.*, p. 578.

As a result, therefore, of papal and imperial approval, and in consequence also of the conditions prevailing in France, Duke William could appeal with some confidence for volunteers from outside his duchy, and that appeal could be made in terms whereby a crude promise of plunder was buttressed by higher considerations of moral right. As will be seen hereafter, the response to that appeal was to be considerable, so that the army which followed the duke across the sea to England was to include numbers of men recruited from outside the Norman duchy. Nor was this all. In consequence of the success of his earlier policy he found himself at this crisis very favourably placed in relation to his more immediate neighbours. Since 1054 Ponthieu had been under his overlordship.[1] Farther to the north-west, Eustace, count of Boulogne, was for the time being disposed to stand by his friend; and his earlier wars had assured him not only of strong support from among the magnates of Brittany, but also of direct assistance from Maine. He was thus singularly well placed for his enterprise, the more especially, as owing to the position he had attained in northern Gaul, he had by 1066 acquired virtual command over every French harbour on the coast stretching from the Couesnon up to the frontier of Flanders.[2]

Control of these harbours was of the utmost importance for the safety of an invading expedition, but a yet more imperative need was for the construction of ships. A permanent Norman fleet existed as early as the time of Duke Robert I,[3] but this must have been of small size, and it was certainly in 1066 quite inadequate to serve for the transport of a large invading force. By the spring of 1066, therefore, active steps were being taken in Normandy for the building of ships,[4] and something is known of the methods by which these were produced. The magnates of Normandy were required severally to make contributions of ships, and these were considerable. The testimony as to certain of the quotas individually imposed is late, and not wholly satisfactory, but it is clear that these varied in size and were imposed in manner not unlike that to be later adopted in respect of the *servitia debita* of the Norman tenants-in-chief in England.[5] In their totality they were sufficient to produce a fleet of various types of vessel whose numbers are variously estimated,

---

[1] Ord. Vit., vol. I, p. 184; vol. III, pp. 237, 238.
[2] Stenton, *op. cit.*, p. 577.   [3] Will. Jum., p. 109.
[4] Will. Poit., p. 190; Ord. Vit., vol. II, p. 134; Bayeux Tapestry, plates XXXVII, XXXVIII (*E.H.D.*, vol. II, p. 257).
[5] The curious text given in Giles, *Scriptores Willelmi* (pp. 21, 22), presents many difficulties, but it may probably be generally relied upon. Cf. Hardy, *Catalogue of Materials*, vol. II, p. 1.

but which was certainly large.[1] Nor is there any reason to doubt the later tradition that the large decorated vessel displayed in the Bayeux Tapestry as carrying the duke to England had been given by his wife Matilda, and was named the *Mora*.[2] The construction of these vessels was pushed forward with the utmost speed in the Norman ports. After May the new ships began to be concentrated in the mouth of the river Dives, where the work was continued without interruption. Nevertheless, despite the zeal displayed in the whole undertaking, it is likely that it was not completed much if at all before the beginning of August.[3] Even so, it was a remarkable achievement.

Events were in fact already demonstrating to Duke William the necessity of speed. Early in May 1066 Tosti, the brother of Harold Godwineson, who in his exile had taken refuge with his relative the count of Flanders, made his expected attempt to return to England by force. He harried the Isle of Wight, then occupied Sandwich, where he enlisted native seamen in his service, and afterwards with a fleet of sixty ships sailed up the east coast to the mouth of the Humber. While raiding in north Lincolnshire, however, his force was cut to pieces by levies raised by Earl Edwin of Mercia, and many of his surviving followers promptly deserted.[4] Tosti thereupon made his way north with a diminished fleet of twelve vessels and took refuge with Malcolm, king of Scotland, with whom he had already entered into a strict alliance.[5] His abortive attempt against England is indeed mainly significant for its bearing on the larger question of the English succession which was every day becoming more clearly the major issue of northern European politics. For Tosti had already made contact with Harold Hardraada. Whether he ever went to Norway himself is uncertain, but the Norwegian king had been made so favourable to his cause that seventeen ships came to his aid from the Orkneys which were then under Harold Hardraada's control.[6] Duke William had likewise taken an active interest in an expedition which was likely to prove embarrassing to his English opponent. A later tradition asserted that Tosti had actually

---

[1] The list of quotas adds up, it seems, to about 777, but the same record gives the total size of the fleet as 1,000 ships. Will. Jum. (p. 134) mentions the figure 3,000. Much exaggeration may here be suspected, but some of the divergence could be due to the extent to which many very small craft were counted.

[2] Giles, *op. cit.*; Bayeux Tapestry, plate XLIII (*E.H.D.*, vol. II, p. 260).

[3] For the dates on the events in 1066, see below, Appendix D.

[4] AS. Chron., 'C', *s.a.* 1066; Stenton, *op. cit.*, p. 578.

[5] *Ibid.* Cf. Simeon of Durham (*Opera*, vol. II, p. 174).

[6] Gaimar (Michel, *Chroniques*, vol. I, pp. 2, 3).

visited Normandy to seek the duke's assistance,[1] and it is probable that at least he received some limited support from the duchy. Certainly Harold Godwineson, reigning precariously as king in England, considered that Tosti's attack was the prelude to a larger invasion from Normandy. He, therefore, moved down to the Isle of Wight and began actively to organize the defence of the south coast against the Norman duke.[2]

During June, July, and August, Duke William could thus watch the rapid development of the situation. In Norway, Harold Hardraada was already known to be making elaborate preparations for invading England, and he was in touch not only with his own magnates in the Orkneys but also with Tosti who was tarrying expectantly at the court of Malcolm of Scotland. These were formidable threats to the English king, but Harold Godwineson was content to give his primary attention to Normandy. Either because he considered that the Norman attack would come first, or because he wished to reserve his full strength for the defence of his own earldom of Wessex, he concentrated his forces on the south coast. The most effective part of his army was his trained corps of housecarls, but he also called out the local levies of the southern counties, and mustered all the ships at his command.[3] It was a large force, and it waited expectantly while William's own preparations were being pushed forward on the other side of the Channel.

William himself was losing no time. His greater vassals were assembling with their own military tenants to form the nucleus of his force, and volunteers were pouring into the duchy from other lands – particularly from Maine, Brittany, and Picardy and Poitou, and probably also from Burgundy, Anjou, and even southern Italy.[4] Some of these men may have been moved by the crusading character which propaganda was giving to the enterprise, but more were moved by the prospect of the plunder which would be the reward of its success. Most of them were, however, simple mercenaries.[5] William of Poitiers speaks of the gifts by which William purchased their services,[6] and the Penitentiary alleged to have been issued in 1070 by Ermenfrid, bishop of Sitten, in respect of the war of 1066 clearly states that among the troops which supported

---

[1] Ord. Vit., interp. Will. Jum., p. 192. [2] AS. Chron., *loc. cit.* [3] *Ibid.*
[4] *Carmen*, vv. 252–260; Ord. Vit., vol. II, p. 125; Will. Poit., pp. 197, 219. Poitou was represented by Aimeri, *vicomte* of Thouars, for whom see H. Imbert, *Hist. de Thouars* (Niort 1871). He was to play an important part in the subsequent events.
[5] J. O. Prestwich, in R. Hist. Soc., *Transactions*, series 5, vol. IV, p. 24.
[6] Will. Poit., p. 150.

the duke on that occasion were not only the feudal levies but also many who were hired to fight.[1] In the spring and early summer of 1066 it was thus William's most urgent task to create a disciplined force out of these miscellaneous contingents and to ensure that they could act in harmony with one another, and with the feudal troops from the duchy. At the same time he forced forward the completion of the ships which were being massed at the mouth of the Dives. By about 12 August[2] this fleet was at last ready, and the rivals thus faced each other across the waters of the narrow seas.

The first crucial stage in the ensuing struggle was reached, and passed, on 8 September 1066,[3] a date of cardinal importance in the history of the Norman conquest of England. The problem of both commanders, William and Harold Godwineson, was to maintain a large force during the prolonged period of preparation without devastating the countryside on which it was quartered, and it was here that the Norman duke obtained his first success over his English opponent. For a whole month, remarks William of Poitiers, the duke 'utterly forbade pillage', and the extent to which his commands were obeyed is a most impressive indication of his personal dominance, and of the disciplined leadership which he was able to exercise of the miscellaneous force which had gathered under his command.

He made generous provision both for his own knights and for those from other parts, but he did not allow any of them to take their sustenance by force. The flocks and herds of the peasantry pastured unharmed throughout the province. The crops waited undisturbed for the sickle without either being trampled by the knights in their pride, or ravaged out of greed by plunderers. A weak and unarmed man might watch the swarm of soldiers without fear, and following his horse singing where he would.[4]

There is of course an element of exaggeration in this statement, but the event was to show the degree to which it was true. For on the other side of the Channel, Harold was unable to match the achievement. After weeks of waiting, it became clear that he could no longer provision, or hold together, his force. On 8 September, therefore, he was compelled to disband it. The Wessex militia was dismissed, and the king with his housecarls retired to London. The ships were also ordered to repair to the capital, and on the way thither many of them were lost.[5] The south

---

[1] Bessin, *Concilia*, pp. 50, 51. I am encouraged by the remarks of F. M. Stenton (*op. cit.*, p. 653) to take this text at its face value. None the less it presents some perplexing features.

[2] Below, Appendix D. [3] AS. Chron, 'C', *s.a.* 1066.

[4] Will. Poit., p. 152. [5] AS. Chron., *loc. cit.*

coast thus became undefended, and four days later Duke William, eager to seize his opportunity, moved his own fleet from the Dives to the mouth of the Somme in order to take advantage of the shorter sea-crossing. It arrived at Saint-Valéry, having sustained some damage in the transit. But it was speedily refitted, and the duke, everything now at last in readiness, only waited for a favourable wind in order to set sail.[1]

The wind, however, continued to blow from the north, and during the same weeks when it kept William pent in the estuary of the Somme, the situation confronting the duke of Normandy was transformed. Harold Hardraada, finding his own preparations at last complete, now launched his own attack upon England – an expedition comparable to the great Viking invasions of the age of Cnut. It is possible, but improbable, that he went first to the Orkneys to gather fresh reinforcements, but it is certain that while William was still waiting at Saint-Valéry, the Norwegian king arrived off the Tyne with no less than three hundred ships.[2] At this point (it would seem) he was joined by Tosti with such support as he had been able to collect in Scotland. Tosti became the man of the Norwegian king, and by 18 September the whole expedition had pushed up the mouth of the Humber, and effected a landing at Riccall on the Yorkshire Ouse. They then marched towards York, and at Gate Fulford outside the city they found their way barred by Edwin and Morcar with a large army summoned from Mercia and the north. There on 20 September was fought the first of the three great English battles of 1066. It was a prolonged and very sanguinary engagement, but at its close Harold Hardraada was completely victorious. Over the wrecked army of the earls he advanced to his objective. York welcomed him with enthusiasm, and after making arrangements for the submission of the city, he withdrew his troops towards his ships which were still at Riccall.[3]

The news must have come to Harold Godwineson in the south as an overwhelming shock. Nevertheless his reaction to the menace was swift. The problem before him was, in fact, clearly posed. Was it possible for him to march north, cope with the Norwegian host, and get back to the south before the wind in the Channel changed sufficiently for Duke William to sail? He attempted the formidable task, and his conduct of the ensuing campaign is a conclusive testimony to his vigour. With a

[1] Will. Poit., p. 160.
[2] Freeman, *Norman Conquest*, vol. III, p. 344; Stenton, *op. cit.*, p. 580.
[3] Freeman, *op. cit.*, p. 711; Stenton, *op. cit.*, p. 581.

full force, he immediately set out for the north. He can hardly have heard reliable news of the Norwegian attack before Harold Hardraada's landing at Riccall, but four days after the battle of Fulford, forced marches had brought him to Tadcaster. The following day he marched through York and came upon the Norwegian host which had now moved from Riccall to Stamford Bridge on the Derwent.[1] He immediately attacked, and before nightfall of 25 September he had gained one of the most complete victories of the Middle Ages.[2] Harold Hardraada and Tosti were among the slain, and the shattered remnants of their defeated host retreated to the ships at Riccall. Harold Godwineson had regained control of the north.

The campaign of Stamford Bridge marks Harold Godwineson as a notable commander. Doubtless, the Norwegian host had suffered heavy losses at Fulford, but it was none the less a formidable army under the leadership of one of the most renowned warriors of the age. Moreover, the force at the disposal of Harold Godwineson had itself been hastily collected, and it had fought under the handicap of several days of forced marches. What, however, stamps the campaign as exceptional is the fact that a commander operating from London was able to achieve surprise against a host whose movements since 20 September had been confined within twenty-five miles of York. The Norwegian king, it is true, had after Fulford been engaged in arranging for the submission of York, in withdrawing his victorious troops to Riccall and then bringing them up again to the road junction at Stamford Bridge, which he probably did not reach until the 24th. Even so, the achievement of Harold Godwineson in coming upon him unawares with an army hastily brought up from the south is very notable. His success was as deserved as it was complete, but it was yet to be seen whether it would be possible for him, after his victory, to return to the south in time to oppose the impending landing of the duke of Normandy.

The uncertain factor was the Channel wind. Duke William was himself fully conscious of this, and contemporary writers describe his supplications for a change in the weather, and picture him during these fateful days as constantly gazing towards the vane on the church tower of Saint-Valéry.[3] The event was to justify his concern. Two days after

[1] AS. Chron., *loc. cit.*

[2] A biography of William the Conqueror need not enter into the controversies respecting the campaign of Stamford Bridge. A good account of the battle is given in F. W. Brooks, *The Battle of Stamford Bridge* (East Yorks. Local Hist. Soc., 1956).

[3] Will. Poit., p. 160; *Carmen*, vv. 50–75.

Stamford Bridge, while Harold was resting his tired troops at York a favourable wind began at last to blow in the Channel. The haste with which the duke immediately started to embark his troops is graphically displayed in the Bayeux Tapestry,[1] and at nightfall on 27 September the fleet put to sea led by the duke's own galley which carried a lantern at its mast-head.[2] In mid-Channel this ship lost touch with the others, and the duke was faced with yet another personal crisis in his adventurous life. He quelled the incipient panic among his crew by supping at leisure and in good spirit 'as if he were in a room of his house at home',[3] and after an interval the remainder of the fleet appeared. The rest of the voyage was accomplished without incident, and early on the morning of 28 September the duke with his troops landed almost unopposed at Pevensey, thus completing what, judged by results, must be regarded as one of the most important amphibious operations in the history of war.

It had been achieved partly by good fortune, for it was clearly to the duke's advantage that Harold Godwineson should have been engaged in the north of England during these critical days. Nevertheless, the transit could never have been effected if the duke had not possessed for at least a number of hours the command of the narrow seas, and his initial success must thus be related both to the progressive reductions in the English royal navy which had taken place in 1049 and 1050,[4] and also to the control which he had obtained of the ports on the south side of the Channel. Even so, the full result would not have been attained had not Duke William been able to keep his force in readiness on his side of the Channel longer than did Harold on the south coast of England. If William was enabled to cross the narrow seas unopposed on the night of 27–28 September, and to land in the morning on an undefended shore, this was due in large measure to the fact that on 8 September Harold Godwineson had been compelled to disperse his militia, and to send his own ships on their unfortunate voyage to London. Finally, it must be noted that in sailing when he did, without further delay, Duke William boldly seized a hazardous opportunity. For when he sailed from Saint-Valéry at nightfall on 27 September he could hardly have known the result of Stamford Bridge, which was not decided until the evening of 25 September. In other words, when he

---

[1] Plates XXXVIII–XLII (*E.H.D.*, vol. II, pp. 258, 259).
[2] Will. Poit., p. 164; Bayeux Tapestry, plate XLIII (*E.H.D.*, vol. II, p. 260).
[3] Will. Poit., p. 165.   [4] AS. Chron., 'C', *s.a.* 1049, 1050.

put to sea on his great adventure, he probably did not know which of the two Harolds would eventually oppose him: the king of Norway, backed by a Scandinavian host with its supporters from the north of England, or Harold Godwineson at the head of troops recruited mainly from Wessex.

He had put his fortunes to the supreme hazard, and in the meantime he must take steps to safeguard his force during the precarious days following his landing in a hostile country. He hastily constructed an inner rampart within the old Roman fort of Pevensey,[1] and then he sought to take advantage of the configuration of the neighbouring coastline which was then different from what it is today.[2] It was essential that he should keep in touch with his ships until he fought the decisive battle, and Hastings he knew to be a considerable port which could provide him with a suitable harbour. Moreover, Hastings was then at the base of a little peninsula which could be defended by a covering action if it became necessary for him to re-embark his force. To the east and west it was protected by the shallow estuaries of the Brede and Bulverhythe which are now dry land, and it was guarded on the north by the resulting isthmus that was dominated by the heights around Telham Hill. Beyond stretched the thickly wooded country of the weald through which troops could only proceed with some difficulty. To Hastings, therefore, Duke William took both his troops and his ships. Within the town he erected a fortification, and there he awaited the outcome of his venture, ravaging the surrounding country in order, if possible, to stimulate his opponent to attack before his own resources were too seriously wasted.[3]

The plan was well conceived, but for its ultimate success the duke was much indebted to the impetuosity of his opponent.[4] Harold's movements at this time are very difficult to elucidate with certainty.[5] It is usually believed that he was at York when he first heard of William's landing, but it is not impossible that when the news reached him he was

---

[1] Will. Poit., p. 168.
[2] Cf. J. A. Williamson, *Evolution of England*, pp. 69–72.   [3] Will. Poit., p. 168.
[4] The battle of Hastings, and the campaign of which it was the climax, have been exhaustively discussed by modern historians, and with much disagreement. Freeman devoted a great part of his third volume to the theme, and the criticisms levelled at his descriptions by J. H. Round would fill a small book. Here I have used with gratitude: W. Spatz, *Die Schlacht von Hastings* (1896); Stenton, *op. cit.*, pp. 584–588; and a stimulating article by R. Glover, 'English Warfare in 1066' (*Eng. Hist. Rev.*, vol. LXVII (1952), pp. 1–18). Reference may also be made to A. H. Burne, *Battlefields of England*, pp. 19–45. I have been particularly indebted to J. F. C. Fuller, *Decisive Battles of the Western World*, vol. I, pp. 360–385.
[5] Below, Appendix D.

already on his way to the south. At all events, he seems to have reached London on, or about, 6 October. He tarried for some days, waiting for the reinforcements which he had summoned, and then on 11 October, accompanied by a force consisting largely of foot-soldiers, he moved southward to Hastings. His courageous response to the Norman challenge must command respect, and it was undoubtedly stimulated (as William had hoped) by a desire to stop the devastation of his earldom. But there is little doubt that his actions were here unwise. He had taken to the north a large part of the armed forces immediately available to him,[1] but such had been the speed on his return south that he had been compelled to leave behind him much of his infantry, and many of his archers. Nor was his pause in London long enough for these to be adequately replaced. Further delay would certainly have served his purpose, for William had everything to lose by procrastination, and Harold would have gained by it. Instead, he resolved on an immediate offensive, and by inviting an early engagement with depleted resources he played into the hands of his opponent.

He evidently wished to repeat the strategy he had employed with such success at Stamford Bridge, namely to take William by surprise and, if possible, by this means to cut him off from his ships. But his march over the fifty-eight miles which separate London from the Sussex Downs again imposed too heavy a strain upon his foot-soldiers. He seems to have reached the Downs during the night of 13–14 October,[2] and in the darkness to have taken up his position near the modern town of Battle. His troops were evidently in a state of great exhaustion, and in sore need of rest. When the news came to William, he realized that he had been given his great opportunity, and he was quick to seize it. He left Hastings very early in the morning of 14 October,[3] and when he reached the summit of Telham Hill he was made aware that Harold was established on the neighbouring summit. It was now 9 am,[4] and he immediately advanced across the intervening valley to attack.[5] He had been given the early battle he desired. And, in the event, it was he and not Harold who achieved surprise. William came upon Harold 'by surprise' says the Anglo-Saxon chronicler, and 'before his army was drawn up in battle array'.[6]

[1] AS. Chron., 'C', s.a. 1066.　　　　[2] Below, Appendix D.

[3] About 6 am, says Colonel Burne. General Fuller (op. cit., p. 377) thinks that the start must have been between 4.30 and 5 am to allow for assembly, the six-mile march, and the deployment.

[4] Flor. Worc., vol. I, p. 227.　　　[5] Will. Poit., p. 185.　　　[6] AS. Chron., 'D', s.a. 1066.

This achievement was, indeed, to be so crucial in determining the issue that it calls for some comment. It can in part be explained by assuming that Harold's force only reached the scene of battle very late in the darkness of 13 October or perhaps even during the small hours of the following morning,[1] and that his tired troops, some of whom may have arrived later than their leader, rested overlong after their forced march:[2] otherwise it is hard to understand why they were only being arranged in battle order as late as 9 am. The implications of the situation, however, stretched wider. It is improbable that when Harold left London he ever contemplated fighting a defensive battle at all. He had little to gain thereby, for even if, in such an engagement, he had been granted any success that was not total, he might still not have been able to prevent William from re-embarking. It is of course easy to criticize a man who was acting under terrible stress after conducting a campaign at the other end of England, and it is also true that the English losses both at Fulford and at Stamford Bridge had been heavy. Nevertheless, Harold still possessed reserves that were denied to his opponent,[3] and his best chance of success would surely have been to wait until he could attack with overwhelming force an enemy who was operating in alien territory. As it was, he was compelled with depleted resources to fight an early defensive battle against an enemy who could not afford delay. He had been out-generalled.

None the less, he was tactically well placed to conduct the defensive action which had been forced upon him. The size of the army under his command has been very variously estimated, but it probably numbered some 7,000 men.[4] Many of these, however, were inadequately equipped, and his real strength lay in the well-armed housecarls, professional warriors of high repute, who had followed Harold and his brothers,

---

[1] Will. Jum. (p. 134) says Harold rode all night and arrived at the battlefield very early in the morning.

[2] The famous story later told by Will. Malms. (*Gesta Regum*, p. 302) that the English spent the night of 13–14 October in feasting and the Normans in prayer may without undue misgivings be dismissed as propaganda. The English had no opportunity for such junketings, and the Normans were probably preparing for the engagement. In view of the self-styled crusading character which had been given to the expedition it is not impossible that William heard Mass before setting out.

[3] Flor. Worc. (vol. 1, p. 227) states that Harold left London before half his army was assembled (cf. Stenton, *op. cit.*, p. 584).

[4] I here follow Spatz (*op. cit.*, p. 33). General Fuller (*op. cit.*, p. 376) makes the interesting calculation that 'if Harold drew up his army in a phalanx of ten ranks deep to allow two feet frontage for each man in the first rank – the shield wall – and three feet frontage for those in the nine rear ranks, then on a 600-yard front his total strength would be 6,300 men, and if in twelve ranks, 7,500'.

Leofwine and Gyrth, to Sussex. Whether all, or some, of these had fought on horseback at Stamford Bridge has been disputed, but now the situation was different. The infantry and archers whom Harold had commanded when on 25 September he had defeated one of the greatest warriors of the age, had for the most part been left behind in the north, and now it was abundantly necessary that the hastily summoned levies who had replaced them should be stiffened by seasoned troops. The housecarls were, therefore, dismounted, and took their place on the hill, supplied with javelins which they could hurl, and armed with the traditional weapon of the battle-axe.[1] Such was the force that Harold had with him on his commanding summit. Its exact disposition has been much debated.[2] Tradition states that he placed his two standards – the Dragon of Wessex and his personal banner of the Fighting Man – on the spot later occupied by the high altar of Battle Abbey, and it is reasonable to suppose that his front extended some 300 yards to the east and west of this, where in each case the ground begins to fall sharply.[3] In this restricted area on the summit, his army was grouped in very close formation, and it was protected in front and on the flanks by the shields of the housecarls.[4] Such a force, so placed, would evidently be very difficult to dislodge. And it blocked the road to London.

It was, thus, against a strong position, formidably defended, that William advanced.[5] His army was probably slightly less numerous than that of Harold, but it contained a higher proportion of professional warriors, and a much larger contingent of archers. It moved forward in three main groups. On the left were the Breton auxiliaries, perhaps under Count Brian. On the right was a more miscellaneous body in which was found Robert of Beaumont and doubtless many knights from the Beaumont manors on the Risle. In the centre was the main Norman contingent with Duke William himself, relics round his neck, and the papal banner above his head.[6] Thus they moved forward and in regular

---

[1] Bayeux Tapestry, plates LXIV–LXV (*E.H.D.*, vol. II, pp. 272, 273).

[2] The site on the Downs was barren, being marked as was said (AS. Chron., 'D', *s.a.* 1066) only by a desolate apple tree.

[3] Cf. Fuller, *op. cit.*, pp. 376, 377.   [4] Will. Poit., p. 186; Spatz, *op. cit.*, pp. 34–46.

[5] Will. Malms. (*Gesta Regum*, p. 303) says that the Norman troops advanced singing a *cantilena* about Roland. This is not unlikely. On the other hand, there is nothing to suggest that this *cantilena* was the 'Song of Roland' as it appears in the earliest complete form known to us. The *Carmen* (vv. 390–400), Henry of Huntingdon (ed. Arnold, p. 202), and Wace (*Roman de Rou*, vv. 8035–8040) say that they were preceded by a minstrel named 'Taillefer', singing and juggling with his sword. It is a good story and it might even be true, though it has the elements of myth (Faral, *Jongleurs de France*, pp. 56, 57). I have commented on this further in *French Studies*, vol. XIV (1960), pp. 99, 100.   [6] Will. Poit., pp. 180–192.

formation. In the van were lightly armed foot-soldiers with slings and spears, and possibly the archers. Then followed other infantry more heavily armed. Finally came the squadrons of mounted knights equipped with hauberks and helmets, and with swords or javelins.[1]

The battle[2] began when William's light armed infantry came within range of the defenders on the hill. They discharged their own missiles and received in return a hail of weapons of all kinds: javelins, hatchets, and stones fastened to pieces of wood. Thus assailed, the attack began to waver, for the English had the advantage of the ground, and if William's archers were now employed, their arrows shot from below must either have struck the shields of the housecarls or passed over their heads. Duke William, therefore, sent in his knights in the hope of giving his mounted men the opportunity to use their swords. Fierce hand-to-hand fighting ensued, consisting mainly of single combats, and it was perhaps at this stage of the battle that Harold's brothers, Gyrth and Leofwine, were killed. But at length it became apparent that the attack had failed in its objective, which was to break the line of Harold's force. William's advancing infantry had been halted, and now his horsemen wavered, and were, at last, turned down the hill in such confusion that their retreat took on the character of a disordered flight.[3]

It was the crisis of the battle, for it would seem that Duke William's army was to some extent demoralized. One picture in the Bayeux Tapestry shows Bishop Odo attempting to rally the fleeing horsemen, and a rumour spread that Duke William himself had been killed.[4] Here perhaps was Harold's last opportunity. For if he had ordered a general advance, and had been able to control it, he might well have put the disorganized enemy to flight.[5] In the event, however, he neither ordered such a general advance, nor could he enforce the discipline necessary for a continued defensive action. Many of his men, thinking victory had been achieved, abandoned the main body on the hill, and started in

[1] Bayeux Tapestry, plates LXIV, LXVI (*E.H.D.*, vol. II, p. 273).

[2] The primary authorities for the battle of Hastings are Will. Poit. and the Bayeux Tapestry. The AS. Chron. only supplies a few incidental details as does Will. Jum. Other authorities which have been used, such as the poem of Baudri of Bourgeuil, are now discredited in this respect. G. H. White, *Complete Peerage*, vol. XII, part I, Appendix L, has argued also that the *Carmen* often attributed to Guy, bishop of Amiens, before 1068 was in fact written later and should likewise be disregarded as an independent source for the battle. Its authorship is certainly open to dispute, and there is undoubtedly some relationship between the *Carmen* and Will. Poit. It is difficult, however, always to be certain who was the copier, and rash to assert that in no case did the later writer add anything from his own independent knowledge. But, certainly, after G. H. White's criticism, the *Carmen* must be used with caution. See further, below, Appendix D.   [3] Will. Poit., pp. 188, 189.

[4] Bayeux Tapestry, plate LXVIII (*E.H.D.*, vol. II, p. 274).   [5] Fuller, *op. cit.*, pp. 378, 379.

pursuit. It was a fatal move, since the mounted knights could take advantage of their superior mobility against the isolated groups which pursued them. They wheeled, and cut them to pieces.[1] So successful, indeed, was this manœuvre that on at least two subsequent occasions it would seem that it was repeated, when the knights by means of feigned flights enticed groups of the defenders from the hill in order to destroy them.[2]

In any case, the attackers had been given an opportunity to recover. Duke William doffed his helmet, and having displayed himself to his men as still alive he succeeded in restoring order among them. The issue was, none the less, still in doubt. Harold's position had been weakened, but it was still strong, and both sides were becoming exhausted. It was at this juncture, apparently, that William introduced a new element into his conduct of the battle. Hitherto the attacks of his horsemen and his footmen had been uncoordinated: now they were to be combined. William, it is said, ordered his archers to shoot from a distance high into the air so that their arrows might fall on the heads of the defenders, and at the same time he sent his weary horsemen once again up the hill for yet another attack.[3] This time they were successful. It was perhaps now that Harold himself was killed,[4] and now the defenders were overwhelmed, and the hill position taken. A group of housecarls managed to rally for a while at a spot unsuitable for cavalry in the rear of the main position, and to inflict damage on their pursuers.[5] But there could no longer be any doubt of the outcome. The flight became general and soon turned into a slaughter, until at last, as darkness was beginning to fall, the duke called off the pursuit and brought his force back to the hill itself. He encamped for the night amid the carnage.[6]

[1] Will. Poit., p. 189.
[2] Will. Poit., p. 194. Colonel Burne and R. Glover are sceptical about the feigned flights. They are, however, well testified, and they were a feature of contemporary tactics. A feigned flight was used, for instance, by Norman knights at an engagement near Messina in 1060 (Waley, 'Combined Operations in Sicily A.D. 1060–1078', Papers of the British School at Rome, vol. XXII (1954), p. 123), and by Robert le Frison at the battle of Cassel in 1071 (Fliche, Philippe I, pp. 252–261).
[3] Will. Poit., p. 196.
[4] On the death of Harold there has been much dispute, and the matter is exhaustively discussed by G. H. White (op. cit.). The tradition that he was killed by a chance arrow is acceptable to Sir Frank Stenton (op. cit., p. 587), but he may have been otherwise slain. The contradictory evidence is supplied by the Bayeux Tapestry (plates LXXI, LXXII; E.H.D., vol. II, pp. 276, 277), by Will. Malms. (Gesta Regum, p. 363) and in the Carmen (vv. 540–550).
[5] Will. Poit., pp. 202–204. The place was afterwards known as 'Malfosse'.
[6] Bayeux Tapestry, plates LXXII, LXXIII (E.H.D., vol. II, pp. 276–278); Will. Poit., p. 204.

The battle of Hastings has been described as 'a victory over infantry won by cavalry supported by the long-range weapon of the archers'.[1] The judgment seems substantially true, but it needs qualification. It should not be taken, for instance, as implying that Harold could at no time in his reign have put armed horsemen into the field, or that if he had moved with less precipitation from the north he might not have had more archers under his command at Hastings. Again, Hastings cannot be considered a typical engagement between cavalry and infantry.[2] There is no suggestion in the evidence of what can be called the 'classic' use of cavalry – that is to say a massed charge of heavily armed horsemen, riding knee-to-knee, using their mounts to overwhelm their opponents, and then attacking with lances and swords. Nor is there any indication of the most effective reply by infantry to such an assault: namely a firm stand in concentrated mass, with a hedge of protecting spears so disposed as to make the horses 'refuse'. On the contrary, at the beginning of the action, both sides seem to have made abundant use of missile weapons which are not naturally to be associated either with attacking cavalry or with defending infantry. The housecarls had their bundles of javelins, and many of the knights were as much concerned to hurl their spears (as javelins) as to strike with them (in true cavalry fashion) as lances.

Nevertheless, though William relied much on mercenaries, it was the Norman knights who, together with the archers, were chiefly responsible for the victory, and their achievement was directly due to the fact that, however rudimentary their knowledge of cavalry tactics as later developed, they were in truth professional warriors trained to fight on horseback. So important were their mounts to their efficiency that these were brought over with them in the little ships.[3] Indeed this transportation of horses deserves note as a factor in the campaign. The Viking ancestors of the Normans had used horses in their raids, but in general they had relied upon finding them in the countries which they invaded. Nor apparently was there any horse transportation in earlier Viking expeditions against the English coast. On the other hand, the presence of horses in the boats which crossed the Channel in 1066 is given great emphasis in the Bayeux Tapestry, as a characteristic feature of the voyage. But the transport of horses in small ships presents great

[1] Douglas, *New English Review*, November 1945, p. 634.
[2] On what follows, see Glover, *op. cit.* Cf. J. W. Hollister, *Anglo-Saxon Military Institutions*, esp. pp. 136–140.
[3] Bayeux Tapestry, plates XLII, XLIII (*E.H.D.*, vol. II, pp. 259, 260).

difficulties; it is an art which needs to be learnt. Consequently it is significant that such transportation had been successfully employed in 1060–1061, by the Normans in Sicily, perhaps as a result of Byzantine instruction, for the carrying of horses by sea, had from an early date been a feature of the strategy of the eastern empire.[1] It is very possible, therefore, that Duke William in 1066 was here deliberately using knowledge recently gained by his compatriots in the Mediterranean, and this in turn may even have been translated into practice by those knights from Apulia and Sicily who accompanied his expedition.

Certainly, the duke placed special reliance upon his mounted men, and in the decisive battle at Hastings these in turn undoubtedly relied to some extent upon the force of their charge. Nor can it be doubted that these men were (in the true manner of cavalry) accustomed to act in concert.[2] They were the companions, and the followers, of the new aristocracy whose recent rise to power was a mark of the duchy from which they came. Many of the greatest figures of that nobility – such as Robert, count of Eu, Hugh of Montfort-sur-Risle, William of Warenne and Robert of Beaumont – are specifically recorded as having been present at Hastings,[3] and it is known that they brought their own knights with them. Each of these groups must have been conscious of its unity, being composed of men who were already associated as members of an honour, as suitors to the court of the same lord, and as wont to fight in company under his leadership. Perhaps it was the cohesion which this implied that enabled the knights to sustain their protracted effort at Hastings during those long and adverse hours when the issue hung in the balance. More particularly did it contribute to the ultimate victory. A feigned flight is one of the most hazardous movements to carry out at the height of an engagement, for simulated panic is very liable to be transformed into a reality of confusion. Yet if

[1] D. P. Waley, *op. cit.*, pp. 118–125.   [2] Stenton, *op. cit.*, p. 585.

[3] Individuals who can, by express evidence, be shown to have been present in William's force at Hastings are not numerous. G. H. White (*op. cit.*; also in *Genealogists' Magazine*, vol. VI (1932), pp. 51–53) gives a list of fifteen names. An independent investigation has led me to believe that it is reasonable to extend this list to thirty-three or thirty-four names ('Companions of the Conqueror', *History*, vol. XXVIII (1943), pp. 130–147). For a further comment, see J. Mason, in *Eng. Hist. Rev.*, vol. LXXI (1956), p. 61. Such measure of difference as there is between Mr White and myself on this matter may be contrasted with our emphatic agreement in repudiating the hundreds of names which have so often been cited. Could the excellent custodians of the castle of Falaise today be persuaded to revise their memorial tablets? To assert that a man 'came over with the Conqueror' is hazardous. The army which sailed from Normandy to England in 1066 was of considerable size. The ascertainable 'Companions of the Conqueror' are few. On this matter, see further A. J. Bliss in *Litera*, vol. III (Valetta, 1956).

the earliest account of the battle is to be believed this perilous device was repeatedly and successfully used. It could never have been conducted with troops who were not acting in concert, and to some extent under discipline.

Discipline, however, in the last resort, depends upon ultimate command, and the more the battle of Hastings is contemplated, the more clearly appears the personal contribution of Duke William to the final result. The quality of his leadership had indeed been displayed from the start of the war. The restraint which he imposed on his troops during the long period of waiting in Normandy enabled him to keep his force in being after Harold had been compelled to disband the *fyrd*, and to disperse his ships; and this in turn had made possible the duke's successful passage across the Channel some weeks later. In the meantime, the duke had transformed a collection of miscellaneous contingents into an army, so that he was able to seize the opportunity afforded him by the change in the wind on 27 September. Between 28 September and 13 October he once again showed himself superior to his opponent whom he successfully provoked (with the minimum of risk to himself) to the early engagement that was essential to his survival. Lastly, in the deciding battle, which he started with the advantage of surprise, the final result (so long in doubt) was first indicated when Harold failed to impose on his troops the discipline which might have turned an initial success into a victory, whilst William was able to rally his forces after their first reverse. When full recognition has been given to the good fortune which attended him, and when all deductions have been made for the exaggerations of panegyrists, who, like William of Poitiers, are ever ready to gild the laurels of victorious commanders, there can be no doubt that Duke William, by his ability, and through his personality, dominated the battlefield of Hastings, and the campaign of which it was the climax. When on the evening of 14 October he rested on the site of his victory, he was at the peak of his career. Outstanding intelligence had brought him from obscurity to be the central figure in a crisis of European history: will and tenacity, which had for so long been his companions, had enabled his cause to survive in the culminating conflict.

After his victory the duke returned to Hastings to rest his troops, and to allow time for offers of submission to come in. But no such overtures were made. Edwin and Morcar were in the capital, and steps were taken by them, by Stigand, and even by Aldred, archbishop of York, with a view to recognizing Edgar Atheling as king.[1] But the northern earls were clearly not enthusiastic over the project, which was also opposed by some of the bishops.[2] Indeed, it was not long before Edwin and Morcar withdrew to their own earldoms, leaving the south to solve its own problems.[3] Once again the political disunion of England became apparent, and after five days Duke William thought it prudent to move. His progress was marked by that blend of ruthlessness and conciliation which had already served him so well in France. Thus an attack on one of his contingents was punished by savage retaliation against Romney, and this severity induced Dover to submit without resistance. From Dover the duke advanced towards Canterbury, and before he reached its gates he was offered the submission of the city.[4] All this apparently took place before the end of October, but then the Norman progress was stayed. Five weeks' hazardous sojourn in a hostile country made it extremely difficult to feed the troops, and it is not surprising that widespread dysentery now assailed them. William himself was stricken, and he was compelled to delay for the space of nearly a month in the neighbourhood of Canterbury.[5] This pause was not, however, without advantage. The full significance of the Hastings battle was becoming more generally appreciated, and the Kentish regions, one after another, began to surrender. Soon, too, a yet more notable success was achieved. Winchester, the ancient capital of the West Saxon kings was at this time held in dower by Edith the widow of the Confessor, and now, perhaps in response to a formal demand from the duke, she offered to William the submission of the city.[6] As November drew to its close, therefore, Duke William could regard himself as master in south-eastern England. Sussex, Kent, and part of Hampshire were under his control. But the attitude of the north was still uncertain, and London lay enigmatic and formidable across his path.

The key to William's success in the campaign of the autumn of 1066 is to be found in his appreciation of the strategic importance of London. London dominated the communications of the country inasmuch as it was the nodal point at which the Roman roads from Yorkshire, the Midlands, and East Anglia converged to cross the Thames and link up with the roads that gave access to the Channel ports that were in turn essential to William's own contact with his duchy. Yet at the same time

---

[1] AS. Chron.; 'D', *s.a.* 1066; Will. Poit. (p. 215) omits the name of Aldred, perhaps rightly.
[2] Will. Malms., *Gesta Regum*, p. 307. [3] Flor. Worc., vol. 1, p. 228. [4] Will. Poit., pp. 210–214.
[5] This place is described by Will. Poit. as the 'Broken Tower'. [6] *Carmen*, vv. 620–630.

London was too large both in area and population for William to contemplate its capture by direct assault with the force that he had at his command. He therefore determined to isolate the capital. He moved up to the south end of London Bridge, where he beat off a body of Edgar Atheling's troops which sallied out to attack him. Then having fired Southwark, he moved westward, devastating northern Hampshire and passing on into Berkshire. Turning north, he then made the crossing of the Thames at Wallingford and thence, in his circuitous movement, he at last came to Berkhampstead.[1] It was a brutal march, but William's military objective had been gained. The capital had been isolated, and the results were immediately to be disclosed.

Already, while William was at Wallingford, Stigand came out from the city to transfer his allegiance to the duke,[2] and then at Berkhamstead: '[William] was met by Archbishop Aldred, and the Atheling Edgar and Earl Edwin and Earl Morcar, and all the chief men of London. And they submitted after most damage had been done . . . and they gave hostages, and he promised that he would be a gracious liege lord.'[3] It was a formal recognition by the chief men of England, and all that remained necessary was for the Norman magnates in their turn to acquiesce in William's assuming the royal title. This recognition too was given after an interval, and thus it was that William was at last enabled, with the support of leading men of England and Normandy, to make a direct advance upon London. Whether any further resistance was offered by the city is uncertain.[4] In any case, no opposition could any longer stand a chance of success, and a few days before Christmas William entered his new capital.

Arrangements were immediately made for his coronation. And at length on Christmas Day 1066 William, duke of Normandy, was hallowed as king of the English in the Confessor's abbey of Westminster according to the ancient English rite, the unction being performed by Aldred, archbishop of York, in place of the schismatic Stigand. As an innovation, however, the new king was presented to the people by Archbishop Aldred, speaking in English, and by Bishop Geoffrey of Coutances, speaking in French. And this provoked a mishap, for the mercenary troops who were guarding the minster, misunderstanding the shouts which marked the acclamation, and thinking a riot

---

[1] AS. Chron., 'D', s.a. 1066.   [2] Will. Poit., p. 216.   [3] AS. Chron., loc. cit.
[4] Will. Jum. (p. 136) suggests a further skirmish outside the walls. Will. Poit. (p. 220) and the AS. Chron. (loc. cit.) imply that the city surrendered without further resistance.

was starting, began to set fire to the neighbouring houses.[1] It was indeed a portentous event, and for a time it caused alarm and confusion within the abbey itself. Nothing, however, could impair the legal consequence of what had taken place. Duke William of Normandy was now king of the English.

The full significance of William's coronation will be discussed here-after.[2] At once it enabled him to assume all the rights and responsibilities of an Old English king, to employ the service of those local officials who were in office, and, though he was as yet in possession of only a portion of the country, to proclaim the king's peace over all England. Much remained, however, to be done before such claims could be translated in practice, and for the moment the military situation demanded the first attention of the new king. He forthwith began to construct the fortress which later became the Tower of London in order to control the capital, and himself moved out with his force to Barking, thus completing the encirclement of the metropolis.[3] At Barking, too, he summoned a further concourse of English magnates from whom he demanded submission and recognition, and to whom in return he gave a fresh pledge of good government. It was the logical termination of the campaign which had started some four months earlier when he had set sail, with so much in doubt, from Saint-Valéry.

The success of that campaign which had been spectacularly demonstrated in the coronation was such that by the beginning of March, within three months of his crowning, William felt it safe to return to Normandy, leaving England in the charge of trusted Norman magnates. William fitz Osbern, his steward, was established at Norwich, or perhaps at Winchester, whilst Odo, bishop of Bayeux, the king's half-brother, was entrusted, in particular, with the castle of Dover and the region of Kent.[4] With them also were Hugh of Grandmesnil from the neighbourhood of Lisieux, and Hugh of Montfort-sur-Risle.[5] Having made these arrangements, the king set off towards the south, and he took with him as hostages a large group of the most important men of England, particularly those who had been among his former opponents. The procession which moved towards the Sussex coast from London, and on past the Downs where the great battle had so recently taken place, included

<hr>

[1] Will. Poit., p. 220.   [2] Below, chap. 10.
[3] Will. Poit., pp. 218, 237. But the possibility of a confusion with Berkhamstead cannot be disregarded.
[4] Will. Poit., p. 238; Stenton, *William the Conqueror*, p. 244.
[5] Will. Poit., p. 240; Ord. Vit., vol. II, p. 167; Douglas, *Domesday Monachorum*, p. 66.

not only the new king's personal entourage, but also Edgar the atheling, the Earls Edwin and Morcar, Waltheof, and Archbishop Stigand.[1] In the king's absence there was to remain in England no obvious leader who could serve as the rallying point of a revolt.

It was in the nature of a triumphal progress, and so it was made to appear. The port appropriately chosen for embarkation was Pevensey, and white sails were fitted to the ships in token of victory and peace. Thus across a calm sea did the new king pass over to his native duchy. The occasion was indeed exactly calculated to fire the Norman imagination. The curious and detailed comparison made by William of Poitiers between the English invasions of William and of Julius Caesar illustrates the kind of impression which might be created in the mind of a man of letters living in Normandy. But less sophisticated individuals had other, and more convincing proofs, of what had been achieved. They could see displayed the treasure in money and in kind which had been brought from England as spoils of victory, and they could watch in the new king's court prominent and powerful men who had recently resisted him. Small wonder that the victorious ruler of Normandy was, on his return, hailed with enthusiastic acclamation, or that the inhabitants of Rouen swarmed out to meet him as he approached. Some of the older among them could recall how sixteen years before he had regained his capital after a long war in which he had barely survived, and in the interval an astonishing transformation had occurred. Only seven months ago Michaelmas had been commemorated in the Rouen churches while the issue of the English enterprise still hung in the balance. Now it was Lent. But a great kingdom had been added to the Norman dominion; and it seemed fitting that preparations should immediately be begun for the celebration of Easter.[2]

Nor was it entirely out of keeping either with the occasion, or with earlier Norman policy, that very much of William's victorious progress through Normandy at this time should have been directed towards the Norman churches. The new king kept Easter 1067 at the ducal monastery of Fécamp, and at the feast the full pageantry of the Conquest was displayed. The court was splendid. It was attended by a very large assemblage of Norman magnates, both lay and ecclesiastical, and also by visiting notables from France such as Ralph of Mondidier, the step-father of the young king of France. A great gathering admired the

---

[1] AS. Chron., 'D', *s.a.* 1066.
[2] Will. Poit., pp. 242–260; Ord. Vit., vol. ii, pp. 167, 168.

stature and bearing of the English nobles who were in gilded captivity, and the spectators were astonished at the richness of the gold and silver vessels, the treasures of metalwork and embroidery which had been brought to adorn the banquets.[1] It was perhaps the climax of the Norman celebration of victory, and it was marked of course by lavish gifts to the monastery itself, for Fécamp had for long been specially interested in the English venture by reason of the possessions it had already acquired in Sussex, and these were doubtless now confirmed. Nor was this the only Norman monastery which was enriched. The chroniclers insist that the royal gifts were lavish and widespread, and some illustration of this largess is to be found in the charters of Holy Trinity, Rouen.[2] By 1 May, William moved on to Saint-Pierre-sur-Dives near to where he had waited through so many anxious weeks during the previous autumn. There the abbey of Saint Mary had been founded by the Countess Lesceline of Eu, whose son, Count Robert, had fought at Hastings, and now the church was formally consecrated.[3] Then the king continued his progress. Towards the end of June he reached Jumièges, where he was met by Maurilius, the aged metropolitan of Rouen, who arrived in time to perform the last public act of his own distinguished career. On 1 July, in the presence of a large company, including the bishops of Lisieux, Avranches, and Évreux, Maurilius solemnly hallowed the abbey-church which had been begun more than twenty years before by Abbot Robert, later archbishop of Canterbury.[4] The king also took part in the ceremony, and it was about this time that by royal charter he gave Hayling Island to the great Norman monastery.[5]

Little further is known about William's acts in his duchy during these months of festival, though he was at this time to sponsor two important ecclesiastical appointments, the one to the metropolitan see of Rouen, and the other to the bishopric of Avranches.[6] But enough testimony has survived to indicate the manner in which his victory was received in Normandy, and how the duchy appears to have been conscious of having been brought to the zenith of its achievement by the greatest

[1] *Ibid.*   [2] *Cart. S. Trin. Roth.*, nos. XLVII, LXIII.
[3] Ord. Vit., vol. II, p. 168; *Gall. Christ.*, vol. XI; *Instrumenta*, col. 153.
[4] Will. Jum., p. 187. The remains of this church can still be seen.
[5] *Chartes de Jumièges*, no. XXIX. The arguments of the editor for dating this deed 'about 1073' seem inadmissible. On the other hand, the absence of prelates among the attestations suggests that it was not given on the occasion of the consecration by Maurilius of the cathedral at Rouen. Perhaps it was given in England either early in 1067 or in 1068 after William's return from Normandy.
[6] Maurilius died 8 August 1067. John, son of Count Rodulf, was translated from Avranches to Rouen. His place at Avranches was taken by an Italian named Michael.

of its dukes. There may well be truth, as well as admiration, in the assertion of the chroniclers that during this time William was particularly zealous in the proclamation of law, and the maintenance of order,[1] for he too had reached a new peak of authority, and, in the plenitude of royalty, he was faced with new opportunities and new obligations. Amid the acclaim of Rouen, and the splendour of the Fécamp feast, during the celebrations on the Dives and at Jumièges, William must surely often have reflected on the astonishing career which had brought him to this pinnacle of power. But he must at the same time have been acutely conscious that the very magnitude of his achievement now confronted him with new and intractable problems. The Anglo-Norman kingdom had been established. But it was still uncertain whether it could endure.

[1] Will. Poit., p. 262.

Chapter 9

THE DEFENCE OF
THE ANGLO-NORMAN KINGDOM

March 1067 – November 1085

In the summer of 1067, as William moved in triumph from Rouen to Fécamp, from the Dives to Jumièges, he was not only, as few of his predecessors had been, effectively master of Normandy, but he was also the consecrated and acknowledged king of the English. None the less his position was by no means secure. In France, Maine and Brittany were restive, and the French monarchy, whose heir was growing up to manhood, was ill-disposed towards its most powerful vassal. In England, only a part of the country was as yet under Norman control, and beyond the English frontiers, which were themselves ill-defined, stood apprehensive the Welsh princes and the Scottish king. Finally, there remained the longstanding opposition of Scandinavia to any control of England by Normandy. The defeat of Harold Hardraada at Stamford Bridge had prepared the way for William's victory, but other northern rulers would not lightly relinquish their ancient claims on a country which had recently formed a part of the Scandinavian political world.

Thus while the decision of 1066 was to mark an epoch, it was not in itself final, and it had to be confirmed. Its fulfilment in fact depended upon three main conditions. It was essential that Norman strength, as developed during the past fifty years, should be maintained, so that the duchy should retain its predominant place among the powers of northern Gaul. Secondly, the conquest of England had to be completed, and the surviving elements of opposition to the new order reduced to obedience. Thirdly, the continuing Scandinavian threat to the Anglo-Norman state had to be withstood. These three problems were, moreover, closely linked, and the manner in which one or other of them was dominant at any period of the reign can be roughly deduced from the movements of William himself. From the end of 1067 to 1072 he was primarily engaged in suppressing English rebellions, and establishing his power. From 1073 to 1085 he spent most of his time in Normandy.

And, throughout, he had constantly to withstand attacks from Scandinavia. These took place, for instance, in 1069 and 1070; the threat appeared again in 1075; and it was the menace of another and very formidable attack which brought the Conqueror back to England towards the end of 1085. Between December 1085 and September 1087 he was to make some of his most lasting contributions to the future development of England, but, none the less, his last days were spent in defensive warfare on the Norman frontiers, and he was to die within sound of the church bells of Rouen.

In 1067, however, it was the English situation which was the most precarious. The task of the regents William fitz Osbern and Bishop Odo was not easy. They had substantial control over the south-east of the country, and the formal submission of the chief English magnates gave them a claim to obedience elsewhere. Nevertheless there were many who were ready to take advantage of the unsettled conditions, and prominent among them was a west-country magnate named Edric the Wild who raised a revolt in Herefordshire, and called to his assistance the Welsh princes, Bleddyn and Riwallon.[1] They did much damage but failed to obtain control of the shire, and retired with their booty back into Wales, where they prepared for further raiding. Meanwhile, a better organized revolt took place in Kent, where the insurgents called to their assistance Eustace, count of Boulogne.[2] It was a strange appeal, since Eustace in the previous year had fought at William's side at Hastings. He may now, however, have been influenced by the death on 1 September 1067 of his overlord Count Baldwin V of Flanders, who in 1066 had been friendly, or at least neutral, towards William.[3] At all events, Eustace, doubtless recalling his earlier adventures in Kent in 1051, crossed over the Channel with a substantial contingent of knights. Both the regents were at that time north of the Thames, and Eustace was enabled to occupy the town of Dover. But he failed to take the newly erected castle, and a sortie from the garrison cut his force to

---

[1] AS. Chron., 'D', s.a. 1067. On Edric the Wild – 'Silvaticus', 'Guilda' – there has been much learning. The curious may be referred to Freeman (*Norman Conquest*, vol. IV, note I), and to Ritchie (*Normans in Scotland*, chap. I). See also Douglas, *Feudal Documents*, pp. xci–xciii. Ordericus (vol. II, p. 166) says he made his submission at Barking. Legends, moreover, gathered rapidly about him. Thus after dinner one night he came on the fairies dancing, and fell in love with one of them whom he married (Walter Map, *De Nugis*, vol. II, p. 12). The king heard of this and ordered her to be brought to court. A conversation between William the Conqueror and the Queen of the Fairies would have been worth hearing.

[2] Will. Poit., p. 264; Will. Jum., p. 138.

[3] Prou, *Rec. Actes – Philippe I*, p. xxxii. If this suggestion were correct, the raid of Eustace took place in the autumn of 1067.

pieces; whereupon he made an ignominious escape across the Channel. Neither of these risings had in fact seriously disturbed the new government. But a threat of more serious danger was already foreshadowed. According to William of Poitiers, overtures were now being made to the Danes,[1] and an invasion of England by Sweyn Estrithson was becoming an imminent possibility. It was in fact probably with this apprehension that on 6 December 1067 William himself came back from Normandy to England.[2]

On his return, however, his immediate attention was directed towards the south-west. The city of Exeter refused to accept the new régime, and sought to form a league of resistance among the neighbouring towns. William's reply was to march at once into Devonshire at the head of a force which included many English mercenaries. The thegns of Devonshire seem to have accepted the new king, but Exeter itself held out against him for eighteen days, and then at last only surrendered on the understanding that its ancient privileges should be confirmed.[3] Thereupon the king built a castle within the city, and proceeded into Cornwall, where was soon to be established his half-brother, Robert, count of Mortain.[4] Resistance in the south-west in fact was everywhere breaking down. To this period must be assigned the submission of Gloucester, and evidently Bristol had also by now accepted the new order.[5] Indeed, in this same summer, when three of the illegitimate sons of Harold came over from Ireland, they were repelled by the citizens of Bristol, and on their retreat their force was routed by the thegns of northern Somerset.[6] William's rapid campaign in the south-west had in fact been so successful that he could return at once towards his capital. He celebrated Easter 1068 at Winchester, and at Whitsuntide he held a great court at Westminster which was attended by many English notables. Thither too came Matilda, his wife, to be solemnly crowned as queen.[7]

These ceremonies were impressive, but the respite they reflected was short-lived. Very soon there were significant desertions from the new king's court. Edgar the atheling had already taken refuge with Malcolm, king of Scotland, and now Earls Edwin and Morcar departed to their

---

[1] Will. Poit., p. 264.   [2] AS. Chron., 'D', 'E', s.a. 1067.

[3] Ibid.; Ord. Vit., vol. II, p. 180; Round, Feudal England, p. 433. Gytha, the widow of Godwine, had taken refuge at Exeter, and on its surrender she went to the island of Flatholme in the Bristol Channel.

[4] Ord. Vit., vol. II, p. 180; Complete Peerage, vol. III, p. 428.

[5] Freeman, op. cit., vol. IV, p. 175.

[6] AS. Chron., loc. cit.   [7] Ibid.; Ord. Vit., vol. II, p. 181; Regesta, vol. I, no. 23.

earldoms. The Norman settlement had as yet barely affected the north, where despite the efforts of Archbishop Aldred a serious movement of resistance was rapidly growing. During the period immediately following King William's accession, Northumbria had been disputed between Osulf, a protégé of Earl Morcar, and Copsige a former adherent of Tosti. Both had perished in the struggle between them, but in 1068 local resistance was forming not only round Earl Morcar himself but also round Gospatric, a descendant of the more ancient Northumbrian house. Appeals were also being made both to Malcolm and to Sweyn Estrithson. In these circumstances, William thought it necessary to move northward at once. He went first to Warwick, where he placed Henry of Beaumont in charge of a newly built castle and then on to Nottingham. From there he moved up into Yorkshire and was able to enter York without a battle. Having received the formal submission of many of the local magnates, he negotiated a temporary truce with the Scottish king, and after erecting a castle on the spot now marked by Clifford's Tower, he turned southward to enforce the submission of Lincoln, Huntingdon, and Cambridge.[1]

William's extraordinary activity during the first nine months of 1068 deserves note, for during this short period he had conducted an almost uninterrupted series of campaigns which had brought him in turn to Exeter, to Warwick, to York, and then through a large part of eastern England. Yet such respite as had thus been gained was to be short-lived, for the north was soon again to demand his presence. Late in 1068 a Norman, Robert de Commines, had been sent, with the title of earl, to restore order north of the Tees. But, on his arrival at Durham, he was, on 28 January 1069, set upon in the streets of that city, and subsequently burnt to death in the bishop's house.[2] The news quickly passed to York, where the Norman garrison was immediately attacked by local insurgents, and on hearing of these events Edgar Atheling at once made preparations to move down from Scotland. King William was thus forced to return to the north with all speed, and his march in this respect deserves some comparison with that of Harold to Yorkshire in 1066. The king was in York before his enemies expected him, and he dispersed the besiegers of the castle, thus taking possession of the city for the second time. On this occasion he took signal vengeance on the rebels, and set up a new castle near the town. Then, doubtless as a temporary

[1] Ord. Vit., vol. II, p. 185; Stenton, *William the Conqueror*, p. 265.
[2] Simeon of Durham, *Hist. Regum* (*Opera*, vol. II, p. 187).

measure, he placed Gospatric in charge of the earldom. But he could not himself afford to delay, and by 12 April 1069 he was back again at Winchester.[1]

Perhaps the most salient feature of the confused events that occurred in England between the beginning of 1067 and the spring of 1069 was the comparative ease with which the king, and his lieutenants, having at their disposal only a limited number of troops in a newly occupied land, were enabled to suppress each rising as it occurred. This may partly be ascribed to the severe losses which had assailed the warrior class in England during the great battles of 1066. Still more must it be attributed to the lack of any common purpose among the insurgents whose efforts were made in isolation and without any contact with one another. Again, there was, almost from the first, a substantial body of opinion which was favourable, or at least not actively hostile, to the new régime. Many of the ecclesiastics who had been appointed during the reign of Edward the Confessor such as Giso, bishop of Wells, William, bishop of London, or Baldwin, abbot of Bury St Edmunds were committed to the cause of the new king, and it is yet more significant that respected English prelates such as Wulfstan of Worcester and Aldred of York were likewise ready to support him. Nor could their example be wholly disregarded by lesser men. The 'Englishmen' who marched under King William to the assault of Exeter in 1068 may have been for the most part adventurers serving for pay, but there were many thegns and local officials who were ready to accept William as their king, and to help carry on the administration which he conducted. It was the thegns of Somerset who repelled the sons of Harold, and sheriffs of native stock found themselves with Bishops Giso and Wulfstan the recipients of the new king's writs.[2]

It was William's achievement to exploit these favourable conditions, by developing such advantages as he possessed in the techniques of war. The trained mounted troops who had stood him in such good stead at Hastings could be employed in effecting the swift reduction of scattered forces in a hostile countryside, but they were little use in operations against cities, and, by themselves, they were ill-adapted for holding down regions whose doubtful submission had only been hazardously acquired. For this purpose the establishment of fortified strong-points was essential, and contemporaries are unanimous in their opinion that much of William's success in these campaigns was due to his use of the

[1] *Regesta*, vol. I, no. 23. [2] *Regesta*, vol. I, nos. 7, 9

castle[1] which, as has been seen, had been consistently developed in Normandy, both by the dukes and by the new aristocracy.

The employment of the castle, not only as a fortified centre of administration but also as a means for conducting a campaign, had already before 1066 become a normal feature of Norman military life. In England, on the contrary, except in Normanized Herefordshire, its use had hardly been adopted, and it was regarded as a continental innovation of doubtful value. To the absence of castles, indeed, Ordericus Vitalis, who is here following William of Poitiers, attributes the lack of success of the opponents of King William in England during this warfare.[2] Such was the English situation. By contrast, William in his English campaigns evidently employed precisely the same device which he had earlier used in France, and the Bayeux Tapestry shows no substantial difference between the castles at Dol, Rennes, or Dinant, and that which was erected at Hastings in 1066.[3] Here, again, the castle is of the typical motte and bailey pattern which was already familiar in the duchy – that is to say, an earthen mound surrounded by a fosse, and surmounted by a palisaded rampart, crowned with a wooden tower. It could be speedily constructed, and it proved highly effective. Castles of this type were thus at once set up at Pevensey, at Hastings, and even at London, where an erection of this type, built about the time of the coronation, preceded the stone fortification which was to be the Tower of London.[4] It was, however, during the campaigns of 1067, and more particularly in 1068, that the Norman castle as an instrument of war was fully used for the first time in England. The surrender of Exeter was marked by the beginnings of 'Rougemont Castle', and as William proceeded northwards the same plan was continued at Warwick and Nottingham. York at this time received its first castle, and on William's return march castles were erected at Lincoln, Huntingdon, and Cambridge.[5]

Some idea of the importance attached to these castles can be obtained by a contemplation of the men to whom they were entrusted. For these were chosen from among the most important of the Norman magnates. Thus Dover, within the special province of Odo of Bayeux, was put

---

[1] See generally, E. S. Armitage, *Early Norman Castles in the British Isles* (1912).
[2] Ord. Vit., vol. II, p. 184.   [3] *E.H.D.*, vol. II, p. 250.
[4] Will. Poit., p. 169; Ord. Vit., vol. II, p. 165; Armitage, *op. cit.*, p. 229. The stone Tower of London was begun about a decade later under the supervision of Gundulf, bishop of Rochester (Hearne, *Textus Roffensis*, p. 212).
[5] Ord. Vit., vol. II, pp. 181–185; Armitage, *op. cit.*, pp. 151, 242.

under Hugh of Montfort-sur-Risle.[1] The castle at Hastings, first given in charge to Humphrey of Tilleul, was soon to be the responsibility of Robert, count of Eu.[2] The castle at Exeter was given to Baldwin of Meules, the brother of Richard fitz Gilbert, later of Clare, and the son of Gilbert of Brionne, the count. Warwick was assigned to Henry of Beaumont, brother of Robert, and son of the veteran Roger of Beaumont, who had in 1066 been left in Normandy as one of the regents.[3] The first castle at York was entrusted to William Malet of Graville-Sainte-Honorine, near Le Havre,[4] and the second castle at York was to be given to William fitz Osbern himself.[5] Soon the Norman castles in England were to multiply, and what in 1068 was essentially a device of war came to be a permanent feature of the new feudal administrative order which the Norman here established. Indeed, before the end of the eleventh century there had been erected in England at least eighty-four castles, and a few of these were even then being reconstructed in stone.[6] Already, however, by the beginning of 1069, the motte and bailey castle, in charge of a trusted lieutenant of the king, was proving itself an essential, and a highly effective, instrument by which the conquest of England might be completed.

Yet, when all is said, much of William's success between January 1068 and the summer of 1069 must be attributed to the phenomenal energy which he personally displayed at this time. To appreciate the quality of his astonishing activity it is, however, necessary also to note the possibility that during these months, possibly towards the end of 1068,[7] but more

[1] Will. Poit., p. 267; Will. Jum., p. 138.

[2] Ord. Vit., vol. II, p. 186; vol. III, p. 111; Mason, *Eng. Hist. Rev.*, vol. LXVI (1956), p. 61.

[3] Ord. Vit., vol. II, pp. 181, 184. Henry must have been very young at the time, for his elder brother Robert was a *tiro* at Hastings.

[4] Ord. Vit., vol. II, 188. William Malet is a difficult personality. He may have been in England before the Conquest, and one report says that the Conqueror entrusted to him the burial of Harold after Hastings (Freeman, *op. cit.*, vol. III, p. 514).

[5] He is back at Winchester on 13 April 1069 (*Regesta*, vol. I, no. 26).

[6] *e.g.* Lincoln, Colchester, Dover, Richmond.

[7] It is usually stated that the Conqueror was continuously in England during 1068. This is doubtless correct, but the matter is by no means clear. Two Norman charters which passed in his presence are dated 1068. The one is for Troarn (Sauvage, *L'abbaye de Troarn, Preuves*, no. II; cf. *Regesta*, vol. II, p. 391); the other is for Saint-Pierre de la Couture (*Cart. S. Pierre*, no. XV). Neither of these texts is wholly satisfactory in its present form, but the main reason why suspicion has fallen upon them is that they conflict with the assumed chronology of William's movements at this time. Recently, however, L. Musset has printed the text of two charters for the abbey of Saint-Gabriel in Calvados. These are stated to have passed in William's presence at Valognes, and they are dated 1069 (*Actes Inédits du XIᵉ Siècle*, pp. 21–23 – *Bull. Soc. Antiq. Norm.*, 1954). If these, in fact, were given at Christmas 1068 they might have been thus dated by a clerk who began the year at Christmas. On this hypothesis, they could be made to supply some confirmation of the other two Norman charters. Too much

probably in the early summer of 1069,[1] he found it necessary to return to Normandy. Perhaps he deemed it necessary at this critical juncture in his affairs to display his authority south of the Channel, and it is at all events certain that about this time Matilda returned to Normandy so that she might be received with royal honours in the duchy.[2] But his sojourn in Normandy, if in fact it occurred, must in any case have been brief,[3] for the English situation demanded his constant vigilance. By the summer of 1069 William might be said to have established himself in effective control over most of England south of the Humber. Now, however, the whole Norman position in England was to be tested more drastically than ever before.

In the summer of 1069 Sweyn Estrithson launched his long antici-pated attack upon England. It was planned on a scale comparable with that of the invasion of Harold Hardraada of Norway three years previously. A fleet of 240 ships sailed under the leadership of King Sweyn's sons, Harold and Cnut, and of Osbern his brother. It brought to England an army of trained warriors which included many men of high rank in Denmark, and the threat of the expedition was enhanced by the fact that it could count on considerable support within those regions of England which had Scandinavian affinities. The ships first appeared off Kent, and then proceeded up the east coast. Raiding parties were thrown off, but were repelled, and at length the fleet reached the safe anchorage of the Humber. Its arrival was the signal for a general rising in Yorkshire. Edgar the atheling, Gospatric, and Waltheof collected a considerable force, and forthwith joined the Danes. Then the whole body marched upon York. The Norman garrisons were unable to hold the castles, and on 19 September they sallied out and started to fire the city. They perished after prolonged fighting, and on

reliance should certainly not be placed on testimony of this character. But the possibility that William may have visited Normandy during the winter of 1068–1069 is not to be wholly disregarded.

[1] Ord. Vit. (vol. ii, p. 189), without giving a precise date, places Matilda's visit to Normandy after William's second campaign in the north; that is to say, between the Easter court at Winchester (4–11 April 1069) and the beginning of the 'Rising of the North' in the early autumn of that year. And the Valognes charters noted above could with equal, or greater, propriety be cited in support of this date.

[2] Ordericus (loc. cit.) lays special emphasis on this point, and it is significant that the charters given at Valognes were there ratified not only by the king but also by the queen.

[3] The only possible times for such a visit (or visits) to Normandy by King William are: (1) very late in 1068, i.e. between the end of the first northern campaign and the opening the second northern campaign in (?) February 1069; or (2) between April 1069 (the Winchester court) and September 1069, by which time William was back in England preparing to withstand the invasion of Sweyn.

20 September York fell. The Danes thereupon repaired to their ships, and, having moved across to the southern shore of the Humber, they fortified the isle of Axholme. Many of their troops dispersed over the countryside of North Lincolnshire, where they were welcomed by the peasantry, and entertained by them at the village feasts.[1]

The whole Norman venture in England had thus been placed in peril, for at last the resistance to William was assuming a coherence which it had hitherto lacked. A strong Scandinavian force was at large in England, and it was supported by a considerable army led by powerful Saxon magnates. Nor is it surprising that the news of these events spread rapidly through England, and gave occasion for revolts elsewhere: in Dorset and Somerset, for example, in Staffordshire and South Cheshire.[2] But the centre of the crisis was in the north. Yorkshire had been lost, and beyond Yorkshire in 'Saint Cuthbert's land', north of the Tees, there was whirling chaos in which was emerging the authority of Malcolm, king of Scotland. The Scottish king had in fact now thrown in his lot with William's opponents in England, and it was probably about this time that, by one of the most influential marriages in English history, he allied himself to Margaret, the sister of Edgar Atheling.[3] The possibilities latent in the developing situation were in fact incalculable, and in the autumn of 1069 it must have seemed possible that a Scandinavian kingdom might once more be established in northern England, or even a realm created for Edgar Atheling, buttressed by the support of Malcolm and Sweyn, and perhaps even to be sanctioned with a separate coronation by a metropolitan archbishop of the distinct ecclesiastical province of York.

The magnitude of this crisis indicates the importance of the ensuing campaign, and explains (though it does not excuse) its terrible sequel. Never did William act with more vigour or at greater risk. He immediately moved up towards Axholme, where his approach caused the Danes to move back again over the Humber into Yorkshire. Then leaving the counts of Mortain and Eu to watch the situation in Lindsey, the Conqueror struck westward to cope with the rebellion which had broken out under Edric the Wild and the Welsh princes. This he suppressed, apparently without much difficulty, and then at once advanced towards Lincolnshire, leaving Geoffrey, bishop of

---

[1] AS. Chron., 'D', 'E', s.a. 1069, 1070; Ord. Vit., vol. II, p. 191; Simeon of Durham, *Hist. Regum* (*Opera*, vol. II, pp. 187, 188).   [2] Ord. Vit., vol. II, p. 194.
[3] AS. Chron., 'D', s.a. 1067 (an interpolation). The marriage probably took place late in 1069. Cf. Ritchie, *Normans in Scotland*, pp. 25, 26.

Coutances, to cope with the Dorset rising that was threatening the newly constructed castle of Montacute. When the king reached Nottingham, however, he learnt that the Danes were preparing to reoccupy York, and so he turned northward. He found the Aire gap defended against him, but after some delay he managed to effect a crossing, and advanced directly on the northern capital which the Danes evacuated once more. On his route he savagely devastated the land through which he passed, sparing no male and leaving nothing behind him which could support life. Just before Christmas he reached York, and there in a burnt city, surrounded by a desolated countryside, he celebrated the Nativity of Christ.[1]

The devastation which the king carried out on his march had been part of a rapid and critical campaign. That which he now ordered was inspired by a more cold-blooded design. The Norman troops split up into smaller bands and carried out a systematic harrying of Yorkshire. So terrible was the visitation that its results were still apparent twenty years later. But the king himself could not tarry in Yorkshire. In appalling weather he moved up to the Tees on a rapid and hazardous raid, and then without pause he set out upon what was probably the most difficult and arduous march of his career. Realizing that the western rebellion was barely suppressed, and that Chester still remained as the one outstanding centre of resistance, the king struck directly right across the Pennine Chain. It was the depth of winter, and the hardships of the route caused even his seasoned troops to threaten mutiny. But he pushed on, harrying as he went, and reached Chester before his enemies were ready to meet him. He occupied the city without difficulty, and placed a castle there, and also at Stafford. The resistance which had so nearly overwhelmed him was finally broken, and the Danish fleet, seeing its English allies defeated, accepted a bribe to depart from the Humber. The king himself moved back to the south. He reached Winchester before Easter 1070.[2]

King William's campaign of 1069–1070 must rank as one of the outstanding military achievements of the age, and it was to prove decisive in ensuring that the Norman domination of England would endure. None the less, the cost of that achievement and its consequences deserve note in any estimate of the Norman impact upon England, and of the character of William the Conqueror. An eleventh-century campaign

[1] AS. Chron., 'D', s.a. 1069; Ord. Vit., vol. II, pp. 192–195.
[2] Ord. Vit., vol. II, p. 197; Simeon of Durham (op. cit., vol. II, p. 198).

was inevitably brutal, but the methods here displayed were widely regarded as exceptional and beyond excuse,[1] even by those who were otherwise fervent admirers of the Norman king.

On many occasions [writes one of these] I have been free to extol William according to his merits, but I dare not commend him for an act which levelled both the bad and the good in one common ruin by a consuming famine . . . I am more disposed to pity the sorrows and sufferings of the wretched people than to undertake the hopeless task of screening one who was guilty of such wholesale massacre by lying flatteries. I assert moreover that such barbarous homicide should not pass unpunished.[2]

Such was the view of a monk in Normandy. A writer from northern England supplies more precise details of the horrible incidents of the destruction, and recalls the rotting and putrefying corpses which littered the highways of the afflicted province. Pestilence inevitably ensued, and an annalist of Evesham tells how refugees in the last state of destitution poured into the little town. Nor is it possible to dismiss these accounts as rhetorical exaggerations, for twenty years later Domesday Book shows the persisting effects of the terrible visitation, and there is evidence that these endured until the reign of Stephen. Yorkshire, whose prosperity was thus destroyed for more than a generation, was, moreover, not the only region to suffer, for the devastation, though to a diminishing degree, spread as far west as Merseyside, and as far south as Derby.[3]

Never again did William in England have to face such perils as those which menaced his rule in 1069–1070, and such subsequent opposition as he encountered was in the nature of an aftermath to the storm which had recently ravaged the country. The continuing centre of disturbance was the Danish fleet which had returned to the Humber. To it in the spring of 1070 came King Sweyn himself, and under his leadership the Danish force sailed southward towards the Wash.[4] The soldiers entered East Anglia, and entrenched themselves in the Isle of Ely, where they were joined by men of the countryside, and in particular by a Lincolnshire thegn named Hereward.[5] The first objective of the

---

[1] Simeon of Durham shows, however, that the crimes committed by Malcolm in the north had been equally horrible (*op. cit.*, vol. II, p. 191).

[2] Ord. Vit., vol. II, p. 196.

[3] Simeon of Durham (*op. cit.*, vol. II, p. 188); *Chronicon de Evesham* (ed. W. D. Macray), pp. 90, 90; Will. Malms., *Gesta Regum*, p. 309; C. Creighton, *History of Epidemics*, vol. I, pp. 27, 29.

[4] AS. Chron., 'E', *s.a.* 1070.

[5] All that is known, or could possibly be surmised, about Hereward is exhaustively discussed by Freeman (*op. cit.*, vol. IV, pp. 454–487). On his alleged descendants, see Round, *Peerage and Pedigree*, vol. II, pp. 259–286.

composite force was the abbey of Peterborough.[1] Brand the abbot, who had supported the cause of Harold, had recently died, and the abbey had been given to a certain Turold, who took possession with a considerable body of troops with which he hoped to hold down the countryside. On 2 June, however, a miscellaneous force composed of Danes and English, called vaguely by the chronicler 'Hereward and his company', entered Peterborough and gave the abbey over to fire and loot. It was an outrage which challenged constituted order in the region, but at first William did not go further than to negotiate with the Danes. Doubtless by means of another bribe, King Sweyn was persuaded to a truce, and at last the great Danish fleet set sail for home laden with booty. It had been off the coasts of England for nearly two years, and its departure marked a definite stage in the final settlement of England.[2]

In particular, the sailing of the Danish fleet was to prove fatal to the cause of Hereward. William, who was at this time preoccupied with the much more formidable threat to his power that was developing on the Continent, did not at first think it necessary to proceed against the outlaw, and his delay made the situation in the Fens more serious than it need otherwise have been, for in the absence of the king, Hereward was now joined by other more prominent men, including Earl Morcar himself. But without Scandinavian support the rising in the Fens was doomed to failure and when William advanced against Ely in person, the rebels surrendered unconditionally. Earl Morcar was taken prisoner, and Hereward, having escaped with difficulty, passed out of history into legend.[3]

The Norman régime in England had thus survived the first disturbances which followed its establishment. The chief English cities had submitted; the north had been subdued; the Fenland rebellion suppressed; Earl Morcar was a prisoner and soon to die; whilst Earl Edwin about this time was killed by his own followers while flying to Scotland. Nevertheless, the problems facing King William had only been partially solved, and indeed they were now in some measure to be increased. To treat the resistance which his government met in England as if it was something to be regarded in isolation is to misconceive the nature of the dominion which he had established. This was a conjoint dominion stretching across the Channel, and politically united under a single rule.

---

[1] The confused chronology of these events is discussed by E. O. Blake (*Liber Eliensis*, pp. lv, lvi).   [2] AS. Chron., *loc. cit.*   [3] *Ibid.*, 'E', *s.a.* 1071.

Any attack upon any of its parts from any quarter was equally a menace to its survival, and both its enemies and its defenders were to show themselves well aware of the fact. Indeed, it was to become a cardinal feature of the policy of King Philip I of France to exploit this situation. The intimate connexion in this respect of English and continental politics between 1067 and 1085 deserves, therefore, more emphasis than it usually receives. The suppression of risings in England was always connected with the imminence of attacks from Scandinavia or Scotland, from Anjou or Maine; and throughout all this period the maintenance of the northern frontier beyond Yorkshire could never be dissociated from concurrent threats from France, from Flanders, or from the Baltic lands. It was only by means of a far-flung and integrated defence that the Anglo-Norman kingdom was to survive under the rule of William the Conqueror.

The freedom from attack enjoyed by Normandy during the period of the English conquest had been a prime factor in its success, but this continued immunity could not be presumed, and it was now to be disrupted. In 1069, even while the king was conducting his desperate campaign in the north of England, the city of Le Mans revolted against Norman rule.[1] The event might doubtless have been expected but it was none the less sudden. Arnold, the bishop who succeeded Vougrin at Le Mans in 1065, was a nominee and partisan of King William, and, to judge from a charter alleged to have been given to the abbey of La Couture in 1068, Norman administration was still operative in Maine in that year.[2] Now, however, a powerful party in Maine supported the citizens of Le Mans in the interests of Azzo, lord of Este in Liguria, who was the husband of Gersendis, the sister of Count Hugh IV. Azzo, who arrived in Maine before 2 April 1069, managed to collect a large body of adherents, and in particular attracted to his cause Geoffrey of Mayenne, the powerful border lord whose influence had so often been decisive in the politics of the *comté*. The confederation thus formed was too strong for the Norman rulers of Maine to resist. A certain Humphrey, described as the *senescallus* of King William was killed, and the Norman knights were expelled, among them being William of La Ferté-Macé, a brother-in-law of Odo, bishop of Bayeux. Azzo, having achieved thus much, now retired to his Italian lordship, leaving in charge of Maine, Gersendis and their young son Hugh, who

[1] Latouche, *Comté du Maine*, chap. V. The chief authority is the *Actus pontificum Cenomannis in urbe degentium* (ed. Busson and Ledru (1902)).　　[2] *Cart. S. Pierre de la Couture*, no. XV.

was recognized as count. Geoffrey of Mayenne, who forthwith took Gersendis for his mistress, remained the dominant figure in the partnership.[1]

From the first it was an unstable government. In March 1070 the citizens of Le Mans revolted once more, this time against Geoffrey, and formed themselves into what was described as a *commune*.[2] They forced Geoffrey to recognize their claims to special privileges, but were unable to maintain their position. Setting out in company with their bishop to reduce the castle of Sillé, which was held against them, they were betrayed by Geoffrey and routed. Geoffrey himself, however, did not think it safe as yet to re-enter the city to rescue the countess. He took refuge therefore in Château-du-Loir, and the young Hugh was sent for safety to his father in Italy. None the less, before the end of the year, the revolt was finally crushed, and the countess and Geoffrey were together re-established in Le Mans.[3]

These events must have caused the greatest concern to King William in England. Within a few months the Norman rule in Maine, which had been operative since 1063, had collapsed, and the disturbance of Maine invited the intervention of some stronger power which as in the past might use the *comté* as the base for an attack upon the duchy. Moreover, before the end of 1070 there had occurred another revolution on the Continent which entailed peril to Normandy. On 16 July 1070, within five weeks of the departure of Sweyn's fleet from East Anglia, there died King William's brother-in-law, Baldwin VI, count of Flanders. A succession question was immediately opened with which Normandy was to be at once concerned. The two young sons of Baldwin VI, namely Arnulf and Baldwin, received respectively Flanders and Hainault, and in view of their youth the government was conducted by their mother, Richildis. Her rule was strongly resisted, particularly in Flanders, and the opposition was headed by Robert, 'le Frison', a son of Baldwin V. Richildis immediately sought the aid of King Philip I and, looking about for further assistance, turned to William fitz Osbern, the closest personal associate at this time of King William. Early in 1071 the king had sent the earl to Normandy, doubtless to watch over the developing danger from Maine, and now Richildis offered herself in marriage to William fitz Osbern, and placed her son Arnulf

---

[1] *Actus*, pp. 376–377; Latouche, *op. cit.*, p. 37; Douglas, *Domesday Monachorum*, pp. 35, 36.
[2] Whether this could with any propriety be called a 'commune' in the later sense of a collective feudal lordship is discussed by Latouche in *Mélanges – Halphen*, pp. 377–383.
[3] *Actus*, pp. 278, 379.

in his wardship. He accepted the offer, and, in support of his ward and of his designated wife, he hastened to Flanders, 'as if to a game', accompanied, as it was said, by only ten knights. The decisive battle was fought at Cassel on 22 February 1071, and it resulted in the overthrow of Richildis, the establishment of Robert le Frison as count of Flanders, and the death of William fitz Osbern.[1] King William thus lost his most powerful secular supporter in England, and, within a few months of Maine slipping from his control, he saw established a hostile power in the Low Countries.

During 1070–1071 the events in Maine and Flanders must have disturbed William far more than the continuing resistance of Hereward in the Fens, and even in Britain there were other matters which were beginning to press more urgently on his attention. The Norman régime which had been established in England confronted both Celtic Wales and Celtic Scotland with a challenge. On the Welsh border the great Norman palatine lordships were about this time being established,[2] and the defeat of Bleddyn and Riwallon set the stage for a new Norman movement westward. But in 1070 it was Scotland that was most immediately affected. Ever since 1066 Scotland had served as a refuge for disinherited English magnates. Edgar Atheling remained an honoured guest at Malcolm's court; and Malcolm had married Edgar's sister Margaret. In these circumstances, the victorious campaigns of William through the north of England during the winter of 1069–1070 was bound to provoke an immediate reaction from Scotland, which now could provide a new and most formidable threat to the Anglo-Norman kingdom.

The situation was, indeed, of wider significance then even these facts would by themselves suggest. Here was a question of frontiers. The centre of Malcolm's dominion was the kingdom of Alban based upon Perthshire, and flanked to the north by the Scandinavian settlements, and to the south by the provinces of Cumbria and Lothian: Cumbria stretching from the Clyde to the Westmorland fells, and Lothian from the Forth southward; and both with their southern boundaries still undefined. Both these provinces were of vital interest alike to Malcolm and to William, and on both of them the impact of the campaigns of 1069–1070 were immediately felt. In this manner there was at once

---

[1] AS. Chron., 'E', *s.a.* 1070; Ord. Vit., vol. II, p. 235; Fliche, *Philippe I*, pp. 252–261. For the date of the battle of Cassel, see J. Tait, in *Essays – Lane Poole*, pp. 151–167.

[2] Below, pp. 295, 296.

posed the question which was to dominate Anglo-Scottish relations for the next quarter of a century. What henceforward were to be the political filiations of Cumbria and Lothian, or (in other words) what was to be the northern frontier of the newly established Anglo-Norman state?[1] That question was not in fact to be even partially resolved before 1095, but in 1070 it was already urgent. The devastation of the north had created, so to speak, a vacuum of political authority in the debatable region, and already in the spring of 1070, almost before William had reached Winchester, Malcolm was carrying out a terrible devastation of Durham and Cleveland, whilst Gospatric, as earl, was taking reprisals against his former Scottish ally in Cumbria.[2] It was a measure of the menace to William from the north.

The problem before the Conqueror at the end of 1071 was in its essence not wholly dissimilar from that which faced Harold Godwineson in the autumn of 1066. The Anglo-Norman state was being threatened on two of its extreme frontiers, and it was a question which danger should first be met. How pressing was the problem, and how closely connected were its two parts, can be judged by the astonishing rapidity of William's movements during the next fifteen months. In the winter of 1071–1072, with the northern menace behind him, he departed for his duchy.[3] His actions in Normandy at this juncture are but sparsely recorded, but it may be assumed that the court he at once held was concerned with the situation in Maine, and it is significant that his half-brother, Odo of Bayeux, was also in the duchy at this time.[4] The king, however, could not tarry long, and before Easter 1072 he was back in England,[5] and there his first action was to begin the extensive preparation essential for coping with the threat from Scotland. The measures he took were in fact to have a considerable influence upon the establishment of the Norman nobility régime in England, and they imposed burdens not only on the Norman magnates but on the bishoprics and abbeys of England.[6] They were also executed with the utmost speed, and during the summer they were completed. In the early autumn therefore he was ready to act, and he forthwith 'led a land force and a naval force to Scotland'.[7]

So began one of the most remarkable of the many military ventures of the Conqueror. His plan was to make a two-pronged thrust by sea

[1] See G. W. S. Barrow, *The Border* (Durham, 1962).
[2] Simeon of Durham (*op. cit.*, vol. II, p. 190). [3] Ord. Vit., vol. II, p. 237.
[4] Ord. Vit., vol. II, p. 238. [5] *Regesta*, vol. I, no. 63.
[6] Below, pp. 325, 326. [7] AS. Chron., 'D', 'E', *s.a.* 1072.

and land into the heart of Malcolm's kingdom. The army, consisting chiefly of horsemen, moved up by the eastern route through Durham, and then on through Lothian, crossing the Forth by the ford near Stirling to turn eastward towards Perth and the upper reaches of the Tay. The fleet, acting in conjunction, sailed up the east coast of Britain and entered the estuary of the Tay to make contact with the land forces. It was a bold plan, and it achieved a hazardous success. Doubtless, the Conqueror hoped for an engagement somewhere in Lothian where his horsemen might be able to show to advantage, but Malcolm was not disposed to afford him this opportunity. He was, however, so daunted by the invasion that he consented to negotiate, and the two kings met at Abernethy within a few miles of the Norman ships. As a result, Malcolm gave hostages to William and became his man.[1] Whether such homage was held to involve the kingdom of Alban itself, or merely lands in Cumbria and Lothian is uncertain. Nor was it of great significance. What was important was that the Scottish king had been brought formally to recognize the new régime in England, and as a token of this, Edgar Atheling was expelled from the Scottish court.

This campaign must be regarded as one of the most bizarre exploits of Norman arms in the eleventh century, and the risk which attended the enterprise of bringing knights from the Risle and the Seine, from the Bessin and the Hiémois up to the gates of the Highlands were very considerable. William, late in a campaigning season, was operating perilously far from his base, and even the ships which might serve in an emergency as a means of retreat could hardly diminish the menace of his isolation. In these circumstances, by securing from Malcolm a pact so far favourable to himself, he made at great risk a notable contribution to the defence of the Anglo-Norman state. Its existence had been formally recognized in the north; a centre for the assembly of its enemies had been neutralized; and its northern frontier had been asserted if not defined.

William's expedition to Scotland must, moreover, be viewed as part of a larger political strategy, and here time was of the essence of his task. The safety of the state he had created now involved a unified defence which stretched from Abernethy to Nonancourt, from Flanders to the boundaries of Brittany, and in the autumn of 1072 events on the Continent had made it imperative not only that a settlement should be obtained in the north, but that this should be accomplished with the

[1] AS. Chron., 'E', *s.a.* 1072; Skene, *Celtic Scotland*, vol. I, p. 424.

minimum of delay. Maine was in revolt; Flanders had become hostile; and William's presence was urgently needed in Normandy. The preservation of the Anglo-Norman state had in fact become a single problem: it was essentially the same whether it was conducted in Britain or in France; and events in either country had immediate repercussions on the other. Immediately after his pact with Malcolm, William therefore moved south with speed. By 1 November he was at Durham.[1] Where he heard the Christmas Mass is not known – but early in 1073 he was back again in Normandy at the head of a large force which he had transhipped from England.

His return was not too soon, for even during the months of his Scottish campaign his position in France had again deteriorated. The instability of the government of Geoffrey of Mayenne invited intervention in Maine by a stronger power, and some time in 1072 a new turn was given to the situation when the citizens of Le Mans invited the help of Fulk le Rechin, count of Anjou. Anjou was no longer the force it had been in the time of Geoffrey Martel, but by 1072 the repulsive Fulk le Rechin had so far overcome the anarchy he had done much to create, that he could no longer be disregarded as an opponent. The invitation to the count was thus of considerable significance in reconstructing an earlier pattern of politics. Nor did Fulk hesitate to accept it. He immediately entered Maine, and advanced towards Le Mans. The citizens rose in his favour, and with the count's aid, Geoffrey of Mayenne was expelled. Once again a count of Anjou had gone some way towards establishing himself on the frontiers of Normandy.[2]

Such was the developing situation which had brought the Conqueror with such haste from Scotland, and the unified character of the defensive campaigns on which he was engaged can be seen in the composition of the force which accompanied him. Even as Norman knights had been concerned in the expedition to Scotland, so now did English troops take part in the campaign in France, and their participation in the warfare which ensued was both noteworthy and noted.[3] Once again, the chief feature of William's plan was speed. Fulk himself seems to have left Anjou at this time, and William did not wait for his return. Although the campaigning season had barely begun he entered Maine by way of the valley of the Sarthe and attacked Fresnay. This stronghold

---

[1] Simeon of Durham, *Hist. Dunelm. Eccl.* (*Opera*, vol. 1, p. 106).
[2] *Actus*, p. 379; Latouche, *op. cit.*, p. 38; K. Norgate, *Angevin Kings*, vol. 1, pp. 219–220.
[3] AS. Chron., 'D', *s.a.* 1074 (equals 1073).

together with the neighbouring fortress of Beaumont surrendered without much resistance, and William then attacked Sillé, which likewise submitted.[1] The way was now open to Le Mans, which William invested and captured. The seizure of the capital entailed the general submission of the *comté*.[2] By 30 March (as it would seem) it was all over, and the Conqueror was back at Bonneville-sur-Touques, having re-established the Norman ascendancy in Maine.[3]

The rapidity with which the successful campaign in Maine followed the expedition to Scotland undoubtedly enabled the Conqueror to escape from a dangerous crisis in his affairs, and by the summer of 1073 his position was much stronger than it had been twelve months before. Nevertheless, the defence of his composite realm could not be relaxed, the more especially as a new factor was beginning to complicate the problem. The French monarchy was emerging from the eclipse into which it had entered with the minority of Philip I. In 1067 the young king left the tutelage of the count of Flanders,[4] and he was now developing an active policy of his own, against Normandy. For that purpose he sought allies, and these were available. He seems in the first instance to have turned towards Flanders. He had, it is true, in 1071 opposed the advancement of Robert le Frison, but when the latter was established, it was apparent that the interests of the Flemish count were here attuned to those of the French king. Robert, with justice, regarded the Norman duke as his most dangerous rival; he had not forgotten the intervention of William fitz Osbern in Flemish affairs; and it is significant that very soon after the pact between William and Malcolm he gave Edgar Atheling asylum in Flanders.[5] Philip, on his side, in dealing with his over-mighty Norman vassal, had obviously much to gain from friendship with the count of Flanders. A *rapprochement* between them therefore rapidly took place, and it was symbolized by the marriage, in or before 1072, of Philip with Bertha of Hainault, who was Robert's half-sister.[6]

Flanders was, moreover, not the only quarter to which the French

---

[1] *Actus*, pp. 380, 381.   [2] Ord. Vit., vol. II, p. 255.
[3] On 30 March 1073 William was at Bonneville-sur-Touques in the company of Arnold, bishop of Le Mans, and there he confirmed the rights in Maine of the abbey of Solesmes (*Cart. S. Pierre de la Couture*, no. IX). It would seem unlikely that he would have issued this charter before he had himself recovered his jurisdiction in Maine, and if this be so, the campaign must have taken place very early in 1073. The matter cannot, however, be taken as certain. A charter for Saint-Vincent du Mans (*Cart. S. Vincent du Mans*, no. 177) probably passed on the same occasion.   [4] Prou, *Rec. Actes – Philippe I*, p. xxxii.
[5] AS. Chron., 'D', *s.a.* 1075 (equals 1074).   [6] Fliche, *Philippe I*, p. 36.

king could turn for help against Normandy. There was also Anjou. Already by 1068, profiting by the war between Fulk and his brother Geoffrey for the Angevin inheritance, he had made a pact with the former by which he obtained the Gâtinais, and there is documentary evidence that in 1069 the relations between Philip and the count were friendly.[1] Fulk's incursion into Maine in 1072 must therefore have been welcome to the French king, and the situation could be developed. The fundamental characteristic of the policy of Philip I during the next twenty years was thus disclosed. It was to be a ceaseless opposition to Normandy, conducted in alliance with Flanders and Anjou. So consistently in fact was this policy pursued that William was compelled henceforth to spend most of his time in Normandy, and the defence of his kingdom for the remainder of his reign was to be concentrated in France, though (as in 1075 and 1085) it had constant repercussions upon England.

It was in fact during 1074 that William's opponents on both sides of the Channel began noticeably to act in concert. Thus in the course of that year Edgar Atheling returned from Flanders to Scotland where he was received with honour,[2] and the French king at once saw how he might be used as a centre for an alliance against Normandy. He therefore offered him the important castle of Montreuil-sur-Mer which would have placed him in a position of great strategic advantage.[3] For Montreuil was the chief Capetian outlet to the English Channel; it was within easy access of Flanders; and it was at the same time a base from the east. It seemed indeed as if Edgar might once again serve as a rallying point for all the enemies of the Anglo-Norman kingdom, and so seriously did William take the threat that he treated with the atheling, and consented to receive him back at his own court.[4] The French king had, therefore, to seek another centre of opposition to William, and he was to find this in Brittany where a situation was arising that could be made highly dangerous to Normandy. It was, indeed, through Brittany that between 1075 and 1077 there was now to develop a movement in which all William's opponents – English, French, and Scandinavian – became once more for a time associated.

As has been seen, William's Breton campaign of 1064 had prevented the establishment of a hostile state on the border of Normandy during the time of the English expedition, and the death of Conan in December

---

[1] Prou, *Rec. Actes – Philippe I*, no. XLI; Fliche, *op. cit.*, pp. 138, 142, 143.
[2] AS. Chron., *loc. cit.*   [3] *Ibid.*   [4] *Ibid.*, 'E', *s.a.* 1074.

1066 had still further reduced the power of the Breton ruling house. He was succeeded by his son-in-law Hoel, count of Cornouailles. The new ruler inherited all Conan's difficulties in coping with the feudal magnates of Brittany. Among these a most important group was established in the northern and eastern part of Brittany facing Normandy. Prominent among them were the members of the cadet branch of the ruling house represented in Eudo of Penthièvre and his sons. Of these, most had already begun their careers in England under King William,[1] but there remained the eldest, Geoffrey Boterel I, whose lordship stretched all along the northern coast, and included wide lands in the dioceses of Dol, Saint-Malo and Saint-Brieuc.[2] Again, there was Geoffrey 'Granon', a bastard son of Alan III, whose lands were likewise concentrated in the diocese of Dol.[3] Finally to the south of these honours was the great lordship of Gael, a compact barony immediately to the west and northwest of Rennes, which at this time included both Montfort and Montauban, and stretched westward as far as Tremorel and Penpont to comprise no less than forty parishes.[4] This lordship of Gael was in 1074 held by Ralph 'de Gael', who together with many other Breton lords had established himself in England, and who, about 1069, had become earl of Norfolk.

Ralph de Gael[5] was in fact to be the central figure in the crisis that now ensued. He had inherited both his Breton lands and his English earldom from his father, also named Ralph, who had served as staller at the court of Edward the Confessor, and who had later assisted the Conqueror in the settlement of England. Ralph de Gael, the son, had therefore both Breton and English connexions, and he was particularly strong in being a natural leader of all those Bretons of middle rank who had followed in the wake of the Conqueror to receive lands in England. It was in fact to them in the first instance that Ralph appealed when in 1075 he conceived the plan of rebelling against the Conqueror in England, and he managed to associate with his rising no less a personage than Roger 'of Breteuil', earl of Hereford, the second son of William fitz Osbern. The precise causes of the rebellion are obscure, but its occasion was the marriage of Ralph with Roger's daughter, and the

---

[1] *e.g.* Brian, Alan the Red, and Alan the Black.
[2] La Borderie, *Histoire de Bretagne*, vol. III, p. 11.
[3] *Chron. S. Brieuc* (*Rec. Hist. Franc.*, vol. XII, p. 566).
[4] La Borderie, *op. cit.*, vol. III, pp. 68, 69. See also the admirable map in the same writer's *Neuf Barons de Bretagne* (1895).
[5] *Complete Peerage*, vol. XI, pp. 573 *et sqq*.

plot was hatched at the wedding feast held at Exning near Newmarket.[1] Further importance was moreover given to the revolt by the fact that Waltheof, son of Earl Siward of Northumbria, and now earl of Huntingdon, and high in the Conqueror's favour, allowed himself to be associated with it.[2] Thus Breton and English opposition to the Conqueror was combined and, as if to make the movement more logically complete, Ralph appealed to Denmark for help.[3] Meanwhile, Ralph's fellow magnates in Brittany were ready to revolt against Hoel, or to raid into Normandy, whilst Count Robert of Flanders, Fulk le Rechin of Anjou, and King Philip were alertly watching the developing situation.

When the rebellion began in England, William was still in Normandy and it is significant that Archbishop Lanfranc, in whose hands he had left the administration of England, wrote at once to the king in order to persuade him not to return.[4] The king's place at this juncture was in Normandy, and it would be a disgrace if his loyal vassals could not by themselves deal with the revolt in England. In the event, they were able to do so without great difficulty. Wulfstan, bishop of Worcester, and Æthelwig, abbot of Evesham, both native prelates, combined with the Norman lords already established in the western Midlands to prevent Earl Roger from advancing out of Herefordshire to join his fellow rebel, whilst Odo, bishop of Bayeux, and Geoffrey of Coutances, Richard, son of Count Gilbert, and William of Warenne in like manner barred the westward progress of Earl Ralph from Norfolk.[5] Ralph thereupon retreated to Norwich, and then, leaving the castle at that place to be defended by his wife, he departed overseas. He may have gone to Denmark to incite his Scandinavian allies to action, and he eventually reached Brittany.[6] Norwich was forthwith besieged and after some resistance surrendered upon terms which allowed the countess and many members of the garrison to depart for Brittany. Meanwhile the expedition had sailed from Denmark. Sweyn Estrithson had recently died, but his son Cnut, accompanied by many Danish magnates, led a great fleet of over two hundred warships to England. It arrived too late. Norwich had already fallen to the king's men, and the Danes

---

[1] AS. Chron., 'E', s.a. 1075. It might have been thought that the marriage was made against the king's prohibition. A letter of Lanfranc (Ep. 39) shows this was not the case. The speeches put into the conspirators by Ord. Vit. (vol. II, pp. 258, 259), though interesting, are imaginative.　　[2] Ord. Vit. (vol. II, p. 260) makes Waltheof agree only reluctantly.

[3] AS. Chron., loc. cit.　　　　　　　　　　　　[4] Ep. 34.

[5] AS. Chron., loc. cit. Flor. Worc. (vol. II, p. 11) says the engagement took place near Cambridge. Ord. Vit. (vol. II, p. 262) puts it at a place he calls 'Fageduna'.

[6] Ord. Vit., vol. II, p. 263.

contented themselves with sailing northward from Norfolk, pillaging the coast-lands, and York. After this, they departed home with their booty by way of Flanders so that Lanfranc could report to his king in Normandy that the south was now in greater tranquillity than at any time since the king's last departure.[1] Thus at Christmas 1075 William could return to a pacified country in order to deal out punishment to the rebels.[2] The Bretons were savagely dealt with, Earl Roger was thrown into captivity, and Earl Waltheof was immediately cast into prison, there to languish for several months until on 31 May 1076 he was beheaded on Saint Giles Hill outside Winchester.[3] By that time, however, William was already back again across the Channel ready for the war in Brittany.

The revolt of the earls is of great interest as illustrating the problems arising from the establishment of Norman feudalism in England, whilst the participation of Earl Waltheof – and his execution – has a considerable bearing upon the policy adopted by the Conqueror towards his English subjects. But in respect of the defence of the Anglo-Norman kingdom, the chief importance of the rebellion of 1075 lies in its connexion with continental politics. The appeal to Scandinavia immediately gave to the English rising a wider significance, and it was in fact this aspect of the situation which most concerned King William, who, while still in Normandy, wrote urgently to Lanfranc, ordering that the east coast should be put in a state of defence.[4] Nor is it only with Scandinavia that this rising must be related. This was a Breton as well as an English revolt; it was the Bretons in England who were appropriately singled out for William's vengeance; and it was in this connexion also that the movement most concerned William's enemies in France. Earl Ralph at once continued the war from his Breton possessions, and if his rebellion should be successful it was clear that William would find a hostile power established on his western frontier. Such a situation, providing constant opportunities for further attack, would be to the advantage of King Philip and his associates. William, on his part, was equally concerned to prevent it.

The war that followed in 1076 had thus wide general implications, and it is not surprising that it attracted the attention not only of Norman and Breton writers, but also of English and Angevin annalists.

[1] Lanfranc, Ep. 40.   [2] AS. Chron., *loc. cit.*

[3] Ord. Vit., vol. II, pp. 265–267. 'It can only be left an open question whether his execution can be justified in morality as well as in law.' (Stenton, *op. cit.*, p. 603.)

[4] Lanfranc, Ep. 35.

Their testimony is not wholly consistent and is difficult to interpret, but the general course of events can be discerned with a reasonable degree of probability.[1] At the time of Earl Ralph's return to Brittany, Count Hoel was already engaged in war with Geoffrey Granon. Earl Ralph, it would seem, joined with Geoffrey Granon, and together the two magnates established themselves in the castle of Dol.[2] It was a situation that King William could not ignore. Dol was near the Norman frontier; its chief defender was the rebel earl of Norfolk, and the whole operation could be regarded as directed as much against William as against Hoel. For this reason, too, the defenders of Dol were early reinforced by a contingent of troops from Anjou.[3] William, therefore, in September advanced against Dol, and, according to Breton writers, he acted in the campaign which followed in close association with Hoel. But despite all the resources of siege-craft Dol held out.[4] And it was then that the French king seized his opportunity. Philip was at Poitou early in October urgently seeking the assistance of Geoffrey, count of Aquitaine,[5] and towards the end of the month he moved at last at the head of a large force to the relief of Dol. His intervention was well timed, and was completely successful. Dol was relieved, and William, having suffered heavy losses in men and material, was forced to retire.[6]

William's defeat at Dol was the first serious military check that he had suffered in France for more than twenty years, and its importance has been unduly minimized.[7] Indeed, his failure in Brittany in 1076 went some way to counterbalance the successful suppression of the rebellion of the earls in England during the previous year. Ralph remained a great lord in Brittany, strongly entrenched in power, and it is significant that during 1077 King Philip was able to consolidate his position in the Vexin without serious opposition from William. William's losses at Dol had been severe,[8] the damage to his prestige considerable, and his opponents were given an opportunity to follow up their success. Thus it was that, probably in the late autumn of 1076, or during the early months of 1077, Fulk le Rechin, with the assistance (as it seems) of Breton as well as Angevin troops took the offensive and attacked John

---

[1] Below, Appendix E.

[2] *Chron. S. Brieuc; Chron. Britannicum* (*Rec. Hist. Franc.*, vol. XI, p. 413; vol. XII, p. 566), Flor. Worc., *s.a.* 1076.

[3] Ann. 'de Renaud' (Halphen, *Annales*, p. 88).   [4] *Ibid.*

[5] Prou, *Rec. Actes – Philippe I*, nos. LXXXIII, LXXXIV.

[6] AS. Chron., 'E', *s.a.* 1076.

[7] Cf. Stenton (*William the Conqueror*, p. 341): 'a small continental war'.

[8] AS. Chron., *loc. cit.*; Ord. Vit., vol. II, p. 291; Prou, *op. cit.*, nos. LXXXIX, XC.

of Le Flèche, one of William's strongest supporters in Maine.[1] John, however, managed to hold out in his castle until William came to his assistance, and Fulk, who appears to have been wounded in the course of the siege, was compelled to withdraw.[2] An uneasy truce was thereupon made. It was marked by a pact between William and Philip (which was certainly ratified in 1077),[3] and secondly by a pact between William and Fulk which may have been made at the same time and which at all events can hardly be placed elsewhere than in 1077 or 1078.[4]

The real victor in the French campaigns of these years was in effect the French king. His policy had attained its first objective. The reverse suffered by William at Dol had been due to Philip's diplomacy and intervention, and William had now been brought to negotiate at a disadvantage. Philip was quick to turn the occasion to his profit, and his opportunity came in the Vexin. There Ralph of Crépi had been succeeded by his son Simon, who had albeit with difficulty maintained his position against the French king. But now he was seized by one of those violent impulses which were so characteristic of the eleventh century. Having obtained in marriage Judith, daughter of Robert II, count of Auvergne, he chose the occasion of his wedding night to vow himself and his bride to continence, and forthwith renouncing the world, he entered the monastery of Saint-Claude in the Jura. The event, which not unnaturally inspired widespread comment, gave King Philip the opportunity he had so long desired. He immediately occupied the Vexin, and thus extended his demesne up to the Norman frontier on the Epte.[5] The act constituted a new menace to Normandy, but Duke William in his present circumstances could do nothing to prevent it. He was perforce to acquiesce in the change, though in the sequel he was to meet his death in trying to reverse it.

Duke William's position in France had in fact been impaired. It is true that he was not himself forced to cede territory, and although the Angevin overlordship over Maine was once more recognized, the Norman administration there was continued under Robert, the duke's son. But the settlement of 1077–1078 was clearly based upon a compromise which could not be expected to endure, and it marked a reverse in William's fortunes. For the first time since 1054 a limit had

---

[1] Ann. Saint Aubin and Saint Florent (Halphen, *op. cit.*, pp. 5, 129).
[2] Halphen, *Comté d'Anjou*, p. 311, no. 233.   [3] AS. Chron., 'E', *s.a.* 1077.
[4] There may be a reference to this in a charter for Saint-Vincent du Mans (*Cart. S. Vincent du Mans*, no. 99). And see below, Appendix E.   [5] Fliche, *Philippe I*, pp. 147, 149.

been placed on the growth of Norman power in France, and it is impossible to escape the impression that from now on until the death of William the Conqueror the initiative of the struggle in France lay with the French king.

King Philip could certainly at once give a new turn to his offensive against William, and he did so by fostering divisions within Normandy, and by exploiting the difficulties latent in the relations between William and his eldest son. Robert had for long been used as a factor in the Conqueror's policy. In 1063 he had been given the title of count of Maine, and this had been confirmed in the arrangements of 1077–1078. Moreover, on more than one occasion he had been formally recognized as his father's heir, and when William returned to England in December 1067 he became permanently associated with the government of the duchy.[1] Thus it was that after Matilda's own departure for her crowning in England in 1068, Robert was made, as it appears, primarily responsible for the Norman administration.[2] His influence steadily grew, and during the ensuing decade he may even on occasion have been recognized as duke of Normandy under his father the king, for in two charters issued in 1096 he seems to reckon his tenure of the duchy from 1077 or 1078.[3]

Such arrangements might well entail a threat to the unity of the Anglo-Norman kingdom unless they were handled with discretion. Much here depended upon Robert himself, and unfortunately the young man's character was ill-suited to the delicate situation in which he was placed. Ordericus Vitalis was in this matter perhaps a harsh critic, but his vivid description of the young count carries conviction.[4] Robert (he says) was personally brave, and very adventurous, a witty talker, and an attractive companion. But his acts were frequently ill-considered. He was extravagant in word and deed, so that he wasted his substance, and was lavish with promises upon which little reliance could be placed. 'Wishing to please everybody, he was too ready to accede light-heartedly to any request.' The portrait is of a young man possessed of the cruder feudal virtues, and it is not surprising that he was very popular among those of like mind to himself. Nor is it without interest that he speedily came to be a firm friend of Edgar Atheling whom Orderic describes in somewhat similar terms. But, equally certainly,

---

[1] David, *Robert Curthose*, pp. 17–41.   [2] Will. Jum., p. 139; Ord. Vit., vol. II, p. 188.
[3] *Gall. Christ.*, vol. XI; *Instrumenta*, col. 76; Haskins, *Norman Institutions*, p. 67.
[4] Ord. Vit., vol. III, p. 262.

Robert was devoid both of statesmanship and sagacity. Impetuous and vain, he was suitably fashioned to be a tool in the hands of men less frank, and more astute, than himself.

In 1077 Robert was not more than twenty-five years of age, and so far he had shown himself a loyal son to his father. Late in that year, however, or possibly in the spring of 1078, the fatal weakness of his character was displayed with lamentable results. Yielding to the flattery of his companions, he now demanded from his father that he should henceforth have independent control of Normandy and Maine.[1] Such a schism within the Anglo-Norman realm would at this juncture have been fraught with peril. William, however, seems to have refrained from any premature action until he was forced to quell a brawl which broke out at Laigle between the followers of Robert and those of his other sons, William and Henry. This brought matters to an open rupture. Robert precipitately withdrew from his father's court, and, accompanied by a large following, he attempted with incredible folly to gain possession of Rouen itself. Roger d'Ivry, the king's butler, who was then in charge of the castle at the capital, was able to withstand the assault, but William realized that the situation demanded prompt action. He ordered the immediate arrest of the insurgents, and he threatened to confiscate their lands. Robert with most of his associates thereupon fled from Normandy.[2]

The full consequences of Robert's action were, however, still to be disclosed. Robert's position within Normandy and Maine had already received recognition, and his personal popularity among the young nobles was so great that he was able to attract to his support many of the cadet members of the greatest houses in Normandy.[3] Chief among these was Robert of Bellême, son of Roger of Montgomery, earl of Shrewsbury, and with him was associated his brother-in-law, Hugh of Châteauneuf-en-Thimerais, whose castles of Châteauneuf, Sorel, and Rémalard thus became ready to provide the fugitives with bases outside the Norman frontiers from which they could conduct operations against the duchy. At this time, too, or perhaps a little later, the rebels were joined by William of Breteuil, the eldest son of William

---

[1] The revolt must have started after 13 September 1077 when Robert was still at his father's court (*Gall. Christ.*, vol. xi; *Instrumenta*, col. 72) and some time before the opening of the siege of Gerberoi about Christmas 1078.   [2] Ord. Vit., vol. ii, pp. 297, 298.

[3] Ord. Vit. gives two lists of the supporters of Robert (vol. ii, pp. 296–298; vol. ii, pp. 380, 381). All of these persons were certainly associated with Robert at one time or another in his revolts against his father.

fitz Osbern, whose brother Roger had forfeited his English earldom after the rebellion of 1075, and who still languished in prison. Yves and Aubrey, sons of Hugh of Grandmesnil, likewise formed part of this company, as did also at some time Roger the son of Richard fitz Gilbert, lord of Tonbridge and Clare. All these were young men, and their action was distasteful to the heads of the great families to which they belonged – men who had achieved the conquest of England and who were even now organizing the settlement of the conquered kingdom. None the less, a threat had developed which menaced the Norman unity which since 1060 had been the chief source of Norman strength.

Such a situation could not fail to attract the attention of William's enemies in Europe, and it is not surprising that Robert's action led to an immediate revival of the coalition which had previously menaced the Anglo-Norman kingdom. Thus, about this time Robert visited the count of Flanders, and perhaps went on to solicit the aid of the archbishop of Trêves.[1] But the most interested party was the king of France, who saw here an admirable opportunity of developing a policy against William which had already achieved much success. Robert evidently sought his aid, and not in vain, and an unnamed 'steward' of the king of France is known at this time to have kept in contact with the rebels. As a result, Robert was joined by contingents from France and Brittany, from Maine and Anjou.[2] The earlier co-operation of William's enemies had in fact been reproduced, but this time its centre was the Conqueror's heir.

William could not afford to delay. At the time of the outbreak, he was apparently engaged against Rotrou I of Mortagne, but he immediately broke off these hostilities and attacked the rebels who were gathered at Rémalard.[3] In this engagement at least one of the chief supporters of Robert was killed,[4] and the rebels forthwith moved from the south-western frontier of Normandy round to its eastern border, establishing themselves at Gerberoi, a castle near Beauvais which had been placed at their disposal by the French king. There Robert was joined not only by a flux of new adherents from Normandy but also by many knights from France.[5] It was a new crisis, and William was constrained to advance at once against the stronghold. The siege of Gerberoi which began shortly after Christmas 1078[6] lasted some three

---

[1] AS. Chron., 'D', *s.a.* 1079; Ord. Vit., vol. II, p. 381.
[2] Ord. Vit., vol. II, p. 296. [3] *Ibid.* The cause of the quarrel is unknown.
[4] It was clearly a local revolt. Villerai is within a few miles of Rémalard, and Rémalard is some ten miles from Mortagne.
[5] Ord. Vit., vol. II, p. 387. [6] Below, Appendix E.

weeks, and it was only terminated when the rebels sallied out to risk a pitched battle. They were unexpectedly successful. William himself was unhorsed, possibly by his son, and wounded in the arm. His life was indeed only saved by one of his English followers, Toki son of Wigot, who was himself killed.[1] Thereafter the king's forces were put to flight, and Robert was left master of the field. It was a reverse for the Conqueror comparable to that which he had sustained in 1076 at Dol, and it was even more damaging to his prestige. William of Malmesbury indeed speaks of it as the greatest humiliation suffered by the Conqueror in his whole career.[2]

After his defeat at Gerberoi, William returned to Rouen, and there he was forced to enter into negotiations with his opponents. An influential group of senior members of the Norman aristocracy including Roger of Montgomery (now earl of Shrewsbury), Hugh of Grandmesnil, and the veteran Roger of Beaumont[3] at once strove to effect a pacification in the interests of Robert and his young associates, many of whom were the sons or younger brothers of the negotiating magnates. King Philip, who had made their cause to some extent his own, supported them,[4] and William was at last forced to treat. Perhaps before the end of 1079, and certainly before 12 April 1080, Robert was reconciled to his father, and William solemnly renewed to him the grant of succession to the Norman duchy.[5] His control over his son had in fact been substantially weakened, and King Philip in particular had good reason to be satisfied with the results of Robert's first rebellion. The separation of Normandy from England – always the fundamental objective of the French king's policy – had been brought a stage nearer. And it is not wholly surprising that it was for a short time to be actually achieved immediately after the Conqueror's death.

William's defence of the dominion he ruled had always to take account of the menace which threatened all its frontiers, and a reverse in one region was almost invariably followed by an attack from elsewhere. Consequently as soon as the news of the engagement at Gerberoi

---

[1] AS. Chron., 'D', s.a. 1079. Toki has been presumed to be the son of Wigot of Wallingford who is frequently mentioned in Domesday Book.

[2] Will. Malms., *Gesta Regum*, p. 317.   [3] Ord. Vit., vol. II, p. 388.

[4] There is a great difficulty here, for a charter of unimpeachable authenticity (Prou, *op. cit.*, no. XCI) shows Philip and William in association outside the walls of Gerberoi. The only hypothesis which I can tentatively advance is that William after his defeat was forced to retreat, and Philip, in return for some concession, mediated on his own terms between Robert and his father, and took steps to enforce some temporary settlement to his own advantage.

[5] Ord. Vit., vol. II, p. 390; vol. III, p. 242. For date, see *Cart. S. Trin. Roth.*, no. LXXXII.

penetrated to the north, Malcolm, king of Scotland, took immediate advantage of William's defeat in France.[1] Between 15 August and 8 September 1079 he ravaged the whole area from the Tweed to the Tees. It was a severe raid which brought the Scottish king much plunder, and the fact that it had for the time being to remain unpunished, stimulated all the latent opposition to Norman rule in Northumbria. All through the ensuing winter it would seem the unrest grew, and in the spring of 1080 a revolt broke out which threatened the whole Norman settlement in the north, and culminated in one of the most horrible crimes of violence that disgraced the age.

In 1071 the bishopric of Durham had been given to Walcher, a clerk from Lorraine. He was in some respects a notable man, and he played a significant part in the monastic revival which took place at this time in his diocese. Moreover, in all his policy he seems to have been disposed to collaborate to some extent with the native magnates, and he is known, for example, to have been on good terms with Earl Waltheof. Indeed, Walcher's prestige had become so high by 1075 that when Earl Waltheof rebelled, and forfeited his possessions for treason, the king was induced to confide to the bishop the Northumbrian earldom itself. Walcher's qualities, however, were not suited to maintain order in a savagely turbulent province. From the first he seems to have compromised, leaving much of the administration to Gilbert, one of his kinsmen, and at the same time seeking to placate local feeling by favouring a certain Ligulf who was a cadet member of the comital house of Siward. Such a policy could hardly hope to succeed, and the inevitable clash occurred. In the spring of 1080 Gilbert overthrew and killed Ligulf with the aid of the bishop's household knights, and with the approval of Leobwin, the bishop's chaplain. Walcher himself, who had probably been guilty of nothing worse than negligence, was thereupon accused of connivance in the crime, and with more candour than wisdom he offered to prove his innocence by oath before an assembly which he summoned to Gateshead. The folly of this proceeding was at once demonstrated when the supporters of Ligulf arrived armed at the meeting and drove Bishop Walcher with Gilbert, Leobwin, and some of his knights into the adjoining church. This was promptly fired, and as the bishop with his followers emerged from the burning building they were severally butchered. The insurgents then proceeded to Durham. They failed to take the castle,

---

[1] AS. Chron., 'E', *s.a.* 1079, implicitly connects Malcolm's invasion with the engagement at Gerberoi.

but the resulting chaos invited a fresh attack from the hostile king of Scotland.[1]

The massacre of Bishop Walcher and his retinue took place on 14 May 1080. William was then still in Normandy, and indeed he was not able to return to England until late in July.[2] In the meantime, however, Odo, bishop of Bayeux, was sent to the north on a punitive expedition, and in the autumn Robert, now reconciled to his father, set out for Scotland with a large force.[3] He pushed north as far as Falkirk, ravaging Lothian on his way, and forced Malcolm to a pact which recalled most of the provisions of the former agreement at Abernethy.[4] Then turning southward he set up a fortress at the place afterwards to be known as Newcastle-on-Tyne.[5] It was a notable expedition, but it achieved no final solution to the problem of the frontier. The selection of Newcastle for Robert's fortress indicated that the country north of the Tyne had still to be regarded as a debatable land, whilst to the west the dominion of the Scottish king extended as far south as Stainmoor.[6] The future filiations of Lothian and Cumbria had been foreshadowed, but they were still undetermined at the Conqueror's death, and the northern boundary of his kingdom never ceased to cause him anxiety.

Indeed, the threat which William constantly experienced from the north can be contrasted with his comparative immunity from attack from Wales. During the Confessor's reign Wales had been dominated by Griffith ap Llewellyn, prince of North Wales, who had been able to take advantage of the rivalries of the English earls.[7] In August 1063, however, he had perished when campaigning against Harold Godwineson, and for the next twenty years there was no one in Wales to take his place. As a consequence 'there was no more heed paid to the Welsh',[8] and the Welsh border in the time of King William constituted for him not so much a problem of defence as an opportunity for Norman expansion. The establishment of the marcher earldoms of Chester, Shrewsbury, and Hereford, which was to be a feature of the Norman settlement of England,[9] marked the beginning of a persistent Norman penetration into Wales. William fitz Osbern, earl of Hereford, for

---

[1] Simeon of Durham, *Hist. Dunelm. Eccl.* (*Opera*, vol. I, pp. 105, 106, 114); *Hist. Regum* (*Opera*, vol. II, p. 200).

[2] William and Robert were still in Normandy on 14 July (*Regesta*, vol. I, no. 135). They must have returned to England very shortly afterwards.   [3] Simeon of Durham, *loc. cit.*

[4] *Ibid.* (*Hist. Regum – Opera*, vol. II, p. 211); *Hist. Mon. Abingdon*, vol. II, pp. 9, 10.
[5] *Ibid.*   [6] Ritchie, *Normans in Scotland*, p. 50.
[7] J. E. Lloyd, *History of Wales*, vol. II, pp. 358–371.
[8] Gaimar, v. 5084.   [9] Below, pp. 294, 295.

instance, planted colonies at Chepstow and Monmouth before his death; Hugh of Avranches, earl of Chester, extended his power as far as the river Clwyd, and provided means for further encroachments by his cousin Robert of Rhuddlan; whilst Roger II of Montgomery, earl of Shrewsbury, had before 1086 acquired much of the county which was afterwards to bear his name. The effects upon Wales of the Norman conquest of England were not, however, to be fully developed until after the Conqueror's death.[1] And during his lifetime Wales added little to his difficulties in defending the Anglo-Norman kingdom.

It was otherwise with Scotland. A threat from the north persisted throughout the Conqueror's reign, and, as has been seen, it could never be dissociated from the attacks made against his dominions in France. It was fortunate, for instance, that Robert's expedition of 1080 permitted the Conqueror to turn his attention across the Channel, for early in the next year Fulk, count of Anjou, doubtless taking advantage of William's absence in England, began a fresh attack on Normandy through Maine.[2] Supported by Count Hoel of Brittany, he advanced again against La Flèche, and this time he took the stronghold and burnt it.[3] Once again, therefore, William was compelled to cross the Channel in haste, and shortly after the fall of La Flèche he was advancing across Maine with a large force composed both of Norman and English troops. According to one account, a great battle impended, but this was averted by certain ecclesiastics who were in the neighbourhood.[4] A new pact was then made between the king and the count. It reproduced the compromise of 1077, and it appears to have been ratified at a place vaguely described by a later chronicler as *Blancalanda* or *Brueria*.[5] Even so, Maine continued to be a source of danger. It was only after controversy and with papal support that in 1081 Hoel, a bishop with Norman sympathies, was appointed to succeed Arnold at Le Mans, and when some years later Hubert, *vicomte* of Beaumont, revolted against the Norman administration it proved impossible even after a lengthy siege to dislodge him from his castle of Sainte-Suzanne except on his own terms.[6]

---

[1] The whole process (which falls outside the scope of this book) is admirably surveyed by Sir Goronwy Edwards in 'The Normans and the Welsh March' (Brit. Acad., *Proceedings*, vol. XLII (1956), pp. 155–177).

[2] Annals of Saint-Aubin, and 'de Renaud' (Halphen, *Annales*, pp. 5, 88).

[3] Ord. Vit., vol. II, p. 256.   [4] Below, Appendix E.

[5] Ord. Vit., vol. II, p. 356. All attempts to identify the place have hitherto proved more interesting than convincing.

[6] Annals of Vendôme (Halphen, *op. cit.*, p. 65); Ord. Vit., vol. III, pp. 194–201; Latouche, *Comté du Maine*, p. 39; David, *Robert Curthose*, p. 35.

At this time, moreover, a new threat to the Conqueror's position came from his own family. It was in 1082 – the year after Fulk's second attack on La Flèche – that there occurred the famous quarrel between William and his half-brother, Odo bishop of Bayeux and earl of Kent. Odo, as has been seen, had been active in support of the king during 1080, and he seems to have remained in England when William was in Normandy in 1081. In 1082, however, he was arrested by the king.[1] The circumstances surrounding this important event are obscure, but according to a later chronicle it would appear that Odo had aspired to the papacy, and that he had also sought to entice some of the more prominent vassals of the king to follow him on fresh adventures to Italy.[2] Certainly, no medieval monarch could afford to countenance this latter project, and it is stated that William forthwith crossed to England, and despite the reluctance of many of his counsellors seized the person of the earl of Kent, and brought him back captive to Normandy. Odo seems indeed to have been kept in prison from this time until the Conqueror's death in 1087, but his possessions were not forfeited, since in Domesday Book he appears, as, after the king, the largest single landowner in England.[3]

The defection of Odo involved a serious menace to the Norman dynasty, and before the end of 1083 this danger was further increased. Shortly after 18 July in that year Robert, whose personal status in Normandy had been much advanced as a result of his first revolt, decided once more to rebel, and departed from the duchy. His movements during the next four years are uncertain, but he remained the ideal agent for the French king, who gave him full support, and he became the centre of all the opposition to the Conqueror in France.[4] As 1084 advanced therefore King William and his realm might be seen to be approaching a new period of peril, and with the two most powerful members of his family in open opposition, the king's sense of isolation must have been acute. Before the end of the year it was made yet more distressful by the death of his wife to whom, according to the widespread opinion of contemporaries, he had been exceptionally attached. Queen Matilda died on 2 November 1083 and was buried in her own nunnery

[1] AS. Chron., 'E', *s.a.* 1082.

[2] Ord. Vit., vol. III, pp. 189–192, 247.

[3] *Ibid.* But the matter is difficult. If *Regesta*, vol. I, no. 147, was issued in England, Odo was in this country in 1082, but he appears also to have witnessed a charter in Normandy in that year (*ibid.*, no. 150). The Durham charter (*ibid.*, no. 148) cited by the *Complete Peerage* (vol. VII, p. 128) is, I think, a forgery.

[4] David, *op. cit.*, p. 36.

at Caen, where one of the finest epitaphs of the eleventh century still testifies to her memory.[1]

Thus at the beginning of 1085 the security of the Anglo-Norman realm was still not assured, and in fact the final crisis of the Conqueror's reign was now at hand.[2] None the less William's achievement in ensuring its survival between 1067 and 1084 (which it has been the purpose of this chapter to watch) is not to be minimized. It was only accomplished despite reverses by means of an unremitting effort which, through two decades, had perforce to be expended over wide areas and against many enemies. Indeed, on looking back on that defence, its chief feature may well seem to have been the close interrelation which throughout existed between all its parts. The defence of the Anglo-Norman kingdom throughout the English reign of the Conqueror must in fact always be viewed as a unity, and the related campaigns which were conducted by William and his lieutenants had a common purpose, whether they were waged in Northumbria or Maine, or were directed against Sweyn Estrithson or Fulk le Rechin, King Malcolm of Scotland, or King Philip of France. Finally the astonishing energy on the part of King William that was involved in this defensive endeavour also deserves emphasis, for only thus can the total achievement of the Conqueror be appraised. The vitally constructive work carried out by King William between 1067 and 1087 (which has now to be considered) was accomplished in the midst of incessant warfare, and in a realm whose ruler was never secure from attack.

[1] Ord. Vit., vol. III, p. 192.   [2] Below, chap. 14.

Part IV

THE KING
IN HIS KINGDOM

Chapter 10

WILLELMUS REX

The coronation of Duke William of Normandy as king of the English on Christmas Day 1066 was the culminating event in the Conqueror's career. It also marked a turning-point in the history both of Normandy and England, and a stage in the development of medieval Europe. To England it gave spectacular illustration alike of the continuance of her identity, and also of the reorientation of her politics, whilst for Normandy its consequences were scarcely less profound, and no kingdom in western Europe was to be unaffected by the new political grouping which it symbolized. Again, the coronation took its place as a crucial episode in an interrelated process of Norman endeavour which within the space of a century was to stretch from Spain to Sicily, from Apulia to Constantinople, and on towards Palestine. Nor was the impact of the coronation restricted to secular affairs. Itself a religious act, it occurred at a moment when the papacy was beginning to effect a radical change in the structure of western Christendom, and when new ideas of political theology were being voiced with ever wider practical consequences. It is small wonder, then, that William's coronation commanded attention. Heralded, as it might seem, by celestial portents, consequent upon a notable feat of arms, and blessed by the Church, it fired the imagination of contemporaries.

Its full implications were not of course immediately apparent, and much of the importance of William's coronation was in fact to depend upon the controversial interpretations which were later placed upon it. In December 1066 the ceremony might well have been regarded as a simple recognition of existing fact: the inexorable result of a conquest effected by superior generalship, superior diplomacy, and superior force. Such, for example, was probably the dominant sentiment of those sorrowing English magnates who, before the Conqueror proceeded to Westminster, came to Berkhamstead, defeated and deeply moved, to make their submission, and who, it is said, were kindly received by William, who promised to be their good lord.[1] Somewhat more complex sentiments are, however, suggested by the debates which are said to

<hr>

[1] AS. Chron., 'D', *s.a.* 1066.

247

have followed. The English are reported to have urged William to take the crown, because they were accustomed to have a king for their lord,[1] and this, as will appear, involved far more than a change of title: it invoked a complex of loyalties, some traditional and some religious, but all emotionally compelling.

To the Normans surrounding William the situation was inevitably different. These men, ruthless and astute, were naturally anxious to push the conquest to its conclusion, but some of them were doubtless apprehensive lest William as king might be able unduly to enlarge in Normandy the rights which he already exercised as duke. At all events, William himself thought it prudent to display some hesitation in the matter, and it is perhaps significant that in the debate which ensued the most strenuous argument in favour of an immediate coronation was made not by a Norman magnate but by the Poitevin, Haimo, *vicomte* of Thouars.[2] In reality, the decision must have appeared to be almost implicit in the facts of the situation. No alternative course readily presented itself. Thus it was with the formal support of leading men both of Normandy and of England that William came at last to his crowning at Westminster. And there it was specifically as king of the English that he was consecrated.

The ceremony which then took place is of the highest interest, and it is fortunate that there have survived not only contemporary descriptions of what took place, but also a text of the *Ordo*[3] which may reasonably be supposed to reflect that used on this occasion.[4] What, moreover, is of particular importance is that these proceedings followed the traditional English pattern so that William was hallowed according to a rite which was substantially the same as that which had been followed in the coronation of English kings from at least the time of Edgar.[5] In this manner, at the solemn inauguration of his reign as king, every effort was made to stress the continuity of English royal rule. It was *Anglo-Saxonici*, it was the *Populus Anglicus*, who were ritually called upon to salute the king as he was consecrated to rule over 'the Kingdom of the Angles and the Saxons'.[6] The claim to be the inheritor of an unbroken royal succession was thus spectacularly made at the very beginning of William's English reign. It was to govern his policy until his death.

None the less, significant changes were made on this occasion. The

[1] Will. Poit., p. 216. [2] *Ibid.*, p. 218.
[3] Printed in *Three Coronation Orders*, ed. J. Wickham Legg (Henry Bradshaw Soc., vol. XIX (1891), pp. 54–64). [4] P. E. Schram, *English Coronation*, p. 234.
[5] *Ibid.*, p. 28. [6] Wickham Legg, *loc. cit.*

circumstances of 1066 obviously called for some special acceptance of the new ruler, and it was forthcoming. Geoffrey, bishop of Coutances (speaking in French), and Aldred, archbishop of York (speaking in English), formally demanded of the assembled congregation whether they would accept the new king.[1] This was an innovation imported from France,[2] and it was to become in due course an integral part of the English coronation rite. Another interesting change occurred in the prayer *Sta et Retine*. In earlier times this had contained a reference to the new king's father, and in 1066 this was clearly inappropriate: the phrase 'by hereditary right' was therefore substituted. Similarly, the position of the queen had to be considered. Matilda was not to be crowned until 1068, but then she received more signal honours than had before been customary. She was acclaimed as having been placed by God to be queen over the people, and hallowed by unction as a sharer in the royal dominion.[3]

The most significant addition to English coronation ritual introduced by the Normans is, however, to be found in the litany which contained the liturgical acclamations known as the *Laudes Regiae*.[4] These *Laudes* (which had been sung at the coronation of Charlemagne) had, before the Conquest, been sung in Normandy on the chief feasts of the Church, and therein, as has been seen, William received as duke the exceptional honour of mention by name.[5] On the other hand, it is doubtful how far, if at all, these *Laudes* had been employed in pre-Conquest England.[6] None the less they were sung, as it seems, at the coronation of Queen Matilda in Winchester at Pentecost 1068,[7] and in due course they were to become a recognized part of the English coronation service. It is, moreover, very probable that they were sung at William's own coronation in 1066, and more certainly they were chanted before the king at the solemn crown-wearings which came to take place regularly at Christmas, Easter, and Pentecost, and which were noted as a characteristic feature of his rule.[8]

The form of these *Laudes* so far as they concerned William was, moreover, now most notably changed. In the pre-Conquest Norman *Laudes*, the duke is named only after the king of France. The saints

---

[1] Will. Poit., p. 221.   [2] Schram, *op. cit.*, p. 151.   [3] *Ibid.*, p. 29.
[4] E. H. Kantorowicz, *Laudes Regiae* (1946).   [5] *Ibid.*, pp. 63, 166, and above, pp. 153, 154.
[6] *Ibid.*, p. 178. But see also Richardson and Sayles, *Governance of Medieval England* (1963), pp. 406–409.
[7] See W. G. Henderson, Surtees Soc., vol. LXI (1875), pp. 279 *et seq.*; Maskell, *Monumenta Ritualia* (1882), vol. II, pp. 85–89.
[8] AS. Chron., 'E', *s.a.* 1087; Kantorowicz, *op. cit.*, pp. 178, 179.

invoked on his behalf come low in the sequence of the litany,[1] and the salutation runs: 'To William Duke of the Normans, health and perpetual peace.'[2] By contrast, in the *Laudes* which were sung after 1066[3] there is no mention of the king of France; the saints now invoked are Our Lady, St Michael, and St Raphael. And the salutation is: 'To the most serene William, the great and peacegiving King, crowned by God, life and victory.'[4] The change is in every way remarkable. *Vita et Victoria* is an old imperial formula, and *serenissimus* is a very old imperial designation.[5] Moreover, the salutation as a whole is one which in the middle of the eleventh century was accorded to no other lay ruler in western Europe save the emperor and the king of France. The implication is clear. In the liturgy of the Church, Duke William of Normandy has now been recognized as a *rex*. He is saluted as of equal status with the French king: one of the chief secular rulers of western Christendom.

The coronation of William gave sanction to the kingship he had won by arms, and was designed to glorify the regality into which he had entered. It was of course true – and it was everywhere apparent – that a revolution had taken place, and that this had been brought about by invasion and battle. But William and those who spoke for him were never content to leave the matter at that point. By contrast, it was continuously argued that William was the legitimate successor of Edward the Confessor after an interregnum caused by usurpation, and that he was king of England not only *de facto* but also *de jure*. The claims put forward by William in this matter are, moreover, not to be dismissed as merely specious arguments designed to justify spoliation after the event. They deserve consideration both for their effect on contemporaries, and in relation to the achievements of William between 1066 and 1087.

The arguments adduced by William to show that the factors normally operating in the succession of a king of England applied to his own situation thus demand attention. Most curious of these was his

---

[1] Saint Maurice; Saint Sebastian; Saint Adrian.

[2] 'Guillelmo Normannorum duci, salus et pax continua.' This beautiful litany is printed in J. Loth, *La Cathédrale de Rouen* (1879), in *Le Graduel de l'église de Rouen au XIIIᵉᵐᵉ siècle*, ed. Loriquet and others (1907), and in Kantorowicz (*op. cit.*, pp. 167, 168).

[3] The text of this second litany is difficult to reconstruct since it derives from Brit. Mus. Cott. MS. Vitellius E. xii, which in 1731 was much damaged by fire. I follow the version given by Henderson in his edition (*op. cit.*, p. 279).

[4] 'Wilhelmo serenissimo a Deo coronato, magno et pacifico regi vita et victoria.'

[5] Kantorowicz, *op. cit.*, p. 29.

emphatic assertion of hereditary right. 'Right of blood' (*jus sanguinis*) was, in fact, placed in the forefront of his justification by William of Poitiers, who buttressed the contention by reference to the Conqueror's relationship with Emma, the daughter of Duke Richard I, and the mother of Edward the Confessor.[1] The argument was, in truth, weak, but it probably appeared less specious in the eleventh century than it would today. Hereditary right lay at the basis of Anglo-Saxon royalty, but it was a hereditary right of the family as a whole, and not specifically of any one of its members.[2] In asserting *jus sanguinis* for himself William was therefore paying deference to ancient Anglo-Saxon (and indeed Germanic) tradition, without necessarily weakening his position against such men as Edgar Atheling who by modern theory were so much closer in the succession.

The royal family's right to the throne was held to be as inviolable as the right of any individual prince to succeed was weak. To belong to the royal stock (*stirps regia*) was an indispensable condition of legitimate kingship. Consequently, William felt constrained to stress at whatever hazard his connexion with the English kingly house, which derived, as it might seem, from Woden himself. That is why the phrase 'by hereditary right' appeared so strangely in the ritual of his coronation. And for the same reason the claim was reiterated in some of his earliest formal acts as king. In a vernacular writ issued between 1066 and 1070 the new king confirmed to the abbey of Bury St Edmunds the rights which had been held by the abbey in the time of Edward 'my kinsman'.[3] And in a charter which was given to Jumièges about the same time, William, using a title derived from the eastern empire, solemnly declared: 'I, William, lord of Normandy, have become King (*Basileus*) over the fatherland of the English by hereditary right.'[4]

In all primitive monarchies dependent upon the rights of the kindred, it was of course necessary to devise some means whereby the undisputed claim of the family to the throne could be translated into the right of a particular individual to succeed. In Anglo-Saxon England two considerations seem here to have been particularly influential. The one was the expressed wish of the reigning king respecting his successor within the royal family; the other was the acceptance of an individual (also within the family) by the magnates, and the recognition of reciprocal

---

[1] Will. Poit., p. 222.   [2] Kern, *Kingship and Law* (trans. Chrimes), pp. 12–21.
[3] Douglas, *Feudal Documents*, p. 48, no. 3.
[4] *Chartes de Jumièges*, vol. I, no. XXIX: Ego Wuillelmus Normannie dominus, jure hereditario Anglorum patrie effectus sum Basileus.

rights and duties between them as ratified by oath. Both these notions were to have some bearing on the legitimacy of the William kingship, and to both of them he was to pay overt respect.

There is no reasonable doubt that, as has been seen, in or about 1051 William received formal designation by the Confessor as his heir, and the question before contemporaries was whether this nomination had ever been formally rescinded. Within a few years of the Confessor's death, it was asserted that Edward on his death-bed had bequeathed the throne to Harold Godwineson, and there is very strong evidence to suggest that this in fact occurred. The matter is not, however, entirely removed from doubt; nor can the possibility be ignored that this promise may have been extracted by duress from a dying man during the last confused moments of his life by the interested group which is known to have surrounded his bedside.[1] Nor is it certain what weight would have been given by contemporaries to a bequest made at such a time to one who was emphatically not of the *stirps regia*, or whether this would have been generally regarded as invalidating the earlier promise to William. At all events, whatever may in fact have happened on 5 January 1066 around the Confessor's death-bed, William never ceased to claim that he had been formally designated by the king as the legitimate successor to Edward the Confessor.

In the matter of recognition by oath he was placed, however, in a more equivocal position. His acceptance as king by the Norman nobles at Berkhamstead followed recognized practice, but in the case of the English magnates it was obvious that he was dealing by constraint with men whom he had recently beaten in battle. None the less, both at Berkhamstead and at Barking, English notables had sworn loyalty to him, receiving in return a promise of good government, and these transactions could be construed, albeit with some difficulty, as following the English tradition that is exemplified, for instance, in the oaths which had been given and exacted by Edmund in 940–946. It is, however, the procedure which was deliberately adopted at the coronation which is here significant. The noteworthy innovation of the questions by the prelates was certainly introduced as an appeal to tradition, and these questions were preceded by the Conqueror pronouncing a coronation oath which is almost identical with that which had been employed at English royal hallowings since the tenth century. It was apparently delivered 'in a clear voice'.[2]

[1] Above, pp. 181, 182. [2] Schram, *op. cit.*, p. 184.

The character of William's kingship was to depend not only on such respect as he could assert for English tradition, but also on such religious sanctions as he could invoke for the royalty he acquired. The coronation of 1066 has in short to be placed in its proper setting of contemporary political theology. In the eleventh century, the notion of Christ-centred kingship was generally accepted in western Europe.[1] Thus Otto II had been depicted in the Aachen Gospels (c. 990) as set high above other mortals and in direct communion with the Godhead, whilst Conrad II had later been hailed as the Vicar of Christ on earth. Nor were such attributes, derived and developed from the age of Charlemagne, restricted to the emperors. In France the house of Capet, similarly adapting Carolingian tradition, formally claimed to rule by the 'grace of God', and their sacred mission was widely asserted.[2] Such sentiments had in fact become so pervasive that William in 1066 by exchanging his title of *dux* for that of *rex* was, by implication, demanding an exaltation of his authority.

For nowhere had the divine right of monarchy been more forcibly emphasized than in England. If William was to be accepted as a lawful king it was as the true successor of Edward the Confessor, and the sacred character of Edward's kingship is notably asserted in his earliest biography. There, for instance, it is stated that Edward ruled 'by the grace of God and by hereditary right' whilst the crown he wore is described as 'the crown of the kingdom of Christ'.[3] 'Let not the King be perturbed even though he has no son, for God will assuredly provide a successor according to His pleasure.' Edward, in fact, had been 'divinely chosen to be King even before his birth, and had therefore been consecrated to his kingdom not by men but by God'.[4] Such statements are not to be dismissed as mere rhetoric. They represent a view of kingship, which was soon to be challenged, but which in the middle of the eleventh century was widely accepted and politically influential. By assuming English royalty, William in 1066 was in fact laying claim to a position which was generally recognized as possessing attributes specially delegated to it by God.

[1] Kantorowicz, *The King's Two Bodies* (1957), chap. III.
[2] M. Bloch, *Les Rois thaumaturges* (1924), pp. 185–215.
[3] William the Conqueror 'had a crown made for himself by a Greek which with its arc and twelve pearls resembled that of Otto the Great' (Leyser, R. Hist. Soc., *Transactions*, series 5, vol. x (1960), p. 65). Was this the crown which was apparently in Normandy in 1087 ('Monk of Caen' – Will. Jum., p. 146), and which was given to William Rufus by the Conqueror on his death-bed? On the Conqueror's crowns, see further Schram, *Herrschafszeichen und Staatssymbolik*, vol. II, pp. 393 *et sqq.*, and Barlow, *Vita Edwardi*, p. 117.
[4] *Vita Edwardi* (ed. Barlow), pp. 9, 13, 27, 59.

The prestige to which he thus aspired could be further illustrated by reference to the thaumaturgic powers attributed to eleventh-century kings.[1] There is no doubt that preternatural powers of healing had been claimed for Robert II of France, and the *Vita Edwardi* recounts several miraculous cures as effected by Edward the Confessor.[2] Later, Philip I of France was credited with the limited power of healing scrofula by touch, and it would seem that the same power was ascribed to Henry I of England.[3] The precise nature of the power thus exercised was, it is true, ill-defined. In the earlier half of the twelfth century the efficacy of the 'touch' of Louis VI was attributed to his heredity as king of France, and that the power was inherent in royalty came later to be accepted in both France and England.[4] During the Investitures controversy, on the other hand, many ecclesiastics were quick to deny any such supernatural attributes to the kingly office, and in consequence to assert that the healing miracles of Robert I and Edward the Confessor were due not to their royalty but to their personal sanctity.[5] No such distinctions were drawn, however, in popular opinion, and William of Malmesbury, writing for sophisticated readers about 1125, was constrained to chide the large public who believed that it was specifically as king that Edward the Confessor had performed his miracles of healing.[6]

The royal state into which William entered was surrounded by a strange atmosphere of veneration. Whether he himself ever 'touched' for scrofula must remain uncertain, but, set as he was between Edward the Confessor and Henry I (both of whom were later credited with thaumaturgic powers), it is not impossible that he did so.[7] Indeed, there is indirect testimony which points, albeit doubtfully, towards this conclusion. About 1080 Goscelin, a monk of Saint-Bertin, who came to England in 1059, composed a Life of St Edith, the daughter of King Edgar, which he dedicated to Lanfranc. In this work, he describes a posthumous miracle performed by the royal saint whereby Ælviva, abbess of Wilton from 1065 to 1067, was cured of a malady affecting her eyes (one of the signs of scrofula), and the disease is described as 'the royal sickness'.[8] Evidently, towards the end of the reign of William the Conqueror, something like the disease later held to be specially susceptible to the royal 'touch' was already being described in England

---

[1] Bloch, *op. cit.*   [2] *Vita Edwardi*, pp. 60–63.   [3] Bloch, *op. cit.*, pp. 31, 46–49.
[4] *Ibid.*, p. 31.   [5] *Ibid.*, pp. 45, 120.   [6] *Gesta Regum*, p. 273.
[7] R. W. Southern, 'The First Life of Edward the Confessor' (*Eng. Hist. Rev.*, vol. LXII (1943), p. 391).
[8] A. Wilmart, *Analecta Bollandiana*, vol. LVI (1938), pp. 294, 295.

as the 'King's Evil'. And, equally certainly, the crown-wearings which William made a regular feature of his English reign, and at which the *laudes regiae* were sung, could have supplied appropriate occasions whereat such ceremonial acts of healing might have been performed.

Whatever place may be assigned to William the Conqueror in the curious history of royal healing there can be no question of the religious attributes of the royalty which was henceforth to be his. It was thus inevitable that he should claim that his kingdom had come to him as a gift of God. The ecclesiastical support accorded to his expedition could be cited in favour of such a view, and Hastings itself might be likened to a trial by battle in which God had delivered a just verdict. William of Poitiers developed this idea,[1] and if he must be regarded as a prejudiced witness, no such criticism can be levelled at Eadmer. Yet Eadmer comments on the battle of Hastings in exactly the same sense. So heavy were the losses inflicted on the Normans, he says, that in the opinion of eyewitnesses William must have been defeated but for the intervention of God. Therefore (concludes Eadmer) William's victory must be considered as 'entirely due to a miracle of God', who was not willing that Harold's perjury should go unpunished.[2] The idea was capable of wide development. As early as 1067 William is formally described in a charter for Peterborough as 'king of the English by the grant of God'.[3] And the claim that William's royalty had in a special way been granted to him by God was not allowed to die.

It was here that the unction accorded to him at the coronation became important, since it emphasized the religious nature of his office, and at the same time indicated the manner in which his power might perhaps in the future be circumscribed. Unction was reserved for priests and kings. No Norman duke had hitherto been anointed. William's unction therefore marked a stage in the growth of his authority, and it thus attracted the attention of contemporaries. The Anglo-Saxon chronicler confines himself to the statement that William was hallowed, but Eadmer calls emphatic attention to the unction, and William of Poitiers insists that it was performed by a prelate of unblemished reputation.[4] The *Carmen* was later to glorify the act in

---

[1] Will. Poit., pp. 171, 206.

[2] Eadmer, *Hist. Novorum* (ed. Rule), p. 9: 'absque dubio soli miraculo Dei ascribenda est'.

[3] *Mon. Ang.*, vol. I, p. 383: 'Dei beneficio Rex Anglorum.' The phrase has feudal connotations.

[4] AS. Chron., 'D', *s.a.* 1066; Eadmer, *Hist. Novorum, loc. cit.*; Will. Poit., p. 220.

rhetorical verse,[1] but among contemporaries it was William of Jumièges who perhaps best summed up what took place. Not only (he says) was William accepted by the Norman and English magnates; not only was he crowned with a royal diadem; but he was also 'anointed with holy oil by the bishops of the kingdom'.[2] In this manner was the change of dynasty in England formally legitimized by one of the most solemn of the rites of the Church.

There was, moreover, a special importance attaching to the anointing of William in 1066. If unction in the eleventh century was regarded as an essential feature of every royal inauguration, it was particularly apposite at a time of dynastic change, since it was part of ecclesiastical doctrine that suitability to rule rather than strict hereditary right must in the last resort be held to justify any sacramental sanctions bestowed by the Church.[3] At the time of the coronation of Pippin in the eighth century, Pope Zacharius is reported to have declared that it were better that he should be called king who possessed the power rather than he who had none, and a parallel might now profitably be sought between Edgar Atheling and Childerich III. In the interval Adémar of Chabannes had stated much the same principle in favour of Hugh Capet,[4] and Gregory VII was himself to repeat the doctrine with perfect clarity.[5] The notion that dynastic change might be formally and solemnly ratified by consecration, and more particularly by unction, was thus peculiarly applicable to the English situation in 1066.

The precise implications of the unction were, however, liable to dispute, and they were later to form part of a great controversy. Two contrasted interpretations of the unction might in fact be made.[6] It might be regarded as a recognition of existing rights pertaining to the divine institution of royalty, or it might be held as the source of those rights. It gave the king a place apart from the laity, and might even vest him with sacerdotal powers. But it might also be held to make his status dependent upon a religious service performed by the clergy. These questions were to loom large in the arguments on the relations between secular and religious power in western Europe which were to begin before the close of William's English reign, and which were to be developed during the Investitures Contest. It is, therefore, appropriate to consider what was William's own situation in this matter on the day

---

[1] *Carmen* (Michel, *Chroniques*, vol. III, p. 38).   [2] Will. Jum., p. 136.
[3] Kern, *op. cit.*, pp. 37–43.   [4] Ed. Chevanon, pp. 150, 151.
[5] *Monumenta Gregoriana* (ed. Jaffé), p. 458.
[6] Bloch, *op. cit.*, pp. 69–74; Kern, *op. cit.*, pp. 27–61.

on which he was solemnly anointed in Westminster Abbey 'by the tomb of Edward the Confessor' on Christmas Day 1066.[1]

It was inevitable that at the time of the Investitures Contest, those ecclesiastics who were concerned to subordinate secular authority to the Church should seek to deny that royal unction was an indelible sacrament, giving the king the status of priest, and though the papalist case in this matter was not to be fully set out until the time of Innocent III, most of the arguments he reviewed had been stated by Hildebrandine writers during the previous century.[2] A denial that royal unction was a sacrament was, indeed, implicit in the claim of Gregory VII to be able to depose anointed kings, and it is therefore not surprising that when in the course of the twelfth century the sacraments of the church were defined, graded, and limited to seven, royal unction found no place among them, though the consecration of priests of course remained. Consequently, there was towards the end of the twelfth century a consistent attempt made to minimize, in the case of kings, the dignity of the anointing ceremony itself. Such contentions indicate the strength of the later ecclesiastical opposition to the notion of the priest-king, which in fact was to wane in political importance during the twelfth century. But they also suggest how general must have been the support for that notion during the previous century.[3]

There can, indeed, be little question of the strength of these ideas in England in the time of King William. It was, in fact, Norman writers who, in all Europe, were to be the most prominent in developing the notion of the priest-king in favour of the Anglo-Norman monarchy he founded. The famous tractates formerly attributed to the Norman 'Anonymous of York'[4] are now generally believed to have been compiled in Rouen about the end of the eleventh century, and it is not impossible that their author was William Bonne-Ame who in 1079 became archbishop of Rouen with the Conqueror's approval.[5] In these tractates, as is well known, the royal office was exalted to extraordinary heights. By unction (it is there asserted) the king is sacramentally transformed; he becomes a *Christus domini*; he becomes a *sanctus*; and there may even be found in his office a reflection of the authority of

---

[1] Ord. Vit., vol. II, p. 156.

[2] Kantorowicz, *King's Two Bodies*, p. 36; Schram, *op. cit.*, p. 120.

[3] Even in the twelfth century, John of Salisbury could complain that ignorant people still thought that kings had the spiritual authority of priests (Southern, *Making of the Middle Ages*, p. 94).

[4] See G. H. Williams, *Norman Anonymous of 1100* (1951).   [5] *Ibid.*, pp. 24–82, 102–127.

God Himself. It must of course be remembered that this author was writing at the beginning of the Investitures Contest, and with the fervour of a controversialist supporting the secular power. But his ideas are generally regarded as having been traditional,[1] and, as has been seen, they reflected sentiments which had been widely current at an earlier date, and particularly in the early biography of Edward the Confessor. They may reasonably be held therefore to represent the view of the English royalty that was in 1066 acquired by the Norman duke, and the effect of such ideas on popular sentiment in both England and Normandy must have been considerable. Lanfranc (it is said) was once constrained to reprove a clerk who, watching William seated in splendour at one of his crown-wearings cried out: 'Behold I see God.'[2]

It would of course be difficult to assess the effect of such sentiments on William's authority, but it might be easy to underestimate their force. They must certainly have contributed to the consolidation of his power during the early years of his English reign, and from the start he attempted to translate them into practice. Claiming the loyalties inherent in English kingship, he began his administration specifically as an English king. An interesting group of charters has survived which were issued very early in his reign. The most famous of these was in favour of the city of London,[3] but others were addressed to various churches: to Westminster, for example, and to Chertsey Abbey; to Saint Augustine's Abbey at Canterbury; to Giso, bishop of Wells; and to Baldwin, abbot of Bury St Edmunds.[4] It will be noted that all these grantees belonged to southern England beyond which the new king's power did not extend. Already, however, the purport of all these charters was that the customs which prevailed under Edward the Confessor are to be preserved. The reign of Harold Godwineson is treated as an interregnum. The Conqueror is made to appear as the direct successor to the Confessor: as the legitimate, and consecrated, holder of all the royal rights of the ancient English dynasty.

Nor can there be any question that the special qualities of the royalty he thus assumed would affect his policy towards the Church at a time when the relations between secular and ecclesiastical authority throughout western Europe were becoming increasingly controverted. Many of

[1] Kantorowicz, *King's Two Bodies*, pp. 42–61.
[2] Milo Crispin, *Vita Lanfranci* (*Pat. Lat.*, vol. CL, col. 53); cf. Williams, *op. cit.*, p. 161.
[3] Liebermann, *Gesetz*, vol. I, p. 286, and elsewhere.
[4] *Mon. Ang.*, vol. I, pp. 301, 431; Elmham, *Hist. monasterii S. Augustini Cantuariensis* (ed. C. Hardwick), p. 36; Douglas, *Feudal Documents*, p. 49, no. 4.

his English predecessors had ruled specifically 'by the grace of God';[1] most of them, including Edward the Confessor, had intervened in the detailed administration of ecclesiastical affairs;[2] and indeed one of them had actually been likened to the Good Shepherd whose sacred duty it was to tend the flock of the faithful. Now, in the coronation *Ordo* which was sung in 1066, it was once more prayed that this new Norman king would foster, teach, strengthen, and establish 'the church of the whole kingdom of the Anglo-Saxons, committed to his charge, and defend it against all visible and invisible enemies'.[3] Such a position, so notably reasserted at a time of violence and change, was fortified by tradition. Not only did it derive strength from the religious sanctions of Old English royalty, but it harmonized with the long-standing claims of Canterbury to leadership over the whole *ecclesia Anglicana* – a term which not only embraced the provinces both of Canterbury and York but might even stretch into Scotland or Ireland. On this matter William, the great king, and Lanfranc, the great archbishop, were to find themselves at one.[4] And in a wider sphere also the impact of these ideas was to be felt. They offered a counterpoise to rising theories, which, while seeking to diminish the sanctity of royalty, at the same time claimed complete freedom for the Church from secular authority. One of the greatest practical advantages which accrued to Christ-centred monarchy was that it legitimized the control by a king over the Church throughout all his dominions.

The chief effects of William's coronation were of course to be felt in England. But its consequences extended to Normandy also. It was not merely that his personal standing was thereby increased so that a wider gulf was henceforth to separate him from even the greatest of the Norman nobles. Nor was it solely that the feudal arrangements of Normandy were to be altered (as will be seen) in William's favour as a result of the conquest of England. It was, also, a matter of prestige. No Norman duke had ever been anointed.[5] No Norman duke had hitherto been saluted with such impressive *Laudes*, and certainly the faithful in Normandy had never before heard their duke mentioned by name as William now was, as king, in every recital of the Canon of the

---

[1] Stenton, *Anglo-Saxon England*, pp. 537, 538.

[2] Apart from his appointment to bishoprics, note his treatment of the nunnery of Leominister (Freeman, *Norman Conquest*, vol. II, note N).

[3] Wickham Legg, *op. cit.*, pp. 54–64.

[4] Below, pp. 321–323.

[5] Schram, *op. cit.*, p. 47; Bloch, *op. cit.*, pp. 496, 497.

Mass.[1] William brought the glory of medieval regality to the Norman ducal dynasty, and his authority in Normandy was inevitably enhanced by the fact.

There was, moreover, a particular reason why in Normandy, at this time, William's acquisition of the kingly dignity must have been especially influential. The manner in which the English expedition had been blessed by the Church was only part of a process whereby during these critical decades the Normans had adopted the notion of a holy war and exploited it in their own interests. Again and again the same theme had been stressed. In 1062–1063 Pope Alexander II had given his blessing and a banner to Norman knights fighting in Sicily. In 1064 the Normans were prominent in the 'crusade' at Barbastro.[2] In 1066 William himself fought in Sussex under a papal banner, and with dedicated relics round his neck. In 1068 Norman knights such as Roussel of Bailleul and Roger Crispin, whose exploits seem to have been known to William of Poitiers,[3] were serving with the eastern emperor against the Turks.[4] In 1070 the religious character of William's own expedition was proclaimed afresh at Windsor, and in 1071 Norman warriors were engaged with the emperor at Manzikiert.[5] In 1072, while William was advancing into Scotland, Roger son of Tancred captured Palermo from the Saracens,[6] and, however mixed the motives which inspired it, the Norman conquest of Sicily resulted in the most important triumph of Christians over Moslems in the eleventh century. These events so closely connected in time were also intimately related in spirit for, as must be emphasized, they were undertaken by men who were brothers and cousins of one another, fully conscious of their kinship, and conscious also of their common and militant purpose. And now this self-styled 'crusading' endeavour which involved so many lands had been crowned by the assumption of divinely sanctioned royalty by a Norman duke.

[1] There seems no doubt of this. The king is mentioned by name in the Canon in the Sarum and Hereford rites after the name of the bishop (Maskell, *Ancient Liturgy of the Church of England*, pp. 82, 83). This is also the formula of the 'Missal of Robert of Jumièges' (Henry Bradshaw Soc., vol. XL, 1896), so presumably it goes back in England before the Norman conquest. For the French practice, see R. Fawtier, *Capetian Kings* (1950), p. 76. The connexions between the rites of Rouen, Salisbury, and Hereford are discussed with a wealth of learning in E. Bishop, *Liturgica Historica*, pp. 276–301.

[2] Setton and Baldwin, *History of the Crusades*, vol. I, p. 21; R. Dozy, *Recherches sur l'histoire de la litterature de l'Espagne*, vol. II, pp. 335–353. The Annals of Saint-Maxence of Poitiers (*Rec. Hist. Franc.*, vol. XI, p. 220) call particular attention to the participation of the Normans in the affair at Barbastro.

[3] Ord. Vit., vol. II, p. 199.   [4] Schlumberger, in *Revue historique*, vol. XVI (1881), pp. 289–303.

[5] Runciman, *Crusades*, vol. I, pp. 66, 67.   [6] Setton and Baldwin, *op. cit.*, p. 64.

How potent might be the effect of these ideas is suggested by a comparison between some of the literary and liturgical texts of this time. The continuous sequence of events of which the Norman conquest of England may be said to have formed a part, is generally held, for instance, to have inspired the *Song of Roland*, which probably assumed its present form towards the close of the eleventh century, or at all events before 1124.[1] But in the *Song of Roland* not only is the notion of the Holy War glorified, but also the conception of the divinely sponsored monarch who is himself both priest and king. The fabled Charlemagne is, there, a man of supernatural age, and of supernatural sanctity; St Gabriel watches over his sleep, and when he fights, the angel of God goes with him. Moreover, he is certainly the priest-king. He gives the priestly blessing; like a priest, he signs with the cross; and, as only a priest can, he pronounces absolution.[2] Now, it is not impossible that the *Roland* assumed its present form under Norman influence,[3] but whether this be so or not, its relevance to the contemporary idea of the Holy War as exploited by the Normans, and to the Christ-centred monarchy to which William aspired, is evident. Indeed, in respect of the latter notion, the closest parallel to the *Roland* in contemporary texts is to be found in those tracts by the Anonymous of Rouen (or of York) which were certainly of Norman origin, and which equally certainly reflected the same ideas of kingship.

The direct bearing of this on the question of William's royalty could be further illustrated by renewed reference to those *Laudes* which were sung before him, most probably at his coronation, and certainly at his subsequent crown-wearings. In 1068 these *Laudes* contained the invocation: 'To all the lords of the English, and to the whole army of the Christians, life and prosperity.'[4] Now, the hail to the 'army of the Christians' is entirely appropriate to the fabled Charlemagne of the eleventh-century *Roland*. And it may have been brought to England by the Normans. Moreover, its particular relevance to the circumstances of 1066 as envisaged by the Normans is made clear by the subsequent history of the *Laudes* in England. For while these continued to be sung in honour of the kings of England until at least the early thirteenth

---

[1] Bédier, *Légendes épiques*, vol. III, pp. 183 *et sqq*. Many of the details of Bédier's magnificent exposition have been questioned, but the central fact seems established.

[2] *Ibid.*, vol. IV, pp. 458, 459.

[3] Cf. Douglas, 'Song of Roland and the Norman Conquest of England' (*French Studies*, vol. XIV (1960), pp. 99–114).

[4] Omnibus principibus Anglorum et cuncto exercitui Christianorum, vita et salus.

century, yet by the middle of the twelfth century the phrase 'army of the Christians' had been replaced by 'army of the English'.[1] The special 'crusading' sentiment characteristic of the Normans in the eleventh century had departed, and its disappearance shows by implication how strong had been that sentiment at the time of William's coronation.[2]

These considerations indicate from a new angle the effect of William's coronation not only on Normandy but on the wider Norman world. For that world towards the end of the eleventh century was in a real sense a unity. Norman prelates such as Geoffrey of Coutances and Odo of Bayeux received contributions from their kinsfolk in Italy to enable them to build their cathedrals at home. The Norman *Laudes* with which England was made familiar after 1066 were to pass on to Apulia,[3] and it was noted as a source of pride that the chant of Saint-Évroul rose to God from the monasteries of Sicily. Not for nothing was Rouen soon to be hailed as an imperial city – as a second Rome – for (as was said) the Norman people had gone out from thence to subdue so many other lands.[4] These were sentiments of the mid-twelfth century, but they reflected an earlier tradition. The Conqueror, it is said, was wont to confirm his courage by recalling the deeds of Robert Guiscard,[5] and his contemporary biographer boasted that the troops he brought to England belonged to the same race that took possession of Apulia, battled in Sicily, fought at Constantinople, and brought terror to the gates of 'Babylon'.[6] Certainly, the Norman world of this age was a reality, proud of its asserted Christian mission, and proud also of its armed might which by 1072 had been made to stretch from Abernethy to Syracuse, from Barbastro to Byzantium, from Brittany to the Taurus. And within this vast zone of interconnected endeavour, William between 1066 and 1087 occupied a special place. He was the only Norman *rex*; he was the only Norman *Christus Domini*. As such, throughout the self-conscious Norman world of the eleventh century he might claim – and he might sometimes be accorded – a unique prestige.[7]

Herein lay the peculiar importance to Normandy and the Normans

---

[1] Kantorowicz, *Laudes Regiae*, p. 236. [2] *Ibid.*, p. 179.
[3] Ord. Vit., vol. II, p. 91; L. T. White, *Latin Monasticism in Norman Sicily*, p. 48.
[4] E. M. Jamison, 'The Sicilian Norman Kingdom in the Minds of Anglo-Norman Contemporaries' (Brit. Acad., *Proceedings*, vol. XXIV (1938), pp. 249–250).
[5] Will. Malms., *Gesta Regum*, p. 320. [6] Will. Poit., p. 228. Where is 'Babylon'?
[7] As early as the eleventh century, chroniclers were saluting William the Conqueror as if he had been in this sense lord not only of Normandy and England but even in some sense also of Apulia and Sicily (Kantorowicz, *Laudes Regiae*, p. 157).

of the act of 1066 by which William, using all the Old English precedents in his support, laid claim to Christ-centred kingship. And for these reasons, also, the same act was to foster a common purpose in both parts of his realm. In England he could call to loyalties which had long been centred on an ancient royal house. In Normandy, as the duke who had risen to royalty, he could appeal to the particular patriotism of a unique province, and also to Norman pride in a far-flung military endeavour that had been linked to a self-asserted Christian purpose. And these sentiments, distinct in England and Normandy, were in some measure fused together by the central religious act of Christmas Day 1066.

In this sense therefore it is appropriate to apply the term 'Anglo-Norman kingdom'[1] to those dominions on both sides of the Channel which, between 1066 and 1087, were united under the rule of King William. Some important qualifications must, however, always be borne in mind when the term is used in this sense. William was not only king: he was more specifically king of the English; and after 1066, as before, he was also duke of the Normans. In charters of Norman provenance between 1066 and 1087 both titles are normally used,[2] and if the ducal style is made to yield precedence to the royal, the double description remained and its implications are not to be ignored. Nor were its political consequences to be negligible. They were at the last to find expression after William's death, when the Conqueror's realm became divided for nineteen years before it was reunited under the rule of one of his sons.[3]

Nevertheless, when all proper qualifications have been made, it remains true that in a real sense the dominions of King William between 1066 and 1087 constituted a single realm and a political unity. Duke William II of Normandy was now King William I of England, but it was equally true that the Norman duchy was now under the rule of a king. And this was to affect his position in Normandy scarcely less than in England. It was as king that he was to hold his courts which, on both sides of the Channel, comprised much the same set of people. It was as a consecrated king that he, and he alone, between 1066 and 1087, attended and dominated the ecclesiastical councils which met

---

[1] The term is, of course, also used to designate, and with perfect propriety, 'The Kingdom of England under the Norman Kings'.
[2] *Rex Anglorum* followed by *Dux* (or sometimes *Princeps*) *Normannorum*. Any charter of Norman provenance purporting to have been issued by William between 1066 and 1087 without the royal style is for that reason highly suspect.　　　　　[3] Below, pp. 360, 361.

both in Normandy and in England. And it was under a single king that a single aristocracy, predominantly Norman in composition, controlled the administration of his conjoint realm. As a result, during this period Normandy and England were to exercise a continual and reciprocal influence on each other, and the transformations which then occurred were always dependent upon the duke who had become a king, and whose royal status was essential to his subsequent achievement. Thus it was that William's coronation in 1066 accurately foreshadowed many of the special characteristics of the realm he ruled, and indicated much of its future history.

Chapter 11

THE FEUDAL POLITY

The coronation of William the Conqueror marked the beginning of a formative period which produced changes of lasting importance to both parts of his conjoint realm, but it was inevitable that England should be the more immediately and the more profoundly affected. Norman influence upon England was now in fact to be fully extended, and on highly individual lines, by a Norman king, and the earlier growth of Norman power and policy already indicated clearly the main directions in which that influence would be most notably felt. Norman power had been based upon a new feudal nobility which now claimed the rewards of conquest. Norman policy had been fortified by a revival in the province of Rouen. The results to England of the Norman conquest might, therefore, be expected to be in the first instance aristocratic and ecclesiastical. And such was in fact to be the case. But even as William had dominated the recent developments in his duchy by adapting more ancient institutions to his purpose, so also might it be anticipated that he would now utilize to the full the traditional powers of the monarchy he had won, and the institutions of the country he had conquered. This also was to take place, with the result that the Norman impact upon England was to be drastically modified by English tradition under the direction of the Norman king.

The political union of Normandy and England under William the Conqueror, and the manner in which it had been consummated, entailed inexorably radical changes in the higher ranks of the social order in both countries. Between 1066 and 1087 Normandy and England were not only brought under the rule of a Norman king, but they were also progressively and together subjected to the dominance of the Norman aristocracy. The results were to be far-reaching. For Normandy it meant that a newly formed aristocratic group was to be vastly enriched, and at the same time brought into more closely defined relations with the duke who had become a king. For England the same process involved nothing less than the destruction of an ancient nobility, and substitution in its place of a new aristocracy imported from overseas. This was, in fact, perhaps the greatest social change which occurred in England during the reign of William the Conqueror, and it was effected to a large extent under his management.

The fate of the Old English nobility during these years was in truth catastrophic, and its downfall is one of the best documented social transformations of the eleventh century.[1] The three great battles of 1066 in England had taken a heavy toll of this class, and those who escaped the carnage of Fulford, Stamford Bridge, and Hastings, the defeated supporters of a lost cause, faced a future which could only be harsh and bleak. Their position after William's coronation was at best precarious, and it soon deteriorated. At first the king was content to make use of English officials and to have at his court magnates such as Edwin, Morcar, and Waltheof. But these earls were soon to disappear from the political scene, and the events of 1068–1071 were to bring fresh calamities to the men whom they might have protected. The early wars of King William in England entailed further widespread destruction to the lives and property of the Old English nobility, and at the same time brought to an end any policy of compromise which the king might perhaps have been disposed to adopt towards them. It was fatal to their fortunes. Many went into exile: to Scotland, to Flanders, or to Byzantium, and those who remained, robbed of their natural leaders, and deprived of their possessions, found themselves powerless in the face of the new aristocracy which was ready to supplant them. Their downfall was all but complete. Domesday Book records all the greater landowners in England in 1086 and it is rare to find an English name among them. By the end of the Conqueror's reign, it has been calculated, only about 8 per cent of the land of England remained in the possession of this class.[2] It had ceased to be a dominant part of English society.

The new aristocracy which supplanted it, though predominantly Norman, was not exclusively so. Many of those who took part in the Conqueror's venture came from other provinces in Europe, and some of these settled in the country they had helped to subdue. An important group of men derived, for instance, from regions to the east of Normandy, and among these were some who were either Flemish in origin, or to some extent dependents of the counts of Flanders. Eustace, count of Boulogne, despite his adventures in 1067 was to establish his family in England, and many lesser landowners in 1086 could similarly be

---

[1] F. M. Stenton, 'English Families and the Norman Conquest' (R. Hist. Soc., *Transactions*, series 4, vol. xxvi (1944), pp. 1–17).

[2] W. J. Corbett, in *Cambridge Medieval History*, vol. v, chap. XV, to which I am particularly indebted.

traced to the Boulonnais.[1] Such, for instance, as Gunfrid and Sigar from Chocques in Hainault, who were established in Northamptonshire, and the family of Cuinchy, who were later to supply earls of Winchester.[2] Similarly, Arnulf from Hesdins, in the Pas-de-Calais, was, in 1086, a tenant-in-chief in many shires, and Gilbert 'de Gand', who likewise received large estates in England, was the son of a count of Alost.[3] But of all this group with Flemish connexions, the most interesting was a certain Gerbod, who was probably *advocatus* of the abbey of Saint-Bertin. Described as *Flandrensis*, he was apparently the son of another *advocatus* of the same name, and in 1070 he was entrusted with the earldom of Chester.[4] At about the same time his brother, named Frederic, received lands in East Anglia while his sister, Gundrada, married William of Warenne.[5] It was an important connexion, and, if it had been established permanently in England, the Flemish element in the settlement might have been larger than in fact it was. But Gerbod, after holding his earldom for less than a year, returned to Flanders, and having fallen into the hands of his enemies, perhaps at the battle of Cassel, passed into obscurity; whilst Frederic seems to have been killed by the followers of Hereward in 1079.[6] None the less, men from Flanders continued to provide a significant element in the new nobility, and when, before the end of 1069, William protected the lands of Aldred, archbishop of York, he did so by means of a vernacular writ which contained a solemn warning to 'Normans and Flemish and English'.[7]

More numerous than the Flemings, were the Bretons. Among these the most prominent were the sons of Eudo, count of Penthièvre. The second of them, Brian, received extensive lands in the south-west and perhaps became earl of Cornwall. He witnessed a charter of the Conqueror for Exeter in 1069, and in the same year he helped to repel the attack of the sons of Harold.[8] But his sojourn in England was apparently brief. His position in Cornwall was soon to be taken by Robert, count of Mortain, and it was not Brian but his brother Alan I,

[1] Round, *Studies in Peerage and Family History*, pp. 142–145.

[2] Farrer, *Honours and Knights' Fees*, vol. I, p. 20; Round, *King's Serjeants*, p. 257; L. C. Loyd, *Anglo-Norman Families*, p. 84.

[3] Stenton, *Anglo-Saxon England*, p. 621; Loyd, *op. cit.*, p. 51.

[4] C. T. Clay, *Early Yorkshire Charters*, vol. VIII, pp. 40–46; C. Waters, *Gundrada de Warenne*, p. 1; *Cart. S. Bertin* (ed. Guerard), pp. 176–184.

[5] Clay, *loc. cit.*; C. Brunel, *Actes – Comtes de Pontieu*, no. IV.

[6] Ord. Vit., vol. II, p. 219; *Liber Monasterii de Hyda* (ed. Edwards), p. 295.

[7] *Early Yorkshire Charters*, vol. I, no. 12; Stenton, *English Feudalism*, p. 24.

[8] J. Tait, in *Eng. Hist. Rev.*, vol. XLIV (1929), p. 86; *Regesta*, vol. I, no. 23; Will. Jum., p. 141.

'the Red', who in fact was the real founder of the English fortunes of the family. This Alan, who served in the Breton contingent at Hastings, was in constant attendance upon the Conqueror, and received more than four hundred manors in eleven shires, his estates being concentrated in Yorkshire, Lincolnshire, East Anglia, and the south-west.[1] At Richmond he built the great castle which dominates the Swale and gave the name to his barony. And after his death about 1093 the extensive 'honour of Richmond' was to pass successively to his brother, Alan II ('the Black'), and Stephen, who at last united the Breton and English possessions of the family.[2]

The establishment on this scale of a cadet branch of the ruling house of Brittany indicates the importance of the Breton element in the feudal settlement of England. The presence of Ralph of Gael as earl of Norfolk during the earlier years of the Conqueror's reign was another sign of the extent of Breton influence, and in truth there was scarcely a shire which was not affected.[3] The lands pertaining to the Richmond fee became thickly studded with Breton names, many of whom were important. Again, Judhael of Totnes possessed in 1086 a large honour in the south-west; Oger 'the Breton', Alfred of Lincoln, and Eudo, son of Spirewic, were established in Lincolnshire; whilst in Essex, Tihel of Helléan gave his name in perpetuity to Helions Bumpstead.[4] Indeed, the assimilation of the Bretons into the new feudal aristocracy of England was not to be completed before the Conqueror's death. Nor was it achieved without difficulty. The close connexion of the rising of Ralph de Gael with the affairs of Brittany has already been noted, and the suppression of that rebellion led to the imposition of fierce penalties against certain of the Bretons in England.[5] It is not impossible that the substitution of Count Robert of Mortain for Count Brian in Cornwall was a consequence of these measures.

Despite the influential groups which derived from Flanders or Brittany, the bulk of the new aristocracy which was established in England under William the Conqueror came from the nobility which

---

[1] A. Wilmart, in *Annales de Bretagne*, vol. xxxviii (1929), pp. 576–602; *Complete Peerage*, vol. x, p. 784; for the family, see Clay, in *Early Yorkshire Charters*, vols. iv and v.

[2] *Complete Peerage*, vol. x, p. 785. That he was the brother of Alan the Red appears from a charter for Bury St Edmunds (Douglas, *Feudal Documents*, p. 152, no. 169). According to St Anselm, the two brothers aspired to marry Gunhild, daughter of King Harold, when she was a nun at Wilton (Southern, *St Anselm and his biographer* (1963), pp. 183–195).

[3] Stenton, *English Feudalism*, pp. 24–26.

[4] *Ibid.* See also Round in Essex Arch. Soc., *Transactions*, vol. viii, pp. 187–191.

[5] AS. Chron., 'D', *s.a.* 1076 (equals 1075).

had arisen in Normandy during the earlier half of the eleventh century. Its rewards were immense. Of all the land in England surveyed in Domesday Book, about a fifth was held directly by the king; about a quarter by the church; and nearly half by the greater followers of the Conqueror.[1] Moreover, this secular aristocracy was not only extremely powerful and predominantly Norman: it was also small. The immediate tenants of the king as recorded in Domesday Book were, it is true, a large and miscellaneous class, but those who were predominant among them were few. Thus about half the land, held by lay tenure in England under the Conqueror, was given by him to only eleven men. These were Odo, bishop of Bayeux and earl of Kent; Robert, count of Mortain; William fitz Osbern; Roger of Montgomery; William of Warenne; Hugh, son of Richard, *vicomte* of the Avranchin; Eustace, count of Boulogne; Count Alan the Red; Richard, son of Gilbert of Brionne the count; Geoffrey, bishop of Coutances, who had a large secular barony in England; and Geoffrey from Manneville in the Bessin.[2] The names may well challenge attention; for all except Eustace and Count Alan were Normans; and all except Geoffrey of Manneville and Count Alan had played a conspicuous part in the history of Normandy between 1040 and 1066. On them nearly a quarter of England was bestowed.

Most of what remained to be distributed among the secular followers of William was likewise acquired by comparatively few persons. Among the men who were lavishly endowed were, for instance, the representatives of the comital dynasties of Évreux and Eu; Roger Bigot from Calvados; Robert Malet from the neighbourhood of Le Havre; Hugh of Grandmesnil; and Robert and Henry the sons of Roger of Beaumont. And to these might be added Walter Giffard from Longueville-sur-Scie, Hugh of Montfort-sur-Risle, and Ralph III of Tosny.[3] It is an impressive list, but while it could of course be supplemented in many directions with names which were later to become famous in English and European history, it could not be immeasurably extended. It deserves emphasis that less than 180 tenants-in-chief are recorded in Domesday Book as possessed of English estates which are rated at an annual value of more than £100.[4] And from among these, the great men – and the great families – stand out to show the manner in which under the direction of the

---

[1] Corbett, *op. cit.*   [2] *Ibid.*
[3] *Ibid.* Cf. *Complete Peerage*, vol. IX, p. 575, and vol. XII, part I, p. 758; Loyd, *op. cit.*, pp. 45, 56; Douglas, *Domesday Monachorum*, pp. 65-71.
[4] Corbett, *op. cit.*

Conqueror the territorial wealth of England was concentrated between 1070 and 1087 into a few very powerful hands.

This small and dominant aristocracy preserved in England the cohesion it had previously attained in Normandy. Not only did inter-marriages between the greater families continue to strengthen the ties between them, but the magnates themselves were able to reproduce in England the close relationship with their dependents which they had established in Normandy before the Conquest. This element in the Norman settlement of England was in fact so important that it perhaps deserves more illustration than it always receives. The great Norman honours in England were, as is well known, widely scattered, but the *tenurial* connexions among their members were very frequently the out-come of earlier *territorial* associations between them in Normandy. In other words, the chief tenants of a Norman magnate in England might be widely separated from one another, holding lands in different shires, but they very often bore territorial names which reveal their families as near neighbours in Normandy. Thus, among the Domesday Book tenants of Robert Malet were men who can be shown to have come from Claville, Colleville, Conteville, and Émalleville, all of which are situated close to Graville-Sainte-Honorine, the centre of the Malet power in Normandy.[1] Again, as tenants in England of Richard fitz Gilbert or his son can be found men who took their names from Abenon, Saint-Germain-le-Campagne, La Cressonière, Fervaques, Nassandres, and La Vespière, all of which are close to Orbec the head of Richard fitz Gilbert's Norman barony.[2] Examples could be multi-plied. As has been seen, the early connexion between Pantulf and Montgomery was reproduced in eleventh-century Shropshire, and the long-standing dependence of Clères upon Tosny was continued in Yorkshire where in the middle of the twelfth century, members of the family of Clères held lands which before the death of the Conqueror had belonged to Berengar 'de Tosny' of Belvoir.[3] Similarly, among the tenants in England of Robert, count of Eu, were men whose names reveal the origin of their families in Creil-sur-Mer, Floques, Norman-ville, Ricarville, Sept-Meules, and Mesnières, which lie in a circle round Eu itself.[4]

The manner in which the Norman aristocracy was introduced into England provides striking testimony to the constructive statesmanship

[1] Loyd, *op. cit.*, pp. 29, 30, 31, 40, 56.   [2] *Ibid.*, pp. 1, 34, 41, 71, 112.
[3] *Early Yorkshire Charters*, vol. 1, nos. 593–596.   [4] Loyd, *op. cit.*, pp. 36, 43, 63, 73, 86, 97.

of the Conqueror. Two urgent tasks were here imposed upon him. On the one hand, it was essential that the establishment of this highly competitive nobility in a recently conquered land should be effected in such a manner that general anarchy should not ensue. On the other hand, it was imperative that the enrichment of the Norman magnates should be made to enhance, and not to diminish, the king's authority and power both in Normandy and in England. These problems were formidable. But upon their solution the survival of the Anglo-Norman state would in large measure depend.

In England, William's claim to rule as the legal and sanctified successor to Edward the Confessor here stood him in good stead. Even so, it was by personal mastery of a difficult situation that he was able generally to insist that his magnates should take up not only the rights, but also the obligations, of their English predecessors. Thus, it became usual for a Norman lord in England to find himself endowed within each shire not with a miscellaneous collection of manors but rather with all the lands which had formerly belonged to one or more pre-Conquest landowners. The consequences of this were to be profound. It has frequently been noted that, with certain exceptions, the lands granted to the king's followers were not as a rule concentrated, but scattered throughout the country. This process has sometimes been attributed to the king's political design, and sometimes to the fact that as the Conquest proceeded piecemeal, so also did the allocation of lands take place gradually as each new region came under the Conqueror's control. Both these views deserve consideration, but by themselves they offer only a partial explanation of what occurred. In the first place, the 'scattering of the manors' can itself be exaggerated, for while one of William's greater followers was normally given land in many shires, it was by no means uncommon for him to acquire a concentration of landed wealth in some particular region in which he was dominant.[1] Again, the large and scattered estate was by no means unknown in England in the reign of Edward the Confessor, where many of the greater nobles possessed wide lands which (like those of their Norman successors) were largely farmed under a system of stock and land leases.[2] In this respect, therefore, the new aristocracy often found little difficulty in adapting themselves, under the king's direction, to earlier conditions.

Moreover, while the transference of possession was of course sometimes accompanied by private violence, it was more often effected

Stenton, *Anglo-Saxon England*, p. 619.   [2] Lennard, *Rural England*, chaps. V, VI, VII.

without disturbance, and it is wholly remarkable how frequently cases of dispute were settled at the king's command by reference to traditional legal process. In the great trials which were a characteristic feature of the Conqueror's reign appeal was regularly made to Anglo-Saxon custom,[1] and one of the objects of the Domesday survey was not only to record the conditions prevailing in the time of Edward the Confessor but also to provide evidence of the legality of such changes as had occurred since his death. Here, again, William was concerned to represent himself as a king of England by due succession, and it was under the guise of an astute conservatism that the redistribution of English lands took place. A declared respect for legal precedent was thus paradoxically made to pervade the whole process whereby within the short space of twenty years a new nobility was given to England, and this in part explains William's success in effecting so great a redistribution of land without provoking irreparable disorder in his kingdom.

The survival of his composite realm depended, however, even more directly upon his ability to make the establishment of this aristocracy itself subserve its military strength. Indeed, this dominant purpose was displayed from the very outset of his reign. At strategic points in his kingdom he at once endowed with compact blocks of territory those members of the Norman nobility who were most deeply committed to his cause. Thus the bulk of Kent was given to his half-brother Odo, and the five rapes of Sussex – Hastings, Pevensey, Lewes, Arundel, and Bramber – were bestowed on the counts of Eu and Mortain, William of Warenne, Roger of Montgomery, and William of Briouze.[2] The Isle of Wight had in 1067 been entrusted to William fitz Osbern, and after 1076 Cornwall was under the dominance of Robert, count of Mortain.[3] Finally, the great marcher earldoms came into being – Hereford, Shrewsbury, and Chester – and these passed to William fitz Osbern, Roger of Montgomery, and Hugh, son of Richard, *vicomte* of Avranches.[4] From Kent round to Chester, in short, the most vital defensive areas were all in due course allotted to the king's half-brothers, and to William fitz Osbern, William of Warenne, the count of Eu, Roger of Montgomery, and Hugh of Avranches – precisely that group of Norman magnates which had most consistently supported William

[1] Below, pp. 305–310. [2] D.B., vol. I, fols. 16–29.
[3] *Complete Peerage*, vol. III, p. 428; and above, p. 267.
[4] Below, pp. 295, 296.

in Normandy, and which now was to receive the largest share of the landed wealth of England.

Of even greater importance, was the fact that everywhere in England the Norman aristocracy was made to receive its land on conditions which increased William's power as king. It was indicative of his personal authority that he was able to make these men from the start his tenants-in-chief in England, holding their lands, not in absolute ownership as spoils of conquest but in return for providing a specified number of knights for the royal service.[1] It was the king, again, who fixed in each case the number of knights required – the *servitium debitum* as it was called – by means of individual bargains which bore no fixed relationship to the amount or value of the lands granted.[2] These arrangements which, as is well known, involved the institution of military feudalism in England, were in short the product of a royal plan, adopted and enforced by King William in the years immediately following the Conquest. Early narratives suggest that it was already used to provide troops for the expedition to Scotland in 1072;[3] a writ from the king to the abbot of Evesham shows the system in operation before 1077;[4] and records of a slightly later date indicate that many of its details had been worked out before the end of the reign.[5]

The successful imposition of tenure by service upon his magnates in respect of their English lands must be regarded as one of the most notable of the Conqueror's achievements. Not only did it establish his followers as a dominant aristocracy in England, but it made their endowment meet the defensive needs of his realm. The conditions under which these men received their lands supplied the king with between 4,000 and 5,000 trained troops,[6] and the fact that the provision of these troops rested in the hands of a comparatively few men, all closely associated with the king, made the arrangements the more efficient. Nor was there any doubt of their necessity. At no time was the Anglo-Norman state immune from attack. Its preservation was, as has been seen, the hazardous result of two decades of almost continuous war.[7] The feudal policy of the Conqueror was thus a response to immediate military needs. The Anglo-Norman polity became an aristocracy organized for war. Only as such was it enabled to endure.

The success of these arrangements depended in large measure on the

[1] Round, *Feudal England*, pp. 225 *et sqq.*   [2] *Ibid.*, p. 261.
[3] *Chron. Mon. Abingdon*, vol. II, pp. 1–5; *Liber Eliensis* (ed. Stewart), p. 274.
[4] Round, *Feudal England*, p. 304.   [5] Douglas, *Domesday Monachorum*, p. 105.
[6] Stenton, *Anglo-Saxon England*, p. 626.   [7] Above, pp. 211–244.

manner in which they were made. Two stages marked their institution. The first was the imposition of the *servitia debita* on the tenants-in-chief, a series of acts by the king which took place shortly after the Conquest, and which were a direct concomitant of the allocation of English lands to his greater followers. The second stage in the process concerned the means taken by the tenants-in-chief to meet the military obligations which had thus been laid upon them. In the earliest days of Anglo-Norman feudalism many of the knights supplied to the king by his tenants-in-chief did not themselves possess land, but discharged their military service as members of the household retinues of their lords.[1] Such, for instance, were the 'armed and mounted men' who rioted outside Westminster Abbey during the coronation of the Conqueror, or the Norman retainers of Abbot Thurstan who, 'fully weaponed', outraged the monks of Glastonbury in the abbey-church in 1083.[2] They were a dangerous class. The knightly retinue of the abbot of Ely caused havoc on the abbey lands about 1070, and the household knights of Walcher, bishop of Durham, precipitated the northern rebellion of 1080.[3] The household knight belongs, in fact, to a state of society which, as between 1066 and 1072, had not yet been perfectly stabilized. When it was no longer necessary for lords to have knights at hand ready for instant defence, the number of household knights began rapidly to decline in England, though they tended to survive longer in such areas as Lincolnshire and East Anglia where sudden attack from Scandinavia might be anticipated.[4] Certainly, the king had no wish to perpetuate the existence of bodies of men who were always liable to cause disorder, and he discouraged the retention of such men by his tenants-in-chief.

Thus it was that during the Conqueror's reign it became progressively the practice of his tenants-in-chief in England to make provision on their own estates for the knights whose service was owed to the king. Early charters of enfeoffment in England are rare, and not always unambiguous, but some survive from the eleventh century.[5] The enfeoffed knight was already a characteristic figure in English society at the time

---

[1] Stenton, *English Feudalism*, pp. 139–141.

[2] Will. Poit., p. 220; AS. Chron., 'E', *s.a.* 1083.

[3] *Liber Eliensis* (ed. F. O. Blake), pp. 216, 217, and above, pp. 240, 241.

[4] Stenton, *op. cit.*, p. 138.

[5] *e.g.* Douglas, *Feudal Documents*, p. 151, no. 168; Galbraith, *Eng. Hist. Rev.*, vol. XLIV (1929), pp. 353–372. The ambiguity of both these instruments is emphasized by their editors. See also A. Robinson, *Gilbert Crispin*, p. 38, for an early Westminster enfeoffment, and compare this with the Abingdon charter commented on by me in *E.H.D.*, vol. II, no. 242.

of Domesday Book;[1] and by the middle of the twelfth century the typical knight in England was a man holding land by primogenital hereditary tenure in return for a liability to special duties and payments. His chief duty remained the performance of specialized military service, or the financing of such, together with attendance at his lord's court. His chief payments were involved in the 'feudal incidents' – sums to be paid on special occasions to his lord.[2] Within a century of the Norman conquest, knighthood in England thus came to be recognized as the badge not merely of military aptitude but of social class characterized by a privileged form of land-tenure.

Such conditions were characteristic not of the eleventh century but of feudal society as fully formed. But the process which was to entail this result was inherent in the military arrangements made by William, and it began during his reign. He encouraged the enfeoffment of knights by his tenants-in-chief, and on occasion he personally intervened in the particular arrangements they made.[3] Nevertheless, it was a gradual development which was by no means complete at the time of William's death. The enfeoffment of knights proceeded sporadically, and no attempt was made to regularize the 'feudal incidents' before the twelfth century.[4] Throughout the Conqueror's reign, the knights in England formed a very miscellaneous class. Alongside humble retainers living within the households of their lords, there were already described as 'knights' important men possessed of large estates who were socially the equals of their lords, and who might hold land directly from the king elsewhere. Such were probably the 'landholding men of account' who attended the famous Salisbury moot in 1086 and there swore direct allegiance to the king.[5]

The establishment of a new aristocracy on a basis of contractual military tenure was the greatest social change effected in England by King William, and no topic has inspired more controversy than the question whether the basic institutions of military feudalism which it involved were themselves introduced into England for the first time by

[1] See the section given to the knights of Lanfranc (D.B., vol. 1, fols. 4, 4b).

[2] On these see Pollock and Maitland, *History of English Law* (2nd ed.), vol. 1, pp. 296–356. The principal items were the *relief* payable when the knight took over his estate, and *aids* liable to be given to the lord on special occasions. The lord was also entitled to *wardship* over a knight who succeeded when under age, and could dispose of the heiress to a knight in *marriage*.

[3] Douglas, *Feudal Documents*, p. xcix; also *Economic History Review*, vol. IX (1939), pp. 130, 131.

[4] See 'coronation charter' of Henry I (Stubbs, *Select Charters* (1913), p. 100).

[5] Stenton, *English Feudalism*, pp. 85 *et sqq.*; and see below.

the Conqueror and his followers. Broadly speaking, until the end of the nineteenth century, it was generally held that the military arrangements made by King William were evolved by adaptation out of the Old English past when many forms of dependent tenure of course existed. Subsequent scholars, following the lead of J. H. Round, and fortified by the erudition of Sir Frank Stenton,[1] have considered that there was here a break in continuity, and that a new phase of social development began when every great lord held his land in return for a direct obligation to provide a recognized amount of military service. The arguments adduced in favour of this interpretation are certainly cogent, and today it is probably true that most students of the subject would accept them, finding it hard to detect any significant trend towards organized military feudalism in Anglo-Saxon England, and regarding the feudal institutions and practices established in England as essentially an importation into England by William the Conqueror. On the other hand, in recent years this view has been vigorously challenged by several scholars who are being led back to the opinion that Anglo-Norman feudalism owed very much to the institutions of Anglo-Saxon England.[2]

This is assuredly not the place to enter into the details of this debate, but some of the points which will need further consideration before these problems are finally solved may here be briefly and neutrally noted in so far as they relate to the personal career of William the Conqueror himself. Thus it is clearly necessary in this matter to distinguish between the imposition of the *servitia debita* and the subsequent enfeoffments. Despite arguments to the contrary,[3] it would seem that there is as yet insufficient evidence to disturb the belief that the allocation of these quotas was an innovation introduced into England by the first Norman king, and one which owed little or nothing to Anglo-Saxon precedent. With regard to the enfeoffments, however, more complex questions arise. In the Confessor's England the typical warrior was the thegn: by the time of William's death he was the knight. A contrast between the thegn and the knight has therefore been a cardinal feature of all theories which regard military feudalism in England as essentially a creation of the Conqueror's reign. The enfeoffed knight (it

---

[1] Round, *Feudal England*, pp. 225–316; Stenton, *English Feudalism*, chaps. I–IV.

[2] The debate is surveyed by C. W. Hollister in *American History Review*, vol. LXVI (1961), pp. 641–665; and by J. C. Holt in *Economic History Review*, vol. XIV (1961), pp. 333–340.

[3] M.Hollings (see below) presents arguments which are relevant to this question. E. John (*Land Tenure in England*, p. 160) is more emphatic.

is said) whose estate varied in size, performed his service in return for the land he held, and he was essentially a man trained to fight on horseback, and possessed of the equipment for so doing. The thegn by contrast (it is added) was normally possessed of an estate of five hides; his military service derived from his rank and not from his tenure; and when he fought he fought on foot.[1]

How far these distinctions (which have been very generally received as true) are in fact valid must be a matter of opinion, since they are today being both defended and denied by expert critics.[2] It may, however, be useful to discriminate among them. Thus it has been suggested that not every thegn in the time of Edward the Confessor would have denied that he owed his service in return for the land he held, and evidence has been adduced to show that on the lands of the bishop of Worcester, the knights' fees created in the Conqueror's reign were based on the five-hide estates which had previously been occupied by thegns.[3] Such testimony deserves weighty consideration, but it must be noted that it relates to but one region of England, and that elsewhere such correspondence is demonstrably lacking.[4] These matters may, therefore, be left in some suspense. But it may be reasonable to suppose that in practice the theoretical distinction between the thegn and the knight may sometimes have loomed less large in the eyes of contemporaries than it has done in the minds of later commentators. In the time of William the Conqueror it was not unknown for the same man to be described both as a thegn (*tainus*) and as a knight (*miles*);[5] and on one of the greatest baronies in England there appear very shortly after the Conquest military tenants of native ancestry and pre-Conquest connexions, alongside Norman magnates some of whom are known to have fought at Hastings.[6]

Perhaps, indeed, the contrast between the mounted knight and the unmounted thegn has itself been somewhat overstressed. It is true that disaster overtook the Herefordshire thegns who in 1055 were made by Earl Ralph the Timid to fight, continental fashion, on horseback,[7] and it is true also that the Norman knights in 1066 brought their horses with

---

[1] Stenton, *op. cit.*, chap. IV, esp. pp. 116, 118, 131.
[2] *e.g.* J. C. Holt and M. Hollings; and H. R. Loyn, *Anglo-Saxon England and the Norman Conquest* (1962), pp. 320–323.
[3] Hollings, 'The Survival of the Five Hide Unit in the Western Midlands' (*Eng. Hist. Rev.*, vol. LXIII (1948), pp. 453–487).
[4] C. W. Hollister, *Eng. Hist. Rev.*, vol. LXXVII (1962), pp. 418–436.
[5] Douglas, in *Economic History Review*, vol. IX (1939), pp. 128–143.
[6] Douglas, *Domesday Monachorum*, pp. 58, 59, 105.   [7] AS. Chron., 'C', *s.a.* 1055.

them, and used them effectively at Hastings. But it is possible that at Stamford Bridge, Harold had mounted troops at his disposal, and used some of them as cavalry during the engagement. Similarly, the conception of the Norman knight as exclusively a mounted warrior appears to break down when reference is made to his subsequent achievements. At Tinchebrai (1106) King Henry made his barons fight on foot; at Brémule (1119) similar methods were used; at the battle of the Standard (1138) the knights fought in close column on foot, sheathed in armour; and at the battle of Lincoln (1141) King Stephen ordered his knights to dismount, and drew them up in close order as infantry.[1] These men were the immediate descendants of the men who effected the Norman conquest of England, and gave the tone to the military organization which resulted therefrom. They may well have learnt much from the military practices which their fathers had found in England, but the extent to which they fought on foot none the less deserves full consideration in any estimate of the techniques which the Conqueror introduced into England. After all, much of the warfare he had waged as duke before 1066 had consisted of attacks on fortified strongholds such as Brionne, Domfront, and Arques; and in such operations mounted troops would have had but a small part to play. Indeed, it is a mark of the military history of the latter half of the eleventh century that infantry and cavalry were being increasingly combined in operations and sometimes with considerable tactical skill.[2] William himself had shown how effectively this could be done. If his victory at Hastings was due in large measure to his having transformed a number of miscellaneous contingents into a disciplined force, so also did it derive from the skill with which he co-ordinated the onslaught of his mounted warriors with the action of his archers.

Moreover, the feudal host of some five thousand knights produced by the establishment of his greater followers in England can never have been sufficient by itself for the king to conduct the defence of his realm over a period of some twenty years. He was bound, therefore, to supplement it from elsewhere, and there seems no doubt that he turned in this matter to the military organization which already existed in England at the time of his coming.[3] He found in this country a royal army – the *fyrd*; he found also forces for local defence organized in the shires of

---

[1] A. L. Poole, *Obligations of Society*, p. 37; David, *Robert Curthose*, p. 247.
[2] J. F. Verbuggen, *De Krijgskunst in West-Europa in den Middeleeuwen* (1954), pp. 148–149.
[3] Hollister, *Anglo-Saxon Military Institutions* (1962), chap. VII.

England. In both of these the duty of service seems to have been assessed in terms of hides or multiples of hides, and indispensable to the system were the thegns, who were the characteristic warriors of the royal host, and also the natural leaders of the local levies.[1] Much is obscure about these arrangements, but there is no doubt that they survived the Conquest, and provided the Norman king with an instrument that he was not slow to use. In 1068 he summoned English troops to his service when he marched against Exeter,[2] and in the same year the men of Bristol, on their own volition, repulsed the sons of Harold, in the same way as the thegns of north Somerset had repelled Harold himself in 1052.[3] In 1073 William took a large force of English to Maine, and in 1075 Lanfranc successfully called out local levies against the rebel earls.[4] In 1079 there was a strong English contingent in William's army at Gerberoi, and in the fighting the king was to owe his life to an English thegn.[5] Such events are important in dispelling the myth that the Norman conquest can be interpreted in terms of nationalism.[6] They are scarcely less significant in illustrating the manner in which the military arrangements of pre-Conquest England were utilized by the Conqueror during the decades when he was establishing in this country the formal institutions of military feudalism.

Nor was it only on the military organization of pre-Conquest England that he relied to supplement his feudal force. Emphatic attention has recently been called to the extent to which he depended upon mercenaries.[7] As has been seen, he used paid troops in his expedition of 1066, and though he disbanded many of these in 1068, he engaged more for his service in 1069–1070.[8] The treasure alleged to have been taken from the churches of England in 1070 was doubtless used to finance the campaigns of the following years, and about 1078 William employed the profits of estates confiscated from his continental enemies to increase the numbers of his own mercenaries.[9] It is not without relevance to this question that the period of the Conqueror's wars saw the rise to some temporary importance of a moneyed class in Normandy which owed its

---

[1] Michael Powicke, *Military Obligations in Medieval England*, pp. 1–25.
[2] Ord. Vit., vol. II, p. 180.   [3] AS. Chron., 'C', *s.a.* 1052; 'D', *s.a.* 1067 (equals 1068).
[4] *Ibid.*, 'E', *s.a.* 1073, 1075.   [5] *Ibid.*, *s.a.* 1079.
[6] In this connexion it may be noted that Earl Ralph from the Vexin, who in 1055 made the thegns of Herefordshire fight, continental fashion, on horseback, had a wife named Gytha and a son named Harold (Barlow, *Vita Edwardi*, p. lxxiv).
[7] J. O. Prestwich, 'War and Finance in the Anglo-Norman State' (R. Hist. Soc., *Transactions*, series 5, vol. IV (1954), pp. 19–43), from which most of the information which here follows is derived.   [8] *Ibid.*, p. 24.   [9] Ord. Vit., vol. II, p. 297.

prosperity to the management of his revenues,[1] and the same circumstances must also be considered in connexion with the process by which the structure of English feudal society was formed. The 'money-fief' has been traced back in England to the reign of the Conqueror.[2] So also has the institution of scutage – the commutation of military obligations into money payments – and it has been suggested that its assessment may not have been wholly unconnected with the hidage system of an earlier age.[3] Be that as it may, the continuous maintenance of a large body of mercenary troops by the Conqueror is certain, and it helps to explain his terribly heavy taxation of England. In 1085 when he returned to England with an exceptionally large force, the problem of finding means to sustain it was one of the causes of the Domesday inquiry into the taxable capacity of England.[4]

Nevertheless, when all qualifications have been made, there can be no question that the destruction of one aristocracy in England and the substitution of another holding its lands by military tenure involved a revolutionary change. Doubtless, the feudal arrangements thus made could not supply all the Conqueror's needs, and all concerned in the operation of the new order had here to make concessions to a strong native tradition of administration which in any case would not be lightly abandoned by a ruler who claimed all the rights of an Anglo-Saxon king. It remains true, however, that by the end of William's reign the whole aristocratic structure of England had been transformed by the action of a Norman king and in favour of Norman magnates. The 'honour' of the tenant-in-chief, created by grant from the Conqueror, and normally comprising land in many shires, had before 1087 become a fundamental unit of English social life.[5] It had its centre – its *caput* – which was the lord's chief residence, and which might be a castle. It had its court – to which the military tenants of the honour owed suit. It was highly organized.[6] A great Norman lord in England might well have a *corps* of officials comparable even to those of the king himself: he might have his steward, his chamberlains, and so forth; he might even have his justices and sheriffs. His household, smaller and less differentiated, might be of the same pattern as that of the king.

---

[1] L. Musset, *Annales de Normandie* (1959), pp. 285–297.

[2] Bruce D. Lyon, *Eng. Hist. Rev.*, vol. LXVI (1951), p. 178.

[3] Hollister, 'The Significance of Scutage Rates in Eleventh and Twelfth Century England' (*Eng. Hist. Rev.*, vol. LXXV (1960), pp. 577–588).

[4] AS. Chron., 'E', *s.a.* 1085, and below, pp. 347–354.

[5] For example, the honour of the archbishop of Canterbury (*c.* 1096) described in *Domesday Monachorum*, p. 105. [6] Stenton, *op. cit.*, pp. 54–58.

His chief military tenants sometimes called themselves 'peers' of the honour,[1] and in the lord's court these men took their share in shaping their lord's policy, settling disputes among his tenants, and generally in giving him counsel and support. The association was close. Liege homage which a man owed to the lord from whom he held his chief tenement was the strongest bond in the feudal world, and it was also the bond which linked the tenants-in-chief to the king.[2] Correspondingly, the honours of the tenants-in-chief set up by the Conqueror in England were in a sense microcosms of the feudal state he ruled.

The feudal practices established by the Conqueror in England between 1070 and 1087 thus not only entailed permanent consequences for this country, but linked England and Normandy together in a single feudal polity subjected to the same king and the same aristocracy. The feudal structure of England was, however, never to become identical with that of Normandy, and this, too, was due in large measure to the problems which faced William during his English reign, and to the manner in which he attempted to solve them. In England he was concerned to establish a completed feudal organization by means of administrative acts: in Normandy he inherited a feudal organization which had slowly developed, and which in 1066 had not yet been fully formed. The Conqueror was thus enabled to assert from the start in England a larger measure of royal control than he had previously possessed over feudal arrangements in Normandy. This was clearly demonstrated in the vital matter of the *servitia debita*. The original assessments in England can be ascertained with some confidence from returns made in 1166 which themselves faithfully reflected conditions prevailing before 1135.[3] The Norman assessments can be calculated, at least approximately, by reference to the list of Norman fees which was drawn up for Henry II of England in 1172,[4] and from a list of Norman fees which was compiled for Philip Augustus between 1204 and 1208,[5] and which can, on occasion, be supplemented from earlier evidence.[6] The contrast that is here revealed is notable. There is nothing in Normandy to compare with the heavy quotas in England. In Normandy

---

[1] Douglas, *Feudal Documents*, no. 122; *Cart. Mon. Rameseia* (ed. Hart), vol. I, p. 133.

[2] Stenton, *op. cit.*, pp. 29, 30.

[3] *Red Book of the Exchequer* (ed. Hall), pp. 186–445. [4] *Ibid.*, pp. 624–647.

[5] *Rec. Hist. Franc.*, vol. XXIII, pp. 705–711. See also the somewhat later lists given *ibid.*, pp. 608 *et sqq.* For the relationship of these texts, see F. M. Powicke, *Loss of Normandy*, pp. 482, 483.

[6] Particularly in the 'Bayeux Inquest', which is best discussed by H. Navel, in *Bull. Soc. Antiq. Norm.*, vol. XLII (1935).

it is rare, indeed, to find any tenant – lay or ecclesiastical – with a service of more than ten knights, but in England before 1135 not less than eleven lay lords owed sixty or more knights, and at least twenty-seven more owed a service of twenty-five knights or over, whilst six bishoprics and three abbeys owed forty knights or more.

The imposition in England of these exceptionally heavy services indicate the strength of William as a feudal king. Scarcely less significant was the relationship in England between the service owed to him by his magnates, and the number of knights whom they actually enfeoffed. It must be recalled that such enfeoffments were in theory, if not always in practice, the affair of the tenant-in-chief who might establish on his own lands sufficient knights to perform the king's service, or more, or less than that number. If less, the tenant-in-chief would be compelled to secure mercenary knights to discharge his duty to the king: if more, he would have a private force at his command in excess of the knights he provided for the king. It was clearly in the interests of any king anxious to possess an efficient fighting force, and at the same time to preserve order in his dominions, that the number of knights owed for the royal service, and the number of knights enfeoffed by his magnates should as nearly as possible correspond. And in England, before the end of his reign, the Conqueror seems to have been able to make a remarkable approach to that ideal.

The measure of his success in this important matter could not be better illustrated than by a further comparison between England and Normandy. In Normandy there was always a marked discrepancy between the amount of service owed and the number of knights enfeoffed. In 1172, for instance, the bishop of Bayeux, whose Norman honour may be traced back at least to the time of Bishop Odo, had in Normandy a *servitium debitum* of twenty knights, but he had enfeoffed no less than one hundred and twenty knights on his lands. The chamberlain of Tancarville who in 1066 was represented by Ralph of Tancarville had instituted ninety-four knights' fees for a service of ten. Nor were these cases exceptional. On most of the larger Norman honours the number of enfeoffed knights was quite commonly five times that of the service owed, and it was comparatively seldom that it fell below three times of that amount.[1] In England, by contrast, the variations between the enfeoffment and the service owed were comparatively insignificant in extent, and they grew less with the progressive dismissal of stipendiary

---

[1] *Red Book of the Exchequer, loc. cit.*; *Rec. Hist. Franc., loc. cit.*

knights between 1070 and 1087. There was never in feudal England anything to compare with the conditions whereby in France, John, count of Alençon, was to have one hundred and eleven knights enfeoffed for a service of twenty; the count of Meulan seventy-three for a service of fifteen; and Robert III of Montfort-sur-Risle forty-four for a service of seven. Such details have in truth a wide general significance. They go far to explain the success of the Conqueror in making private war in England a cause of forfeiture, whereas, in Normandy, it continued to be regarded as part of a knight's duties to fight in the private battles of his lord.[1]

None the less, despite these significant and important contrasts, the reciprocal influence between the kingdom and duchy in the formation of the feudal structure of the Anglo-Norman state is not to be disregarded. If English feudalism was essentially Norman, so also was Norman feudalism by the end of the eleventh century, in some sense, English. In Normandy feudal institutions, which had slowly grown up, had not, even in 1066, been brought fully under ducal control, and even the essential principle of the *servitium debitum*, with which Normandy was of course familiar, as has been seen, does not seem at that date to have been uniformly applied to all the greater Norman baronies. Now, between 1070 and 1087, in England, a feudal order was established in which the rights of the prince were from the outset legally recognized and rigidly enforced. But the same families were involved in the feudal arrangements on both sides of the Channel, and their overlord was in each case the same. If, therefore, the rights of the king as overlord in England were asserted with special emphasis, recognition of such rights was bound to spread also in the duchy. And so it was. In 1050, whatever may have been the ducal theory, it is very doubtful whether such great families as Beaumont, Tosny, and Montgomery would have admitted that they held their lands by conditional tenure from the duke. During the Conqueror's English reign, however, these three houses, and many others, became tenants-in-chief in England, and there submitted to large *servitia debita*. And by 1087 no Norman lord would have been so bold as to claim that he did not hold his lands conditionally by service, although such service was in Normandy less onerous than in England. The Normans gave the essentials of feudal organization to England, but the completion of feudal organization in Normandy was none the less due to the conquest of England.

[1] Stenton, *op. cit.*, p. 14; Douglas, *Domesday Monachorum*, p. 72.

The feudal unity of the Anglo-Norman state was thus conditioned by the influence on each other of the duchy and the kingdom under the guidance of a king who assumed special rights within the feudal organization he controlled, and who claimed, in addition, the full prerogatives of the English royalty he had won. It was based, moreover, upon that community of interest between king and aristocracy which William as duke had been so successful in creating in Normandy before 1066. As the feudal pattern of the Anglo-Norman kingdom was dependent by the settlement in England of the Norman aristocracy under conditions which were specially advantageous to the king, so also was its government to depend in the first instance upon the relationship between that nobility and the Conqueror.

The central institution of William's government was his court, and the king's court – the *curia regis* – could from one point of view be regarded simply as the court of the greatest feudal honour in the land. The duty of the feudal vassal everywhere included attendance at the court of his lord, and this duty was shared by the king's own tenants. When the *servitia debita* had been imposed by the king upon ecclesiastics as well as upon lay lords, the feudal character of his court became still more pronounced, and though the principle was never exclusively applied, the *curia regis* of the Conqueror could without much distortion be viewed as composed of men who were linked to the king by the conditions under which the Norman aristocracy held its lands in the duchy and in the kingdom. In this sense, therefore, the *curia regis* which regularly met under William as king did not differ in essence from the *curia ducis* which before 1066 had surrounded him as duke. In both courts could be found members of his family – his wife and sons – together with his chief magnates, lay and ecclesiastical. The great court which met at Laycock towards the end of the Conqueror's reign[1] was, if larger, very similar in character to the court which in 1051 had ratified the privileges of Saint-Wandrille,[2] or that which before 1066 had met at Fécamp to assert the rights of Saint-Florent of Saumur,[3] or that again which in 1063 passed a notable charter for Saint-Ouen of Rouen.[4]

The sessions of this feudal court under King William, which took place in England between 1066 and 1087, did not, however, imply so abrupt a transition in English practice as might have been imagined. For in England William found already in existence a royal council of ancient origin, which, though formed according to different principles,

Regesta, vol. I, no. XXXII.   [2] *R.A.D.N.*, no. 126.   [3] *Ibid.*, no. 199.   [4] *Ibid.*, no. 158.

constituted an assembly of magnates not unlike that which had surrounded the duke in his duchy. The *witan* of Edward the Confessor in its fullest sessions had likewise consisted of the greater ecclesiastics and lay lords (particularly the earls), together with such other notables as the king might order to attend.[1] Like William's ducal court in Normandy before the Conquest, it was an assembly of magnates summoned by a ruler who needed their continuous support, and it is little wonder therefore that the Conqueror was at first ready to accept it. The councils which witnessed his greater English charters in 1068–1069 were thus very comparable with the larger *witans* of the Confessor's reign. In them William fitz Osbern and Roger of Montgomery, for example, took their place alongside Edwin, Morcar, and Waltheof; Saxon and Norman prelates attended in company; and among the officials present were several who had served the Confessor.[2]

These early courts of William's English reign are of peculiar interest in illustrating his policy of making what was to prove a fundamental constitutional change, both smooth and efficacious. Not until after 1070 did personnel of his *curia* become radically altered. Then, however, the development was rapid as the substitution in England of the new aristocracy for the old was inexorably reflected in the composition of the *curia*. In the greater courts towards the end of the reign it is rare indeed to find an important English name. The transformation might thus seem to have been made almost complete, but even so its constitutional significance needs to be carefully appraised. Despite the introduction of new men and new feudal ideas, the court of William the Conqueror even at the end of his reign might still in one sense be found comparable to the *witan* of Edward the Confessor, since in 1080 as in 1050 this court consisted of the monarch and members of his family, the great ecclesiastics and lay lords, and certain officials. Nor was William, posing always as the Confessor's rightful successor, ever likely to forget the special position he occupied by virtue of his English royalty. On the other hand, it remains true to say that by the time of the Conqueror's death, the *curia regis* had become Norman in personnel, and Norman also in the fact that its members attended by reason of a military tenure which the Normans had made a normal feature of English aristocratic life.

This *curia* met with considerable frequency. But already before 1087

---

[1] J. T. Oleson, *Witenagemot in the Reign of Edward the Confessor* (1955).
[2] *Regesta*, vol. I, nos. 22, 23, 28.

there was a tendency to hold its full sessions at Christmas, Easter, and Pentecost, and such occasions were always marked by magnificent ceremonial and lavish entertainment. Indeed no more effective illustration of the character of Anglo-Norman monarchy, or of its relationship to the men on whose support it depended, could be found than in a full meeting of William's court at one of the great festivals of the Christian year. Here, for instance, was the occasion for a crown-wearing, which as has been seen, formed so essential a part of the manifestation of eleventh-century kingship in its sacred and secular dignity. Seated in majesty, clad in full regalia with his lords and prelates around him, the king's authority was exalted and the ultimate sanctions of his power displayed. At the same time, the intimate connexion between the king and his immediate vassals, and their common interests were asserted. These assemblies permitted the effective rulers of Normandy and England to maintain personal contact with each other, and they enabled the king to become acquainted with all the regions of his realm through intercourse with the men who were directly responsible for their administration. Such, for example, was the atmosphere which surrounded the 'deep speech' held by the Conqueror in his Christmas court at Gloucester in 1085, when the Domesday inquest was planned, and an assembly of this nature might well include magnates whose interests covered the whole of England.[1]

It was not, however, only on such occasions of special magnificence that King William sought counsel with his magnates. His *curia* was often of smaller dimensions consisting only of such men on whose advice the king particularly depended. Thus Archbishop Lanfranc, and the king's half-brothers, Odo and Robert, together with Alan of Brittany, Richard fitz Gilbert, Roger of Montgomery, and William of Warenne seem to have formed, as it were, an inner circle of advisers whose presence the king very frequently demanded. Here, again, there is a comparison to be made between English and Norman usage, for both before, and after, the Conquest, William's *curia* in Normandy likewise expanded and contracted in this way. Moreover, after 1070, the chief personalities in William's court, on both sides of the Channel, were substantially the same. Local officials varied, of course, on each occasion, and men concerned with particular business were drawn from the localities which were most affected. But the greater magnates moved with the king. Men such as Robert and Henry of Beaumont, Roger of Montgomery,

---

[1] AS. Chron., 'E', *s.a.* 1085.

Robert, count of Mortain, and Richard fitz Gilbert – all great land-owners in England – appear at least as often in the Norman as in the English courts.[1] Keeping company with the king on his transits across the Channel, they gave to the royal *curia* the same essential character, whether it was held in Normandy or in England.

Nor was the business which occupied the Conqueror's court in England essentially different from that which, at least since 1054, had concerned his court in the duchy. As in Normandy during the decades preceding the Conquest, so now, the majority of the instruments which passed in the *curia* in England between 1070 and 1087 were concerned with confirmations of land or privilege, and, as a consequence, with judicial decisions relating to the settlement of claims. In England, the circumstances of the Conquest, and of the ensuing settlement, made this task of special importance, and, as will be seen, special machinery was frequently employed to deal with it. Nevertheless, the normal work of the feudal court of the Conqueror continued to be the same, both in Normandy and in England. The trial at Laycock,[2] which lasted from dawn to dusk before the full royal *curia*, might be taken as an example of the practice in England, but it could be paralleled in Normandy. It was before a full court held at Rouen between 1072 and 1079 that the king heard a suit between Ralph Tesson and the abbey of Fontenay,[3] and a similar court held in 1080 gave judgment in favour of Holy Trinity, Rouen, against the bishop of Évreux.[4] Examples could be multiplied. No court on either side of the Channel was more notable than that which in 1080 adjudicated between the family of Creully and the abbey of Fécamp,[5] or that which on 5 September 1082 vindicated at Oissel the judicial privileges of the abbot of Saint-Wandrille against William, archbishop of Rouen.[6]

It would, however, be unwise to particularize too closely upon the functions of the Conqueror's court. The essence of his government was a personal monarchy whose power stretched over Normandy and England. The king ruled his realm, and summoned to his assistance those members of the Anglo-Norman aristocracy, lay and ecclesiastical, who best could help him in his work. The duty of his council was, therefore, in the most general sense, to advise the king; and the king on his part would always wish to secure the support of the men who

[1] *e.g. Regesta*, vol. I, nos. 69, 72, 73, 117, 121.
[2] *Op. cit.*, vol. I, no. XXXII. [3] *Gall. Christ.*, vol. XI; *Instrumenta*, cols. 61–65.
[4] *Cart. S. Trin. Roth.*, no. LXXXIV. [5] *Cal. Doc. France*, no. 1410.
[6] Lot, *Saint-Wandrille*, no. 39.

alone could make his rule effective. There was thus as yet no differentiation of governmental function, and not until after William's death was there to be evolved out of his court specialized bodies composed of men charged with particular fiscal and judicial duties. As is well known, the exchequer and the later courts of law were offshoots of the *curia*, as was also the chancery as a distinct office. In the Conqueror's reign, government was still viewed in a simpler way. The king ruled the land, and his feudal vassals were called upon to assist him in his task: to offer him counsel, and to support his executive acts.

The feudal organization of King William's realm thus served to link together Normandy and England, and to join together in a common purpose the Anglo-Norman king and the Anglo-Norman aristocracy. The very survival of that aristocracy, particularly in England where it constituted a small minority, depended upon its members co-operating with one another, and with their king. It was as much to the interest of these men as to that of William himself that such inevitable rebellions as might occur – such as that of 1075 – should be suppressed as quickly as possible, and the history of the Normans in England, especially during the reign of the Conqueror, is never to be explained by an inherent opposition between 'king' and 'baronage'. More legitimately is it to be considered as a feudal settlement of a recently conquered country by an exceedingly able group of men with the king at their head. For their ideas of government were fundamentally the same. All alike inhabited a feudal world, which in England was largely their own creation, and they believed that it was to the advantage of everyone in this feudal world, including the king, to hold fast to his proper rights, and not to encroach upon the rights of others. The definition of feudal rights and obligations might cause dispute, but their ultimate sanction was not denied. It was a common acceptance of feudal principle by both king and magnates, in both Normandy and England, which permitted the survival of the Anglo-Norman kingdom, and went far to determine its character. It was to modify at every turn the operations of local government, and the fortunes of humbler folk whose lives were everywhere to be affected by the interrelations of great families. And it was to provide the essential background for the developing administration of a great king who exalted the royal power.

Chapter 12

THE ROYAL ADMINISTRATION

It is no part of the purpose of this book to re-tell the constitutional history of England between 1066 and 1087, but a study of William the Conqueror cannot wholly avoid the task of attempting to isolate the Norman factor in such changes as then occurred, and of estimating the personal contribution which was made by the king in bringing them about. Yet even if the problem be thus rigorously restricted, it does not admit any easy solution. The institutional developments of these years, and their social consequences, were due to a bewildering interplay of Norman and English influences. In governing his conjoint realm William found himself at the mercy of distinct and often opposed traditions, and he was faced also with the results of powerful social and economic tendencies which the Norman conquest had set in motion or accelerated.

Nevertheless, it would be rash to minimize the king's own importance in instigating or deflecting the developments which ensued. It was a personal monarchy which he exercised, and his personal influence was here always potent, and sometimes decisive. He was feudal overlord with direct and compelling rights over his greater vassals: he was a sanctified king, inheriting the prestige of the Old English monarchy, and the administrative machinery which that monarchy had created. He was placed at the very centre of power, and it is inconceivable that a king of dominating will and political genius should not have wished to seize the opportunities offered by such a position. Any consideration of his administration, or of the influence he individually exercised on the social changes which he witnessed, must, therefore, begin with the king himself and with the officials who were the chief executive agents of his will.

It was in the king's household that the king's most intimate and trusted servants were to be found. It is fortunate therefore that there has survived a document of slightly later date – the *Establishment of the King's Household*[1] – which reflects what must have been the organization of the

---

[1] 'Constitutio Domus Regis': for text, see C. Johnson, *Dialogus de Scaccario* (1956). A commentary is given by G. H. White in R. Hist. Soc., *Transactions*, series 4, vol. xxx (1948), pp. 127–155.

Conqueror's household, and reveals the primitive notions of government still prevailing in his time. As was proper to a personal monarchy, the king's administration could still be regarded as the responsibility of the king's personal servants. In the household, as described in this text, the chancellor will be found in the company of personal servants such as the king's huntsmen, while important officials bear such titles as steward, butler, and chamberlain. The holders of these offices were none the less among the most important men of the land. Many, if not all, of their purely domestic duties were discharged by deputy, and they themselves were directly responsible for much of the royal administration. The development of the royal household under the Conqueror is thus of considerable importance since it contributed substantially to the efficiency of his rule, and since it was to entail extensive constitutional consequences in the future. And the process will be found once again to illustrate the Conqueror's policy of effecting a major change with the least possible disturbance of English usage.

William had found established in England a royal household which was not dissimilar from the ducal household in Normandy, but the men who surrounded the Confessor were designated by titles unknown to Latin Europe, and the widespread use of the Danish term 'staller' to describe any 'placeman' makes it impossible to distinguish with any precision among the duties discharged by his household officials.[1] There were, however, at the Confessor's court men of standing who were content to hold domestic titles as a mark of honour, and the rough equivalents of the butler, the chamberlain, and the marshal, as these offices were understood in Normandy, could already, before 1066, be found in England. It was possible for William to retain in his household during the early years of his reign several laymen who had been officials at the Confessor's court. Bundi the staller was one of these; so possibly was Ednoth the staller; and so, certainly, was Robert 'fitz Wimarc', a man of Breton origin, and perhaps of royal connexions, who served both the Confessor and the Conqueror.[2] Very soon, however, William began, in his household, to replace men of native English ancestry by members of the Norman aristocracy who had risen to power during his reign as duke. Haimo, who was a steward in England as early as 1069, was the son of Haimo *dentatus* who was killed at Val-ès-Dunes; Roger Bigod who was prominent in the Cotentin before 1064 possibly acquired

---

[1] L. M. Larson, *King's Household* (1904); Stenton, *Anglo-Saxon England*, p. 632.
[2] *Regesta*, vol. I, nos. 7, 18, 23, 29; Round, *Feudal England*, pp. 330, 331.

during the reign of William the Conqueror the stewardship he subsequently held; and Eudo *dapifer*, already a steward in England from about 1072, was the son of that Hubert of Ryes who gave sanctuary to the young Duke William in 1047.[1] The advancement of these men was typical of a policy which by the time of the Conqueror's death was almost fulfilled. By 1087 the household of the king of England was overwhelmingly Norman in *personnel*.

Such men, scions of the new Norman nobility, brought to the offices they held the traditions with which they had been made familiar at the Norman court. Indeed, many of them had already held office in the ducal household. Chief among these was William fitz Osbern, who, already steward before 1066, retained the office even after he had become an English earl.[2] Despite his exceptional power, however, he was representative of an aristocratic group who performed service in the Conqueror's court both before and after the Conquest. Similarly, Hugh of Ivry succeeded to the office of butler before 1066 and retained the title until after 1082.[3] Finally there is the constableship, which in this respect is particularly significant.[4] For the constable was essentially the man in charge of the household knights of his lord, and the military organization of England in the time of the Confessor had as yet given no occasion for such an officer to be established at his court. The office, however, already existed in Normandy, where it was held by Hugh II of Montfort-sur-Risle, and this man, who fought at Hastings, retained the position after the Conquest, receiving the 'Honour of the Constable' for his services.[5]

It would, moreover, be rash to assume that during the Conqueror's reign there was any rigid separation between his household in England and his household in Normandy.[6] The instance of the chamberlain is here of interest. The office, it will be recalled, had been held in Normandy as early as 1034 by a certain Ralph, whose son Ralph of Tancarville was William's chamberlain both before and after 1066, passing on the office after his death in 1079 to the great family he founded.[7] Now, Ralph of Tancarville does not appear ever to have come to England, so that some distinction between the two households might here be

---

[1] *Regesta*, vol. i, nos. 26, 63, and p. xxiv.
[2] Douglas, *Eng. Hist. Rev.*, vol. LIX, pp. 77–79.   [3] White, *op. cit.*, p. 141.
[4] White, *Genealogist*, New Series, vol. XXXVIII (1922), pp. 113–127; Stenton, *loc. cit.*
[5] Douglas, *Domesday Monachorum*, pp. 65–70.
[6] White, R. Hist. Soc., *Transactions*, series 4, vol. XXX, p. 127.
[7] *Complete Peerage*, vol. x, Appendix F.

suspected. On the other hand, no master chamberlain appears to have been appointed in England during William's reign, and it is therefore probable that Ralph's duties in England were discharged by deputy.[1] At all events, his case was in some respects exceptional, and in general it would appear that these household officials of the Conqueror served the king wherever he went. Whether there was as yet any settled order of precedence among them is hard to determine. The steward, the butler, the chamberlain, and the constable seem to have retained in varying degrees the prominence which they had enjoyed before 1066, and among these offices there were distinctions, which, likewise, appear to have derived from earlier Norman traditions. Thus, between 1070 and 1087, as in pre-Conquest Normandy, there normally existed simultaneously in the household two or more stewards, and two or more constables, but the offices of butler and chamberlain were not so divided, so that the titles of master butler and master chamberlain were employed to distinguish their holders from their subordinates.[2]

Alike in its organization, in its personnel, and in the titles of its chief officers, the royal household of King William at the close of his reign resembled in most respects the earlier ducal household. Nevertheless, one important development within the household at this time derived from English precedent. No man in Normandy between 1035 and 1066 bore the title of chancellor, though the office was between 1060 and 1067 becoming fully established in the court of Philip I.[3] Nor did the ducal chaplains during these years form a highly organized *scriptorium*. In England, however, the case had been very different. The short sealed writs, uniform in character, which were issued with great frequency by Edward the Confessor,[4] presuppose a body of royal clerks who had developed settled traditions of administrative practice. Nor is there much reason to doubt that from time to time one of these chaplains obtained within the royal *scriptorium* a position of control, and he may have been entrusted with the great seal which the Confessor is known to have possessed.[5] That any of Edward's chaplains was ever styled chancellor is, however, extremely doubtful, though a certain Regenbald, who survived the Conquest and received grants from King William, was subsequently referred to under this title and may have discharged

---

[1] *Complete Peerage*, vol. x, Appendix F. [2] White, *op. cit.*, p. 128.
[3] Prou, *Rec. – Actes Philippe I*, p. lxvii.
[4] On all that concerns the Anglo-Saxon Writ, see M. E. Harmer, *Anglo-Saxon Writs* (1952), which may be supplemented by T. A. M. Bishop and P. Chaplais, *Facsimiles of English Royal Writs to 1100* (1957). [5] Harmer, *op. cit.*, pp. 101–105.

some at least of the duties which were to be associated with the chancellor's office during the Conqueror's reign.[1]

The first man certainly to be styled chancellor in England was Herfast, whose career as one of Duke William's chaplains has already been noted, and who in 1069 is described as chancellor in a charter for Exeter.[2] There was, however, at first little change in the *scriptorium* over which he presided, for between 1066 and 1070 there continued to be issued in England writs in the vernacular, which are indistinguishable in form from those of Edward the Confessor, and which are unlike any documents produced then, or at any previous time, in Normandy.[3] Nor was this continuity of practice substantially broken even in 1070 when Herfast was promoted to the see of Elmham. Nevertheless, under his successor, Osmund, likewise styled chancellor,[4] certain significant changes began to appear.[5] Henceforward, the Conqueror's writs were, generally speaking, couched not in the vernacular but in Latin, and they were progressively employed to transact a wider variety of business. The writs of the Confessor normally recorded a grant of land or rights: the later writs of the Conqueror were increasingly used to announce commands or prohibitions. They became, in short, the most characteristic expression of the king's administrative will; and the office of chancellor, now firmly established, was filled in a continuous succession through the reign.[6] Thus Herfast who became bishop of Elmham in 1070 was succeeded by Osmund who received the see of Salisbury in 1078; he in turn was replaced by Maurice who was made bishop of London in 1085, and Maurice was followed by Gerard who was still chancellor at the end of the reign. These chancellors remained, however, simply officials of the king's household, whose services after a few years were normally rewarded with a bishopric. The separation of the chancery from the household, and its development as a great judicial office, only took place at a later date.

Under the Conqueror, the king's household officials directed the royal administration in all its aspects, but the application of that administration to the kingdom at large was in other hands, and the most crucial point in the blending of Norman and English traditions took place in the sphere of local government. Here the Conqueror found at his disposal not only the great feudal families he had established in

[1] *Ibid.*, pp. 29, 60; R. L. Poole, *Exchequer in the Twelfth Century*, p. 25, no. 2.
[2] *Mon. Ang.*, vol. ii, p. 531; *Regesta*, vol. i, no. 28.
[3] Bishop and Chaplais, *op. cit.*, p. xiii.   [4] *Cart. S. Vincent du Mans*, no. 177.
[5] Bishop and Chaplais, *op. cit.*, pp. xiii, xiv.   [6] Stenton, *op. cit.*, *p.* 634.

England, but also operative units of local administration – the shires and the hundreds – which had pursued a vigorous life before ever he came to this island. It was in harmonizing these elements of social life under the control of a monarchy which had direct relations with both, that some of the greatest achievements of the Anglo-Norman dynasty were later to be made. But the process which was to entail such lasting results was begun under the Conqueror, and its later successes owed much to his initiative.

The character of the transformation of aristocratic power in England, and its effects upon English local government under the direction of the first Norman king, could not be better illustrated than by reference to the curious history of the English earldoms and of the English shrieval-ties in his time. England before 1066 had been familiar with earls and sheriffs: Normandy with counts and *vicomtes*. By the end of William's reign these offices were all possessed by men of the same aristocracy, and they were, moreover, in the Latin documents of the age described in identical terms. Both the earl in England and the count in Normandy were designated *comes*: both the sheriff and the *vicomte* appear in the texts as *vicecomes*. The fact deserves some emphasis. King William was never indifferent to English traditions, nor were the clerks who drafted his official acts lacking either in knowledge or a desire for precision. That they found no difficulty in describing offices, whose earlier history had been different, by identical names, tempts speculation how far, owing to the Norman settlement, the earls and sheriffs in England were made to approximate as to status and function, to the counts and the *vicomtes* of Normandy.

The question is made more interesting when reference is made to the personalities most directly concerned with the transition. Norman counts took a large part in the the conquest of England, and received a large share of the spoils. But with one doubtful exception, no Norman count (*comes*) became during the Conqueror's reign at any time an earl (*comes*) in England. Neither Robert, count of Eu, nor Richard, count of Évreux, received an English earldom, and it is unlikely (though not impossible) that Robert, count of Mortain, was ever earl of Cornwall.[1] By contrast it was a bishop of Bayeux who in 1067 became earl of Kent; and William fitz Osbern who at about the same time was made earl of Hereford was never a count in Normandy. An equally striking situation is revealed in connexion with the shrievalty. The

---

[1] *Complete Peerage*, vol. III, p. 428.

Norman aristocracy was to take possession of this office. But no Norman *vicomte* (*vicecomes*) became a sheriff (likewise *vicecomes*), whereas two members of notable vice-comital dynasties – to wit, Hugh of Avranches and Roger II of Montgomery – became earls in England.[1]

During the reign of the Conqueror, the position of the earl within the English polity was so transformed that it came to approximate more closely to that of the pre-Conquest Norman count than to that of the pre-Conquest English earl. In the time of Edward the Confessor almost the whole of England had been divided into earldoms, and although the notion that the earl was a royal official had never been allowed to die, in practice the politics of the reign had been dominated by the quasi-independent rivalries of the great comital houses. The events of 1066 were, however, fatal to these powerful families. After the battle of Hastings no member of the house of Godwine remained with authority, and there were to be no more earls of Wessex. Edwin and Morcar, earls at that time of Mercia and Northumbria, were likewise disinherited, and after a few years of political insignificance they passed finally from the scene, the one by death and the other through perpetual imprisonment. In the far north, Gospatric was only briefly titular earl of a truncated Northumbrian earldom, and Waltheof son of Earl Siward was to survive but for a short time. His execution for treason in 1076 brought to an end the tradition of the Old English earldoms.

William had no intention of allowing them to revive. He had no desire to see his kingdom parcelled out afresh into semi-independent princedoms, and instead, while exercising great caution, he reverted in his English policy to notions consonant with his experience of the Norman *comté*. The Norman counts before the Norman conquest had all been closely connected with the ducal dynasty, and their *comtés*, smaller in size than the English earldoms, had been situated in regions specially important to the defence of the duchy. Similar conditions were now to be reproduced in England. Thus the bestowal in 1067 of the earldom of Kent upon his half-brother Odo, and, in the same year, of the earldom of Hereford on William fitz Osbern were clearly defensive measures, and the early establishment of the earldom of Norfolk was certainly inspired by the need of protection against the Danes. Similarly, the earldoms of Chester and Shrewsbury which before 1077 had passed into the hands of Hugh of Avranches and Roger II of Montgomery[2]

[1] *Ibid.*, vol. III, p. 165; vol. XI, p. 685.
[2] Chester before 1077; Shrewsbury between 1 and 4 November 1074 (*Complete Peerage*, vol. XI, Appendix K – by L. C. Loyd).

were constructed to guard the Welsh frontier. These special creations, important as they were, covered, moreover, only a fraction of the territory which had been held by the great earls of the Confessor's reign, and they were soon to be yet further diminished. After the forfeiture of Ralph Gael in 1075 the earldom of Norfolk was not to be revived during the Conqueror's reign, and after the disgrace of Odo in 1082 the earldom of Kent was allowed to lapse. By the end of the Conqueror's reign, therefore, a remarkable transformation had here been effected. Whereas in 1065 almost the whole of England had been subjected to the rule of earls drawn from three dominant familes, in 1087 the only earldoms in being were a small region in the extreme north which in 1080 or 1081 had been entrusted to Robert of Montbrai, and the three palatine earldoms of Chester, Shrewsbury, and Hereford, one of whose holders, Roger of Breteuil, had languished in prison since 1075.[1] The earldom which in 1065 had been in England the normal unit of provincial government had by 1087 become an exceptional jurisdiction created like the Norman *comtés* on certain frontiers for special purposes of security and defence.

If the approximation of English to Norman usage thus resulted in a diminution of the importance of the earl within the English polity, a similar approximation in the case of the sheriff entailed a directly opposite result.[2] No English sheriff in pre-Conquest England had the standing or power of the great hereditary Norman *vicomtes* such as those of the Cotentin, the Avranchin, or the Bessin. The sheriff under Edward the Confessor was a landowner of the second rank whose status depended upon his being the agent of the king. By the end of William's reign his place had been taken by men who, like the earlier Norman *vicomtes*, were among the most powerful members of the aristocracy. Moreover, just as the Norman *vicomte* had been subordinate not to a local count but to the duke, who was also count of Rouen, so also did these men, as sheriffs, enter into a transformed political structure where, unlike their English predecessors, they normally found no earl as their immediate superior. It is small wonder, therefore, that there came to be 'a strong likeness between the English sheriff and the Norman *vicomte*', and indeed contemporaries found little difficulty in describing English shires as *vicomtés*.[3] The earlier history of the two offices had of course been

---

[1] *Complete Peerage*, vol. IX, p. 568.

[2] On everything connected with the Anglo-Norman sheriff, see W. A. Morris, *The Medieval English Sheriff* (1927), chap. III.

[3] *Ibid.*, p. 41; *Miracula S. Eadmundi* (Liebermann, *Ungedruckte*, p. 248).

different, but the functions, and status, of their holders in the Anglo-Norman state were made to some degree to correspond, and when all proper qualifications are made it remains true to say that 'the sheriffs of the half century succeeding the Conquest resemble their French contemporaries much more than either their English successors, or the shire-reeves of the Anglo-Saxon period'.[1]

The assimilation of the two offices (which was never to be complete) was none the less gradual. In the opening years of his English reign, William turned naturally to the existing sheriffs as primary agents of the royal power, and some of his earliest writs were addressed (in the vernacular) to sheriffs such as Edric of Wiltshire or Tofi of Somerset, who had been in office during the old régime.[2] Not until after 1070 was there any consistent attempt to replace sheriffs of native ancestry by men of a different type recruited from the duchy. Then, however, the process was rapid, and it became an essential part of William's policy to place prominent men from the new aristocracy in an office which provided so powerful a means of giving effect to the royal will. Such, for instance, were Haimo, sheriff of Kent, the son of Haimo *dentatus* who fought at Val-ès-Dunes, or Baldwin of Meules, sheriff of Devon, the son of Gilbert of Brionne, the count.[3] Such, too, were Hugh of Port-en-Bessin, sheriff of Hampshire, Urse of Abetôt, sheriff of Worcester, and Robert Malet, sheriff of Suffolk, who in Normandy was lord of the honour of Graville-Sainte-Honorine.[4] And the importance of Geoffrey of Manneville, sheriff of Middlesex, Roger Bigot, sheriff of Norfolk, Edward 'of Salisbury', sheriff of Wiltshire, and Durand, sheriff of Gloucestershire, is indicated by the fact that the heirs of all of them became, within two generations, earls in England.[5]

The acquisition of the office of sheriff by men of this importance could only be made of service to the king if they were themselves subjected to his control and made to serve, like their humbler Saxon predecessors, as royal agents. To achieve this object was not, however, easy. The office provided great opportunities for the enrichment of its holders, and many of the Norman sheriffs of this period became notorious for their depredations. Churches and monasteries were particularly loud in their complaints: Urse of Abetôt had robbed the churches of Worcestershire,

[1] Stenton, *William the Conqueror*, p. 422.
[2] Round, *Feudal England*, p. 422; Hunt, *Two Cartularies of Bath*, p. 36.
[3] Douglas, *Rise of Normandy*, p. 19.
[4] Douglas, *Domesday Monachorum*, p. 54; Loyd, *Anglo-Norman Families*, p. 56.
[5] Morris, *op. cit.*, p. 49.

Pershore, and Evesham, whilst Ely had suffered heavy losses at the hands of Picot, sheriff of Cambridgeshire.[1] Such protests could, however, only be made by the strong and influential. It was, therefore, of high importance that the king himself should strive to check abuse by his sheriffs of the great powers they wielded. In 1076 or 1077 he set up a commission which included Lanfranc, Robert, count of Eu, and Richard fitz Gilbert to inquire into the conduct of sheriffs throughout England, ordering them in particular to make restitution of any lands which had been seized from the church. Surviving writs show the attempt to give effect to this decision,[2] and in many of the great trials of the reign sheriffs came up for judgment. In its turn the Domesday inquisition was to entail the restitution of many estates which had been wrongfully acquired by the sheriffs.[3] The essential part played by the Conqueror's sheriffs in the Norman settlement of England depended, however, less upon such specific control than on the loyalty which they normally displayed towards the king. The acquisition of the English shrievalty by the Norman aristocracy thus in its turn contributed substantially to the Conqueror's policy of establishing that aristocracy in his kingdom without too great a disruption of existing institutions of local government.

For the Anglo-Norman sheriffs took over all the duties of their Anglo-Saxon predecessors.[4] They were responsible for the collection of the royal revenue; they were the executants of royal justice; they controlled the local courts of shire and hundred. In addition, they performed as in the keeping of castles, some of the functions associated in the duchy with the *vicomte*; and like the Norman *vicomtes*, many of them became specially connected with the royal court. They brought to their position in England the prestige of great feudal magnates, and this, added to the royal authority which they represented, gave them the power to enforce the king's orders, even when these might affect the greatest man in the land. It was through them that the Norman king was able to give new vitality to an ancient English office, and to bring the strength latent in Anglo-Saxon local institutions to the service of the feudal polity he founded.

Nowhere was this to prove more important than in the essential matter of finance, and here too it was William's policy to take over what

---

[1] 'Heming's Cartulary' (ed. Hearne), vol. I, pp. 253, 257, 261, 267–269; M. M. Bigelow, *Placita Anglo-Normannica*, p. 22; E. Miller in *Eng. Hist. Rev.*, vol. LXII (1947), pp. 441 *et sqq.*
[2] *E.H.D.*, vol. II, nos. 38, 39, 40.   [3] *e.g.* D.B., vol. I, fols. 208, 375–377.
[4] Morris, *op. cit.*, pp. 54 *et sqq.*

was best in the traditions of the duchy and the kingdom. The development of the fiscal system of Normandy before the Norman conquest has already been noted, and, as has been seen, its organization had been sufficient to provide the duke before 1066 with a revenue superior to that of most of his neighbours in Gaul.[1] Its most characteristic feature was the assessment of taxes on administrative areas rather than on individual estates, and the farming of the *vicomtés* by the *vicomtes*. At the same time the utilization of the ducal revenues had become the responsibility of the ducal *camera* whose existence can be traced back to Duke Richard II, and which during the Norman reign of Duke William was under the control of the chamberlain. Many of the details of the fiscal arrangements of pre-Conquest Normandy are obscure, but they had certainly provided Duke William before 1066 with the exceptionally large resources which had been necessary to enable him to make his great adventure overseas in that year. Now, they might be expected to offer the Conqueror indispensable financial support in the tasks which confronted him as king.

In England, William inherited a distinct financial system and one which was in many respects unique. Like the Norman duke, the English king had drawn his revenue from many sources. He had his customary dues; he had the profits of coinage and of justice; and he had the revenues from his own estates which were frequently farmed by his sheriffs. But in addition the king in England had for long exercised the right to levy a general tax over the whole country, which was described as a 'geld', and this geld was based upon an assessment which, while it varied in detail from region to region, was everywhere organized upon similar principles.[2] Each shire was assessed a round number of geldable units, which in Wessex and the southern Midlands were called 'hides'; the assessment was then subdivided within each shire among the hundreds; and the quota of the hundred was then repartitioned once more among the villages usually in blocks of five or ten hides. The system was undoubtedly cumbrous, but it enabled the king to impose a roughly uniform tax over the whole realm, and it has been described as 'the first system of national taxation known to western Europe'.[3]

William was quick to take advantage of it. The vernacular Northamptonshire Geld Roll, drawn up as it seems between 1072 and 1078,[4] shows

[1] Above, pp. 133–135.   [2] Stenton, *Anglo-Saxon England*, pp. 635–639.
[3] *Ibid.*, p. 636.   [4] A. Robertson, *Anglo-Saxon Charters*, pp. 230–235 (*E.H.D.*, vol. II, no. 61).

that the Conqueror was already utilizing the Old English geld arrangements for his own purpose; and there has also survived a group of Latin records, collectively known as the *Inquisitio Geldi*, which describes the manner in which a levy was made over the five western shires.[1] The Conqueror, in fact, imposed these gelds at fairly regular intervals during his reign, and the importance he attached to them is strikingly illustrated in the great survey which marked its close. Domesday Book is not simply a geld book, but one of its chief purposes was to record the liability to geld throughout England, and it is from this survey, drawn up by the first Norman king, that most of our knowledge of the geld system of Anglo-Saxon England is derived.[2]

William, in fact, brought under a single political domination two countries whose individual fiscal arrangements were relatively well developed, and it is therefore of interest to consider how far, under his direction, these were made to influence each other. There is no evidence that the English methods of geld assessment were ever in his time transported to Normandy. On the other hand, the central control of all the royal and ducal revenues continued to be in the *camera*, which after the Conquest, as before, remained under the supervision of master chamberlains of the house of Tancarville. It is not, however, certain whether during the Conqueror's reign the process had begun whereby the treasury, under an independent treasurer, was to be established as an office separate from the *camera*, or how far this development had been foreshadowed before 1066 in either Normandy or England.[3] A certain Henry, holding lands in Hampshire, was in Domesday Book (1086) styled 'the treasurer' and this Henry (though without the title) is independently recorded as having held land in Winchester, where from the time of Cnut the royal treasure, or part of it, was stored.[4] Again, the family of Mauduit, which, at a later date, held one of the chamberlainships of the exchequer, can likewise be traced to Winchester in 1086.[5] It would, none the less, be rash to draw too precise conclusions from such testimony. There is a distinction between a treasury which is a mere storehouse, and a treasury which is an office concerned, also, with dealing with the king's creditors, and with adjudicating on financial disputes.[6] The most that

---

[1] These records have been assigned to 1084 (Stenton, *op. cit.*, p. 636, note 2) and connected with the levy of the previous year. V. H. Galbraith (*Eng. Hist. Rev.*, vol. LXV (1950), pp. 7–15) places them in 1086 and connects them with the Domesday Inquest.

[2] Below, pp. 347–355.   [3] T. F. Tout, *Chapters in Administrative History*, vol. I, p. 86.

[4] R. L. Poole, *Exchequer in the Twelfth Century*, p. 35.

[5] Round, *Commune of London*, pp. 81, 82.   [6] Tout, *op. cit.*, vol. I, pp. 74, 75.

can be said is that, within twenty-five years of the Conqueror's death, some progress had been made towards the latter conception. Domesday Book was kept in the treasury from an early date, and between 1108 and 1113 an important plea was held 'in the treasury at Winchester'.[1]

It would be irrelevant, therefore, in this context to attempt any precise answer to the controversial question how far, if at all, the origins of the later exchequer can be traced to the Conqueror's reign. As is well known, the twelfth-century exchequer consisted of two related bodies: the upper exchequer which was a court controlling financial policy, and the lower exchequer which was concerned with the receipt and payment of money. It is the lower exchequer that has been derived from the treasury, which in some form or another as distinct from the *camera* has been detected in the time of the Conqueror, and even perhaps in that of the Confessor. Some of the later practices of the exchequer, such, for instance, as the blanching or assaying of money, were apparently used under the Confessor and extended under the Conqueror. Again, the importance of treasuries as recognized royal storehouses – particularly those of Winchester and Rouen – was much enhanced under William. Finally, the methods of accounting later used in the exchequer – the abacus and the careful accounts recorded on rolls – were probably of foreign origin, and may have owed something to Norman practices and officials introduced into England by the Conqueror.[2]

Whatever conclusions may be drawn about the origins of the twelfth-century exchequers of Normandy and England, the general character of William's fiscal policy is clear, and the manner in which he here blended the distinct traditions of his duchy and his kingdom, combining them efficiently into a single operative system. So far as England is concerned, this result depended directly on the fact that, as has been seen, the shrievalty during his reign was taken over so completely by the Norman aristocracy. For the sheriff remained, after 1066 as before, the chief royal finance officer.[3] He collected the royal dues; he collected fines such as the *murdrum*; and each Michaelmas he helped to supervise the payment of 'Peter's Pence'. He collected the profits of justice for the king, and was probably responsible for seeing that the feudal obligations of the king's tenants were properly discharged. He exploited the royal manors

---

[1] Round, *Feudal England*, p. 143; *Chron. Mon. Abingdon*, vol. ii.
[2] All these questions have, however, recently been ventilated afresh in Richardson and Sayles, *Governance of Medieval England* (1963), pp. 216–251.   [3] Morris, *op. cit.*, pp. 62–69.

within his shire, and took into his keeping any estates that had been for-feited to the king. Under William, moreover, it was the sheriff who was ultimately responsible for the collection of the geld. How far the later practice whereby the sheriff farmed his shire was developed by William is uncertain. There is at least one case of a farm of a shire by a sheriff before 1066, but it would be rash to assert that the practice was then general in England, or even to conclude that the system had been fully established by 1087.[1] Before the death of William, however, the practice had certainly been widely extended, and here the example of the farm-ing of the Norman *vicomtés* by the *vicomtes* may perhaps have been influential.

Of the efficiency of William's financial administration, and of its success, there can be no doubt. The revenues which as duke he had drawn from his duchy were exceptionally large for a province of Gaul, and after 1066 these were vastly increased. Together with his half-brothers he owned directly nearly half the land in England, and he drew a very large annual revenue therefrom through his sheriffs. Again, the circumstances in which the new honours had been established not only gave him very lucrative rights in respect of the feudal incidents in England, but enabled him to enforce a stricter payment of these dues in connexion with the Norman honours which were held by the same men. Profits of justice in their turn had always been a source of wealth to the duke, and now these profits were also drawn from all over England. More important still was the English geld which he must have regarded as one of the most valuable legacies which he inherited from his royal Anglo-Saxon predecessors. Four times at least he is known to have raised this tax from all over England, and the imposition was very heavy. To judge from later practice it was normally levied at the rate of two shillings for every hide of land, but on rare occasions the rate was even higher, and in the notorious geld of 1083 the assessment was at six shillings a hide.[2] It is true that many estates, particularly those of the church, were exempted from this savage tax, but even so the amount collected must have been enormous.

Nor were these the only sources from which William drew his revenue. Before the Conquest he had acquired an extensive income from taxes on Norman trade, and when he became king he could vastly increase this by similar taxation in England. By the Conquest he acquired a kingdom which was rich not only in its landed wealth

---

[1] Morris, *op. cit.*, p. 29.   [2] AS. Chron., 'E', *s.a.* 1083.

but also in respect of its trade.[1] London especially was a trading centre of high importance. To it in the time of the Confessor there came merchants from Normandy and northern France, from the Low Countries, and the Rhineland. A trade with Sweden was conducted from York, Lincoln, and Winchester, and perhaps to a lesser degree from Stamford, Thetford, Leicester, and Norwich. Chester was a centre of a trade in furs; English cheese was exported to Flanders; and both Droitwich and Norwich were important salt markets. All this activity now came under the control of the Norman king and could be taxed for his profit. It is true that the Conquest to some extent disrupted the flow of English overseas trade, but even so William's revenue from this source must have been very large. And from the towns themselves, in which it was centred, he derived great wealth. The boroughs of Anglo-Saxon England were too diverse in character to allow easy generalization to be made about them. But a greater borough normally belonged to the king in respect of two-thirds of the profit to be extracted from it, and such revenue, deriving perhaps from a mint, and more certainly from burgage tenements and from market tolls, might be very extensive.[2] It undoubtedly contributed substantially to the Conqueror's wealth and power.

It must be remembered also that such economic losses as England sustained as an immediate result of the Conquest were often made for the benefit of Normandy, and thus in turn added to William's resources. The treasure brought back to Normandy from England in 1067 attracted attention,[3] and much of the development of Normandy during the next decades was undoubtedly financed out of wealth taken from England. There was much direct spoliation of England for the sake of the duchy, but in general it was in a more indirect way that after 1066 the wealth of Normandy was increased. Norman abbeys and Norman lords had become possessed of English lands, and as these were exploited, a financial basis was supplied for the extension of Norman commerce. The material prosperity of the abbey of Fécamp under the wise rule of Abbot John is well attested,[4] and elsewhere there is testimony of a great expansion of Norman trade. The tolls levied by Geoffrey, bishop of Coutances, increased fourteen times between 1049 and 1093, and it has been estimated that a similar increase took place in the tolls of

---

[1] Darlington, in *History*, vol. XXIII (1938), pp. 141–150; H. R. Loyn, *Anglo-Saxon England and the Norman Conquest*, esp. chaps. II, III, and IX. [2] Loyn, *op. cit.*, p. 383.
[3] Will. Poit., pp. 256–258. [4] L. Musset, *Fécamp – XIIIe centenaire*, p. 79.

Caen and perhaps of Bayeux.[1] As for Rouen, the development was even more striking. The prosperity of the city as a trading port was now further enhanced, with the result that the wealth of its merchants became notorious, and a mercantile aristocracy was in process of formation.[2] By 1091 a certain Conan, who was a member of the powerful civic family of the Pilatins, was famed for his riches, and these were in fact so great that out of his own resources he could hire a considerable force of mercenaries in support of William Rufus.[3]

All this activity on both sides of the Channel was to the king's advantage, and particularly in respect of the increased flow of money which it stimulated. William had claimed as duke, and he was to retain as king, a monopoly of coinage. In the duchy there were but two mints, those of Bayeux and Rouen, but the importance of these was now naturally much increased. And in England, William found here a more notable source of revenue. In England it had been characteristic of a borough to have its mint, and coins are known to have been struck for King Harold during his short reign at no less than forty-four minting places.[4] The exclusive right of William to mint money thus became after the Conquest of the first importance, and the Norman moneyers of the king were men of substance whose management of the royal finance enabled them to amass their own considerable fortunes. The activities of Rannulf, the minter, in Normandy, before the Conquest have already been noted. His sons inherited and increased their father's wealth, and one of them, Waleran, himself a moneyer, extended his operations to England with such effect that he acquired lands in Cambridgeshire, Suffolk, Essex, and Hertfordshire, and also a house in Wood Street, London.[5]

It is impossible to estimate with any accuracy the precise amount of the annual revenue which William collected from Normandy and England. Figures are difficult to obtain, and when available it is hazardous to express them in terms of modern money. But the total sum by contemporary standards was extremely large. William was known as a wealthy prince, and when he died his financial position was perhaps stronger than that of any other ruler in western Europe. Moreover, though he left treasure to his successors, he himself never needed to be

[1] Musset, *Annales de Normandie* (1959), p. 297.
[2] S. Dek, *Annales de Normandie* (1956), pp. 345–354.
[3] *Ibid.* Cf. Prestwich, R. Hist. Soc., *Transactions*, series 5, vol. IV, p. 27.
[4] Stenton, *op. cit.*, p. 573.
[5] Musset, *op. cit.*, pp. 293, 294; *Actes – Henri II*, vol. I, nos. CLII, CLIV.

parsimonious.[1] The splendour of his court and the lavishness of his alms were notorious. His son-in-law rated his largess as second only to that of the emperor of Byzantium, and, according to William of Malmesbury, the crown-wearings which he instituted were so costly that Henry I effected a considerable economy by discontinuing them.[2] More particularly, the constant wars waged in defence of his kingdom could only have been financed out of a large revenue. Inheriting financial organizations of considerable efficiency in both parts of his realm, he developed these to such purpose that the resources of Normandy and England could be exploited to subserve the political needs of the Anglo-Norman kingdom. Indeed, the survival of that kingdom was to depend in large measure on the wealth he came to control.

The ultimate test of the government of any medieval king must, however, always be sought in connexion with the administration of justice, and here the quality of the Conqueror's statesmanship was displayed with especial clarity in both parts of his realm. As has been seen, the *curia regis* of William as king was, like the *curia ducis* over which he had earlier presided as duke, essentially a feudal court endorsing feudal law and custom; and some account of its operation between 1066 and 1087 has already been given.[3] But just as in Normandy, William had used his *vicomtés* as units of local justice, so also in England did he find, in the shires and hundreds, local courts of ancient origin, and these too he at once began to use in an attempt to make his justice pervade the kingdom he had conquered. Nowhere, indeed, in the Conqueror's England was the blend of Norman feudal ideas with pre-feudal English traditions to be more apparent than in his utilization of local courts to supplement the jurisdiction of his central *curia*.

The chief agent in forging this link which was so essential to the Conqueror's policy was undoubtedly the sheriff. Before the end of his reign the sheriff had become a great feudal magnate, and as such he was personally vested with judicial rights. But he was also by virtue of his office placed in a special relation to the courts of shire and hundred, and it was natural that he should, as his Saxon predecessors had done, hear pleas concerning the king and the kingdom in those courts.[4] He may, it is true, have shared these duties with others. The office of local

---

[1] Ord. Vit., vol. IV, pp. 87, 88.
[2] Runciman, *Crusades*, vol. I, p. 168; Will. Malms., *Gesta Regum*, p. 488.
[3] Above, pp. 284–288. [4] Morris, *op. cit.*, pp. 54–56.

justiciar[1] was established in England before the end of the reign of William Rufus, and it is not impossible that it existed sporadically, and at intervals of time, in England during the reign of the Conqueror. Æthelwig, abbot of Evesham, clearly had some official judicial position in the western shires in 1072, and so also did other men elsewhere at later times in his reign, though these were seldom specifically named as justiciars of particular shires. Nevertheless, whatever other expedients William may have used to introduce his justice into the shire courts of England, it was the sheriff who in this matter remained the natural executant of the king's will, and it was to the sheriff that the king's writ ordering some particular plea to be held was normally addressed. At the same time William exercised a more direct intervention in local justice by the dispatch of members of his own court to conduct local trials of particular importance. As will be seen, many of the chief members of the Norman aristocracy, both ecclesiastical and lay, were employed in this way by the Conqueror as itinerant justices, and among them Geoffrey, bishop of Coutances, was to be the most active in this work.

The success with which the ancient local courts of England were brought to the service of the first Norman king, and the extent to which they were made to uphold tradition at a time of change deserve to be reckoned as among the greatest of the Conqueror's achievements, and in no other matter was his statesmanship to be more influential on his English posterity. His policy in this respect thus deserves some illustration, and it could not be better exemplified than by reference to some of the great trials which were so marked a feature of his English rule.[2] Thus in his time a series of pleas were held respecting certain estates which were alleged to have been wrongfully taken from the abbey of Ely.[3] Between 1071 and 1074, for instance, a great inquiry, held before the united courts of the neighbouring shires, was conducted by the bishops of Coutances and Lincoln, Earl Waltheof, and the sheriffs Picot and Ilbert. Judgment was given for the abbey, but at least one, and probably two, more trials concerning the Ely lands occurred during the Conqueror's reign. Some time between 1080 and 1084, for instance, a

[1] On all that concerns the local justiciar, see H. A. Cronne, in *University of Birmingham Historical Journal*, vol. VI (1958), pp. 18–38.

[2] These have attracted much attention. Much of the evidence is in Bigelow, *Placita Anglo-Normannica* (1879). For a commentary, see G. B. Adams, *Councils and Courts in Anglo-Norman England* (1926), pp. 70–98.

[3] E. Miller, 'The Ely Land Pleas in the Reign of William I' (*Eng. Hist. Rev.*, vol. LXII (1947), pp. 441 *et sqq.*).

great plea was conducted at Kentford by Geoffrey, bishop of Coutances, in the presence of many of the king's tenants-in-chief, and before a combined session of the courts of the three adjacent shires, and once again judgment was given in favour of the monastery. These Ely pleas were, indeed, notable occasions, but even more spectacular, perhaps, was the trial held, either in 1072 or between 1075 and 1076, at Pinnenden Heath in Kent to adjudicate between Archbishop Lanfranc and Bishop Odo of Bayeux respecting lands which the bishop was said to have taken from the see of Canterbury.[1] This trial, also, was held under the presidency of Geoffrey, bishop of Coutances, before an assembly of the king's tenants-in-chief, meeting this time within the shire court of the county of Kent. Lanfranc obtained judgment in his favour, but the execution of the verdict seems to have been delayed, since many of the disputed estates were still in Odo's possession in 1086.[2] Finally may be mentioned the plea relating to a dispute between Wulfstan, bishop of Worcester, and Walter, abbot of Evesham, over their respective rights in the manors of Bengeworth and Great Hampton.[3] Once again the presiding judge was Geoffrey of Coutances, and the trial was held at a session of neighbouring shire courts.

These are the best reported trials of the reign, but they were certainly representative of many others, and they may fairly be taken to illustrate the general principles of the Conqueror's administration of justice. The king's direct interest in them is evident. They were instituted by royal writ, and the presiding judge was in every case the king's deputy.[4] At Pinnenden Heath, Geoffrey of Coutances is described as representing the king, whilst in the Worcestershire plea he was bidden by the king to act *in meo loco*.[5] Odo of Bayeux conducted a later Evesham plea in the same capacity, and he likewise presided for the king at a trial between Bishop Gundulf of Rochester and Picot the sheriff concerning land at Freckenham in Norfolk.[6] The presence of these men as royal *missi* – or commissioners – marks these occasions as trials before the king's court, and to that court there came, as in feudal duty bound, tenants-in-chief of the lord king, men who might sometimes be drawn from outside the shires which were more particularly affected.[7]

---

[1] J. F. Le Patourel, in *Studies – F. M. Powicke*, pp. 15–26; *E.H.D.*, vol. II, no. 50.
[2] Douglas, *Essays – James Tait*, pp. 54, 55.
[3] 'Heming's Cartulary' (ed. Hearne), vol. I, pp. 77–83.
[4] Adams, *op. cit.*, p. 71; Miller, *op. cit.*, pp. 446–448.
[5] Le Patourel, *op. cit.*, p. 23; 'Heming's Cartulary', vol. I, p. 77.
[6] Bigelow, *op. cit.*, pp. 34–36.   [7] Adams, *op. cit.*, p. 75.

Nevertheless, in these trials use was also made of specifically English institutions. The pleas were held in full sessions of the shire courts, and to these meetings there came not only the *francigenae* of the shire but also Englishmen. And the shire courts, as such, together with the sheriffs, played a vital part in the trials themselves. The Worcestershire plea was tried by the barons with the witness of the whole county, and at Kentford the verdict was formally recorded as being also the judgment of the shires.[1] Just as the Ely plea was ordered to be held 'by several shire courts before my barons', so also was the Freckenham suit heard by the king's command 'in a combined session of four shire courts in the presence of the Bishop of Bayeux and others of my barons'.[2] By holding his feudal courts in assemblies of the English shires William was grafting the royal rights of a Norman king of England on to the ancient institutions of the land he had conquered.

Nor was this merely a matter of expediency. Nothing is more remarkable in these trials than the king's desire that the traditional legal customs of England should be maintained. The bishop of Worcester was allowed to produce witnesses of native origin to testify to his established rights, and at Kentford the English took a significant part in the inquiry.[3] At Pinnenden Heath there were assembled together 'not only all the Frenchmen in the shire but also, and more especially those English who were well acquainted with the laws and customs of the land'.[4] In particular there came to this trial Æthelric, a former bishop of Selsey, 'a man of great age, and very wise in the law of the land, who by the king's command was brought to the trial in a waggon in order that he might declare and expound the ancient practice of the laws'.[5] Such acts possess more than merely antiquarian interest. Lanfranc, archbishop of Canterbury, was the king's principal adviser, whilst Odo, bishop of Bayeux, was the king's half-brother and one of the most powerful of his subjects. A dispute between them might well threaten the whole fabric of the newly established Anglo-Norman state. It is therefore noteworthy that such a controversy at such a time could, by the king's order, have been adjudicated by reference to traditional English customs. Few conquerors, medieval or modern, have shown more statesmanlike concern for the traditions of countries recently won by the sword.

The procedure adopted in these trials also calls for comment. The

---

[1] D.B., vol. I, fol. 175b; Bigelow, *op. cit.*, p. 22.   [2] Bigelow, *loc. cit.*
[3] Bigelow, *op. cit.*, p. 22; *E.H.D.*, vol. II, no. 52.   [4] Le Patourel, *op. cit.*, p. 22.   [5] *Ibid,*

method of the ordeal, which was still employed, had long been used on both sides of the Channel, as also had been the inquiries by means of witnesses or by the production of charters.[1] On the other hand, the Conqueror's practice of sending commissioners to hold his local courts was substantially an innovation in England and it was to prove, under William's successors, a powerful agency for developing the royal power. Not only, moreover, did these men bring the king's authority more directly than ever before into the shire courts of England, but in their conduct of the pleas over which they presided they made use of a method of proof which was to have the most extensive influence upon English judicial practice at a later date. For it was in these trials that use was, for the first time, consistently made of the jury as 'a group of men appointed by a court to give a collective verdict upon oath'.[2]

The origin of this institution has been much debated. Traces of it have been found in the Danish districts of England before the Norman conquest,[3] but, according to many scholars, it was introduced into England by the Normans, who developed it out of the sworn inquests which had been used by the Carolingian kings.[4] The matter may, therefore, here be left in suspense. What is certain, however, is that William employed such juries more consistently, and to greater effect, than had ever before been the case in England, and between 1066 and 1087 their use became a characteristic feature of his judicial administration. Such a jury can, for instance, probably be seen at Kentford, whilst in the Freckenham plea Odo, bishop of Bayeux, used two juries in an attempt to ascertain the facts under dispute.[5] Similarly, in Normandy, at a trial held before the king between 1072 and 1079, the rights of the priory of Bellême were vindicated by what appears to have been a collective verdict delivered by a jury composed of men of great age.[6] The practice was evidently becoming more general, and soon it was to be spectacularly extended. The Domesday inquest, which was not wholly unconnected with the earlier litigation, was itself in 1086 to be conducted largely by means of sworn verdicts given by juries up and down the land.[7] All England was thus to be made familiar with this institution which the Conqueror had established as a regular part of the

---

[1] Adams, *op. cit.*, pp. 77, 78, 97, 98; Haskins, *Norman Institutions*, p. 35.
[2] Stenton, *op. cit.*, p. 642.   [3] *Ibid.*, p. 649.
[4] Pollock and Maitland, *History of English Law* (2nd ed.), vol. I, pp. 141–142.
[5] Stenton, *op. cit.*, p. 642; Bigelow, *op. cit.*, pp. 34–36.
[6] Lechaudé d'Anisy, *Grands Rôles*, pp. 196, 197.
[7] Douglas, *Essays – James Tait*, pp. 56, 57.

royal administration. It was not the least of his contributions to the future development of English justice.

The royal administration conducted by King William entailed many consequences which were not to be fulfilled until long after his death, and it would be hard to assess what were its immediate effects upon the daily lives of the people over whom he ruled. The establishment of the Anglo-Norman kingdom wrought no such changes on peasant life as it produced in the higher ranks of society. The rural conditions prevailing in Normandy do not appear to have been substantially modified during the third quarter of the eleventh century,[1] and though the Conquest, and the disturbances which followed it, brought havoc and destruction to many English villages, the agrarian structure of England was not essentially different at the end of the Conqueror's reign from what it had been in 1066.[2] The new rulers of England seem to have been unwilling, or unable, to modify the varieties of peasant organization which existed in pre-Conquest England, and nothing is more remarkable than the persistence during these decades of diverse provincial traditions. The village customs of Kent and Northumbria were, for example, to remain distinct, and there is ample evidence that the peasantry of East Anglia and the North Mercian Danelaw still possessed after twenty years of Norman rule an exceptional degree of personal freedom.

The rural organization of eleventh-century England has been exhaustively discussed by a long succession of scholars,[3] and it needs notice in this place only so far as it was affected by the personal administration of William as king. In this connexion it is significant that the bulk of our knowledge of English peasant life in the time of Edward the Confessor derives from the great survey that was compiled by his Norman successor, and it is likewise significant that the men who drew up that survey applied to England the same terms that they used in describing the peasantry of Normandy. The Latin terms used in Domesday Book undoubtedly lack precision, but they reveal a rural society which is not essentially different from that which is described in pre-Conquest texts in the vernacular, such as the treatise on estate management known as the *Rights and Ranks of People*.[4] The categories of peasants which appear in Domesday Book are not strictly defined or mutually exclusive, but,

---

[1] L. Delisle, *Classe agricole*, pp. 1–26.   [2] Stenton, *op. cit.*, p. 473.

[3] For the latest work, see R. Lennard, *Rural England* (1959); and Loyn, *op. cit.* (1962).

[4] Liebermann, *Gesetze der Angelsachsen*, vol. I, p. 442; and see the translation by S. I. Tucker, in *E.H.D.*, vol. II, no. 172. It is usually referred to by the title of the early Latin translation: *Rectitudines Singularum Personarum*.

as in the earlier record, they range from men whose obligations, though manifold, were not incompatible with personal freedom, to heavily burdened cottagers, and to slaves who might be regarded as human chattels. Intermediate among them was the villein – the central figure of peasant society. He was the peasant with a share in the open fields of the village, who despite elements of freedom in his condition was subjected to heavy services. He performed forced labour on several days each week on his lord's land, was liable to forced payments in money or in kind, and, when he died, his possessions were legally forfeit to his lord.

The essential continuity of English rural life during the latter half of the eleventh century has long been recognized, and all that has been noted of William's administration suggests that his influence was directed to maintain it. Such changes as here took place during his reign might perhaps be briefly summarized as having occurred in two main directions. The first is the rapid decline between 1066 and 1086 in the number of slaves in England. In the time of Edward the Confessor slavery had been a characteristic feature of English village life, and it has been calculated, though with some uncertainty, that on the eve of the Norman conquest about one in every eleven persons in England was a slave.[1] By 1086 this proportion (whatever its accuracy) had been so drastically reduced that a modern commentator has found here 'the most vivid feature of change revealed in Domesday Book'.[2] It is not altogether easy to explain. Doubtless, economic factors played their part, and the new landlords, rapacious and avaricious, may have found it more profitable to exploit their estates by means of the forced labour of a dependent peasantry than by the work of slaves whose food they might have to provide. Again, the influence of a vigorously reformed church should not be ignored. But when all is said, some credit in this matter may reasonably be assigned to William's own administration. A very strong tradition, which probably at least partially reflects the truth, asserts that there was little in pre-Conquest Normandy to correspond to the widespread prevalence of slavery – and of the slave trade – in pre-Conquest England.[3] And William may perhaps have been influenced by this. He is known, for example, to have striven – albeit without much success – to suppress the Bristol slave trade,[4] and

---

[1] Loyn, *op. cit.*, pp. 350–352.　　　[2] *Ibid.*, p. 328.
[3] Pollock and Maitland, *History of English Law* (2nd ed.), vol. 1, p. 77: 'Such evidence as we have tends to show that the Conqueror left a land where there were few slaves for one in which there were many, for one in which the slave was still treated as a vendible chattel, and the slave trade was flagrant.'　　　[4] *Vita Wulfstani* (ed. Darlington), pp. 43, 91.

one of the laws later attributed to him specifically forbids the sale of one man by another outside the country.[1] At all events, it deserves note that, for whatever reasons, slavery in England rapidly declined during the reign of William the Conqueror, and within half a century of his death it had virtually disappeared from the English countryside.[2]

The other broad change in English peasant life which was characteristic of these years was in the opposite direction. The more independent of the English peasantry, normally described in Domesday Book as 'freemen', or 'sokemen', sank rapidly in the social scale. The consequences of such organized devastations as took place in the north in 1069 and 1070 may easily be imagined, and even in areas which were not so tragically affected it is not uncommon to find villages where the whole population had deteriorated in economic status between 1066 and 1086. It would, doubtless, be rash to generalize too freely from isolated examples, for every village was a flux of rising and falling fortunes. But the changes which, during these years, took place among the landowners of England must often have afflicted the peasantry. The new aristocracy, possessed of large and scattered estates, which they were concerned to exploit, were harsh landlords, and their stewards, moving from region to region, tended to enforce a uniformity of subjection which operated to the disadvantage of the more favoured villagers.[3] Inheriting the rights of their Saxon predecessors, these men possessed also the feudal superiorities they had acquired from the Norman king. And at the same time the Norman legal theory that peasant status should be determined not by inherited political right but in relation to services performed, cut at the root of such traditional claims to personal freedom as were still precariously asserted by the more independent peasants. For these reasons, while slavery began to disappear from England under Norman rule, predial servitude increased.

The reign of William the Conqueror undoubtedly witnessed very great distress among the English peasantry who comprised some nine-tenths of the population of England. Their existence was at best precarious, for they had few reserves. The failure of a crop could produce immediate scarcity, and two successive bad harvests might bring on one of those terrible famine pestilences which were so marked a feature of the age.[4] Yet such distressful conditions, in which life and

[1] Stubbs, *Select Charters* (ed. 1913), p. 99; *E.H.D.*, vol. II, no. 18.
[2] Vinogradoff, *Growth of the Manor*, p. 337.   [3] Lennard, *Rural England*, p. 33.
[4] C. Creighton, *History of Epidemics in Britain* (1891), vol. I, chap. I.

health might be preserved only with difficulty, were not the product of the Norman conquest, and it is doubtful whether they were much aggravated by it. When all allowance has been made for the inevitable hardships falling on the less fortunate during a period of political change, it remains true that there was no fundamental break in the continuity of English peasant life under the administration of William the Conqueror.

Nor was the impact of his rule markedly different on the inhabitants of the English towns.[1] The king's interest in English trade and the boroughs in which it was concentrated, has already been noted, but for the men who lived in these places the period was full of hazard. Sometimes sheer disasters occurred. The successive sackings of York, for instance, must have entailed terrible distress, and the practice of erecting castles in the chief cities of England often provoked something like a catastrophe, as at Lincoln where no less than one hundred and sixty houses were destroyed to make way for the new stronghold.[2] For these and other causes, the urban proletariat was increased during these years by men who had recently been impoverished. None the less, the growth of English municipal life was not in its essentials disrupted. During the Conqueror's reign it continued to suffer from the shock and disturbance of the Conquest, and its recovery was not complete in 1086.[3] Yet within sixty years of the Conqueror's death the towns of England were enjoying a more flourishing life than ever before, and this development probably owed something to Norman direction, and to William's policy of conservation.[4] Much of the municipal organization characteristic of twelfth-century England had existed in embryo in the time of Edward the Confessor, and William preserved and developed it. It is noteworthy how many of the Anglo-Norman charters to English towns are retrospective in character.

The composition of the English urban population does not appear to have been substantially modified as an immediate result of the Norman conquest. But the beginnings of one development which was to entail

[1] Darlington, in *History*, vol. xxiii (1938), pp. 141–150; J. Tait, *Medieval English Borough* (1936); Carl Stephenson, *Borough and Town* (1933). I prescind the controversy between Tait and Stephenson on English municipal development.
[2] J. W. F. Hill, *Medieval Lincoln*, p. 54.   [3] Loyn, *op. cit.*, p. 377.
[4] Loyn, *op. cit.*, p. 324. 'Trade did not flourish immediately as a result of the Conquest, though increased regular contact with the Continent and an infusion of new blood were both characteristics that promised well for the future.' This seems to accord with the conclusion of Tait (*Medieval English Borough*, p. 36) 'that the Norman Conquest ultimately gave a great impulse to English trade and urban development is not in dispute'.

wide future consequences can perhaps be traced to the Conqueror's acts.[1] It is doubtful whether before the Conquest there had been any permanent Jewish settlements in England, but the existence of a Jewish community in Rouen during the central decades of the eleventh century is certain. Nor is there much doubt that a colony of these Rouen Jews came to England in the wake of the Conqueror, and was there established at his instigation.[2] It was rapidly to increase in importance, and by 1130 it was evidently a settled and prosperous community.[3] On the other hand, it would be erroneous to postulate for the eleventh century anything corresponding to the widespread Jewish activity characteristic of Angevin England. The consequences of William's acts in this respect were thus to lie in the future. He facilitated the advent of Jews into England, and Jewry in England was throughout the twelfth century to retain not only a predominantly French character, but also special connexions with the Anglo-Norman monarchy.[4] But if this process began in the Conqueror's reign, and under his administration, it was not far advanced during his life, and it is doubtful whether in his time there was a settled Jewish colony in any English town except London.[5]

The daily life of the people of England depended in the eleventh century very directly upon customs and traditions which William was consistently concerned to maintain. For this reason his administration, harsh and brutal as it was, probably did something to mitigate the distress which fell on the humbler of his subjects at a time of upheaval. The English peasantry had reason to be thankful that the new aristocracy was established without wholesale disturbance, and the litigation which is recorded in Domesday Book shows many cases when some restitution was made to native tenants who had been dispossessed by the new landowners or by rapacious sheriffs. The peasantry on their part were to gain in the long run from the king's rigorous supervision of local policing.[6] Here again he followed his normal practice of adapting

---

[1] On all that follows in this paragraph, see H. G. Richardson, *The English Jewry under Angevin Kings* (1960), and particularly pp. 1-5, 23-25.

[2] *Ibid.*, pp. 1-2: 'That the London community was an offshoot of the community at Rouen is hardly open to dispute: in any case the Jews of England were so closely allied to those of Normandy that there can be no doubt of their country of origin.'

[3] *Ibid.*, p. 25.   [4] *Ibid.*, p. 3.   [5] *Ibid.*, p. 8.

[6] William is known, for instance, to have developed the system of the tithing already existing in certain parts of England, whereby men were organized in groups of ten which could be made collectively responsible for their good behaviour. The part he played in making this institution more effective, and wider spread, is a matter of some dispute, but all the evidence points to the Conqueror's reign as having been a critical period in the development of what afterwards became the institution of frankpledge (W. A. Morris, *The Frankpledge System*, chap. I).

existing institutions to his purpose. Thus by a famous ordinance he made the hundred corporately responsible for the murder of any of his followers, commanding that if the murderer was not apprehended by his lord within five days the hundred in which the crime was committed should collectively contribute such part of the very heavy *murdrum* fine of forty-six marks of silver as the lord might be unable to discharge.[1] Order, thus maintained, was, in truth, bought at a heavy price, but its benefits were recorded by William's contemporaries on both sides of the Channel. An Englishman gratefully noted the good order he established,[2] and Norman chroniclers are unanimous in lamenting the disintegration of public security which occurred in the duchy after his death.[3]

The administration of his conjoint realm by William the Conqueror was in every way remarkable. Harsh and brutal, it was never blindly tyrannical. Frequently repulsive in its cruder applications, it was adapted to Norman and English conditions, and, particularly in the spheres of justice and finance, it was to entail enduring consequences. Nor should it be forgotten that its operations stretched uniformly over his whole dominion. His court moved with the king wherever he went, and the development of royal justice was to follow much the same course in Normandy and England. Again, William's chancellors were concerned with business in both parts of his realm, and often accompanied the king to and fro across the Channel. Herfast was connected with charters relating both to Normandy and England,[4] Osmund was frequently in the duchy in his official capacity,[5] and so also was Maurice.[6] While, therefore, between 1066 and 1087 every department of English administration was affected by Norman influence, English administrative practices were in their turn often transported across the Channel. And certainly the disorders which began in Normandy immediately after William's death serve to demonstrate that the more stable conditions which prevailed in the duchy between 1066 and 1087 were due in large measure to the efficiency of his rule.

It was inevitable that the advent into England of a Norman king should have produced greater administrative changes in the land he conquered than in the duchy from which he came. But it is the quality of these changes that challenges attention, for in England the

---

[1] Stenton, *op. cit.*, p. 676.
[2] AS. Chron., 'E', *s.a.* 1086 (equals 1087).
[3] Haskins, *Norman Institutions*, pp. 62–64.
[4] *Regesta*, vol. I, nos. 22, 28.
[5] *Cart. S. Vincent du Mans*, no. 177; *Cart. Bayeux*, no. III.
[6] *Gall. Christ.*, vol. XI; *Instrumenta*, col. 266.

Conqueror's genius was displayed as much in adaptation as in innovation, and it was his personal achievement that in the midst of the confusions attendant upon conquest he never disrupted the administrative framework of the kingdom he acquired. This in turn may partly explain why the administrative developments which he sponsored proceeded without substantial interruption despite the king's own long absences from England. Between 1066 and 1087 William spent more time in France than in England, and it is a measure of his prestige that he could trust others to carry on the highly individual policy he inaugurated. As has been seen in 1066 he confidently entrusted the government of Normandy to Matilda, Roger of Montgomery, and Roger of Beaumont, and in 1067 Odo of Bayeux, William fitz Osbern, and Hugh II of Montfort-sur-Risle were left in charge of England.[1] Later, in England, it was most frequently Archbishop Lanfranc who was commissioned to act for the king, but Odo,[2] and also many laymen from the great Norman houses, such as William of Warenne and Richard fitz Gilbert, likewise served in this capacity, and with success.[3]

Here again the unity of the Anglo-Norman feudal polity created by the Conqueror was displayed, and the extent to which this fostered the influence of Normandy and England upon each other. When, after William's death, Normandy and England were divided, the administrative consequences to both were to be unfortunate. And when, after 1106, they were once more united, the administrative conditions established by the Conqueror were to be restored, and in consequence the reign of Henry I was to witness important developments in the spheres of justice and finance on both sides of the Channel.

[1] Will. Poit., p. 226.
[2] *Regesta*, vol. I, nos. 78–85; Ord. Vit., vol. III, p. 244; Macdonald, *Lanfranc*, p. 73.
[3] Will. Malms., *Gesta Regum*, p. 334; *Sir Christopher Hatton's Book of Seals* (ed. L. C. Loyd), plate VIII.

Chapter 13

THE KING IN THE CHURCH

No aspect of the career of William the Conqueror is of more interest – or of more importance – than the part he played in the history of the western Church between 1066 and 1087. His policy in this respect thus invites particular attention, but if his personal contribution to the ecclesiastical life of his age is here to be appraised, it must be viewed in its totality and placed in its contemporary setting. Thus the enduring results of his work on the Church in England cannot be explained without reference to the earlier and continuing ecclesiastical development of Normandy; and neither the Church in Normandy nor the Church in England at this time can be properly envisaged unless they are also to be seen as integral parts of the Church in Europe. William's victory in 1066 had brought together under a single temporal domination the three ecclesiastical provinces of Rouen, Canterbury, and York; and also two parts of the western Church which in Normandy and England had hitherto responded to different influences. The Conquest was thus to alter the political balance of western Christendom which at this same time was itself under papal direction, passing through a crisis.

The ecclesiastical consequences of the Norman conquest were thus to be widespread, and need to be considered against a background of conflicting loyalties. Between 1066 and 1087 the ecclesiastical influence on the province of Rouen was in England brought to bear on a Church which cherished its own individual traditions. Again, William, as king, showed himself resolute not only to retain his royal rights in the Church, but also to discharge what he conceived to be his ecclesiastical duties. And he was to do this at a time when the papacy, sponsoring the reforms which had already permeated the province of Rouen, was also seeking to free the Church from secular control. Finally (as must be emphasized), this same Norman king of England, and all his subjects both Norman and English, lived in a world in which the Church was recognized as an all-embracing unit whose claims to spiritual authority were unquestioned. For William, as for his contemporaries, the conception of Christendom was neither a pious aspiration nor a threat to national independence. It was a factor of practical politics.

These contrasting loyalties, sincerely held and courageously sustained, colour the ecclesiastical politics of this age, and the inherent interest of William's policy in respect of them is further enhanced if reference be made to the chief personalities it was to involve. Thus the papacy which since 1049 had emerged from political eclipse was, during these years, occupied by two men who could not be ignored. Alexander II (1061–1073) was a vigorous pontiff whose activities were widespread, whilst Gregory VII (1073–1086) must on all grounds be adjudged to have been one of the most dominating personalities ever to occupy the chair of Saint Peter. Again, in 1066 the archbishopric of Rouen passed to John, bishop of Avranches, a cadet of the Norman ducal house whose previous career had been distinguished, and who was to leave his mark, both on the politics and on the literature of his age.[1] Finally, in 1070, as an inevitable consequence of the Conquest, the schismatic Stigand was deposed from the see of Canterbury, and there replaced by Lanfranc, now abbot of Saint Stephen's, Caen, who had already by his previous career at Le Bec, and elsewhere, won for himself an acknowledged reputation as one of the outstanding ecclesiastical figures of the age. He had previously refused the see of Rouen, and his appointment to Canterbury was undoubtedly due in the first instance to William himself.[2] Henceforth, their association was to be so close that it is always difficult, and sometimes impossible, to decide whether the policy, which, in England, they jointly implemented, was inspired by the one or the other.

The great king was thus matched by a great archbishop.[3] When he reached Canterbury, Lanfranc was not less than fifty-five years of age, and famed as a lawyer, a controversialist, a diplomatist, and a teacher. His greatest achievements were, however, still to come. His character is best displayed in his acts, but his letters, which are models of their kind, reveal something of the man who wrote them.[4] Concise and decisive, they are informed with authority, and inspired with sound judgment. Though tenderness and affection are not lacking, these letters more frequently convey advice with prudence, admonition with severity, or commands with force. An authoritative and intensely able man

---

[1] *Gall. Christ.*, vol. XI, cols. 31, 32; and above, pp. 122–124.

[2] Milo Crispin, *Vita Lanfranci* (Giles, *Lanfranci Opera*, vol. I, p. 291).

[3] On Lanfranc, see A. J. Macdonald, *Lanfranc* (ed. 1944), and Knowles, *Monastic Order*, pp. 85–145.

[4] They are edited in Giles, *Lanfranci Opera*, vol. II, and in *Pat. Lat.*, vol. CL. They are here cited by number as given in *Pat. Lat.*, or from the translations (by G. W. Greenaway) given in *E.H.D.*, vol. II, nos. 89–106.

stands revealed, a prelate in power who with all his knowledge of the management of men was himself sincere. Nor does Lanfranc's public life, taken as a whole, belie this impression. His monastic vocation was undoubtedly genuine, and there is no reason to question the sincerity of his expressed reluctance to be archbishop. Nevertheless, after 1070, though still a monk and a friend of monks, it was as a statesman that he shone. Contemporaries were impressed by his sagacity, his political sense, and his capacity for leadership. He could ruthlessly chastise political rebels or contumacious monks,[1] but his sense of justice was constant, as was his devotion to the Church. He could adapt his policy to changing circumstances, but it was pursued with inflexible purpose. His association with William the Conqueror was thus in the conditions of the time to entail far-reaching results in England. 'It may be doubted' – remarks a modern authority – 'whether of all the eminent men who filled the see of Canterbury between Augustine and Cranmer any individual save only Theodore of Tarsus had a greater share than Lanfranc in organizing the Church in this country.'[2]

The policy which in conjunction with the king he was to implement in England depended directly upon the development of the Church in Normandy, which has been noted as having taken place during the Conqueror's Norman reign. The special character of the province of Rouen had already been fixed before the Norman conquest, and when in 1066 its influence was extended overseas by force of arms it underwent no essential change. The Norman episcopate, for example, continued throughout most of this period to be dominated by men who had risen to power before the Conquest. The appointment of John of Avranches to Rouen in 1067 merely gave greater scope to the activities of a notable prelate; and the bishoprics of Bayeux and Coutances were held until after the death of the Conqueror by Odo and Geoffrey, though both of these extraordinary men now devoted most of their energies to the secular affairs of England. Hugh of Lisieux was to survive, honoured and respected, until 1072, and was succeeded by Gilbert Maminot of Courbépine, a member of a substantial Norman family of the middle rank, whilst on the death of Yves, the bishopric of Sées, wrested at last from the family of Bellême, passed to a brother of Eudo the steward.[3]

---

[1] *Acta Lanfranci* (Earle and Plummer, *Two Saxon Chronicles Parallel*, vol. I, p. 220); AS. Chron., 'E', *s.a.* 1075.

[2] Knowles, *op. cit.*, p. 143.

[3] *Gall. Christ.*, vol. XI, cols. 681, 770; Ord. Vit., vol. II, p. 311; Hommey, *Diocèse de Sées*, vol. II, p. 331; Douglas, *Domesday Monachorum*, p. 29.

The appointment of Baldwin, one of the duke's chaplains, to Évreux in 1066 was an innovation inspired by English example, but Baldwin's successor in 1071 was another man of illustrious Norman connexions.[1] In short, after 1066 as before, the Norman episcopate was overwhelmingly representative of the Norman secular aristocracy.[2] William Bonne Ame, himself, who in 1079 passed from the cloister to become an admirable archbishop of Rouen was a nephew of Gerard Fleitel, and the son of a former bishop of Sées.[3]

A similar continuity can be seen in the monastic life which continued to supply the greatest element of distinction to the Norman church. There were, it is true, fewer new foundations, and not all the appointments to abbacies were happy. But some of the great figures from the past survived. John of Fécamp did not end his astonishing career until 1079, and Le Bec had still to reach the zenith of its greatness under Saint Anselm. And there were some other monasteries in the province which were not wholly unworthy to be associated even with Le Bec. The picture painted by Ordericus Vitalis of Saint-Évroul as a home of piety and learning in his time is both convincing and attractive. In short, though there were to be both episcopal and monastic scandals in Normandy between 1066 and 1087, as elsewhere in the Church, and though reforms were both needed and undertaken, it remains true that the high prestige of the province of Rouen was enhanced rather than diminished during these years. The bishops carried on an efficient administration for the benefit of their sees. Conciliar activity was, as will be seen, vigorous and constant. And the continuing momentum of that astonishing monastic revival which had marked the reign of William as duke may be judged by the fact that between 1066 and 1087 Norman monasteries were to give no less than twenty-two abbots and five bishops to England.[4]

The province of Rouen was not, however, unaffected by the Conquest. Its material resources were much increased. There is no doubt, for instance, that both Odo and Geoffrey brought wealth from England to enrich their sees, and before 1086 more than twenty Norman monasteries, of both ducal and private foundation, had received land in twenty-five English shires.[5] Some of these endowments were small, but

---

[1] *Gall. Christ.*, vol. xi, cols. 571, 572.

[2] The chief exception is Avranches which in 1067 was given to Michael, an Italian, with apparently no Norman connexions.

[3] Ord. Vit., vol. ii, pp. 64, 213, 336. [4] Knowles, *op. cit.*, p. 704.

[5] See D. Matthew, *The Norman Monasteries and their English Possessions*.

the English lands acquired, for instance, by Fécamp, Grestain, Saint-Wandrille, Saint-Évroul, Troarn, and the two houses at Caen were in bulk considerable. At the same time the ecclesiastical power of the secular ruler over the Norman church was fortified, in being now exercised by a consecrated king. In Normandy every appointment to a bishopric between 1066 and 1087 was directly dependent on William's decision, and throughout all the canons of the council of Lillebonne in 1080 there runs the assertion of the ultimate authority of the duke who had become a king.[1] In England the situation was the same, though the circumstances were very different. Ecclesiastical appointments remained in the king's hands, and the prelacy which he was to establish in the land he conquered was brought ever more closely under his control by being subject to the feudal obligations he was to impose.

In England, moreover, the king's ecclesiastical dominance was to be exercised in such close association with Lanfranc that the essential preliminary to the policy which they were jointly to base on Norman example was the assertion by Lanfranc of primacy over the whole Church in England. The famous controversy between Canterbury and York which this assertion was to involve began in fact within four years of the battle of Hastings.[2] In May 1070 the king gave the archbishopric of York, made vacant by the death of Aldred, to Thomas, a canon of Bayeux, on the understanding that he should later receive consecration from Lanfranc. Lanfranc's own consecration as archbishop of Canterbury took place on 29 August 1070, but when Thomas came south to be consecrated Lanfranc refused to perform the rite unless he was given a written profession of obedience from Thomas.[3] Thomas, pleading the privileges of his own church, at first refused to supply this. According to some accounts, he furthermore appealed to the king who, after some hesitation, supported Lanfranc.[4] At all events, Thomas at length submitted, albeit with some reservations, and was duly consecrated. This was, however, by no means the end of the matter. In the autumn of 1071 both archbishops went to Rome to receive their *pallia*, and when at the papal court Thomas not only reopened the question of the primacy but claimed that the sees of Worcester, Dorchester, and Lichfield belonged to the northern province. The pope referred the matter to an English

---

[1] L. Valin, *Duc de Normandie*, p. 72; Haskins, *Norman Institutions*, p. 32.

[2] On this see Böhmer, *Kirche und Staat*, pp. 86–126; Z. N. Brooke, *English Church and the Papacy*, pp. 112–126; Macdonald, *op. cit.*; and R. W. Southern, 'The Canterbury Forgeries' (*Eng. Hist. Rev.*, vol. LXVIII (1958), pp. 193–226).   [3] *Acta Lanfranci.*

[4] *Hugh the Chanter* (ed. Johnson), pp. 2–7; Will. Malms., *Gesta Pont.*, p. 40.

council, and at Winchester in 1072 the whole matter was formally debated. At length, judgment was given in favour of the archbishop of Canterbury on all essential points.[1] The disputed bishoprics were assigned to the southern province; the right of the archbishop of Canterbury to a profession of obedience from the metropolitan of York was held to be established; and Lanfranc was recognized as primate of England. Lanfranc had in fact made good his claim. Only formal confirmation by the papacy was needed to make his victory complete. But this, as will be seen, he was never to obtain.

The details of this notable controversy (which has here been very briefly summarized) are, however, of far less importance than the issues which were involved, and the manner in which Lanfranc's case was presented and sustained. The king's own interest in the matter became apparent at a very early stage. William had been able to appreciate, as duke, the advantage of ruling over a country which was a single ecclesiastical province, and the division of England into two such provinces he could only regard as a source of weakness. Indeed, it is not impossible that his support of Lanfranc may, in the circumstances of 1070, have been due in part to his apprehension that a metropolitan archbishop of York, acting as head of an independent province not yet fully under Norman control, might seek to buttress his own position by crowning a rival king – perhaps a Scandinavian prince or a member of the Old English royal house – as a legitimate ruler in the north of England.

But such considerations, weighty as they may seem, only touched the fringes of the issue. What was far more significant was that Lanfranc, supported by the Norman king, here saw fit to base his case on English tradition. He found at Canterbury strong claims to primacy, and he appealed to English precedent, citing in his favour the writings of Bede, the acts of early English church councils, and a long series of early papal letters. Some of these letters were undoubtedly forgeries, and Lanfranc's complicity in their concoction has been much debated.[2] Most scholars would now acquit him of the charge, and it is more probable that he relied (perhaps too readily) upon a brief which had been prepared for him by the monks of his cathedral church at Canterbury. The matter need not here be reconsidered. What is in point is the character of Lanfranc's argument, and the nature of William's support of it. In order to give effect to an essentially Norman policy, this Norman

---

[1] Wilkins, *Concilia*, vol. 1, p. 324; Stenton, *Anglo-Saxon England*, p. 657.
[2] The whole controversy is surveyed by Southern (*op. cit.*).

prelate of Italian birth utilized an English tradition to which he gave fresh vitality. The character of the Norman impact upon England could hardly be better exemplified.

Western Christendom was also involved. Lanfranc's assertion of primacy entailed rights comparable to those which had in the remote past been exercised, for instance, by sees such as Milan, Carthage, and Toledo. But the whole policy of the centralizing papacy in the latter half of the eleventh century was directed against such superiorities. It is true that in 1079 Gregory VII sought for the benefit of Gebuin to erect the archbishopric of Lyons into a primatial see with jurisdiction over Sens and Rouen.[1] But the scheme, which was successfully resisted, was not really a deflection of papal policy in this matter, since it was inaugurated in the interest of a particular individual, and was assumed to be revocable at any time by papal action. The claims of Lanfranc were of a wholly different nature, for they challenged at a vital point the policy of popes who were striving with some success to make the ecclesiastical province, and not the kingdom, the essential unit of the church. It is not surprising, therefore, that William and his archbishop failed to obtain formal confirmation of the Canterbury primacy at Rome. Indeed the nature of the situation was clearly revealed in the sequel. It was not for a new grant that the appeal had been made, but for the recognition of an existing right, and when that recognition was refused, the right was none the less continuously exercised. Linking his position to the fullest imperial pretensions ever made by the Old English monarchy which the Norman king had acquired, Lanfranc asserted an authority which could be extended over all England and even beyond its bounds.[2] It was thus a matter of right that he later intervened in the ecclesiastical affairs of Ireland and still more notably, through Saint Margaret the Queen, in those of Scotland.[3]

In these circumstances, and through this agency, the Norman impact on the Church in England was made, and there is no mistaking either its nature or its force. During the reign of William the Conqueror the church in England underwent changes whose effects endured, and while the results of these changes have been diversely judged, the source of their inspiration is not to be questioned. The expressed policy of the Conqueror was here 'to sustain in England the same usages and laws

---

[1] Fliche, *Réforme grégorienne*, vol. ii, pp. 230–232. Also below, pp. 338, 339.
[2] Southern, *op. cit.*
[3] Epp. nos. 36, 37, 38, 51; *Acta Lanfranci*; A. Gwynn, *Irish Eccl. Rev.*, vol. LVII, p. 213.

which he and his ancestors had been wont to observe in Normandy',[1] and the statement aptly summarized the transformation which took place in his time. The earlier development of the Church in Normandy we have found to have been achieved under ducal control: the changes which overtook the church in England during his reign as king were royal in direction and Norman in inspiration.

The process was marked in the first instance by a change in the prelacy of England comparable to that which had taken place in the secular aristocracy. Stigand, who had held the sees of Canterbury and Winchester in plurality was, of course, destined for deposition, and his replacement by Lanfranc at Canterbury in 1070 might be regarded as an inevitable political consequence of the Norman conquest. But many of the other English bishops were in hardly better case. Æthelmær of Elmham was Stigand's brother; Æthelric of Selsey had been closely associated with him; and Leofwine the married bishop of Lichfield was to be condemned by Lanfranc.[2] It is thus hardly surprising that all three were to vacate their sees before 1070, Æthelric and Æthelmær by formal deposition, and Leofwine by resignation.[3] In the north, Aldred of York was a prelate of a very different type, but he died on 11 September 1069, and left the way open for a new appointment, whilst the confusion of the see of Durham also invited drastic action. From the early years of his reign, therefore, William found himself in a position to begin the Normanization of the episcopacy of England, and this policy he was consistently to pursue. By 1080 Wulfstan of Worcester was the only bishop of English birth left in England, and, of the remaining occupants, all save one[4] were of Norman birth or training.

The same policy was adopted in respect of the English abbeys. In 1066 there were thirty-five independent Benedictine houses in England, and many of the greater abbots were to show themselves hostile to William from the start. Ælfwig of New Minster in Winchester who was Harold's uncle fell on the field of Hastings. Leofric of Peterborough, who was cousin to Edwin and Morcar, also died as a result of wounds received in the battle, and his successor Brand, who was uncle to Hereward the Wake, made immediate overtures to Edgar Atheling on

---

[1] Eadmer, *Hist. Novorum*, p. 9.

[2] Will. Malms., *Gesta Pont.*, p. 150; Freeman, *Norman Conquest*, vol. II, pp. 414, 557.

[3] Wilkins, *Concilia*, vol. 322; Knowles, *op. cit.*, p. 103.

[4] Giso, bishop of Wells, who was a Lotharingian. Peter of Lichfield would seem to have been a Norman and so was probably the physically afflicted Hugh of Orival, who succeeded to the see of London in 1075 (Will. Malms., *Gesta Pont.*, pp. 145, 308).

his appointment.[1] Æthelsige of Saint Augustine's, Canterbury, helped to organize the Kentish resistance, and William had good reasons for suspecting the disaffection of Æthelnoth of Glastonbury, of Godric of Winchcombe, of Sihtric of Tavistock, and of Wulfric, Ælfwig's successor at New Minster.[2] It was natural, therefore, that within six years of William's coronation all these men should have been removed, and their places were filled in every case by men from overseas.[3] Such acts were, moreover, part of the Conqueror's general policy. Of the twenty-one abbots who attended the council of London in 1075, only thirteen were English, and only three of these remained in office at the time of the Conqueror's death.[4]

The Normanization of the prelacy in England was a cardinal feature of the Conqueror's rule, and it is not difficult to assess the motives which inspired it. The prelates of England were, as of right, among the closest counsellors of the king. The bishops were great servants of state by reason of their office, and though the monasteries varied in importance many of them were extremely rich, and together they possessed perhaps a sixth of the landed wealth of England.[5] Moreover, the prelates themselves were soon to become among the most important of the king's tenants-in-chief responsible for a large section of the feudal array. William, as has been seen, had already before 1066 subjected many, but not all, of the Norman monasteries to knight-service, and now in, or shortly after, 1070 he imposed the same tenure on the bishoprics and on most of the abbeys of England, adopting the same methods as he had employed in the case of his lay magnates. The quotas imposed varied greatly in size. The sees of Canterbury and Winchester and the abbeys of Peterborough and Glastonbury had each, for instance, to provide sixty knights, whilst the bishopric of Chichester was assessed at only two and the wealthy abbey of Ramsey at only four. These assessments were moreover to prove final; generally speaking, they were not subsequently altered; and what is more remarkable, abbeys founded after the Conqueror's reign do not appear to have been subjected to the obligation at all.[6]

William himself must thus be held responsible for imposing on the

---

[1] Knowles, *op. cit.*, pp. 103, 104.   [2] *Mon. Ang.*, vol. I, p. 3; vol. II, pp. 297, 430.
[3] Thurstan at Glastonbury; Galland (probably a Norman) at Winchcombe; Ruallon (possibly a Breton) at New Minster; and Geoffrey at Tavistock.
[4] Wilkins, *Concilia*, vol. I, p. 364; Stenton, *op. cit.*
[5] Corbett, *Camb. Med. Hist.*, vol. V, p. 509.
[6] Round, *Feudal England*, pp. 221 *et sqq.*; Chew, *Ecclesiastical Tenants in Chief* (1932); Knowles, *op. cit.*, p. 609.

Church in England this burden which in its totality was to prove very heavy. At first, as on many of the lay lordships, the obligation was discharged by stipendiary knights, but widespread sub-infeudation rapidly took place and the consequences were far-reaching. Bishops and abbots were at once involved more closely than ever before in secular affairs, and in the case of the abbeys a division was normally made between the land of the abbot and that of the monastery, so that the abbot as a great feudal lord became removed from the life of his monks.[1] The full implications of this were not to be revealed until after the Conqueror's death. But the imposition by him of tenure by knight-service on the bishoprics and abbacies of England must, none the less, be regarded as one of the most important – and perhaps the most deleterious – results of his ecclesiastical policy in England.

In these circumstances it was clearly impossible for William to retain in high ecclesiastical office men who had committed themselves to the régime he had supplanted, or who were personally hostile to himself; and it was natural that he should turn for their successors towards the province from which he came. It would, none the less, be wrong to conclude that the Conqueror was here guided solely by motives of political expediency. William had some excuse for believing that a transportation from Normandy, and particularly from the Norman monasteries, would be of benefit to the Church in England; and he is known to have taken ecclesiastical advice in this matter from prelates of high repute, such as Hugh, abbot of Cluny, and John, abbot of Fécamp.[2] Nor did he act here without discrimination. The most notable occupants of English sees at the beginning of his reign were Giso of Wells, a Lotharingian, and Leofric of Exeter, who had been educated in Lorraine, together with the more outstanding prelates of English birth – Aldred, archbishop of York, and Wulfstan, bishop of Worcester. All of these were retained in office until death, and the Englishmen, in particular, received much of the Conqueror's favour. Nor would it be easy to criticize very severely the Norman appointments to English bishoprics which he made. The gift of the see of Lincoln to Remigius of Fécamp was a return for political service, and William was to continue the earlier English practice of rewarding with bishoprics clerks from the royal *scriptorium*.[3] But Remigius served Lincoln well, and of the

[1] Knowles, *op. cit.*, pp. 395–411, 614.
[2] *Pat. Lat.*, vol. cxlix, cols. 923, 927; Robinson, *Gilbert Crispin*, p. 1.
[3] Remigius had apparently made a contribution of ships to the expedition of 1066 (Giles, *Scriptores Willelmi*, p. 22).

household officials only Herfast was a discreditable bishop. For the rest, the bishops whom the Conqueror established in England were, generally speaking, hard-working men, good administrators, and often great builders, and many of them left a fine reputation behind them. Osmund of Salisbury (later to achieve canonization), Gundulf of Rochester, and Walcher of Durham were remembered for their personal sanctity, whilst Robert of Hereford was renowned for his learning. All of these left a permanent mark on the sees they ruled.

Similar conclusions may also be drawn concerning the Conqueror's monastic appointments. With the exception of Æthelwig, abbot of Evesham, who was honoured by William and kept in office until his death in 1077,[1] the English abbots as a body were undistinguished at the beginning of William's reign[2] – some of them like Sihtric of Tavistock were disreputable[3] – and their replacement by monks from the reformed Norman monasteries could be defended for ecclesiastical as well as political reasons. There were here of course some serious mistakes. Turold from Fécamp, successively abbot of Malmesbury and Peterborough, was a soldier rather than a monk and no friend to the monasteries over which he presided, whilst Thurstan from Caen who became abbot of Glastonbury treated his monks with such violent harshness that he provoked a scandal.[4] These were, however, exceptional, and the majority of William's abbots in England discharged their duties with distinction. The future greatness of Saint Albans dated from the time of Abbot Paul from Caen, who was a nephew of Lanfranc. Simeon from Saint-Ouen who was set over Ely won the admiration of his monks for his administration of their affairs through a period of difficulty. Serlo, who came from Le Mont-Saint-Michel to Gloucester, not only rebuilt the abbey-church but introduced a new spirit of devotion into his monastery. But perhaps none of the English abbeys was better served in this period than the Confessor's own foundation of Westminster. Nothing but good is known of Vitalis, who arrived there from Bernay in 1075, and his successor Gilbert Crispin, a member of a great Norman family who came from Le Bec in 1085, must on all grounds be adjudged as one of the outstanding abbots of the age.[5]

These Norman abbots brought to England 'a new discipline and a

---

[1] On him, see R. R. Darlington, in *Eng. Hist. Rev.*, vol. XLVIII (1933), pp. 1–22, 177–198.
[2] Stenton, *op. cit.*, p. 652.
[3] He left his abbey to join the sons of Harold in piracy (Will. Malms., *Gesta Pont.*, p. 204).
[4] AS. Chron., 'E', *s.a.* 1083; Knowles, *op. cit.*, p. 114.
[5] *Liber Eliensis*, pp. 253, 261; Will. Malms., *Gesta Pont.*, p. 293; Robinson, *op. cit.*, pp. 1–8.

new or at least a revitalized, observance',[1] and the character of their
influence can be illustrated by reference to the 'constitutions' which
Lanfranc himself drew up for the guidance of his monks at Christ
Church, Canterbury.[2] In these *consuetudines* the monk-archbishop embodied what he found to be best in the reformed Norman and continental usage, and adapted this to the particular needs of England. The
consuetudines of Lanfranc were never to be imposed as a code, but they
came throughout England to be highly influential on the activities of
the new Norman abbots. It was thus in relation to the general tone of
English monastic life rather than through any multiplication of houses
that the Norman influence is here to be discerned.[3] William, it is true,
founded the abbey of Battle to commemorate his victory, and filled it
with monks from Marmoutier, whilst between 1078 and 1080 William
of Warenne established at Lewes the first Cluniac monastery in this
country.[4] But apart from these, there were few important new foundations in England at this time. On the other hand, there is little reason
to question the general belief of contemporaries that during these years
there occurred a quickening of the momentum of English monastic life.
The opinion might, indeed, be further supported by reference to the
remarkable monastic revival which took place in the north during the
Conqueror's reign. This was due in the first instance to Reinfrid, a
Norman knight who had become a monk at Evesham, and to Eadwine,
an English monk at Winchcombe. They settled with a few followers at
Bede's ruined church at Jarrow, and in 1083, after diverse experiences,
their community, which now numbered twenty-three persons, was
transferred to Durham by Bishop William of Saint-Calais to take charge
of his cathedral church.[5]

The Norman influence on the English bishoprics was scarcely less
remarkable. Its most notable feature was the transference of English
sees to the cities, where they were to remain for centuries. Already in
1050 Leofric had transferred his see from Crediton to Exeter, and in
1075 the council of London authorized the removal of the sees of
Lichfield, Selsey, and Sherborne to Chester, Chichester, and Salisbury.[6]
A few years earlier Herfast had removed the see of Elmham to Thetford,

---

[1] Knowles, *op. cit.*, p. 121.

[2] Edited in 1956 with a translation and a critical commentary by M. D. Knowles, *The Monastic Constitutions of Lanfranc*, from which is derived what here follows.

[3] The houses of Shrewsbury, Wenlock, Tewkesbury, and Selby ought, however, here to be mentioned.

[4] *Early Yorkshire Charters* (ed. C. T. Clay), vol. VIII, pp. 59–62.

[5] Knowles, *op. cit.*, pp. 165–172. [6] Wilkins, *Concilia*, vol. I, pp. 363, 364.

whence it was soon to be transferred to Norwich, while Remigius moved his own see from Dorchester to Lincoln.[1] Scarcely less important than this was the remodelling of the cathedral constitutions of England. Here Lanfranc found two principal types of organization in being. On the one hand, by an arrangement which was almost unique, four of the English cathedrals – namely Canterbury, Winchester, Worcester, and Sherborne – were served by monks.[2] On the other hand, in several cathedrals where regular monks had not been introduced an attempt had been made to compel the canons to live a communal life under a rule which enjoined not only celibacy but the use of a common dormitory and refectory. How far this practice had been extended is not wholly clear, but several English cathedrals had by 1066 been affected by it.[3]

For the former of these practices Lanfranc had great sympathy, although it was different from anything he had known in Normandy. He was himself a monk, and he watched with approval the appointment of monks as bishops in England, and now the number of monastic cathedrals in England was likewise to be increased. Norwich under Herfast, Rochester under Gundulf, and Durham under William thus all received monastic constitutions in his time.[4] By contrast the see of Sherborne lost its monastic constitution after its removal to Salisbury, but after a brief dispute Winchester remained monastic, and before the end of the reign there were thus six monastic cathedrals in England.[5] In respect of the secular cathedrals the development was equally striking. Full emphasis has been given to the manner in which the cathedral chapters and the cathedral dignitaries were established in Normandy in the decades immediately preceding the Conquest.[6] Now this same type of organization was to be brought to England, and in the case of the secular cathedrals it replaced any communal constitutions that may previously have existed. In due course there thus came to be nine English secular cathedrals served by chapters and dignitaries similar to those which had existed in Normandy before the Norman conquest. These were Salisbury, London, Lincoln, York, Exeter, Hereford, Lichfield, Chichester, and Wells; and they were later to be known as cathedrals of the 'Old Foundation'.[7]

[1] J. W. F. Hill, *Medieval Lincoln*, pp. 76–81.   [2] Knowles, *op. cit.*, pp. 129, 619.
[3] Darlington, *Eng. Hist. Rev.*, vol. LI (1936), pp. 403–404.   [4] Knowles, *op. cit.*, pp. 131–134.
[5] Canterbury, Winchester, Worcester, Durham, Rochester, Norwich. Wells (with Bath) and Lichfield (with Chester) stand by themselves.
[6] Above, pp. 122, 123.   [7] Edwards, *English Secular Cathedrals*, p. 12.

The manner in which this took place is, however, somewhat obscure. It was once thought that the constitution characteristic of English secular cathedrals based upon the four greater dignitaries of dean, precentor, chancellor, and treasurer had been imported to England from Bayeux, where Thomas I, archbishop of York, had been a canon.[1] It would, however, appear unlikely that either Bayeux or Rouen in the eleventh century could have supplied the precise model for this constitution.[2] None the less the basic principles of the constitution of the English secular cathedrals of the Middle Ages derived from changes brought about by the Norman conquest. It is true that the earliest definite evidence of this secular organization is not earlier than 1090–1091 when Osmund of Salisbury, Remigius of Lincoln, and Thomas of York reconstituted their chapters, but these prelates had all been appointed by William, and they must have derived their general ideas on this matter from the duchy from which they came. At all events, as a result of changes introduced under the Conqueror, the organization of the bishoprics of England, both secular and monastic, was within a generation of William's death to assume the form it preserved until the Reformation.

The position of the bishop within the English polity was thus substantially modified during the Conqueror's reign. He had been brought under the closer supervision of his metropolitan, and as a great feudal lord he had been absorbed into the military structure of the land. At the same time, the redistribution of the sees and the reorganization of the chapters had given great scope for his administration. A notable feature of this was, for example, the emergence at this time in England, as in pre-Conquest Normandy, of the archdeacon as the bishop's regular agent in all matters of discipline and justice. Within six years of the battle of Hastings a council at Winchester ordered all bishops to appoint archdeacons,[3] and in view of the earlier Norman development the command is significant. It marked a change. Archdeacons were not unknown in England during the reign of Edward the Confessor,[4] but references to them are rare; and it was not until after the Norman conquest that they became, in England as previously in Normandy, a normal part of the administrative hierarchy of the Church. Here, therefore, may be seen another illustration of the importation of Norman organization into

---

[1] Bradshaw and Wordsworth, *Statutes of Lincoln Cathedral*, vol. 1, pp. 33–36, 101–113; G. W. Prothero, *Memoir of Henry Bradshaw*, p. 345.

[2] Edwards, *op. cit.*, pp. 14–17, based on material supplied by L. C. Loyd.

[3] Wilkins, *Concilia*, vol. 1, p. 363.   [4] Harmer, *Anglo-Saxon Writs*, p. 530.

England, and other changes in the conduct of ecclesiastical justice followed naturally as a consequence of the same tendency. The famous writ issued by William in, or shortly after, 1072 removing ecclesiastical pleas from the hundred courts was avowedly inspired by his conviction that the litigation which it fell to bishops to conduct had not previously been properly administered in England.[1] Henceforth, spiritual pleas were to be heard not in the hundred courts but by bishops and their archdeacons in their own courts, and the resulting conditions might be aptly compared with those envisaged in the regulations concerning episcopal jurisdiction set out in 1080 in the canons of the council of Lillebonne.[2]

The expansion of Norman influence on the Church throughout William's dominions, and the character of its effect upon England, could not in fact be better indicated than by reference to the ecclesiastical councils which were held in Normandy and in England at this time. The conciliar history of this age will not be written with confidence until the completion of investigations now proceeding of the manuscript evidence upon which it is based. In particular some of the dates generally assigned to these assemblies may stand in need of revision. But in the meantime a comparison of the material printed by Bessin for Normandy[3] and by Wilkins for England[4] may prompt some interesting reflections. There may have been conciliar activity in the Confessor's England, but there is no evidence of it, and at this time the metropolitan authority of Canterbury was notoriously weak. On the other hand, there is abundant testimony to show that councils were regularly held in Normandy from 1040 to 1080, and in England provincial councils became, after 1066, a regular feature of English church life. The point is sufficiently important to deserve a brief illustration. Councils were held at Rouen about 1046, at Caen in 1047, at Lisieux in 1054 or 1055, at Rouen in 1063, and again at Lisieux in 1064 – and this at a time when no comparable activity is recorded for England.[5] After 1066 the Norman councils continue with equal regularity, at Rouen for example in 1069–1070, again in 1072, and apparently also in 1074, and at Lillebonne in 1080.[6]

---

[1] Stubbs, *Select Charters* (ed. 1913), pp. 99–100.

[2] Bessin, *Concilia*, pp. 67–71, esp. canons III and XLVI.

[3] *Concilia Rotomagnensis Provinciae* (1717). This book is a kind of new edition, much augmented, of the *Sanctae Rotomagensis Ecclesiae Concilia*, produced by Jean Pommeraye in 1677.

[4] *Concilia Magnae Britanniae et Hiberniae*, 4 vols. (1737). For the relation of this to earlier work on the subject, see F. M. Powicke, 'Sir Henry Spelman and the "Concilia"' (Brit. Acad., *Proceedings*, vol. XVI, 1930).

[5] Above, pp. 130–132.   [6] Bessin, *Concilia*, pp. 52–72.

But now the Norman activity was fully reflected in England. Councils met at, as it would seem, Winchester in 1070 and 1072, at London in 1075, and at Winchester again in 1076. And while no record of their acts has survived, Lanfranc is known to have held at least three other councils before the end of the reign, at London in 1077–1078 and at Gloucester, both in 1080–1081 and in 1085.[1] Making all allowance for evidence still to be discovered, or freshly appreciated, it is surely impossible to escape the conclusion that under Norman influence there occurred after 1066 a marked revival of conciliar activity in England.

The significance of this conclusion is, moreover, much enhanced if reference be made to the matters discussed in these councils. In the first place it deserves more emphasis than it usually receives that there was in this respect no break in 1066 in the province of Rouen. It is surely noteworthy that Archbishop Mauger, a prelate generally condemned for his mundane activities, should have convoked a reforming council at Rouen at least seven years before Leo IX launched his own reforming programme at the council of Rheims, and the same preoccupation with the reforms continued in Normandy without interruption. The canons of the council of Rouen in 1072 are expressly referred to those enacted at Lisieux in 1064, and the council of Lisieux in 1080 made direct reference to conditions established in the time of William as duke.[2]

Equally significant in this respect was the closer relationship between the enactments of the Norman and English councils during the reign of William as king. Between 1066 and 1087 the Church in England and the Church in Normandy were faced in common with western Europe by similar problems in respect of the reforms, and adopted similar measures for solving them. Prominent among the abuses which called for redress was, for instance, that of 'simony'; that is to say, the traffic for money in ecclesiastical offices – and here a remarkable parallel is to be observed between Normandy and England. In Normandy, simony had been attacked as early as the time of Archbishop Mauger, and now simony became the object of vigorous legislation alike at Rouen between 1072 and 1074 and at London in 1075.[3] A similar unity of purpose can be seen in respect of the burning question of ecclesiastical celibacy which occupied so much of the attention of the reforming party, and which

---

[1] Wilkins, *Concilia*, vol. 1, pp. 323, 325, 362–370. A valuable commentary on the arrangement of this material is given in the footnotes to Stenton, *Anglo-Saxon England*, pp. 657–659.
[2] Bessin, *Concilia*, p. 56; Haskins, *Norman Institutions*, pp. 30–35.
[3] Bessin, *Concilia*, p. 64; Wilkins, *Concilia*, vol. 1, p. 363.

met with such resistance both in England and in Normandy.[1] The council of Rouen, assigned to 1072, repeated and hardened the orders on celibacy made in 1064 at the council of Lisieux,[2] and in 1076 the council of Winchester issued important decrees relating to this matter in England.[3] In England, however, there was apparently some concession to earlier custom. The rule was to be strictly enforced on canons and the higher clergy, and it was commanded that in the future no priest should be ordained without a declaration of celibacy. But parish priests who were already married were not compelled to put away their wives. Here clearly there was an effort at compromise, but none the less the spirit of the regulations was the same in England and Normandy, and even in England a strict interpretation of them was sometimes attempted. The stark alternative presented by Bishop Wulfstan to the married clergy of the diocese of Worcester to choose between their churches and their wives is in strict conformity with the 13th canon of the council of Rouen of '1072'.[4]

The wide scope of the ecclesiastical legislation on both sides of the Channel during William's reign also calls for comment. As has been seen, the judicial powers of the bishops were reviewed in much the same sense at Winchester in 1076, and at Lillebonne in 1080. But in the middle years of the reign conciliar legislation was concerned more especially with the lower ranks of the hierarchy, and even with the laity. The simoniacal practices denounced at Rouen between 1072 and 1074 were referred, particularly, not to bishoprics but to archdeaconries and parish churches, and more than half the conciliar activity in Rouen during these years was devoted to the parochial clergy.[5] Similarly, the concern of the council of Winchester in 1076 with the concubinage of parish priests formed part of a policy which aimed at strengthening the parochial organization of the Church in England. The protection of the parish priest against his manorial lord whose rights in the revenues of the manorial church were recognized was particularly necessary at a time when a new secular aristocracy was assuming power in the country, and it was equally necessary in a time of change to safeguard the parish priest against those who might intrude upon his spiritual functions.[6]

---

[1] Archbishop John was stoned by the canons of Rouen when he bade them put away their concubines (Ord. Vit., vol. II, p. 171).
[2] Bessin, *Concilia*, p. 56 (canons XIII, XVII); Delisle, *Journal des Savants* (1901), pp. 516–521.　　　　[3] Wilkins, *Concilia*, vol. I, p. 367.
[4] *Vita Wulfstani* (ed. Darlington), pp. 53, 54; Bessin, *Concilia*, p. 56.
[5] Bessin, *Concilia*, pp. 54–56.　　　　[6] Stenton, *op. cit.*, p. 661.

These enactments have, moreover, to be viewed against a wider background. In many parts of England wide areas were still served by communities of priests attached to ancient minster churches, but during these years further progress was made towards replacing this system by parishes each served by a single priest, supported by revenues of a single church and normally coincident with the villages of which they were the ecclesiastical counterparts.[1] Thus was the reign of William the Conqueror to witness a significant stage in the evolution of the English parish.

The interconnexion between the ecclesiastical affairs of Normandy and England during these years in the matter of reform is in part to be explained by the great reforming decrees which were issuing from Rome at this time, and which, particularly after 1073, were naturally reflected in the legislation of the Church on each side of the Channel. But this continuous activity which found expression year after year, now in Normandy and now in England, was also inspired by the common concerns of a Church which was now under a single secular domination, and which was administered by a hierarchy which was throughout predominantly Norman. Apart from their joint acceptance of common doctrine and of papal direction, the chief connecting link between the Churches of Normandy and England during these years was William himself, and any survey of the councils of the time indicates how closely he was personally responsible for their activities. He attended their meetings whether they were held in Normandy or England. Thus in 1070 he took a prominent part at the council of Winchester, and in 1072, once more at Winchester, he presided over the meeting which settled the dispute between Lanfranc and Thomas.[2] Again, the council of Rouen which is assigned to 1074 is expressly stated to have met under his presidency, and he was likewise present at the council of Winchester of 1076.[3] Perhaps, however, it was in 1080 that his interest in the affairs of the church in both parts of his realm was most notably displayed, for at Pentecost in that year he presided over the great council which met at Lillebonne, while seven months later the council of Gloucester met in connexion with the session of his Christmas court. Finally, the ecclesiastical council of Gloucester in 1085 was held in connexion with the meeting of the royal court which planned the Domesday survey.[4]

[1] Cf. Douglas, *Domesday Monachorum*, pp. 7–12.
[2] Ord. Vit., vol. II, p. 199.
[3] Wilkins, *op. cit.*, vol. I, p. 369.
[4] *Acta Lanfranci*; Darlington, *op. cit.*

William's personal supervision of the ecclesiastical councils of Normandy and England at this time is in every way notable. He alone was present at these assemblies on both sides of the Channel. Lanfranc never attended a provincial council in Normandy after he became archbishop, and there is no evidence that an archbishop of Rouen was ever in England during the Conqueror's reign. Odo of Bayeux and Geoffrey of Coutances, being closely connected with the king's secular administration, passed frequently with him between England and Normandy, but no other Norman bishop is known to have witnessed a royal charter in England between 1070 and 1087,[1] and no occupant of an English see attended a Norman ecclesiastical council during these years. The two hierarchies, although both predominantly Norman in origin, remained distinct so far as ecclesiastical councils were concerned. When Geoffrey, bishop of Coutances, attended the council of London in 1075 he was pointedly described as a 'bishop from overseas', and his presence on that occasion was probably due to the fact that he was the recognized agent of the king deputed to supervise any transference of property that might be decreed.[2]

It was the king – and the king alone – who both in Normandy and in England took part in this connected series of ecclesiastical councils whereat a reforming programme was successively decreed in canons which were alike in spirit, and often alike even in the words in which they were expressed. William was in fact an active and co-ordinating agent in promoting the reforms throughout the Church in his conjoint realm. He assumed responsibility for the welfare of the Church throughout all his dominion, and he claimed also full authority as king in directing its affairs.

The ecclesiastical authority exercised by William both in Normandy and England was pervasive. In the duchy it derived from earlier conditions which the Conquest altered, if at all, only in the Conqueror's interest. In the kingdom it was buttressed not only by Norman precedent but also by William's royal consecration as the Confessor's legitimated heir. Prelates on both sides of the Channel were after 1070 subject to him as feudal lords, and no episcopal or important abbatial appointment during his reign was made except at his command,

---

[1] Hugh, bishop of Lisieux, perhaps escorted Queen Matilda to England in 1068 (Round, *Commune of London*, pp. 30–35), and Baldwin, bishop of Évreux, was present at the Conqueror's court at Winchester in the next year (*Regesta*, vol. 1, no. 26), but these were exceptional events and they were not to be repeated.

[2] Wilkins, *Concilia*, vol. 1, p. 363; Stenton, *op. cit.*, p. 658.

THE KING IN HIS KINGDOM

or at least with his consent. Again, while the jurisdictional rights
of bishops were strengthened, as at Winchester in 1076 and as at Lillebonne in 1080, it was assumed that these should be exercised by virtue
of the royal 'concession'.[1] It was the king who should intervene if
episcopal justice was lax or ineffective, and it was the king, likewise,
who might, and who did, decide in his own court disputes between
prelates, or disputes between prelates and laymen.[2] When, in 1073,
controversy broke out between John, archbishop of Rouen, and
Nicholas, abbot of Saint-Ouen, both prelates were summoned to the
royal court, and the ensuing riots in the city were quelled by the
vicomte.[3] Similarly, in 1079 a dispute between Bishop Robert of Sées
and the canons of Bellême was heard in the first instance in the royal
court before William and Matilda, and a few years later the litigation
between William, abbot of Fécamp, and William of Briouze respecting
land in Sussex was decided at a meeting of the royal court held at
Laycock.[4]

The dominant position occupied by William in the Church throughout his conjoint realm, and the extent to which he used this to foster the
reforms, goes far to explain the special nature of his relations with the
papacy between 1066 and 1087. Indeed, those relations derived naturally from earlier Norman policy and its later application to England.
The king did not differ from his contemporaries in recognizing the
ecclesiastical cohesion of western Christendom under papal leadership.
Moreover, the close interdependence between papal and Norman policy
which had already been achieved in secular affairs had created a situation from which neither party could escape. The papacy had since 1054
come to rely on Norman support in its relations with the eastern empire,
and the Normans had gained solid advantages by posing as the champions in a holy war. The English expedition had itself been made to
fit into this pattern, and it had moreover given to the Norman duke a
kingdom whose own previous relations with the papacy had been close,
and which was particularly characterized, along with Poland and the
Scandinavian lands, by the annual payment of 'Peter's Pence'.[5] It is
not surprising therefore that immediately after the Conquest a close
harmony should have prevailed between the papacy and the Norman

[1] Wilkins, *Concilia*, p. 363; Bessin, *Concilia*, pp. 65–71.
[2] Will. Poit., pp. 124–126; Bessin, *Concilia*, pp. 71, 77 (canon III).
[3] *Gall. Christ.*, vol. XI, cols. 23, 34.
[4] Hommey, *Diocèse de Sées*, vol. II, p. 145; *Regesta*, vol. I, no. 127.
[5] *E.H.D.*, vol. II, nos. 74–76; Southern, *Making of the Middle Ages*, p. 27.

duke who had become king. His new status, hallowed by consecration, was to be specially proclaimed by papal legates. In 1067 Alexander's approval was given to the promotion of John of Avranches to Rouen, and in 1070 not only did the deposition of Stigand take place in full accord with papal policy, but the transference of Lanfranc from Caen to Canterbury was effected with the pope's support. And when at the end of 1071 the new archbishop visited Rome for his *pallium* he was received with exceptional honour.[1]

This underlying accord deriving from earlier Norman policy, and implicit in the circumstances of the Conquest, deserves some emphasis, for though it was later to be strained almost to breaking-point, it always persisted, and it was never, during the Conqueror's reign, to be disrupted. The crucial point of contact lay in the reforms, and the new Norman king had therefore some justification in claiming that after 1066 he was the proper agent for promoting the reforms which he had previously sponsored in Normandy, and which the papacy was now assiduously fostering throughout western Christendom. As time went on, however, the papacy, particularly in the person of Gregory VII, came to insist with ever greater precision that the reforms could never be made effective unless the Church itself was to be freed from secular control in the matter of appointments, and unless the hierarchy should be submitted to the papacy not only in all spiritual but also in many temporal matters. The ultimate merits of this policy need not be debated. But it is fair to remark that in the third quarter of the eleventh century it represented an innovation on existing practice. William between 1066 and 1087 claimed no ecclesiastical powers that he had not previously exercised in Normandy to the benefit of the Church, and no rights which had not been asserted, for example, by Henry III in the empire, or indeed by Edward the Confessor in England. There was certainly ground here for controversy, but the implication of such disputes as arose should be clearly envisaged. Before 1089 such differences as occurred between the Norman king and the papacy can for the most part be legitimately regarded as concerning the means by which might best be implemented a reforming programme which, generally speaking, they held in common.

The latent tensions were thus only gradually to be displayed. The advent of Gregory in 1073 imparted a new precision to papal policy, and it was soon apparent that the Canterbury primacy was not going

---

[1] Macdonald, *op. cit.*, p. 64; Eadmer, *Hist. Novorum*, p. 11.

to be confirmed by Rome. Nor should the sequel be viewed out of relation to political events. It was between 1076 and 1080 that Gregory VII advanced through Canossa to the peak of his political power. And it was precisely during these same years that, as has been seen, William suffered his greatest reverses. A dispute about the see of Dol occurred within weeks of William's defeat outside its walls,[1] and the most intransigent of Gregory's demands were made in the months following the Conqueror's reverse at Gerberoi. It was in fact between 1079 and 1081 that the issues between the pope and the king became formidably acute. William was determined to assume responsibility for the Church within his dominions, and to prevent his bishops from becoming subject to a dual claim upon their loyalty. The pope was equally determined to override divisions within the Church, and to exercise, either directly or through his legates, a detailed supervision of all matters of ecclesiastical discipline and appointments. During these thirty months, therefore, when Gregory was reaching the climax of his power he made a concerted effort to overthrow the barriers which William set up around the Anglo-Norman church. It was made, moreover, in three principal directions. Gregory sought to enforce the regular attendance at Rome of the prelates of Normandy and England. He endeavoured to diminish the authority of the metropolitan see of Rouen. And finally he attempted to establish a claim of fealty to the papacy from William as king of England. These three endeavours were all part of a single policy, which it was William's aim successfully to resist.

The demand for the regular attendance of the Anglo-Norman prelates at Rome was made in a series of letters which beginning on 25 March 1079 continued with increasing severity until at last Lanfranc was himself threatened with deposition.[2] These letters were ineffective, but a breach between king and pope was none the less avoided. William, though firm in his refusal, acted with commendable caution, and the pope, though indignant, refrained from putting his threats into execution. A similar situation arose in connexion with the move made by the papacy about this time to diminish the jurisdictional authority of the see of Rouen. As has been seen, in April 1079 Gregory, curiously claiming to be reviving the institutions of imperial Rome, sought to confer on Gebuin, archbishop of Lyons, a primacy over the three ancient Roman

---

[1] In 1076 Gregory wrote to the king announcing the deposition, for good reason, of Bishop Juhel, who was a partisan of William. The king resisted the deposition, and in consequence Juhel, though excommunicate, was still in precarious possession of his see a year later (Jaffé, *Monumenta Gregoriana*, pp. 318–320, 541).　　　[2] *Ibid.*, pp. 377, 494.

provinces of the Lyonnaise, namely Lyons, Rouen, and Sens.[1] The motives which animated the pope in this matter were complex, and the scheme was probably as impractical as it was ambitious. Its inception, however, imperilled William's authority in Normandy by menacing the structure of the Norman church which had always been closely knit under the control of the duke and the metropolitan see. It is small wonder that the papal plan was rejected out of hand by William, who naturally also found no difficulty in preventing the Norman bishops from conforming to it. The scheme in fact never became operative.[2]

It had, however, one immediate result. Gebuin, the archbishop of Lyons, by virtue of the primatial authority conferred upon him, saw fit in 1079 to depose both Arnold, bishop of Le Mans, and Juhel, abbot of La Couture in the same city, in consequence of a quarrel between them.[3] There was no doubt that conditions in Le Mans at this time were such that the action could be justified, and on general grounds it could hardly be resisted with conviction. But it none the less offered a challenge to William. He could not allow without protest an archbishop of Lyons, with or without papal approval, to depose a prelate in his own realm without his consent, and the matter was complicated by the fact that Arnold, who had originally been appointed as the Norman nominee in opposition to Anjou, had always shown himself one of William's most zealous supporters.[4] The matter therefore was one of great delicacy, and it was further exacerbated by the situation which now developed at Rouen. As early as 1078 John the archbishop was stricken with paralysis and unable properly to carry on his duties.[5] The pope, therefore, had here some reasons for complaint, and after John's death on 9 September 1079 he hesitated to recognize William Bonne-Ame whom the king nominated to the see.[6] It seemed an impasse, but once again no overt rupture was allowed to take place. Early in 1080 William sent a conciliatory mission to Rome, and the pope evidently thought it inadvisable to break with the reforming king of England. The bishop and the abbot at Le Mans were both reinstated by papal order, and William Bonne-Ame received recognition as archbishop of Rouen.[7]

---

[1] *Ibid.*, p. 370; Fliche, *op. cit.*, vol. II, pp. 230–232.   [2] Fliche, *loc. cit.*
[3] See letter of Gebuin to Raoul, archbishop of Tours (*Rec. Hist. Franc.*, vol. XIV, p. 668).
[4] Latouche, *Comté du Maine*, pp. 79, 86, 87.
[5] Ord. Vit., vol. II, p. 310.
[6] Jaffé, *Monumenta Gregoriana*, pp. 315, 380.
[7] *Rec. Hist. Franc.*, vol. XIV, p. 648; Gregory's letter to William of 1081 (Jaffé, *op. cit.*, p. 469) implies that the recognition had already been given. See further, Brooke, *English Church and the Papacy*, p. 140.

Finally, it was probably in 1080 that Gregory made – or repeated – his famous demand that William should do him fealty in respect of the kingdom of England.[1] The demand was apparently conveyed verbally on the pope's behalf by the legate Hubert of Die, and it was made, as it would seem, not specifically in virtue of the pope's spiritual authority, which was recognized in England as elsewhere, but rather on certain other grounds, alleged to relate especially to England. Weight may have been given in this respect to the 'False Decretals' now receiving increasing attention in Rome, and more especially to the 'Donation of Constantine'. More importance was, however, probably attached to Peter's Pence which, it was asserted, represented tribute and denoted dependency. But the main reason for the demand was undoubtedly connected with William's own application for papal support in 1066.[2] The king stated that on that occasion he had never proffered homage to the pope in the event of his success, but this disclaimer was not accepted in Rome, and here it is important to note that Gregory's demand was in this respect no novelty since a similar claim had as it seems been previously made by Alexander II.[3] Gregory's action, however, brought the vexed question to an issue, and William's reply was clear, terse, and final. He admitted the obligation to Peter's Pence, and promised that henceforth it should be paid with greater regularity. But he denied that this payment betokened temporal subjection, and he concluded:

Your legate . . . has admonished me to profess allegiance to you and your successors, and to think better regarding the money which my predecessors were wont to send to the Church of Rome. I have consented to the one but not to the other. I have not consented to pay fealty, nor will I now because I never promised it, nor do I find that my predecessors ever paid it to your predecessors.[4]

It was explicit and decisive. Nor was the issue raised again during the remainder of William's reign. After 1081, indeed, Gregory was hardly in a position to revive the matter even if he had wished to do so. In January 1081 he revoked the sentences of suspension passed on the Norman bishops by his legates at the council of Saintes, and thereafter

---

[1] In this matter I follow Brooke (*op. cit.*, pp. 139–142), who there summarizes and supplements the conclusions of his classic article on the subject (*Eng. Hist. Rev.*, vol. XXVI (1911), pp. 225–238). The dating of Gregory's demand in 1080, though extremely probable, is perhaps not finally determined (cf. Stubbs, *Constitutional History*, vol. I, p. 285, note 1).
[2] Brooke, *op. cit.*, p. 142.   [3] *Ibid.*, p. 141.   [4] *E.H.D.*, vol. II, no. 101

he was to find himself ever more disastrously engaged in his struggle with the emperor until his death in exile from Rome in 1085.[1]

Interesting as they are, the disputes which occurred in 1079 and 1080 must not be regarded as typical of the relations between the Conqueror and the papacy, for, speaking generally, those relations were constructive and co-operative. Nothing occurred after the Conquest to mar the close association between William and Alexander II, and in 1073 William had found no difficulty in sending immediate congratulations to Gregory on his succession. It was to be remembered that Hildebrand as archdeacon had made a personal contribution to William's success in 1066, and if he was perhaps prone to exaggerate the debt that the king had thereby incurred, he never seems to have considered that his support on that occasion had been misplaced. His first letter to William as pope in 1074 was cordial, and even in 1080 at the height of their disagreement he could refer to the Conqueror as a 'jewel among princes'.[2] On at least two occasions he restrained his legates when they acted against the king of England, and he was quick to distinguish William from his fellow rulers in Europe by virtue of the king's prudence, probity, and justice. The authentic expression of his attitude to William, and of the quality of their relationship, is indeed to be found in a confidential letter which the pope sent to two of his legates within a year of William's rejection of his demand for fealty, and both the date and the words of this missive deserve careful attention:

Although in certain matters the king of the English does not comport himself as devoutly as might be wished, nevertheless he has neither destroyed nor sold the Churches of God; he has taken pains to govern his subjects in peace and justice; he has refused his assent to anything detrimental to the Apostolic See, even when solicited by certain enemies of the cross of Christ; he has compelled priests on oath to put away their wives and the laity to forward the tithes they were withholding from us. In all these respects he has shown himself more worthy of approbation and honour than other kings. . . .[3]

It was an accurate summary of the underlying accord which, despite difficulties, persisted between the reforming pope and the reforming king.

William the Conqueror and Gregory VII stand out from among their contemporaries as the two great constructive statesmen of the age. Both

---

[1] Macdonald, *Hildebrand*, pp. 227–241.
[2] Jaffé, *Monumenta Gregoriana*, pp. 89, 414.
[3] *E.H.D.*, vol. II, no. 102.

were men of iron determination; both were sincere; and together they were among the makers of medieval Europe. The wonder is not that there was a clash between their dominant personalities, but that they worked together so much in unity for a common purpose. The extent of their co-operation does credit to both of them, and it is not perhaps too much to assert that they recognized each other's greatness across the welter of lesser rulers by whom they were surrounded. William never ceased to foster the reforms that were the special concern of the papacy, and as late as 1082 he was asking Gregory for advice respecting the affairs of the see of Durham.[1] Gregory on at least two occasions rescinded the acts taken by his legates against William. How much controversy was in fact avoided can be guessed by a comparison between the Anglo-Norman kingdom and the rest of western Europe. The papal decree against lay-investiture which was published in Rome in 1074 did not enter England before the end of the eleventh century, despite the fact that every bishop appointed in Normandy and England between 1070 and 1087, except only Ernost and Gundulf of Rochester, received his pastoral staff from the king.[2] There was never an 'investitures contest' in the Anglo-Norman kingdom during the reign of William the Conqueror.

William's own conception of his rights as king within the Church were to be aptly summed up in the 'customs' which a writer of the next generation attributed to him.[3] As king he would perform his duty of securing the welfare of the Church within his dominions, and as king he would resist any division of loyalty among his subjects. Thus in the case of a disputed papal election no pope was to be recognized within his realm without his consent; no papal letter was to be received without his permission; no ecclesiastical council within his kingdom was to initiate legislation without his approval; and no bishop must excommunicate any of his officials or tenants-in-chief without his leave. It was a clear-cut position, but it was traditional rather than anti-papal. When Lanfranc about 1081 stated in a letter to Gregory, 'I am ready to yield obedience to your commands in everything according to the canons',[4] he was perfectly sincere, and he was voicing the views of his royal master. But the canons, as interpreted by Lanfranc and by William,

---

[1] Simeon of Durham (*Opera*, vol. I, p. 121). It should be noted that in 1084 Lanfranc, although with some detachment, declined to endorse the criticisms of Gregory made by the supporters of the anti-Pope Clement (*E.H.D.*, vol. II, no. 106).

[2] Brooke, *op. cit.*, p. 138; Macdonald, *Lanfranc*, p. 212.

[3] Eadmer, *Hist. Novorum*, p. 9. [4] *E.H.D.*, vol. II, no. 103.

were different in emphasis from the canon law beginning to be propounded at Rome by Gregory VII. William took his stand on a theory of royalty, and of its obligations, which had been current in the previous century, and to which expression had been given at his coronation. The king had his special duties towards the Church, and he would fulfil them. William's ecclesiastical policy was thus throughout (in the admirable phrase of Professor Z. N. Brooke) 'entirely natural and regularly consistent'.[1]

In view of the theory of royalty which he embodied, and in view also of the practical use he made of it with regard to the Church, William must himself be held very responsible for the ecclesiastical changes which marked his reign. As has been seen, most of those changes took place in Normandy before 1066, whilst in England they occurred after that date when the king's policy was influenced and sometimes modified by Lanfranc. It would be wrong, however, to distinguish between William's ecclesiastical policy as expressed before and after 1066. In this respect, also, it was 'regularly consistent'. William had been brought up in the midst of an ecclesiastical revival in his duchy which he had some share in promoting. He carried its principles to England to such purpose that between 1070 and 1087 the Church in England was made to conform to the continental pattern and subject to the reforming ideas which were permeating western Europe. Thus William, who 'never tried to create a national or independent church', 'brought the English church out of its backwater into the regular current once more'.[2]

It is no part of the present study to pass judgment on the condition of the late Old English church, the more especially as scholars find themselves much divided on the subject. Some commentators are still disposed to give credence to the adverse criticisms made, for example, by William of Malmesbury,[3] whilst others, though properly cautious of accepting them at their face value, are none the less chary of eulogy.[4] By contrast an emphatic and erudite protest has been made against the notion that the Church in England between 950 and 1050 was 'decadent' or that it stood in any special need of reforms imported from overseas.[5] The matter may here, therefore, properly be left in suspense with the

[1] Brooke, op. cit., p. 134.
[2] Ibid., p. 136.
[3] Will. Malms., Gesta Regum, p. 305.
[4] Brooke, loc. cit.; Knowles, Monastic Order, p. 94.
[5] R. R. Darlington, 'Movements of Reform in the late Old English Church' (Eng. Hist. Rev., vol. LI (1936), pp. 385–428); cf. also History, vol. XXII (1937), pp. 1–13. See also the judicious survey now supplied by Professor F. Barlow in The English Church, 1000–1066 (1963).

remark that it was inevitable that such widespread changes as have been outlined in this chapter should have entailed loss as well as gain. The feudalization of the church in England was in the future to produce unhappy consequences, and whatever may be thought of the discipline, the organization, and the spirituality of the late Old English church, it cannot be regarded as having been ineffective in the sponsorship of art and literature. In this respect, at least, England in 1050 was in no sense a backward country. Her metal-work was famous, and her coinage was fine. English embroidery was particularly esteemed, and English book production, particularly that of the Winchester school, of outstanding excellence.[1] It has even been asserted that in respect of the minor arts the Norman conquest was 'little short of a catastrophe', and if the glories of the Romanesque architecture which the Normans brought to England are apparent to any traveller, it would be rash to disparage the ecclesiastical building which took place in England during the earlier half of the eleventh century, most of which has failed to survive.[2] Finally, it needs no emphasis that in the decades preceding the Norman conquest, England was continuing to produce a literature in the vernacular, which in this respect was without parallel in contemporary Europe.[3]

This vernacular culture, between 1066 and 1087, received a lethal blow, and its place was taken in England by a culture which drew its inspiration in art and literature from the vivid intellectual interests of Latin Europe, which had already permeated the province of Rouen. Henceforth for more than a century, with rare exceptions, whatever was thought and written by Englishmen was thought and written in Latin, and the English contributions to philosophy and theology were to form part of controversies which were common to the Continent. Despite the irreparable damage that had been inflicted upon the earlier indigenous endeavour, England had therefore been brought by political events in a special sense into the main stream of European development. And this had occurred at a propitious time of reformation and revival. For thereby England was, in the near future, enabled to take her full share in the renaissance of the twelfth century which has been justly described

[1] See generally R. W. Chambers, 'The Continuity of English Prose' (*Early English Text Soc.*, vol. 186), and more particularly the fine essay by Professor F. Wormald on 'Style and Design' in *The Bayeux Tapestry* (ed. Stenton), pp. 25–36.
[2] A. W. Clapham, *English Romanesque Architecture before the Norman Conquest*, esp. p. 117.
[3] Chambers, *op. cit.*; K. Sisam, in *Review of English Studies*, vol. VII, p. 7; vol. VIII, p. 51; vol. IX, p. 1.

as marking one of the brightest epochs in the history of European civilization. She was to make her notable and highly individual contribution to all those great movements in art, in literature, in scholarship, and in education, which were characteristic of western Christendom at the zenith of its medieval achievement.

A final assessment of the gain and loss that was here involved is probably impossible. Certainly, it has still to be made. There can, however, be no doubt that between 1070 and 1087 the Church both in Normandy and England was brought ever more firmly under the control of 'a ruler who was resolved of set purpose to raise the whole level of ecclesiastical discipline in his dominions'.[1] Nor can there be much question of William's success in implementing that resolve. During these years he carried the revival, which had previously marked the Norman duchy, to its logical conclusion, and he gave to the Church in England the character it was to retain for the remainder of the Middle Ages. At a time of revolutionary ecclesiastical change in Europe he acted, moreover, with such circumspection, and with such regard for tradition, that he postponed for his lifetime any crisis in the relations between temporal and spiritual authority within his realm. Nor can his ecclesiastical policy be regarded as other than sincere and constructive, for although he was of necessity occupied incessantly with the acquisition and retention of power, he never allowed himself to be wholly immersed in secularity. His motives were undoubtedly mixed, but he made his own enduring contribution to the movement of ecclesiastical reform that marked the age, and which was itself a potent factor in the formation of medieval Europe.

[1] Knowles, *op. cit.*, p. 93.

Chapter 14

THE END OF THE REIGN

Christmas 1085 – 9 September 1087

The last two years of William's life possess a special interest for his biographer. In one sense they represent the epilogue to a great career, but in another they can be regarded as embodying the final crisis of his reign wherein all its chief characteristics were displayed in conjunction. The twenty-four months that elapsed between the autumn of 1085 and William's death in September 1087 saw the revival of a hostile confederation against the Anglo-Norman kingdom in a form reminiscent of earlier decades. They witnessed the continuation of William's previous defence of that kingdom, though this time by exceptional means. And they witnessed, also, the Conqueror's greatest administrative achievement. These months were all spent by him either in war or in active preparation for war, but they also included the taking of the Domesday survey which was the most noteworthy illustration of what his government involved. Nor can these events be dissociated from each other. Throughout his life, war and a struggle for survival had formed the background, and the essential condition, of his constructive acts. They continued to do so until death.

The beginning of this crisis is aptly recorded in the Anglo-Saxon Chronicle for 1085: 'In this year people said, and declared for a fact, that Cnut, king of Denmark, son of King Sweyn was setting out towards England, and meant to conquer that land with the aid of Robert, count of Flanders.'[1] The traditional enemies of the Anglo-Norman kingdom were thus all becoming arrayed against it. St Cnut (Cnut IV), son of Sweyn Estrithson, was reviving the Scandinavian claims on England which had been asserted with such force, and with such long-standing sanctions, not only by his father but also by Harold Hardraada and Magnus. Robert of Flanders, whose sister had married the Danish king, was again in the field as in 1074. In France, King Philip with the memories of Dol and Gerberoi in his mind was actively supporting

[1] AS. Chron., 'E', *s.a.* 1085. Cnut IV became king of Denmark in 1080 in succession to his brother Harold 'Hein'. He had taken part in the expeditions against England in 1069 and 1075.

346

William's son Robert, who remained in open enmity with his father, while Odo, bishop of Bayeux, although in captivity, could incite the treason of William's English and Norman subjects. Finally, Malcolm stood hostile on the Scottish border, and Fulk le Rechin of Anjou was ready to turn the situation to his advantage. Such was the threat which William now had to meet, and his personal circumstances must have imposed an additional strain upon him. He was ageing, and had recently been bereft of his wife to whom he had been devoted. There were few members of his own family on whom he could rely, and his own health was failing inasmuch as he was becoming increasingly – even notoriously – corpulent. The energy with which he faced the coalition of his enemies in the closing months of his reign is thus not the least notable illustration of his fortitude and determination.

As soon as he was aware of Cnut's threatened invasion, he acted with speed and vigour. He caused certain of the coastal districts of England to be laid waste in order to deny provisions to any invading force. For his own part, leaving to others the defence of Normandy, he crossed the Channel 'with a larger force of mounted men and foot-soldiers than had ever come into this country'. The statement made by an English writer who may well have been alive in 1066 challenges attention, and itself testifies to the magnitude of William's preparations. It merits, however, some further analysis. There is little doubt that this great force was largely composed of mercenaries, and William's ability to pay them is remarkable, and must surely be related to the great geld which he had levied on England during the previous year. Even so, the maintenance of such a host created difficulties. 'People wondered how this country could maintain all that army.' In the event William dispersed them over the estates of his vassals, compelling these to provision them according to the size of their lands. It was a drastic act, yet it may be doubted whether by itself it was sufficient, even though some of the mercenaries were later disbanded. The next two annals of the native chronicle are understandably full of laments about the heavy taxation which was being levied on the land.[1]

It was in these circumstances that at Christmas 1085 William came to Gloucester to hold his court. There he 'had much thought and very deep discussion with his council about this country – how it was occupied, and with what sort of people'.[2] And the result was the taking of the Domesday survey. So noteworthy was this vast undertaking, and

[1] AS. Chron., 'E', s.a. 1085, 1086.   [2] *Ibid.*, s.a. 1085.

so important was the result, that every detail of the process by which the inquiry was conducted, the motives which inspired it, and the record which was produced have been the object of erudite and controversial comment.[1] The general course of events was, however, succinctly described by early writers in words which though familiar deserve quotation.[2] The chief of these notices is contained in a famous passage of the Anglo-Saxon Chronicle itself:

[The king] sent his men over all England into every shire and had them find out how many hundred hides there were in the shire, or what land and cattle the king himself had in the country, or what dues he ought to have annually from the shire. Also, he had a record made of how much land his archbishops had, and his bishops and his abbots and his earls – and though I relate it at too great length – what or how much everybody had who was occupying land in England, in land and cattle, and how much money it was worth. So very narrowly did he have it investigated that there was no single hide nor a yard of land nor indeed (shame it is to relate it but it seemed no shame to him to do) was one ox or one cow or one pig left out, that was not put down in his record. And all these writings were brought to him afterwards.[3]

In many particulars this statement is less precise than might be desired, but its general purpose is clear, and it is fortunate that it can be supplemented by another contemporary notice of equal authority. This is contained in a passage written by Robert Losinga, bishop of Hereford from 1079 to 1095, who was almost certainly present himself at the deep speech that was held at Gloucester:

In the twentieth year of his reign, by order of William, King of the English, there was made a survey of the whole of England, that is to say of the lands of the several provinces of England, and of the possessions of each and all of the magnates. This was done in respect of ploughlands and of habitations,

---

[1] It need hardly be said that no attempt is here made to review these theories in detail. The important recent works to which I have been particularly indebted are (in order of publication): *Domesday Rebound* (H.M. Stationery Office, 1954); R. Welldon Finn, *The Domesday Inquest* (1961); and V. H. Galbraith, *The Making of Domesday Book* (1961). The earlier erudition will best be found in J. R. Round, *Feudal England* (1895), and in F. W. Maitland, *Domesday Book and Beyond* (1897). These two great books, though savagely handled by Professor Galbraith, still retain much of their value, and of their power to inspire. Reference may also be made to Douglas, in *History*, vol. XXI (1936), pp. 249–257; in *Domesday Monachorum* (1944), pp. 16–30; and in *E.H.D.*, vol. II, pp. 847–893. Bibliographies will be found at pp. 802–811 of the last-named work, in A. Ballard, *The Domesday Inquest* (ed. 1923), and in V. H. Galbraith, *op. cit.*, pp. 231–233.

[2] In addition to the passages quoted, see Flor. Worc. (vol. II, pp. 18, 19); Will. Malms., *Gesta Regum*, p. 317; and the Worcester Annalist printed by Liebermann(*Anglo-Normannische Geschichtsquellen*, p. 21). Other early references to the Domesday survey are given in *E.H.D.*, vol. II, nos. 198–204.   [3] AS. Chron., 'E', *s.a.* 1085.

and of men both bond and free, both those who dwelt in cottages, and those who had their homes and their share in the fields; and in respect of ploughs and horses and other animals; and in respect of the services and payments due from all men in the whole land. Other investigators followed the first; and men were sent into provinces which they did not know, and where they were themselves unknown, in order that they might be given the opportunity of checking the first survey, and if necessary, of denouncing its authors as guilty to the king. And the land was vexed with much violence arising from the collection of the royal taxes.[1]

It would appear, moreover, that for the purposes of this investigation England was divided up into seven or more circuits to each of which a separate panel of these royal commissioners was assigned.[2] And the method and scope of their inquiries are succinctly stated in a record known as the 'Ely Inquiry' (*Inquisitio Eliensis*). The Domesday inquest, it is there stated, was:

... the inquiry concerning lands which the king's barons made according to the oath of the sheriff of the shire, and of all the barons and their Frenchmen, and of the whole hundred court – the priest, the reeve and six men from each village. They inquired what the manor was called, and who held it in the time of King Edward; who holds it now; how many hides there are; how many ploughs in demesne; and how many belonging to the men; how many villeins; how many cottars; how many slaves; how many freemen; how many sokemen; how much woodland; how much meadow; how much pasture; how many mills; how many fisheries; how much has been added to, and how much taken away from the estate; what it used to be worth altogether; what it is worth now; and how much each freeman and sokeman had and has. All this to be recorded thrice: to wit, as it was in the time of King Edward; as it was when King William gave the estate; and as it is now. And it was also noted whether more could be taken from the estate than is now being taken.[3]

---

[1] Added by the author as a note to the Chronicle of Marianus Scotus. First printed by W. H. Stevenson, in *Eng. Hist. Rev.*, vol. XXII (1907), p. 74.

[2] The late Carl Stephenson (*Medieval Institutions* (ed. Bruce D. Lyon, 1954), p. 188) reconstructed these circuits as follows:

(1) Kent, Sussex, Surrey, Hampshire, Berkshire.
(2) Wiltshire, Dorset, Somerset, Devonshire, Cornwall.
(3) Middlesex, Hertford, Buckingham, Cambridge, Bedford.
(4) Oxford, Northampton, Leicester, Warwick.
(5) Gloucester, Worcester, Hereford, Stafford, Shropshire, Cheshire.
(6) Huntingdon, Derby, Nottingham, Rutland, York, Lincoln.
(7) Essex, Norfolk, Suffolk.

The names of some of the Domesday commissioners are known. Chief of them would appear to have been Geoffrey, bishop of Coutances. For Worcestershire the commissioners would seem to have been Remigius, bishop of Lincoln, Walter Giffard, Henry of Ferrières, and Adam, son of Hubert of Ryes (cf. Galbraith, *op. cit.*, pp. 8, 36).

[3] *E.H.D.*, vol. II, no. 215.

The magnitude of the undertaking needs no further emphasis. And in general – with certain modifications – the resulting texts, now collectively known as Domesday Book, reflect fairly faithfully the answers to these questions.

Domesday Book consists of two volumes of somewhat different character now preserved in the Public Record Office in Chancery Lane.[1] One of these (vol. II, or the 'Little Domesday') relates to Norfolk, Suffolk, and Essex. The other (vol. I, or the 'Great Domesday') deals with all the rest of England that was surveyed. There are, however, other texts which were also the product of this inquiry, and chief of these is that known as the Exon Domesday, now preserved in the cathedral library at Exeter, which relates to the five south-western shires.[2] These three volumes all possess individual characteristics. In particular both the Little Domesday and the Exon Domesday are more inchoate in form and contain more detailed information than the Great Domesday. On the other hand, all these three volumes clearly derived from the same inquest, and they all conform to the same fundamental plan. They are territorial in arrangement in so far as the information they supply is presented shire by shire; and they are feudal in arrangement in that, within each shire, the information is given under the holdings therein of the king and his tenants-in-chief.

The chief difficulty in ascertaining the manner in which William caused this vast investigation to be made consists in discerning how the mass of information obtained by the Domesday commissioners was digested into the 'books' which were eventually compiled. A record known as 'The Cambridgeshire Inquest'[3] indicates that in that shire an inquiry was made in court whereat jurors from the several hundreds gave sworn testimony, and it has been very generally believed that this procedure was adopted throughout England; that the 'writings' which were in due course brought to the king were the returns thus elicited; and that only subsequently were they rearranged according to a feudal plan at Winchester.[4] It has, however, been recently suggested with

---

[1] Edited by Abraham Farley, and printed in two folio volumes in 1783 by the Record Commission. Translations for various counties are included in the *Victoria History of the Counties of England*.

[2] Printed by the Record Commission as a supplementary volume to their edition of Domesday Book (vol. III, 1816). The shires considered are Wiltshire, Dorset, Somerset, Devonshire, Cornwall.

[3] *E.H.D.*, vol. II, no. 214; *Victoria County History*, Cambridgeshire, vol. I, pp. 400–437.

[4] This, crudely stated, is the theory developed with a wealth of erudition by Round, *op. cit.*, pp. 3–147.

authority[1] that such inquiries before jurors of the hundreds formed only one part of the Domesday inquisition;[2] that the original returns from the shires were compiled locally according to a feudal plan; and that it was these feudal returns (*breves*) of the fiefs within each shire of the king and his tenants-in-chief, which were brought in due course to Winchester. In this way, it is said, the differences as well as the similarities between the three Domesday 'books' can best be explained. The Exon Domesday was a first draft of one collection of these feudal *breves*, which in due course was summarized and digested into the Great Domesday, whereas the Little Domesday was another of these drafts which, for reasons unknown, never received such treatment, and thus remained in its original form.[3]

Every theory as to the making of Domesday Book has some difficulties to overcome. But whatever may have been the exact process by which Domesday Book was compiled, it remains an astonishing product of the Conqueror's administration, reflecting at once the problems with which he was faced, and the character of his rule. It was imperative that he should know the resources of his kingdom, for his need of money was always pressing, and never more so than in 1085. He sought therefore to ascertain the taxable capacity of his kingdom, and to see whether more could be exacted from it. The elaborate calculations, running throughout the whole survey, of hides and carucates in their fiscal connotation as geld paying units, is by itself evidence of this, as is also the prevalence throughout the south and west of England of assessments in multiples of five hides.[4] In Domesday Book there is in fact sure testimony of the manner in which William took over (as has been seen) the taxational system of the Old English state, and used it to his own advantage. It is small wonder, therefore, that this was the aspect of the matter which most impressed – and distressed – contemporary observers. The term *descriptio*[5] which they normally used in referring to the survey itself indicates an assessment to public taxation, and fear of the consequences was everywhere apparent. In fact, the whole inquiry was clearly most unpopular. It provoked violent opposition, and even bloodshed.[6]

---

[1] V. H. Galbraith, *op. cit.* The full scope of this 'hypothesis' and its implications can only be appreciated by reference to the detailed evidence on which it is based.

[2] Perhaps their chief function was in adjudicating on disputed claims.

[3] These 'books' might thus perhaps be held to be based on circuits (2) and (7) as indicated above.

[4] Round, *loc. cit.*   [5] D.B., vol. II, fol. 450: the colophon to the 'Little Domesday'.

[6] Robert Losinga (see above, p. 349); the Worcester Annalist (Liebermann, *op. cit.*, p. 21) refers to 'multis cladibus'.

Yet if the need for a more efficient collection of revenue supplied the chief motive prompting King William to this great endeavour, his purpose in the undertaking should not be too rigidly circumscribed. William was lord of a feudal kingdom which was threatened with attack, and its feudal resources had to be deployed to the utmost advantage. The court which had decided on the great inquest was a feudal court, and the arrangement of the survey was, within each shire, according to the great fiefs. And this was what might have been expected. It was important for the king (as 'Florence of Worcester'[1] observed in describing the survey) to ascertain how much land each of his barons possessed, for they were responsible for the provision of the enfeoffed knights who were necessary for the defence of the realm. And if Domesday Book gives little information about feudal organization as such, since for the most part it omits to indicate the amount of knight-service owed to the king by his tenants-in-chief, it none the less supplied William with more detailed feudal information than he had possessed at any time since his coming to England. It gave him for the first time a comprehensive account of how the land of England had been allocated among his greater followers. Domesday Book, in fact, assumed throughout the existence of the newly established feudal order and indicated its territorial basis.

Domesday Book was not, however, merely a fiscal record (though that was its primary purpose), nor was it in addition merely a feudal statement, though that, to a lesser degree, it also served to supply. In yet another way did it offer a further illustration of the authority which William assumed in the country he had conquered. Throughout his reign, from the time of his coronation, he had claimed to be regarded as the legitimate successor of Edward the Confessor, and this claim was reflected throughout Domesday Book. No feature of the survey is more noteworthy, or more significant, than its design to record conditions not only as they were in 1066 and 1086, but also as they had been in the time of King Edward. And in this connexion the survey could be regarded as in a sense the result of a judicial inquiry and related to the earlier litigation of the Conqueror's reign.[2] In many districts a continuous process of litigation had led up to the Domesday inquest, and the Domesday commissioners, who had themselves often, like Geoffrey of Coutances, conducted the previous trials by the same method of the sworn inquest, were frequently, in 1086, dealing with matters which

---

[1] s.a. 1086. [2] Douglas, Essays – James Tait, pp. 47–57.

were still in dispute. William, regarding himself as the Confessor's successor, evidently wished for a complete record of English conditions before his coming, and he also desired to legalize the great changes which the Conquest had caused. Domesday Book thus bears unmistakable traces of being connected with the controversies respecting ownership and possession which had marked the two previous decades. Individual entries often describe, and attempt to reconcile, contesting claims by reference to the past, and the accounts of Yorkshire, Lincolnshire, and Huntingdonshire record the *clamores* or disputes which came up for settlement at the time of the Domesday inquisition.[1]

The character of Domesday Book and the achievement it embodied can, in truth, only be appraised by reference to William himself. Indeed, perhaps the most remarkable fact about the Domesday inquest is that it was ever undertaken, and ever successfully completed. As Professor Galbraith observes, 'it is our best evidence of the iron will of the Conqueror, and the measure of the difference between the authority wielded by him and even the greatest of his predecessors'.[2] His personality and his purpose are reflected on every page of Domesday Book. A country had been conquered, and since that conquest the king had been compelled to spend most of his time outside England. Very much concerning England, and the Norman settlement therein, must still have remained unknown to him, and the information he required was essential to his government and to the defence of his realm. He desired, therefore, to know everything that men could tell him about his new kingdom, its inhabitants, its wealth, its provincial customs, its traditions, and its tax-paying capacity. As a result, the record, so astonishing in its scope, escapes classification since it subserved so many needs. Consequently, while Domesday Book has some of the characteristics of a geld inquest, of a feudal record, and of a judicial statement, its special nature must never be forgotten. It is a record without parallel. It is not simply a geld book since it is unlike all other geld books. It is not a true feodary for it is unlike all other feodaries. It is not simply the result of a great judicial inquiry for its scope was much wider. It was the unique product of a unique occasion. The events of 1085 gave urgency to the desire of a great king to obtain the fullest possible amount of information about the kingdom he had won, and the result was the most remarkable statistical record ever produced in any medieval kingdom.

[1] *e.g.* D.B., vol. 1, fols. 207, 208, 375–378.   [2] *Op. cit.*, p. 215.

Such was the prestige which soon came to attach to Domesday Book that there is some danger that its importance may even be exaggerated. Throughout the Middle Ages, and beyond, men turned to the great survey as to a court of appeal, and in more recent times some scholars have been prone to seek in it for information which it could hardly be expected to supply.[1] In truth, of course, Domesday Book was not made to provide later historians with material for their interpretations of the past, but to subserve the administrative purposes of the king who created it. It should be remembered, also, that not the whole of England was covered by the inquiry, for the royal commissioners did not extend their investigations north of the Tees or the Westmorland fells. Nor was Domesday Book itself as infallible as some were tempted to suppose; there are to be found within it both duplications and inaccuracies, and since its compilers were frequently 'describing an alien society in alien terms',[2] it is not always to be relied upon in respect of the technical classifications it attempts of estates, of status, and of tenure.

Yet when all proper deductions are made, the king's achievement which is embodied in Domesday Book remains astonishing, and recent scholars have paid full tribute to it. 'As an administrative achievement,' writes Sir Frank Stenton, 'it has no parallel in medieval history.'[3] It is a supreme demonstration of the efficiency of those who served the Conqueror, and of the energy with which at the close of his life he could still enforce the execution of a great design. Nor must it be forgotten that all this was done in the teeth of opposition from a reluctant country. And the final product was commensurate with the strength of will that created it. Domesday Book has been correctly and strikingly described by another authority as 'marking an epoch in the use of the written word in government'.[4] And it is scarcely an exaggeration to add that there had been 'nothing like it since the days of imperial Rome'.[5]

After the momentous decisions of his Gloucester court at Christmas 1085, William moved through southern England during the months when the Domesday inquest was being conducted. He heard the Easter

[1] Cf. Douglas, in *History*, vol. XXI (1936), p. 255.

[2] Stenton, in *Eng. Hist. Rev.*, vol. XXXVII, p. 250.

[3] Stenton, *Anglo-Saxon England*, p. 610.

[4] Galbraith, *Studies in the Public Records*, p. 90.

[5] It is interesting to note that a Winchester annalist (*Annales Monastici*, vol. II, p. 34) alludes to the survey thus: 'Edictum a rege exiit ut tota Anglia describeretur.' This is clearly an echo of the Gospel for the First Mass of Christmas: 'Exiit edictum a Caesare Augusto ut describeratur universus orbis.'

Mass of 1086 at Winchester, and at Pentecost he was at Westminster, where he conferred knighthood on his son Henry. And then he

. . . travelled about so as to come to Salisbury at Lammas, and there his councillors came to him, and all the people occupying land who were of any account over all England whosoever's vassals they might be; and they all submitted to him, and swore oaths of allegiance to him that they would be faithful to him against all other men.[1]

It was the second of the great administrative acts of these critical months.

The Oath of Salisbury[2] is deservedly famous. But there have been some who have sought to invest it with a constitutional significance which it can hardly have possessed. It has even been suggested that there came to Salisbury on this occasion 'not only every feudal dependent of the king, but every freeman and freeholder whatsoever'.[3] It is, however, beyond the bounds of possibility that an assembly of this nature could have been brought together at Salisbury in August 1086, and even the knights who had been enfeoffed by that time over all England were probably too numerous, and in many cases of too little social importance, for the king to have wished for them all to attend a meeting of his court. Undoubtedly, the Salisbury court was one of exceptional size and splendour, but the 'landowning men of any account' were probably the more important mesne tenants of the great honours, men of similar social standing as their lords, the 'peers' of the honours whose special role in the feudal administration of England has already been noted.[4] Such an assembly, though large and imposing, would not have been of inordinate size, and it would precisely have served the king's immediate purpose.

None the less, while William is not to be credited with having on this occasion attempted to substitute some more modern conception of sovereignty for the position he held as king in the feudal state, his acts, on this occasion, were exceptional in their nature, and of high importance. The special position of the king in the feudal order of Anglo-Norman England, and the reasons for it, have already been analysed, and the proceedings at Salisbury in 1086 did something to make the

---

[1] AS. Chron., 'E', s.a. 1085 (equals 1086).
[2] The most important recent discussions are in Stenton, *English Feudalism*, pp. 111–113 and H. A. Cronne, in *History*, vol. XIX (1934), pp. 248–252.
[3] Stubbs, *Constitutional History*, vol. I, p. 299.
[4] Above, pp. 275, 280, 281.

royal authority more effective. The measures taken by the king were certainly unprecedented, and were regarded as such, but they were not 'anti-feudal' in their purpose. Rather, they were designed to give additional strength to the feudal organization which in England, from the circumstances of the Conquest, already possessed special features. The Salisbury oath, like the Domesday inquest, of which it was in some sense the counterpart, was the king's response to a challenge. The Anglo-Norman kingdom was facing a crisis, and it was clearly important that its ruler should establish a close relation with all the great men in England with a view to fortifying the military organization on which he relied. Once again the personal dominance of King William was displayed.

The crisis itself might now, however, seem to be passing. Cnut had assembled a large army, and collected a great fleet in the Limfjord to transport it to England. But throughout the period of his preparations he was faced with disaffection among his subjects, and in the ensuing disturbances he was himself captured and in July 1086 he was murdered in the church of Odensee.[1] His death meant that the expedition had to be abandoned, and the immediate threat of an invasion of England from Scandinavia was removed. But the situation none the less remained perilous. Robert, the king's son, was in revolt, and Odo, his half-brother, was fostering treason. Robert, count of Flanders, was a declared enemy, and at home Edgar Atheling showed himself so disaffected that the king thought it prudent to allow him to depart for Apulia with no less than two hundred followers. Moreover, the former pattern of the attacks on the Anglo-Norman kingdom was now reproduced. During 1086 William's attention had inevitably been concentrated on England, and this gave King Philip the opportunity to renew operations in France. It is not surprising therefore that, very shortly after the Salisbury court, the Conqueror made preparations to return to Normandy. He is reported to have gone to the Isle of Wight, and to have been vigorous at this time in collecting additional taxes, doubtless to pay for more mercenary troops. About the end of 1086 he crossed over to France, but where he spent the last Christmas of his life is not known.[2]

William's movements during the early months of 1087 are, in fact, highly obscure. The chroniclers are silent on the matter, and the documentary evidence is difficult to interpret. It was doubtless during the meeting of the Salisbury court that the king issued two writs in

[1] Stenton, *William the Conqueror*, p. 364.   [2] AS. Chron., 'E', *loc. cit.*

favour of Maurice, the newly appointed bishop of London,[1] and it was probably at some later date that he gave to the abbey of Westminster two further writs,[2] one of which is dated 'after the survey of the whole of England'. Finally, there is extant a confirmation made about this time in favour of the nunnery of Saint-Amand at Rouen,[3] and this, which was given in the presence of a considerable number of notable witnesses, may be presumed to have been issued after the king's return to Normandy. These texts have an exceptional interest as being among the last documentary products of the Conqueror's rule, but they supply little information about his activities during the closing months of his reign.

There can be no doubt, however, that his main preoccupation continued to be with defence, and it is not surprising that his attention should have been directed once more to the long-standing threat latent in the French king's control of the Vexin, which William had been forced to accept in 1077.[4] In the interval, moreover, there had taken place in this region a change which was favourable to William's prospects. Some time between July 1080 and Christmas 1081 the comté of Meulan situated towards the south of the Vexin had passed by marriage into the hands of Robert of Beaumont, one of the duke's most trusted and powerful supporters, so that he now possessed a strong ally in the debatable region.[5] For these reasons, when in the late summer of 1087 the French king's garrison at Mantes crossed over into the Evreçin and began to pillage Normandy, William decided to retaliate in force.[6] Before August 15 he launched an expedition designed to regain the Vexin for Normandy, and particularly the towns of Mantes, Chaumont, and Pontoise.[7]

[1] Gibbs, *Early Charters of St Paul's*, nos. 5, 12. Maurice became bishop of London in or about April 1086, and the mention in both documents of Osmund, bishop of Salisbury, perhaps suggests the occasion when these writs were issued.

[2] These are given in facsimile as plates XXIV and XXV in Bishop and Chaplais, *English Royal Writs to A.D. 1100*. The editors show conclusively that both these writs were issued by the Conqueror. They place them in 1087. This is probably correct, but it may be remarked that both these writs are English in origin, and that one of them is in the hand of a known scribe in the English chancery. Does this suggest that the king was himself in England when they were given? If so, it might be necessary either to place them at the end of 1086, or, alternatively, to postulate a visit by the king to England in the spring of 1087. In the absence of any evidence to the contrary it is usually, and doubtless correctly, assumed that William crossed the Channel (to Normandy) for the last time about the end of 1086.

[3] Le Cacheux, *Histoire de Saint Amand*, p. 252, no. 13.

[4] Above, p. 234, 235.

[5] *Complete Peerage*, vol. VII, p. 524; J. Depoin, *Cart. de S. Martin de Pontoise*, pp. 308–316.

[6] Ord. Vit., vol. III, p. 222.

[7] AS. Chron., 'E', *s.a.* 1085 (equals 1086). Ord. Vit. (vol. III, p. 225) says that the expedition started in the last week of July.

The campaign which followed was not only the last, but also one of the most brutal of the Conqueror's reign. He crossed the Epte, and with a large force harried the countryside up to Mantes. Then, when the garrison sallied out without due precaution, he fell upon them with a surprise attack. They retreated in confusion into the city hotly pursued by William's troops, and a terrible destruction followed.[1] Mantes itself was so completely burnt that even today it is hard to find in the town any traces of eleventh-century buildings.[2] Such barbarity was inexcusable, but it raises the question whether William now, as on previous occasions, meant his ruthlessness to be a preparation for more extensive operations. His campaign of 1087 is usually, and perhaps rightly, dismissed as an unimportant episode notable only because of its tragic personal sequel. But Mantes is only some thirty miles from Paris, and William with his great resources of men and money might conceivably have followed up his success with far-reaching consequences to the future of the French monarchy. Such speculations are, however, profitless, for the conclusion was very different. The sack of Mantes was the last military act of the Conqueror, since as he rode through the burning streets of the town, calamity came suddenly upon him. Some say that his horse, taking fright from the burning embers, threw the corpulent king with such force against the high pommel of his saddle that he was lethally ruptured; others affirm that he was suddenly afflicted with some violent intestinal complaint. At all events he was incapacitated. In the greatest pain he returned from the devastated Vexin through the summer heat to Rouen. There he rested. But his illness and discomfort increased daily, and he found the noise of the city intolerable. After some days, he gave orders that he should be carried to the priory of Saint-Gervais on a hill in the western suburbs, and there he went, attended by Gilbert Maminot, bishop of Lisieux, and Gontard, abbot of Jumièges, both of whom were reputedly skilled in medicine. He was obviously dying.[3]

Two accounts of what transpired during the last days of the Conqueror's life have survived. The one was written by an anonymous monk of Caen shortly after the event.[4] The other is from the gifted pen of Ordericus Vitalis who wrote some fifty years later. Ordericus Vitalis

---

[1] Ord. Vit., vol. III, p. 225.   [2] Freeman, *Norman Conquest*, vol. IV, pp. 701–703.

[3] Will. Malms., *Gesta Regum*, pp. 336, 337; AS. Chron., *loc. cit.*; Ord. Vit., vol. III, pp. 226, 227.

[4] Printed by J. Marx in his edition of Will. Jum. A translation is given in *E.H.D.*, vol. II, no. 6.

was concerned to give a full description of what he rightly considered to be a most noteworthy occasion, and he adopted the device of making the dying king review his life in a long speech which is in itself a notable summary of the Conqueror's career.[1] The speech itself is clearly imaginative, but it may safely be held to reproduce the authentic atmosphere of the scene, and the background painted by Ordericus bears all the marks of authenticity, since the writer, who was himself an acute observer, was familiar with Norman traditions and had, besides, many contacts with those who had been closely concerned.[2] Indeed, his elaborate descriptions can often in their essentials be confirmed by the more laconic statements of the monk of Caen.

It was a large company which gathered round the dying king at the priory of Saint-Gervais, but the two most prominent members of his family were significantly absent. Robert, his eldest son, was in revolt and keeping company with his father's chief enemy King Philip, whilst Odo, the powerful bishop of Bayeux, was still being held in captivity in Rouen. Lanfranc too was absent, since, loyal to the last, he was looking after the king's interests in England. But the king's other surviving sons were there, and with them was his half-brother Robert, count of Mortain, William Bonne-Ame, archbishop of Rouen, and many others, including Gerard, his chancellor, and the chief officials of his household. The great king was slowly dying in harrowing circumstances, but on his death-bed he was surrounded by an assemblage which was not essentially different from one of the great courts which had supported so many of the major decisions of his reign. It was thus to a concourse of magnates who had shared in his work that he was able to make his final dispositions, for, to the end, though in increasing pain, he preserved the clearness of his mind and his power of speech.[3]

In his extremity he was not unnaturally anxious to mend his soul, and though the scene may have been overcoloured by later writers for the purposes of edification, there is no reason to question the piety he exhibited, or the penitence he expressed, particularly for the bloodshed that had been the inevitable price of his achievement. He made his confession, and received absolution. Then he commanded a lavish distribution of alms, and made the attendant clerks record with particularity those who were to benefit from his gifts. He made a special

[1] Ord. Vit., vol. III, pp. 228–243.
[2] Ordericus had, for instance, close connexions with the diocese of Lisieux, and Gilbert, who was bishop of Lisieux from 1077 to 1101, was in close attendance on the Conqueror during his last days.   [3] Monk of Caen; Ord. Vit., vol. III, p. 228.

distribution to the clergy of Mantes to restore what he had burnt, and he exhorted those present to have a care after his death for the maintenance of justice and the preservation of the faith. Finally, he commanded that those whom he held in prison should be set free, with the single exception of the bishop of Bayeux. Here he found himself faced with the opposition of those who surrounded him, and Robert, count of Mortain, was particularly pressing in demanding his brother's release. The argument was prolonged, and at length the king in sheer weariness gave way, though not without insisting on the fell consequences likely to ensue. Odo was therefore released, and very soon he was to be present at the Conqueror's funeral.[1]

The disposal of the realm was a matter of greater moment. William expressed himself with justifiable bitterness against his son Robert whose disloyalty had dishonoured his father's age, and whom he judged to be unfit to rule unless constantly admonished and controlled. But once again, as in 1080, the Norman magnates sought to heal the breach between father and son, and at last the king, having expressed his forgiveness, consented to honour his former promises, and formally committed the duchy of Normandy to Robert, his first-born son. The case of England was, however, different. The motives here ascribed to the Conqueror at a later date by Ordericus Vitalis are interesting. According to this highly coloured account,[2] the king was conscious that he had acquired his royalty not by hereditary right but by judgment of battle, and at the expense of countless lives. He dared not, therefore, leave a kingdom thus won elsewhere than to God. But he hoped that God would grant it to his second surviving son, William, to whom he gave his sceptre, his sword, and his crown.[3] Conscious, moreover, of the disturbances which would inevitably follow his death, he addressed to Lanfranc in England a sealed letter confirming his acts, and he ordered William to depart without delay. The young man thereupon promptly left his father's death-bed, and riding in haste had already reached Wissant en route for England when he heard of the Conqueror's death. Finally, the king gave to his son Henry a considerable sum of money, and he too immediately left Saint-Gervais in order to secure it.[4]

These arrangements which were directly to affect the future deserve some comment. For instance, the gift of money made to Henry has sometimes been regarded as meagre and inadequate, whereas in truth,

---

[1] Monk of Caen; Ord. Vit., vol. III, pp. 228, 245, 248, 251.
[2] Ord. Vit., vol. III, pp. 242, 243.   [3] Monk of Caen.   [4] Ord. Vit., vol. III, p. 244.

viewed in relation to eleventh-century values, it was substantial.[1] The treatment accorded to Robert and William might likewise be misunderstood. The motives here assigned to the Conqueror by Ordericus contain curious hints, both of what might have been English feeling in the matter, and also of royalty conceived as a God-given dignity. But the king's action could be further explained by reference to contemporary circumstances. As has been seen, the succession of Robert to Normandy had been prepared by a long series of events, and it was not only his incompetence and disloyalty which prevented his succession to England. The Conqueror was here following the established practice of the Norman aristocracy which was that the Norman lands of a family (the lands of inheritance) should pass to the eldest son, whereas the English lands (the lands of conquest) should devolve on the second son. This usage had been very generally adopted,[2] and it was a custom which in any event William might have found it hard to ignore. None the less, the result was a set-back to the Conqueror's policy. The separation of Normandy from England had for long been a prime objective of King Philip of France, which William had consistently opposed.[3] Now that objective seemed to have been attained, and the dying king must have felt that he had here suffered a last reverse.

Having made his dispositions, William was anointed, and received the sacrament from the archbishop of Rouen,[4] and the final scene of his life is described in a famous passage from Ordericus Vitalis, which, though doubtless overcharged with emotion, may none the less be accepted as trustworthy in its main outlines. The king passed the night of 8 September in tranquillity, and awoke at dawn to the sound of the great bell of Rouen Cathedral.

On his asking what it signified, his attendants replied: 'My lord, the bell is ringing for Prime in the church of Saint Mary.' Then the king raised his eyes and lifted his hands and said: 'I commend myself to Mary the holy Mother of God, my heavenly Lady, that by her intercession I may be reconciled to her Son our Lord Jesus Christ.' And having said this he died.

Immediate confusion followed his passing, and some of the attendants behaved as if they had lost their wits.

---

[1] The sum given was £5,000. Perhaps this might be multiplied by seventy or eighty to give a modern valuation, but the reckoning is in no way precise.

[2] Examples could be multiplied. The instances of fitz Osbern, Montgomery, Harcourt, and Montfort-sur-Risle come to mind.

[3] Above, chap. 9.

[4] Monk of Caen.

Nevertheless, the wealthiest of them mounted their horses and departed in haste to secure their property. Whilst the inferior attendants, observing that their masters had disappeared, laid hands on the arms, the plate, the linen, and the royal furniture, and hastened away, leaving the corpse almost naked on the floor of the cell.[1]

William the Conqueror – Duke William II of Normandy, and King William I of England – died early in the morning of Thursday, 9 September 1087.[2]

The blend of the earthy and the sublime in these descriptions of the Conqueror's death were even more blatantly displayed in the circumstances of his burial. It was decided that he should be interred in the monastery of Saint Stephen which he had founded at Caen, but it would appear that there was at first some difficulty in making arrangements for the suitable transportation of the body. None the less it was in due course borne down the Seine and then transported by land to the outskirts of Caen, where it was met by a distinguished company of mourners. But the pomp of the procession was interrupted by an accidental fire which broke out in the town. At last, however, the church was reached, and there a notable company assembled to hear Mass, and to listen to a sermon by Gilbert, bishop of Lisieux. The king's son, Henry, and many lay magnates were present, together with all the Norman bishops and many Norman abbots, including the aged Nicholas of Saint-Ouen, and also Anselm from Le Bec. Thus at his funeral the Conqueror was once again surrounded by a Norman court comparable to those which had so often graced his reign.[3]

The dignity of the occasion was, however, soon disrupted. One Ascelin, a local worthy, protested that he had been robbed of the ground in which the king was to be buried, and claimed compensation, which he received.[4] And then a still more macabre episode took place, for the attendants actually broke the unwieldy body when trying to force it into the stone coffin, and such an intolerable stench filled the church that the priests were forced to hurry the service to a close.[5] Nor

[1] Ord. Vit., vol. III, pp. 248, 249.

[2] The Monk of Caen gives 10 September, but 9 September is given by the AS. Chron. and by Ord. Vit. 9 September is certainly correct. The anniversary was celebrated at Jumièges on 9 September as is indicated by the necrology of that abbey (*Rec. Hist. Franc.*, vol. XXIII, p. 421).

[3] Monk of Caen; Ord. Vit., vol. III, p. 251. All these came to the obsequies of this 'renowned baron' (*famosi baronis*). The phrase is strictly reminiscent of the 'Song of Roland'.

[4] Ord. Vit., vol. III, pp. 252, 253; Will. Malms., *Gesta Regum*, pp. 337, 338.

[5] Ord. Vit., vol. III, pp. 254, 255. The repulsive story is only given by Ord. Vit., but it can hardly have been invented.

was even this the last outrage to be inflicted on the Conqueror's body. His son William caused a fine memorial to be erected by Otto the goldsmith, and this with an inscription by Thomas II, archbishop of York, was to survive undisturbed until 1522.[1] In that year, however, the tomb was opened on instructions from Rome, and the body having been examined was reverently reinterred.[2] But in 1562 a complete devastation took place at the hands of the Calvinists. The tomb was rifled, the monuments destroyed, and the remains, with the exception of one thigh bone, scattered and lost.[3] The single remaining relic was, however, preserved, and in 1642 it was reburied under a new monument which about a century later was replaced by a more elaborate structure. But even this was not allowed to endure.[4] It was demolished in the revolutionary riots of 1793, and today a simple stone slab with a nineteenth-century inscription records what was the burial place of William the Conqueror.

[1] Monk of Caen; Ord. Vit., vol. III, p. 356. For Otto the Goldsmith and his possessions in England, see Douglas, *Feudal Documents*, no. 20, and D.B., vol. II, fols. 97b, 286b. Henry I of England also contributed to the monument (Will. Malms., *Gesta Regum*, p. 337).

[2] C. Hippeau, *L'abbaye de Saint-Étienne de Caen* (1855), pp. 169, 170.

[3] *Ibid.*, p. 181.

[4] *Ibid.*, p. 354. Where is the thigh-bone now? Freeman (*op. cit.*, vol. IV, p. 273) states that it was destroyed in 1793. But opinion in Caen today is that it is still in the grave.

EPILOGUE

EPILOGUE

Thus ended the life of William the Conqueror, 'and this was the last end of all that was mortal in him besides his fame'.[1] A biographer is always apt to exaggerate the importance of the man he portrays, and undoubtedly the main interest of the historical process which has here been surveyed lies outside the career of any individual, however eminent. The Norman conquest of England (which was the central event in that process) was perhaps the most revolutionary event in English history between the Conversion and the Reformation. It gave to England a new monarchy, a feudal polity of a special type, a reconstituted Church, and a changed concentration on a new set of political and intellectual ideas. But, at the same time, it was so achieved as to ensure the essential continuity of English life. By combining much that was new with the revival of much that was old, it went far to determine the highly individual character of medieval England.

Transformations of this magnitude cannot be referred simply to a single personality. Still less are they to be assessed by means of judgments inspired by the preoccupations of later periods – the more especially as these may often depend upon religious political and social criteria which are themselves open to dispute. By what ultimate standard should one compare the Church of Lanfranc with that of Aldred, the spirituality of John of Fécamp with that of Wulfstan, the virtues and vices of the Anglo-Norman aristocracy with those of their predecessors in England? How should one judge with any finality the relative merits of English political connexions in the Middle Ages with France and Scandinavia? How – again – should one place in the balance the literary production of Ælfric with that of St Anselm, or weigh the merits of the vernacular annals of the Anglo-Saxon chronicler against those of the great Latin history of Ordericus Vitalis, monk of Saint-Évroul who, be it said, was also *Anglicanus*? The most that can be done towards assessing these changes is to place them in their contemporary setting. The Norman conquest of England was prepared by previous history; it depended upon the developing power and policy of a unique province; and it derived from a complex of political relations which

[1] John Hayward, *The Lives of the III Normans, Kings of England* (1613), p. 22.

before 1066 had come to enmesh France, Scandinavia, Italy, and much of western Europe. Its results (for good or ill) were not only political and mundane: they were also social, ecclesiastical, and cultural. And they stretched wide. The establishment of the Anglo-Norman kingdom altered the political balance of Europe. It conditioned much of the future history of France. And it modified the internal structure, and the external influence, of western Christendom in the Middle Ages.

The prolonged crisis of the central decades of the eleventh century – so complex in its causes and so pervasive in its results – far transcends in importance the exploits of any one man. Nevertheless, when all proper qualifications have been made, it still remains difficult to explain the momentous developments which then took place without reference to William's own influence on every one of the political movements which have here been examined. A man's place in history depends on the extent to which he can mould, and also respond to, the needs of his time. But his ability to do so derives from his own qualities, and his opportunities in this respect are enhanced in an age when government is essentially personal. For these reasons, if for no others, William's character and personality must challenge attention, since they were among the factors in the making of England and of Europe.

What did he look like – this man who made such a profound impression on his contemporaries? The representations of William in the Bayeux Tapestry, on his seal in England, and on the coins which were struck for him as king, are too stylized to give any clear idea of his personal appearance. But the literary evidence is more illuminating. A Norman monk, who may well have seen him, described him as a burly warrior with a harsh gutteral voice, great in stature but not ungainly.[1] Writers in England say that he was majestic, 'both when seated and standing', though the excessive corpulence which later disfigured him doubtless began in his middle years.[2] He enjoyed remarkably good health, we are told, until the very end of his life, and his exceptional physical strength is often noted. William of Poitiers and William of Jumièges dilate on his prowess in the field of battle, and there are plenty of examples of his capacity to endure great physical hardship.[3]

[1] Monk of Caen.
[2] Will. Malms., *Gesta Regum*, p. 335; AS. Chron., *s.a.* 1086 (equals 1087).
[3] Will. Poit., pp. 36, 196–199; Will. Jum., pp. 122, 123; Will. Malms., *loc. cit.*

It is a composite description which, drawn from so many sources, inspires confidence.

It can, moreover, be supplemented by testimony of a special character. When in 1522 William's tomb at Caen was opened for the first time, the body in its original stone coffin was found to be in a state of good preservation, and, according to an early account, it was that of a large man with notably long arms and legs.[1] This detail also can be confirmed. For the single femur which escaped the subsequent destructions by Calvinists, when measured, was found to indicate a man who must have been some five feet ten inches in height.[2] Finally, there is yet another piece of evidence to record. When the tomb was first opened in 1522 a portrait was drawn from the remains, and this, painted on wood, was hung over the sepulchre. In due course it too was destroyed, but there survives at Caen an extraordinary picture made early in the eighteenth century which may well be a copy of the sixteenth-century painting.[3] This depicts a large and dominating monarch, massive in bulk, with full-fleshed face and russet hair. He is dressed in the manner of a sixteenth-century king, and he resembles closely the famous contemporary portraits of Henry VIII of England. Too much reliance must obviously not be placed upon a picture of this character and of this date.[4] But taken in conjunction with the other evidence it may not unreasonably be supposed to reflect in some measure what was in fact the personal appearance of William the Conqueror.

This portly warrior, robust and domineering, may be contrasted physically with the wife whom he won with such difficulty, and with whom he was so closely associated. Contemporaries, who were fully conscious of her influence speak frequently of her virtues, but seldom of her appearance, but here too it is possible to utilize some special testimony. Matilda's tomb in the church of Holy Trinity, Caen, suffered devastation comparable to that which destroyed the sepulchre of her husband in Saint Stephen's. The original coffin was thus destroyed, but in her case the bones were saved, and having been placed in a small casket they were reburied under the original and beautiful stone slab which, with its inscription, still remains in the church.[5] In 1961,

---

[1] C. Hippeau, *L'abbaye de Saint-Étienne de Caen* (1855), pp. 169, 170, 181.

[2] *Ibid.*, p. 182.   [3] *Ibid.*, pp. 181, 182; de Bouard, *Guillaume le Conquérant*, p. 124.

[4] It will be recalled that Henry VIII had visited France in 1520 for the 'Field of the Cloth of Gold'.

[5] Reproduced in J. S. Cotman, *Architectural Antiquities of Normandy* (1822), as plate XXXIII in vol. 1.

moreover, this casket was itself disinterred, and its contents examined with remarkable results.[1] For the bones proved to be those of an extremely small woman whose height can hardly have exceeded fifty inches. The picture thus suggested is surely challenging. Nor is it without interest to reflect that the famous duchess and queen, who could act as one of William's regents in Normandy, and who on at least one occasion opposed the will of her formidable husband, may have been a lady of this diminutive size. William and his wife when throned and adorned at one of their solemn crown-wearings, surrounded by the great Norman ecclesiastics, and the Norman warrior aristocracy, must in truth have appeared a remarkable couple.

As to William's personal character there is no need to repeat the astonishingly diverse judgments which propaganda has inspired over the centuries.[2] It is fortunate, however, that there have survived two contemporary descriptions made by men who knew him. One of these was written shortly after his death by a monk at Caen, and it deserves quotation:

This king excelled in wisdom all the princes of his generation, and among them all he was outstanding in the largeness of his soul. He never allowed himself to be deterred from prosecution of any enterprise because of the labour it entailed, and he was ever undaunted by danger. So skilled was he in his appraisal of the true significance of any event, that he was able to cope with adversity, and to take full advantage in prosperous times of the fickle promises of fortune. He was great in body and strong, tall in stature but not ungainly. He was also temperate in eating and drinking. Especially was he moderate in drinking, for he abhorred drunkenness in all men, and disdained it more particularly in himself and at his court. He was so sparing in his use of wine and other drink that after his meal he rarely drank more than thrice. In speech he was fluent and persuasive, being skilled at all times in making known his will. If his voice was harsh, what he said was always suited to the occasion. He followed the Christian discipline in which he had been brought up as a child, and whenever his health permitted he regularly and with great piety attended Christian worship each morning and evening, and at the celebration of Mass.[3]

[1] Information supplied by Professor de Bouard.

[2] Apart from the two contemporary accounts, perhaps the best descriptions of William the Conqueror are to be found in the magnificent death-bed speech put by Ordericus into the mouth of the dying king (Ord. Vit., vol. II, pp. 401–418), and the estimate which Lord Lyttleton included in his *History of King Henry II*, vol. I (1767), pp. 49–52. I confess, moreover, to admiration for the lapidary conclusion of Professor Southern. 'William had an undaunted mastery of the problems of the secular world – that is to say of other men's wills – in both fighting and ruling unapproached in creative power by any other medieval ruler after Charlemagne' (*Saint Anselm and his Biographer* (1963), p. 4).

[3] Printed in Will. Jum. at p. 145. Translated in *E.H.D.*, vol. II, no. 6.

This remarkable description echoes an earlier account of Charlemagne himself, which in its turn is dependant on Suetonius, and while it must of course be received with proper discrimination,[1] it is not to be set aside. It must be regarded as an impressive tribute made by a man who was in a position to know the facts.

It needs, however, to be compared with the estimate of the Conqueror made about the same time by an Englishman who had 'looked upon him and once lived at his court'.[2] Here again William appears as 'a very wise man, and very powerful and more worshipful and stronger than any predecessor of his had been'. But he is shown also as a harsh and violent oppressor, and as one who was himself brutal, avaricious, and cruel. The balanced nature of this notable assessment is indicated by its conclusion. 'These things we have written about him both good and bad.'

These early accounts of William the Conqueror are of the highest interest, and it is important to consider how far they can be confirmed. There is no doubt, for instance, that William shared in the savagery which marred so many of the secular rulers of his age, and in one respect he was held in England to have been exceptional in his wanton disregard of human suffering. There is no reason to question the tradition that the New Forest was made at his instigation, and writers of the twelfth century found little difficulty in asserting that it was divine vengeance for this crime which caused so many members of his family to perish at that place: his second son Richard about 1075; his third son William in 1100; and his grandson Richard (Robert's bastard) at some other date.[3] The amount of devastation which was in fact involved has perhaps been exaggerated,[4] but certainly many villages were depopulated and there was doubtless some destruction of church property.[5] And even more to be deplored were the savage penalties threatened

---

[1] The author was a Norman proud of the Norman achievement which William had brought to fulfilment. He was also a monk of an abbey which William had founded.

[2] AS. Chron., 'E', s.a. 1086 (equals 1087).

[3] Cf. Will. Malms., Gesta Regum, pp. 332, 333.

[4] Possibly by Ord. Vit. (vol. IV, p. 32), certainly by Freeman (Norman Conquest, vol. IV, pp. 611–613).

[5] The chief authority is F. Baring (Eng. Hist. Rev., vol. XVI (1901), pp. 427 et sqq.; and ibid., vol. XXVII (1912), pp. 513 et sqq.). His conclusions are summarized by C. Petit-Dutaillis (Studies Supplementary to Stubbs' Constitutional History, vol. II, p. 171) thus: 'William I found in a corner of Hampshire 75,000 acres of almost deserted country, and of this he made a forest. He added, however, fifteen or twenty thousand acres of inhabited land on which there were a score of villages and a dozen hamlets; and doubtless through fear of poaching, he evicted 500 families numbering about 2,000 persons.'

against those who robbed the royal game. The Anglo-Saxon chronicler breaks into doggerel verse at this point to vent his indignation:

> He made great protection for the game
> And imposed laws for the same
> That who slew hart or hind
> Should be made blind
> He preserved the harts and boars
> And loved the stags
> As if he were their father.[1]

It is in fact a sorry indictment, and there is moreover no doubt that the forest law which came to be characteristic of medieval England was in its essentials an importation from Normandy.[2] None the less, the matter should be placed in its context. William came from a province which, then as now, was plentifully filled with forests, and the ducal rights therein are attested in eleventh-century charters.[3] But in England, too, before the Conquest, the royal forest artificially created and fiercely protected was a familiar institution.[4] Cnut laid heavy penalties on those who hunted in his forests, and Edward the Confessor shared in the passion for the sport. The Conqueror undoubtedly increased the royal forests in England, and with callous cruelty, but he did not create the conditions which made such acts possible, nor was he alone in their perpetration.

A more serious indictment against William in this respect could indeed be made in connexion with the brutality which marred so many of his campaigns. The horrors at Alençon in 1051 were matched by those at Mantes in 1087, and the march round London in 1066 was accompanied by wholesale devastation. Yet if these acts are not to be palliated, they were not wanton or purposeless. The sack of Alençon ended the resistance of Domfront; in 1066 the destruction of Romney made possible the bloodless occupation of Dover; the isolation of London in the same year could be defended as a strategic measure; and after the surrender of Exeter in 1068 William successfully prevented plundering by his troops. The devastation of the north of England in 1069–1070 was of course of a more lethal and terrible character, and it is hard to find any excuse for it even by reference to the crisis which then threatened the Anglo-Norman kingdom from Northumbria and

---

[1] AS. Chron., 'E', s.a. 1086 (equals 1087); translated by S. I. Tucker.
[2] Petit-Dutaillis, *loc. cit.*   [3] L. Delisle, *Classe agricole*, pp. 334 *et sqq.*
[4] Stenton, *Anglo-Saxon England*, p. 674.

from Scotland, Norway, and Maine. William was without doubt, on occasion, bestially cruel. But it might, none the less, be possible to indulge here in too complacent a condemnation. He was not the first king of England – nor the last – to lay waste a countryside for his sport, and the twentieth century has perhaps little right to sit in judgment on the eleventh in the matter of ruthless warfare.

William was stained with blood. But his avarice was almost equally repulsive. This appears in most of the accounts, and England was of course the chief victim. It is true that his greed was occasioned chiefly by his need for mercenaries, but even so his rapacity was infamous, and the distress it caused widespread. The ruthlessness with which he exacted money from England must be set against the efficient administration he provided. His taxes were savage, and they were imposed without mercy and often without equity:

> He had castles built
> And poor men hard oppressed
> This king was so very stark
> And deprived his subjects of many a mark
> Of gold and more hundreds of pounds of silver
> That he took by weight and with little justice
> From his people with little need
> For such a deed
> Into avarice did he fall
> And loved greediness above all.[1]

No wonder that the Domesday inquiry in 1086 caused riots, for he then 'acted according to his custom, that is to say he obtained a very great amount of money wherever he had any pretext for it whether just or otherwise'.[2]

The other side of the picture is, however, not to be ignored. It was this same Englishman who after describing the harshness of William's government noted his patronage of the Church; the majesty of his crown-wearings; his regal dignity and the respect it inspired; and above all the good order promoted by his stern administration. 'No one however powerful dared do anything against his will', and as a result 'any honest man could travel over his kingdom without injury with his bosom full of gold, and no man dared strike [?or kill] another'. This was a strong and pitiless king. But he was not simply a self-regarding tyrant, nor was

---

[1] AS. Chron., 'E', s.a. 1086 (equals 1087); translated by S. I. Tucker.
[2] Ibid., s.a. 1085 (equals 1086).

he regarded as such by those he ruled. The severity of his administration they had felt for themselves, but having experienced also 'the good security he made in this country', they left it to God to judge his ruthless suppression of disorder.[1]

It was a charitable verdict, for the personal portrait which emerges is undoubtedly repellent. It was, however, a duty imposed upon medieval royalty to provide strong justice, and any eleventh-century king must have had much ado to save his soul. Nor in contemplating William's career is it possible not to share, in some measure, the admiration felt by contemporaries for the courage and determination which informed it. William displayed the ineluctable connexion between personality and power, and demonstrated how, in the shaping of events, decision and fortitude may be of more importance than material resources, and how purpose, if it be inflexible, may prove ultimately decisive. Doubtless, his character had been bitterly annealed during his terrible childhood, and during the years when in youth he had waged against odds his long war for survival. But there must have been a wonderful strength in this man which enabled him to rise from his bastard beginnings to a plenitude of power, and to elicit from the hard-faced men who surrounded him the support which alone made possible his success. Only thus was this Norman duke enabled to reach a dominant position in the crisis which overtook western Christendom in his time, so that he could make his own contribution towards linking the destinies of medieval England with those of Latin Europe at a moment when its political and ecclesiastical structure was being formed (partly through his acts) into the pattern characteristic of the high Middle Ages.

His energy likewise deserves some commemoration. Between 1051 and 1054, for example, when still in his twenties he conducted a campaign in Maine; he took possession of Rouen; he captured Arques; he quelled a great rebellion in Upper Normandy; he organized the defence of his duchy against the full strength of the French king; he convoked the council of Lisieux; and he deposed an archbishop of Rouen. Throughout his life his activity was constant and he was ever on the move. Thus his great war in Maine in 1073 followed very closely upon his campaign late in the previous year on the threshold of the Highlands, and his frequent passages to and fro across the Channel were probably more numerous than those which can be specifically recorded. Of the quality of his vigorous leadership there can be no

[1] AS. Chron., 'E', s.a. 1086 (equals 1087).

doubt, and something of its nature can be seen in many of the incidents of his life. As when, for instance, he prevented a large force of undisciplined mercenaries from plundering the Norman countryside, or when on that fateful night of 27 September 1066 he lost touch with his fleet, and finding himself alone in mid-Channel, with all his fortunes in the balance, he thereupon feasted 'as if at home' to restore the courage of his men.[1] Inherent authority made him a master of men.

Assuredly he was a man to fear. 'Earls he had in his fetters – he expelled bishops from their sees, and abbots from their abbacies; he put thegns in prison and finally he did not spare his own brother Odo.'[2] On the other hand, with the exception of Waltheof, the justice of whose fate remains a subject of controversy, few if any of the magnates who unsuccessfully opposed him in Normandy, or England, before or after 1066, suffered death after they were delivered into his hands. The stories later circulated that he resorted to poison are certainly apocryphal,[3] and no violent death ever alleged against William is so horrible as the butchery of the atheling Alfred in 1036, or the disgusting murder in 1049 of Beorn in the ships of Sweyn.[4] On occasion, too, the Conqueror could be surprisingly lenient to opponents who came into his power. His treatment of Nigel of Saint-Sauveur, or of Count William of Arques, or of Edgar the atheling might even be described as generous.

There was in fact an element of paradox in his character. His brutalities, his avarice, and his oppressions speak for themselves, and they were lamentable. But it would be wholly false to regard him as a crude ruffian, or as simply a sanguinary brute. It was not merely because of his overt patronage of the Church that he won the respect of many of his most illustrious contemporaries. His ecclesiastical appointments were, generally speaking, good; his co-operation with Lanfranc did credit to them both; and the pope whom he opposed paid tribute to his respect for religion. His personal piety was undoubtedly sincere; he was abstemious in the matter of food and drink; and his continence was regarded as exceptional. He was capable of affection, and sometimes able to inspire it. He could on occasion even be affable and generous. Indeed, it was this surprising trait in his character that came prominently into the minds of that little group which assembled in an upper room at Caen after his funeral to reflect upon the vicissitudes of his

---

[1] Will. Poit., p. 163.   [2] AS. Chron., 'E', *loc. cit.*   [3] Below, Appendix F.
[4] AS. Chron., 'C', *s.a.* 1036; 'D', *s.a.* 1050 (equals 1049). Earl Godwine was later held to have been responsible for the murder of Alfred (below, pp. 412, 413), and this Sweyn was Godwine's son and the elder brother of King Harold.

astonishing career.[1] He remains then something of an enigma: admirable; unlovable; dominant; distinct.

His private character was reflected in his public policy, and few students of the events which have here been recorded will be tempted to underestimate his personal contribution to the history of his age. As duke, the concentration of Norman power and the development of Norman policy owed much to his direction. In 1066 his diplomacy was as notable as was his military capacity. As king of England he established without anarchy, though by spoliation, a new feudal order. He helped to transform the conditions of English ecclesiastical life. Finally he not only preserved the kingdom he had won, but he vitalized many of its ancient institutions. He made his mark on all the countries he ruled, and his death, when it came, was widely held to presage disaster. It was not for nothing that so many of his greater followers then left the world to spend their last days in monastic seclusion, or that a great fear spread among lesser folk who apprehended the disturbances that would follow his passing.

He was, of course, the product of his time, and his achievement was dependent upon developments in Normandy and England, in France and Italy over which he had little control. But it was the mark of his constructive statesmanship that he attuned his purpose to the conditions of the critical age in which he lived. He bestrode his generation, but he also served it: he seized, as well as created, opportunities. If he magnified the might of Normandy he derived from the Norman past, and if he conquered England he resuscitated many English traditions. His essential greatness is to be found in the permanence of what he achieved. The Norman conquest would have been impossible without him, and without him its results would have been very different. The future history of England and of Europe was substantially modified by his acts:

Verely, he was a very great Prince: full of hope to undertake great enterprises, full of courage to atchieue them: in most of his actions commendable, and excusable in all. And this was not the least piece of his Honour, that the kings of England which succeeded, did accompt their order onely from him: not in regard of his victorie in England, but generally in respect of his vertue and valour.[2]

So, in 1613, wrote John Hayward of William the Conqueror. And his words – those of a contemporary of Shakespeare – may aptly serve as a conclusion to this book.

[1] Hugh of Flavigny (*Mon. Germ. Hist. Scriptores*, vol. VIII, p. 407).
[2] John Hayward, *The Lives of the III Normans, Kings of England* (1613), p. 122.

APPENDICES

APPENDICES

The birth of William the Conqueror, and the connexions of Herleve

William the Conqueror was the bastard son of Robert I, duke of Normandy. He was born at Falaise, and his mother was Herleve, a girl of that town.

If, however, these facts respecting William's birth may be thus baldly stated, it must be added that all the circumstances surrounding the event are obscure, and that the evidence relating to it is tenuous and contradictory. Thus, William of Poitiers has here no precise information to impart; William of Jumièges merely records Robert's paternity; and William of Malmesbury, who gives a graphic account of Robert's first encounter with William's mother, does not mention her name or the place where the meeting took place.[1] Herleve's name seems to have been supplied for the first time by Ordericus Vitalis;[2] and that William was born at Falaise appears first to have been categorically asserted by writers of the twelfth century.[3] There was, indeed, a later legend that Herleve was of Flemish stock, and that William was born at Rouen.[4] But such stories have nothing to commend them.[5] The tradition that the Conqueror was born at Falaise is very strong, and can (as will be seen) be supported by circumstantial evidence. It may be accepted without undue misgiving.

The origins of Herleve were humble. Contemporary writers are discreetly silent about her father, but Ordericus Vitalis gives his name as Fulbert, and also tells that when at a later date William was besieging Alençon, the defenders waved hides and skins from the walls to taunt the duke with the fact that his mother's relatives were *polinctores*.[6] The very firm tradition that Herleve's father was a tanner is thus supported, and the tanneries of Falaise were famous. It must, however, be noted that the word *polinctor* could more readily be translated as embalmer.[7]

[1] Will. Jum., p. 115; Will. Malms., *Gesta Regum*, p. 285.
[2] Interp. Will. Jum., p. 157.
[3] Wace, *Roman de Rou* (ed. Andresen), vol. II, p. 204; Benoit (ed. Michel), vol. II, p. 555.
[4] Cf. J. Depoin, *Congrès millenaire normand*, vol. I, pp. 305–309.
[5] H. Prentout, *Guillaume le Conquérant: légende et histoire* (Caen, 1927), pp. 20–23.
[6] Interp. Will. Jum., p. 171.
[7] *Complete Peerage*, vol. XII (I), Appendix K, p. 30. The matter is further confused by the fact that Wace (*Roman de Rou*, vol. II, p. 204) calls Fulbert *parmentier* which might be rendered 'tailor'.

The conclusion would seem to be that Herleve's father was very probably named Fulbert, and that Fulbert was very probably a tanner, but perhaps a man who prepared corpses for burial.

The date of William's birth has been exhaustively discussed. I have accepted the conclusions of M. Henri Prentout, as reinforced by the testimony examined by Mr L. C. Loyd and Mr G. H. White in the *Complete Peerage*.[1] The evidence is, however, not as conclusive as might be wished. In the death-bed speech, which Ordericus Vitalis puts into the mouth of William the Conqueror, it is stated that at that time (i.e. 9 September 1087) William was sixty-four years of age, and this would put his birth in or about 1023.[2] In view of other testimony, this may be confidently set aside. William of Malmesbury remarks that when Robert I departed on pilgrimage, that is to say in January 1035 or at the very earliest at the end of 1034, the Conqueror was seven years old,[3] and Ordericus says that he was then a boy of eight years.[4] These remarks would place William's birth in 1027 or early in 1028. Similarly, William is said to have been eight years old when Robert died in July 1035.[5]

It will appear how difficult it is to give precision to these remarks, many of which might be translated with almost equal propriety as 'in his seventh (or eighth) year', or 'seven (or eight) years old'. Ordericus, and indeed Wace, are, moreover, self-contradictory. An early narrative *De Obitu Willelmi*[6] written by a monk of Caen before the end of the eleventh century states, however, that in September 1087 William was in the fifty-ninth year of his life.[7] This statement carries higher authority than the others which have been cited. If taken literally, it would place William's birth between 9 September 1028 and 9 September 1029. In view, however, of the other testimony which inclines to an earlier date, I am myself disposed to place the Conqueror's birth early within these limits. A date during the autumn of 1028 has therefore here been adopted, but the matter cannot be regarded as finally settled.

It is probable, though not certain, that Herleve bore to Robert another child – a girl named Adelaide who in due course married (i) Enguerrand, count of Ponthieu; (ii) Lambert of Lens; and (iii) Odo,

---

[1] Prentout, 'De la Naissance de Guillaume le Conquérant' (*Études sur Quelques Points d'Histoire de Normandie* (Caen, 1927), pp. 73–89); *Complete Peerage*, vol. XII (1), Appendix K, where all the testimony is assembled.　　　　[2] Ord. Vit., vol. III, p. 228.

[3] Will. Malms., *Gesta Regum*, vol. II, p. 285: habebat tunc filium septennem.

[4] Ord. Vit., vol. III, p. 229: puer utpote octo annorum.

[5] Ord. Vit., vol. II, p. 11: tunc octo annorum erat.

[6] Will. Jum., pp. 145–149.　　　　　　　[7] anno vitae suae quinquagesimo none.

count of Champagne.[1] It is certain that the Conqueror had a sister, or half-sister, of this name, and with this career; it is also certain that she was not the daughter of Herleve's husband, Herluin, *vicomte* of Conteville. She may, however, have been the daughter of Robert by some mistress other than Herleve, but it is perhaps more probable that she was the Conqueror's sister of the whole blood.

Herleve's career advanced the fortunes of her kinsfolk. It seems that the obscure Fulbert became in due course a *cubicularius* in the ducal household,[2] and something is known of Herleve's brothers. Charter evidence gives their names as Osbern and Walter.[3] Walter, moreover, is stated to have watched over the future Conqueror during his perilous childhood, and on one occasion to have saved his life by snatching the lad from his cot and carrying him for safety into the 'dwellings of the poor'.[4] This Walter had at least two daughters. One named Clara became a nun at Montivilliers.[5] The other, Matilda, married Ralph Tesson.[6] The Tessons were a very considerable family in Middle Normandy, and this marriage further illustrates the advancement of Herleve's relatives.

Some time after the Conqueror's birth, Herleve was married to Herluin, *vicomte* of Conteville, and to him she was to bear two famous sons, Odo, bishop of Bayeux, and Robert, count of Mortain, and at least one daughter who married William, lord of La Ferté-Macé.[7] Ordericus states that Herluin's marriage to Herleve took place after 1035,[8] but though the statement has won some credence, it is open to grave objections. Odo became bishop of Bayeux between October 1049 and 23 April 1050,[9] and if Ordericus's assertion were accepted, Odo would then have been barely fourteen. Such an appointment would hardly have passed without notice by Odo's hostile critics, who would certainly have called attention to such a scandal at the beginning of his career. Much interest therefore attaches to the remark of William of Malmesbury that Herleve was married off to Herluin *before* the death of Robert.[10] And I have myself very little doubt that the marriage took

---

[1] *Rot. Scacc. Norm.*, vol. II, p. xxxi; *Complete Peerage, loc. cit.*

[2] Ord. Vit., interp. Will. Jum., p. 157.

[3] *R.A.D.N.*, no. 134 (Signum Walteri avunculi comites). This may legitimately be placed beside the list of witnesses given in Lot, *Saint-Wandrille*, no. 17 (Osbernus avunculus comitis. Walterius frater eius).

[4] Ord. Vit., vol. III, p. 229.

[5] *Gall. Christ.*, vol. XI; *Instrumenta*, col. 329.

[6] *Ibid.*, col. 65a.

[7] L. C. Denis, *Chartes de Saint-Julien de Tours*, nos. 24, 29; Douglas, *Domesday Monachorum*, pp. 35, 36.

[8] Interp. Will. Jum., p. 157.

[9] *Gall. Christ.*, vol. XI, col. 353.

[10] *Gesta Regum*, p. 333.

place very soon after the birth of the Conqueror; and that Odo, being born about 1030, was some nineteen years old when he became a bishop.

Besides Herleve, Herluin married a certain Fredesendis, and there seems little doubt that she was his second wife.[1] From this union there were at least two children, Ralph and John, the former of whom may possibly be the Radulfus de Contivilla who held lands in Somerset and Devon in 1086.[2]

Some inferences are possible respecting the date of Herleve's death. Towards the end of his life, Herluin founded the abbey of Grestain,[3] and Robert of Torigny asserted that both he and Herleve were buried there.[4] It is, however, most improbable that Herleve was buried at Grestain,[5] and the absence of her name from the list of benefactors to that abbey, and the presence therein of the name of Fredesendis,[6] suggests very strongly that Herleve died before Herluin founded the monastery.[7] The foundation of Grestain is, moreover, usually placed in or shortly after 1050.[8]

If Herleve, in fact, died, as is here suggested, about 1050, she can hardly have been more than forty years of age at the time of her death. Yet she had accomplished much. In view of her humble origins, her career and connexions[9] may even now challenge some attention. She was a remarkable girl.

---

[1] Douglas, *Domesday Monachorum*, p. 34.

[2] Bréard, *L'abbaye Notre-Dame de Grestain*, nos. I, II; Douglas, *loc. cit.* But there are several Contevilles.   [3] Bréard, *loc. cit.*

[4] Ed. Delisle, vol. II, p. 202. There is – or was recently – an inscription among the ruins to this effect.   [5] *Gall. Christ.*, vol. XI, col. 83.   [6] Bréard, *op. cit.*, nos. I, II.

[7] Herluin was alive in 1059 (Chevreux et Vernier, *Archives de Normandie*, plate V), but since none of his gifts to Grestain were in England it is probable that he died before, or very shortly after, the Conquest.   [8] Bréard, *op. cit.*, p. 20.   [9] Below, Table 6.

The chronology of Duke William's campaigns between 1047 and 1054

The very difficult chronology of Duke William's wars during these years has been considered with great learning and with contrasted results by several continental scholars, such as L. Halphen,[1] R. Latouche,[2] and J. Dhondt,[3] and I have been particularly indebted to the remarkable appendix which Henri Prentout added to his essay on the early life of Duke William, which was published posthumously in 1936.[4] As will be seen, I have been able gratefully to accept, with only slight modifications, most of Prentout's conclusions on this matter, but the subject has been, and still is, so much a subject of controversy that it is necessary here to set out the evidence which has led me to adopt the dating of these events, which has been given in the preceding pages.

There is fortunately no need to question the accepted date of 1047 for the battle of Val-ès-Dunes. It must, however, be remarked that annals of Caen, and of Lire, give 1046, as does also Robert of Torigny in his supplement to the chronicle of Sigebert of Gembloux.[5] It is not wholly impossible that this variation may perhaps have been due to an employment of the Lady Day reckoning for the beginning of the year which would here be relevant since the battle was evidently fought, as will be seen, before 25 March. Be that as it may, the date of 1047 is well attested. It is given, for instance, in the annals of Jumièges,[6] of Saint-Évroul,[7] and of Sainte-Colombe of Sens.[8] Moreover, Ordericus Vitalis not only gives the year 1047 in his interpolations to William of Jumièges, but repeats this in his own history, where he relates the date convincingly to other events.[9] The battle of Val-ès-Dunes may thus be assigned without undue hesitation to 1047, or more precisely (bearing in mind the normal practice of beginning the year at Christmas) to

[1] *Comté d'Anjou* (1906), pp. 70–80.   [2] *Comté du Maine* (1910), pp. 27–32.
[3] 'Les Relations entre la France et la Normandie' (*Normannia*, vol. XII (1939), pp. 465–486); 'Henri Iᵉʳ, l'Empire et l'Anjou' (*Revue belge de Philologie et d'Histoire*, vol. XXV (1946), pp. 87–109).
[4] *Histoire de Guillaume le Conquérant – Le Duc De Normandie* (*Mém. Acad. Nat. de Caen*, vol. VIII, 1936). This is an incomplete work issued posthumously.
[5] *Rec. Hist. Franc.*, vol. XI, pp. 166, 366.   [6] Ed. J. Laporte, p. 55.
[7] Ord. Vit., vol. V, p. 157.   [8] *Rec. Hist. Franc.*, vol. XI, p. 292.
[9] Will. Jum., p. 171; Ord. Vit., vol. I, p. 182; vol. II, p. 373; vol. III, p. 159.

some time after 25 December 1046; and it is in every degree probable that it occurred early in that period. The flooded waters of the Orne which played so large a part in the victory would be consistent with a date in winter or in very early spring.[1]

Although Henry I himself retired from Normandy after the battle, the war is known to have continued without interruption. Guy of Burgundy fortified himself at Brionne, and the siege of that castle began. Both William of Poitiers and William of Jumièges state that the defence was very stubborn,[2] but give no precise indication of its duration. Ordericus Vitalis on the other hand states that the siege lasted 'for three years' (*per triennium*),[3] and that this is not a mere verbal flourish is shown in another passage in his *History*, where alluding to Duke Robert II (the Conqueror's son) he speaks of 'Brionne . . . which his father with the aid of the French king could scarcely subdue in three years when Guy the son of Rainald of Burgundy defended it after the battle of Val-ès-Dunes.'[4] It is of course possible to suggest that there might here be exaggeration,[5] but to do so would be flying in the face of the evidence. There seems in fact no warranty for disregarding these curiously precise statements of an informed writer, and it appears impossible to avoid the conclusion that the siege of Brionne continued at least until the end of 1049.

These considerations have, moreover, some bearing on the most important and the most difficult question in this chronology, namely the date of William's campaigns during this period in Maine. A very strong tradition has assigned the warfare between the duke and Geoffrey Martel round Domfront and Alençon to 1048–1049, and this dating was endorsed in the brilliant reconstruction of this campaign made in 1906 by Louis Halphen in his notable book on the history of Anjou in the eleventh century.[6] There it is suggested that the hostilities between the count and the duke began shortly after Geoffrey's attack on Château-du-Loir and the capture of Gervais, bishop of Le Mans, so that 'before the autumn' of 1048 Duke William and King Henry were together engaged in attacking Mouliherne in Anjou, and after October the duke on his own account captured Alençon and besieged Domfront, completing the operation in the early months of 1049. Though this was a very early book by this great scholar, published when its author was only

---

[1] Above, p. 50.
[2] Will. Poit., pp. 19–21; Will. Jum., p. 123.
[3] Ord. Vit., vol. IV, p. 335.
[4] *Ibid.*, vol. IV, p. 335.
[5] Cf. Freeman, *Norman Conquest*, vol. II, p. 262; Stenton, *William the Conqueror*, p. 85.
[6] *Op. cit.*, pp. 70–73.

twenty-six years of age, his detailed conclusions on this chronology have been accepted by nearly all subsequent writers on the subject. Nevertheless, before 1936 Henri Prentout had boldly challenged the accepted view, and placed the fighting round Alençon and Domfront in the winter of 1051–1052.[1] Prentout's arguments (which do not appear to be widely known in England)[2] seem to the present writer to be so compelling that they warrant a reconsideration of the matter.

It must immediately be emphasized how scanty is the positive evidence that can be adduced in favour of the traditional view. The warfare is not mentioned by the Angevin chroniclers, and it receives no notice in the early Norman annals. It is, therefore, necessary to depend in the first instance on the accounts given by William of Jumièges and William of Poitiers,[3] and neither of these writers supplies a date. One difference between them may, moreover, be noted: William of Poitiers gives some prominence to a siege of Mouliherne by King Henry assisted by Norman troops, whilst William of Jumièges makes no mention of this episode. The two narratives, however, have this in common. They both place these events in their sequence between the capture of Brionne (which can hardly have fallen much if at all before the beginning of 1050), and the revolt of Count William of Arques which, as will be seen, began some time in the course of 1052. Whilst, therefore, the chronological arrangement of both William of Poitiers and William of Jumièges leaves very much to be desired, their testimony (for what it is worth chronologically) would seem to point to a date for these campaigns later than that which has traditionally been assigned to them.

Nor is the other evidence which has been cited in favour of the date of 1048–1049 for this war unequivocal.[4] It is very reasonable to suggest that the capture of Gervaise at Château-du-Loir early in 1048 may have provoked hostilities between the king and the count of Anjou, but this does not necessarily imply that the duke of Normandy's expedition against Domfront occurred in that year. Finally, an allusion made by Anselm the monk in his description of the council of Rheims (1049) to hostilities then taking place between the king of France and his magnates, which has been held to refer to the war between Henry and Geoffrey, might with equal propriety be made to apply to almost any contemporary disturbance in the dominions of the king, and there was

[1] *Op. cit.*, pp. 140–144.

[2] I note, however, that de Bouard places the action round Domfront, without further comment in 1050–1051 (*Guillaume le Conquérant*, p. 41).

[3] Will. Jum., pp. 125–127; Will. Poit., pp. 23, 37–39.   [4] Cf. Prentout, *loc. cit*.

in fact in 1049 a siege of Neufchâtel-sur-Aisne near Rheims where the monk was writing.[1] On all grounds it would seem that the theory which place William's campaign round Alençon and Domfront in 1048–1069 is at best a plausible hypothesis which is inadequately supported by the surviving testimony.

This being so, it becomes imperative to consider whether some other interpretation will not better conform to the known facts. And in this connexion the blockade of Mouliherne falls for separate consideration, since scholars have perhaps been too hasty in treating it as inevitably part of the same question as that involving Domfront and Alençon.[2] There is, in truth, nothing in William of Poitiers (the sole authority) to warrant this assumption. The arrangement of his treatise at this point merits in fact careful note.[3] The passage respecting Mouliherne follows immediately after the account of the fall of Brionne. Then comes an account of the rising enmity of Geoffrey of Anjou towards Duke William. Then ensues a long passage about the accession of Edward the Confessor to the English throne, and not until after all this does there begin the description of the war round Alençon and Domfront. Moreover, Mouliherne is far removed from the scene of these latter campaigns: it is beyond Maine itself and in Anjou. The date of the blockade of Mouliherne must therefore be considered by itself. It may conceivably have occurred in 1048 for it is not far distant from Château-du-Loir. On the other hand, a letter from Geoffrey of Anjou to Pope Leo IX, the text of which has survived albeit in a late copy,[4] suggests that the king's war against the count entered a new phase in 1051 and the Mouliherne blockade could thus be placed in the spring of that year. In that event the operations conducted by Duke William around Domfront (which occurred after the Mouliherne episode) would also fall inevitably in 1051. While, however, it is probable that the Mouliherne blockade did in fact take place in the spring of 1051, it is not impossible that it was further distinct in time from Duke William's later war in Maine.

Note must now be taken of certain dates in Angevin history which can be regarded as firmly established. These are:

Early 1048, or   Assault on Château-du-Loir by Geoffrey Martel,
possibly late 1047   and imprisonment of Gervais.[5]

---

[1] *Ibid.* Cf. *Rec. Hist. Franc.*, vol. XI, p. 465.
[2] I am not wholly convinced by Prentout's argument in this sense (*ibid.*, p. 142).
[3] Will. Poit., pp. 22–40.   [4] Sudendorf, *Berengarius Turonensis* (1851), Appendix VIII.
[5] *Actus Pont. Cenomm.*; Halphen, *op. cit.*, p. 71; Latouche, *op. cit.*, p. 28.

October 1049	Opening of the council of Rheims.
	Geoffrey is threatened with excommunication for his treatment of Bishop Gervais.[1]
1050	Geoffrey is excommunicated.[2]
26 March 1051	Death of Hugh, count of Maine.[3]
Shortly after 26 March 1051 }	Geoffrey Martel takes possession of Le Mans.[4]
Shortly after 26 March 1051 }	Release of Bishop Gervais who forthwith goes to the Norman court.[5]
15 August 1052	Henry I and Geoffrey, count of Anjou, having been reconciled, are in company at the royal court at Orléans.[6]

Now, if these dates be considered it will appear that there is one time, and one time only, in this sequence when it might seem overwhelmingly probable that Geoffrey of Anjou, having at last established his position in the south of Maine, should direct his operations northward towards the Norman frontier, and that is in the period following his own establishment at Le Mans (March–April 1051). And there is, moreover, a considerable amount of converging testimony that this in fact occurred, provoking the retaliation of Duke William and the consequent war round the border fortresses. Thus Geoffrey's own letter to Leo IX, to which reference has already been made, specifically says that at this time Bishop Gervais, having obtained his release, broke faith with the count and went to Normandy where he urged the duke, and also the king, to take action in Maine. Duke William with the siege of Brionne now over, would at last be able, and doubtless ready, to respond. Indeed William of Poitiers says that he did so, strong in the knowledge that the domestic disturbances in Normandy were ended[7] – a remark which would not have been appropriate had Brionne still be holding out.

Finally the same conclusion is imposed if the campaign round Domfront and Alençon is brought into relation with the subsequent revolt of Count William of Arques. One of the most significant events of the war in Maine was the sudden desertion of the duke by the count

---

[1] Above, p. 58.
[2] Ann. S. Maxence (Marchegay et Mabille, *Chroniques des Églises*, p. 398).
[3] *Necrologie de la Cathédrale du Mans* (ed. Busson and Ledru), p. 72.
[4] *Actus Pont. Cenomm.*   [5] *Ibid.*, and Sudendorf, *loc. cit.*
[6] *Rec. Hist. Franc.*, vol. XI, p. 590; Soéhnée, *Cat. Actes, Henri I*, no. 91.
[7] Will. Poit., p. 65.

of Arques. At a critical moment in the siege of Domfront, we are told, he renounced his vassalage and departed, doubtless to organize his own rebellion in eastern Normandy.[1] A remarkable chronological conformity thus seems to be here revealed, indicating afresh that the Domfront operation must surely have taken place in 1051–1052. For as late as the beginning of 1051, the count of Arques, still in possession of his dignity, was still in official harmony with the duke, having been then associated with him in the issue of grants for Saint-Wandrille,[2] so that his renunciation of vassalage can hardly have taken place before 1051. On the other hand, the count's desertion from Domfront during the winter of 1051–1052 would be the natural prelude to the count's own rebellion which, as will be seen, must have begun in the summer or autumn of the latter year.

The rebellion of Count William of Arques which was connected with the reconciliation between King Henry and Geoffrey Martel[3] took place between the capture of Domfront by Duke William and the battle of Mortemer. The battle of Mortemer can, moreover, be precisely dated. Neither William of Poitiers nor William of Jumièges supplies a date, but Ordericus Vitalis in interpolating the latter gives 1054[4] and in his own *History* he not only states that the battle occurred in 1054, but that it was fought *in hieme ante quadragesimam*.[5] Now, Ash Wednesday in 1054 fell on 16 February and Quadragesima Sunday on 20 February. The battle of Mortemer must thus be placed early in February 1054.

Two other events connected with the hostilities preceding the battle of Mortemer can also be dated with some precision. The reconciliation between Henry and Geoffrey Martel took place before 15 August 1052, since a dated charter shows them together at Orléans in amity on that day.[6] Secondly, the obituaries of Saint-Wulfram and Saint-Riquier unite in placing the death of Enguerrand, count of Ponthieu, on 25 October,[7] and this supplies also the date of the action at Saint-Aubin where Count Enguerrand was killed.[8] Now, as will be seen from the preceding argument, there are only two years to which this obituary could be assigned – 1052 and 1053. Of these 1052 is theoretically possible and should not be absolutely discarded. On the other hand, 1053 is much more probable, for the siege of Arques is known to have been very protracted, and

---

[1] Will. Poit., p. 63.
[2] Chevreux et Vernier, *Archives*, plate IV.
[3] Ord. Vit., vol. i, p. 184.
[4] Will. Jum., p. 180.
[5] Ord. Vit., vol. iii, pp. 160, 237.
[6] Soéhnée, *op. cit.*, no. 91.
[7] C. Brunel, *Rec. Actes des Comtes de Ponthieu* (1930), p. iv.
[8] Will. Jum., p. 120.

the action at Saint-Aubin apparently came late in these operations. There are, it is true, discrepancies in the various accounts of this war. According to William of Poitiers,[1] Duke William originally came to Arques to place his own garrison there, and the fortress was later betrayed to the count; thereupon Duke William came again to Arques, fought an action in front of the castle, and left Walter Giffard to besiege it; and only after this did King Henry and the count of Ponthieu come to its relief with the consequent affray at Saint-Aubin. On the other hand, William of Jumièges omits any reference to the first betrayal of the castle, and Ordericus Vitalis speaks only of one march by Duke William into Talou.[2] But whatever version of these events be accepted, it will be seen that before the eventual fall of Arques there occurred at least one and possibly two expeditions by Duke William, not to mention the engagement which involved the death of Hugh of Morimont, and the action at Saint-Aubin which cannot have occurred later than 25 October 1053. It seems, therefore, impossible to escape the conclusion that the rebellion of William of Arques must have begun in 1052, and since the rebels appealed to King Henry[3] it should be related to the reconciliation between the French king and Count Geoffrey which was complete by 15 August of that year.

After a review of the evidence, and with all possible reserve in view of its difficult nature, I have therefore adopted the following chronology for these events. The battle of Val-ès-Dunes took place very early in 1047, and thereafter ensued the siege of Brionne which lasted until the end of 1049. In the meantime Geoffrey of Anjou (late 1047 or early 1048) had attacked Château-du-Loir and captured Bishop Gervais. It is possible, though unlikely, that the king with Norman assistance blockaded Mouliherne about this time, but that event should more probably be assigned to the spring of 1051. In March–April 1051 Geoffrey Martel occupied Le Mans, and thereafter moved up to the Norman frontier. Duke William, urged on by Bishop Gervais, who was now in Normandy after his release, thereupon in the autumn of 1051 came to the relief of Domfront and Alençon. The siege of Domfront lasted through the winter months, and was concluded early in 1052. During the siege Count William of Arques renounced his vassalage, went eastward to prepare his own rebellion. He appealed to the king of

---

[1] Will. Poit., pp. 55–61.
[2] Will. Jum., p. 119; Ord. Vit., vol. III, pp. 42, 232, 233.
[3] *Ibid.*, vol. I, p. 184.

France, who became reconciled to Geoffrey Martel before 15 August 1052. The war involving the siege of Arques began in the summer or autumn of 1052, and was still continuing on 25 October 1053. The castle fell very late in 1053, and early in the next year King Henry launched his double invasion of Normandy which was repelled at the battle of Mortemer in February 1054.

The marriage of William and Matilda

Few episodes in the Conqueror's life have given rise to more controversy than his marriage to Matilda, daughter of Baldwin V, count of Flanders, by Adela, daughter of Robert I, king of France. Even the precise date of the marriage is uncertain. It was projected in or before 1049, but it had not taken place by the autumn of that year when it was forbidden by Leo IX at the time of the council of Rheims.[1] On the other hand, it had been celebrated before the end of 1053, in which year Matilda appears as the duke's consort in a dated charter given to Holy Trinity, Rouen.[2] Within these dating limits it is, however, very hard to particularize. The annals of Tours, themselves an unreliable compilation in this matter, were erroneously cited by Freeman in favour of 1053,[3] but the date itself is not impossible, for the imprisonment of Leo IX by the Normans after the battle of Civitate (June 1053)[4] might have provided an occasion for defying the papal prohibition. On the other hand, there are reasons for placing the marriage earlier, and for viewing it in connexion with the transformation in the relations between the duke of Normandy and the king of France which took place in 1051–1052. Thus Mlle Foreville gives 1051–1052 for the marriage,[5] and Professor de Bouard places it *sans doute en 1050 ou peu après*.[6] These opinions carry conviction, and some of the facts in the early career of Robert, William's eldest son, can be cited in its support. Robert was Matilda's eldest child, and he was born in wedlock. His birth has been placed *circa* 1054, but it is not impossible that he was born earlier.[7] He is described as having been *adolescens* in 1066,[8] and in that year also he was cited as confirming a charter for Marmoutier *quia scilicet maioris iam ille aetatis ad praebendum spontaneum auctoramentum idoneus esset.*[9] Although therefore the tender age of Matilda (see below) must be taken into account in assigning a date

---

[1] Hefele-Leclerc, *Histoire des Conciles*, vol. IV, part II, p. 1018.
[2] *Cart. S. Trin. Roth*, no. XXXVII.
[3] Freeman, *Norman Conquest*, vol. IV, note O.
[4] Chalandon, *Domination normande*, vol. I, p. 137.
[5] Ed. Will. Poit., pp. 46, 61.
[6] *Guillaume le Conquérant*, p. 36.
[7] David, *Robert Curthose*, p. 5.
[8] Will. Malms., *Gesta Regum*, p. 450.
[9] Bertrand de Broussillon, *Maison de Laval*, vol. I, p. 45, no. 30.

for her first pregnancy, it seems not unreasonable to place her marriage in 1050–1051,[1] but definite proof of this is lacking.

The view once held that Matilda was already married when William sought her hand, and was then the mother of a daughter, Gundrada, later the wife of William of Warenne, has now been conclusively disproved by the researches of Chester Waters[2] and Sir Charles Clay.[3] There is no reason to suppose that Gundrada was the daughter either of William or Matilda. Moreover, it is unlikely that Matilda herself was of an age to be a mother in 1049 when the papal ban was pronounced. Her age cannot be precisely ascertained but the marriage of Baldwin V to her mother, Adela, was apparently not consummated until 1031, for William of Jumièges states that this was one of the factors in stimulating Baldwin V's rebellion against his father in that year.[4] On this showing Matilda could not have been more than seventeen in 1049, and she may have been younger since there is no evidence to show that she was the eldest of the four children given by Adela to Baldwin V.

All theories respecting the reasons of the papal prohibition of the match between William and Matilda are therefore now based on the suggestion that (as hinted by Ordericus Vitalis)[5] the parties were within the prohibited degrees. Scholars, however, have differed sharply as to the nature of the alleged relationship between them. Three views on the matter may be briefly noted:

1. It has been suggested[6] that the prohibition was due to a marriage between Duke Richard III of Normandy and Matilda's mother, Adela of France. There are, however, objections. Certainly, Richard III married a woman named Adela, but it is doubtful if this was Adela of France, and, in any case, a marriage between Richard III and Adela of France could not have been consummated.[7]

2. It has been suggested[8] that the ban was based on a common descent of William and Matilda from Rolf the Viking, which would

---

[1] *Handbook of British Chronology* (R. Hist. Soc. (1961), p. 31).
[2] *Gundrada de Warenne* (Exeter, 1884).   [3] *Early Yorkshire Charters*, vol. VIII, pp. 40–46.
[4] Will. Jum., pp. 103–104.   [5] Interp. Will. Jum., pp. 181–182.
[6] W. H. Hutton, in *Dict. Nat. Biog.*, sub. 'Mathilda'.
[7] Adela of France was brought to the Flemish court when the girl was *in cunis*, and she was kept there for some years – annos usque ad nubiles – until the marriage could be consummated, an event which apparently occurred in 1031 (Will. Jum., p. 103). But Richard III was duke from 1026 to 1028 and on this reckoning Adela of France could then have been little more than an infant.
[8] Prentout, 'Le marriage de Guillaume le Conquérant' (*Études sur quelques points d'histoire de Guillaume le Conquérant*, Caen, 1930) – a most valuable article which discusses much of the evidence here considered.

have made them cousins in the fifth degree. Whether this descent (which is itself not beyond question) would have been sufficient for the prohibition even if it had been known in Rome is perhaps somewhat doubtful.

3. It has been held on the authority of William of Jumièges[1] that Baldwin IV of Flanders married not only Ogiva, daughter of Richard, duke of the Ardennes, who was the mother of Baldwin V, but also a daughter of Richard II of Normandy. This marriage, if it occurred, might perhaps have been made to serve as a reason for the ban.

All these theories are open to some criticism, and despite the erudition that has been lavished upon them, the question cannot be regarded as settled.

The marriage of William and Matilda was by all accounts very happy, and it was certainly fruitful. Matilda bore her husband four sons and at least five daughters.[2] The sons were Robert, later duke of Normandy; Richard; and William and Henry, subsequently kings of England. Richard was accidentally killed in the New Forest at an early age.[3] The date of the mishap is not known, but since he was young at the time, and since he was Matilda's second son (though not necessarily her second child), his death can reasonably be placed between 1070 and 1080, and perhaps *circa* 1075.

The question of the daughters of William and Matilda is more complicated, and the essential evidence may be briefly tabulated as follows:

A. *William of Poitiers* states:[4] (i) that a daughter of William (unnamed) was betrothed to Herbert, count of Maine; (ii) that a daughter of William (unnamed) was sought for in marriage by two rival kings of Spain who were brothers, one of whom has been reasonably identified as Alphonso IV, later king of Leon; and (iii) (by implication) that a daughter of William (unnamed) was at one time betrothed to Harold of Wessex.

B. *Ordericus Vitalis*[5] mentions five daughters of William's marriage whom he names and describes as follows: (i) Agatha, who was betrothed successively to Harold of Wessex and Alphonso of Spain. She protested

---

[1] Will. Jum., p. 88.
[2] Freeman, *Norman Conquest*, vol. IV, note O; *Handbook of British Chronology, loc. cit.*
[3] Will. Malms., *Gesta Regum*, p. 332.   [4] Will. Poit., pp. 89, 143, 230.
[5] Ord. Vit., vol. II, pp. 189, 391, 392; vol. III, p. 159.

vigorously against going to Spain, and died a virgin, being buried at Bayeux; (ii) Adeliza, who undertook religious vows early in life and lived under the protection of Roger of Beaumont; (iii) Constance, who married Alan IV of Brittany; (iv) Adela, who married Stephen I, count of Blois; and (v) Cecily, who became abbess of Holy Trinity, Caen.

C. *William of Malmesbury*[1] mentions five daughters, namely Cecily, Constance, and Adela as above, and two other daughters (unnamed), one of whom, he says, was betrothed to Harold, and the other to Alphonso.

D. *Robert of Torigny*[2] at a later date speaks of four daughters, Cecily, Constance, and Adela as above, and also 'Adeliza', who according to him was betrothed to Harold.

E. *Domesday Book*[3] mentions a daughter of William named Matilda.

Both the similarities and the contradictions in these accounts are interesting. Cecily, Constance, and Adela are well known from their subsequent careers. Agatha and Adeliza have on the evidence been thought to represent only one person.[4] It may be so, but I am personally inclined here to accept Ordericus's curiously precise statement about Adeliza at its face value. The remark of William of Poitiers at least helps to confirm his statement that one of these daughters was betrothed to Alphonso of Spain, though whether one of them was betrothed to Herbert of Maine as well as to Harold of Wessex must remain in doubt. It will be noted further that none of these chroniclers mentions Matilda, and it might be tempting to doubt her existence or her legitimacy were it not that a Caen narrative apparently mentions her in connexion with both her mother and her sister Cecily, thus confirming the reference in Domesday Book.[5]

It may therefore be concluded that William and Matilda had four sons, born in the following order:

1. Robert, later duke of Normandy. Born 1051–1054. Died 10 February 1134.
2. Richard. Born before 1056. Died *circa* 1075?
3. William, later king of England. Born 1056–1060. Died 2 August 1100.
4. Henry, later king of England. Born late 1068. Died 1 December 1135.

[1] *Gesta Regum*, p. 333. [2] Interp. Will. Jum., pp. 317, 318.
[3] D.B., vol. 1, fol. 49. [4] *Handbook of British Chronology*, loc. cit.
[5] Freeman, *Norman Conquest*, loc. cit.

It would appear also that William and Matilda may have had six daughters who (without reference to seniority) might be enumerated as follows:

1. Agatha, betrothed successively to Harold, earl of Wessex, and to Alphonse of Leon (and possibly previously to Herbert, count of Maine). Died a virgin.
2. Adeliza.
3. Cecily, born before 1066, subsequently abbess of Holy Trinity, Caen. Died 1127.
4. Adela, married, 1080, Stephen I, count of Blois. Died 1137.
5. Constance, married, 1086, Alan IV, count of Brittany. Died 1090.
6. Matilda.

Dogmatism would here, however, be out of place. The separate existence of Agatha and Adeliza is not certain, and the evidence about Matilda is less than satisfactory.[1] The relative ages of the daughters is moreover not known, and one at least of them, Cecily, was born before Henry I. Finally, it may deserve a note of surprise (and admiration) that a lady of such diminutive size as was William's wife[2] should have produced so large a family before her own death in 1083.

[1] The matter is complicated by the fact that Ordericus (vol. II, p. 182) says that one of William's daughters was betrothed to Edwin of Mercia.
[2] Above, pp. 369, 370.

APPENDIX D

The sequence of events in 1066

The purpose of this note is *not* to dispute the accepted chronology for the principal events of this crucial year. The object of the following remarks is merely to indicate the evidence upon which that chronology is based and to suggest a distinction between those dates for which the testimony seems conclusive, and those for which it appears to be less than completely satisfying. Otherwise there may in the future (as in the past) be some danger of undue dogmatism.

The chronology (which has been followed in this book) may be set out as follows:

Thursday, 5 January. Death of King Edward.[1]
Friday, 6 January. Burial of King Edward.[2] Coronation of Harold.[3]
May. Tosti attacks the Isle of Wight.[4]
Sunday, 18 June. Duke William at Caen.[5]
Saturday, 12 August. William's fleet assembled in the Dives.
Friday, 8 September. Harold disbands the *fyrd*.[6]
Tuesday, 12 September. William's fleet at Saint-Valéry.
Wednesday, 20 September. Battle of Fulford.[7]
Sunday, 24 September. Harold at Tadcaster.[8]
Monday, 25 September. Battle of Stamford Bridge.[9]
Wednesday, 27 September. Change in the Channel wind. Embarkation of the Norman fleet at nightfall.
Thursday, 28 September (early morning). William's landing at Pevensey.
Friday, 29 September. William occupies Hastings.
Friday, 6 October. Harold in London.
Wednesday, 11 October. Harold leaves London.
Friday night, 13–14 October. Harold on the Sussex Downs.
Saturday, 14 October. Battle of Hastings.[10]
Sunday, 15 October–Friday, 20 October. William at Hastings.
Friday, 20 October. William storms Romney.

[1] AS. Chron., 'E', *s.a.* 1066.   [2] *Ibid.*   [3] Will. Poit., p. 146.
[4] AS. Chron., 'C', 'D', *s.a.* 1066 – 'soon after' 24 April.
[5] *R.A.D.N.*, no. 231.   [6] AS. Chron., 'C', *s.a.* 1066.
[7] *Ibid.*, 'D', *s.a.* 1066.   [8] *Ibid.*, 'C', *s.a.* 1066.
[9] *Ibid.*   [10] *Ibid.*, 'D', 1066.

396

Saturday, 21 October. Submission of Dover.

Saturday, 21 October–Saturday, 28 October. William at Dover.

Sunday, 29 October. Submission of Canterbury.

All November. William at 'Broken Tower' outside Canterbury.

First half of December. William's march round London–Surrey–North Hampshire–Wallingford–Berkhamstead.

Monday, 25 December. Coronation of Duke William as king of England in London.[1]

As will be seen from the foregoing citations, many of these dates would seem to be established beyond any reasonable doubt. For others, however, the evidence appears to be less conclusive than might be desired.

For instance, even the cardinal date of Duke William's crossing of the Channel presents some difficulty. Thus we have the following statements in the Anglo-Saxon Chronicle:[2]

D	E
Then Count William came from Normandy to Pevensey on Michaelmas Eve, and as soon as they were able to move on they built a castle at Hastings.	Count William landed at Hastings on Michaelmas Day.

At first sight, there might seem here to be a discrepancy, and indeed some scholars of repute have concluded (following 'E') that William sailed on the night of 28 September (not 27), and landed on the morning of Michaelmas Day (not Michaelmas Eve).[3] The difficulty may most probably be resolved by reference to William of Jumièges, who states that the Conqueror landed at Pevensey, where he set in hand the construction of a castle, and then leaving this in the hands of some of his troops himself hurried on to Hastings.[4]

Both Freeman[5] and Stenton[6] place the landing at Pevensey (following 'D') on the morning of 28 September, and the occupation of Hastings on 29 September. There seems little doubt that this is correct. None the less it remains curious that 'E', the Canterbury chronicler, should either (i) have been ignorant of the true date of the crossing, or (ii) have ignored the landing at Pevensey and spoken of the landing only in connexion with the subsequent occupation of Hastings.

[1] *Ibid.* [2] *Ibid.*, 'D' and 'E', *s.a.* 1066. [3] *e.g.* Ramsay, *Foundation of England*, vol. II, p. 19.
[4] Will. Jum., p. 134. [5] *Norman Conquest*, vol. III, p. 733. [6] *Anglo-Saxon England*, p. 583.

Some of the dates previous to the crossing are less securely determined. They appear to be derived in the first instance from a couplet which occurs in the *Carmen* attributed to Guy, bishop of Amiens, respecting the time spent by William's fleet at Saint-Valéry. This states (according to one reading) that William remained at Saint-Valéry, waiting for a favourable wind for 'thrice five days' – *ter quinque dies*.[1] Accepting the evening of 27 September for the crossing of the Channel, this would bring the arrival of the fleet at Saint-Valéry to 12 September, which fits in very well with Harold's disbanding the *fyrd* on 8 September. And since according to William of Poitiers the fleet was in the Dives for a month, 12 August is suggested for its completion. It is all very probable, and, doubtless, at least approximately, correct. Nevertheless the positive testimony remains fragile. The *Carmen* has recently been impugned as an original authority for the events of 1066,[2] and even if that criticism be not fully accepted, the couplet in question is itself somewhat equivocal, since the key words *ter quinque* are apparently only one reading, the other, according to two editors,[3] being *tum quinque*, which would supply a very different basis for calculation. It may also be remarked that William of Malmesbury asserts that the fleet arrived at Saint-Valéry as early as August.[4]

No part of the chronology of 1066 presents more difficulties than the sequence of Harold's actions between Stamford Bridge and Hastings. The problem may be summarized as follows:

The battle of Hastings began about 9 am[5] on 14 October. Harold must therefore have reached the Downs on 13 October, or during the night of 13–14 October. The site of the battle of Hastings is some fifty-eight miles from London, and if Harold left London with a force consisting mainly of foot-soldiers on the 11th there would be time, though none to spare, for him to have covered the distance. Harold is, moreover, stated to have spent six[6] or possibly five[7] days in London, which would place his arrival in the capital on 5 or 6 October. But a tradition which is generally accepted is that he only moved south after he had heard of William's landing and that this news reached him when

---

[1] Ed. Henry Petrie, *Monumenta Historica Britannica*, vol. I (1848), p. 857:
    Nam ter quinque dies complesti finibus illis
    Expectans summi Judicis auxilium.
[2] G. H. White, *Complete Peerage*, vol. XII, part I, Appendix L.
[3] Michel, *Chroniques anglo-normandes*, vol. III, p. 4; J. A. Giles, *Scriptores Willelmi*, p. 29. I am disposed to accept Petrie's reading.   [4] *Gesta Regum*, p. 293.
[5] Flor. Worc., vol. I, p. 227.   [6] Ord. Vit., interp. Will. Jum., p. 196.
[7] Gaimar (Michel, *Chroniques*, vol. I, pp. 6–7).

he was still at York.[1] The news could hardly have reached York before the evening of 1 October.[2] To arrive in London even by 6 October he would thus have to have covered some one hundred and ninety miles in five days, which would be good going even if he were accompanied only by a small force of mounted men, and quite impossible for an army of foot-soldiers.

Such then is the problem, and no solution to it can command full confidence. The weakest point in the accepted story may lie in the statement that Harold received the news of William's landing when still at York. The twelfth-century tradition that this was so is certainly strong, but it is not impregnable, and it contains some contradictory elements.[3] It is thus not impossible that Harold was already on his way south when he heard the news, and in that case some (though not all) of the difficulties would be removed. It has also been asserted that Harold left London not on 11 October but on 12 October,[4] and here an additional complication is supplied by the statement of William of Jumièges that Harold 'after riding all night appeared on the field of battle early in the morning'.[5] In view of the distance to be covered, I cannot, however, myself believe that Harold left London as late as 12 October, even if he resorted to a night march, or even if it were assumed[6] that his force of foot-soldiers became so straggled over the Sussex countryside that a portion of it may not even have arrived in time for the opening of the engagement.

I have, therefore, though with considerable hesitation, thought it plausible to believe: (i) that wherever it was that Harold heard the news of William's landing, he probably reached London with a small force of mounted men on 6 October; (ii) that he left London with his newly collected army, consisting mainly of foot-soldiers, on 11 October; and (iii) that he reached his position on the Downs during the night of 13–14 October.[7] Any reconstruction of these events depends, however,

[1] Henry of Huntingdon, *Historia Anglorum* (ed. Arnold), bk. VI.

[2] Stenton, *op. cit.*, p. 584, note 1.

[3] Henry of Huntingdon (*loc. cit.*) says that he received the news of William's landing in the evening of Stamford Bridge – that is to say, before it had ever taken place!

[4] Freeman, who gives 11 October in a valuable appendix (*op. cit.*, vol. III, note FF) contradicts this in the body of his book (*ibid.*, vol. III, p. 437) where he makes William leave London on 12 October. In this he is followed by Colonel Burne (*Battlefields of England*, p. 20).

[5] Will. Jum., p. 134: tota nocte equitans in campo belli mane apparuit.

[6] Burne, *loc. cit.*

[7] This would to some extent allow for the remark of Will. Jum. More particularly would it help to explain the fact that William came up on Harold 'by surprise before he had drawn up his army in battle array' (AS. Chron., 'D', *s.a.* 1066). Harold's weary troops had arrived late during the night and had perhaps rested overlong on the summit.

partly on unconfirmed hypotheses, and it needs emphasis that many of the most widely received narratives of what happened during this momentous fortnight imply a certainty which the available evidence does not justify.

The dates of the events between Hastings and the coronation, as indicated above, accord with those given in Freeman's book, but though very plausible and probably correct, they, too, are not fully vouched for by the existing testimony, and it is noteworthy that Sir Frank Stenton at this point in his standard history[1] wisely refrains from supplying detailed information. William of Poitiers, who may here be followed with confidence, gives the sequence: Romney–Dover and the submission of Canterbury.[2] He also records that William spent eight days at Dover.[3] Greater precision can only be attempted by further reference to the *Carmen*. Thus, belief that William spent five days at Hastings immediately after the battle derives from this source.[4] It is, however, plausible, and if taken with the other evidence it would bring William to Canterbury early in November. The *Carmen* also states that William spent a month in the neighbourhood of that city,[5] and this assertion may be legitimately connected with the sickness that William of Poitiers says afflicted his troops about this time.[6] If it be accepted, the campaign round London would fall in the first fortnight of December. The famous negotiations followed, and William was crowned on Christmas Day.

[1] *Op. cit.*, p. 588.   [2] Will. Poit., p. 210.   [3] *Ibid.*, p. 212.   [4] vv. 598, 599.
[5] v. 624: per spatium mensis cum gente perendinat illic.   [6] Will. Poit., p. 212.

The chronology of King William's campaigns
between 1073 and 1081

The chronology of the Conqueror's campaigns between 1073 and 1081 is beset with difficulty, and it has engaged the attention of many scholars as distinguished as Freeman, Miss Norgate, Louis Halphen, Sir Frank Stenton, M. Latouche, A. Fliche, and Professor C. W. David. Since, however, among these scholars there has been considerable disagreement, the matter may properly be ventilated afresh. Though in debt to all these authorities in what follows, I am myself inclined to accept, although with some modifications, the solution propounded in 1906 by Halphen,[1] and developed later by Fliche[2] and Professor David.[3] The matter is, however, sufficiently complicated to warrant the evidence being restated.

An essential part of the problem concerns the question of how far, if at all, the statements of Ordericus Vitalis on this matter can be accepted.

Apart from two detached notices concerning the revolt of Robert and the battle of Gerberoi,[4] the narrative of Ordericus of these campaigns is contained in his *History* in Book IV, chapters XII, XIII, XIV, and XVII.[5] Chapters XV and XVI contain a long digression inspired by the notice of the death of Earl Waltheof at the end of chapter XIV. The whole thus forms a unity, and begins shortly after Ordericus has lost the support in his narrative of the lost portion of the history of William of Poitiers.

The sequence of events given by Ordericus is as follows:

1. William's campaign in Maine. Entry into Le Mans.
2. Fulk le Rechin attacks La Flèche. (According to Ordericus, Fulk is supported by 'Count Hoel' with a large force of Bretons. William leads an army of Normans and English against him. A great battle is averted by the intervention of clerics.)
3. A pact is arranged between William and the count of Anjou. (According to Ordericus this was concluded at a place called *Blancalanda*

---

[1] *Comté d'Anjou*, esp. pp. 181–183.   [2] *Philippe I*, pp. 271–274.
[3] *Robert Curthose*, chaps. I and II.   [4] Ord. Vit., vol. II, pp. 294–298, 386, 387.
[5] *Ibid.*, vol. II, pp. 254–267, 290–292.

vel Brueria, and the writer adds that this peace remained unbroken until the death of the Conqueror.)

4. The revolt of the earls in England and the death of Waltheof.

5. William's campaign in Brittany, culminating in his unsuccessful siege of Dol. (According to Ordericus, Dol was relieved by Alan Fergant, 'count of Brittany'. William was compelled to retreat and Alan Fergant married Constance, William's daughter.)

William's campaign in Maine (O. V. 1) can be precisely dated: it occurred in 1073 and probably before 30 March of that year.[1] Similarly, there is no question that the revolt of the earls (O. V. 4) took place in 1075.[2] These notices by Ordericus thus need no further comment in this place. The remainder, however, call for careful examination and criticism.

In the first place, the campaign of William in Brittany needs consideration. The Anglo-Saxon, Breton, and Angevin annals, together with the charters of Philip I, make it quite certain that this campaign and William's defeat at Dol took place in September – early November 1076:[3] the campaign followed indeed logically upon the revolt of Earl Ralph in England, and it was connected also with Count Hoel's warfare with the rebel magnates of Brittany.[4] This being so, the narrative of Ordericus at this place becomes at once unintelligible for the following reasons:

(i) He makes no mention of King Philip's intervention at Dol, which certainly took place and was probably decisive.

(ii) Count Hoel did not die until 1084,[5] and it was then that he was succeeded by his son Alan Fergant. Unless Ordericus has here given Alan the comital style simply as a tribute to birth, his bringing him into the story in this manner, in 1076, would seem to be an error.

(iii) It is in the highest degree unlikely that Constance married Alan Fergant in 1076 or 1077. Ordericus, himself, seems elsewhere to imply that she was still unmarried in 1081, and there is positive evidence to suggest that her marriage to Alan Fergant took place

---

[1] AS. Chron., 'E', *s.a.* 1073; *Regesta*, vol. I, nos. 67, 68.

[2] AS. Chron., 'E', *s.a.* 1075.

[3] AS. Chron., 'E', *s.a.* 1076; *Chron. Britannicum* and *Chron. S. Brieuc* (*Rec. Hist. Franc.*, vol. XI, p. 413; vol. XII, p. 566); Annales Saint-Aubin and Annales 'de Renaud' (printed in Halphen, *Annales Angevines*, pp. 5, 88); Prou, *Rec. Actes – Philippe I*, no. LXXXII.

[4] Ann. S. Brieuc (*Rec. Hist. Franc.*, vol. XI, p. 413).

[5] Clay, *Early Yorkshire Charters*, vol. IV, p. 84.

in 1086.[1] It may be further noted that Ordericus is not, in general, very sure about Alan Fergant, since elsewhere he calls him count of Nantes, whereas he was the son of Hoel, count of Cornouailles.[2]

(iv) If, as the Breton annals assert, Hoel acted in alliance with William at the time of the siege of Dol, it would be very unlikely (though not impossible) that Alan Fergant should have acted against his father in this campaign, and this improbability is enhanced by the fact that in 1077 Alan rescued his father from the Breton rebels.[3]

Some of these difficulties were well appreciated by Freeman in a remarkable appendix,[4] whose value is only partially vitiated by a misconception of the dating of one of the Angevin annals.[5] His guess that Alan Fergant may have been betrothed to Constance in 1077, and only married to her nine years later,[6] would not, however (even if it were plausible), bring Ordericus's account into line with the other sources. Indeed, Freeman himself hazarded the suggestion (which had before been made by Lobineau)[7] that Ordericus was here referring to some warfare in Brittany at a later date. Either this was so – and there is no other evidence to support it – or Ordericus was here relying on erroneous information. In any case, his account adds nothing of value to our knowledge of the campaign in Brittany in 1076. It can be set aside.

Further difficulties arise in connexion with the account given by Ordericus of the attack on La Flèche by Fulk. As will be seen, Ordericus in his narrative places this after the campaign in Maine and the fall of Le Mans.[8] For this reason, Freeman, Stenton, and (with some hesitation) Miss Norgate place the attack on La Flèche in 1073.[9] It would seem, however, that Ordericus himself does not give warranty for this conclusion. After speaking of the fall of Le Mans, he suggests that an interval may have occurred before the subjugation of Maine,[10] and in any

---

[1] Ord. Vit., vol. III, p. 28; Rec. Hist. Franc., vol. XII, pp. 559, 562, 563.

[2] Ord. Vit., vol. II, p. 392; Clay, loc. cit.

[3] Rec. Hist. Franc., vol. XI, p. 413; vol. XII, p. 566; Morice, Hist. de Bretagne, Preuves, vol. I, p. 102; Chron. Quimperlé (Rec. Hist. Franc., vol. XII, p. 561).

[4] Norman Conquest, vol. IV, p. 817.

[5] As shown by Marchegay and Mabille (Chroniques des Églises, p. 12) the entry MDLXXXVI in the Annales 'de Renaud' is a scribal error for MDLXXVI.

[6] Freeman, loc. cit.   [7] Histoire de Bretagne, vol. I, p. 104.   [8] Ord. Vit., vol. II, p. 255.

[9] Freeman, Norman Conquest, vol. IV, p. 561; Stenton, William the Conqueror, p. 313; K. Norgate, Angevin Kings, vol. I, p. 257.

[10] Ord. Vit., vol. II, p. 255.

case the affair at La Flèche (as described by Ordericus) is made by that writer to lead directly up to the pact between William and Fulk at *Blancalanda vel Brueria*.[1] Thus, even if the narrative of Ordericus was here to be taken at its face value, it would be reasonable to place the episode he describes as taking place at La Flèche at any time between the fall of Le Mans (spring, 1073) and the pact at *Blancalanda vel Brueria* for which he supplies no date.

In face of such obscurity it is necessary to turn to other evidence.

The Angevin annals make it clear that there were two attacks about this time by Fulk Rechin on La Flèche. The first (which was unsuccessful) occurred in 1076, 1077, or possibly 1078.[2] The second (which was successful and involved the burning of the castle) took place in 1081 – that is to say after the revolt of Robert, and William's reverse at Gerberoi.[3] It would seem, therefore, that Ordericus's account must refer to one or other of these, unless (as is very probable) he has confused the two. It will be recalled, moreover, that he places his notice immediately before, and in connexion with, the pact between William and Fulk at *Blancalanda vel Brueria*. The date of the pact thus described, therefore, needs to be settled, and here the description given by Ordericus of Fulk's army during the attack on La Flèche is relevant. He remarks that Fulk on this occasion was assisted by 'Count Hoel' and 'a very large force of Bretons'.[4] Now, it is likely enough that Breton troops should have supported their Angevin allies in Brittany in following up their success at Dol, but these would have been from among the Breton rebels who in 1076 had been fighting not only against William but against Hoel.[5] It seems, in short, inconceivable that Hoel should have attacked La Flèche and the Normans in Maine in conjunction with Fulk at any time during 1076 or 1077: indeed, during the latter year he himself fell a prisoner to the Breton rebels and was only rescued by his son Alan Fergant.[6] Two alternative conclusions seem thus to be imposed. Either Hoel must be eliminated from Ordericus's story, or the treaty which he describes between Fulk and William must be connected with the second attack on La Flèche – that is to say, in 1081. Consequently it is important that the annals 'of Renaud' specifically speak of a pact between William and Fulk in 1081, and in terms which appear

[1] Ord. Vit., vol. ii, p. 258.
[2] Halphen, *Comté d'Anjou*, p. 311, no. 233; Halphen, *Annales*, pp. 5, 119; David, *Robert Curthose*, p. 32, note 71.
[3] Halphen, *Annales*, pp. 5, 88. [4] Ord. Vit., vol. ii, p. 256.
[5] Above, pp. 233–235. [6] *Rec. Hist. Franc.*, vol. xii, p. 561.

to supplement Ordericus's description.[1] Not only, as Ordericus says, was there a general amnesty, and the performance of Robert's homage to Fulk *ut minor majori*, but, as the annals 'of Renaud' would add, William had to offer hostages to Fulk.[2] Finally, the remark of Ordericus that this pact gave peace between Anjou and Normandy until the death of the Conqueror,[3] though in no case fully accurate, would be understandable in relation to a treaty ratified in 1081, but quite incomprehensible in connexion with a treaty made in 1076–1078 when Robert's rebellion, and the battle at Gerberoi, and the second attack on La Flèche were still to come. On all grounds it seems impossible (or at least very hazardous) to place the so-called 'treaty of Blanchelande' elsewhere than in 1081.

What, then, happened between William and Fulk in 1077–1078? It is certain that in 1077 there occurred a treaty between William and King Philip 'which did not last long',[4] and it would seem unlikely that the French king (so soon after the events in Brittany in the autumn of 1076) would here have acted without associating his Angevin vassal and ally in any arrangements which were then made. It is thus improbable that Fulk's first attack on La Flèche occurred after the pact between William and Philip, and equally unlikely that it took place before the end of the Breton campaign in early November 1076. The Angevin annals, it will be recalled, give three dates for this attack – 1076, 1077, and 1078. The last year is given in the annals of Saint-Florent of Saumur, but these are often a year in error,[5] and for the reasons given above I am inclined to reject it.[6] MS. 'D' of the annals of Saint-Aubin gives 1076, but since the numeral occurs twice in the manuscript, it has the appearance of a repeated entry, and MSS. 'B', 'C', and 'A' of these annals give 1077, which would also be more in keeping with the circumstantial evidence.[7] I, therefore, place the first attack of Fulk on La Flèche early in 1077 or perhaps very late in 1076.[8]

This unsuccessful operation by Fulk might well have resulted in some temporary agreement between him and William, made in conjunction with the pact entered into between William and King Philip in 1077. It is therefore significant that a charter for Saint-Vincent-du-Mans given about this time is dated by reference to a pact being made

---

[1] Halphen, *Annales*, p. 88; *Comté d'Anjou*, pp. 183, 184.
[2] Halphen, *Annales*, p. 88; Ord. Vit., vol. II, p. 257.
[3] Ord. Vit., vol. II, p. 258.   [4] AS. Chron., 'E', *s.a.* 1077.
[5] Halphen, *Annales*, p. 119.   [6] But see David, *op. cit.*, p. 32, note 71.
[7] Halphen, *Annales*, p. 5.   [8] Contrast Halphen, *Comté d'Anjou*, p. 182.

between King William and Count Fulk at a place called *Castellum Vallium*.[1] This charter certainly passed before 5 November 1080, for it is witnessed by William as abbot of Saint-Vincent, and this William was at that date appointed bishop of Durham. Consequently, if the so-called 'treaty of Blanchelande' was made, as has been here suggested, in 1081, this truce must be distinct from it. It would thus seem reasonable to place it in 1077–1078, and in direct relation to the pact of 1077 made between King William and Philip.

There only remain to be considered the events between 1077 and 1081. Malcolm's invasion of northern England is fixed by the Anglo-Saxon Chronicle as having occurred between 15 August and 8 September 1079.[2] Again, Robert's counter-raid on Scotland is firmly placed by 'Simeon of Durham' in 1080, and it must have occurred after 14 July of that year when Robert and his father were still in Normandy.[3] The dates of Robert's first rebellion against his father, and of the battle of Gerberoi present, however, some difficulties. Freeman assigned the siege of Gerberoi to the winter of 1079–1080;[4] this, however, is demonstrably wrong. Ordericus Vitalis states that the siege (which lasted some time) began immediately after Christmas, and the Anglo-Saxon Chronicle (which normally begins the year at Christmas) places it in 1079.[5] The significance of this combined testimony is, moreover, conclusively confirmed by a charter of King Philip I of France[6] which is witnessed by Robert the steward, and which not only refers to the siege of Gerberoi as in progress, but contains a dating clause[7] which could indicate Christmas 1078, but could not possibly indicate Christmas 1079 – indeed during the course of 1079 Robert was to be replaced as steward by Adam.[8] The siege of Gerberoi thus took place in the last days of 1078 and was concluded during the first weeks of January 1079.

Robert's first quarrel with his father obviously broke out some time before this, but it occurred later than 13 September 1077, when Robert took part with his father at the dedication of Saint-Stephen's, Caen.[9]

---

[1] *Cart. S. Vincent du Mans*, no. 99. This passed 'eo tempore quo Willelmus rex Anglorum cum Fulcone Andavagensi comite juxta castellum Vallium trevisam accepit'.

[2] AS. Chron., 'E', *s.a.* 1079: 'between the two feasts of Saint Mary'.

[3] *Opera*, vol. II, p. 211; *Gall. Christ.*, vol. XI; *Instrumenta*, col. 266.

[4] *Op. cit.*, pp. 646, 647.

[5] Ord. Vit., vol. II, p. 387; AS. Chron., 'E', *s.a.* 1079.

[6] Prou, *Rec. Actes – Philippe I*, no. XCIV.

[7] Actum publice in obsidione predictorum regum videlicet Philippi regis Francorum et Guillelmi Anglorum regis circa Gerborredum, anno Incarnati Verbi, millesimo septuagesimo VIII, anno vero regni Philippo regis Francorum XIX.   [8] Prou, *op. cit.*, no. XCVII.

[9] *Gall. Christ.*, vol. XI; *Instrumenta*, col. 72; *Regesta*, vol. I, no. 96.

His rebellion must, therefore, have begun either very late in 1077, or, more probably, early in 1078. After Gerberoi, he was in due course reconciled with William, and, certainly, this reconciliation took place before 12 April 1080, when he is to be found once again at his father's court.[1]

The chronology of these events is so obscure, and so many points respecting it still await full elucidation, that it would be signally rash to dogmatize too confidently about it. These remarks will, however, explain why, with whatever hesitations, I have adopted the following sequence in this book:

1073   (? before 30 March) William's campaign in Maine. Fall of Le Mans.

1073   (30 March) William at Bonneville-sur-Touques.

1074   Edgar Atheling goes to Scotland; is offered Montreuil-sur-Mer by Philip; is reconciled to William.

1075   Revolt of the earls in England.

1076   (September to early November) Campaign in Brittany. William's defeat at Dol.

1077   (early, or perhaps very late, in 1076) Fulk le Rechin's first attack (unsuccessful) on La Flèche.

1077   Hoel captured by the Breton rebels, and rescued by Alan Fergant.

1077   William's pact with Philip I.

1077   (or perhaps 1078) First pact between Fulk and William (possibly at *Castellum Vallium*).

1078   (early, or possibly late, 1077) Robert's quarrel with his father and first revolt.

1079   (January) William's defeat at Gerberoi.

1079   (15 August–8 September) Malcolm's invasion of northern England.

1079   (12 April 1080) Robert is reconciled to his father.

1080   (14 July) William and Robert together at Caen.

1080   (late summer or autumn) Robert invades Scotland. Foundation of 'New Castle'.

1081   (spring) Robert and William still in England.

1081   Second attack by Fulk on La Flèche. This is successful and the castle is burnt.

1081   Second pact between William and Fulk (possibly at *Blancalanda vel Brueria*).

[1] *Cart. S. Trin. Roth.*, no. LXXXII.

On poisoning as a method of political action in eleventh-century Normandy

No estimate of early Norman history or of the character of William the Conqueror can afford to neglect the possibility that poisoning was rife in the duchy in his time. Steenstrup in fact called attention to this point, and examined some of the testimony which relates to it.[1] Nevertheless, the subject invites further consideration in this place. Among the persons intimately connected with Norman history who are alleged to have perished by poison are the Dukes Richard III and Robert I; Alan III and Conan II, counts of Brittany; Walter, count of the Vexin, and Biota his wife; Robert, son of Geré; Arnold of Échauffour; and Gilbert, brother of Roger II of Montgomery. The list is, indeed, astonishing, and if it reflected the truth it would throw a lurid light on Norman conditions. The subject has therefore its own importance, and its consideration may have some relevance to the development of Anglo-Norman chronicles. It merits, therefore, some examination.

Duke Richard III's death is attributed to poison by William of Jumièges, albeit with a certain reservation: 'Many people say that he died from poison.'[2] And William of Malmesbury in due course elaborates this by adding that the instigator of the crime was Duke Robert I: 'There is certainly a widespread rumour that he was poisoned with the connivance of his brother Robert.'[3] The same story is given in the *Gesta Consulum Andegavorum*[4] – and it appears once (but only once) in the numerous references to Duke Richard III in the *History* of Ordericus Vitalis.[5] The evidence that a crime was committed cannot therefore be regarded as strong, and weaker still is the testimony that Duke Robert was the culprit. On the other hand, it deserves emphasis that a belief that poison was here used was current at a very early date, for the assertion appears in Adémar of Chabannes, who wrote before William of Jumièges, and indeed very shortly after the event. He baldly states:

[1] *Normandiets Historie*, p. 284.
[2] Will. Jum., p. 100.
[3] *Gesta Regum*, p. 211.
[4] Ed. Halphen and Poupardin, p. 50.
[5] Ord. Vit., vol. II, p. 366.

'Richard succeeded [to the duchy of Normandy] . . . and not long after he perished by poison.'[1]

Duke Robert I died at the Bythinian Nicaea on one of the first three days of July 1035; and some time before 1060 it was being reported that he had been poisoned. The author of the *Miracula S. Wulframni* remarks (again with some reservation): 'As we are told, he died from poison at Nicaea.'[2] Later, William of Malmesbury, relying apparently on some rumour which convinced him, not only repeated the story, but added to it many circumstantial details:

On his return home, Robert ended his life at Nicaea, a city of Bythinia. He died, it is said, by poison administered to him by an official named Ralph Mowin. This Ralph committed the crime in the hope of obtaining the dukedom, but when he came home his offence became known, and, shunned by all, he departed into exile.[3]

Both the name of the alleged culprit and the motive ascribed to him prompt the liveliest scepticism, and it is noteworthy that Rodulf Glaber, who was much nearer the event and who was himself deplorably avid of scandal, never mentions venom in connexion with the death of Duke Robert I.[4] It was left to Wace and his successors to develop the tale.[5]

Alan III, count of Brittany, died as it seems on 1 October 1040, and Ordericus, three times in his *History*, asserts that he was poisoned.[6] The story was later to be repeated, but I have found no reference to it before the time of Ordericus, and its credibility would seem further to be weakened by the treatment accorded by Ordericus to the death of Alan's son, Conan II. Here he twice suggests that Conan also was poisoned and at the instigation of Duke William himself. Thus in his *History* he makes the rebels of 1075 state that Duke William 'poisoned Conan, the valiant count',[7] and in an interpolation to William of Jumièges he expands the story yet further. Conan is here alleged to have refused to join the expedition in 1066 because of the poisoning of his father, Alan, by the Normans at Vimoutiers, and 'when Duke William heard this he was much troubled':

But God soon deigned to free him from the threat of his enemies. For one of the Breton lords who was a vassal both of Conan and William, and who acted as an intermediary between them, smeared with poison Conan's hunting

[1] Ed. Chavanon, p. 189. [2] Soc. Hist. Norm., *Mélanges*, vol. XIV (1938), p. 47.
[3] *Gesta Regum*, p. 212. [4] Ed. Prou, p. 108.
[5] *Roman de Rou* (ed. Andresen), vol. II, p. 159; Benoit (ed. Michel), vol. II, p. 574.
[6] Ord. Vit., vol. II, pp. 252, 369; vol. III, p. 225. [7] *Ibid.*, vol. II, p. 259.

horn, the reins of his horse, and his gloves. . . . Conan was at this time laying siege to Château-Gonthier. . . . Having put on his gloves and touched the reins of his horse, he unfortunately raised his hands to his lips, and thus became infected with poison. He died soon afterwards. . . . The man who had betrayed him, seeing that his purpose had been achieved, left Conan's force and went to tell Duke William of his death.[1]

The tale itself hardly commands credence, and it seems unsupported by any adequate testimony. Moreover, Conan did not die until 11 December 1066;[2] that is to say, considerably after the expedition to England had taken place. His death is concisely recorded in the necrology of Chartres Cathedral: *III Idus Decembris: Obit Conanus Britannorum comes.*[3]

The case of Walter, count of the Vexin, and his wife Biota presents somewhat similar features. This man, who was nephew to Edward the Confessor, married a daughter of Herbert 'Wake-Dog', count of Maine, and in due course laid claim to Maine against Duke William.[4] There-upon (says Ordericus) '. . . the noble duke attacked the rebels, and while the warfare was continuing with varying fortunes, Walter and Biota his wife died as a result, it is said, of poison treacherously given them by their enemies'.[5] The caution of 'as they say' should be noted, and also the discretion with which Ordericus here refrains from assigning the crime specifically to the duke. Nevertheless, he makes the particular accusation through the mouths of the rebellious earls of 1075 who are made to declare of Duke William: 'He caused to perish by poison on one and the same night Walter, count of Pontoise, nephew of King Edward, and Biota his wife, and this while they were both his guests at Falaise.'[6] Though M. Latouche accepts the story at its face value,[7] it may be doubted whether Ordericus himself fully believed in the tale, which in any case is out of character and otherwise un-confirmed.

When individually considered, all these accounts tend to invite scepticism to a greater or lesser degree. There is a similar pattern to be discerned in many of them, and often the earliest mention of venom is accompanied by some phrase suggesting uncertainty. It is not quite true to say with Steenstrup[8] that all the accounts are somewhat late, for the testimony of Adémar of Chabannes and the *Miracula S. Wulframni*

---

[1] Will. Jum. (ed. Marx), pp. 193, 194. [2] Lobineau, *Histoire de Bretagne*, vol. I, p. 97.
[3] *Cart. Notre-Dame de Chartres*, vol. III, p. 220. [4] Above, pp. 174, 175.
[5] Ord. Vit., vol. II, p. 102. [6] *Ibid.*, vol. II, p. 259.
[7] *Comté du Maine*, p. 34. [8] *Op. cit.*, p. 290.

as cited above is reasonably early. None the less, it is from the twelfth century that most of the stories of eleventh-century Normandy poisonings derive. Moreover, the practice of Ordericus in becoming more definite in the words he puts into the mouths of his characters than when speaking in his own person is also significant. Nor should the lamentable conditions of eleventh-century hygiene and eleventh-century diet be forgotten in considering the bodily disorders of that age. The dysentery which afflicted the army of William the Conqueror after Hastings is easily explicable, and sometimes (as may be suspected) a less criminal interpretation than that of deliberate poisoning can be placed on some of these deaths from illness. The last hours of King Henry I were described in almost embarrassing detail.[1] His death was evidently due to a commonplace mishap: a dose of purgative physic, honestly if over-enthusiastically prescribed, carelessly dispensed and injudiciously administered – a routine hazard, at all times, of any sick-bed.

Yet, if it would be hard to find any particular case of alleged poisoning in eleventh-century Normandy where the evidence is wholly convincing, the frequency with which this accusation was made must of itself challenge attention. It might almost seem that any writer on Norman affairs was prone to attribute to venom any sudden death that could not be explained by reference to more obvious violence, and the regularity with which this was done invites comment.

It is here that a comparison with contemporary England becomes instructive. Here an accusation of poisoning was very rare. There were, moreover, between 1042 and 1057 at least three notable and sudden deaths in England which might have invited suspicion, and would undoubtedly have done so if they had occurred in Normandy. These were the deaths of Harthacnut, of the atheling Edward, and of Earl Godwine. Concerning Harthacnut, two versions of the Anglo-Saxon Chronicle remark:

[Harthacnut] was standing at his drink, and he suddenly fell to the ground with fearful convulsions, and those who were near caught him, and he spoke no word afterwards. He died on 8 June.[2]

Here, as will be seen, there is no suggestion of poisoning, and the account falls rather into line with an earlier tradition of continental writing, as when Richer of Rheims attributed the death of Duke Richard I of

---

[1] Ord. Vit., vol. II, p. 79; interp. Will. Jum., p. 185.
[2] AS. Chron., 'C', 'D', s.a. 1042.

Normandy in 996 to 'the minor apoplexy'.[1] And even more significant was the case of the atheling Edward whose death occurred suddenly after his return to England in 1057, and in circumstances which undoubtedly contained an element of mystery:

We do not know for what reason it was brought about that he was not allowed to visit his kinsman King Edward. Alas, that was a miserable fate and grievous to all his people that he so speedily ended his life after he came to England – to the misfortune of this poor realm.[2]

The author is puzzled, but the obvious temptation to speak of venom (which few Norman writers would have repelled) is here firmly resisted.

There remains the case of Earl Godwine whose death in 1053 occurred in circumstances which might have seemed to call for an accusation of venenation. The *Vita Edwardi Regis*, however, merely remarks: 'There died the earl of happy memory.'[3] But the Anglo-Saxon Chronicle is fuller:

On Easter Monday, as he was sitting with the king at a meal he suddenly sank towards the footstool bereft of speech, and deprived of all his strength. Then he was carried to the king's private room, and they thought it was about to pass off. But it was not so. On the contrary, he continued like this without speech or strength right on to the Thursday, and then departed this life.[4]

Such are the earliest accounts, and they voice no suspicion of foul play. Nor does any such appear in the twelfth-century elaboration which Ailred of Rievaulx supplies in a remarkable passage which for more than one reason merits some attention:

One day which was a popular festival, the king was sitting at table, and Earl Godwine was in the royal company. During dinner a waiter in his haste struck one foot against some obstacle, and nearly fell. But advancing his other foot, he recovered his balance, and remaining upright, he suffered no mishap. Many of those present exclaimed at the incident saying how right it was that one foot should help another. The earl jokingly cried out: 'So should one brother help another, and a man support his friend in time of need.' To which the king, turning towards him, immediately replied: 'So would *my* brother have helped *me* if Godwine had allowed it.' At this Godwine turned pale, and with a distorted countenance he exclaimed: 'Well do I know O king that in your mind you hold me guilty of your brother's death. Well do I know, also, that you do not disbelieve those who say I was a traitor to him and to you. But let God who knows all secrets be my judge! May this crust

[1] Ed. Waitz (1877), p. 180.   [2] AS. Chron., 'D', *s.a.* 1057.
[3] Ed. Barlow, p. 30.   [4] AS. Chron., 'C', *s.a.* 1053.

which I hold in my hand pass through my throat and leave me unharmed to show that I was guiltless of treason towards you, and that I was innocent of your brother's death!' He spoke; and putting the crust into his mouth he thrust it into the midst of his gullet. He tries to push it further and cannot. He then tries to pull it out but it sticks ever more firmly. The passage of his breathing soon becomes choked; his eyes turn up; and his limbs grow rigid. The king watches him die thus miserably, and, conscious that the divine vengeance has been fulfilled, he says to those standing by: 'Drag out that dog.'[1]

The description, whose dramatic power may appear even in a transla-tion, is an obvious elaboration connected with the developing cult of Saint Edward.[2] On the other hand, certain of the details, notably the picture of the tripping waiter and the jokes which followed his mishap, possess an actuality which it is hard to ascribe to pure imagina-tion. What, however, is important, in the present context, is that in all these accounts of the death of an English magnate when feasting in hostile company, there is no suggestion whatever of poison having been either contemplated or administered. The contrast with the narratives relating to Normandy is very striking.

Why then was the suspicion of poison so readily entertained respect-ing any sudden death in eleventh-century Normandy whereas, in respect of England there was apparently little disposition to indulge in these accusations? Was it because the fear of venom was, during the eleventh and twelfth centuries, wider spread in the duchy than in the kingdom? And was there any special justification for these apprehensions in Normandy?

Perhaps certain stories related by Ordericus Vitalis have some relevance to any attempt to answer these questions. Thus of Robert, son of Geré, who died in 1060, he says:

He was at table, and snatched an apple which his wife held. It was poisoned, and he died five days after eating it.[3]

And, later, Ordericus expatiates on this fatal consequence of such deplorable table-manners:

One day when [Robert son of Geré] was sitting happily by the fire, he watched his wife, Adelaide, holding in her hand four apples. He playfully snatched two of these from her, and ignorant that they were poisoned, he ate

---

[1] *Historiae Anglicanae Scriptores X* (Twysden), 1632, cols. 294, 395.
[2] See F. Barlow, *Vita Edwardi regis*. Appendix 'D'.
[3] Ord. Vit., vol. II, p. 28.

them despite his wife's protests. The poison soon took effect – and after five days he died.[1]

Whatever the insinuation, there is no necessary implication of foul play in a death following the over-hasty eating of rotten apples. But another story from Ordericus is more sinister. Mabel of Bellême, wife of Roger II of Montgomery (we are told), plotted to poison her husband's enemy, Arnold of Échauffour. She prepared the lethal dose, and placed it in readiness. But Gilbert, her husband's brother, returning heated from riding, drained off the poisoned goblet, and in consequence perished. Nor was this all. After this abortive attempt which ended so disastrously, Mabel is stated to have bribed the chamberlain (*cubicularius*) of Arnold, and entrusted to him poisons to be offered to his master. This time her plans were successful, with the result that, 'after some days', Arnold died.[2]

To accept these tales at their face value would indeed be rash. But it might be possible to underestimate their significance. Ordericus, if credulous, was neither malicious nor a liar; and these accounts concerned people of whom he had special knowledge. Both Arnold of Échauffour and Robert, son of Geré, played an important part in the history of Saint-Évroul where Ordericus was a monk, and Ordericus had himself been brought up in the household of Mabel's husband, Roger II of Montgomery, where his father held a position of trust.[3] Ordericus may even, when a boy at Shrewsbury, have seen Mabel of Bellême of whom he paints a convincing portrait. It is thus noteworthy that he did not expect such stories concerning the wife and brother of his father's lord to be received with incredulity or with indignation. They evidently did not appear either to Ordericus or to his readers as too monstrous to be believed.

In this connexion it is perhaps relevant to repeat another story relating to the family of Montgomery in which poisoning is neither mentioned nor implied. The Lady Mabel (we are told) was wont constantly to visit the abbey of Saint-Évroul with an over-large retinue which she expected to be lavishly entertained. The abbot's protests were disregarded, and at length:

[the abbot] warned her that such folly must stop. To this Mabel angrily replied: 'When next I come my retinue will be much more numerous.' Whereupon the abbot said: 'Believe me, unless you repent of this wickedness

---

[1] Ord. Vit., vol. II, p. 73.   [2] *Ibid.*, vol. II, pp. 106, 107.   [3] *Ibid.*, vol. II, pp. 220, 416–420.

you will suffer something you don't like.' And so it happened. For that very night she suddenly became ill and began to suffer great pain. Immediately she caused herself to be carried out of the abbey, and hurrying from the estates of Saint-Évroul she passed by the house of a certain man called Roger Suisnar. She ordered that his baby girl should be made to suck her paps which were causing her particular pain. This was done. The baby gave suck, and soon afterwards died. . . . But Mabel got better and returned to her own home.[1]

The story is highly coloured, but circumstantial physical details perhaps carry some conviction. It would, doubtless, be uncharitable to suppose that the abbot had doctored the lady's supper,[2] but the possibility cannot be wholly set aside.

A review of the available evidence may therefore suggest that in no case is it safe to accept without the utmost reserve any assertion that a particular Norman magnate during the earlier half of the eleventh century perished as a result of deliberate poisoning. Each surviving accusation when individually tested fails to carry conviction. On the other hand, the exceptional frequency with which such accusations were made respecting Normandy (by contrast, for example, with England) deserves note. It might even suggest that such crimes were held to be possible, and might even be expected. Did an apprehension of venom haunt the households of the Norman aristocracy between 1035 and 1066 when Normandy was rising to greatness in the age of William the Conqueror, Lanfranc, and Saint Anselm?[3]

[1] *Ibid.*, vol. II, pp. 52, 53.

[2] Cf. G. H. White, R. Hist. Soc., *Transactions*, series 4, vol. XXII, p. 87.

[3] The subject of medieval poisoning is inexhaustible, and its fascination has to be experienced to be believed. I cannot, however, risk robbing my readers of possible entertainment by failing to cite O. Sheperd, *The Lore of the Unicorn* (1930), or the fantastic but erudite *Chronicles of the House of Borgia* (1901), written as was said by 'Baron Corvo', but in reality by Frederick Rolfe in circumstances that are felicitously described by A. J. A. Symons in *The Quest for Corvo* (1935).

SELECT CHART PEDIGREES

1. The Norman ducal dynasty: A.
2. The Norman ducal dynasty: B.
3. The Old-English royal dynasty in the period of the Norman conquest.
4. The Scandinavian interest in the succession to the throne of England, as illustrated in the connexions of Emma.
5. The counts of Évreux and the counts of Eu, with some of their connexions.
6. Some connexions of Herleve (to illustrate Appendix A).
7. The counts of Maine and the counts of the Vexin.
8. The family of William fitz Osbern in relation to Anglo-Norman history, 1035–1075.
9. The Anglo-Norman connexions of counts of Brittany and lords of Richmond in the eleventh century.

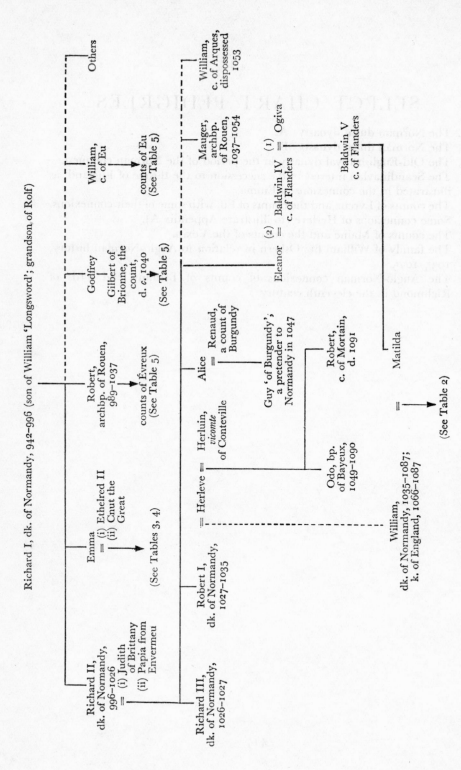

Table 1. The Norman ducal dynasty in the eleventh century: A.

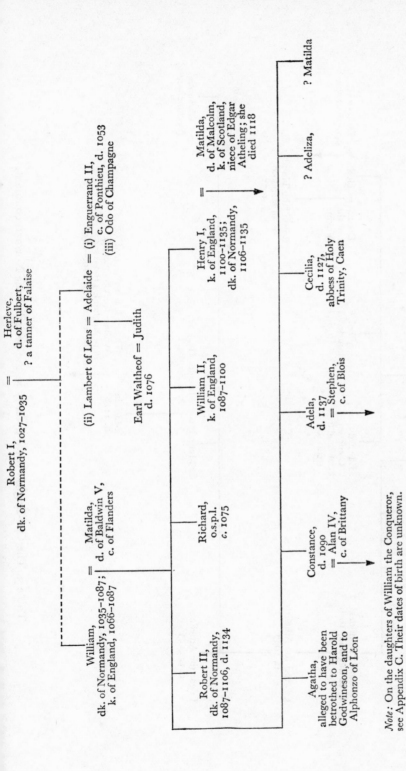

Table 2. The Norman ducal dynasty in the eleventh century: B.

Robert I, dk. of Normandy, 1027–1035 = Herleve, d. of Fulbert, ? a tanner of Falaise

William, dk. of Normandy, 1035–1087; k. of England, 1066–1087 = Matilda, d. of Baldwin V, c. of Flanders

Adelaide = (i) Enguerrand II, c. of Ponthieu, d. 1053
(ii) Lambert of Lens
(iii) Odo of Champagne

Earl Waltheof = Judith
d. 1076

Robert II, dk. of Normandy, 1087–1106, d. 1134

Richard, o.s.p.l. c. 1075

William II, k. of England, 1087–1100

Henry I, k. of England, 1100–1135; dk. of Normandy, 1106–1135 = Matilda, d. of Malcolm, k. of Scotland, niece of Edgar Atheling; she died 1118

Agatha, alleged to have been betrothed to Harold Godwineson, and to Alphonzo of Léon

Constance, d. 1090 = Alan IV, c. of Brittany

Adela, d. 1137 = Stephen, c. of Blois

Cecilia, d. 1127, abbess of Holy Trinity, Caen

? Adeliza,

? Matilda

Note: On the daughters of William the Conqueror, see Appendix C. Their dates of birth are unknown.

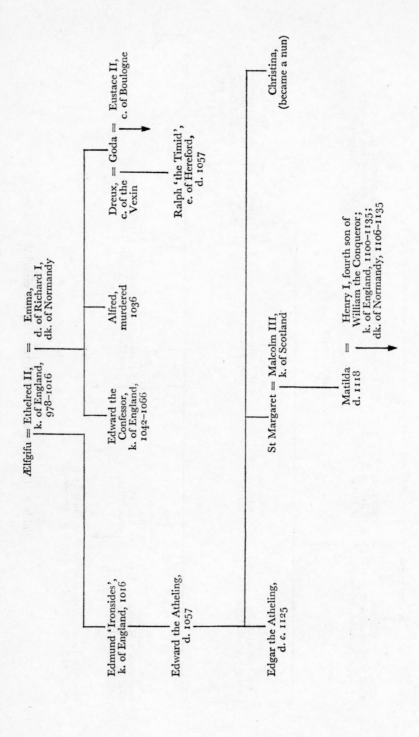

Table 3. The Old-English royal dynasty in the period of the Norman conquest.

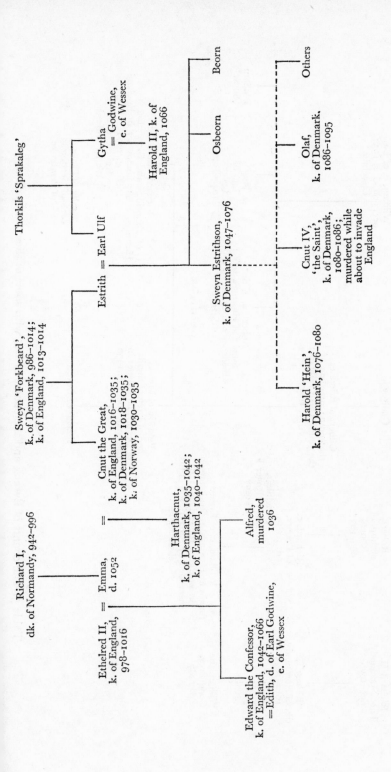

Table 4. The Scandinavian interest in the succession to the throne of England as illustrated in the connexions of Emma.

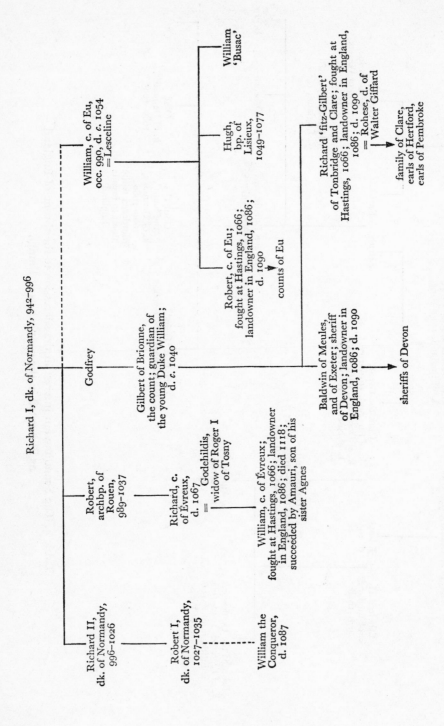

Table 5. The counts of Évreux and the counts of Eu, with some of their connexions.

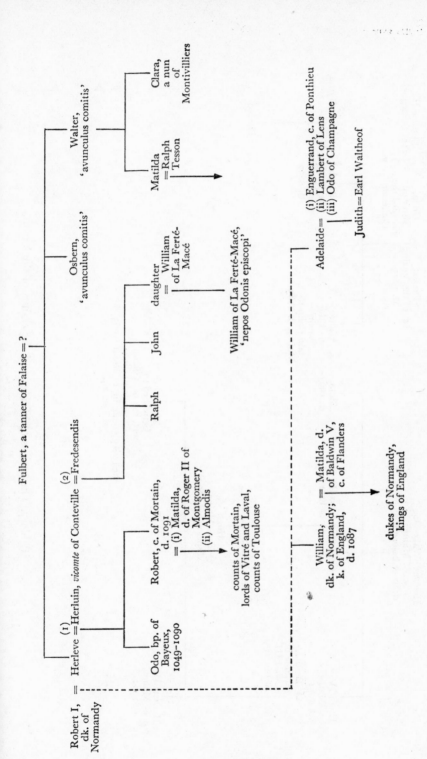

Table 6. Some connexions of Herleve. (To illustrate Appendix A.)

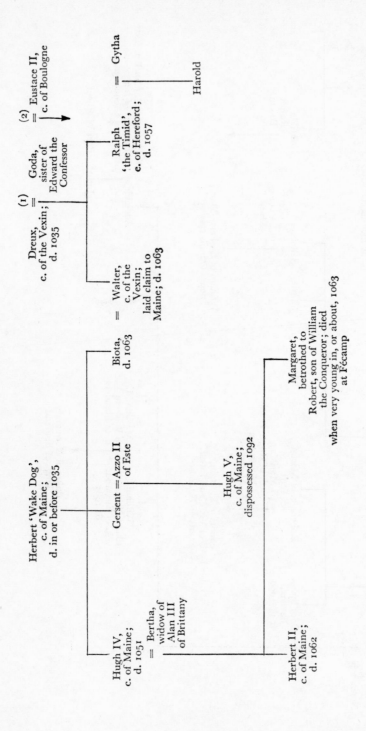

Table 7. The counts of Maine, and the counts of the Vexin.

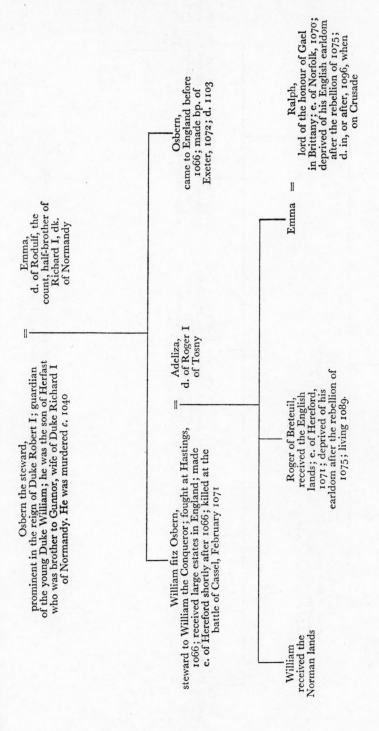

Osbern the steward,
prominent in the reign of Duke Robert I; guardian
of the young Duke William; he was the son of Herfast
who was brother to Gunnor, wife of Duke Richard I
of Normandy. He was murdered c. 1040

=

Emma,
d. of Rodulf, the
count, half-brother of
Richard I, dk.
of Normandy

William fitz Osbern,
steward to William the Conqueror; fought at Hastings,
1066; received large estates in England; made
e. of Hereford shortly after 1066; killed at the
battle of Cassel, February 1071

=

Adeliza,
d. of Roger I
of Tosny

Osbern,
came to England before
1066; made bp. of
Exeter, 1072; d. 1103

William
received the
Norman lands

Roger of Breteuil,
received the English
lands; e. of Hereford,
1071; deprived of his
earldom after the rebellion of
1075; living 1089.

Emma   =   Ralph,
lord of the honour of Gael
in Brittany; e. of Norfolk, 1070;
deprived of his English earldom
after the rebellion of 1075;
d. in, or after, 1096, when
on Crusade

Table 8. The family of William fitz Osbern in relation to Anglo-Norman history,
1035–1076.

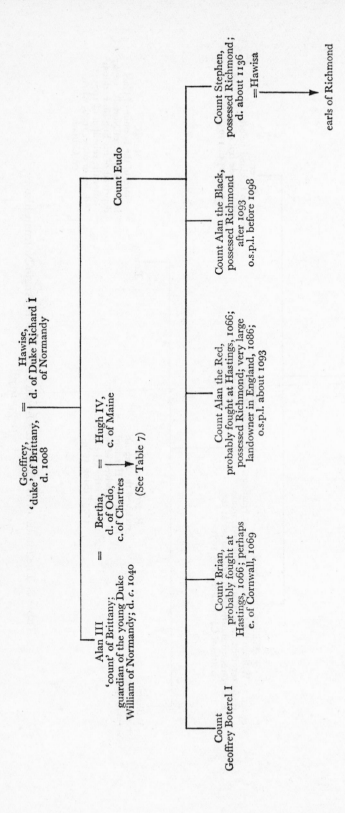

Table 9. The Anglo-Norman connexions of counts of Brittany, and lords of Richmond in the eleventh century.

SELECT BIBLIOGRAPHY

The list which follows is in no sense to be regarded as a full bibliography for the history of William the Conqueror and his times. Its purpose is simply to give further precision to the citations supplied in the footnotes to this book; to direct attention to some of the principal authorities on which the author has relied; and to indicate, if only in part, his debt to his fellow-scholars. The conventional distinction between primary and secondary authorities has been retained, but it must be emphasized that many of the works given in the latter category contain texts of original documents, and are often here included for that reason. The editions quoted are normally those which have been cited in the footnotes. Volumes in the 'Rolls Series' are marked by the letters 'RS'; publications of the *Société des Antiquaires de Normandie* and of the *Société de l'Histoire de Normandie* are indicated respectively by the letters 'SAN' and 'SHN'. Other abbreviations used will be found on pp. vii–viii.

I

PRIMARY SOURCES

A. CHRONICLES AND NARRATIVES

Acta Archiepiscoporum Rothomagensium (*Rec. Hist. France*, vol. xi, pp. 70–73).

Acta Lanfranci (Earle and Plummer, *Two of the Saxon Chronicles Parallel*, vol. i, pp. 283–292).

Actus pontificum Cenomannis in urbe degentium, ed. G. Busson and A. Ledru (Le Mans, 1902).

Anglia Sacra sive Collectio Historiarum de Archiepiscopis et Episcopis Angliae, ed. H. Wharton, 2 vols. (London, 1691).

Anglo-Saxon Chronicle, a revised translation, edited by D. Whitelock with D. C. Douglas and S. I. Tucker (London, 1961).

——, *Two of the Saxon Chronicles Parallel*, ed. J. Earle and C. Plummer, 2 vols. (Oxford, 1892, 1898).

Annales de Saint-Aubin, de Saint-Serge, de Saint-Florent, et de Vendôme, ed. L. Halphen and R. Poupardin (Paris, 1913).

Annales Fontanellenses priores (Saint-Wandrille), ed. J. Laporte (SHN, *Mélanges*, vol. xv, 1951).

Annales Gemmeticenses (Jumièges), ed. J. Laporte, 1954.

Annales du Mont-Saint-Michel, ed. L. Delisle (*Robert de Torigni*, vol. ii, pp. 207–236).

Annales Rothomagenses (Rouen), ed. Holder Egger (*Mon. Germ. Hist. Scriptores*, vol. xxvi, pp. 488–500).

Benoit, *Chronique des Ducs de Normandie*, ed. F. Michel, 3 vols. (Paris, 1836–1843).

Brevis Relatio de origine Willelmi Conquestoris, ed. J. A. Giles (*Scriptores Willelmi*, pp. 1–23).

Carmen de Hastingae Proelio, ed. F. Michel (*Chroniques anglo-normandes*, vol. III, pp. 1–38); also, ed. H. Petrie (*Monumenta*, pp. 850–872).

Chabannes, Adémar of, *Chronicon*, ed. J. Chavanon (Paris, 1897).

Chanson de Roland, ed. J. A. Jenkins (Oxford, 1929).

Chronicon Monasterii de Abingdon, ed. J. Stevenson, 2 vols. (RS, 1858).

Chronicon Monasterii de Bello (Battle Abbey) (London, 1846).

Chronicon Britannicum (Morice, *Histoire de Bretagne, Preuves*, vol. I, cols. 1–8).

Chronicon Abbatiae de Evesham, ed. W. D. Macray (RS, 1863).

Chronicon Namnetense (Nantes), ed. R. Merlet (Paris, 1896).

Chroniques anglo-normandes, ed. F. Michel, 3 vols. (Rouen, 1836–1840).

Clare, Osbert of, *The Letters of Osbert of Clare*, ed. E. W. Williamson (Oxford, 1929).

Dudo of Saint Quentin, *De Moribus et Actis primorum Normanniae Ducum*, ed. J. Lair (SAN, 1865).

Durham, Simeon of, *Opera Omnia*, ed. T. Arnold, 2 vols. (RS, 1882, 1885). [Includes the *Historia Dunelmensis Ecclesiae* and the *Historia Regum*.]

Eadmer, *Historia Novorum*, ed. M. Rule (RS, 1884).

——, *Vita Anselmi*, ed. R. W. Southern (Edinburgh, 1962).

Edward the Confessor, *Lives of Edward the Confessor*, ed. H. R. Luard (RS, 1858).

——, *Vita Ædwardi Regis qui apud Westmonasterium requiescit*, ed. F. Barlow, Edindurgh, 1962).

Emma, queen of England, *Encomium Emmae*, ed. A. Campbell (London, 1949).

Flavigny, Hugh of, *Chronicon* (*Mon. Germ. Hist. Scriptores*, vol. IX, p. 317).

Flodoard, *Annales*, ed. P. Lauer (Paris, 1906).

Fécamp, abbey of, *Liber de Revelatione* (*Pat. Lat.*, vol. CXLI, cols. 702–704).

Gaimar, Geoffrey, *L'estoire des Engles*, ed. T. D. Hardy and C. T. Martin, 2 vols. (RS, 1888, 1889).

Gesta Francorum et aliorum Hierosolimitanorum, ed. R. Hill (Edinburgh, 1962).

Gesta pontificum Cameracensium (*Mon. Germ. Hist. Scriptores*, vol. VII, pp. 389–439).

Gesta sanctorum patrum Fontanellensium coenobii, ed. F. Lohier and J. Laporte (SHN, 1936).

Glaber, Rodulf, *Francorum Historia*, ed. M. Prou (Paris, 1886).

Hariulf, *Chronicon centulense*, ed. F. Lot (Paris, 1894).

Harold II, king of England, *Vita Haroldi*, ed. W. de G. Birch (London, 1885).

Herluin, abbot of Le Bec, *Vita Herluini*, ed. J. A. Robinson, in *Gilbert Crispin*, pp. 87–110.

Herman, *Miracula Sancti Edmundi*, ed. F. Liebermann (*Ungedruckte*, pp. 203–279).

Historiae Anglicanae Scriptores X, ed. R. Twysden, 2 vols. (London, 1652).

Historiae Normannorum Scriptores antiqui, ed. A. Duchesne (Paris, 1619).

Hugh the Chanter, *History of the Church of York*, ed. C. Johnson (Edinburgh, 1961).

Huntingdon, Henry of, *Historia Anglorum*, ed. T. Arnold (RS, 1879).

Inventio et miracula sancti Vulframni, ed. J. Laporte (SHN, *Mélanges*, vol. XIV, 1938).

Jumièges, William of, *Gesta Normannorum ducum*, ed. J. Marx (SHN, 1914).

Lanfranc, *Opera Omnia*, ed. J. A. Giles, 2 vols. (Oxford, 1844).

——, *Vita Lanfranci*, auct. Milo Crispin (*Pat. Lat.*, vol. CL, cols. 19–98).

——, *Epistolae* (*Pat. Lat.*, vol. CL, cols. 515–624).

Liber Eliensis, ed. E. O. Blake (London, 1962).

Lisieux, Arnulf of, *Letters*, ed. F. Barlow (London, 1939).

Malmesbury, William of, *De Gestis Pontificum Anglorum*, ed. N. E. S. A. Hamilton (RS, 1870).

——, *Gesta Regum Anglorum*, ed. W. Stubbs, 2 vols. (RS, 1887, 1889).

——, *Historia Novella*, ed. K. R. Potter (Edinburgh, 1955).

——, *Vita Wulfstani*, ed. R. R. Darlington (London, 1928).

Miracula sancti Audoeni (*Acta Sanctorum*, August, vol. IV, p. 834).

Miracula sancti Wulframni (SHN, *Mélanges*, vol. XIV, 1938).

'Monk of Caen', *De Obitu Willelmi*, ed. J. Marx (in *Gesta* of William of Jumièges, pp. 145–149).

Monumenta historica Britannica, ed. H. Petrie, vol. I (London, 1848).

Neustria Pia, ed. A. du Monstier (Rouen, 1663).

Ordericus Vitalis, *Historia Ecclesiastica*, ed. A. Le Prévost and L. Delisle, 5 vols. (Paris, 1838–1855).

——, Interpolations to the *Gesta* of William of Jumièges (ed. Marx, pp. 151–198).

Poitiers, William of, *Gesta Guillelmi ducis Normannorum et regis Anglorum*, ed. R. Foreville (Paris, 1952).

Recueil d'annales angevines et vendômoises, ed. L. Halphen (Paris, 1903).

Recueil des Historiens des Gaules et de la France ('Dom Bouquet'), 24 vols., 1738–1904 [contains also charters and obituaries].

Rievaulx, Ailred of, *De Vita et miraculis Edwardi Confessoris* (R. Twysden, *Historiae Anglicanae Scriptores*, vol. I, cols. 370–414).

Richer of Rheims, *Historiae*, ed. G. Waitz (Hannover, 1877).

Scriptores rerum Danicarum medii aevi, ed. J. Langebek and others, 9 vols. (Copenhagen, 1772–1878).

Scriptores rerum gestarum Willelmi Conquestoris, ed. J. A. Giles (London, 1845).

Snorri, Sturlason, *Heimskringla*, ed. E. Monsen and A. H. Smith (Cambridge, 1932).

Torigny, Robert of, *Chronique de Robert de Torigni suivie de divers opuscules historiques de cet auteur*, ed. L. Delisle, 2 vols. (SHN, 1872, 1873).

——, *De Immutatione Ordinis Monarchorum* (*Chronique*, ed. Delisle, vol. II, pp. 181–206).

——, Interpolations to *Gesta* of William of Jumièges, ed. Marx, pp. 199–341.

Wace, *La Conception Notre-Dame dite la Fête aux Normands*, ed. G. Mancel and G. S. Trebutien (Caen, 1842).

Wace, *Roman de Rou et des Ducs de Normandie*, ed. H. Andresen, 2 vols. (Heilbronn, 1877); also, ed. F. Pluquet, 2 vols. (Rouen, 1827).

Worcester, Florence of, *Chronicon ex Chronicis*, ed. B. Thorpe, 2 vols. (London, 1848, 1849).

B. DOCUMENTS AND RECORDS

(Cartularies and collections of charters are normally listed under the name of the king, the monastery, or the region to which they particularly relate.)

Angers, *Cartulaire de l'abbaye de Saint-Aubin d'Angers*, ed. Bertrand de Broussillon, 3 vols. (Paris, 1903).

——, *Cartulaire noir de la Cathédrale d'Angers*, ed. D. Urseau (Angers, 1908).

Anglo-Saxon Charters, ed. A. J. Robertson (Cambridge, 1939).

Anglo-Saxon Laws, *Die Gesetze der Angelsachsen*, ed. F. Liebermann, 3 vols. (Halle, 1903–1916).

Anglo-Saxon Wills, ed. D. Whitelock (Cambridge, 1930).

Anglo-Saxon Writs, ed. F. Harmer (Manchester, 1952).

Archives de Normandie et de la Seine-Inférieure: Recueil de Facsimilés d'écritures, ed. P. Chevreux and J. Vernier (Rouen, 1911).

Bath, *Two Chartularies of the Priory of St Peter at Bath*, ed. W. Hunt (Somerset Record Society, 1893).

Bayeux, *Antiquus cartularius ecclesiae Baiocensis (Livre Noir)*, ed. V. Bourrienne, 2 vols. (SHN, 1902, 1903).

Bayeux Tapestry, ed. F. M. Stenton and others, 1957 (also in *E.H.D.*, vol. II, pp. 232–278).

Beaumont-le-Roger, *Cartulaire de l'église de la Sainte-Trinité de Beaumont le Roger*, ed. E. Deville (Paris, 1911).

Benedictional of Archbishop Robert, ed. H. A. Wilson (H. Bradshaw Society, vol. XXIV, 1903).

Book of Fees, commonly called the Testa de Nevill, 3 vols. (Public Record Office, 1920–1931).

Bury St Edmunds, *Feudal Documents from the Abbey of Bury St Edmunds*, ed. D. C. Douglas (British Academy, 1932).

Caen, *Analyse d'un ancien cartulaire de l'abbaye de Saint-Étienne de Caen*, by E. Deville (Évreux, 1905).

Calendar of Charter Rolls (Public Record Office, 1903 – in progress).

Calendar of Documents preserved in France, illustrative of the history of Great Britain and Ireland, ed. J. H. Round, vol. I (Public Record Office, 1899).

Canterbury, *An Eleventh Century Inquisition of St Augustine's, Canterbury*, ed. A. Ballard (British Academy, 1902).

——, *Cartulary of the Priory of St Gregory, Canterbury*, ed. A. M. Woodcock (London, 1956).

——, *The Domesday Monachorum of Christ Church, Canterbury*, ed. D. C. Douglas (London, 1944).

Cartulaire normand de Philippe-Auguste, Louis VIII, Saint Louis et Philippe-le-Hardi, ed. L. Delisle (SAN, 1852).

Channel Islands, *Cartulaire des Îles normandes* (Jersey, 1918–1924).

Charles III, king of France, *Recueil des Actes de Charles III (le Simple)*, ed. P. Lauer, 2 vols. (Paris, 1940, 1949).

Chartres, *Cartulaire de Notre-Dame de Chartres*, ed. E. de Lepinois and L. Merlet, 3 vols. (Chartres, 1861–1865).

——, *Cartulaire de l'abbaye de Saint-Père de Chartres*, ed. B. E. C. Guérard, 2 vols., 1840.

Château du Loir, *Cartulaire de Château-du-Loir*, ed. M. E. Vallée (Le Mans, 1905).

Cluny, *Charters and Records among the Archives of the ancient Abbey of Cluny*, ed. G. F. Duckett, 2 vols. (Lewes, 1888).

Codex diplomaticus aevi Saxonici, ed. J. M. Kemble, 6 vols. (London, 1839–1848).

Colchester, *Cartularium Monasterii Sancti Iohannis Baptistae de Colecestria* (Roxburghe Club, 1897).

Consuetudines et Iusticie (Haskins, *Norman Institutions*, pp. 277–284).

Coutumes de Normandie, *Le très ancien coutumier de Normandie*, ed. E.-J. Tardif, 2 vols. (SHN, 1881, 1903).

——, *Summa de Legibus Normanniae*, ed. E.-J. Tardif (SHN, 1896).

Concilia Rotomagensis Provinciae, ed. G. Bessin (Rouen, 1717). [This is in the nature of a new edition, much augmented, of the *Concilia* published by F. Pommeraye in 1677.]

Concilia Magnae Britanniae et Hiberniae, ed. David Wilkins, 4 vols., 1737.

Constitutio Domus Regis (in *Dialogus de Scaccario*, ed. C. Johnson).

Craon, family of, *La Maison de Craon. Étude historique accompagnée du cartulaire de Craon*, ed. Bertrand de Broussillon, 2 vols., 1893.

Dialogus de Scaccario, ed. A. Hughes, C. G. Crump, and C. Johnson (Oxford, 1902); also ed. C. Johnson, 1950.

Domesday Book, ed. Record Commission, vols. I and II, 1783.

English Historical Documents, ed. D. C. Douglas; vol. I (*c.* 500–1042), ed. D. Whitelock; vol. II (1042–1189), ed. D. C. Douglas and G. W. Greenaway (London, 1955 and 1953).

'Exon Domesday', included in vol. IV of the Record Commission's edition of Domesday Book (London, 1816).

Eynsham Cartulary, ed. H. E. Salter, 2 vols. (Oxford, 1907, 1908).

Facsimiles of English Royal Writs to 1100 A.D., ed. T. A. M. Bishop and P. Chaplais (Oxford, 1957).

Facsimiles of Royal and other Charters in the British Museum, vol. I, ed. G. F. Warner and H. J. Ellis (London, 1903).

Fontenay-Le-Marmion, *Cartulaire de la Seigneurie de Fontenay le Marmion*, ed. G. Saige (Monaco, 1895).

Gallia Christiana, vol. XI (Paris, 1759). [About half of this large volume consists of *Instrumenta* relating to Normandy and England.]

Gloucester, *Historia et Cartularium Monasterii S. Petri Gloucestriae*, ed. W. H. Hart (RS, 1863–1867).

Gregory VII, Pope, *Monumenta Gregoriana*, ed. P. Jaffé (Berlin, 1865).

——, *Registrum Papae Gregorii VII*, ed. E. Caspar (Berlin, 1893).

Hatton, C., *Sir Christopher Hatton's Book of Seals*, ed. L. C. Loyd and D. M. Stenton (Oxford, 1950).

Henry I, king of France, *Catalogue des Actes d'Henri Ier, roi de France*, ed. F. Soehnée (Paris, 1907).

Henry I, king of England, *Les Diplômes de Henri Ier, roi d'Angleterre, pour l'abbaye de Saint-Pierre sur Dive*, ed. R. N. Sauvage (SHN, *Mélanges*, vol. XII, 1933).

——, see also, *Regesta Regum Anglo-Normannorum*, vol. II.

Henry II, king of England, *Recueil des Actes de Henri II, roi d'Angleterre, concernant les provinces françaises*, ed. L. Delisle, 4 vols., 1909–1927. [Contains much material relating to the eleventh century.]

Hyde Abbey, *Liber Monasterii de Hyda*, ed. E. Edwards (RS, 1866).

Inquisitio comitatus Cantabrigiensis; subjicitur Inquisitio Eliensis, ed. N. E. S. A. Hamilton (London, 1876).

Jumièges, *Chartes de l'abbaye de Jumièges*, ed. J. J. Vernier, 2 vols. (SHN, 1916).

Lanfranc, *Decreta Lanfranci Monachis Cantuariensibus transmissa*, ed. M. D. Knowles (Edinburgh, 1951).

Laval, family of, *La Maison de Laval. Étude historique accompagnée du cartulaire de Laval et de Vitré*, ed. Bertrand de Broussillon, 5 vols. (Paris, 1895–1903).

Leges Willelmi (Stubbs, *Select Charters*, ed. 1913, pp. 98–99).

Le Mans, *Cartulaire de Saint-Victeur au Mans*, ed. Bertrand de Broussillon (Paris, 1905).

——, *Cartulaire de Saint Vincent du Mans*, ed. R. Charles and Menjot d'Elbenne, 2 vols. (Le Mans, 1886, 1913).

Le Tréport, *Cartulaire de l'abbaye de Saint-Michel du Tréport*, ed. P. Laffleur de Kermingant (Paris, 1880).

Lewes, *The Chartulary of the Priory of St Pancras et Lewes*. Sussex portion, ed. L. F. Salzmann (2 vols., Sussex Record Society, 1932, 1934); Cambridgeshire portion, ed. J. H. Bullock and W. M. Palmer (Cambridge, 1938); Yorkshire portion, ed. C. T. Clay (Yorkshire Archaeological Society *Journal*, 1933).

Liber Niger Scaccarii, ed. T. Hearne, 2 vols. (Oxford, 1728).

Lincoln, *The Registrum Antiquissimum of the Cathedral Church of Lincoln*, ed. C. W. Foster and K. Major (Lincoln Record Society, 1931, etc.).

——, *Statutes of Lincoln Cathedral*, ed. H. Bradshaw and C. Wordsworth, 3 vols. (Cambridge, 1882–1897).

Lincolnshire Domesday and Lindsey Survey, ed. C. W. Foster and T. Longley (Lincoln Record Society, 1924).

London, *Early Charters of the Cathedral Church of St Paul*, ed. M. Gibbs (London, 1939).

Longueville, *Chartres du Prieuré de Longueville*, ed. P. le Cacheux (SHN, 1934).

——, *Newington-Longueville Charters*, ed. H. E. Salter (Oxfordshire Record Society, 1921).

Lothair, king of France, *Recueil des Actes de Lothaire et de Louis V, rois de France*, ed. L. Halphen (Paris, 1908).

Louviers, *Cartulaire de Louviers*, ed. Th. Bonnin, 5 vols. (Louviers, 1870–1883).

Magni Rotuli Scaccarii Normanniae sub Regibus Angliae, ed. T. Stapleton, 2 vols. (London, 1840, 1844).

Meulan, *Recueil des Charles de Saint-Nicaise de Meulan*, ed. E. Houth (Pontoise, 1924).

Missal of Robert of Jumièges, ed. H. A. Wilson (H. Bradshaw Society, vol. XI, 1896).

Monasticon Anglicanum (W. Dugdale): new edition, 6 vols. in 8 (London, 1817–1830).

Monasticon Diœcesis Exoniensis, ed. G. Oliver (Exeter, 1846).

Northamptonshire, *Facsimiles of Early Charters from Northamptonshire Collections*, ed. F. M. Stenton (Northamptonshire Record Society, 1930).

Oxford, *Facsimiles of Early Charters in Oxford Muniment Rooms*, ed. H. E. Salter (Oxford, 1929).

Philip I, king of France, *Recueil des Actes de Philippe I, roi de France*, ed. M. Prou (Paris, 1908).

Placita Anglo-Normannica, ed. M. M. Bigelow (Boston, U.S.A., 1879).

Pontefract, *The Chartulary of St John of Pontefract*, ed. R. Holmes, 2 vols. (Yorkshire Archaeological Society, 1899, 1902).

Ponthieu, *Recueil des Actes des Comtes de Pontieu*, ed. C. Brunel, 1930.

Pontoise, *Cartulaire de l'abbaye de Saint-Martin de Pontoise*, ed. J. Dehorne, 2 vols. (Pontoise, 1895, 1900).

Pouillés de la Provence de Rouen, ed. A. Longnon, 1903 (*Rec. Hist. Franc.*, 4to continuation).

Ramsey Abbey, *Cartularium Monasterii de Rameseia*, ed. W. H. Hart, 3 vols. (RS, 1884–1893).

Recueil des Actes des Ducs de Normandie de 911 à 1066, ed. M. Fauroux (SAN, 1961).

Recueil de Facsimilés de Chartes normandes, ed. J. J. Vernier (SHN, 1919).

Red Book of the Exchequer, ed. H. Hall, 3 vols. (RS, 1896).

Redon, *Cartulaire de l'abbaye de Redon*, ed. A. de Courson (Paris, 1863).

Regesta Regum Anglo-Normannorum, vol. I, ed. H. W. C. Davis (Oxford, 1913); vol. II, ed. C. Johnson and H. A. Cronne (Oxford, 1956).

Registrum Honoris de Richmond, ed. R. Gale (London, 1722).

Robert II, king of France, *Catalogue des Actes de Robert II, roi de France*, ed. W. M. Newman (Paris, 1837).

Rochester, *Registrum Roffense*, ed. J. Thorpe (London, 1769).

——, *Textus Roffensis*, ed. T. Hearne (Oxford, 1720).

Rouen, monastery of Holy Trinity, *Chartularium Monasterii Sanctae Trinitatis de Monte Rothomagi*, ed. A. Deville. This is pp. 402–487 of *Cartulaire de Saint Bertin*, ed. B. Guérard (Paris, 1841).

Saint-Calais, monastery of, *Cartulaire de l'abbaye de Saint-Calais*, ed. L. Froger (Le Mans, 1888).

Saint-Leu d'Esserent, priory of, *Cartulaire*, ed. E. Muller (Pontoise, 1901).

Saint-Michel de l'abbayette, *Cartulaire de Saint-Michel de l'abbayette*, ed. Bertrand de Broussillon (Paris, 1894).

Saint-Pierre de la Couture, *see* Solesmes.

Saint-Wandrille, abbey of, charters of, *see below*, Lot, F.

Saint-Ymer en Auge, *Cartulaires de Saint-Ymer en Auge, et de Bricquebec*, ed. C. Bréard (SHN, 1908).

Salisbury, *The Register of St Osmund*, ed. W. H. R. Jones, 2 vols. (RS, 1883, 1884).

Saumur, *Chartes normandes de l'abbaye de Saint-Florent près Saumur* (SAN, 1880).

Savigny, *Cartulaire de l'abbaye de Savigny*, ed. A. Bernard, 2 vols. (Paris, 1853).

Scotland, *Early Scottish Charters*, ed. A. C. Lawrie (Glasgow, 1905).

Sele, *The Chartulary of the Priory of St Peter at Sele*, ed. L. F. Salzmann (Cambridge, 1923).

Solesmes, *Cartulaire des abbayes de Saint-Pierre de la Couture, et de Saint-Pierre de Solesmes* (Le Mans, 1881).

Three Coronation Orders, ed. J. Wickham Legg (H. Bradshaw Society, vol. xix, 1891).

Tours, *Chartes de Saint-Julien de Tours*, ed. L. Denis (Laval, 1913).

Vendôme, *Cartulaire de l'abbaye cardinale de la Trinité de Vendôme*, ed. C. Metais, 5 vols. (Paris, 1893–1900).

Whitby, *Cartularium Abbathiae de Whiteby*, ed. J. C. Atkinson, 2 vols. (Surtees Society, 1879, 1881).

Worcester, *Hemingi Chartularium ecclesiae Wigorniensis*, ed. T. Hearne, 2 vols. (Oxford, 1723).

Yorkshire, *Early Yorkshire Charters*, ed. W. Farrer and C. T. Clay, 11 vols. (Edinburgh, and Yorkshire Record Society, 1914–1955).

II

SECONDARY AUTHORITIES AND WORKS OF REFERENCE

Adams, G. B., *Councils and Courts in Anglo-Norman England* (New Haven, U.S.A., 1962).

Adigard des Gautries, L., *Les Noms de lieux du Calvados – de l'Eure – des Îles normands – de la Manche – de la Seine-Maritime – attestés entre 911 et 1066*. (In *Annales de Normandie* continuously from 1951 to 1959.)

Andrieu-Guitrancourt, P., *Histoire de l'Empire normand et de sa civilisation* (Paris, 1952).

Annales de Normandie, a quarterly review (Caen, 1951), in progress.

Ancestor, The, a quarterly review (London, 1902–1905).

Armitage, E. S., *The Early Norman Castles of the British Isles* (London, 1912).

(L') Art de Verifier les Dates, 3 vols. (Paris, 1783–1787).

Ballard, A., *The Domesday Inquest* (London, 1906).

Barlow, E., *The Feudal Kingdom of England* (London, 1961).

——, *The English Church, 1000–1066* (London, 1963).

Barrow, G. W. S., *The Border* (Durham, 1962).

Bédier, J., *Les Légendes épiques*, 4 vols. (Paris, 1908–1913).

Bentham, J., *History and Antiquities of the Conventual and Cathedral Church of Ely*, 2 vols. (Cambridge-Norwich, 1771, 1817).

Béziers, M., *Mémoires pour servir à l'état historique et géographique du Diocèse de Bayeux*, ed. G. Le Hardy, 3 vols. (SHN, 1894–1896).

Bigelow, M. M., *History of Procedure in England* (London, 1880).

Bishop, Edmund, *Liturgica Historica* (Oxford, 1962).

Bishop, T. A. M., 'The Norman Settlement of Yorkshire' (*Studies – F. M. Powicke*, pp. 1–14).

Bliss, A. J., 'The Companions of the Conqueror' (*Litera*, vol. III, Valetta, 1956).

Bloch, M., *La Société féodale*, 2 vols. (Paris, 1939, 1940).

——, *Les Rois thaumaturges* (Strassburg, 1924).

——, 'La vie de Saint Édouard le Confesseur par Osbert de Clare' (*Analecta Bollandiana*, vol. XLI (1923), pp. 5–131).

Blosseville, Marquis de, *Dictionnaire topographique du Département de l'Eure* (Paris, 1877).

Bodin, R., *Histoire – de Neufchâtel-en-Bray, suivie du – cartulaire*, ed. F. Bouquet (SHN, 1885).

Böhmer, H., *Kirche und Staat in England und in der Normandie* (Leipzig, 1899).

——, *Die fälschungen Erzbishof Lanfranks von Canterbury* (Liepzig, 1902).

Bonnenfant, G., *Histoire générale du diocèse d'Évreux*, 2 vols. (Paris, 1933).

Bouard, Michel de, 'De la Neustrie carolingien à la Normandie féodale: continuité ou discontinuité' (*Bulletin of the Institute of Historical Research*, vol. XXVII (1955), pp. 1–14).

——, 'Le Duché de Normandie' (F. Lot and R. Fawtier, *Institutions françaises*, vol. I, pp. 1–33).

——, 'La Chanson de Roland et la Normandie' (*Annales de Normandie*, 1952, pp. 34–38).

——, *Guillaume le Conquérant* (Paris, 1958).

——, 'Sur les origines de la Trêve de Dieu en Normandie' (*Annales de Normandie*, 1959, pp. 169–189).

Boussard, J., 'La seigneurie de Bellême aux Xe et XIe siècles (*Mélanges – Halphen*, pp. 43–55).

Bradshaw, H., *Collected Papers* (Cambridge, 1889).

Bréard, C., *L'abbaye de Notre-Dame de Grestain* (Rouen, 1904).

British Academy, *Proceedings*, 1904 – in progress.

Brooke, Z. N., *The English Church and the Papacy from the Conquest to the Reign of John* (Cambridge, 1931).

——, 'Pope Gregory VII's Demand for Fealty from William the Conqueror' (*Eng. Hist. Rev.*, vol. XXVI (1911), pp. 225–258).

Brossard de Ruville, *Histoire de la ville des Andelis*, 2 vols. (Les Andelys, 1863, 1864).

Burne, A. F., *The Battlefields of England* (London, 1951).

Caumont, A. de, *Statistique monumentale du Calvados*, 5 vols. (Paris, 1848–1867).

Chalandon, F., *Histoire de la domination normande en Italie et en Sicile*, 2 vols. (Paris, 1907).

Charpillon and Carème, *Dictionnaire de toutes les communes du Département de l'Eure*, 2 vols. (Les Andelys, 1868, 1879).

Chesnel, P., *Le Cotentin et l'Avranchin sous les ducs de Normandie* (Caen, 1912).

Chew, H. M., *The English Ecclesiastical Tenants-in-Chief* (Oxford, 1932).

Chibnall, M., *The English Lands of the Abbey of Bec* (Oxford, 1946).

Clapham, A. W., *English Romanesque Architecture after the Conquest* (London, 1934).

Clay, C. T., *A Worcester Charter of Thomas II, Archbishop of York* (*Yorkshire Archaeological Society Journal*, vol. xxvi, 1945).

Cleveland, duchess of, *The Battle Abbey Roll with some Account of the Norman Lineages*, 3 vols. (London, 1889).

Cochet, J. B. D., *Répertoire archéologique du département de la Seine-Inférieure* (Paris, 1871).

Complete Peerage of England, Scotland, Ireland, Great Britain, and the United Kingdom, by G.E.C.: new edition, revised and much enlarged, 13 vols. in 14 (1910–1959).

Congrès du Millénaire de la Normandie: Compte-rendu des Travaux, 2 vols. (Rouen, 1912).

Coquelin, F.-B., *Histoire de l'abbaye de Saint-Michel du Tréport*, ed. C. Lormier, 2 vols. (SHN, 1879, 1888).

Corbett, W. J., 'The Development of the Duchy of Normandy, and the Norman Conquest of England' (*Cambridge Medieval History*, vol. v (1926), chap. XV).

Cotman, John Sell, *Architectural Antiquities of Normandy, accompanied by Historical and Descriptive Notices by Dawson Turner*, 2 vols. (London, 1822).

Cottineau, L. H., *Répertoire topo-bibliographique des abbayes et prieurés*, 2 vols. (Mâcon, 1936, 1937).

Creighton, C., *A History of Epidemics in Britain from A.D. 664 to the Extinction of Plague* (Cambridge, 1891).

Cronne, H. A., 'The Office of Local Justiciar in England under the Norman Kings' (*University of Birmingham Historical Journal*, vol. xi (1957), pp. 18–38).

——, 'The Salisbury Oath' (*History*, vol. xix (1934), pp. 248–253).

Darlington, R. R., 'Aethelwig, abbot of Evesham' (*Eng. Hist. Rev.*, vol. xlviii (1933), pp. 1–22, 177–198).

——, 'Ecclesiastical Reform in the late Old English Period' (*Eng. Hist. Rev.*, vol. li (1936), pp. 385–428).

——, 'The Early History of the English Towns' (*History*, vol. xxiii (1938), pp. 141–150).

——, 'The Last Phase of Anglo-Saxon History' (*History*, vol. xxii (1937), pp. 141–150

Dauphin, H., *Le Bienheureux Richard, abbé de Saint Vannes* (Louvain, 1946).

David, C. W., *Robert Curthose, Duke of Normandy* (Harvard U.P., Cambridge, U.S.A., 1920).

Davis, G. R. C., *Medieval Cartularies of Great Britain* (London, 1858).

Debidour, L., *Essai sur l'histoire de l'abbaye benedictine de Saint-Taurin d'Évreux* (Évreux, 1908).

Défense des Titres et des Droits de l'abbaie de S. Ouen (Paris, 1743).

Delamare, R., *Le 'De Officiis ecclesiasticis' de Jean d'Avranches, archevêque de Rouen* (Paris, 1908).

Delisle, L., *Châteaux de la Manche* (Saint-Lô, 1922).

——, *Études sur la condition de la classe agricole et l'état de l'agriculture Normandie au Moyen Age* (Évreux, 1851; Paris, 1903).

——, *Histoire du Château et des Sires de Saint-Sauveur-le-Vicomte suivie de pièces justificatives* (Paris, 1867).

——, 'Matériaux pour l'édition de Guillaume de Jumièges preparée par Jules Lair' (*Bibliothèque de l'École de Chartes*, vol. LXXI (1910), pp. 481–526).

——, 'Des Revenus publics en Normandie au XIIᵉ siècle' (*Bibliothèque de l'École de Chartes*, vol. X (1848); vol. XI (1849); vol. XIII (1853)).

——, 'Canons du Concile tenu à Lisieux en 1064' (*Journal des Savants*, 1901, pp. 516–521).

——, 'Mémoire sur d'anciens sacramentaires' (*Mémoires de l'Institut*, vol. XXXII (1886), pp. 57–423).

Depoin, J., *Études préparatoires à l'histoire de familles palatines* (Paris, 1908).

Deslandes, R., *Étude sur l'église de Bayeux – antiquité de son céremonial son chapitre – disposition du chœur de la cathédrale* (Caen, 1917).

Desroches, M., *Notice sur les manuscrits de la bibliothèque d'Avranches* (SAN, *Mémoires*, vol. XI (1840), pp. 70–156).

Deville, A., *Histoire du Château et des Sires de Tancarville* (Rouen, 1834).

——, *Essai historique et descriptif sur l'église et l'abbaye de Saint-Georges de Boscherville* (Rouen, 1827).

——, *Histoire du Château d'Arques* (Rouen, 1839).

Deville, E., *Notices sur quelques manuscrits normands conservés à la Bibliothèque Sainte-Genevieve*, 6 parts (Évreux, 1904, 1905).

Devoisin, A. J., *Histoire de Notre-Dame du Désert* (Paris, 1901).

Dhondt, J., 'Henri I, l'Empire et l'Anjou' (*Revue belge de Philologie et d'Histoire*, vol. XXV (1947), pp. 87–109).

——, 'Les Relations entre la France et Normandie sous Henri I' (*Normannia*, vol. XII (1939), pp. 465–486).

——, 'Quelques aspects du règne d'Henri I' (*Mélanges – Halphen*, pp. 199–208).

Domesday Rebound (Public Record Office, 1954).

Douglas, David C., 'Ancestors of William fitz Osbern' (*Eng. Hist. Rev.*, vol. LIX (1944), pp. 62–79).

——, 'Companions of the Conqueror' (*History*, vol. XXVIII (1943), pp. 129–147).

——, 'The Earliest Norman Counts' (*Eng. Hist. Rev.*, vol. LXI (1946), pp. 129–156).

——, 'Edward the Confessor, Duke William of Normandy and the English Succession' (*Eng. Hist. Rev.*, vol. LXVIII (1953), pp. 526–545).

——, *English Scholars* (London, 1951).

Douglas, David C., 'The First Ducal Charter for Fécamp' (*Fécamp – XIII*^e *Centenaire*, pp. 45–53).

——, 'Les Evêques de Normandie 1035–1066' (*Annales de Normandie*, vol. III, pp. 88–102).

——, *The Norman Conquest and British Historians* (Glasgow, 1946).

——, 'The Norman Conquest and English Feudalism' (*Economic History Review*, vol. IX (1939), pp. 128–143).

——, 'Odo, Lanfranc and the Domesday Survey' (*Essays – James Tait*, pp. 47–57).

——, 'Robert de Jumièges et la Conquête de l'Angleterre' (*Jumièges – XIII*^e *centenaire*, pp. 282–287).

——, 'The Rise of Normandy' (British Academy, *Proceedings*, vol. XXXIII (1947), pp. 101–131, and separately).

——, 'Rollo of Normandy' (*Eng. Hist. Rev.*, vol. LVII (1942), pp. 417–436).

——, *The Social Structure of Medieval East Anglia* (Oxford, 1927).

——, 'Some Problems of Early Norman Chronology' (*Eng. Hist. Rev.*, vol. LXV (1950), pp. 289–303).

——, 'The Song of Roland and the Norman Conquest of England' (*French Studies*, vol. XIV (1960), pp. 99–116).

Dozy, R., *Recherches sur l'histoire de la litterature de l'Espagne*, 2 vols. (Paris, 1881).

Drogereit, R., 'Gab es eine angelsächsische Königskanzlei?' (*Archiv für Urkundenforschung*, vol. XIII (1935), pp. 335–446).

Ducarel, A. C., *Anglo-Norman Antiquities considered in a Tour through Part of Normandy* (London, 1767).

Duchesne, L., *Les premiers temps de l'état pontifical* (Paris, 1911).

Dugdale, W., *The Baronage of England*, 3 vols. (London, 1675, 1676).

Dumaine, L. V., *Tinchebrai et sa Région au Bocage normand*, 3 vols. (Paris, 1883–1885).

[Du Plessis, Toussaints], *Description géographique et historique de la Haute Normandie*, 2 vols. (Paris, 1740).

Dupont, E., *La participation de la Bretagne à la conquête de l'Angleterre par les Normands* (Paris, 1911).

Durtelle de Saint Sauveur, E., *Histoire de Bretagne*, 2 vols. (Paris, 1935).

Edwards, J. G., 'The Normans and the Welsh March' (British Academy, *Proceedings*, vol. XLII (1956), pp. 155–179).

Études Lexoviennes, 3 vols. (Paris, 1915–1928).

Eudeline, P., *Hauville: monographie paroissiale* (Évreux, 1918).

Faral, E., *Les Jongleurs de France* (Paris, 1910).

Farcy, P. de, *Abbayes de l'évêché de Bayeux* (Laval, 1887).

Farin, F., *Histoire de la ville de Rouen*, 3rd ed., 2 vols. (Rouen, 1738).

Fauroux, M., *see: Recueil des Actes des Ducs de Normandie*.

Fawtier, R., 'Les reliques rouennaises de Sainte Catherine d'Alexandrie' (*Analecta Bollandiana*, vol. XLII (1923), pp. 357–368).

Fécamp, abbey of, *Ouvrage scientifique du XIII*^e *centenaire* (Fécamp, 1958).

Finn, R. W., *The Domesday Inquest and the Making of Domesday Book* (London, 1961).

——, *An Introduction of Domesday Book* (London, 1962).

Flach, J., *Les Origines de l'ancienne France*, 4 vols. (Paris, 1886–1917).

Fliche, A., *Le Règne de Philippe I, roi de France* (Paris, 1912).

——, *Le Réforme grégorienne*, 2 vols. (Paris, 1924, 1925).

Foreville, R., 'Aux origines de la legende épique: Guillaume de Poitiers' (*Moyen Age*, vol. LXI (1950), pp. 95–219).

——, 'Guillaume de Jumièges et Guillaume de Poitiers' (*Fécamp – XIIIᵉ Centenaire*, pp. 643–653).

Formeville, H. de, *Histoire de l'ancien évêché-comté de Lisieux*, 2 vols. (Lisieux, 1873).

Freeman, E. A., *The History of the Norman Conquest of England*, 5 vols., and index vol. (Oxford, 1870–1879).

——, *The Reign of William Rufus*, 2 vols. (Oxford, 1882).

——, *Sketches of Travel in Normandy and Maine* (London, 1897).

Frère, E., *Manuel du Bibliographe normand*, 2 vols. (Rouen, 1858, 1860).

Fuller, J. F. C., *Decisive Battles of the Western World*, vol. II (London, 1954).

Galbraith, V. H., 'The East Anglian See and the Abbey of Bury St Edmunds' (*Eng. Hist. Rev.*, vol. XL (1925), pp. 222–228).

——, 'An episcopal land-grant of 1085' (*ibid.*, vol. XLIV (1929), pp. 353–372).

——, 'Girard the Chancellor' (*ibid.*, vol. XLVI, 1931).

——, 'The Making of Domesday Book' (*ibid.*, vol. LVII (1942), pp. 161–177).

——, *The Making of Domesday Book* (Oxford, 1961).

——, 'The Literacy of Medieval English Kings' (British Academy, *Proceedings*, vol. XXI (1935), pp. 201–238).

——, 'Monastic Foundation Charters of the Eleventh and Twelfth Centuries' (*Cambridge History Journal*, vol. IV (1934), pp. 205–222, 296–298).

Ganshof, F. L., *Qu'est-ce que la Féodalite?* (Brussels, 1947).

Genestal, R., *Du Rôle des Monastères comme établissements de crédit* (Paris, 1901).

Geslin de Bourgoyne, J., and Barthélemy, A. de, *Anciens Évêchés de Bretagne*, 6 vols. (Paris, 1855–1879).

Giry, A., *Manuel de Diplomatique* (Paris, 1894).

Glanville, L. (Boistard) de, *Histoire du prieuré de Saint-Lô de Rouen*, 2 vols. (Rouen, 1890, 1891).

Gleason, S. E., *An Ecclesiastical Barony of the Middle Ages: the Bishopric of Bayeux, 1066–1204* (Harvard U.P., Cambridge, U.S.A., 1936).

Glover, R., 'English Warfare in 1066' (*Eng. Hist. Rev.*, vol. LXVII (1952), pp. 1–18).

Goebel, J., *Felony and Misdemeanour* (New York, 1937).

Goujou, A., *Histoire de Bernay et de son canton* (Évreux, 1875).

Grierson, P., 'The relations between England and Flanders before the Norman Conquest' (R. Hist. Soc., *Transactions*, series 4, vol. XXIII (1941), pp. 71–113).

Grosse-Duperon, R., *L'église Notre-Dame de Mayenne, Notes et Documents*, 2 vols. (Mayenne, 1911, 1912).

Guéry, Ch., *Histoire de l'abbaye de Lire* (Évreux, 1917).

Guillhiermoz, P., *Essai sur l'origine de la noblesse en France au Moyen Age* (Paris, 1902).

Guitard, M., *Documents normands conservés à Londres* (Rouen, 1934).

Gurney, D., *The Record of the House of Gournay*, 2 vols. (London, 1848, 1858).

Halphen, L., *Le comte d'Anjou au XIe siècle* (Paris, 1906).

——, *Mélanges d'histoire du Moyen Age – dediés à L. Halphen* (Paris, 1915).

Handbook of British Chronology, ed. F. M. Powicke and E. B. Fryde (R. Hist. Soc., 1961).

Harcourt, Vernon, *His Grace the Steward and Trial by Peers* (London, 1907).

Hardy, T. D., *Descriptive Catalogue of Materials relating to the History of Great Britain and Ireland*, 3 vols. in 4 (RS, 1862–1871).

Haskins, C. H., *Norman Institutions* (Harvard U.P., Cambridge, U.S.A., 1918).

——, *The Normans in European History* (New York, 1915).

——, *Anniversary Essays presented to C. H. Haskins* (New York, 1929).

Hayward, John, *The Lives of the III Normans, Kings of England* (London, 1613).

Hefelé-Leclerc, *Histoire des Conciles*, vols. IV and V (Paris, 1911, 1913).

Hill, C., 'The Norman Yoke' (*Puritanism and Revolution*, London, 1958).

Hill, J. W. F., *Medieval Lincoln* (Cambridge, 1948).

Hippeau, C., *L'Abbaye de Saint-Étienne de Caen* (Caen, 1855).

——, *Dictionnaire topographique du département de Calvados* (Paris, 1866).

Hollings, M., 'The Survival of the Five Hide Unit in the Western Midlands' (*Eng. Hist. Rev.*, vol. LXIII (1948), pp. 453–487).

Hollister, C. W., *Anglo-Saxon Military Institutions* (Oxford, 1962).

——, 'The Norman Conquest and the Genesis of English Feudalism' (*American Historical Review*, vol. LXVI (1961), pp. 641–664).

Holtzmann, W., *Papsturkunden in England*, 3 vols. (Berlin, 1930–1952).

Hommey, L., *Histoire générale ecclésiastique et civile du diocèse de Sées*, 5 vols. (Alençon, 1898–1900).

Hunger, V., *Histoire de Verson* (Caen, 1908).

Huynes, J., *Histoire générale de l'abbaye du Mont-St-Michel*, ed. E. de R. de Beaurepaire, 2 vols. (SHN, 1872, 1873).

Imbert, H., *Histoire de Thouars* (Niort, 1871).

Inman, A. H., *Domesday and Feudal Statistics* (London, 1900).

Jamison, E., 'The Sicilian Norman Kingdom in the mind of Anglo-Norman Contemporaries' (British Academy, *Proceedings*, vol. XXIV (1938), pp. 237–286).

Jumièges, *Histoire de l'abbaye royale de Saint-Pierre de Jumièges par un religieux bénédictine de la Congrégation de Saint Maur*, ed. Julien Loth, 3 vols. (SHN, 1872–1875).

——, *Jumièges: Congrès scientifique du XIIIe centenaire* (Rouen, 1955).

Kantorowicz, Ernst H., *Laudes Regiae: a study in Liturgical Acclamations* (University of California, 1946).

——, *The King's Two Bodies: a Study in Medieval Political Theology* (Princeton University Press, 1957).

Kelham, R., *Domesday Book Illustrated* (London, 1788).

Kern, F., *Kingship and Law in the Middle Ages*, trans. S. D. Chrimes (London, 1939).

Knowles, M. David, *The Monastic Order in England* (Cambridge, 1940).

——, 'Les Relations monastiques entre la Normandie et l'Angleterre', (*Jumièges – XIIIᵉ centenaire*, pp. 261–267).

Knowles, M. David, and Hadcock, R. N., *Medieval Religious Houses in Englan and Wales* (London, 1953).

La Borderie, A. le M. de, *Étude historique sur les Neuf Barons de Bretagne* (Rennes, 1895).

La Borderie, A. le M. de, and Poquet, B., *Histoire de Bretagne*, 6 vols. (Rennes, 1896–1914).

Laheudrie, E. de, *Histoire du Bessin*, 2 vols. (Caen, 1930).

Lair, J., *Guillaume Longue-Epée* (Paris, 1893).

La Morandière, G. de, *Histoire de la Maison d'Estouteville en Normandie* (Paris, 1903).

Langlois, P., *Nouvelles recherches sur les bibliothèques des archevêques et du chapitre de Rouen* (Rouen, 1854).

La Roque, G.-A. de, *Histoire généalogique de la Maison de Harcourt*, 4 vols. (Paris, 1663).

Larson, L. M., *The King's Household in England before the Norman Conquest* (Madison, U.S.A., 1904).

Latouche, R., *Histoire du Comté du Maine pendant les Xᵉ et XIᵉ siècles* (Paris, 1810).

Lauer, P., *Le Règne de Louis IV, d'Outre Mer* (Paris, 1900).

Le Baud, P., *Histoire de Bretagne* (Paris, 1638).

Lebeurier, P. F., *Notice sur l'abbaye de la Croix-Saint-Leufroy* (Paris, 1866).

Le Brasseur, P. P., *Histoire civile et ecclésiastique du Comté d'Évreux* (Nevers, 1722).

Le Cacheux, M. J., *Histoire de l'abbaye de Saint-Amand de Rouen* (Caen, 1937).

Le Cacheux, P., 'Une charte de Jumièges concernant l'épreuve par le fer chaud' (SHN, *Mélanges*, vol. XI (1927), pp. 203–217).

Lecanu, C. A. F., *Histoire du diocèse de Coutances et Avranches*, 2 vols. (Coutances, 1877, 1888).

Lechaudé-d'Anisy, *Les anciennes abbayes de Normandie* (SAN, *Mémoires*, vols. VII, VIII).

——, *Grands Rôles des Echiquiers de Normandie* (Caen, 1846).

Leclercq, I. J., et Bonnes, J. P., *Un maître de la vie spirituelle au XIᵉ siècle: Jean de Fécamp* (Paris, 1946).

Lemarignier, J.-F., 'Autour de la royauté française du IXᵉ au XIIIᵉ siècle' (*Bibliothèque de l'École de Chartes*, vol. CXIII, 1955).

——, 'La dislocation du Pagus et le problème des Consuetudines' (*Mélanges – Halphen*, pp. 401–411).

——, *Recherches sur l'hommage en marche et les frontières féodales* (Paris, 1945).

——, *Les Privilèges d'exemption et de jurisdiction ecclésiastique des abbayes normandes* (Paris, 1937).

Lennard, R., *Rural England, 1086–1135* (Oxford, 1959).

Le Noir, J. L., *Preuves généalogiques et historiques de la Maison de Harcourt* (Paris, 1907).

Le Patourel, J. H., 'Geoffrey, Bishop of Coutances' (*Eng. Hist. Rev.*, vol. LIX (1944), pp. 129–140.

——, 'The Reports of the Trial on Pennenden Heath' (*Studies – Powicke*, pp. 15–26).

Le Prévost, A., 'Les anciennes divisions territoriales de la Normandie' (SAN, *Mémoires*, vol. XI (1840), pp. 1–59).

——, *Mémoires et Notes de M. Auguste Le Prévost pour servir à l'histoire du département de l'Eure*, 3 vols. (Évreux, 1862–1869).

Le Roux de Lincy, A. J. V., *Essai historique et littéraire sur l'abbaye de Fécamp* (Rouen, 1840).

Le Roy, T., *Livre des curieuses recherches du Mont-Saint-Michel* (1647), ed. E. de R. Beaurepaire (SAN, *Mémoires*, vol. XXIX (1877), pp. 223–246).

Licquet, F. T., *Histoire de Normandie*, 2 vols. (Rouen, 1835).

Liebermann, F., *Ungedruckte Anglo-Normannische Geschichtsquellen* (Strassburg, 1879).

——, *see also;* Anglo-Saxon Laws, *Die Gesetze der Angelsachsen.*

Lobineau, G. A., *Histoire de Bretagne*, 2 vols. (Paris, 1707). [The second volume contains the *Preuves.*]

Lot, F., *L'art militaire et les armées au moyen âge* (Paris, 1946).

——, 'Études sur les légendes épiques françaises V : La chanson de Roland' (*Romania*, vol. LIV (1928), pp. 357–378).

——, *Fidèles ou Vassaux?* (Paris, 1940).

——, *Études critiques sur l'abbaye de Saint-Wandrille* (Paris, 1913).

——, *Mélanges d'histoire – offerts à F. Lot* (Paris, 1925).

Lot, F., and Fawtier, R., *Histoire des Institutions françaises au Moyen Age*, 3 vols. (Paris, 1958–1963).

Loth, J., *La Cathédrale de Rouen* (Paris, 1879).

Lottin de Laval, V., *Bernay et son arrondissement* (Bernay, 1890).

Loyd, L. C., *The Origins of some Anglo-Norman Families* (Harleian Society, vol. CIII, 1951).

——, 'The Origin of the Family of Warenne' (Yorkshire Archaeological Society *Journal*, vol. XXXI (1933), pp. 97–159).

Loyn, H. R., *Anglo-Saxon England and the Norman Conquest* (London, 1962).

Luchaire, A., *Histoire des Institutions monarchiques de la France (987–1180)*, 2 vols. (Paris, 1891).

Lyon, B. D., *From Fief to Indenture* (Cambridge, U.S.A., 1957).

——, 'The Money Fief under the English Kings' (*Eng. Hist. Rev.*, vol. LVI (1941), pp. 161–193).

—— (editor), *Medieval Institutions* (Cornell University Press, 1954).

Mabillon, J., *De Re Diplomatica*, 1681 ; supplement, 1704.

Macdonald, A. J., *Lanfranc : a Study of his Life and Writing* (Oxford, 1944).

Maclagan, E., *The Bayeux Tapestry* (King Penguin Books, 1943).

Madox, T., *Baronia Anglica* (London, 1736).

——, *Formulare Anglicanum* (London, 1702).

Maitland, F. W., *Domesday Book and Beyond* (Cambridge, 1897).

——, *Collected Papers*, 3 vols. (Cambridge, 1911).

Martène, E., and Durand U., *Thesaurus novus anecdotorum*, 5 vols. (Paris, 1717).

Martin-du-Gard, Roger, *L'abbaye de Jumièges* (Montdidier, 1909).

Marx, J., 'Guillaume de Poitiers et Guillaume de Jumièges' (*Mélanges –* F. Lot, pp. 515–542).

Maskell, W., *Ancient Liturgy of the Church of England* (London, 1846).

——, *Monumenta ritualia ecclesiae anglicanae* (Oxford, 1882).

Mason, J. F. A., 'The Companions of the Conqueror: an additional name' (*Eng. Hist. Rev.*, vol. LXVI (1956), pp. 61–69).

Matthew Donald, *Norman Monasteries and their English Possessions* (Oxford, 1962).

Merlet, L., *Dictionnaire topographique du Département d'Eure et Loir* (Paris, 1861).

Morgan, J. F., *England under the Norman Occupation* (London, 1858).

Morice, P. H., *Histoire ecclésiastique et civile de Bretagne*, 5 vols. (1742). [The last three vols. contain the *Preuves*.]

Monstier, A. du, *see: Neustria Pia*.

Morris, W. A., *The Medieval English Sheriff to 1300* (Manchester, 1927).

Musset, L., 'Actes inédits du XIᵉ siècle' (SAN, *Bulletin*, vol. LII, pp. 117–155; vol. LIV, pp. 115–154; 1952–1955).

——, 'Les destins de la propriété monastique devant les invasions normandes' (*Jumièges – XIIIᵉ centenaire*, pp. 48–55).

——, 'Les domaines de l'époque franque et les destinées du régime domanial du IXᵉ au XIᵉ siècle' (SAN, *Bulletin*, vol. XLIX (1942–1945), pp. 7–97).

——, 'La vie économique de l'abbaye de Fécamp sous l'abbatiat de Jean de Ravenne' (*Fécamp – XIIIᵉ centenaire*, pp. 67-79).

——, 'A-t-il existé en Normandie au XIᵉ siècle une aristocratie d'argent?' (*Annales de Normandie* (1959), pp. 285–299).

Navel, H., 'L'enquête de 1133 sur les fiefs de l'évêché de Bayeux' (SAN, *Bulletin*, vol. XLII (1935), pp. 5–80).

——, 'Recherches sur les institutions féodales en Normandie' (SAN, *Bulletin*, vol. LI, 1953).

Nicole, J., *Histoire – des évêques d'Avranches*, ed. Ch.-A. de Beaurepaire (SHN, *Mélanges*, vol. IV (1898), pp. 1–110).

Norgate, K., *England under the Angevin Kings*, 2 vols. (London, 1887).

Nouveau Traité de Diplomatique, 6 vols. (Paris, 1750–1765).

Offler, H. S., 'The Tractate, De Iniusta Vexacione Willelmi episcopi' (*Eng. Hist. Rev.*, vol. LXVI (1951), pp. 321–341).

Oleson, T. J., *The Witenagemot in .he Reign of Edward the Confessor* (Oxford, 1955).

——, 'Edward the Confessor's Promise of the Throne to Duke William of Normandy' (*Eng. Hist. Rev.*, vol. LXXII (1957), pp. 221–228).

Oliver, G., *Lives of the Bishops of Exeter* (Exeter, 1861).

Petit-Dutaillis, C., *Studies and Notes Supplementary to Stubbs's Constitutional History*, 3 vols. (Manchester, 1908–1929).

Pezet, R. A. L., *Les barons de Creully* (Bayeux, 1854).

Pfister, C., *Étude sur le règne de Robert le Pieux* (Paris, 1885).

Philpot, J. H., *Master Wace: a Pioneer in Two Literatures* (London, 1925).

Pigeon, E. A., *La Diocèse d'Avranches*, 2 vols. (Coutances, 1887, 1888).

Pluquet, F., *Notice sur la vie et les écrits de Robert Wace* (Rouen, 1824).

Pocock, J. G. A., *The Ancient Constitution and the Feudal Law* (Cambridge, 1957).

Pollock, F., and Maitland, F. W., *The History of English Law before the time of Edward I*, 2nd ed., 2 vols. (Cambridge, 1898).

Pommeraye, F., *Histoire de l'abbaye royale de Saint Ouen de Rouen – ensembles celles des abbayes de Sainte Catherine et de Saint Amand* (Rouen, 1662).

——, *Histoire des Archevêques de Rouen* (Rouen, 1667).

——, *Histoire de l'église cathédrale de Rouen* (Rouen, 1686).

Poole, A. L., *Obligations of Society in the Twelfth and Thirteenth Centuries* (Oxford, 1946).

Poole, R. L., *The Exchequer in the Twelfth Century* (Oxford, 1912).

——, *Chronicles and Annals* (Oxford, 1926).

——, 'Leopold Delisle' (British Academy, *Proceedings*, vol. v, 1911).

——, *Studies in Chronology and History* (Oxford, 1934).

——, *Essays in History Presented to Reginald Lane Poole* (Oxford, 1927).

Porée, A. A., *Histoire de l'abbaye du Bec*, 2 vols. (Évreux, 1901).

Pottier, A., *Revue rétrospective normande* (Rouen, 1842).

Powicke, F. M., *The Loss of Normandy* (Manchester, 1913).

——, 'Sir Henry Spelman and the "Concilia"' (British Academy, *Proceedings*, vol. xvi (1930), pp. 345–382).

——, *Studies in Medieval History presented to F. M. Powicke* (Oxford, 1948).

Powicke, M., *Military Obligation in Medieval England* (Oxford, 1962).

Prentout, H., *Essai sur les origines et fondation du Duché de Normandie* (Paris, 1911).

——, *Étude critique sur Dudon de Saint-Quentin* (Paris, 1916).

——, *Études sur quelques points de l'histoire de Guillaume le Conquérant* (Caen, 1930).

——, *Études sur quelques points de l'histoire de Normandie* (Caen, 1926; *Nouvelle Séries*, Caen, 1929).

——, *La Normandie* ('Régions de la France', 1910).

Prestwich, J. O., 'War and Finance in the Anglo-Norman State' (R. Hist. Soc., *Transactions*, series 5, vol. iv (1954), pp. 19–44).

Richard, A., *Histoire des Comtes de Poitou*, 2 vols. (Paris, 1903).

Richardson, H. G., 'The Coronation in Medieval England' (*Traditio*, vol. xvi (1960), pp. 111–202).

Richardson, H. G., and Sayles, G., *The Governance of Medieval England from the Conquest to Magna Carta* (Edinburgh, 1963).

Rickard, P., *Britain in Medieval French Literature* (Cambridge, 1956).

Ritchie, R. L. G., *The Normans in England before Edward the Confessor* (Exeter, 1948).

——, *The Normans in Scotland* (Edinburgh, 1954).

Robinson, J. A., *Gilbert Crispin, Abbot of Westminster* (Cambridge, 1911).

——, *Somerset Historical Essays* (British Academy, 1911).

Round, J. H., *The Commune of London, and other Studies* (London, 1899).

——, *Family Origins and other Studies* (London, 1930).

——, *Feudal England* (London, 1895).

——, *Geoffrey de Mandeville* (London, 1892).

——, *Peerage and Pedigree*, 2 vols. (London, 1910).

——, *Studies in Peerage and Family History* (London, 1901).

——, see also: *Calendar of Documents preserved in France.*

Royal Historical Society; *Transactions*, 5 series (in progress).

Runciman, Steven, *A History of the Crusades*, 3 vols. (Cambridge, 1951–1954).

Sackur, E., *Die Cluniacenser*, 2 vols. (Halle, 1892, 1894).

Sauvage, H., *Les Chartes de fondation du Prieuré de Bacqueville-en-Caux: Étude critique* (Rouen, 1882).

——, *Note sur les manuscrits anglo-saxons et les manuscrits de Jumièges conservés à la Bibliothèque municipale de Rouen* (Le Havre, 1870).

Sauvage, R. N., *Les fonds de l'abbaye de Saint-Étienne de Caen aux Archives de Calvados* (Caen, 1911).

——, *L'abbaye de Saint-Martin de Troarn* (Caen, 1911).

Schlumberger, G., 'Deux chefs normands des armées byzantines' (*Revue historique*, vol. XVI, 1881).

Schram, P. E., *History of the English Coronation* (Oxford, 1937).

Setton, K. M., and Baldwin, M. W. (editors), *A History of the Crusades*, vol. I: 'The First Hundred Years' (Philadelphia, 1955).

Sion, J., *Les Paysans de la Normandie orientale* (Paris, 1909).

Sisam, K., 'Ælfric's Catholic Homilies' (*Review of English Studies*, vol. VII, pp. 7–22; vol. VIII, pp. 51–68; vol. IX, pp. 1–11; 1931–1933).

Skene, W. F., *Celtic Scotland*, 3 vols. (Edinburgh, 1876–1880).

Social Life in Early England, ed. G. Barraclough (London, 1960).

Société des Antiquaires de Normandie: *Mémoires*, 1825 – in progress.

Société de l'Histoire de Normandie: *Mélanges*, 1891 – in progress.

Southern, R. W., 'The Canterbury Forgeries' (*Eng. Hist. Rev.*, vol. XXIII (1958), pp. 193–226).

——, 'The English Origins of the "Miracles of the Virgin"' (*Medieval and Renaissance Studies*, vol. IV (1958), pp. 176–216).

——, 'The First Life of Edward the Confessor' (*Eng. Hist. Rev.*, vol. LVII (1943), pp. 385–400).

——, 'Lanfranc of Bec and Berengar of Tours' (*Studies – Powicke*, pp. 27–48).

——, *Saint Anselm and His Biographer* (Cambridge, 1963).

Spatz, W., *Die Schlacht von Hastings* (Berlin, 1896).

Stapleton, T., see: *Magni Rotuli.*

Steenstrup, J., *Normandiets Historie under de syv første hertuger* (Copenhagen, 1925).

Stein, H., *Bibliographie générale des cartulaires français* (Paris, 1907).

Stenton, F. M., *Anglo-Saxon England* (Oxford, 1943).

Stenton, F. M., 'The Danes in England' (British Academy, *Proceedings*, vol. XIII (1927), pp. 203–246).

——, *The Free Peasantry of the Northern Danelaw* (Lund, 1926).

——, *The Latin Charters of the Anglo-Saxon Period* (Oxford, 1955).

——, 'The Development of the Castle in England and Wales' (*Social Life in Early England*, pp. 96–123).

——, 'Norman London' (*ibid.*, pp. 179–207).

——, *Types of Manorial Structure in the Northern Danelaw* (Oxford, 1910).

——, *William the Conqueror and the Rule of the Normans* (London, 1908).

Stephenson, C., 'Feudalism and its Antecedents in England' (*American Historical Review*, vol. XLVIII (1943), pp. 245–265).

Stevenson, W. H., 'A Contemporary Description of the Domesday Survey' (*Eng. Hist. Rev.*, vol. XXII (1907), pp. 74–78).

——, 'An Old-English Charter of William the Conqueror' (*ibid.*, vol. XI (1896), pp. 731–744).

Stubbs, W., *The Constitutional History of England*, 3 vols. (many editions).

——, *Select Charters and other Illustrations of English Constitutional History* (many editions).

Studi Gregoriani, ed. G. S. Borino, 3 vols. (Rome, 1947).

Tait, J., 'An Alleged Charter of William the Conqueror' (*Essays – R. L. Poole*, pp. 151–167).

——, *The Medieval English Borough* (Manchester, 1933).

——, *Historical Essays in Honour of James Tait* (Manchester, 1933).

Tardif, E.-F., 'Études sur les sources de l'ancien Droit normand et spécialment sur la législation des ducs de Normandie' (*Congrès millénaire – Normandie*, vol. I, pp. 570–619).

Tolhurst, J. B. L., 'An examination of two Anglo-Saxon MSS. of the Winchester School: the Missal of Robert of Jumièges and the Benedictional of St Æthelwold' (*Archaeologia*, vol. LXXXIII (1933), pp. 27–49).

Toustain de Billy, R., *Histoire ecclésiastique du Diocèse de Coutances*, ed. F. Dolbet, 3 vols. (SHN, 1874–1886).

Tout, T. F., *Chapters in the Administrative History of Medieval England*, 6 vols. (Manchester, 1920–1937).

——, *Essays in Medieval History presented to T. F. Tout* (Manchester, 1925).

Turner, G. Dawson, *Account of a Tour in Normandy*, 2 vols. (London, 1820).

Ullmann, W., *Medieval Papalism* (London, 1949).

Vacandard, E., 'Un essai d'histoire des archevêques de Rouen au XIe siècle' (*Revue catholique de Normandie*, vol. III (1893), pp. 117–127).

——, 'Liste chronologique des archevêques de Rouen' (*Revue catholique de Normandie*, vol. XIII (1904), pp. 189–202).

Valin, L., *Le Duc de Normandie et sa cour* (Paris, 1910).

Vaultier, F., 'Recherches historiques sur l'ancien pays de Cinglais' (SAN, *Mémoires*, vol. X (1837), pp. 1–296).

Vigfusson, G., and Powell, F. York, *Corpus Poeticum boreale*, 2 vols. (Oxford, 1883).

—— *Origines Islandicae*, 2 vols. (Oxford, 1905).

Verbuggen, J. F., *Die Krijskunst in West-Europa in de middeleeuwen* (Brussels, 1954).

Villars, J. B., *Les normands en Méditerranée* (Paris, 1951).

Vinogradoff, P., *English Society in the Eleventh Century* (Oxford, 1908).

Waley, D. P., 'Combined Operations in Sicily A.D. 1060–1078' (*Papers of the British School of Rome*, vol. XXII, 1954).

Waters, R. E. C., *Genealogical Memoirs of the Counts of Eu* (London, 1886).

—, *Gundrada de Warenne* (Exeter, 1884).

Wharton, H., *see: Anglia Sacra.*

White G. H., 'The Battle of Hastings and the Death of Harold' (*Complete Peerage*, vol. XII, part I, Appendix L).

——, 'The Conqueror's Brothers and Sisters' (*ibid.*, Appendix K).

——, 'Marshals under the Conqueror' (*ibid.*, vol. XI, Appendix E).

——, 'The Household of the Norman Kings' (R. Hist. Soc., *Transactions*, series, 4, vol. XXX (1948), pp. 127–145).

——, 'The First House of Bellême' (*ibid.*, series 4, vol. XXII (1940), pp. 68–99).

——, 'The Sisters and Nieces of Gunnor, Duchess of Normandy' (*Genealogist*, new series, vol. XXXVII, 1920).

White, T. L., junr., *Latin Monasticism in Norman Sicily* (Cambridge, U.S.A., 1938).

Wilkins, D., *see: Concilia.*

Wilkinson, Bertie, 'Freemen and the Crisis of 1051' (*Bulletin John Rylands Library*, vol. XXXIV (1938), pp. 368–387).

——, 'Northumbrian Separatism in 1065 and 1066' (*ibid.*, vol. XXXII (1936), pp. 504–526).

Williams, G. H., *The Norman Anonymous of 1100 A.D.* (Cambridge, U.S.A., 1951).

Williams, Watkin, 'William of Dijon' (*Downside Review*, vol. LII (1934), pp. 520–545).

Wilmart, André, *Auteurs spirituels et textes dévots du Moyen Âge* (Paris, 1932).

——, 'Alain le Roux et Alain le Noir' (*Annales de Bretagne*, vol. XXXVIII (1929), pp. 576–602).

Yver, J., 'Le bref anglo-normand' (*Revue Historique de Droit*, vol. XXIX, 1962).

——, 'Les Châteaux forts en Normandie jusqu'au milieu du XIIe siècle' (SAN, *Bulletin*, vol. LIII, 1955).

——, 'Le Développement du pouvoir ducal en Normandie de l'avènement de Guillaume le Conquérant à la mort d'Henri I' (*Atti del Convengno internationale di Studi Ruggeriani*, Palermo, 1955).

——, 'L'interdiction de la guerre privée dans le très ancien droit normand' (*Travaux de la Semaine de Droit normand*, Caen, 1928).

SCHEDULE OF SELECTED DATES

The list which follows sets out some of the principal dates which have been adopted in this book. Where no precise date has been suggested in the text, this has been indicated by a question mark. No finality is claimed for this list, since the chronology of the age of William the Conqueror is beset with difficulties, and, even in respect of some of the most important events, the evidence is less conclusive than might be desired. Many of the questions here involved have been considered above in the appendices.

1028? (autumn)[1] Birth of William the Conqueror.

1031   Duke Robert I of Normandy supports King Henry I of France in the latter's war to obtain his kingdom.

1035   (July) Death of Duke Robert I in Bithynia: accession of William as duke of Normandy.
       (12 November) Death of Cnut the Great.

1036   Murder of the atheling Alfred (brother of Edward the Confessor).

1037   (16 March) Death of Archbishop Robert I of Rouen: his successor was Mauger, William's uncle.

1040   (23 February) Consecration of the abbey-church at Le Bec.
       Geoffrey II (Martel) becomes count of Anjou.

1040? Count Alan III of Brittany, Count Gilbert of Brionne, and Osbern the steward (William's guardians) die at various dates by violence.

1041   (or 1042) Unsuccessful attempt to introduce the Truce of God into Normandy.

1042   (after June) Accession of Edward the Confessor as king of England.

1043   Coronation of Edward the Confessor.

1044? Lanfranc becomes prior of Le Bec.

1045   (January) Marriage of Edward the Confessor to Edith, daughter of Earl Godwine of Wessex.
       Threatened invasion of England by Magnus, king of Norway.

1046? Ecclesiastical council at Rouen.

1046   (late) Revolt of the western *vicomtes* and Guy of Burgundy in Normandy. King Henry intervenes on behalf of William.

1047   (January) Battle of Val-ès-Dunes.
       (October) Ecclesiastical council near Caen (William present). Proclamation of the Truce of God in Normandy.
       (25 October) Death of Magnus, king of Norway.

1048   (late) Leo IX becomes pope.

1049   (October) Opening of the council of Rheims.
       (late – early 1050) William recaptures Brionne.

1050   (early) William re-enters Rouen.

[1] See Appendix A.

1051   (? January) Robert, formerly abbot of Jumièges, now bishop of London, becomes archbishop of Canterbury.

(26 March) Death of Hugh IV, count of Maine.

(shortly after 26 March) Le Mans surrendered to Geoffrey, count of Anjou.

Unsuccessful rebellion by Earl Godwine of Wessex and his sons against Edward the Confessor; they are sent from England into exile. About this time William is promised the succession to the kingdom of England.

(summer – ? February 1052)[1] Warfare between William and Geoffrey, count of Anjou, round Domfront and Alençon.

1051 or 1052?[2] Marriage of William to Matilda, daughter of Baldwin V, count of Flanders.

1052   (summer) Outbreak of the rebellion of William, count of Arques.

(15 August) Count Geoffrey of Anjou and King Henry of France, having been reconciled, are together at Orléans.

(before September) Return by force to England of Earl Godwine and his sons Harold and Leofwine. They are re-established in their earldoms. Expulsion of many Normans from England, including Robert, archbishop of Canterbury. Stigand is given the archbishopric of Canterbury.

1053   (13 April) Death of Earl Godwine of Wessex.

(June) Battle of Civitate.

(November or December) Capture of Arques by William.

(December–January 1054) King Henry summons levies from France. There follows his invasion of the Évreçin, while Odo, his brother, with his associates invades eastern Normandy.

1054   (1–20 February) Battle of Mortemer.

(later) Ecclesiastical council at Lisieux (William present). Deposition of Mauger, archbishop of Rouen: he is succeeded by Maurilius.

1055   Death of Siward, earl of Northumbria.

1056? Robert, William's half-brother, becomes count of Mortain.

1057   (January–March) King Henry and Count Geoffrey of Anjou in association.

(August) King Henry invades Normandy. Battle of Varaville.

Return to England from Hungary of the atheling Edward (son of Edmund Ironsides), together with his children, Margaret, Edgar, and Christina. He dies shortly after his arrival.

1057   (30 September) Death of Leofric, earl of Mercia.

(22 December) Death of Ralph the Timid, earl of Hereford.

1058   (17 March) Malcolm III (Canmore) becomes king of Scotland.

Capture of Thimert by William. Beginning of the siege of Thimert by King Henry.

---

[1] I do not absolutely exclude the possibility that (as frequently asserted) these campaigns took place in 1048–1049, but I consider this to be highly improbable. See Appendix B.

[2] See Appendix C.

Attack on England by Magnus, son of Harold Hardraada, king of Norway.

1059   Synod of Melfi.

1060   (4 August) Death of King Henry I of France; he is succeeded by Philip I, then a minor.

(14 November) Death of Count Geoffrey of Anjou.

1061   (October) Alexander II becomes pope.

1062   (9 March) Death of Herbert, count of Maine.

1063   Invasion and conquest of Maine by William. Death of Walter, count of Maine, and his wife Biota.

1064   Visit of Harold Godwineson to Normandy.

William invades Brittany.

Ecclesiastical council at Lisieux (William present).

'Crusade' of Barbastro.

1065   (autumn) Revolt in Northumbria. Exile of Earl Tosti Godwineson.

1066[1] (5 January) Death of Edward the Confessor.

(6 January) Coronation as king of Harold Godwineson.

(spring) Norman mission to Rome under Gilbert, bishop of Lisieux, seeking papal support.

(May) Tosti attacks Isle of Wight.

(July) Ecclesiastical council at Caen (William present).

(September) William's fleet assembles in the Dives.

(8 September) Harold Godwineson in southern England disbands his army.

(September) William's fleet at Saint-Valéry-sur-Somme.

(September) Invasion of northern England by Harold Hardraada, king of Norway, supported by Tosti Godwineson.

(20 September) Battle of Fulford.

(25 September) Battle of Stamford Bridge.

(28 September) William lands at Pevensey.

(29 September) William occupies Hastings.

(6 October) Harold Godwineson in London.

(14 October) Battle of Hastings.

(21 October) Submission of Dover.

(29 October) Submission of Canterbury.

(Most of November) William in neighbourhood of Canterbury.

(first half of December) William's march round London.

(25 December) Coronation of William as king of the English in London.

1067   (*circa* 1 March–6 December) William in Normandy.

(1 July) Death of Maurilius, archbishop of Rouen; he is succeeded by John, bishop of Avranches.

(autumn) Raid on Kent by Eustace, count of Boulogne.

Odo, bishop of Bayeux, becomes earl of Kent.

William fitz Osbern becomes earl of Hereford.

[1] See Appendix D.

1068 (early) Subjection of Exeter.
   (summer) William's first entrance into York.
   Occupation of Warwick, Lincoln, Huntington, Chester, etc.

1069 (February–April) York rebels, and is retaken by William.
   Revolt in Maine: loss of Le Mans.
   (summer) Invasion of Yorkshire by Sweyn Estrithson, king of Denmark; general rising of the north supported by Malcolm III, king of Scotland.
   (20 September) Occupation of York by the rebels.
   (before Christmas) William retakes York.

1069? Marriage of King Malcolm to Margaret, sister of Edgar the atheling.

1069 or 1070 Ecclesiastical council at Rouen.

1070 (January–March) 'Harrying of the North'; William's campaign in Teesdale; his march over the Pennines; occupation of Chester and Stafford.
   (4 April) William at Winchester.
   (April) Ecclesiastical council at Winchester (William present); deposition of Stigand.
   (15 August) Lanfranc becomes archbishop of Canterbury.
   (summer) King Malcolm ravages northern England.

1071 (22 February) Battle of Cassel; death of William fitz Osbern.
   (16 April) Capture of Bari by the Normans.
   (19 August) Battle of Manzikiert.
   (summer) Departure of the Danish fleet from the English coast.
   (October) End of Hereward's resistance in the Fens.

1072 (January) Capture of Palermo by the Normans.
   (April) Ecclesiastical council at Winchester (William present).
   (autumn) William's invasion of Scotland; pact of Abernethy.
   (1 November) William at Durham.

1072? Ecclesiastical council at Rouen.

1073 (perhaps before 30 March) William invades and reconquers Maine.
   (30 March) William at Bonneville-sur-Touques.
   (21 April) Death of Pope Alexander II: he is succeeded by Gregory VII.

1074 Edgar the atheling is offered Montreuil-sur-Mer by King Philip I.
   Ecclesiastical council at Rouen (William present).

1075 Revolt of the earls in England.
   (August–October) Ecclesiastical council at London (William present).

1076 (April) Ecclesiastical council at Winchester (William present).
   (31 May) Execution of Waltheof.
   (September–early November) Campaign in Brittany. William defeated at Dol.

1077 (early) First attack (unsuccessful) on La Flèche by Fulk le Rechin, count of Anjou.

Pact between William and King Philip.

(December) Roger II of Montgomery becomes earl of Shrewsbury.

1078 (early or perhaps late – 1077) First pact (? at *Castellum Vallium*) between Fulk le Rechin and William.

First revolt of Robert, William's eldest son, against his father.

1079 (January) William defeated at Gerberoi.

(15 August–8 September) Devastation of northern England by Malcolm, king of Scotland.

(9 September) Death of John, archbishop of Rouen: he is succeeded in the next year by William Bonne-Ame.

1080 (early – or perhaps late, 1079) Robert is reconciled to his father.

(Pentecost) Ecclesiastical council at Lillebonne (William present).

(late summer or autumn) Robert invades Scotland: foundation of 'New Castle'.

(Christmas) Ecclesiastical council at Gloucester (William present).

1080? Gregory VII makes (or repeats) a demand to William for fealty in respect of the English kingdom. This is refused.

1081 Second (and successful) attack on La Flèche by Fulk le Rechin.

Second pact between William and Fulk (possibly at *Blancalanda*).

1082 Imprisonment of Odo, bishop of Bayeux, and earl of Kent.

1083 (after 18 July) New revolt of Robert against his father.

(2 November) Death of Matilda, wife of William the Conqueror.

1084 (?Pentecost) William at Westminster.

(19 June) William at Rouen.

1085 (25 May) Death of Pope Gregory VII.

Cnut IV, king of Denmark, prepares to invade England with the support of Robert, count of Flanders, and others.

(December) William holds his Christmas court at Gloucester, whereat the Domesday survey is planned.

1086 (July) Murder of Cnut IV, king of Denmark.

(August) Assembly at Salisbury; 'The Salisbury Oath'.

(later) William crosses to Normandy.

1087 (summer) King Philip raids the Évreçin. William invades the Vexin and sacks Mantes.

(9 September – very early in the morning) William the Conqueror dies at Saint-Gervais outside Rouen.

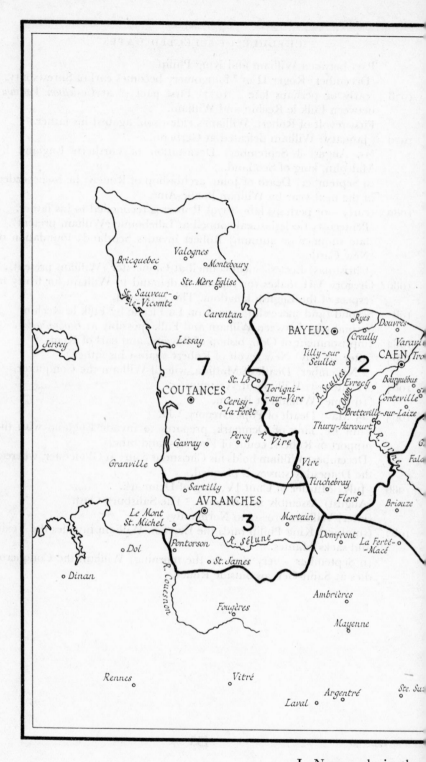

I. Normandy in the

The Norman bishoprics: 1. Rouen. 2. Bayeux. 3. Avranc

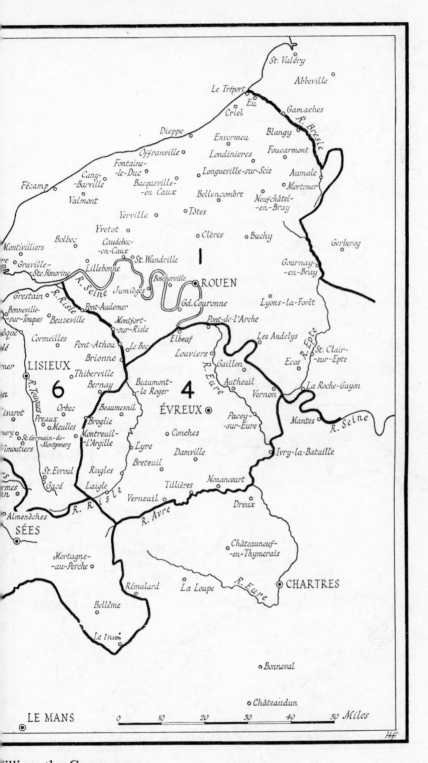

St. Valéry
Abbeville
Le Tréport
Eu
Criel
Gamaches
R. Bresle
Dieppe
Envermeu
Blangy
Offranville
Londinieres
Foucarmont
Fontaine-
-le-Duc
Cany-
-Barville
Bacqueville-
-en Caux
Longueville-sur-Scie
Aumale
Mortemer
Fécamp
Valmont
Bellencombre
Neufchâtel-
-en-Bray
Yerville
Tôtes
Montivilliers
Bolbec
Yvetot
Clères
Buchy
Gerberoy
Caudebec-
-en-Caux
Graville-
-Ste Honorine
Lillebonne
St. Wandrille
Boscherville
I
Gournay-
-en-Bray
Grestain
R. Seine
Jumièges
ROUEN
R. Risle
Pont-Audemer
Gd. Couronne
Lyons-la-Forêt
Bonneville-
-sur-Touques
Beuzeville
Montfort-
-sur-Risle
Pont-de-l'Arche
Cormeilles
Pont-Athou
Le Bec
Elbeuf
Les Andelys
R. Epte
St. Clair-
-sur-Epte
LISIEUX
Brionne
Louviers
Ecos
6
Thiberville
R. Touques
Bernay
Beaumont-
-le Roger
4
Gaillon
La Roche-Guyon
Autheuil
Vernon
ivarot
Orbec
Préaux
Beaumesnil
ÉVREUX
Pacey-
-sur-Eure
Mantes
R. Seine
nery
Meulles
St. Germain-de-
-Montgomery
Broglie
Montreuil-
-l'Argille
Conches
Lyre
Damville
Ivry-la-Bataille
imoutiers
St. Evroul
Gacé
Rugles
Breteuil
Laigle
R. Eure
Tillières
Nonancourt
emes
Verneuil
Dreux
Almenêches
R. Risle
R. Avre
SÉES
Châteauneuf-
-en-Thymerais
Mortagne-
-au-Perche
Rémalard
La Loupe
R. Eure
CHARTRES
Bellême
Le Hu..
Bonneval
Châteaudun
LE MANS
0   10   20   30   40   50 Miles

illiam the Conqueror.
reux. 5. Sées. 6. Lisieux. 7. Coutances.

II. England and Normandy in the time of William the Conqueror.

INDEX

Abenon, 270

Abernethy, pact of, 227, 241

Abingdon, abbey of, 241

Adela, d. of William the Conqueror, 393–395

Adelaide, sister of William the Conqueror, 380

Adeliza, ?d. of William the Conqueror, 393–395

Adso the *vicomte*, 143

Ælfgar, e. of Mercia, 172
  Edith, d. of, 183
  Edwin (q.v.), son of
  Morcar (q.v.), son of

Æthelric, bp. of Selsey, 308, 324

Æthelwig, abbot of Evesham, 232, 273, 306

Agatha, ?d. of William the Conqueror, 393–395

Aimeri, *vicomte* of Thouars, 248

Airan, 49, 91

Alan III, c. of Brittany, 29, 33, 34, 37–40, 163, 178, 231, 408, 409

Alan IV (Fergant), c. of Brittany, 401–403

Alan the Black, c. of Brittany, lord of Richmond, 267, 268

Alan the Red, c. of Brittany, lord of Richmond, 267–269, 286

Aldred, archbp. of York, 182, 183, 204, 206, 207, 249, 267, 367

Alençon, 42, 58–60, 372, 379–380, 384–386, 389

Alexander II, Pope, 187–190, 260, 318, 337, 340, 341

Alfred the atheling, 144, 145, 162–164, 171, 375

Alfred the giant, 26, 141

Alfred of Lincoln, 268

Almenèches, monastery at, 91, 113, 114

Ambrières, 71, 174

Angers, *see* Anjou

Anglo-Norman history,
  earlier interpretations of, 3–7
  evidence for, 10–12

Anglo-Norman kingdom,
  character of, 263–264

defence of, 211–244
establishment of, 181–218
unity of, 222–224, 264, 284

Anglo-Saxon Chronicle, 10, 255, 347–350, 367, 371, 412, 413

Anjou, 54–76, 110, 191, 223, 228–244, 383–391, 402–407
  annals of, 233, 244, 384–388, 402–407
  counts of, *see* Fulk Nerra; Fulk le Rechin; Geoffrey Martel

Anschitil the *vicomte*, 28, 93

Anselm, St, 116, 120, 127, 320, 362

Apulia, 90, 203, 247, 356

Archdeacons,
  in England, 330, 331
  in Normandy, 27, 122, 123

Argentan, 46

Ari the learned, 24

Arnold, bp. of Le Mans, 223, 339

Arques, 25, 26–27, 64–66, 374, 386–390
  count of, *see* William
  vicomtes of, *see* Godfrey; Rainald

Arras, monastery of St Vedast at, 110

Arundel, rape of, 272

Ascelin of Caen, 362

Athelstan, k. of England, 159

Auffay, family of, 65
  Gulbert of, 65

Avejot, bp. of Le Mans, 58

Avranches, 19
  bishopric of, 19, 90, 119–132, 151, 186, 209
  bishops of, *see* John; Michael

Avranchin, 20, 26, 27, 54, 93, 144
  vicomtes of, *see* Hugh, e. of Chester; Rannulf Meschin; Richard

Avre, river, 17, 25

Axholme, 219

Azzo d'Este, c. of Maine, 223–224
  Gersendis, wife of, 223, 224

Bailleul, Roussel of, 260

Baldwin IV, c. of Flanders, 35, 77, 392, 393
  Judith, d. of, *see* Tosti
  Ogiva, wife of, 77, 393

Baldwin V, c. of Flanders, 46, 75–80, 175, 180–182, 188, 212, 392, 393
  Adela, wife of, 76, 392, 393
  Matilda, wife of William the Conqueror (q.v.), d. of
Baldwin VI, c. of Flanders, 224
  Arnulf, son of, 224
  Baldwin, son of, 224
  Richildis, wife of, 224, 225
Baldwin, bp. of Évreux, 320
Baldwin, chancellor of King Philip I, 145
Barbastro, 'crusade' of, 260
Barfleur, 18
Barking, 207, 212, 252
Bastembourg, Thurstan of, 88
Battle Abbey, 199, 328
Baudry of Bourgueil, 200
Bauptois, 27
Bayeux, 17, 19, 22, 72, 176, 304
  abbey of Saint-Vigor at, 114, 117
  bishopric of, 19, 88, 113, 119, 149, 330
  bishops of, see Hugh; Odo
Bayeux Tapestry, 10, 175–177, 182, 190, 195, 200, 216
Beaufou, Roger of, 151
Beaumont, family of, 86–87, 102, 137, 283
  Roger of, 85, 102, 113, 115, 137, 143, 144, 151, 185, 394
  Robert of, son of Roger, 85, 86, 186, 199, 203, 269, 286, 287, 357
  Henry of, son of Roger, 85, 86, 217, 269, 286
  see also Vieilles, Humphrey of
Beaumont-en-Auge, monastery at, 112, 117
Beaumontel, 90
Beaurain, 176
Bec (Le), abbey of, 86, 87, 116–118, 126–130, 320
  see also Anselm; Herluin; Lanfranc
Bede, 322, 328
Bellême, family of, 42, 57, 58
  see also Mabel; William Talvas; Yves, bp. of Sées
Bellencombre, 92, 99, 100
Bengeworth, 307
Berkhampstead, 206, 247, 252
Berkshire, 206
Bernay, abbey of, 89, 91, 105, 109, 112–115, 327

Bessin, 18, 26, 27
  vicomtes of, see Rannulf I; Rannulf II; Rannulf Meschin
Bessin, Guillaume, 3, 331
Bishoprics,
  in England, 325–331
  in Normandy, 19, 23, 27, 118–127, 319, 321
Blancalanda, 242, 403–407
Bleddyn, 212, 225
Blois, 56
  Odo, c. of, 57, 68
  Stephen, c. of, 393–395
  Adela, d. of William the Conqueror (q.v.), wife of Stephen
Böhmer, Heinrich, 4
Bolbec, 92
Bonneville-sur-Touques, 114, 176, 184, 229
Borbillon, 51
Bosham, 167, 175
Bouard, Michel de, 4, 370, 391
Bourgueil, monastery at, 110
Bramber, rape of, 272
Brand, abbot of Peterborough, 221, 324
Brecknock, 37
Brémule, battle of, 278
Bresle, river, 17, 18
Breteuil, 70, 90, 102
  Roger of, e. of Hereford, 231–234, 296
  William of, 237, 238
Bretons in England, 230–233, 267–269
Brian, c. of Brittany, 199, 267
Brionne, 25, 34, 41, 55, 70, 75, 278, 384–386, 389
  see also Gilbert of, the Count
Briouze, William of, 272, 336
Bristol, 213, 311
Brittany, 18, 54, 191, 230–235, 402–407
  annals of, 233, 234, 402–407
  counts of, see Alan III; Alan IV; Alan the Black; Alan the Red; Brian; Eudo of Penthièvre; Geoffrey; Geoffrey 'Granon'; Hoel of Cornouailles; Stephen
  feudalism in, 178
  Solomon, k. of, 18
Brooke, Z. N., 4, 342, 343
Bruges, 79
Buckinghamshire, 172
Bundi the staller, 290
Burghill, 167

Burgundy, 17, 110, 191
Bury St Edmunds, abbey of, 251, 258
  Baldwin, abbot of, 215
Butler, office of, 146
  see also Ivry, Hugh of

Caen, 48, 72, 80, 111, 117, 134, 150, 244,
    304, 360–363, 369, 383, 394, 396
  councils at, 51–52, 131, 172, 185, 331–
    333
  origins of, 56
  William's connexions with, 56
  see also Holy Trinity abbey; St
    Stephen's abbey
Cambridge, 214, 216
Cambridgeshire, 166, 304
  Picot (q.v.), sheriff of
  Survey of, 350
Canossa, 338
Canterbury, 205, 329, 337, 397
  archbishops of, see Lanfranc; Robert
    of Jumièges; Stigand
  primacy of, 259, 321–323, 334
  province of, 317–345
  see also St Augustine's abbey
Carlyle, Thomas, 6
Carmen de Hastingae Proelio, 200, 255,
    398–400
Cartularies, 11–12, 430–434
Cassel, battle of, 201, 225, 267
Cassian, John, 126
Castellum Vallium, 234, 405, 406
Castles, 42, 140–142, 215–217
Cathedrals,
  of Old Foundation, 329
  monastic, 329
Cathedrals, capitular organization of,
  in England, 329, 330
  in Normandy, 123–127
Catherine, St, relics of, 111
Cavalry, use of, 49, 198–203
Celibacy of clergy, 332, 333
Cerisy-la-Forêt, abbey of, 23, 105, 109,
    113–117, 150
Chabannes, Adémar of, 22, 256, 409, 410
Chamberlain, office of, 146, 291
  see also Tancarville
Chambrais (now Broglie), 89
Chancellor, office of, 146–148, 292, 293
  in England, 147, 292, 293
  in France, 146

Charlemagne, 261
Charles III, Emperor, 16, 28
Charters, 10–12
  English, 10, 430–434
  Norman, 11, 12, 430–434
  see also Writs
Chartres, 16, 26, 46, 71, 74
  cathedral of, 410
  see also Saint-Père de Chartres
Château-du-Loir, 58, 59, 224, 385–389
  Haimo of, 58
Château-Gonthier, family of, 57
Châteauneuf-en-Thimerais, 237
Châtillon (Conches) monastery at, 96,
    112–114, 117, 150
Chaumont, 357
Chepstow, 242
Cherrieux, 141
Chertsey, abbey at, 258
Cheshire, 219
Chester, 220, 303
  earldom of, 328
  earls of, see Gerbod; Hugh
Chichester, 167
  bishopric of, 325, 328, 329
Childerich III, 256
Chocques, 267
  Gunfrid of, 267
  Sigar of, 267
Christina, d. of Edgar the atheling, 171
Christus vincit, 154
Cinglais, district of, 48, 115
Civitate, battle of, 188
Clare, family of, see Richard fitz Gilbert
Claville, 270
Clay, C. T., 392, 402, 403
Clères, family of, 42, 95, 96, 270
  Roger of, 95, 150
  Gilbert of, 95
Cleveland, 226
Cluny, abbey of, 23, 107, 108, 117, 118,
    124, 125, 328
  Hugh, abbot of, 326
  Maieul, abbot of, 108
  Odilon, abbot of, 44
Cnut the Great, k. of England, 160–163,
    167, 372
  Emma (q.v.), wife of
  Harold 'Harefoot' (q.v.), son of
  Harthacnut (q.v.), son of
Cnut IV, k. of Denmark, 218, 232, 346,
    347, 356

Cocherel, 89
Coinage, see Mints
Colchester, 217
Colleville, 267
Comet, 181
Commines, Robert de, e. of Northumbria, 214
'Companions of the Conqueror', 203n.
Conan II, c. of Brittany, 178, 179, 230, 408–410
Conches, see Châtillon
Conrad II, Emperor
Constable, office of, 146, 291
  see also Montfort-sur-Risle
Constance, d. of William the Conqueror, 393–395
  see also Alan IV, c. of Brittany
Constance, wife of Robert I, k. of France, 29
Constantinople, 247, 266
Constitutio Domus Regis, 289–291
Conteville, vicomté of, 142
  see also Herluin, vicomte of
Coquainvilliers, 88
Cormeilles, monastery at, 112, 113, 117
Cornouailles, see Hoel
Cornwall, 166, 213, 267, 272, 294
Coronation,
  of Harold Godwineson, 182
  of William the Conqueror, 206, 207, 247–264
Cotentin, 18, 26, 27, 92, 141, 144, 160
  see also Nigel, vicomte of
Coudres, 161
Couesnon, river, 17, 18, 25, 178
Coulombes, abbey of, 146, 149
Councils, ecclesiastical,
  in England, 331–336
  in Normandy, 129–132, 331–336
Count, office of, in Normandy, 23–26, 138, 139
  comparison of, with earldoms in England, 26, 295, 296
Coutances,
  bishopric of, 19, 20
  bishops of, see Geoffrey; Robert
Craon, family of, 57
Creil-sur-Mer, 270
Crépi, Ralph of, 174, 235
  Simon of, 235
  Judith, wife of Simon, 235

Creully, family of, 48, 93, 114, 287
Crispin, family of, 46, 150
  see also Gilbert; Milo; Roger
Croix-Saint-Leuffroi, monastery of, 86, 113, 117
Croth, priory of, 97
Crown-wearings, 255
Crusade, notion of, 187, 188, 260–264
Cuinchy, family of, 267
Cumbria, 225, 226
Curia Regis, 284–288

Danelaw, 20, 159, 165
Darlington, R. R., 4, 343, 344
David, C. W., 401–407
Delisle, L., 3
Denmark, see Cnut IV; Sweyn Estrithson
Derby, 221
Deux-Jumeaux, monastery of, 109
Devon, 91, 213
  Baldwin of Meules (q.v.), sheriff of
Dhondt, J., 383
Die, Hubert of, 340
Dijon, William of, 23, 107–109, 117, 125
Dinant, 178, 216
Dives, river, 184, 190, 193, 210
Dol, 178, 216, 231–236, 338, 401–403
  Riwallon of, 178
Domesday Book, 10, 12, 87, 221, 243, 266, 269, 280, 298, 300, 301, 309–313, 334, 347–354, 373, 394
  character of, 351–353
  controversies respecting, 348
  making of, 348–352
  motives inspiring compilation of, 351–353
Domfront, 58–60, 70, 151, 278, 372, 284–386, 389
'Donation of Constantine', 340
Dorchester, bishopric of, 167, 321, 329
  Ulf (q.v.), bp. of
Dorset, 219
Douvrend, 90
Dover, 88, 168, 169, 205, 207, 216, 372, 397
Dreux, 46, 74
Dreux, c. of the Vexin, 73, 74, 167
  Goda (q.v.), wife of
  Ralph the Timid (q.v.), son of
  Walter, c. of the Vexin (q.v.), son of
Droitwich, 303
Dublin, 173

Ducal court in Normandy, 148–151
Duchesne, André, 3
Dudo of Saint-Quentin, 22
Dugdale, William, 3
Dunstan, 107
Durham, 214, 226, 228, 240–241
  bishopric of, 324, 328, 329, 342
  bishops of, see Walchere; William
  Simeon of, 10

Eadmer, 10, 255
Earl, office of,
  in pre-Conquest England, 165, 166
  change in character after Norman
    conquest, 294–296
  comparison of, with Norman counts,
    26, 295, 296
East Anglia, 166, 172, 221, 268, 274
Échauffour, 141
  Géré of, 42, 88
  Robert, son of Géré, 408, 413, 414
Écquetôt, Osbern of, 97
Edgar the atheling, 171, 182, 205–221,
  225–229, 236, 251, 256, 356, 375
Edith, d. of Earl Godwine, wife of
  Edward the Confessor, 166–168, 205
Edmund Ironsides, k. of England, 171
Edric the Wild, 212, 219
Edward the atheling, 171, 172, 411, 412
  Agatha, wife of, 171
  children of, see Christina; Edgar the
    atheling; Margaret
Edward the Confessor, 74, 78
  birth and parentage, 160
  exile in Normandy, 144, 164
  king of the English, 164–180, 372
  favours Normans, 166–170
  relations with Earl Godwine, 164–171,
    411–413
  relations with Harold Godwineson,
    166–180
  bequeathes kingdom to William the
    Conqueror, 168–170
  relations with church, 166–170, 259,
    337
  relations with Scandinavia, 164–180
  court of, see Witan
  household of, 290, 291
  scriptorium of, 147, 292–294
  writs of, 293–295
  death of, 181, 182, 252, 396
  cult of, 253–254, 257, 412, 413

Edwin, e. of Mercia, 179, 183, 190–193,
  204, 208, 213, 222, 285, 295, 324,
  395
Elmham, bishopric of, 324
  Æthelmær, bp. of, 324
  see also Herfast
Ely, 221, 222, 298
  abbey of, 274
  trials relating to, 306–308
  Simeon, abbot of, 325
  see also Inquisitio Eliensis
Émalleville, 270
Emma, d. of Duke Richard I, 128, 160,
  161, 165, 167
  see also Cnut the Great; Ethelred II
Empire, eastern, 7, 203, 251, 305, 336
Empire, western, see Conrad II; Henry
  III; Henry IV; Otto II
England,
  unity of, 180
  divisions in, 180
  O.E. aristocracy in, 265–271
  church in, before 1066, 4, 5, 9, 322–
    327, 343–345
  earldoms in 1065–1080, 293–296
  military organization of, before 1066,
    275–279
  introduction of feudalism in, 265–283
  fiscal organization of, 298–303
  trade of, 302–303
  wealth of, 297–304
  cultural achievements of, 343, 345
  towns in, 302, 303, 313, 314
  hundreds of, 299, 300, 314, 315, 349,
    350
  shires of, 305–309, see also Sheriff
  peasantry of, 310–313
  prelacy in, 317–331
  Normanization of, 332–335
  bishops in, 324–335
  change in sees of bishops, 328, 329
  monasteries of, 324, 325
  persisting traditions in, 275–279, 289–
    316, 319, 320, 375, 376
Enguerrand II, c. of Ponthieu, 63, 380,
  388
Epte, river, 17, 235, 358
Erchembald the vicomte, 26, 97, 187
  Gulbert, son of, 97
Ermerfrid, bp. of Sitten, 69, 191
  penitentiary of, 191, 192
Ernald of Bayeux, 134, 135

Ernost, bp. of Rochester, 342
Esclavelles, 65
Essex, 166, 268, 304
Eudo the Steward (q.v.), sheriff of
Ethelred II, k. of England, 21, 159–162, 167, 171
  Alfred the atheling (q.v.), son of
  Edward the Confessor (q.v.), son of
  Emma (q.v.), wife of
Eu, 17, 18, 26, 27, 76, 176
  counts of, see Robert; William
  see also Hugh, bp. of Lisieux; Lesceline
Eudo, son of Spiriwic, 268
Eudo of Penthièvre, c. of Brittany, 29, 39, 178, 179, 231
  Alan the Black (q.v.), son o
  Alan the Red (q.v.), son of
  Brian (q.v.), son of
  Stephen (q.v.), son of
Eudo the Steward, 48, 290, 319
Eure, river, 89
Eustace, c. of Boulogne, 66, 168, 172, 212, 266, 267, 269
  Goda (q.v.), wife of
Evesham abbey, 298, 328
  Æthelwig (q.v.), abbot of
Évreçin, 27, 68, 97, 387
Évreux, 17, 32, 33
  bishopric of, 19, 119–132, 209
  bishops of, see Baldwin; Hugh; William
  counts of, see Richard; William
  monastery of Saint-Taurin at, 91, 124
  see also Robert, archbp. of Rouen
Ewias, Harold, 167
Exeter, 213, 214, 216, 217, 279, 372
  bishopric of, 293, 329
  bishops of, see Leofric; Osbern
Exmes, see Hiémois
Exning, 232
'Exon Domesday', 351–354

Fageduna, 232
Falaise, 15, 46, 48, 72, 141, 203, 379–381, 410
Falkirk, 241
Fauroux, M., 3
Fécamp, abbey of, 23, 105–117, 125, 126, 149, 162, 166, 186, 209, 210, 284, 303, 320, 321
  abbots of, see William of Dijon; John; William of Rots

Ferrières, family of, 89, 92
  Walkelin of, 42, 88
Fervaques, 270
Feudalism,
  growth of in Normandy, 27, 84–103
  origins of in England, 100, 103, 273–283
  variations of, 84, 98, 100, 103, 275–283
'Feudal Incidents', 97, 275
Fitz-Osbern, family of, 89, 90, 361
  Osbern the Steward (q.v.)
  Emma (q.v.), wife of Osbern
  William fitz Osbern (q.v.), son of
  see also Bretueil; Herfast
Five-hide estates, 276–279
Flanders, 35, 46, 51, 76–80, 106–109, 169–182, 223–225, 288–244
  counts of, see Baldwin IV; Baldwin V; Robert le Frison
  see also Matilda, wife of William the Conqueror
Flavigny, Hugh of, 33
Flemings in England, 266, 267
Fliche, A., 401
Flodoard, 16
Floques, 270
Florence, abbey of St Mary at, 121
'Florence of Worcester', 10, 182, 352
Fontanelle, see Saint-Wandrille
Fontenay, abbey of, 112–115, 118, 140, 287
France, 7, 9, 16, 28–30, 44, 47, 53–78, 160–162, 189, 249, 253
  kings of, see Henry I; Hugh Capet; Lothair; Louis d'Outre-Mer; Louis VI; Philip I; Robert II
Frankpledge, 314
Freckenham, 307, 309
Freeman, E. A., 3, 6, 396–403
Fresnay, 115, 228
Fulbert, grandfather of William the Conqueror, 15, 379–381
Fulford, battle of, 193, 198, 396
Fulk Nerra, c. of Anjou, 35
Fulk le Rechin, c. of Anjou, 228–234, 238–244, 347, 401–408
'Fyrd', 278, 279

Gacé, Ralph of, 33, 40–43, 46
Gael, lordship of, 231
  see also Ralph of Gael

Galbraith, V. H., 134, 348, 350, 353
Gateshead, 240
Gâtinais, 230
Gelds, 299–302
Gembloux, Sigebert of, 383
Geoffrey, bp. of Coutances, 119–132,
    206, 207, 232, 249, 269, 303, 306–
    310, 319, 320, 335
Geoffrey Boterel, c. of Brittany, 231
Geoffrey, c. of Aquitaine, 234
Geoffrey, c. of Brittany, 29, 35
    Hawisa, wife of, 29
Geoffrey Flaitel, bp. of Lisieux, 320
Geoffrey 'Granon', c. of Brittany, 231–
    234
Geoffrey Martel, c. of Anjou, 56–78, 173,
    384–391
Gérard de Broigne, 23, 106, 107
Gerard the chancellor, 293, 359
Gerberoi, siege of, 238, 239, 279, 405–407
Gerbod, e. of Chester, 267
    Frederic, brother of, 267
Gersendis of Maine, 223, 224
Gervais, bp. of Le Mans and archbp. of
    Rheims, 58, 71, 144, 384–387, 389
Ghent, abbey of St Peter at, 23, 106
Giffard, Walter, 68, 269, 386
Gilbert of Brionne, the Count, 25, 37–41,
    45, 91, 116
    Baldwin of Meules (q.v.), son of
    Richard fitz Gilbert (q.v.), son of
Gilbert Crispin, abbot of Westminster,
    46, 127, 327
Gilbert Crispin, 46, 150
Gilbert 'de Gand', 267
Gilbert Maminot, bp. of Lisieux, 319,
    359, 362
Giso, bp. of Wells, 215, 258
Gisors, 17, 21
Giverville, 186
Glastonbury, abbey of, 129, 274, 325, 327
    Æthelnoth, abbot of, 325
    Thurstan, abbot of, 129, 274, 325,
    327
Glos-la-Ferrières, Bjarni of, 42
Gloucester, 168, 213, 286, 334, 348, 354
    see also Serlo
Gloucestershire, 87, 167
    Durand, sheriff of, 297
Goda, sister of Edward the Confessor, 171
    see also Dreux, c. of the Vexin; Eustace,
    c. of Boulogne

Godfrey, the Count, 25
    Gilbert of Brionne (q.v.), son of
Godfrey, vicomte of Arques, 94
Godwine, e. of Wessex, 6, 78, 163–171,
    411–413
    Gytha, wife of, 213
    children of, see Edith; Gyrth; Harold;
    Leofwine; Sweyn; Tosti
Goscelin, vicomte of Rouen, 94, 111, 115,
    140
    Emmeline, wife of, 111, 115
Goscelin of Saint-Bertin, 254
Gospatric, e. of Northumbria, 214, 215,
    218, 226, 295
Grandmesnil, family of, 114, 117, 137
    Hugh of, 207, 238, 269
    Aubrey, son of Hugh, 238
    Yves, son of Hugh, 238
    Robert of, 114, 117
Graverie, 135
Graville-Sainte-Honorine, 217, 270
Great Hampton, 307
Gregory VII, Pope, 187, 318–345
    character of, 341–342
    demands fealty from William the
    Conqueror, 340, 341
    policy of, 256, 257, 318–341
Grestain, abbey of Notre-Dame at, 112,
    113, 117, 321
Griffith-ap-Llewellyn, 172, 183, 241
Grimoald of Plessis, 48, 102
Guazo, 97
Guernsey, 150
Gundulf, bp. of Rochester, 327, 329
Gunhild, d. of Harold Godwineson, 268
Gunnor, wife of Duke Richard I, 34, 88,
    145
    her sisters and nieces, 89–90
Guy, bp. of Amiens, 200
Guy, c. of Ponthieu, 67, 176, 177
Guy 'of Burgundy', 31, 38, 47–55, 87,
    141
Guy-William, c. of Aquitaine, 67, 71
Gyrth, 172, 199, 200

Hague, 27
Haimo, 'dentatus', 290
    the Steward, son of, 290, 297
Halberstadt, 119
Halphen, L., 383, 385, 401
Hampshire, 205
    Hugh of Port-en-Bessin, sheriff of, 297

Harfleur, 17

Harold Godwineson, k. of England, 6,
182–241, 258, 304, 394, 396–400
takes part in rebellion of 1051, 167–169
relations with Edward the Confessor,
166–180, 252
takes oath to William the Conqueror,
175–178
character of, 182, 184
military abilities of, 194
campaign against Harold Hardraada,
193, 194
campaign in Sussex, 197–198
at battle of Hastings, 198–201
death of, 201
sons of, 213, 267
Gunhild, d. of, 268

Harold Hardraada, k. of Norway, 173,
180, 181, 183, 190–194

Harold 'Harefoot', k. of England, 163,
164

'Harrying of the North', 219–221, 372

Harthacnut, k. of England, 163, 164, 411

Haskins, C. H., 3, 98

Haspres, 106

Hastings, 196, 216, 217, 272, 396
battle of, 49, 198–202
rape of, 272

Havre (Le), 92, 217, 269

Hawisa, d. of Duke Richard I, 29

Hayling Island, 209

Hayward, John, 367, 376

Helions Bumpstead, 268

Héllean, Tihel of, 268

Henry I, k. of France, 29, 38, 44–53, 173,
383–391, 408, 411

Henry I, k. of England, 254, 305, 306

Henry II, k. of England, 54

Henry III, Emperor, 78, 337

Henry IV, Emperor, 188

Henry of Beaumont, see Beaumont

Herbert 'Wake-Dog', c. of Maine, 57
Gersendis (q.v.), d. of

Herbert II, c. of Maine, 73, 74, 173, 393

Hereford, 167, 212, 216, 232, 241, 272,
277, 294, 295
bishopric of, 260, 329
bishop of, see Robert Losinga
earldom of, see Breteuil, Roger of;
Ralph the Timid; William fitz
Osbern

Hereward the Wake, 221, 222, 267, 324

Herfast, chancellor and bp. of Elmham,
147, 293, 313, 327, 329

Herfast, father of Osbern the Steward,
89, 90, 145

Herleve, mother of William the Conqueror, 15, 31, 112, 379–382
see also Fulbert (father); Herluin
(husband); Odo, bp. of Bayeux
(son); Osbern (brother); Robert I,
dk. of Normandy; Robert, c. of
Mortain (son); Walter (brother)

Herluin, abbot of Le Bec, 116, 117, 132

Herluin, vicomte of Conteville, 15, 112,
381
Fredesensis, wife of, 382
Herleve (q.v.), wife of
sons of, see Odo; Robert

Hertfordshire, 304
Ilbert, sheriff of, 306

Hesdins, Arnulf of, 267

Hiémois, 25, 27, 32, 46, 94, 95

Hildebrand, see Gregory VII, Pope

Hoel, bp. of Le Mans, 242

Hoel of Cornouailles, c. of Brittany,
231–235, 242, 401–404
Alan IV, c. of Brittany (q.v.), son of

Holy Sepulchre, 36

Holy Trinity, Caen, abbey of, 80, 109,
111, 149, 185, 186, 321

Holy Trinity, Rouen, abbey of, 23, 63, 87,
110–115, 117, 124, 145, 146, 209,
287, 391
Isembard, abbot of, 128

Honours,
establishment of, in England, 273–283
organization of, 280–281

Hope, 167

Horses, transport of, by sea, 202, 203

Housecarls, 191–194, 199, 202

Hugh I, archbp. of Rouen, 85, 90, 107

Hugh, bp. of Bayeux, 35, 39, 42, 90

Hugh, bp. of Évreux, 143

Hugh, bp. of Lisieux, 69, 119–132, 144,
150, 209, 319, 335

Hugh IV, c. of Maine, 57–59, 73, 144

Hugh V, c. of Maine, 223

Hugh, e. of Chester, 26, 54, 186, 242, 269,
272, 295

Hugh Bardo, 97

Hugh Capet, 28, 256

Hugh the Great, 28

Hugleville, Richard of, 65

Humber, river, 180, 190–194, 218
Hundred courts, 305–310, 313, 314
Huntingdon, 166, 214, 232

Inquisitio Eliensis, 349
Inquisitio Geldi, 300
Investitures controversy, 254–258, 342
Ireland, 173, 259, 323
Isle of Wight, 190, 191, 272, 356
Italy, 188, 191, 243
    Normans in, 7, 32, 102, 188, 203
Ivry, 26, 35, 42, 90, 102
    Hugh of, 146, 150, 291
    Roger of, 237
    see also Hugh, bp. of Bayeux; Rodulf

Jerusalem, 35, 36
Jews, 313, 314
John XV, Pope, 159
John, abbot of Fécamp, 108, 111, 112,
    303, 320, 367
John, bp. of Avranches, and archbp. of
    Rouen, 90, 102, 119–132, 144, 151,
    318, 319, 326, 336, 337
Jouy, 90
Judhael of Totnes, 268
Judith of Brittany, 15, 29, 89, 109, 115
    see also Richard II, dk. of Normandy
Jumièges, abbey of, 16, 23, 63, 86, 105–
    118, 127, 128, 134, 146, 176, 209,
    210, 383
    Gontard, abbot of, 358
    see also Robert of, archbp. of Canter-
    bury
Jumièges, William of, 11, 85, 91, 124–
    128, 209, 251, 256, 368, 379–394,
    397
Jurisdiction,
    ducal, 133, 150–153
    royal, 305–310
    ecclesiastical, 330, 331
    see also Curia Regis; ducal court;
    hundred courts; shire courts; trials
Jury, use of, 309, 310
Justiciars, 305–307

Kent, 166, 172, 205, 207, 212, 213, 272,
    294, 307
    earldom of, *see* Odo
    Haimo, sheriff of, *see* Haimo the
    Steward
Kentford, trial at, 307–309

Knighthood,
    characteristics of, 97, 273–274
    obligations of, 97, 273
Knights, 97, 98
    differences among, 97, 98, 275–278
    enfeoffed, 275–277
    stipendiary, 274–275
    serve as cavalry, 203, 204, 277
    serve on foot, 278
Knights' fees, 275–277
Knowles, M. D., 4, 115–118, 343–345

Lacman, 21
La Cressonière, 270
La Ferté-Macé, family of, 223
    William of, 223, 381
Laigle, 141
Lambert of Lens, 380
Lanfranc,
    early career of, 79, 116, 128, 137, 138
    prior of Le Bec, 79, 116, 137
    abbot of St Stephen's, Caen, 186, 308
    archbp. of Canterbury, 254, 258, 318–
    323
    ecclesiastical policy of, 259, 318–345
    convokes councils, 331–335
    vindicates primacy of Canterbury,
    321–323
    co-operates with William the Con-
    queror, 286, 298, 308, 359
    regent for the king, 232, 233, 279, 359
    relations with English bishoprics, 321–
    333
    relations with English monasteries,
    321–333
    barony of, 277
    consuetudines of, 328
    character of, 318, 319
Latouche, R., 383, 401
Laudes Regiae, 154, 249–250, 255, 261–262
Laval, family of, 57
    Guy de, 86
La Vespière, 270
Laycock, trial at, 284, 286, 336
Le Homme, 141
Leicester, 87, 303
Le Mans, 17, 59, 174, 223, 224, 228, 229,
    386, 387, 402–404
    bishopric of, 58, 339
    bishops of, *see* Arnold; Avejot; Ger
    vais; Hoel; Siffroi; Vougrin

Le Mans, *contd.*
see also Saint-Vincent; Saint-Pierre-
de-la-Couture
Leo IX, Pope, 56, 76–78, 131, 386
Leobwin, 240
Leofric, bp. of Exeter, 326, 328
Leofric, e. of Mercia, 166, 168, 171
Leofwine, Godwineson, 169, 172, 199, 200
Le Prévost, A., 3
Les Andelys, 17
Lesceline, countess of Eu, 97, 112, 124,
150, 209
Lessay, abbey of Holy Trinity at, 112,
114, 125
Lewes, 328
priory at, 328
rape of, 272
Lichfield, bishopric of, 321, 324, 328
Leofwine, bp. of, 324, 329
Liége, 121, 129
Liege-homage, 281
Lieuvin, district of, 89
Ligulf, 240
Lillebonne, 17, 184
council of, 51–52, 140, 321, 331–335
Limfjord, 356
Lincoln, 214, 216, 278, 303
bishopric of, 329
bishop of, see Remigius
Lincolnshire, 190, 219, 268, 274
Lire, monastery at, 112, 113, 117, 125
Lisieux, 19, 207
bishopric of, 19, 119–132
bishops of, see Gerard; Gilbert; Hugh;
Roger
councils at, 69, 131, 132, 331–335
Gilbert, archdeacon of, 187
Lobineau, G. A., 403
Loire river, 57
London, 168, 182, 195, 197–207, 216,
303, 329, 372, 396–399
bishops of, see Maurice; Robert;
William
councils at, 325, 332–335
strategic importance of, 205–206
Tower of, 207, 216
trade of, 303, 304
Longueville-sur-Scie, 92, 269
Lothian, 225, 227
Lothair, k. of France, 21, 106, 107
Louis d'Outre-Mer, k. of France, 21, 23,
28, 159

Louis VI, k. of France, 254
Loyd, L. C., 270, 330
Lugdunensis Secunda, 18, 19
Lyons, 17, 323, 338, 339
Gebuin, archbp. of, 323, 338, 339

Mabel of Bellême, 60, 414–415
see also Roger II of Montgomery;
William Talvas
Mabillon, Jean, 12
Magnus, k. of Norway, 164, 165
Mainard, 23, 107
Maine, 57–61, 70–73, 86, 110, 173–175,
191, 223–244, 279, 373, 383–391,
401–408
counts of, see Azzo d'Este; Herbert
'Wake-Dog'; Herbert II; Hugh
IV; Hugh V; Walter
Malcolm III (Canmore), k. of Scotland,
190–192, 213–228, 347, 406, 408–
410
Malet, Robert, 269, 270, 297
William, 217
'Malfosse', 201
Malmesbury, William of, 6, 10, 149, 184,
254, 305, 380
Manneville, Geoffrey of, 269, 297
Mantes, 17, 357, 358, 360
Manzikiert, battle of, 260
Margaret (St), d. of Edward the
atheling, 171, 219, 323
see also Malcolm III, k. of Scotland
Marmoutier, abbey of, 71, 147, 151, 185,
328, 391
Bartholomew, abbot of, 185
Marseilles, 17
Marshall, office of, 148
Martainville, 87
Matilda, wife of William the Conqueror
47, 75–80, 185, 213, 236, 243, 249
335, 369–370, 391–395
see also Baldwin V, c. of Flanders
Matilda, d. of William the Conqueror,
394, 395
Maud, d. of Rannulf, *vicomte* of the
Avranchin, 93
Maudit, family of, 300
Mauger, archbp. of Rouen, 38–43, 69,
70, 116, 119, 120, 131, 148
Maurice, chancellor and bp. of London,
293, 315, 357

Maurilius, archbp. of Rouen, 69, 120–132, 134, 143, 209
Mayenne, family of, 57, 71, 174
  Geoffrey of, 71, 174–176, 223, 224, 228
Melfi, synod of, 188
Mercenaries, employment of, 191–193, 213, 215, 279, 280, 347, 348
Mercia, earldom of, 165–168, 171–173, 180
  earls of, see Ælfgar; Edwin; Leofric
Mesnières, 270
Messina, 221
Meules, Baldwin of, 91, 113, 217, 297
Mezidon, 49
Michael, bp. of Avranches, 209
Middlesex, 297
  Sheriff of, see Manneville, Geoffrey of
Milo Crispin, 116
Milton, John, 6
Mints, 133–135, 304
Miracula Sancti Wulframni, 409, 410
Monasteries,
  in England, 322–328
  in Normandy, 105–118
Monastic cathedrals, 328, 329
Mondidier, Ralph of, 208
Money-fief, 280
'Monk of Caen', 358–363, 380, 381
Montacute, 220
Mont Barbet, 71, 174
Montbrai, Robert of, e. of Northumbria, 296
Monte Gargano, 36
Montfort-sur-Risle, family of, 88, 92, 144, 291, 361
  Hugh I of, 42
  Hugh II of, 88, 203, 207, 217, 291
  Hugh III of, 269
  Robert III of, 283
  see also Bastembourg, Thurstan of
Montgomery, family of, 32, 91, 92, 114, 137, 283, 361
  Roger I of, 91, 95
  Roger II of (q.v.)
  Robert of Bellême, son of Roger II, 237
Montivilliers, nunnery of, 109–113, 125, 150
Montreuil, 176, 230

Montreuil l'Argille, 141
Mont-Saint-Michel (Le), abbey of, 16, 21, 23, 34, 71, 88, 105–117, 124, 140, 149, 151, 162, 327
  Rannulf, abbot of, 151
Mora, the, 190
Morcar, e. of Northumbria, 179, 180, 183, 193, 204, 208, 213, 214, 222, 285, 295, 324
Mortain, 26
  counts of, see Robert; William Werlenc
Mortemer,
  battle of, 53, 67–76, 80, 103, 171, 173, 383, 389
  family of, 68, 99
  Hugh of, 102
  Roger of, 100
Mouliherne, 59, 384–386
Moulins, 67
Murdrum fine, 314, 315
Musset, L., 4

Nassandres, 270
Neufchâtel-en-Bray, 68
Neufchâtel-sur-Aisne, 386
Neufmarché, family of, 37, 65
  Bernard of, 37
  Geoffrey of, 65
  see also Turchetil
Neustria, 19–28
Newcastle-on-Tyne, 241
New Forest, 371–373
New Minster, abbey of, 324
  Ælfwig, abbot of, 324
  Wulfric, abbot of, 325
Nicaea, 37, 409
Nicholas II, Pope, 76, 80
Nicholas, abbot of Saint-Ouen, 32, 38, 41, 336, 362
Nigel, vicomte of the Cotentin, 39, 48, 54, 92, 140–142, 150, 375
Nonancourt, 17, 227
Norfolk, 232–234, 297
  earl of, see Ralph of Gael
  sheriff of, see Roger Bigot
Norgate, Kate, 401
Norman conquest,
  contrasted interpretations of, 2–4
  propaganda respecting, 4–6
Normandy,
  annals of, 11
  unity of, 80, 110, 136, 137, 154, 159

Normandy, *contd.*
 divisions in, 17–19, 26, 28
 physical structure of, 17–19
 ducal power in, 22–30, 42, 43, 133–155
 dukes of, *see* Richard I; Richard II;
  Richard III; Robert I; Robert II;
  Rolf; William 'Longsword'; William
  the Conqueror
 Carolingian traditions in, 22–30, 42–
  43
 Scandinavian influence on, 19–22, 29,
  30
 bishoprics of, 19–23, 118–132, 319–321
 monasteries in, 25, 105–132
 ecclesiastical revival in, 105–132
 secular aristocracy in, 27, 97–104,
  281–283
 counts in, 23–26, 294–296
 vicomtes in, 26, 27, 92–95, 136–142,
  295–297
 peasantry in, 52, 310, 311
 place-names of, 22, 23
 fiscal organization of, 134–136
 wealth of, 133–135
 see also William the Conqueror
Norman tractates, 257, 258, 261
Normanville, 270
Northampton, 179
Northamptonshire Geld Roll, 299, 300
Northumbria, earldom of, 165–166, 171,
  179–180, 214–221, 240, 244
 earls of, *see* Commines, Robert de;
  Gospatric; Morcar; Siward; Tosti;
  Walchere; Waltheof
Norway, 190–192
Norwich, 232, 233, 303
 bishopric of, 329
Nottingham, 216, 220

'Oath of Salisbury', 275, 355, 356
Odensee, 356
Odo, bp. of Bayeux, and e. of Kent, 15,
  119–132, 136, 144, 200, 207, 212,
  216, 223, 243–245, 269, 294–296,
  307–309, 319, 335, 359, 360, 381,
  382
Odo, c. of Blois, 67, 68, 381
Oger the Breton, 268
Oise, river, 73
Oissel, trial at, 287
Olaf (St), 21, 23, 161, 173

Orbec,
 honour of, 270
 vicomté of, 142
Ordericus Vitalis, 11, 127, 216, 236, 320,
  358–363, 379–380, 383–395, 401–
  414
Orkneys, 190, 191, 193
Orléans, 17, 57, 62
 council at, 19
Orne, river, 49–51, 53, 384
Osbern the Steward, 34, 37, 42, 89, 90,
  145
 Emma, wife of, 89, 90, 145
 Osbern, bp. of Exeter (q.v.), son of
 William fitz Osbern (q.v.), son of
Osbern, bp. of Exeter, 166
Osbern the *vicomte*, 96
 Ansfrid, son of, 96
Osbern, brother of Sweyn Estrithson, 218
Osbern the moneyer, 136
Osmund, bp. of Salisbury, 293, 315, 327,
  329
Osmund de Bodes, 187
Otto II, Emperor, 253
Otto the Goldsmith, 363

Pacy, 90
Pagi, 27, 28
Palermo, 260
Pantulf, family of, 95, 270
Papacy,
 alliance of, with Normans in Italy,
  187, 188
 supports Norman invasion of England,
  187–188, 192–198
 reforming policy of, 318–345
 relations with William the Conqueror,
  336–343
 see also Alexander II; Gregory VII;
  John XV; Leo IX; Nicholas II;
  Zacharias
Paris, 17, 46, 57, 358
Parish priests, 43, 333, 334
Parker, Matthew, 5
Passais, district oi, 60
Penpont, 231
Perche, 18
Pershore, abbey of, 298
Peterborough, abbey of, 221–222, 255
 abbots of, *see* Brand; Leofric; Turold
'Peters Pence', 336, 340

Pevensey, 195, 216, 397
rape of, 272
Philip I, k. of France, 77, 175, 188, 223–244, 292, 346, 356–361, 401–407
Bertha of Hainault, wife of, 229
Picardy, 106, 110, 191
Picot, sheriff of Cambridgeshire, 298, 306, 307
Pilatins, family of, 304
Pilgrimages, 35, 36
Pinnenden Heath, trial at, 307, 308
Plessis, 102
Poisoning, 408–415
Poissy, 48
Poitiers, William of, 11, 52, 68, 142, 143, 191, 213, 216, 260, 368, 379–393, 401
Poitou, 57, 110, 191
Pommeraye, Jean, 3, 331
Pont-Audemer, Thorold of, 86
Pont-Authou, 88
Ponthieu, 63
counts of, see Enguerrand; Guy
Pontoise, 357
Port-en-Bessin, 297
Hugh of, sheriff of Hampshire, 297
Pouancé, 129
Préaux,
monastery of Saint-Pierre at, 109, 112
nunnery of Saint-Léger, at 109, 112
Prentout, H., 3, 383–385
Provence, 110

Radbod, bp. of Sées, 119
Rainald, c. of Clermont, 67, 68
Rainald, vicomte of Arques, 93
Godfrey, son of, 94
Rainald, dk. of Burgundy, 31
Adeliza, d. of, 31
Guy of Burgundy (q.v.), son of
Ralph of Gael, e. of Norfolk, 232–234, 268, 296
Ralph the staller, 231
Ralph the Timid, e. of Hereford, 167–171, 277, 278
Ramsey, abbey of, 282
Rannulf I, son of Anschitil, vicomte of the Bessin, 48–51, 54, 92, 136
Rannulf II, vicomte of the Bessin, 54, 92, 140
Maud, wife of, 93, see also Richard, vicomte of the Avranchin

Rannulf Meschin, e. of Chester, 93
Rannulf the moneyer, 136, 304
Rectitudines Singularum Personarum, 310
Regenbald, 292, 293
Reinfrid, monk of Evesham, 328
'Relief', 98
Rémalard, 237, 238
Remigius, bp. of Lincoln, 306, 326, 329
Rennes, 129, 178, 216, 231
Marbod, bp. of, 129
Rheims,
council at, 76, 131, 385, 387
Gervais (q.v.), archbp. of
Rhuddlan, Robert of, 242
Ricarville, 270
Riccall, 193, 194
Richard I, dk. of Normandy, 16, 20, 23, 28, 91, 106, 107, 411
Gunnor (q.v.), wife of
Hawisa, d. of, 29
children of, 25
Richard II, dk. of Normandy, 15, 16, 25, 31, 44, 77, 150, 160–162
Judith of Brittany (q.v.), wife of
Papia, wife of, 38
children of, 31
Richard III, dk. of Normandy, 15, 27, 31, 32, 65, 77, 141, 408–409
Adela, wife of, 27, 77
Nicholas, abbot of Saint-Ouen (q.v.), son of
Papia, d. of, 65
Richard, son of William the Conqueror, 371, 393, 394
Richard, c. of Évreux, 85, 113, 294
Godehildis, wife of, 85, see also Tosny
William, c. of Évreux, son of, 269, 272
Richard, vicomte of the Avranchin, 92, 139, 145
Hugh, e. of Chester (q.v.), son of
Maud, d. of, 93
Richard, abbot of Saint-Vannes, 36, 44, 51, 109, 118
Richard fitz Gilbert, 232, 238, 269, 270, 286, 288, 298
Roger, son of, 238
Richard 'Pentecost', 167
Richard, son of Scrob, 167
Richard, son of Tescelin the vicomte, 26, 140
Richmond (Yorks), honour of, 217, 268
see also Alan the Black; Alan the Red

Rievaulx, Ailred of, 412, 413
Risle, river, 87, 89, 113, 126, 199
Riwallon of Wales, 212, 225
Robert II, k. of France, 46, 76, 161, 254
  Constance, wife of, 29
  Adela, d. of, 76
  Henry I, k. of France (q.v.), son of
Robert I, dk. of Normandy, 15, 31–37, 44, 60, 87, 102, 103, 109–111, 144, 161–163, 189
  William the Conqueror (q.v.), son of
  see also Herleve
Robert II, dk. of Normandy, son of William the Conqueror, 73, 143, 174, 185, 236–244, 347, 348, 356, 359–362, 391–393, 404–409
  Richard, son of, 371
Robert I, archbp. of Rouen, 25, 32–39, 119, 120, 128, 161, 164
  Ralph of Gacé (q.v.), son of
  Richard, c. of Évreux (q.v.), son of
  William, son of, 33
Robert, bp. of Coutances, 90
Robert of Jumièges, bp. of London and archbp. of Canterbury, 128, 144, 167–170
Robert Losinga, bp. of Hereford, 327, 348, 349
Robert, c. of Eu, 68, 112, 203, 209, 219, 269, 272, 294, 298
Robert, c. of Mortain, 15, 112, 136–138, 143, 213, 219, 267–269, 272, 294, 360, 381
Robert le Frison, c. of Flanders, 201, 224, 225, 229, 244, 346, 347, 356
Robert of Beaumont, see Beaumont
Robert Bertram, 112, 117, 140
Robert fitz Wimarc, 290
Robert Guiscard, 262
Rochester, 329
  Ernost, bp. of, 342
  Gundulf, bp. of, 307, 329, 342
Rodulf Glaber, 409
Rodulf of Ivry, the Count, 89, 90, 102, 119, 145
  Emma, d. of, see Osbern the Steward
  Hugh, bp. of Bayeux (q.v.), son of
  John, archbp. of Rouen (q.v.), son of
Roger, bp. of Lisieux, 160
Roger of Beaumont, see Beaumont
Roger Bigot, 269, 290, 297

Roger Crispin, 260
Roger, e. of Hereford, see Breteuil
Roger II of Montgomery, 60, 61, 91–95, 99, 136, 143, 144, 186, 237, 239, 269, 285, 287
  vicomte of the Hiémois, 93–95, 139, 144
  e. of Shrewsbury, 94, 295
  Mabel of Bellême (q.v.), wife of
Roger, son of Tancred, 260
Rögnvald, e. of Möre, 16
Rolf (Rollo), dk. of Normandy, 16–17, 20, 21, 77, 92, 106, 153, 159, 392
Rome, 76, 342, 393, see also Papacy
Romney, 205, 396
Rotrou, c. of Mortagne, 238
Rouen, 16–30, 55, 56, 76, 85–87, 93–99, 113, 134, 135, 176, 179, 185, 208–210, 212, 237, 239, 257, 287, 304, 314, 358
  archbishopric of, 16, 32–40, 119–132, 153, 154, 209, 318, 323, 330, 339, 374
  cathedral of, 89, 90, 123–125, 209, 260, 330, 361
  councils at, 131, 132, 331–333
  province of, 19, 105–132, 170, 317–345
  archbishops of, see John; Mauger; Maurilius; Robert; William 'Bonne-Ame'
  abbeys in, see Holy Trinity; Saint-Amand; Saint-Ouen; Saint-Gervais
Round, J. H., 4, 276
Royalty,
  divine right of, 253–264
  nomination to, 251–252
  hereditary succession to, 250–252
  sanctity of, 253–264
  unction of, 255–260
Ryes, Hubert of, 48, 290
  Eudo the Steward (q.v.), son of

Saint Albans, abbey of, 327
  Paul, abbot of, 327
Saint-Amand (Rouen), nunnery of, 105, 109, 110, 113, 307
Saint-Aubin, 65, 67, 388, 389
Saint Augustine's abbey, Canterbury, 258, 325
  Æthelsige, abbot of, 325
Saint-Bertin, abbey of, 267

Saint-Brieuc, 231

Saint-Clair-sur-Epte, pact at, 16

Saint-Claud, monastery of, 235

Saint-Évroul, abbey of, 86, 113–115, 127, 321, 383, 415
  Thierry, abbot of, 127

Saint-Fromond, monastery of, 109

Saint-Gabriel, monastery of, 114, 217, 358

Saint-Georges-de-Boscherville, abbey of, 134, 148

Saint-Gervais (Rouen), monastery of, 358–362

Saint-James-de-Beuvron, 141, 178

Saint-Lô, 20

Saint-Malo, 231

Saint-Marculf, monastery of, 109

Saint-Martin-de-Sées, abbey of, 113, 114

Saint-Martin-de-Troarn, abbey of, 113, 114, 117, 217, 321
  Durand, abbot of, 128

Saint-Martin-du-Bosc, monastery of, 114

Saint-Michel de l'Abbayette, monastery of, 71

Saint-Michel-du-Tréport, abbey of, 112, 114, 124

Saint-Ouen (Rouen), abbey of, 16, 22, 23, 63, 105–113, 117, 124, 125, 134, 327
  Nicholas (q.v.), abbot of

Saint-Père de Chartres, abbey of, 33, 87, 90, 97, 123

Saint-Philibert,
  honour of, 89, 90, 102, 151
  monastery of, 109

Saint-Pierre-de-la-Couture, abbey of, 151, 217, 223, 229, 339
  Juhel, abbot of, 339, 340
  Reinald, abbot of, 151

Saint-Sauveur, family of, see Cotentin, vicomtes of

Saint Stephen's, Caen, abbey of, 80, 88, 117, 131, 139, 186, 318, 321
  Lanfranc (q.v.), abbot of

Sainte-Suzanne, 242

Saint-Valéry, family of, 65

Saint-Valéry-sur-Somme, 193, 194, 207, 396, 398

Saint-Victor-en-Caux, monastery at, 112, 117

Saint-Vincent-du-Mans, abbey of, 123, 229, 405

Saint-Wandrille, abbey of, 23, 63, 87, 88, 94, 105–118, 134, 145, 149, 162, 287, 321, 388
  Gerbert, abbot of, 128
  Robert, abbot of, 152

Saint-Ymer-en-Auge, abbey of, 88, 124

Saintes, council at, 340

Saintonge, 110

Saire, 27

Salisbury,
  assembly at, 275, 355, 356
  bishopric of, 260, 329
  see also 'Oath of Salisbury'; Osmund

Samson, bp. of Worcester, 130

Sandwich, 190

Saracens, 260

Sarthe, 228

Saumur, abbey of Saint-Florent at, 284

Scandinavia,
  influence on England, 20, 21, 156–180
  influence on Normandy, 19–22, 29, 30, 156–180
  threat to William the Conqueror from, 211–244, 274, 347, 348, 356, 374

Scotland, 214, 225–228, 238–244, 259, 266, 273, 323, 374
  see also Malcolm III; Margaret

Scriptorium, royal, in England, 292, 293

Scrofula, the 'King's Evil', 254, 255

Scutage, 280

Sées, 17, 19, 20
  bishopric of, 19, 119–132
  bishops of, see Radbod; Yves
  see also Saint-Martin-de-Sées

Segré, 179

Seine, river, 16, 18, 28, 68, 113

Selden, John, 3

Selsey, bishopric of, 383

Sélune, river, 17

Sens, abbey of Sainte-Colombe at, 383
  bishopric of, 32, 329

Sept-Meules, 270

Serlo, abbot of Gloucester, 327

Serqueville, 49

Servitium debitum,
  in England, 189, 273–283, 335
  in Normandy, 101–103, 282–283, 335
  imposition of, on bishoprics and abbeys, 325–326

Sherborne,
  bishopric of, 328, 329
  Æthelsige, bp. of, 160

Sheriff, office of, 296
  change in character after Norman
    conquest, 297–299, 301–308
  comparison of, with office of *vicomte*,
    296–298, 302, 307
Ships and fleets, 189–193, 226, 227
Shire courts, 305–310
Shrewsbury, earldom of, 94, 241, 272, 295
  see also Roger II of Montgomery
Sicily, 188, 203, 247, 260
Sierville, 87
Siffroi, bp. of Le Mans, 68
Sigy, priory of, 41
Sihtric, 21
Sihtric, abbot of Tavistock, 325
Sillé, 229
Simony, 131, 132, 333
Siward, e. of Northumbria, 86, 166, 168,
    171
Slavery, 311–312
Solesmes, abbey of, 229
Somerset, 213, 215, 219, 279
  Tofi, sheriff of, 297
Somme, river, 293
Song of Roland, 10, 129, 199, 261
Sorel, 237
Sotteville-les-Rouen, 187
Southern, R. W., 7, 321–323
Southwark, 206
Spain, 85
  Alphonzo, k. in, 393
  Normans in, 85, 188, 247
Spelman, John, 3
Staffordshire, 219, 220
Stainmoor, 241
Staller, office of, 290
Stamford, 303
Stamford Bridge, battle of, 193, 194,
    198–199, 396
Standard, battle of the, 278
Stapleton, Thomas, 3
Steenstrup, J., 3, 408, 410
Stenton, F. M., 4, 192, 234, 276, 354,
    400, 403
Stephen, c. of Brittany, 268
Steward, office of, 145, 146
  see also Eudo; Haimo; Osbern;
    Stigand; William fitz Osbern
Steyning, 166, 167, 186
Stigand, bp. of Winchester and archbp.
    of Canterbury, 169–170, 204, 206,
    324

Stigand the Steward, 145, 150
  Odo, son of, 145
Suffolk, 297, 304
Surrey, 206
Sussex, 199, 205, 209, 272
  rapes of, 272
Sweyn Estrithson, k. of Denmark, 164–
    166, 213–222, 346
  Cnut IV (q.v.), son of
  Harold, son of, 218
  Osbern, brother of, 218
Sweyn 'Forkbeard', k. of Denmark, 160
Sweyn Godwineson, 35, 166, 171, 374

Tadcaster, 395, 396
'Taillefer', 199
Talou, 27, 92, *see also* Arques
Tancarville, family of, 146, 150, 282,
    291, 300
  Gerald of, 146
  Ralph I of, 146
  Ralph II of, 146, 291
Taxation,
  in England, 299–303, 351, 352, 373
  in Normandy, 133–136
Tay, river, 227, 228
Tees, river, 214, 219, 220
Telham Hill, 196
Telonarii, 135, 197
Tenants-in-chief,
  establishment of, in England, 265–288
  obligations of, 273–288
Tesson, family of, 48, 112, 381
  Ralph, 48, 112, 115, 140, 144, 287, 381
Thames, river, 205, 206, 212
Thegns, 276–279
Thetford, bishopric of, 303
Thimert, siege of, 74
Thomas I, archbp. of York, 129, 130,
    321–323, 329, 334
Thomas II, archbp. of York, 363
Thurstan, abbot of Glastonbury, 129,
    274, 325, 327
Thurstan Goz, *vicomte*, 42, 43, 46, 93, 141
  Richard, *vicomte* of the Avranchin
    (q.v.), son of
Thury, 115
Tilleul, Humphrey of, 203
Tillières, 17, 42, 45, 46, 70, 74
Tinchebrai, battle of, 278
Toki, son of Wigot, 239

Tonbridge, 238
Torigny, Robert of, 85, 89, 112, 383
Tosny, family of, 85–91, 95, 96, 137, 150, 270, 283
  Berengar of, 270
  Ralph II of, 85, 90, 91
  Roger I of, son of Ralph II, 42, 85, 96, 112
  Godehildis, wife of Roger I, 85
  Ralph III of, son of Roger I, 68, 85, 95, 96, 113, 269
  Ralph IV of, 86
Tosti Godwineson, e. of Northumbria, 78, 172, 179–181, 191–194
  Judith, wife of, 78, see also Baldwin IV
Touques, river, 113
Tours, 17, 57
  Hildebert, bp. of, 129
Tower of London, 216
Treasuries, 150, 300, 301
Trémorel, 231
Tréport (le), see Saint-Michel-du-Tréport
Trials,
  in England, 305–310
  in Normandy, 141–151, 307–310
  see also Jurisdiction
Troarn, 91, see also Saint-Martin-de-Troarn
Truce of God, 43, 44, 51–52, 133, 140, 152, 153
Turchetil of Neufmarché, 37
Turold, abbot of Peterborough, 221, 222
Tyne, river, 241

Ulf, bp. of Dorchester, 167
Urse of Abetôt, sheriff of Worcestershire, 297

Vains, 139, 151
Val-ès-Dunes, battle of, 49–54, 69, 93, 383, 384, 389
Vallombrosa, 121
Valmeraye, 49
Valognes, 48, 217, 218
Varaville, battle of, 53, 72, 73
Verneuil, 17
Vernon, 17, 41, 92, 110
  family of, 87–89
  Hugh of, 87
  William of, 87

Vexin, 17, 73–74, 110, 174, 235, 357
  counts of, see Dreux; Ralph of Crépi; Walter
  see also Ralph the Timid
Vicomte, office of, 27, 92–95, 136–142
  comparison with office of sheriff in England, 295–297
Vieilles, Humphrey of, 42, 86–89, 112, 115
  Roger of Beaumont (q.v.), son of
Villeray, 238
Vimoutiers, 91, 409
Vire, river, 17, 18, 48
Vita Edwardi regis, 10, 412
Vitalis, abbot of Westminster, 327
Vitré, family of, 57
Vitré-aux, Loges, 62
Volpiano, William of, see Dijon, William of
Vougrin, bp. of Le Mans, 71, 223

Wace, 26, 50, 51, 68, 184, 409
Walchelin, bp. of Winchester, 329
Walchere, bp. of Durham, e. of Northumbria, 240, 241, 274, 327
Waleran, c. of Meulan, 144
Wales, 37, 172, 173, 211, 212, 225, 241, 242
Wallingford, 206
Walter, abbot of Evesham, 307
Walter, brother of Herleve (q.v.), 15, 381
Walter, c. of the Vexin, and c. of Maine, 73, 74, 144, 171, 172, 408, 410
  Biota, wife of, 174, 408, 410
Waltheof, son of Siward, e. of Northumbria, 86, 218, 232, 233, 285, 295, 306, 401
Warenne, family of, 92, 93, 99, 100, 267
  Rodulf of, 96, 100
  William of, 68, 76, 100, 101, 203, 232, 267, 269, 272, 328
  Gundrada, wife of, 76, 267, 392
Warwick, 87, 214, 216, 217
Waters, Chester, 392
Wells, bishopric of, 329, see also Giso
Wessex, earldom of, 165–171, 191, 192
  see also Godwine; Harold Godwineson
Westminster abbey, 46, 80, 127, 182, 206, 207, 247, 248, 256, 357
  abbots of, see Gilbert Crispin; Vitalis
White, G. H., 89, 200, 398
Wilkins, David, 3, 331

WILLIAM THE CONQUEROR

Career

birth and parentage, 15, 16, 379–382

boyhood, 31, 32, 162

accession as duke, 35–37

guardians of, 36–39

minority of, 36–52

vassal of the French king, 38–60

faces rebellion of Guy of Burgundy and the *vicomtes*, 47–50

appeals to Henry I, 48

at battle of Val-ès-Dunes, 48–51

attends council at Caen, 51, 52

besieges Brionne, 54–56, 384

re-enters Rouen, 56

favours Caen, 56, 57

supports Henry I against Geoffrey Martel, 58, 385–388

captures Domfront and Alençon, 59, 60, 384, 385

marries Matilda, 76–78, 391–395

receives nomination as successor to Edward the Confessor, 169

faces hostile coalition in France, 1051–1054, 62–63

does not visit England in 1051, 169

captures Arques, 65, 66, 387, 388

sends William, c. of Arques, into exile, 66

strengthened by Norman victory at Mortemer, 69

secures deposition of Archbp. Mauger, 69

favours appointment of Archbp. Maurilius, 69, 121

garrisons Mont Barbet and Ambrières, 71

disinherits William Werlenc, c. of Mortain, 138, 139

faces invasion of Normandy, 1057, 71

at battle of Varaville, 72

captures Thimert, 74

conquers Maine, 1063, 173, 174

receives oath from Harold Godwineson, 176, 177

invades Brittany, 177, 178

receives news of Harold's succession as k. of England, 181, 182

prepares to invade England, 182–192

takes counsel with Norman magnates, 184, 185

builds fleet, 189

negotiates with pope and emperor, 186–188

collects mercenaries and disciplines them, 189–190

at Saint-Valéry-sur-Somme, 192–196

crosses Channel and lands at Pevensey, 194–196

consolidates position in Sussex, 196, 197

forces early action on Harold, 198

at battle of Hastings, 199–204

takes Canterbury, 205, 396

isolates London, 205, 206, 396, 397

holds council at Berkhampstead, 206

receives submission of English magnates, 206, 207

is crowned king of the English, 209, 247–264

holds council at Barking, 207

returns to Normandy, 207–210

captures Exeter, 213

occupies York, 214

receives submission of many English cities, 213, 214

builds castles, 215, 217

faces rising of the North, 218–220

retakes York, 220

harries the North, 220–222

campaign beyond the Tees, 220

marches across the Pennines, 220

takes Chester, 220

receives further submissions, 220, 221

suppresses rising of Hereward, 221

faces revolt in Maine and attack from Scotland, 223–229

invades Scotland, 226–228

makes pact at Abernethy with Malcolm III, 227

recaptures Le Mans, 228

faces hostility of Philip I and of Anjou, 229–244, 401–408

faces revolts in England and Brittany, 230–234

orders execution of Waltheof, 233

defeated at Dol, 234, 404

loses control of the Vexin, 235

faces revolt of his son Robert, 236–239, 404–408

defeated at Gerberoi, 239

makes pacts with Fulk le Rechin and Philip I, 239, 240, 404–408

WILLIAM THE CONQUEROR, *contd.*
Career, contd.
reconciled to Robert, 240
orders invasion of Scotland, 240, 406
at council of Lillebonne (1080), 51,
52, 140, 321, 331–335
refuses demand for fealty from
Gregory VII, 340, 341
imprisons Odo of Bayeux, 243, 244
faces new rebellion of Robert, 242
attacks Sainte-Suzanne, 242
faces invasion from Cnut IV of
Denmark, 346, 347, 356
holds court at Gloucester, 1085, 347
orders Domesday survey, 347–354
receives 'Oath of Salisbury', 355, 356
invades Vexin, 357
sacks Mantes, 358
mortally wounded, 358
returns to Rouen, 358
disposes of his dominions, 359–361
dies, 362
funeral of, 363
children of, 393–395

Government and Administration
political inheritance of, 16–30
his charters and writs, 144–153, 263,
313
his court, 148–155, 284–288
his household, 142–148, 289–292
his powers as duke, 133–155
his status as king, 247–264
his realm a political unity, 263–264
crown-wearings, 254, 255, 286, 305
fiscal administration, 133–136 299–
302
feudal policy, 96–104, 265–288
judicial acts, 148–151, 305–310
ecclesiastical policy, 105–132, 317–345
presides at church councils, 130–132
holds pleas in England, 305–310
his respect for English traditions, 9,
258, 272, 290, 305–310, 322, 323
his use of English institutions, 289, 316,
347–354

Policy respecting
Church in England, 317–345
English earls and sheriffs, 294–298
English aristocracy, 265, 266, 284, 285,
290, 291

English military institutions, 278–280
English peasantry, 310–315
Jews, 313, 314
feudalism in Normandy, 3, 92–130
Norman aristocracy, 92–104
Norman counts and *vicomtes*, 92–95,
136–142
Norman bishoprics, 118–130
Norman monasteries, 105–117

Personal relations with
Alexander II, 187, 260, 318, 337, 340,
341, 389
Cnut IV, 218, 232, 346–356
Edgar Atheling, 171, 182, 214–231,
225–230, 251–256, 356, 375
Edward the Confessor, 162–180
Fulk le Rechin, 228–244, 347, 401–
408
Geoffrey Martel, 56–78, 384–391
Gregory VII, 318–345
Guy of Burgundy, 47–55
Harold Godwineson, 175–201
Henry I, k. of France, 44–53, 152,
383–391, 408, 411
Lanfranc, 79, 137, 138, 232, 233, 279,
317–344
Malcolm, k. of Scotland, 190–192,
213–218, 239–244, 408–410
Maurilius, archbp. of Rouen, 120–134,
143, 209
Odo, bp. of Bayeux, 119–136, 243–244,
294–296, 307–309, 360, 382
Philip I, k. of France, 223–244, 356–
361, 401–407
Robert, his son, 236–244, 348–362,
379–393, 404–409
Sweyn Estrithson, 164–166, 213–222
Waltheof, 232–233, 285, 295, 306, 401
William, c. of Arques, 38–42, 62–66,
385–389

Political relations with
Anjou, 56–78, 218–244, 401–408
Brittany, 37–46, 230–235
French monarchy, 44–53, 356–361,
383, 391, 408–410
Maine, 57–61, 70–73, 173–175, 233–
244, 383–391, 401–408
Papacy, 77–80, 187, 188, 318–345
Scandinavia, 211–244, 347, 348
Scotland, 190–192, 213, 218, 408–410

WILLIAM THE CONQUEROR, *contd.*
Vexin, 73, 74, 110, 174, 235, 357
Wales, 172, 173, 211, 212, 241, 242

Characteristics and reputation
avarice, 302, 373
courage in adversity, 64, 65, 83, 84, 195, 201, 374, 375
continence, 375
cruelty, 58–60, 206, 219–221, 371–372
contemporary opinions of, 83, 84, 369–371
contrasted judgments on, 3–5
diplomatic skill, 175–179, 184–189
dignity, 370, 371
genius for leadership, 83, 84, 133–148, 192, 201, 374, 375
military ability, 55–60, 83, 191–204
personal appearance, 83, 368–369
subject of legends, 12, 212
subject of propaganda, 5
piety, 373
energy, 374
statesmanship, 99–103, 131–149, 305–310, 347–354
strength of will, 370–373
William II, k. of England, 304, 360, 361, 363, 371
William 'Longsword', dk. of Normandy, 16, 17, 21, 23, 24, 106, 153, 159
William 'Bonne-Ame', archbp. of Rouen, 119, 127, 257, 320, 339, 359
William, bp. of Évreux, 119, 124, 144, 150
William, bp. of London, 167, 170, 215
William of Saint-Calais, bp. of Durham, 328, 329
William, c. of Arques, 25, 38–42, 62–66, 99, 113, 149, 375, 385, 386, 389
Walter, son of, 63
William, c. of Eu, 25
Lesceline (q.v.), wife of
Robert, c. of Eu (q.v.), son of
William Werlenc, c. of Mortain, 25, 99, 138
William of Rots, abbot of Fécamp, 129,

William Bertram, 88
William fitz Osbern, e. of Hereford, 61, 70, 86, 90, 99, 112, 113, 136–138, 143–150, 184, 224, 225, 269, 272, 285, 294
William of Breteuil, son of, 237
Roger of Breteuil (q.v.), son of
William Talvas of Bellême, 42, 60
Wilton, nunnery of, 254
Ælviva, abbess of, 254
Wiltshire, 297
Edric, sheriff of, 297
Winchcombe, abbey of, 325
Godric, abbot of, 325
Eadwine, monk of, 328
Winchester, 205, 213, 233, 249, 299–301, 350, 351
bishopric of, 170, 324, 329
bishops of, *see* Stigand; Walchelin
councils at, 322, 330, 332, 334, 336
see also New Minster
Witan, 284–286
Worcester,
bishopric of, 321, 329
bishops of, *see* Samson; Wulfstan
Worcestershire, 167, 297, 307, 308
sheriff of, *see* Urse of Abetôt
Writs,
character of, 292
English origin of, 292, 293
Norman use of, 293, 294
Wulfric, abbot of New Minster, 325
Wulfstan, bp. of Worcester, 183, 215, 232, 307, 308, 324, 367

York, 183, 193, 194, 214–220, 233, 303, 329, 399
archbishops of, *see* Aldred; Thomas I; Thomas II
province of, 180, 219, 317, 321–323
Yorkshire, 214–220, 268
Yver, Jean, 4
Yves, bp. of Sées, 58, 119, 123, 319

Zacharias, Pope, 256

DAVID C. DOUGLAS is one of the most distinguished English medievalists now active in research. He is a Fellow of the British Academy and Emeritus Professor of History in the University of Bristol. In 1963 he was Ford's Lecturer to the University of Oxford, his lectures being on William the Conqueror and the Norman conquest. He is general editor of the series of studies of English monarchs of which the present volume is the first to be published. (Details of the series are given on the back of this jacket.)

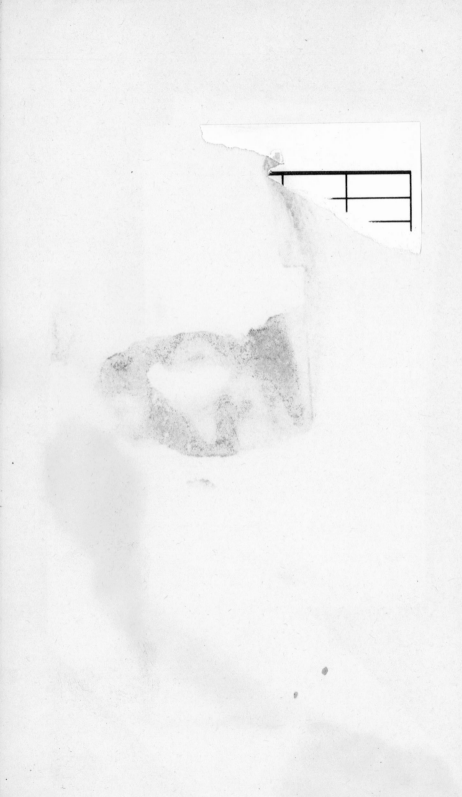